From Subject to Citizen

THE SECOND EMPIRE AND
THE EMERGENCE OF
MODERN FRENCH DEMOCRACY

Sudhir Hazareesingh

PRINCETON UNIVERSITY PRESS

PRINCETON, NEW JERSEY

Library of Congress Cataloging-in-Publication Data

Hazareesingh, Sudhir.
From subject to citizen : the Second Empire and the emergence
of modern French democracy / Sudhir Hazareesingh.
p.   cm.
Includes bibliographical references and index.
ISBN 0-691-01699-2 (cloth : alk. paper)
ISBN 0-691-05848-2 (pbk. : alk. paper)
1. France—History—Second Empire, 1852–1870.   2. Political
culture—France—History—19th century.   3. Democracy—
France—History—19th century.   I. Title.
DC277.H39   1998   944.07—dc21   97-44318

This book has been composed in Sabon

For Thara

With love and gratitude

CONTENTS

Illustrations   ix

Preface   xi

INTRODUCTION
Democracy and Citizenship in Nineteenth-Century French
Political Culture   3

CHAPTER 1
The Paradoxes of Bonapartist Democracy   29

CHAPTER 2
Tradition and Change: Legitimist Conceptions of
Decentralization   96

CHAPTER 3
Between Hope and Fear: The Limits of Liberal Conceptions
of Decentralization   162

CHAPTER 4
The Path Between Jacobinism and Federalism:
Republican Municipalism   233

CONCLUSION
The Second Empire and the Emergence of Republican
Citizenship   306

Bibliography   323

Index   357

ILLUSTRATIONS

1. Principaux Fonctionnaires de l'Empire Français, Imagerie
   d'Epinal, no. 529. Bibliothèque Nationale, Paris   34
2. Défilé des Députations des Communes de la Savoie devant
   Leurs Majestés à Chambéry. From *L'Illustration*, 8
   September 1860   47
3. Jean Gilbert Victor Fialin, Duc de Persigny, lithography
   Bornemann. Bibliothèque Nationale, Paris   74
4. Photograph of Louis Veuillot. Bibliothèque Nationale,
   Paris   108
5. Comte Alfred de Falloux, lithography. Bibliothèque
   Nationale, Paris   113
6. Duc Victor de Broglie, lithography Grégoire et Deneux.
   Bibliothèque Nationale, Paris   170
7. Lucien-Anatole Prévost-Paradol, lithography Lemoine.
   Bibliothèque Nationale, Paris   180
8. Charles de Rémusat, lithography Auguste Bry.
   Bibliothèque Nationale, Paris   201
9. Jules Simon, lithography Perdriau et Leroy. Bibliothèque
   Nationale, Paris   241
10. Pierre Clément Eugène Pelletan, lithography Perdriau et
    Leroy. Bibliothèque Nationale, Paris   256
11. Corps Législatif, 1869, Députés de la Seine, photograph
    by Appert. Bibliothèque Nationale, Paris   302

PREFACE

THIS BOOK began its life as a short piece of research at the Archives
Nationales in Paris on the subject of administrative decentralization in
mid- to late-nineteenth-century France. The more I read about the matter, however, the better I came to appreciate that discussions about local
liberty and communal democracy were fundamentally enmeshed in
deeper ideological controversies about the exercise of state power, the
role of universal suffrage, the relationship between town and country,
and the nature of citizenship in France. Two years later this short article
had become a book; institutional and administrative analysis had been
reinforced by elements drawn from intellectual history and political theory; and an ideographic piece about the French state had been turned
into a general argument about the origins of democracy in modern republican France.

None of the above would have been possible without the encouragement and generosity of colleagues on both sides of the Atlantic, who all
made time to read the whole or parts of my manuscript. In Oxford,
Vincent Wright inspired me to reexamine the politics of the Second Empire and selflessly shared his encyclopedic knowledge of its history,
which he has done so much to revolutionize; John Burrow supplied wise
counsel about how intellectual history should be approached and narrated; Martin Ceadel plucked out inconsistencies and ambiguities in the
text and sensibly directed me to pay greater attention to the material
and historical contexts of my argument; Michael Freeden's scholarly
writings helped to formulate my ideas about ideology and political culture; Freeden also provided an extremely valuable comparative perspective on the chapter on liberalism; Robert Gildea's sharp eye saved me
from a number of errors, and his judicious advice helped to recast the
argument in crucial places; Ruth Harris brought her acute analytical
powers to bear on the manuscript and supplied invaluable assistance in
thinking through its broader implications; the chapter on republicanism
benefited enormously from the insights of Colin Lucas, especially into
the relationship between the political culture of the revolutionary era
and later-nineteenth-century republicanism; and Adam Swift attempted
to bring me up to the standards of analytical rigor and intellectual clarity exemplified in his own writings.

In the United States, I am deeply grateful to Stanley Hoffmann at
Harvard University, who took time out of his extremely busy schedule

to offer critical comments on the entire manuscript; Philip Nord at Princeton University, whose recent book on nineteenth-century France was an inspiration and who raised a number of probing questions about several aspects of my argument (not all of which, alas, have been adequately answered in the pages that follow); and Tony Judt at New York University, whose intellectual generosity was — as ever — exemplary and whose searching comments helped to make this a better book than it otherwise would have been. Finally, I would also like to record my thanks to Judith Stone of the University of Western Michigan, who read the manuscript for Princeton University Press, offering constructive advice and raising a number of useful points. All of the above are of course in no way to blame for whatever deficiencies remain in this book, for which I alone am responsible.

I am also obliged to colleagues who helped with various forms of moral and material support: Theodore Zeldin by encouraging me to tread down the path long ago opened by his outstanding scholarship on the Second Empire and the Third Republic; Vincent Wright by handing over an impressive variety of dog-eared documents on nineteenth-century France; Natalie Zemon Davis by putting me in touch with Philip Nord and providing inspiration during her all-too-short Eastman year at Balliol College in 1994–95; Suzanne Berger by helping me to gain access to the Widener Library during a visit to MIT; Julia Hore by miraculously supplying the keys to the Balliol photocopying room at a crucial stage in the production of the manuscript; and Jack Hayward, Ruth Harris, and Howard Machin by assisting with an application for a research grant. I owe special tribute to Richard Cobb, with whom I enjoyed wonderful conversations about French railways, Polish Communists, and members of the Jockey Club de l'Ile Maurice. He possessed an extraordinary understanding of the fortitudes and frailties of the human condition and was unceasingly generous with his advice and encouragement. This book will always remind me of his impish smile and the malicious glint in his eye.

Institutional support also played a major role in enabling me to write this book. I am profoundly indebted to Oxford University for granting me a Special Lecturership in 1993–94, which allowed me to spend an entire research term in Paris; the Master and Fellows of Balliol for the benefit of a sabbatical in Michaelmas Term 1995, during which the first draft of this book was completed; and the British Academy, which generously awarded me a Research Grant for travel and maintenance during the summer of 1996. For the material on which this book is based I consulted a number of archives and libraries, whose staff I would also like to thank: the Archives Nationales; Bibliothèque Nationale; Bibliothèque Historique de la Ville de Paris; Archives du Grand-Orient de

France; Archives de la Préfecture de Police; and Institut des Etudes Politiques (all in Paris); the Widener Library at Harvard; and the Archives Départementales de Loire-Atlantique (Nantes) and Lot (Cahors). Last, but not least, I am grateful to Brigitta van Rheinberg, my editor at Princeton University Press, her assistant Alessandra Phillips, my production editor, Karen Verde, and my copy editor, Dalia Geffen, for presiding over the material production of the book with efficiency and courtesy. Finally, the index was expertly compiled by Frank Pert, to whom I would like to express my warm gratitude.

The most fundamental acknowledgment always comes last. Not a page of this book could have been written without Karma Nabulsi, who bestowed upon me a rich harvest of love, *complicité*, and intellectual companionship. Her presence at my side is a blessing for which I shall forever be thankful.

S. H.
Balliol College, Oxford
24 December 1997

From Subject to Citizen

Introduction

DEMOCRACY AND CITIZENSHIP
IN NINETEENTH-CENTURY
FRENCH POLITICAL CULTURE

ATTENDING TO questions of origins is a natural part of the political and intellectual historian's trade. In France, however, this is not a mere matter of abstract speculation: lineage is indeed regarded as a critical determinant of contemporary political identities. Hence the obsessive and often feverish controversies over the commemoration of past events. For the act of remembrance is rarely devoid of ideological connotations: in choosing to celebrate the French Revolution, the martyrdom of Joan of Arc, the baptism of Clovis, or the founding of the Capet monarchy, public authorities and political groups explicitly seek to appropriate a specific heritage, and in so doing to marginalize and even exclude others from it. At the same time, the object is often to privilege one particular historical narrative over competing versions; here, the aim is to confer the seal of universality on a distinct (and often mythical) representation of the past. "Origins" are in both these senses not at all part of "history"; they are deeply embedded in the ideological universe of the present.[1]

In this context, few subjects are more ideologically loaded than the question of the origins of the "modern" French polity. History is written by victors, and the political history of how France became a modern political democracy has largely been perceived through republican eyes.[2] Taking a broader approach, this book reconsiders the importance of mid-nineteenth-century political culture for the emergence of the modern republican conception of citizenship. This reassessment will be done through an analysis of the politics of the Second Empire, in particular its debate on territorial government and decentralization, which dominated much of local and national public life in France between 1852 and 1870. My conclusion, based on a detailed analysis of these discussions, is that the Second Empire marked a turning point in the intellectual articulation of the French political community as we know it today;

---

[1] See Robert Gildea, *The Past in French History* (London: Yale University Press, 1994).

[2] On the institutionalization of republican political culture since the Revolution, see Pierre Nora, ed., *Les lieux de mémoire*, vol. 1 (Paris: Gallimard, 1984).

more specifically, it was from the ideological crucible of the 1860s that the modern republican notion of citizenship later came to be formulated.

The Origins of the Modern French Polity

Attempting to identify the political origins of "modern" France naturally presupposes some definition of its essential qualities. Among the key characteristics of the French polity we might reasonably include its constitution, its public and administrative institutions, its distinct democratic and republican political culture, and its collective sense of national identity. The conceptual link between these different elements lies in the notion of citizenship, a concept that has been the subject of renewed attention in the 1990s.[3]

The common property of historians, political scientists, jurists, philosophers, and sociologists, the notion of citizenship has been widely used to analyze the various ways in which conditions of membership in Western polities have evolved since antiquity.[4] In its more narrow sense, a normative theory of citizenship defines the rights and duties of individuals within the political community: what specific entitlements and guarantees they can secure from the collectivity, and conversely what expectations the collectivity may legitimately have of them. In a broader sense, the notion of citizenship identifies the intelligibility of the political order: the concept acquires its full meaning when members of a political community come to share a broadly similar understanding of the purposes of their public institutions and of their own place within them.[5]

I will use the concept of citizenship in both dimensions in the course of this book: in the first, as a means of spelling out the specific ways in which different political groups defined individual and collective rights and duties; in the second, as a way of assessing how far these different views cohered in an overall conception of the necessary properties of civic and political life in nineteenth-century France.

[3] For an analysis of recent works, see Will Kymlicka and Wayne Norman, "Return of the Citizen: A Survey of Recent Work on Citizenship Theory," in *Theorizing Citizenship*, ed. Ronald Beiner (Albany: State University of New York Press, 1995), 283–322.

[4] On Roman notions of citizenship, see Claude Nicolet, *Le métier de citoyen dans la Rome républicaine* (Paris: Gallimard, 1976). For a broad overview of the modern concept, see Brian Turner and Peter Hamilton, eds., *Citizenship*, 2 vols. (London: Routledge, 1994); see also J. M. Barbalet, *Citizenship: Rights, Struggle and Class Inequality* (Stratford, England: Open University Press, 1988); Pierre Birnbaum and Jean Leca, eds., *Sur l'individualisme: Théories et méthodes* (Paris: Presses de la Fondation Nationale des Sciences Politiques, 1986).

[5] Richard Vernon, *Citizenship and Order: Studies in French Political Thought* (Toronto: University of Toronto Press, 1986), 2–3.

For a long time, the origins of the modern French polity — in all of its facets — were traced to one emblematic occurrence: the 1789 Revolution. Throughout the nineteenth century, this epic event (or rather series of events) appeared to most observers as the inexorable moment at which the old France gave way to something qualitatively modern. Writing in the late nineteenth century, Hippolyte Taine noted:

> In the organization that France gave itself then, all the general lines of its contemporary history can be traced: political revolutions, social utopias, class divisions, the role of the church, the conduct of the nobility, the bourgeoisie, or the people; developments and changes in philosophy, letters, and arts.[6]

There is no denying that the Revolution was a founding moment, which had dramatic and sometimes irreversible effects on all the elements of French collective life mentioned by Taine.[7] However, if the seeds of France's modern political culture were undoubtedly sown in the late eighteenth century, the germinating process was long and often tortuous. If we take three of the Revolution's major republican values to be secularism, political democracy, and social equality, fundamental questions about the first were still being asked up to 1905, and about the second as late as 1940; as for the third, only with the decline of the Parti Communiste Français (PCF) and the relative dissipation of the cleavage between the Left and the Right has this aspect of the Revolutionary heritage been partly eroded.[8]

Born with the Revolution, the modern French polity was thus fashioned during an incremental process that stretched across the nineteenth and twentieth centuries. Given that, it is legitimate to inquire whether this process was even and continuous or whether it was marked by sharp accelerations and historical turning points. A related but distinct question is whether this modern political community emerged in France through the transhistorical practices of modern state- and nation-building or whether it was defined and constructed relatively autonomously of institutional developments at the center.

The prevailing answer to both questions — among French historians as well as historians of France — has generally favored rupture rather than continuity, as well as the conclusion that the political community

---

[6] Hippolyte Taine, *Les origines de la France contemporaine* (Paris: Robert Laffont, 1986), 1:5.

[7] See Ferenc Feher, ed., *The French Revolution and the Birth of Modernity* (Berkeley: University of California Press, 1990).

[8] For a strong (but not entirely convincing) statement of this case, see Henri Mendras, *La seconde révolution française, 1965–1984* (Paris: Gallimard, 1988); and François Furet and Pierre Rosanvallon, *La république du centre* (Paris: Calmann Lévy, 1988).

was fashioned "from above"; in the words of Theodore Zeldin, "The politicians were the principal architects of national unity."[9] The rupture is generally seen to occur in 1870–71, with the end of the Second Empire and France's humiliating military defeat by Prussia. In the words of Daniel Halévy, these two years marked "the end of an epoch, the end of a certain France that was already disappearing, of the insolent nation that during three centuries had ruled Europe unchallenged."[10]

The consensus has been that the modern French polity — with its necessary myths[11] — was created during the last three decades of the nineteenth century, under the Third Republic (1875–1940).[12] In political and institutional terms, this was the "apogee of political democracy,"[13] with the emergence of liberal democratic institutions and the crystallization of the geographical divide between left- and right-voting regions.[14] No less important, under the Third Republic France apparently ceased to be, in Eugene Weber's celebrated terms, "a country of savages." In his estimation, "The ideology of the nation was still fragmented and informal in the middle of the nineteenth century. French culture became truly national only in the final years of the nineteenth century."[15] The 1870s and 1880s are also presented as critical turning points in the modernization of French political culture in regional studies[16] and histo-

---

[9] Theodore Zeldin, *France, 1848–1945*, vol. titled *Intellect and Pride* (Oxford: Oxford University Press, 1979), 3.

[10] Daniel Halévy, *La fin des notables* (Paris: Grasset, 1930), 15.

[11] On the "invented" character of French national unity, see Eric Hobsbawm, "Mass-Producing Traditions: Europe, 1870–1914," in *The Invention of Tradition*, ed. Eric Hobsbawm and Terence Ranger (Cambridge: Cambridge University Press, 1983), esp. 264–65.

[12] One of the most engaging accounts of the origins of the Third Republic is by Gabriel Hanotaux, *Histoire de la fondation de la Troisième République, 1870–1873* (Paris: Plon, 1925). See also Alexandre Zévaès, *L'Histoire de la Troisième République* (Paris: Georges-Anquetil, 1926); Halévy, *La fin des notables*, and *La République des ducs* (Paris: Grasset, 1937); François Goguel, *La politique des partis sous la Troisième République* (Paris: Editions du Seuil, 1956); and Jacques Chastenet, *L'enfance de la Troisième République, 1870–1879* (Paris: Hachette, 1952).

[13] Steven Englund, "Le Théatre de la Démocratie Française," in *Une histoire de la démocratie en Europe*, by Antoine de Baecque (Paris: Editions Le Monde, 1991), 125.

[14] Hervé Le Bras and Emmanuel Todd, *L'invention de la France* (Paris: Librairie Générale, 1981), 33.

[15] Eugène Weber, *La fin des terroirs* (Paris: Fayard, 1983), 691. For a recent response, see James Lehning, *Peasant and French: Cultural Contact in Rural France during the Nineteenth Century* (Cambridge: Cambridge University Press, 1995). On the broader historiographical debates about the origins of the "French nation," see Suzanne Citron, *Le mythe national: L'histoire de France en question* (Paris: Editions Ouvrières, 1989).

[16] For example, Alain Corbin, *Archaïsme et modernité en Limousin au XIXeme siècle*, 2 vols. (Paris: Marcel Rivière, 1975).

ries of the peasantry,[17] as well as by leading historians of the French Left.[18]

This sense of collective identity is largely seen as a product of the republican education system, which was founded in the early 1880s as a centralist means of disseminating the key values of the new republican order.[19] This "Jacobin" project, whose premises had to accepted even by those in the periphery who opposed its ideological and cultural content, is broadly seen to define the modern cultural notion of Frenchness.[20] In this respect, some have gone one step further and have traced back to this particular period the ascendancy of a dominant bourgeoisie, whose exclusive political and economic interests the new republican order is seen to serve.[21] By the emphasis it gave to creative and cultural life, the late-nineteenth-century Republic is also regarded as the progenitor of the intellectual, a social and political figure whose fate is inextricably linked with the emergence of modern republicanism in France.[22]

Hence — and as the logical culmination of all these developments — the prevailing conclusion that it was also under the Third Republic that the contours of a democratic, republican, individualist, and secular notion of citizenship were fully defined.[23] In this reading of French history, modern French citizens thus appear as creations of the democratic and republican state; they identified with its conception of the nation, espoused the hegemonic values of its dominant bourgeois class, and in short acquired a complete sense of their civic identity and political purpose under the strong but paternal influence of France's new republican masters.

[17] See Pierre Barral, *Les agrariens français de Méline à Pisani* (Paris: Armand Colin, 1968).

[18] For instance, Tony Judt, *Socialism in Provence, 1871–1914: A Study in the Origins of the Modern French Left* (Cambridge: Cambridge University Press, 1979).

[19] The proximate intellectual origins of republican secularism are analyzed by Katherine Auspitz. See *The Radical Bourgeoisie: The Ligue de l'Enseignement and the Origins of the Third Republic, 1866–1885* (Cambridge: Cambridge University Press, 1982).

[20] On the "mediating" influence of religion in the making of national identity in late-nineteenth- and early-twentieth-century Brittany, see Caroline Ford, *Creating the Nation in Provincial France: Religion and Political Identity in Brittany* (Princeton: Princeton University Press, 1993).

[21] Sanford Elwitt, *The Making of the Third Republic* (Baton Rouge: Louisiana State University Press, 1975), 305.

[22] On the origins of the phenomenon, see Christophe Charle, *Naissance des "intellectuels," 1880–1900* (Paris: Editions de Minuit, 1990).

[23] Dominique Schnapper, *La communauté des citoyens* (Paris: Gallimard, 1994).

French Citizenship in Historical Perspective

It would be invidious to deny the part the Third Republic played in the emergence of the modern democratic polity. It remains, however, that this story has been primarily narrated by French republicans, in an interpretation that was often colored by their strong ideological values (and prejudices).[24] Indeed, the argument of this book is that the predominant focus on the post-1870 decades has produced an unduly narrow account of the intellectual and political forces that have fashioned France's democratic modernity.[25] As David Thomson long ago noted in his classic (and in many respects still unsurpassed) work *Democracy in France*, modern French democracy emerged in the nineteenth century through an "accumulative" process,[26] to which all post-Napoleonic regimes made significant contributions. I will illustrate this claim principally in relation to the Second Empire, during which many basic parameters of the modern French notion of citizenship were defined.

The portrayal of how the principles of citizenship became entrenched in French political culture has in many ways followed the broader trend identified here. For a long time, the focus was directed at the French Revolution, which was regarded as the founding moment of the modern republican notion of citizenship.[27] But however much it may have contributed to defining its ideological and juridical framework,[28] the Revolution could not really be regarded as the moment at which these norms

[24] For classic accounts of the origins of republicanism, see Charles Seignobos, *Histoire de la France contemporaine*, vol. 7 (Paris: Hachette, 1921), and Jacques Chastenet, *La République des républicains* (Paris: Hachette, 1954). Two exceptions to this general view are Pierre Barral's pioneering work *Les fondateurs de la Troisième République* (Paris: Armand Colin, 1968), which by a judicious selection of speeches and writings of leading republican figures traces the emergence of an "ideologically coherent" republican doctrine from the 1860s to the 1880s; and Raymond Huard's *La naissance du parti politique en France* (Paris: Presses de la Fondation Nationale des Sciences Politiques, 1996), which recognizes the importance of the Second Empire in the emergence of democratic practices and institutions in France.

[25] For a review of the debate on the social forces underlying the "modernization" of rural France in the nineteenth century, see Ted Margadant, "Tradition and Modernity in Rural France during the Nineteenth Century," *Journal of Modern History* (December 1984): 667–97.

[26] David Thomson, *Democracy in France* (London: Oxford University Press, 1946), 17.

[27] For recent discussions, see Renée Waldinger, Philip Dawson, and Isser Woloch, eds., *The French Revolution and the Meaning of Citizenship* (Westport, Conn.: Greenwood Press, 1993), and Charles Tilly, "The Emergence of Citizenship in France and Elsewhere," *International Review of Social History* 40, no. 3 (1995): 223–36.

[28] For a critique of the revolutionary application of the concept, see Olivier le Cour Grandmaison, *Les citoyennetés en révolution, 1789–1794* (Paris: Presses Universitaires de France, 1992).

became collectively accepted in France—especially as many had to be substantially revised by later generations.[29] Here again, with the exception of a few regional studies highlighting the importance of the political culture of the Second Republic,[30] the general consensus has been that it was in the later parts of the nineteenth century that this critical ideological modernization took place.[31] The Third Republic codified the distinct republican conception of nationality, which blended *ius soli* with the traditional notion of *ius sanguinis*.[32] This was also the polity whose schools disseminated an individualistic and secular conception of civic identity, largely in opposition to the communitarian alternatives offered by populists, royalists, and Catholics.[33]

However, this emphasis on its Third Republican origins overlooks the fact that the notion of citizenship was securely established in nineteenth-century political discourse long before the 1880s. As with the prerevolutionary era, when the concept was more widely diffused than is generally believed,[34] the intellectual history of this nineteenth-century notion of citizenship has yet to be written. For there is much evidence for the view that large sections of the French political community (and not just republicans) thought about each other as citizens throughout this period. Indeed—and this clearly marks the difference from the an-

[29] Notably the distinction between active and passive citizens, which was inconsistent with the universalist thrust of modern republicanism. See William Sewell Jr., "Activity, Passivity, and the Revolutionary Concept of Citizenship," in *The French Revolution and the Creation of Modern Political Culture*, ed. Colin Lucas (Oxford: Pergamon Press, 1988), 2:105–23.

[30] See in particular Philippe Vigier's *La Seconde République dans la région alpine*, 2 vols. (Paris: Presses Universitaires de France, 1963), and Maurice Agulhon's *La république au village: Les populations du Var de la Révolution à la Seconde République* (Paris: Plon, 1970). See also A. Bergerat, "La radicalisation politique des paysans de l'Allier sous la Seconde République," *Cahiers d'Histoire de l'Institut Maurice Thorez*, no. 27 (1978): 114–73. A more recent argument on the formative influence of the Second Republic, based on an analysis of the peasant revolts of 1851, is Ted Margadent's *French Peasants in Revolt: The Insurrection of 1851* (Princeton: Princeton University Press, 1979).

[31] See Claude Nicolet, *L'idée républicaine en France* (Paris: Gallimard, 1982).

[32] Pierre Guillaume, "L'accession à la nationalité: Le grand débat, 1882–1932," in *Citoyenneté et nationalité*, ed. Dominique Colas, Claude Emeri, and Jacques Zylberberg (Paris: Presses Universitaires de France, 1991), 137–48.

[33] On the pedagogy of the principles of good citizenship, see, for example, Jules Simon, *Le livre du petit citoyen* (Paris: Hachette, 1880); Gabriel Compayré, *Eléments d'éducation civique et morale* (Paris: Garcet, 1880); Jules Steeg, *Instruction morale et civique* (Paris: Fauvé et Nathan, 1883); and Paul Bert, *L'instruction civique à l'école* (Paris: Picard-Bernheim, 1883). For a critical examination of these writings, see Raoul Allier, *La formation du futur citoyen à l'école primaire publique* (Paris: Fernand Nathan, 1924).

[34] See the insightful chapter by Lucien Jaume, "Citoyenneté et souveraineté: Le poids de l'absolutisme," in *The French Revolution and the Creation of Modern Political Culture*, ed. Keith Michael Baker (Oxford: Pergamon Press, 1987), esp. 1:518–19.

cien régime — the decades after 1814 witnessed the growing use of the term not only in intellectual writings but also in official political and juridical discourse.

If we consult France's diverse constitutions, for example, we find explicit references to the term *citoyen* in the 1814 Charter,[35] in Bonaparte's Additional Act of 1815,[36] and in the 1830 Charter.[37] The 1848 constitution stated emphatically that "reciprocal duties bind citizens to the republic, and the republic to its citizens."[38] Finally, the first article of the 1852 constitution of the Second Empire spelled out the regime's adherence to the "great principles proclaimed in 1789, [which] are the foundation of the public rights of Frenchmen."[39] By the 1850s and 1860s, therefore, the notions of citizen and citizenship were in extensive use, not only in official political and juridical language but also in a wide variety of discursive contexts.

In his analysis of French political vocabulary between 1869 and 1872, Dubois notes an impressive range of formulations; we thus encounter the "good" and "virtuous" citizen, but also the "honest" citizen, the "citizen-President," the "citizen-soldier," the "citizen-king," the "citizen-bourgeois," the "citizen-worker," and even the "citizen-subject."[40]

An objection to this claim might be that usage is not synonymous with common understanding, let alone agreement. Political and intellectual elites may well have referred extensively to the notion of citizenship between 1848 and 1870, but (as for example with the notion of liberty) there could have been heavy dissonances in their cognitive understanding of its meaning and scope. In this book, however, I intend to suggest precisely the opposite view. I will show that by the late 1860s, despite some continuing differences over its specific attributes, there was a broad agreement among mainstream political elites over the general

[35] Article 11: "The search for opinions and votes carried out before the restoration is forbidden. The same disregard is recommended to tribunals and to the citizens" (Charles Debbasch and Jean-Marie Pontier, eds., *Les Constitutions de la France* [Paris: Dalloz, 1989], 116).

[36] The text was strongly influenced by Benjamin Constant, who rallied to the emperor after the flight of the Bourbons; its title 6 contained nine articles on the rights of citizens (ibid., 129).

[37] Article 66: "The present charter and all the rights it confers are entrusted to the patriotism and courage of the national guards and all French citizens" (ibid., 138).

[38] Chapter 2 also contains sixteen articles defining the rights of citizens guaranteed by the constitution (ibid., 144–46).

[39] Ibid., 165.

[40] The latter was probably a legitimist construct, as we will note in chapter 2. See Jean Dubois, *Le vocabulaire politique et social en France de 1869 à 1872* (Paris: Larousse, 1962), 245–46.

principles that should define membership in the French political community. In reaching this conclusion, my analysis will diverge in several respects from existing accounts of the origins of citizenship in France.

Above all, this book strongly challenges the prevailing notion that modern French citizenship was essentially an invention of the elites of the Third Republic.[41] The debates of the Second Empire will show that all political groups had clear and strong views on the matter; the subject was therefore at the center of political debate long before the advent of opportunist and radical elites in the 1880s and 1890s. By highlighting this range of views before the Third Republic, I will also explode what might be called the myth of republican agency: the notion that the modern paradigm of citizenship was the creation of republicans *alone*.[42] A number of political groups in the Second Empire also shared many key notions about civic and political life (such as political freedoms, mass participation, local democracy, and political accountability). Indeed, the ideological framework of republican municipalism, which I will define in chapter 4, will emerge as the product of an encounter between the classic principles of republican ideology and the broader political culture of the Second Empire.

In this book on the political culture of the Second Empire I will also extend the intellectual framework within which the notion of citizenship is conventionally discussed, in two ways. Those who view the Third Republic as the defining moment for the emergence of the modern citizen tend to offer a bipolar account of its genesis: a secular, democratic, and individualist republican paradigm is thus typically contrasted with a religious, authoritarian, and communitarian construct.[43] The point of my argument is to show that the range of ideological views about membership of the political community was much broader in nineteenth-century French political culture; an important object is precisely to recover some of these debates in all their richness and complexity.[44] For there were not only Bonapartist, legitimist, Catholic, liberal, and republican approaches to citizenship before 1870 but also vibrant (and often deeply frenetic) arguments within each of these political traditions over the question.

A second aspect of this intellectual broadening bears on the types of

[41] For a typical example of this approach, see Serge Berstein and Odile Rudelle, eds., *Le modèle républicain* (Paris: Presses Universitaires de France, 1992), esp. 11–128.

[42] For an example of this republican exclusivism, see Odile Rudelle, "La tradition républicaine," *Pouvoirs*, no. 42 (1987): 31–42.

[43] See Yves Déloye, *Ecole et citoyenneté: L'individualisme républicain de Jules Ferry à Vichy* (Paris: Presses de la Fondation Nationale des Sciences Politiques, 1994).

[44] For a similar emphasis on the ideological diversity of nineteenth-century French political culture, see Robert Tombs, *France, 1814–1914* (London: Longman, 1996), 86.

issues that historians and political scientists conventionally deem relevant to identifying the principles of good citizenship. Given that this concept is largely about defining what keeps a political community together, the natural tendency has been to focus on debates about the nation as the fulcrum of its emergence. Indeed, in many writings, no real distinction is made between the concepts of nation and citizen.[45] To define citizenship, from this angle, is to identify the ways in which the French state created a sense of collective identity, either in political and juridical terms or through the establishment of distinct cultural norms.[46]

Although the Jacobin project of nation- and state-building undoubtedly played a central role in the development of the modern French polity,[47] this was not the only way in which France came to acquire a sense of collective identity. Indeed, such feelings can emerge alongside and even independently of the state-led process of bureaucratic incorporation of different social groups into one community.[48] For being part of the same political community is also about living together in a localized space: defining proper relations with one's neighbors, creating institutions of sociability, administering communal properties, electing local councillors and representatives, and articulating the relationship between localities and the political and administrative center. In short, powerful notions of the rights and duties of citizens are embedded in experiences (and expectations) about local and territorial collective life. Indeed, I would go so far as to argue that the notion of citizenship — in both its historical and its theoretical dimension — cannot be understood properly without addressing these essential facets of local collective life.

In this book I will uncover precisely these modes of political and territorial identity. My account of the political culture of the Second Empire will support the conclusions of those who argue for the "growing importance of the nation-state in local society and politics" between 1852 and 1870.[49] I will also argue that French local and national elites

[45] "Modern national citizenship was an invention of the French Revolution" (Rogers Brubaker, *Citizenship and Nationhood in France and Germany* [Cambridge: Harvard University Press, 1992], 35). The same point is made by Jean Leca, in "La citoyenneté en question," in *Face au racisme*, ed. Pierre-André Taguieff, ed. (Paris: Editions La Découverte, 1991), 2:314.

[46] See Max Silverman, "The Revenge of Civil Society," in *Citizenship, Nationality, and Migration in Europe*, ed. David Cesarani and Mary Fulbrook (London: Routledge, 1996), 146–48.

[47] For an overview, see Pierre Rosanvallon, *L'Etat en France de 1789 à nos jours* (Paris: Editions du Seuil, 1990).

[48] On the notion of bureaucratic incorporation, see Anthony D. Smith, "The Origins of Nations," in *Nationalism*, ed. John Hutchinson and Anthony D. Smith (Oxford: Oxford University Press, 1994), 147–51.

[49] Bernard Rulof, "Popular Culture, Politics, and the State in Florensac (Hérault) during the Second Empire," *French History* 5, no. 3 (September 1991): 299.

had come to a broadly convergent view concerning the core principles of public life by the late 1860s. This agreement was expressed inter alia in a common emphasis on a particular interpretation of the heritage of the 1789 Revolution; the importance of mass participation in civic life; the inalienable quality of individual freedoms; the rejection of bureaucratic oppression; and the need for a state that was strong and decisive but also politically accountable.

This ideological convergence was manifested in large measure through discussions on the territorial organization of the French polity. There was general agreement over how municipal and departmental institutions should be organized and reformed, what degree of freedom communes should be granted, and how the proper relationship between central and local government should be articulated. This agreement demonstrated that a strong sense of what held France together as a political collectivity was already present by the late 1860s. Although this intellectual consensus was not uncontested (but when was it ever?), it suggests that France had acquired a coherent notion of its core political characteristics long before the epic battles over the definition of its republican and national identities in the late nineteenth century.

Redefining Citizenship: The Second Empire and the Problem of Decentralization

In the remainder of this introduction I will consider how and why the principles of good citizenship came to be redefined during the Second Empire. The short answer is that French political elites were driven to reconsider the basic principles of collective life in the course of a wide-ranging public discussion about the shortcomings of centralization. This debate convinced these elites of the need to devolve greater political powers to communal and departmental institutions. Decentralization thus became a central focus of intellectual reflection between 1852 and 1870. Alongside the notion of citizenship, decentralization thus constitutes the second major theme of this book. Indeed, the two concepts represent different sides of the same coin, for it was through their cogitations about territorial politics that political elites and intellectuals came to rethink the principles of good citizenship.

The notion of decentralization obviously presupposes the existence of its opposite: centralization. Although it was argued—most notably by Guizot and Tocqueville—that the phenomenon of centralization was largely a creation of the ancien régime rather than the Revolution,[50] the term appeared for the first time during the Revolutionary era. Alphonse

[50] For an analysis and critique of the liberal historiography of the Revolution, see Eric Hobsbawm, *Echoes of the Marseillaise* (London: Verso, 1990), 1–31.

Aulard dated it around 1799–1800, when police reports began to mention the term explicitly.[51] Although significantly influenced by the Jacobins' legacy, the concept first made its appearance — fittingly enough — under Napoleon Bonaparte, who soon established an imperial political system that enshrined the principles of political and administrative centralization.[52] This body of practices came to be seen as the source of many of the evils of public life in France during the nineteenth century, most notably the absence of a civic sense among the French.[53]

Indeed, a measure of the problematic nature of citizenship was the frequency with which French political and intellectual elites engaged with the question of decentralization after 1815.[54] In the early years of the Restoration, Jean-Marie Duvergier de Hauranne denounced what he called "the unduly exaggerated system of centralization."[55] His liberal colleague Pierre Royer-Collard reminded the royalist government that "the commune, like the family, comes before the state."[56] In one of the defining books of the "Great Debate" of the 1820s,[57] Prosper de Barante demanded greater local liberties but also attacked the isolation and complacency of the provincial aristocracy.[58] Under the July Monarchy, efforts were made to develop a coherent municipal framework that specified a limited range of rights to communes,[59] but these changes fell

[51] Alphonse Aulard, "Origines du mot *centralisation*," *La Révolution Française* (July–December 1902): 175.

[52] On the centralization of the First Empire, see Alphonse Aulard, "La centralisation napoléonienne," in *Etudes et leçons* (Paris: Alcan, 1913), 7:113–95; Félix Ponteil, *Napoléon 1er et l'organisation autoritaire de la France* (Paris: Armand Colin, 1956); and Georges Lefevre, *Napoléon* (Paris: Presses Universitaires de France, 1969), esp. 79–94.

[53] On the revolutionary theory and practice of centralization, see Yann Fauchois, "Centralisation," in *Dictionnaire critique de la Révolution Française: Idées*, ed. François Furet and Mona Ozouf (Paris: Flammarion, 1992), 67–85.

[54] See, for example, *Réflexions sur l'organisation municipale par un membre de la Chambre des Députés* (Paris: Delaunay, 1818); Baron Pierre-Paul-Nicolas Henrion de Pansey, *Du pouvoir municipal* (Paris: Barrois, 1820); Comte Des Garets, *Mémoires sur l'administration* (Paris: Le Normant, 1821); Claude René Bacot de Romand, *Observations administratives* (Paris, 1822); and Alexandre-Pierre Barginet, *De la centralisation* (Paris: Delaunay, 1828).

[55] Jean-Marie Duvergier de Hauranne, *Réflexions sur l'organisation municipale et sur les conseils généraux de département* (Paris: Delaunay, 1818), 106.

[56] Quoted in *Le self-government local en France*, by Paul Loppin (Paris: Pedone, 1908), 94.

[57] This debate — and its implications for liberal political thought in France — is assessed by Larry Siedentop, *Tocqueville* (Oxford: Oxford University Press, 1994), 20–40.

[58] *Des Communes et de l'aristocracie* was first published in 1822 and reissued in 1829. His grandson Robert de Nervo published it again in 1866 under the title *La décentralisation en 1829 et 1833* (Paris: Douniol, 1866).

[59] The Orleanist legislation on municipalities is analyzed by Louis de Cormenin, *Recueil sur l'administration municipale* (Paris: Dupont, 1838).

well short of the aspirations of radical advocates of decentralism, notably the legitimists.[60] A legitimist pamphlet thus defined centralization as a new form of feudalism, which brought in its wake "the destruction of communal institutions, the alienation of its properties, and the misappropriation of charitable foundations, its revenues arbitrarily taken by the Treasury, its local resources diverted to employ a large cohort of employees and functionaries, inopportune or tardy expenses, a general disorder."[61] During the agitated years of the 1840s, finally, there were numerous projects for local government reform,[62] culminating in the inconclusive discussions of the decentralization commission set up by the National Assembly.[63]

Thus there were a number of historical antecedents of the arguments of the Second Empire. Indeed, there were many subsequent attempts to revive the discussions under the Third Republic, notably around the turn of the century.[64] However, the discussions of the 1860s were far more comprehensive in range and scope than anything that had preceded (or would succeed) them. This was partly because of the sense that centralization had reached its climax under the Second Empire:

[60] See Jean-Baptiste Villèle, *Projet d'organisation municipale, départementale, et régionale* (1834; reprint, Paris: Plon, 1874), and Comte de Coëtlognon, *Appel aux Bretons pour la revendication des principes monarchiques et des libertés nationales* (Paris: Sapia, 1844).

[61] *Association pour l'émancipation politique et la réforme parlementaire contre le serment, le monopole et la centralisation administrative* (Paris: Gazette de France, 1833), 43. For further opposition views, see also *Appel à la France contre les divisions des opinions* (Paris: Gazette de France, 1831); Comte de Saint-Clou, *Des maux produits par la centralisation* (Paris: Dentu, 1831); Pierre Hauser, *De la décentralisation* (Paris: Paulin, 1832); and Francisque Bouvet, *Du principe de l'autorité en France et de la limite des pouvoirs* (Paris: Pagnerre, 1839), 31.

[62] See, for example, Gustave Boulay, *Réorganisation administrative* (Paris: Michel Lévy, 1840), and Louis Florent-Lefebvre, *De la décentralisation* (Paris: Marescq, 1849).

[63] Pierre Bodineau and Michel Verpeaux, *Histoire de la décentralisation* (Paris: Presses Universitaires de France, 1993), 50.

[64] Among the notable contributions were Henri Charriaut, *Enquête sur la décentralisation* (Paris: Nouvelle Revue Internationale, 1895); De Lucay, *La Décentralisation* (Paris: Guillaumin, 1895); Paul Deschanel, *La décentralisation* (Paris: Berger-Levrault, 1895); J. Ferrand, *Un avant-projet de décentralisation administrative* (Amiens: Jeunet, 1895); Ange Benedetti, *La décentralisation et la commission départementale* (Aix: Barthélémy, 1897); Alfred Guignard, *Le self-government ou la décentralisation* (Paris: Ligue Nationale de Décentralisation, 1897); Jean Imbart de La Tour, "Décentralisation et liberté dans la commune," *Revue Politique et Parlementaire* (October 1899); Jean de Loris, *L'idée de la décentralisation* (Besançon: Imprimerie du Progrès, 1900); Jean-René Aubert, *Enquête sur la décentralisation artistique et littéraire* (Paris: Bibliothèque de l'Association, 1902); Henri Le Brun, *Essai de politique administrative* (Paris: Didier, 1902); and Vincent Constant, *De la décentralisation dans la commune* (Aix: Niel, 1905). A monarchist overview of the nineteenth century as a whole was presented by Charles Maurras, *L'idée de décentralisation* (Paris: Revue Encyclopédique, 1898).

mayors were appointed by the government, the cities of Paris and Lyon were denied an elected municipal authority, local government councils were placed under the tutelage of state officials, national and local elections were manipulated, and freedom of association was severely restricted.[65]

Opposition movements (legitimists, liberals, and republicans) campaigned for greater political liberties, and eventually the Empire recognized the necessity of reforming the system of local democracy and territorial government. The sheer volume of writings on local liberty thus distinguished the Second Empire's debates on decentralization from all others.

Also, unlike in previous decades, decentralization was not the doctrinal preserve of any single party or school but a common object of discussion for all mainstream political movements. A further distinctive feature of the debate was its ubiquity: it was conducted in both houses of parliament (the Legislative Corps and the Senate), within different branches of the imperial state, at national conferences and international congresses, in hundreds of books, journals, and pamphlets, and in the Parisian and provincial press.[66] A plethora of schemes for reconstituting the relationship between the state and its citizens were thus generated — most serious, some eccentric; some short and compact, others dense and developed; some terse and pedagogical, others bombastic and lyrical; some modest and incremental, others radical and even utopian. These diverse proposals provoked furious controversies, also in many dimensions: within the imperial state; in the press and among thinkers and intellectuals; between provincial writers and the Parisian elites; between the imperial state and all opposition parties; within political movements (most notably the Bonapartists and the republicans); and, finally, among opposition parties (for example, between the legitimists and the republicans).

So much was decentralization in the public mind that it inspired the Montpellierian lawyer Henri Bernard to write a five-act comedy on the subject.[67] This masterpiece was later overshadowed by an evocatively

[65] For good summaries of the imperial system of territorial government, see Maurice Bourjol, *Les institutions régionales de 1789 à nos jours* (Paris: Berger-Levrault, 1969), and François Burdeau, *Histoire de l'administration française du XVIIIeme au XXeme siècle* (Paris: Editions Montchrestien, 1989).

[66] For a detailed study of the treatment of decentralization in the Parisian press, see Elzéar Lavoie, "La décentralisation discutée dans la presse politique Parisienne de 1860 à 1866" (Ph.D. diss., University of Paris, 1963).

[67] Henri Bernard, *La décentralisation ou la province: Comédie en cinq actes* (Montpellier: Boehm, 1862).

entitled play performed at Nantes which lampooned governments' repeated failures to advance the cause of local liberty.[68]

DECENTRALIZATION AND CITIZENSHIP: THE IMPORTANCE OF IDEOLOGICAL ANALYSIS

Although there is no specific monograph on the subject of decentralization under the Second Empire, the period covered in this book has been
examined in several broader studies of modern French administrative
history.[69] Distinctive to my approach, however, is the attempt to identify
the political and ideological principles that underlie the formation of
various doctrines of local democracy and territorial government.

This method is fundamentally different from the dominant approach
to questions of local liberty in the literature on public and territorial
institutions. Administrative historians generally treat decentralization in
an essentially formalistic way. This is reflected in a predominant emphasis on positive law and a tendency to separate administrative rules
from their political and philosophical contexts.[70] However, contending
conceptions of local democracy cannot be understood in exclusively juridical or formalistic terms. This is not to belittle the importance of
studying territorial politics in terms of rules and laws but merely to say
that these principles are devised and applied by men. As demonstrated
in Le Clère and Wright's classic work on the prefects of the Second
Empire,[71] these men were products of a particular historical period and
bearers of distinct and often contradictory social values and political
assumptions. But principles do not appear *ex nihilo*. A corpus of administrative rules and codes also presupposes a political philosophy.

As I will note throughout this book, the debate about local democracy forced all the major political movements to define and reexamine
their core principles and values. To explain why one particular scheme
of local liberty was preferable to any other, a clear notion of the concept

---

[68] *Leçon de décentralisation, de garde nationale, d'horlogerie et d'archéologie comparées en Deux Actes et Sept Tableaux, par le rural Petitjean-Bonaventure-Grospierre*
(Nantes: Libraros, 1871).

[69] See Christian Gras and Georges Livet, *Régions et régionalisme en France* (Paris:
Presses Universitaires de France, 1977); François Burdeau, *Libertés, libertés locales
chéries!* (Paris: Cujas, 1983), and Reinhard Sparwasser, *Zentralismus, Dezentralisation,
Regionalismus und Föderalismus in Frankreich* (Berlin: Duncker and Humblot, 1986).

[70] One of the classic nineteenth-century juridical accounts is by Léon Aucoc, "Les controverses sur la décentralisation administrative," *Revue Politique et Parlementaire* (April–
May 1895).

[71] Bernard Le Clère and Vincent Wright, *Les préfets du Second Empire* (Paris: Armand
Colin/Presses de la Fondation Nationale des Sciences Politiques, 1973).

of freedom had to be posited, but also a defensible and coherent range of views about history, human nature, equality, justice, morality, power, authority, and even God. Hence the essential connection between decentralization and the theme of citizenship; views about how local politics should be conceived, both in its own terms and in relation to the national political framework, were deeply embedded in general theories of the good life. In other words, different notions of decentralization were expressions of a wider set of assumptions about citizenship which were inherently ideological.

The notion of ideology provides a useful instrument for gauging the character and substance of different views about local democracy and citizenship under the Second Empire.[72] It helps to demonstrate, first and most obviously, that although most politicians agreed on the necessity of decentralization during the 1860s, none of them had quite the same conception of citizenship. Thus, for the Bonapartists, decentralization was a matter of transferring decisional power from ministries to local bureaucratic agencies, but without substantively increasing the degree of public involvement in the life of the city. For most of the opposition, by contrast, a genuine measure of decentralization required handing over administrative powers to elected councils, thereby giving the citizenry a greater element of control over its own affairs. But ideological analysis also shows that even when there was a consensus on defining a set of liberties in a particular way, agreement could not be reached because of differing priorities. Bonapartists and republicans, for example, had exactly the same definition of freedom of expression. The former, however, attached greater importance to order and stability than to liberty and therefore, until the late 1860s, refused to grant the political rights of expression and association that the republicans demanded.

Thinking about local liberty as part of a wider scheme of values also offers an opportunity to test the intellectual coherence of the various proposals for political reform. In this respect, the pages that follow show that contradiction is a fundamental law of politics. Bonapartists believed in a depoliticized system of local government but also in the growing necessity of political competition through universal suffrage; legitimists demanded decentralization in the name of one conception of liberty but tried to define social and political membership of society in terms of its opposite; liberals insisted that citizens should enjoy individual liberties but appealed to traditional social authority to preserve order; and the republican municipalists sought to involve the citizenry in public life on the basis of civil and political equality but hoped to turn

---

[72] On the concept of ideology, see Michael Freeden, *Ideologies and Political Theory: A Conceptual Approach* (Oxford: Oxford University Press, 1996).

to bourgeois notables to confirm the legitimacy of their communal institutions.

Yet, despite — or perhaps because of — these and other contradictions, what also emerges from my analysis is the richness and intricacy of these ideologies. This complexity appears in three dimensions: in the number and density of subcultures within each ideology, particularly within republicanism, but also within Bonapartism, liberalism, and even legitimism; in the sophistication and inventiveness of these ideologies, as reflected in their ability to construct a cohesive political identity that reconciled future aspirations, present imperatives, and past lineages; and, last but not least, in their capacity to perform an essential function of ideological discourse: the justification of particularist interests in a rhetoric of universality.[73]

Finally, viewing the question of local democracy through the prism of citizenship enables the transcendence of the sterile dichotomy between governmental rejection and oppositional advocacy of decentralization. One of the conventional wisdoms about local democracy in nineteenth-century France is that political groups always demanded it when out of power but immediately abandoned it the moment they attained public office. Royalists thus often supported substantive local liberties under the Revolution and Empire but retained the centralized system of territorial politics after 1815.[74] As we will note later, the same charge was leveled at the republican party after 1877. Conversely, liberals rejected decentralization during the first half of the nineteenth century, when they were in government, and passionately embraced it after 1851, when they were excluded from office.[75] Such patterns have led to the frequent perception of decentralism as a largely rhetorical exercise, used by opposition groups merely to unsettle and embarrass established authority.

Viewing decentralist schemes exclusively through such instrumental lenses is crudely reductionist. Such an approach ignores what often makes the advocacy of local liberty an interesting object of study: what it reveals about the broader political values and ideological assumptions of a political movement. It also makes the classic mistake of judging the past status of a political doctrine in the light of its subsequent fate. Most important, it misses out the explicit link between notions of local liberty and broader conceptions of citizenship. Indeed, contrary to the

---

[73] On the functions of ideology, see my *Political Traditions in Modern France* (Oxford: Clarendon Press, 1994), 5–32.

[74] Tombs, *France, 1814–1914*, 98–99, 340.

[75] Jean-Marc Ohnet, *Histoire de la décentralisation française* (Paris: Librairie Générale, 1996), 72–77.

common view that the debates on decentralization simply fizzled out after 1870, I will show that many of the ideas and themes of the 1860s decisively influenced the formulation of the republican notion of citizenship under the Third Republic.

REVISITING NINETEENTH-CENTURY
FRENCH POLITICAL CULTURE

As mentioned earlier, in this book I also challenge a number of orthodox assumptions about nineteenth-century French political life, by a thorough reevaluation of the political culture of the Second Empire, especially its relationship with the republican order that appeared in France in the 1880s.

The Bonapartist regime is now beginning to reemerge from the long purgatory imposed by generations of hostile socialist and republican historians.[76] Marx's heavy sarcasms[77] and Victor Hugo's derision[78] have been replaced by a number of works stressing the positive features of Louis Napoleon's reign. The economic successes of the regime,[79] its efforts to develop social legislation for workers,[80] and the moral and political qualities of the emperor:[81] all have received attention in recent decades. Without necessarily endorsing these revisionist claims or indeed overlooking the numerous failings of the Bonapartist regime, I also argue for a reconsideration of the political significance of Louis Napoleon's reign. More particularly, my analysis highlights the vibrancy and dynamism of the political culture of the Second Empire—an aspect of nineteenth-century political life that is receiving increasing scholarly attention.[82] I will outline some of the striking features of this era in the final part of the introduction.

[76] On the transformation of Second Empire historiography since 1945, see the proceedings of the 1971 colloquium at Aix-en-Provence, in *Revue d'Histoire Moderne et Contemporaine* (January–March 1974).

[77] Karl Marx, *Le dix-huit brumaire de Louis Bonaparte* (Paris: Editions Sociales, 1979).

[78] Victor Hugo, *Napoléon-le-Petit: Histoire d'un crime* (Paris: Ollendorf, 1907).

[79] Georges Pradalié, *Le Second Empire* (Paris: Presses Universitaires de France, 1979), 123.

[80] For an early attempt to rehabilitate the emperor on this score, see Etienne Lamy, *Etude sur le Second Empire* (Paris: Calmann Lévy, 1895), 3–130; see also Adrien Dansette, *Du 2 Décembre au 4 Septembre* (Paris: Hachette, 1972), 431, and William H. C. Smith, *Napoléon III* (Paris: Hachette, 1982), 265.

[81] Louis Girard, *Napoléon III* (Paris: Fayard, 1986), 516; Philippe Séguin, *Louis Napoléon le Grand* (Paris: Grasset, 1990), 331–32; and James McMillan, *Napoleon III* (London: Longman, 1991), 167.

[82] See most notably Philip Nord, *The Republican Moment: Struggles for Democracy in Nineteenth-Century France* (Cambridge: Harvard University Press, 1995).

It is now increasingly recognized that a profound social and economic revolution was set in motion sometime between 1850 and 1875, fundamentally and irreversibly altering individual and collective mentalities in France. Indeed, economic and social historians view the 1860s in particular as a turning point — and not for France alone.[83] The expansion of France's internal market and the development of its road and rail networks broadened the economic and social horizons of millions and began "a major transformation of the way of life of the people of France."[84]

One of the most striking manifestations of this change was the acceleration of rural migration. After slowing down during the first half of the nineteenth century, mass movement into towns and cities took a qualitative leap in 1850–65. In the estimation of Philippe Ariès, this period effectively marked the beginning of the classic era of rural depopulation in France, which continued well into the twentieth century.[85] However, this broad phenomenon was also consistent with an increase in agricultural revenues, especially in the 1860s and early 1870s;[86] the Second Empire is thus generally remembered as a period of great agricultural prosperity.[87]

Rural migration went hand in hand with urban development, which was particularly conspicuous during the Second Empire. Several dimensions are especially noteworthy: the growth in population of towns and cities, which steadily ingested the migratory flows from rural France,[88] and the no less spectacular infrastructural development of the urban landscape, of which Haussmann's Paris was the most striking example.[89]

[83] For a comparative European view, see C. Pouthas et al., *Démocratie, réaction, capitalisme, 1848–1860* (Paris: Presses Universitaires de France, 1983), 577, and Christophe Charle, *Les intellectuels en Europe au XIXeme siècle* (Paris: Fayard, 1996).

[84] See Roger Price, *The Modernization of Rural France: Communications Networks and Agricultural Market Structures in Nineteenth-Century France* (London: Hutchinson, 1983), 398.

[85] Philippe Ariès, *Histoire des populations françaises* (Paris: Editions du Seuil, 1971), 284; see also Didier Blanchet and Denis Kessler, "La mobilité géographique de la naissance au mariage," in *La société française au XIXeme siècle*, ed. J. Dupaquier and D. Kessler (Paris: Fayard, 1992), 343–69. For a nineteenth-century view, see Alfred Legoyt, "Du mouvement de la population en 1854," *Journal des Economistes* (April–June 1858): 360–79, and his longer work *Du progrès des agglomérations urbaines et de l'émigration rurale en Europe et particulièrement en France* (Marseilles, 1867).

[86] Annie Moulin, *Les paysans dans la société française* (Paris: Editions du Seuil, 1992), 66–69.

[87] Georges Duby and Armand Wallon, eds., *Histoire de la France rurale* (Paris: Editions du Seuil, 1976), 3:202–31.

[88] Françoise Bourillon, *Les villes en France au XIXeme siècle* (Paris: Ophrys, 1992), 103–5.

[89] On the principles of Haussmanization, see Maurice Agulhon, ed., *Histoire de la France urbaine* (Paris: Editions du Seuil, 1983), 4:77–117. More generally, see Louis Girard, *La politique des travaux publics du Second Empire* (Paris: Armand Colin, 1952).

The growth of communications, the mass movement into towns and cities, and the extension of the urban fabric all contributed to the broader phenomenon of industrialization, which also received a strong impetus during the 1850s and 1860s.[90] Although uneven and comparatively fragile, the expansion of French industry was effectively launched during the Second Empire, with an increased focus on heavy industry and the modernization of production methods,[91] as well as the first attempt systematically to integrate industrial concentration and working-class habitat.[92] A small but telling symbol of these new departures in both production and consumption was the appearance of the department store: the Bon Marché opened its doors in 1852, the Louvre and Printemps stores in 1855, and the Samaritaine in 1869.[93]

All these changes had important consequences for the French class structure, notably with the growth of the middle classes and the emergence of an urban proletariat.[94] The general prosperity of the Second Empire benefited all social categories (although some clearly more so than others) but also transformed collective mentalities. Better rail and road networks, greater commercial exchanges, and higher levels of literacy reduced physical and mental distances between regions and gave peasants and urban dwellers a better sense of the world that lay beyond their localities.

This understanding was not always positive; for example, peasant migration and urban development strongly accentuated existing rural feelings of resentment against "the city"; as we will note, Paris occupied a particularly prominent place in this rural (and provincial) demonology. At the same time, towns and cities saw the emergence of increasingly confident bourgeois elites, wielding significant economic influence and social authority. This sense of confidence was often translated into the creation of diverse associations (ranging from mutual aid to intellectual, artistic, and sporting groups), which began to take off in France in the

[90] Jean-Pierre Rioux, *La révolution industrielle, 1780–1880* (Paris: Editions du Seuil, 1971), 84–92.

[91] Jean-Charles Asselain, *Histoire économique de la révolution industrielle à la première guerre mondiale* (Paris: Presses de la Fondation Nationale des Sciences Politiques, 1985), 106; Albert Broder, *L'économie française au XIXeme siècle* (Paris: Ophrys, 1993), 82–83.

[92] The exemplary model was Le Creusot, which was dominated by the impressive Eugène Schneider, member of the Legislative Corps, and later its vice-president and president. See Christian Devillers and Bernard Huet, *Le Creusot: Naissance et développement d'une ville industrielle* (Seyssel: Champ Vallon, 1981), 58–59.

[93] Alain Beltran and Pascal Griset, *La croissance économique de la France, 1815–1914* (Paris: Armand Colin, 1994), 88.

[94] Christophe Charle, *Histoire sociale de la France au XIXeme siècle* (Paris: Editions du Seuil, 1991), 130–33.

early 1860s.[95] All of these developments acted as a powerful stimulus for a redefinition of the concept of citizenship by the elites of the Second Empire.[96]

A New Political Culture

This reconsideration was facilitated by a turning point for what might be termed the culture of politics in France: the way in which a public domain of political intercourse was defined and actualized by national and local elites during the Second Empire. Literacy levels increased during this period, a phenomenon that partly explained the advent of cheap newspapers (such as the *Petit Journal*). These publications brought "a new vision of the world" to every corner of France,[97] and especially a sense of events and issues occurring beyond the limits of locality. Indeed, the debate on decentralization and citizenship was one of the first examples of a new departure in the articulation and presentation of ideas to the wider public. During this period what might be called a modern culture of journalism developed in France,[98] with not only the appearance of a broad range of newspapers but also the attribution of a distinctive status to journalistic elites.[99]

This process was intimately linked to the dynamics of political change. With the restoration of male universal suffrage in 1851, constitutionalist political ideas and values no longer could be expressed exclusively within the narrow confines of the Parisian elite; they had to be clearly defined and transmitted to the educated (and even the noneducated) adult population constituting the electorate. This required a subtle form of vulgarization, involving among other things the calibration of a political message according to the nature and sophistication of its intended readers. The development of republican support in provincial (and especially rural) parts of France in the 1860s was often directly connected to the establishment of local newspapers, which acted as an effective conduit for the dissemination of new political ideas.[100]

---

[95] See Annie Grange, *L'apprentissage de l'association, 1850–1914* (Paris: Mutualité Française, 1993), 36.

[96] I am grateful to Tony Judt for highlighting the importance of these social and economic changes for my general argument.

[97] Roger Price, *A Social History of Nineteenth-Century France* (New York: Holmes and Meyer, 1987), 178.

[98] See Georges Weill, *Le journal* (Paris: La Renaissance du Livre, 1934), 231.

[99] For an evocative account of the journalistic figures of the time, see Comte Maurice Fleury and Louis Sonolet, *La société du Second Empire* (Paris: Albin Michel, 1914), 3:149–87; Jean Morienval, *Les créateurs de la grande presse en France* (Paris: Spes, 1934).

[100] For a documentation of the republican advance in rural parts of the Nièvre after

It may be retorted that this intellectualization of politics had been going on in France for at least a hundred years before the Second Empire. This is true, but not in the form that it definitively acquired during the 1860s, with the liberalization of the strict controls imposed on the press. Hence the distinct importance of a large number of writers, thinkers, and pamphleteers who appear in this book. Their role was not to formulate original political thoughts (even though some did) but rather to represent an existing stock of political and cultural ideas to a larger and varied audience. This conception of politics reached its maturity in the late nineteenth century, with the emergence of nationalist and republican politics and the notion of the intellectual.[101] This book provides compelling evidence that many of the assumptions and practices embedded in this notion effectively came of age under the liberal Empire.

The Modernization of the Revolutionary Heritage

The dynamism of imperial political culture also appears in the continuing and multifarious presence of the French Revolution in its debates. Whereas the place of the Revolution in the historical and public imagination during the early and later parts of the nineteenth century has been analyzed,[102] the pivotal importance of the period between 1852 and 1870 has not been completely appreciated.[103] Yet the two decades of the Second Empire were extremely important for the mythological character of the Revolution; all republicans and most liberals, for example, articulated their political opposition to the Second Empire by invoking the "principles of 1789." But this was also a period of fierce disputes over the ideological heritage of the Revolution. Indeed, at probably no other time in nineteenth-century French history was the mantle of the Revolution coveted by so many different groups.[104] These battles over the legacy of 1789 appeared in many dimensions: between the Bona-

---

1863, see Marcel Vigreux, "Les élections de 1869 dans le Morvan nivernais," *Revue d'Histoire Moderne et Contemporaine* 25 (July–September 1978): 443–69.

[101] On the emergence of intellectuals in France in the late nineteenth century, see Pascal Ory and Jean-François Sirinelli, *Les intellectuels en France, de l'Affaire Dreyfus à nos jours* (Paris: Armand Colin, 1986), 13–60; Charle, *Naissance des "intellectuels."*

[102] On the first half of the nineteenth century, see François Furet, "French Historians and the Reconstruction of the Republican Tradition, 1800–1848," in *The Invention of the Modern Republic*, ed. Biancamaria Fontana (Cambridge: Cambridge University Press, 1994), 173–91.

[103] The intrarepublican debate on Jacobinism is presented in François Furet, *La gauche et la révolution au milieu du XIXeme siècle* (Paris: Fayard, 1986).

[104] For an overview, see Dominique Aubry, *Quatre-vingt-treize et les Jacobins: Regards du dix-neuvième siècle* (Lyon: Presses Universitaires de Lyon, 1988).

partist regime and the republicans; between liberals and republicans; and, often with exceptional intensity, within the republican party itself.

Yet across this torrent of celebrations, commemorations, and re-criminations, it is possible to detect the crystallization of a liberal con-sensus over the definition of the Revolution: its key values and princi-ples appear as individual liberty, justice, and civil equality, and its social thrust is limited to the promotion of education and equality of oppor-tunity. This ideological convergence brought together (in an intellectual, not political, sense) a motley crowd of liberal legitimists, Saint-Simo-nians, left-wing Bonapartists, liberal Protestants, moderate and demo-cratic socialist republicans, and Orleanist liberals. It was vehemently rejected both by the radical and revolutionist republican Left and by the religious and counterrevolutionary Right. With some adjustments (and subsequent additions), this precise coalition of intellectual forces would later underpin the new republican order.

The Second Empire was thus an important moment in the formation of a particular — and enduring — conception of France's political iden-tity. This era was also, as I will argue in chapter 4, of critical impor-tance in the internal history of the republican movement in France: it represented the moment during which French republican ideology made the intellectual transition from the problematic of Revolution to the modern concerns of democratic citizenship.

THE DILEMMAS OF LIBERALISM

The period between 1852 and 1870 also provides an intriguing picture of the ambivalent growth of French liberalism during the nineteenth century.[105] The debate over territorial government and civic virtues was in one sense a story of the rise — and indeed triumph — of liberal politi-cal values in French political culture. By the late 1860s, significant forces in each major political movement professed their adherence to liberalism, specifically to such values as freedom of expression, civil and political rights, and a law-based and procedurally impartial state.

This success, however, was ambivalent. Even within these different liberal subcultures of republicanism, Orleanism, legitimism, and Bona-partism, constant forces were at work to undermine this apparent legit-imation of liberalism. The benign instincts of liberal Bonapartists and Orleanists were often tempered by a fear of anarchy and social revolu-tion; liberal legitimists were frequently constrained by the weight of tra-

---

[105] For an interesting historical analysis of the problems confronting the liberal tradition in the later nineteenth century, as seen through the writings of Emile Durkheim, see Rich-ard Bellamy, *Liberalism and Modern Society* (Oxford: Polity Press, 1992), 58–104.

dition and social hierarchy; and municipalist republicans often disregarded the principles of tolerance and pluralism when it came to discussing the religious question.

In short, the liberalism of the Second Empire (rather like the short-lived liberal Empire itself) was thus an uncertain and somewhat stilted phenomenon. But this was part of a much longer story that—like most narratives in nineteenth-century France—began in 1789. The Revolution created a liberal tradition in France but at the same time reinforced institutional structures and political mentalities which constantly undermined that tradition. The Second Empire provided graphic evidence of the continuing force of this dialectic. Indeed, these tensions did not disappear with the advent of the Third Republic, which was in many senses the most overtly liberal regime to govern France in the nineteenth century. Yet this liberal regime also systematically excluded a number of social and political groups (women, workers, and Catholics) from full membership in the political community.[106] The ideological sources and multiple manifestations of this paradox of liberal citizenship in France are fully explored in this book.[107]

THE EMERGENCE OF DEMOCRACY

Finally, the vibrancy and complexity of imperial political culture appear most emphatically in the question that provides the central focus of this book: local democracy. Despite the claims of orthodox republican historiography,[108] the Second Empire was the period in which universal suffrage acquired a preeminent position in the French political system. This did not mean that it was accepted by all; nor even that it gained an irreversible place in the hearts and minds of the political elite. Simply, all political parties were forced to recognize its presence at the center of the political process and draw appropriate lessons from this fact. This gave rise to a large, varied, and interesting literature on the subject. Some of this material is discussed in this book insofar as it bears directly on questions of local democracy and citizenship; however, this

---

[106] See Robert Gildea, *France, 1870–1914*, 2d ed. (Harlow: Longman, 1996), 83.

[107] I am indebted to Ruth Harris for underlining this point.

[108] For recent examples, see Pierre Miquel, *La Troisième République* (Paris: Fayard, 1989), 20; Alain Garrigou, *Le vote et la vertu: Comment les Français sont devenus électeurs* (Paris: Presses de la Fondation Nationale des Sciences Politiques, 1992), 51–52. A somewhat less blinkered assessment of the Second Empire's contribution to modern democracy can be found in François Caron, *De l'Empire à la République* (Paris: Fayard, 1985), esp. 179–96.

body of writing often tends to be overlooked in studies of the history of electoral politics in nineteenth-century France.[109]

The dynamism of the Second Empire goes even deeper. The Second Empire restored male universal suffrage in France in December 1851, thus abolishing the restrictions introduced by the reactionary republican majority in 1850.[110] The regime also practiced democracy in a frequent and almost feverish way: between 1852 and 1870, there were frequent countrywide elections at national, cantonal, and municipal levels, without forgetting the plebiscites. Voting thus became a common experience for increasingly large numbers of citizens.[111] From this I may offer support for Blanchard's "sacrilegious" hypothesis that the Second Empire as a whole (and not just the liberal Empire) was a crucial moment in the historical construction of democratic practices in France.[112] The archives of the Ministries of the Interior and Justice show that millions of people not only acquired the habit of voting regularly during these years but also came to express their political preferences in an increasingly independent manner — two key preconditions of republican citizenship. Theodore Zeldin noted in his classic work on the imperial regime: "[The Second Empire] disciplined the electorate and thus enabled universal suffrage to be practiced without violence and to become ingrained in the habits of the nation."[113]

The decline of the phenomenon of "official" candidacies during the 1860s is in this respect highly instructive. This is not to say that the regime's practices in the democratic arena were irreproachable. Many of

---

[109] A typical recent example is Pierre Rosanvallon's *Le sacre du citoyen: Histoire du suffrage universel en France* (Paris: Gallimard, 1992), which purports to provide a general history of universal suffrage in France. The account leaps directly from 1851 to 1870; the development of the mass vote under the Second Empire is not systematically assessed. The same absence of reference to the Second Empire is notable in Rosanvallon's more recent piece, "The Republic of Universal Suffrage," in *The Invention of the Modern Republic*, ed. Fontana, 192–205.

[110] Robert Gildea, *Barricades and Borders: Europe, 1800–1914* (Oxford: Oxford University Press, 1987), 176–77.

[111] Extremely high in the first two legislative elections of the Second Empire in 1852 and 1857 (36.7 percent and 35.5 percent), the abstention rate dropped markedly in 1863 (to 27.1 percent) before falling to 21.9 percent in 1869. See Raymond Huard, "Comment apprivoiser le suffrage universel," in *Explication du vote: Un bilan des études électorales en France*, ed. Daniel Gaxie (Paris: Presses de la Fondation Nationale des Sciences Politiques, 1985), 142.

[112] Marcel Blanchard, *Le Second Empire* (Paris: Armand Colin, 1956), 211–12. Raymond Huard has also argued this view, in *Le suffrage universel en France, 1848–1946* (Paris: Aubier, 1991), 86.

[113] Theodore Zeldin, *The Political System of Napoleon III* (London: Macmillan, 1958), 98.

the opposition's strictures against the Empire's corrupt electoral practices were entirely justified. Even more important, the regime's denial of a democratically elected municipal authority to the capital city deprived Paris of the moderating and consensual municipal culture that was beginning to emerge in the rest of France. From this perspective, the Empire's paternalistic local government regime was partly responsible for the violent and destructive passions that eventually consumed the Paris Commune in 1871.

The reverse side of the coin also needs to be examined. During the Second Empire the French nation began to experience the practice of democracy and to build the foundations of a civic culture — a fact that, as we will see later, was quietly recognized even by the republicans in their more sober moments. The debates over local democracy and citizenship were in this sense not of parochial significance but went to the heart of the question of how to give substance and meaning to the notion of political community in France. In an age when nation-states in Europe and elsewhere are in the process of identifying (or rethinking) the principles and values that hold them together, many of the conclusions their French predecessors reached more than a century ago are still refreshingly relevant.

Chapter 1

THE PARADOXES OF BONAPARTIST DEMOCRACY

As NOTED in the introduction, the Second Empire was long demonized in French republican historiography. Later generations of historians typically remembered the circumstances of the founding of the regime, the brutal and repressive nature of its authoritarian phase, the decadent frivolity of its court, and the humiliating defeat of French troops at Sedan.[1] Prefacing his *Histoire du Deuxième Empire* in 1874, Charles Barthélémy commented that France had been governed by a "diseased dreamer"; the reign of Napoleon III had simply been "a lie that lasted eighteen years."[2] Writing in 1886, Augustin Challamel summed up the Second Empire as the era of the "absorption of the rights of a nation into the interests of one man."[3]

No less damning was the general verdict on imperial elites, whose shadowy status was immortalized in Haussonville's contemptuous image of men standing "barefoot in patent-leather boots."[4] Equally flattering was Prince Napoleon, who told his cousin the emperor that his ministers seemed to dress like "coachmen or cooks."[5] In the Orleanist writer Xavier Marmier's memoirs, we find the dignitaries of the Empire "avid for fat salaries, hungry for profits, and eager to derive every possible advantage from their position, whether with dignity or indignity, by fair means or foul." Such men were nothing but vain and unscrupulous adventurers, who were incapable of the slightest elevation of spirit or thought.[6] In Louise Colet's republican satire *Ces petits messieurs*, the spirit of the late Second Empire is painted in equally somber tones: the predominant qualities attributed to the agents of Empire are cynicism, moral callousness, coarseness, and incompetence.[7]

In recent decades, a growing number of works on the Second Empire have attempted to correct this negative impression. The overall me-

---

[1] See, for example, Augustin Regnault, *La France sous le Second Empire, 1852–1870* (Paris: Vanier, 1907), 308–10.

[2] Charles Barthélémy, *Histoire du Deuxième Empire* (Paris: Blériot, 1874), x–xi.

[3] Augustin Challamel, *Histoire de la liberté en France* (Paris: Jouvet, 1886) 2:318.

[4] Quoted in Alain Plessis, *The Rise and Fall of the Second Empire, 1852–1870* (Cambridge: Cambridge University Press, 1987), 31.

[5] Quoted in Blanchard, *Le Second Empire*, 147.

[6] Xavier Marmier, *Journal, 1848–1890* (Geneva: Droz, 1968), 2:128.

[7] Louise Colet, *Ces petits messieurs* (Paris: Dentu, 1869).

chanics of the imperial political system have been reassessed, and its key agents have emerged as dynamic and purposeful figures, whose will was indeed often autonomous of that of their political and administrative masters.[8] Biographical studies have emphasized the managerial talents of the emperor's ministers and advisers;[9] erudite monographs have underlined the devotion to the public good of his prefects and councillors of state;[10] dictionaries have brought attention to the wealth of individual and collective accomplishments between 1852 and 1870;[11] copious articles have underscored the professional qualities of the imperial police;[12] and (perhaps most startlingly of all) private letters have revealed that even the austere members of the elite Finance Inspectorate were "men of flesh and blood."[13] Yet, for all these welcome additions to our knowledge, Second Empire Bonapartism remains somewhat underconceptualized. In his classic book *Les droites en France*, René Rémond points to the political originality of Bonapartism and stresses three key elements in its ideological "system": the reference to 1789, the principle of authority, and the constant search for "glory."[14] Rémond distinguishes between a right- and left-wing tendency within Bonapartism and notes the preponderance of the former by 1870. However, there is no development of his conceptual analysis or an explanation of how this ideological divide might relate to other types of Bonapartism he identifies. In a wide-ranging study of Bonapartism between 1800 and 1850, Frédéric Bluche also notes certain elements of continuity (most notably the revo-

---

[8] Zeldin, *The Political System of Napoleon III*.

[9] See, most notably, Joseph Durieux, *Le Ministre Pierre Magne, 1806–1879*, 2 vols. (Paris: Champion, 1929); Albert Duchêne, *Un ministre trop oublié: Chasseloup-Laubat* (Paris: Société d'Editions Géographiques, Maritimes, et Coloniales, 1932); Jean Maurain, *Baroche, ministre de Napoléon III* (Paris: Félix Alcan, 1936); Robert Schnerb, *Rouher et le Second Empire* (Paris: Armand Colin, 1949); Honoré Farat, *Persigny, un ministre de Napoléon III* (Paris: Hachette, 1957); Gerda Grothe, *Le Duc de Morny* (Paris: Fayard, 1966); *Eugène Rouher: Journées d'étude, 16–17 Mars 1984* (Clermond-Ferrand: Institut d'Etudes du Massif Central, 1985); Edouard Bornecque-Winandy, *Achille Fould, Ministre de Napoléon III* (Neuilly, 1989).

[10] See Vincent Wright, *Le Conseil d'Etat sous le Second Empire* (Paris: Armand Colin, 1972); Le Clère and Wright, *Les Préfets du Second Empire*; Jean-Pierre Defrance, "Janvier de la Motte," *Administration*, no. 160 (1993).

[11] William Echard, *Historical Dictionary of the French Second Empire* (London: Aldwych, 1985); Jean Tulard, *Dictionnaire du Second Empire* (Paris: Fayard, 1995).

[12] See, for example, Terry W. Strieter, "The Faceless Police of the Second Empire: A Social Profile of the *gendarmes* of Mid-Nineteenth Century France," *French History* 8, no. 2 (June 1994): 167–95.

[13] See Pierre-François Pinaud, "La vie quotidienne de l'Inspection des Finances sous le Second Empire," *Revue Historique* (January–March 1987): 65.

[14] René Rémond, *Les droites en France* (Paris: Aubier, 1982), 106–7.

lutionary legacy) but concludes with the "permanent ambiguity" of the Bonapartist phenomenon.[15]

The ambivalent quality of Bonapartism is undeniable. The image of heterogeneity it has left behind is partly the product of Napoleon III's reluctance to form a distinct Bonapartist party or even to establish a doctrinal review.[16] With reference to the Second Empire alone, contemporaries and later historians have identified a wide range of manifestations of the Bonapartist phenomenon — authoritarian and liberal, nationalistic and chauvinistic, but also conservative and rural,[17] notabilist,[18] Orleanist and neolegitimist,[19] democratic and popular,[20] red and white,[21] clerical and anticlerical, technocratic and Saint-Simonian,[22] and even socialist.[23] The mere distinction between liberal and authoritarian Bonapartism is therefore manifestly insufficient to make sense of this social and intellectual diversity. At the same time, it is perhaps going too far to argue, as Rothney does, that "one could speak of an entire Bonapartist spectrum ranging from extreme left to extreme right."[24] This claim is acceptable only in the sense in which it might apply to all other broad political families during the Second Empire. As we will see in the rest of this book, liberals, republicans, and even legitimists were broad churches, within which a wide ideological spectrum could be distinguished. But this view is not to be confused with the location of these specific ideologies on a more general political spectrum. Indeed, the claim that Bonapartism (or any other political grouping, for that matter) occupies the entire political spectrum is unhelpful, because it shies away from addressing the necessary question of its core ideological principles.

The underconceptualization of Bonapartism is apparent in another

[15] Frédéric Bluche, *Le bonapartisme: Aux origines de la droite autoritaire* (Paris: Editions Latines, 1980), 336.

[16] Frédéric Bluche, *Le bonapartisme* (Paris: Presses Universitaires de France, 1981), 96.

[17] Philippe Vigier, "Le bonapartisme et le monde rural," in *Le bonapartisme, phénomène historique et mythe politique*, ed. Karl Hammer and Peter Claus Hartmann (Munich, 1977).

[18] Rémond, *Les droites en France*, 110.

[19] See Bernard Ménager, "1848–1871: Autorité ou Liberté," in *Histoire des droites en France*, ed. Jean-François Sirinelli (Paris: Gallimard, 1992), 1:107–27.

[20] Corbin, *Archaïsme et modernité*, 908.

[21] Georges Lachaud, *Bonapartistes blancs et bonapartistes rouges* (Paris: Dentu, 1885).

[22] Georges Weill, "Les Saint-Simoniens sous Napoléon III," *Revue des Etudes Napoléoniennes* 3 (1913): 391–406.

[23] Gustave de Bernardi, *La Révolution* (Paris: Albanel, 1875), 43.

[24] John Rothney, *Bonapartism After Sedan* (New York: Cornell University Press, 1969), 22.

dimension. Many areas of Bonapartist writing continue to be exempted from any manner of ideological analysis. In particular, there is a continuing tendency to downplay — if not altogether to disregard — the ideological aspects of the Bonapartist conceptions of the state, largely because its Jacobinism is simply taken for granted. Thus, in his analysis of Bonapartist administrative institutions under the Second Empire, Guy Thuillier exemplifies this atheoretical approach by arguing that the development of the imperial administration between 1852 and 1870 occurred without any theoretical or ideological guiding principles.[25] In short, the reassessment of the history of the Second Empire has yet fully to come to terms with the richness and diversity of Bonapartist ideology. The dominant view now seems to be that however discerning and effective they may have been as statesmen and administrators, the men of Empire were mere empiricists whose actions were guided by a mixture of public interest and opportunism rather than ideology.

One of the primary purposes of this chapter is to correct this view, by offering a broad analysis of Bonapartist discourse on centralization. This analysis serves two revisionist purposes: first, to demonstrate clearly the existence of Bonapartist theories of the state and public administration, which were formulated and argued over among Bonapartist elites (as well as with other political groups); second, to bring to light a range of Bonapartist writings on decentralization. In traditional approaches to the French Right, this aspect of Bonapartism is generally passed over in silence.[26] For their part, historians of decentralization tend to regard the advocacy of greater local liberty during the Second Empire as the exclusive preserve of opposition groups. From their perspective, decentralism appears primarily as a revisionist — and even subversive — enterprise orchestrated by political movements to undermine the power and authority of the Napoleonic regime.[27] Even those historians of the Second Empire who recognize the regime's commitment to liberal reform during the 1860s often ignore the phenomenon of Bonapartist decentralization, or else they present it as an opportunistic response to the clamors of opposition groups and public opinion more generally.[28]

---

[25] Guy Thuillier, "Administration," in *Dictionnaire du Second Empire*, ed. Tulard, 6.

[26] Jean-Christian Petitfils, *La Droite en France de 1789 à nos jours* (Paris: Presses Universitaires de France, 1989), 44–49. In his chapter on Bonapartism in *Les droites en France*, Rémond does not discuss the internal debate over decentralization.

[27] See, for example, Rosanvallon, *L'Etat en France*, 79–80; and André-Jean Tudesq, "La Décentralisation et la droite en France au XIXeme siècle," in *La Décentralisation, Colloque d'Histoire*, Faculté des Lettres et Sciences Humaines d'Aix-en-Provence, 1–2 Décembre 1961 (Aix-en-Provence: Editions Ophrys, 1964), 55–67.

[28] See, for example, Blanchard, *Le Second Empire*, 140–41; Georges Pradalié, *Le Sec-*

None of these approaches, therefore, seriously entertains the notion of a genuinely Bonapartist form of decentralization. Yet during the 1860s the regime of Napoleon III took a number of political and legislative initiatives to promote greater local liberty in France. The last of these measures was the creation of an extraparliamentary commission of inquiry in February 1870, whose wide-ranging discussions were interrupted only by the outbreak of the war with Prussia. The promotion of local liberty therefore became an integral part of the Bonapartist regime's discourse. In this chapter I will assess the nature and extent of its commitment to the cause of decentralization and will offer three general conclusions. First, decentralization was a response to a growing internal crisis produced by the contradictions of the imperial political and administrative system. However, divisions within the Bonapartist movement prevented this response from developing to its full potential, which explains the limited progress that the promotion of decentralist legislation had achieved by the time the Second Empire collapsed in September 1870. At the same time, civic and political practices evolved significantly in the direction of greater local autonomy, to such an extent that the local government regime of 1870 in effect bore little resemblance to the centralist order that the Empire had sought to promote in 1852.

Second, the debates over decentralization also provide an illustration of the problematic nature of local politics for the Bonapartist state. Considerations of administrative efficiency had to be reconciled with political and ideological imperatives; for example, the regime was eager to derive its legitimacy from male universal suffrage, which was restored in December 1851.[29] At the same time the Second Empire sought to maintain close administrative control over the communes and departments and to promote a depoliticized conception of communal citizenship. The regime was also torn between its instinctive desire to preserve order and stability in the provinces and a genuine aspiration to breathe life into the quiescent structures of municipal and departmental administration. Finally, there were conflicts of interest between different branches of the imperial state (especially between the prefects and the elected representatives). The question of decentralization thus exposed a number of critical problems the regime faced in its attempts to reconstruct the machinery of the state and redefine the nature of citizenship. Despite its failure to maintain itself after 1870, however, the Bonapartist regime played an important role in preparing the terrain for the irruption of democratic politics in France in the later nineteenth century.

---

ond Empire (Paris: Presses Universitaires de France, 1969), 40–43; and Octave Aubry, Le Second Empire (Paris: Club du Livre, 1956), 429–41.

[29] Huard, Le suffrage universel, 69–73.

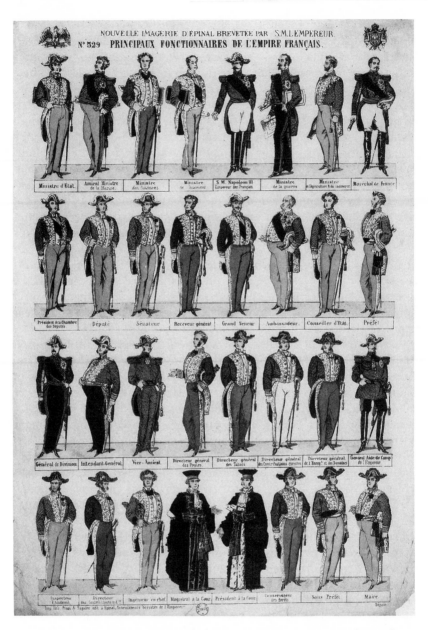

Fig. 1. Principaux Fonctionnaires de l'Empire Français, Imagerie d'Epinal, no. 529, Bibliothèque Nationale, Paris. A good representation of the Bonapartist administrative hierarchy. Worth noting is the ambiguous relationship between prefects and councillors of state on one hand and deputies and senators on the other; both groups are on the same line. Also of interest is the lowly place assigned to the mayor (bottom right-hand corner).

This chapter begins with a description of the philosophy and practice of Bonapartism, particularly its attachment to centralization under the Second Empire. This account is followed by an analysis of the political utility of centralization for the Bonapartist regime. I then examine the dysfunctions of the local government system and the social, political, and institutional reasons that impelled the Empire to put forward decentralist proposals. These measures and their justifications are subsequently contrasted with the views of authoritarian and centralist Bonapartists, who fiercely opposed any scheme that devolved substantive powers to the departments and communes. This conflict between centralist and decentralist views was played out fully in the workings of the 1870 extraparliamentary commission, whose inconclusive efforts demonstrated the limits of the Bonapartist conception of decentralization. My analysis ends with an overall assessment of the empire's record in local politics and the promotion of principles of good citizenship.

BONAPARTISM: UNITY AND DIVERSITY

The common ideological core of Second Empire Bonapartism was based almost exclusively on an interpretation of the achievements of the emperor Napoleon. As a Bonapartist weekly put it in 1850, "The Napoleonic cause is the same in 1848 as in 1802."[30] This lineage was further emphasized after the reestablishment of the empire in 1852. In the words of a Bonapartist pamphleteer, "The eternal honor of the great emperor is to have understood the great Revolution, to have adopted its principles, to have proclaimed and sanctioned them, covering them with the authority of his genius."[31]

These key Bonapartist principles of the Revolution were the abolition of feudalism, the introduction of civil equality, the principle of taxation, the admission of all citizens to public offices, and the subordination of the church to the state.[32] All Bonapartists also recognized the strategic importance of cultivating the rural world; in the words of one of the emperor's most proficient ministers, "It is in this milieu that are preserved a pure sense of morals and a strong devotion to the empire."[33] Although the Bonapartist vision of the rural world stressed the importance of the values of "authority, order, and hierarchy,"[34] it was distinct from traditionalist and clericalist conceptions in that it saw itself as a

[30] *Le Napoléon*, 6 January 1850.

[31] Henry d'Escamps, *Du rétablissement de l'Empire* (Paris: Plon, 1852), 9.

[32] Ibid., 10–11.

[33] Durieux, *Le Ministre Pierre Magne*, 1:336–37.

[34] Auguste Guyard, *Lettres aux gens de Frotey sur une commune modèle* (Paris: Dentu, 1863), 33–34.

progressive force; one rural Bonapartist declared his commitment to "the moral revolution brought about by progress."[35] Provincial Bonapartists also welcomed the spread of education and were often suspicious of clerical and noble influences. Thus in 1869 Ernest de Bouteiller, the official candidate in the constituency of Metz (Moselle), underscored his commitment to "the propagation of education for all" and the "moral and material improvement of the condition of France."[36]

As noted earlier, historians have identified divisions between progressive and authoritarian subcultures within Bonapartism—in the political terminology of the time, between "liberals" and "Arcadians."[37] The latter have been seen to favor order, religion, military glory, and social conservatism and to depend for their support on traditional social elites. The former are said to stress the popular and democratic aspect of the Bonapartist tradition, which was attached to civil equality and universal suffrage.[38] But this dichotomy often obscures rather than illuminates the reality of Second Empire Bonapartism. The attachment to order and authority appears as a characteristic feature of all Bonapartists, who commonly subscribed to the view that "nothing can be created, live, and develop without order and regularity."[39] Indeed, such views served as the basis for the justification of Louis Napoleon's coup in 1851.[40] At the same time, this dichotomy does little to capture the place of the Bonapartist ideologue Persigny, whose political instincts were nothing if not authoritarian but who nonetheless—and unlike many Bonapartists of this variety such as Jérôme David, Boilay, and the Cassagnacs—regarded the principle of universal suffrage as a core component of Bonapartist ideology.[41]

Indeed, Bonapartists and republicans often expressed a common attachment to universal suffrage; however, there were differences in the manner in which it was conceived and practiced. Republicans tended to stress the civic and participationist advantages of universal suffrage,

[35] Paul David, *La commune rurale* (Toulouse: Savy, 1863), ix.
[36] Quoted in *Les élections dans le département de la Moselle*, vol. 2 (Metz: Faculté des Lettres et Sciences Humaines de Strasbourg, 1971).
[37] Rémond, *Les droites en France*, 121.
[38] In the words of a Bonapartist pamphleteer in 1852, "There is no sovereignty without direct and universal suffrage. There is no constitution without direct and universal suffrage" (Maximilien Tallès, *L'Empire c'est la souveraineté du peuple* [Paris: Garnier, 1852], 59).
[39] Charles Merruau, *Souvenirs de l'Hôtel de Ville de Paris, 1848–1852* (Paris: Plon, 1875), 61.
[40] Louis Véron, *Mémoires d'un bourgeois de Paris* (Paris: Librairie Nouvelle, 1856), 5:302–3, and *Nouveaux Mémoires d'un Bourgeois de Paris* (Paris: Librairie Internationale, 1866), 442.
[41] Farat, *Persigny*, 279.

whereas Bonapartists saw it as an "essentially conservative" instrument.[42] Bonapartists also rejected the republican emphasis on representative and deliberative forms of democracy; in the words of the imperialist poet Mérimée, "Parliamentary democracy is one of the worst governments for a country that lacks a strong aristocracy."[43] Hence the Bonapartist fondness for plebiscites.[44] Furthermore, it is difficult to locate Saint-Simonian or technical approaches, which were embraced by many Bonapartist elites, within the strict dichotomy between liberalism and authoritarianism. Indeed, many Bonapartists advocated a technical conception of politics as opposed to an ideological one, in which greater emphasis was placed on good management and sound finance; as with figures such as Eugène Rouher, there was often an element of intellectual flexibility—if not opportunism—in the demeanor of these Bonapartists.[45] Finally, to complicate matters even further, the antielitist strand in the Bonapartist tradition, which often expressed strong hostility to traditional notables and religious institutions, was by no means the exclusive property of liberals.

The issue of centralization will underscore the somewhat precarious nature of the classification between liberal and authoritarian Bonapartism. Generally speaking, liberal Bonapartists were in favor of a moderate form of decentralization, whereas their authoritarian counterparts tended to defend political and administrative centralization. But these positions were sometimes inverted. Despite their commitment to greater political liberty, not all liberal imperialists were advocates of decentralization, and some authoritarian Bonapartists were strongly committed to the extension of local liberties, provided they were thought not to interfere with the general interest. In the final analysis, it will emerge that it was these divisions over the nature of citizenship, more than any intrinsic Bonapartist commitment to centralism, that contributed to the failure of the regime to advance the cause of decentralization beyond the limited steps taken by the summer of 1870.

BONAPARTIST CENTRALISM: POLITICAL AND ADMINISTRATIVE DIMENSIONS

As with all French regimes since the Revolution, the territorial units of the commune, the canton, and the department constituted the principal

---

[42] Ernest Merson, *Confessions d'un journaliste* (Paris: Savine, 1890), 301.

[43] Letter, 22 May 1869, in *Lettres à M. Panizzi, 1850–1870*, by Prosper Mérimée (Paris: Calmann Lévy, 1881), 2:362.

[44] Jules Amigues, *Lettres au peuple* (Paris: Amyot, 1872), 20–21.

[45] For a somewhat different perspective on Rouher's politics, see Schnerb, *Rouher et le Second Empire*, 161–67.

basis upon which the administrative territorial order of the Second Empire was founded. Distinct to the imperial regime, however, was a particular conception of the vertical relationship between higher and lower administrative bodies. This approach was largely based on the principles of political and administrative centralization, which were directly inherited from the Bonapartist tradition. For Bonapartists, society was a construct whose primordial feature was not sociability but power. In the words of the journalist Adolphe Granier de Cassagnac, "Power is the first of social necessities; it is reflected, as a consequence of its principle, in the origin, nature, and purpose of all societies."[46]

This philosophy was strongly articulated during the early years of the Second Empire. At a speech delivered at the opening of the Legislative Corps in January 1858, Napoleon III had categorically asserted that "the empire requires a strong state, capable of overcoming the obstacles that might impede its advance, for, let us not forget, the progress of every new regime is a long struggle."[47] To this Bonapartist lineage was added the influence of Saint-Simonian ideas on Napoleon III,[48] as typified in the following paternalistic view of the role of the state: "A government is not a necessary ulcer, but rather the beneficial motor of every social organism."[49] Hence the ideological justification of centralization, loftily spelled out by a Bonapartist councillor of state:

> "What does this word [centralization] mean in its general and summary definition? It means: a government far removed from the men it governs. This distance is necessary so that the law can be fair and impartial; nothing is as odious and unfair as a fragmented government, where particular interests are all-powerful, and where the wounds inflicted by a superior on his subordinate are constantly irritated and even exacerbated by the very presence of the master; man only submits himself and accepts a superior in a sphere more elevated than his own; from this height, he obeys an order because he feels it dictated by a hand that has not been implicated in the miserable passions surrounding him.[50]

The local political and administrative arrangements that the Second Empire aspired to maintain operated around the simple precepts of or-

[46] *Le Réveil*, 8 January 1859.

[47] Louis Napoléon [Napoléon III], *Discours, messages, et proclamations de l'Empereur* (Paris: Plon, 1860), 373.

[48] See Girard, *Napoléon III*, 177.

[49] Louis Napoléon [Napoléon III], *Oeuvres de Napoléon III* (Paris: Plon, 1856), 1:11, 21. On the influence of Saint-Simonism during the Second Empire, see Georges Weill, *L'école Saint-Simonienne* (Paris: Alcan, 1896), 236–53, and Sébastien Charléty, *Histoire du Saint-Simonisme* (Paris: Hachette, 1896).

[50] Edouard Boinvilliers, *Paris souverain de la France* (Paris: Dubuisson, 1868), 19.

der, harmony, and depoliticization. An illustration is provided in the following excerpt from the newspaper *L'Ariégois*, here narrating a visit by Adolphe Billault, president of the Legislative Corps (and a future interior minister of the Empire), to the *chef-lieu* of his department in August 1853:

> The functionaries, mayors of rural communes, and notables of the town have paid homage to His Excellency, who for all has managed to find words whose frankness and judiciousness will leave indelible impressions.
> . . . Everything is ready: our town has its physiognomy of solemn days; in the middle of the elegant bridge across the Ariège an *arc-de-triomphe* is raised, and on its pediment can be read these words: Long Live Napoleon III, to M. Billault, President of the Legislative Corps and Deputy of the Ariège. . . .
>   The crowd mingles happily and unfolds along the avenues and quays. No military machinery, no constraint, no official formalities, can deny this reception the status of a family gathering; all is calm and dignified; this is a spontaneous homage, a sympathetic and respectful demonstration in tribute to an eminent personality, honored by the trust of the head of state and the esteem of all parties, an eminent man to whom the Ariège entrusts its future.[51]

The symbolic order of the commune was clearly revealed here. In the eyes of the Bonapartists, the local polity was likened to a family, whose destiny was not troubled by any destructive passions and where sentiments of respect and loyalty predominated. The depoliticization of public life was a consistent theme of Bonapartist ideology: "Let us not be Orleanists, legitimists, republicans, or even Bonapartists; let us only love our country."[52] The commune was also presented as a festive locality, in which social and political contradictions were forgotten and even transcended. Last but not least, the commune was part of an elaborate hierarchy, whose paternalism offered all the requisite guarantees of order, discipline, and rationality. A Bonapartist notable carried the metaphor to its logical conclusion: "What will therefore be the best model to follow so as to make our administrative organization as perfect as possible? Need it be said that it is the army?"[53] Solidarity, harmony, hierarchy: the local government regime inaugurated by Napoleon III in the laws of July 1852 and May 1855 bore the centralist imprint of the Bonapartist tradition in a number of key respects.[54] First, the leading

---

[51] *L'Ariégois*, 27 August 1853.

[52] E. Chérot, *La bourgeoisie et l'Empire* (Paris: Dentu, 1860), 30.

[53] Comte Rodolphe d'Ornano, *De l'administration de l'Empire* (Paris: Dentu, 1860), 6.

[54] See Edme Simonot, *Le suffrage universel et l'existence communale sous le régime de*

figures in local assemblies (the mayor and the assistant mayor) were
appointed by the state rather than chosen by their respective councils.[55]
The president and executive officers of the General Council were also
chosen by the state. In Paris, Lyon, and all the communes of the Seine, the
entire municipal council (as well as the mayor) was appointed by the
emperor. In Paris the regime consistently opposed all demands for municipal elections. An internal memorandum argued as follows in 1864:

> The greater part of the Parisian electorate has no real municipal sense.
> Floating masses of workers who arrive one day and are ready to leave the
> next, of families whose members are dispersed by the nature of their work
> in different parts of the city, of nomadic tenants who necessarily transport
> themselves from district to district without finding a preferred locality or a
> patrimonial state, this accumulation of men, estranged from one another, is
> seized only by political ideas and gives in easily, when it is not dominated
> by a great national sentiment, to the most deplorable suggestions.[56]

Second, the executive powers of the commune and the department
were constrained by statutory provisions that severely limited their ability to initiate and execute policies independently of the wishes of central
government. Municipal councils lost the powers of nomination that
some had fleetingly exercised during earlier regimes.[57] For much of the
Second Empire, the General Council enjoyed less power and autonomy
than its counterpart under the July Monarchy.[58]

Third, the activities of the municipality and the General Council were
carried out under the watchful surveillance of the prefect, the representative of central government in each department and often the dominant
figure in local political life.[59] Nominations of mayors were generally

---

la loi de 1855 (Paris: Firmin Didot, 1861); more generally, see Henry Berton, *L'évolution
constitutionnelle du Second Empire* (Paris, 1900), 144–45.

[55] Mayors of large cities were chosen by central government, and those of smaller towns
and villages (those with fewer than ten thousand inhabitants) were appointed by prefects.
By virtue of the laws of 21 March 1831 and 5 May 1855, the government had the discre-
tionary right to terminate the functions of mayors. After 1855, prefects also appointed
assistant mayors.

[56] Archives Nationales, Papiers Eugène Rouher, 45 AP 19, "De l'organisation municipale de la ville de Paris," 13 January 1864.

[57] For example, the right to elect the mayor and to be consulted over the choice of the
local schoolteacher.

[58] Félix Ponteil, *Les institutions de la France de 1814 à 1870* (Paris: Presses Universitaires de France, 1966), 372–73.

[59] See Le Clère and Wright's *Les Préfets du Second Empire*, which demolishes the myth
of prefectoral omnipotence during the Second Empire. Nonetheless, the powers of the
prefects remained considerable when compared with those wielded by their successors in
the Third Republic.

made on the recommendation of prefects. Under the terms of the 1855 law, the prefects also had the power to suspend municipal councils and dismiss mayors. Between 1852 and 1870, 323 mayors were dismissed, often to the intense fury of the political opposition. But this figure represented less than half the number of mayors dismissed by the July Monarchy.[60]

One of the most important and politically useful instruments available to prefects was the power of apportionment—the division of communes into sections. Throughout the Second Empire, these powers were used to undermine and frustrate the representation of opposition groups in local councils.[61] Fourth, local and central administrative institutions were given explicitly political functions of control, surveillance, and repression. These powers were exercised against individuals and groups who engaged in activities deemed hostile to the interests of the Empire. In the immediate aftermath of the coup d'état in 1851, the prefect of the Rhone wrote to his mayors: "I am depending on your zeal on the day of battle to ensure the support of all honest people to Louis Napoleon. . . . Exercise the utmost vigilance, and if you discover any agitators roaming your commune, do not hesitate to have them arrested."[62]

The elimination of political dissent was part of a broader conception of public life in the provinces. As the description of Billault's visit suggested, the ideal of local life put forward by the central government was essentially apolitical. Representative institutions were presented as administrative rather than political bodies, whose deliberations were not allowed to enter the public domain. As a circular letter from the minister of the interior made clear to all prefects, "The most serious considerations require that municipal discussions be contained within the sphere of purely administrative interests; they should be prevented from being perverted either by the dangerous provocations of external passions or by regrettable appeals to a vain popularity."[63] Similar considerations applied to the departmental councils: "Members of the General

[60] Eight hundred fifty-three mayors were revoked between 1830 and 1848. See Elzéar Lavoie, "La révocation des maires, 1830–1875," in *Europe et Etat: Actes du Colloque de Toulouse, 11–13 Avril 1991* (Aix-en-Provence: Presses Universitaires d'Aix-Marseille, 1992), 61.

[61] In the 1865 municipal elections in Marseille, the prefect announced the division of the city into twenty-one sections only eight days before polling day, to the great anger of opposition groups. Similar practices were carried out in Auxerre, Bordeaux, and Lille and denounced by Armand le François in *Le Temps*, 16 July 1865. More generally, see Baron de Layre, *Les minorités et le suffrage universel* (Paris: Dentu, 1868).

[62] Baron de Vincent, 15 December 1851, quoted in *Histoire de la France contemporaine*, ed. Jean Elleinstein (Paris: Editions Sociales, 1979), 3:194.

[63] *Bulletin Officiel du Ministère de l'Intérieur*, circular of minister on the publication of the deliberations of municipal councils, 16 September 1865, 632.

Councils should be above all wise and prudent men, impervious to party intrigue and devoted to the government."[64] Indeed, mayors and presidents of the General Councils were generally chosen on the basis of technical proficiency and local prestige rather than ideological ortho-doxy. Legislation adopted in the early days of the Empire forbade the General Councils from expressing political views.[65] Municipal councils deemed to be governed by unruly political passions were dissolved.[66] At the same time, local assemblies were presented as performing a useful civic role, notably in educating the citizenry in the virtues of sound administration. In his opening speech at the session of the General Council of the Puy-de-Dôme in August 1864, Eugène Rouher delineated the following Bonapartist conception of the educative function of de-partmental administrative councils:

> These assemblies are in all of France a great technical school that facilitates the deeper study of our administrative, economic, and financial organiza-tion in which the politician prepares or completes his education and ac-quires the experience and maturity necessary to face on a greater stage those higher-order struggles in which more considerable interests are at stake. . . . Politics and its irritant passions are banished from these sur-roundings so as to preserve a greater purity in the atmosphere.[67]

Local public life, in sum, was about fostering a distinct type of citi-zenship, which was concerned with technical means rather than ideo-logical ends and thus administration rather than politics. It also sought to unite the citizenry behind issues of common interest rather than to appeal to the demons of class, religion, and ideology. Yet, even though every attempt was made to keep political conflict out of the communes and departments, the Empire sought to legitimize its authority through universal suffrage—an eminently political instrument. Persigny, the ide-ologue of the regime, sought to overcome the contradiction.

> Universal suffrage, that is, the collective will of an entire people, which has constituted public authority in the person of the emperor, engenders in its turn all liberties: communal liberty in the municipal council alongside the mayor, the representative of authority; departmental liberty in the General

[64] Archives Nationales [henceforth abbreviated as Arch. Nat.] F1c IV 8, circular of min-ister of interior to all prefects, 7 July 1852.
[65] In 1870, 60 percent of all general councillors were apolitical; only 15 percent were clearly defined as hostile to the Empire. See Louis Girard et al., *Les conseillers généraux en 1870* (Paris: Presses Universitaires de France, 1967), 133.
[66] Thus, between 1860 and 1865 there were 63 dissolutions of municipal councils. See a defense of the practice by Vuitry, in *Annales du Sénat et du Corps Législatif: Compte-rendu analytique des séances*, session of 13 April 1867 (Paris: Panckoucke, 1867), 130.
[67] Arch. Nat., Papiers Eugène Rouher, 45 AP 19.

Council, with the prefect at its side; and national liberty in the Legislative Corps, beside the sovereign . . . By ensuring the reciprocal independence of authority and liberty, instead of subordinating the one to the other, Napoleonic theory has virtually resolved the problem of liberty in France.[68]

The Bonapartist conception of the relationship between local and central institutions was thus doubly hierarchical.[69] Representative institutions at the center (the Legislative Corps and the Senate) were clearly ranked above their counterparts in the departments and communes, whose functional attributes were considerably more restricted. In this respect, as I noted in the introduction, the Second Empire merely reaffirmed a Jacobin commitment to a unitary conception of the state (and a rejection of federalism), which was common to all regimes since the French Revolution, whether monarchical or republican. Furthermore, each of these deliberative bodies exercised its respective mandate under the scrutiny of a higher administrative body: the Council of State (and ultimately the emperor himself) for the Legislative Corps[70] and the Senate,[71] and the prefectorate for the departmental assemblies and the municipalities. The Second Empire's local government regime was thus centralist not only in its commitment to functional and territorial unity but also in its intended subjection of political representation to administrative control.[72]

This approach found favor with both the authoritarian and the liberal wing of the Bonapartist movement. For authoritarians such as Persigny, Rouher, and Jérôme David, a centralized regime was justified because they believed it delivered political stability, maintained social cohesion, and protected the country from the subversive inclinations of revolutionary socialism. For liberal Bonapartists such as Prince Napoleon, centralization was an essential means of creating a sense of national identity and unity and of breaking down the particularist attachments that often tied peasant communities to local social elites. In sum, authoritarian Bonapartists welcomed centralization as a means of preserving order, whereas their liberal counterparts viewed it as a way of upholding the Napoleonic principles of civil and political equality. Ultimately, however, the real devotees of administrative power were the authoritarian Bonapartists. In the course of sketching a comparison with

[68] From a speech given at a banquet of the Loire General Council, in *Courrier de Saint-Etienne*, 25 August 1864.

[69] Auguste Pougnet, *Hiérarchie et décentralisation* (Paris: Germer Baillière, 1866), 135.

[70] On the legislative role of the Council of State, see Wright, *Le Conseil d'Etat*, 109–11.

[71] On the role of the Senate, see Henri Perceau, *Le Sénat sous le Second Empire* (Paris: Jouve, 1909).

[72] Maurice Pain, "Le Second Empire et ses procédés de gouvernement," *Revue Politique et Parlementaire* (June 1905): 574–77.

the British nobility, Persigny underlined the essential role of the administration in France:

> In the place of a great aristocracy covering the land with vast domains
> immobilized by the regime of substitutions and disposing of enormous
> means of influence, we have an administrative hierarchy, which alone constitutes the entire political organism of our democracy; outside it there are
> nothing but grains of sand without cohesion or common purpose.[73]

THE UTILITY OF CENTRALISM

The benefits derived from such a centralist regime for local government appeared obvious enough, and during the first decade of the Second Empire the political system operated according to the logic prescribed by its authors. The subordination of elected bodies to the administration initially insulated local politics from the passions of public life. The repression that followed the 1851 coup d'état severely undermined the political and organizational strength of the republicans, Orleanists, and legitimists. Many of the latter compounded their isolation by voluntarily abstaining from participation in local political life during the first decade of the Empire.[74] Local elections, with the exception of those held in legitimist and republican heartlands, took on a largely apolitical character.

Furthermore, the government's appointment of the mayor ensured that the state's interests were represented and defended in most of the communes of France. Although the mayor was both an agent of the government and a representative of the commune, in the Bonapartist scheme of things the former function clearly took precedence over the latter. This role was particularly important in the rural communes (by far the most numerous),[75] where the mayor was often the only resident representative of the state. He was thus the only person vested with the powers of publicizing laws, executing measures of public safety, revising electoral lists, and carrying out recruitment operations for the army. In this sense, the control of the appointment of mayors was intended to ensure that the regime's administrative will was carried out in all corners of the territory. It was also part of a constant exercise in the supervision of territorial agents. Reports on the activities of mayors were

[73] "Discours sur les principes politiques de l'Empire," 26 August 1863, in *Le Duc de Persigny et les doctrines de l'Empire*, ed. Joseph Delaroa (Paris: Plon, 1865), 163.

[74] Rémond, *Les droites en France* , 104–5.

[75] According to the 1866 census, of the 37,548 communes of France, 16,674 had fewer than 500 inhabitants, and 15,976 had between 501 and 1,500 inhabitants. At the other end of the scale, only 45 communes had more than 30,000 inhabitants. A copy of the census is in Arch. Nat. C2866 (Commission de Décentralisation).

filed by a number of administrative agents; they ranged from enthusiastic endorsements to severe condemnation. The mayor of Montricoux was thus denounced to the prefect of Tarn-et-Garonne by the local schoolteacher: "The mayor is always opposed to what is good; always in a state of intoxication, he has banned his municipal council from the municipality; he rejects everything he should approve, so much so that in the commune nothing can be done any longer. I shall not speak of the harm he has done, I would need a volume . . . everything is falling into ruin."[76]

But the mayor was also a political agent of the government, and this aspect of his role came into full view during electoral consultations. It was the mayor's duty to rally the support of the inhabitants of his commune for the official candidate. Mayors thus issued colorfully alarmist electoral proclamations denouncing the candidates of the opposition. The mayor of Jouvelle beseeched the inhabitants of his commune not to vote for the liberal monarchist candidate for the Legislative Corps, the marquis d'Andelarre, in 1863. Andelarre, he alleged, was not only an enemy of the Empire but also a "protector of the party of the nobility and the clergy, that is, the party that would like to see the return of the times when our ancestors were summoned in turn to beat the water and silence the frogs, in order that Monsieur and Madame la Marquise could sleep peacefully."[77]

If the mayor was the foot soldier of the regime in the provinces, the real strategists of the Empire were the prefects. Cherished figures of Bonapartist administrative ideology,[78] their powers were increased considerably under the local government decrees of 1852 and 1855; additional powers were conferred in 1861 and 1867. Although the prefects became the primary targets in the opposition's demonology of the administration, local resentment was often particularly directed at their subordinates the subprefects, who adopted a higher profile in the communes. As a report from the *procureur-général* of Seine-et-Marne made clear in 1861, "Here one must *belong* to Monsieur le sous-Préfet, obey him everywhere and in all matters; it is the only way to remain on good terms with the administration and not to make irreconcilable and powerful enemies."[79] Together with the local judiciary, the prefects and subprefects provided the principal source of information to central government concerning the activities of opposition groups, the political at-

[76] Archives Départementales Tarn-et-Garonne, 1 M 314, letter dated 7 October 1866.

[77] Jules Ferry, *La lutte électorale en 1863* (Paris: Dentu, 1863), 148–49. This dramatic reminder of past indignities proved ineffectual; the marquis was comfortably elected.

[78] See V. des Aubiers, *De l'administration et de ses réformes* (Paris: Dupont, 1852), 101–38.

[79] Arch. Nat. BB30–426; emphasis is in the text.

titudes of the clergy, and the general balance of opinion in the departments.

This regular supply of information served several key purposes in the Empire's political management of the provinces. First, it enabled the regime to keep a close eye on local political developments and particularly to gauge the impact of national and even international events on domestic opinion.[80] Knowledge of the local political terrain was also a necessary condition for maintaining a close eye on the Empire's opponents. The reports of the prefects and procureurs-généraux present a graphic phenomenology of the hostile activities of individuals, members of the clergy, organized groups such as syndicalists and regionalists, political movements, and newspapers. Most of this information was simply digested by the Ministry of the Interior and the Ministry of Justice, sometimes providing the basis for reports to the emperor himself.[81] Repressive action, however, was not infrequent and could take a wide variety of forms. In the immediate aftermath of the coup d'état and the proclamation of the Empire, the regime used terror and repression on a wide scale to destroy all forms of organized opposition.[82] But even after the regime consolidated its power, it was possible for one individual to be sentenced to eight months' imprisonment for publicly insulting the emperor.[83] Until the liberal reforms of the late 1860s, newspapers and public meetings could also be banned, and known political opponents could be threatened and intimidated. Enemies of the regime who were deemed to pose a threat to public order were regularly brought before the courts.[84] All this activity was made possible by the elaborate network that sent a constant stream of information back to Paris from the provinces.

Above all, the centralization of information enabled the Empire to select its national and local political elites, through the system of official candidacies. These figures were chosen by the government on the basis of information provided by prefects, who then attempted to ensure that the full weight of the local administration was thrown behind the candidates.[85] The justification of the practice of selecting official candidates

[80] The bimonthly reports of the prefects in 1861–62 thus contain much information about public attitudes toward the Roman question, as well as the free trade treaty signed with Britain in 1860. See Arch. Nat. F7 12243.

[81] For example, a detailed account of hostile activities of the clergy was compiled in the aftermath of the 1863 elections and passed on to Napoleon III (see Arch. Nat. BB30–426).

[82] See H. C. Payne, *The Police State of Louis Napoleon Bonaparte, 1851–1860* (Seattle: University of Washington Press, 1966).

[83] Arch. Nat. BB30–389, report by the procureur-général of Aix, October 1868.

[84] On the system of justice, see Pierre Guiral, "Réfléxions sur la justice du Second Empire," in *La France au XIXeme siècle* (Paris: Sorbonne, 1973), 109–18.

[85] Rosanvallon, *Le sacre du citoyen*, 311.

Fig. 2. Défilé des Députations des Communes de la Savoie devant Leurs Majestés à Chambéry, from *L'Illustration*, 8 September 1860. The annexation of the Savoie in 1860 gave Napoleon III an opportunity to reaffirm his centralist conception of the relationship between Paris and the provinces.

for legislative, cantonal, and municipal elections was pragmatic rather than ideological. First, universal suffrage was a new and relatively untested political instrument, whose use needed to be explained carefully to the public. Second, the regime believed that candidates could not be expected to gain public esteem without the patronage of the administration. In a note to his prefects in January 1852, Morny warned that universal suffrage was "easy to win over to a glorious name, unique in history, representing authority and power in the eyes of the population, but difficult to attach to lesser individualities."[86] Finally, and most important, the regime invoked considerations of order. In the immediate aftermath of the coup d'état, the country was deemed to be threatened by subversion. In these circumstances, the electorate could not be left to its own devices. As the procureur-général of Colmar noted in August 1860, apparently unaware of the double entendre of his proposition, "Universal suffrage could become a dangerous weapon in the hands of skillful and malicious agitators."[87]

[86] Fondation Thiers, Papiers Baroche, 1132, Morny circular, 8 January 1852.
[87] Arch. Nat. BB30–426.

Coercion and repression were not the only (and indeed not even the principal) methods the Empire used to manage its political relationship with the provinces. Winning over the confidence of the local populations required the cultivation of a relationship based on mutual interest and advantage, and the institutions of local government played an important role in this process in a number of ways. First, the regime consciously attempted to enhance the prestige of local office. Thus, rural mayors were awarded the Legion of Honor under the Second Empire for the first time since its creation by Napoleon, in a deliberate attempt to raise the regime's profile in the countryside.[88] As mentioned earlier, the emperor also rejected proposals to create a Bonapartist party; instead he made a calculated choice to attempt to use the local government system to rally the support of influential local notables.[89] Thus Haussmann, during his spell as prefect of the Gironde, adopted an open policy toward the selection of official candidates for municipal and cantonal elections: "It seemed politic to me to maintain in their functions all the former mayors and deputy mayors who had not previously been noticed for their extreme republican zeal, and who could be considered as having rallied the government without ulterior motives."[90] As the regime consolidated its power by the late 1850s, memories of the repression directed at the forces of "order" immediately after the coup d'état began to recede. The Empire sought to win over those conservative forces which were prepared to accept the new dynasty, recognize the regime's achievement in defeating the forces of "movement," and sympathize with some of its political and economic objectives. After his return to the Ministry of the Interior in November 1860, Persigny sent a circular letter to his prefects underlining the point:

Many honorable and distinguished men from earlier governments, while paying tribute to the emperor for all his great achievements, are still keeping themselves out of public life, out of a sentiment of personal dignity. Show them the consideration they deserve. Do not neglect any opportunity to urge them to give the country the benefit of their wisdom and experience, and remind them that although it is noble to cultivate past memories, it is even more noble to serve one's country.[91]

[88] The decree of 9 August 1854 awarded the Legion of Honor to "MM. Duval, mayor of Soncourt (Vosges), 62 years of service as mayor of the commune; Berton, mayor of Saint-Vaize (Charente-Inférieure), mayor without interruption over the past 58 years; and Desquennoy, mayor of Lawarde-Mauger (Somme), 58 years of service as deputy mayor of this commune" (*Annuaire du Ministère de l'Intérieur*, 1854, 346–47; see also André Chandernagor, *Les maires en France* [Paris: Fayard, 1883], 199–202).

[89] Ménager, "1848–1871," 114–15.

[90] Baron Georges Haussmann, *Mémoires* (Paris, 1890), 1:551.

[91] Arch. Nat., Papiers Eugène Rouher, 45 AP 11, Persigny to prefects, 5 December 1860.

This strategy (directed principally at the former Orleanist elites) met with only limited success at the national level, but there were numerous instances of *ralliement* of monarchists and republicans at the local level. The governments of the 1860s kept up the policy of recruiting local notables, even though the figures chosen were not always received with great enthusiasm by local Bonapartist activists. But the centralization of local government hindered rather than helped this strategy, as the Empire had little to offer to potential recruits by way of substantive local powers.

Second, the Empire attempted to use its considerable powers of patronage to draw local populations into a collaborative relationship with the state. Here is the characteristically impetuous assessment of Persigny:

> The patronage powers of the government are immense. By the eighty thousand remunerated positions of which it disposes, by the funds of all types that it can distribute as assistance to communes, to different establishments, to churches, to presbyteries, to schools; by the favors of all kinds that its decisions can procure, by its honorific and other rewards, by the very manner — more or less gracious, more or less favorable, more or less prompt — in which it decides the matters with which it is referred, it is possessed of enormous means of influence, and no government in history ever disposed of such powers.[92]

Although this power of patronage was exercised by administrative as well as political elites (to the great chagrin of Persigny, who lamented the growing appropriation of this instrument by local notables), its effectiveness was undeniable and was partly the cause of the inflated growth in the number of public servants during the Second Empire.[93] The institution of universal suffrage enhanced both the necessity and the scope for patronage. For example, the development of railway networks during the 1860s was accelerated by the public clamor for ever more local lines and stations, a theme that dominated local and often national election campaigns.[94] The cultivation of strong links between the imperial state and rural populations thus became a strategic necessity for the Empire, and the regime exploited its appeal to the full. The genuine popularity of the regime in rural France was partly a function of its cultivation of the Bonapartist myth through the elaborate and

---

[92] Fialin de Persigny, *Mémoires du duc de Persigny* (Paris: Plon, 1896), 313.

[93] The number of public functionaries (excluding the clergy) rose from 477,000 in 1851 to almost 700,000 in 1870. See Alain Plessis, *Nouvelle histoire de la France contemporaine* (1852–71; reprint, Paris: Editions du Seuil, 1979), 9:59.

[94] See Ferry, *La lutte électorale*, 48–49.

extravagant spectacles of the imperial court.[95] It also mattered that the regime was able to satisfy the material interests of the population and exorcise the specter of social revolution. The construction of a comprehensive network of local roads, promoted by imperial initiatives in 1861 and 1867, also did much to improve conditions for local agriculture.[96] But, as the procureur-général of Aix noted in 1870, the Empire also embodied a number of key principles that appealed to the peasants: "The respect of rights, the principle of equality before the law—this is where the Bonapartist tradition still has its deepest roots."[97] The celebration of the collective virtues of rural France, often in contrast with the crudeness and amoralism of urban existence, thus became one of the dominant themes of Bonapartist ideology. In a speech given at a regional agricultural competition in May 1864, Persigny drew a sharp contrast between urban and rural public opinion.

> One has to take account of the influence of agglomerations of populations on public opinion; for it is certain that great crowds sometimes have the ability to exalt the sentiments of men beyond the limits of reason. In the provinces and in the countryside, although the populations are more scattered, everyone knows each other and each person is appreciated to his true value. Indeed, what characterizes the agricultural class . . . is that it more easily resists attempts to divide it. In the big cities and towns, however, although all are concentrated in one area, the different strata of the population are estranged from one another and live in a state of isolation, which easily allows their defiance to be aroused. . . .
>
> In a word, in the provinces and in the countryside, public opinion, whether liberal or conservative, is truly the expression, the product, of the ideas and sentiments of the whole society, that is, of all social classes; this is evidently the most enlightened opinion. In the great centers of population, by contrast, because it is always the deplorable principle of class conflict, the eternal bane of big cities, that replaces notions of public interest, it is often the case that the more enlightened sections of the population are dominated by their lesser counterparts.[98]

Urban opinion was thus conflictual, often irrational, and therefore open to the influence of demagoguery. In the countryside, however, the picture was entirely different: class conflict and political subversion

---

[95] On the imperial court, see Vicomte de Beaumont-Vassy, *Histoire intime du Second Empire* (Paris: Sartorius, 1874); Comte de Maugny, *Souvenirs du Second Empire* (Paris: Kolb, 1889), 3–101; Louis Girard, "La Cour de Napoléon III," in *Hof, Kultur, und Politik im 19. Jahrhundert*, ed. Karl Ferdinand Werner (Bonn: L. Rohrscheid, 1985), 155–65.

[96] Hippolyte Roche, *Napoléon et les communes* (Paris: Lainé, 1869), 2.

[97] Arch. Nat. BB30-390.

[98] Arch. Nat., Papiers Eugène Rouher, 45 AP 19.

were largely absent, and public opinion was thus more enlightened. A more cynical way of expressing the same thought was Madame Baroche's following reflection after the Empire's triumph in the legislative elections of 1857: "All things considered, there was no middle; universal suffrage had to populate the country either with wolves or with sheep; praise be given to the countryside where there are only sheep."[99]

THE DYSFUNCTIONS OF CENTRALISM

Even during the first decade of the regime, the centralist system that governed the Second Empire's management of the provinces did not fully serve the political and administrative purposes for which it was established. Municipal and departmental assemblies did not always operate within their restricted legal frameworks. Ideological conflict was not altogether absent from communal and cantonal elections, even though rural contests generally assumed an apolitical character. It is true that a vertical chain of administrative command was established, which was broadly successful in maintaining order in the provinces. Furthermore, the system of official candidacies helped to produce overwhelming majorities for the government in the Legislative Corps in 1852, 1857, and 1863. But a number of serious problems also emerged very rapidly, even in the relatively placid political climate of the 1850s.

Repression was not always enthusiastically carried out by those entrusted with its execution (prefects, magistrates, members of the police, and mayors). In any event, the regime could not plausibly expect to build a partnership with social groups through coercive methods alone. The relationship between the administrative and elective bodies did not always proceed smoothly. Prefects and elected notables fought fierce battles for the control of local power bases. In 1855 Morny, president of the Legislative Corps, bitterly complained to Minister of Interior Billault that many of his deputies were being "persecuted" by the prefects.[100] Furthermore, despite the apolitical nature of local administration, the regime did not entirely succeed in eliminating political conflict from local public life. Thus, for example, prefects who found themselves in legitimist or republican departments often had to negotiate (and indeed compromise) with local opposition forces.[101]

The nominating powers of the regime were also a source of problems. Communes were often bitterly divided into rival factions (almost always

---

[99] Madame Jules Baroche, *Second Empire: Notes et souvenirs* (Paris: Crès, 1921), 79.

[100] Arch. Dépt. Loire-Atlantique, Papiers Billault, 20 J 20, Morny to Billault, 14 July 1855.

[101] Le Clère and Wright, *Les Préfets du Second Empire*, 131.

on the basis of purely local considerations), and currying favor with one camp could often result in alienating the opposite side from the regime altogether.[102] To compound the problem, the regime did not always find it easy to recruit local elites. The weak version of the problem was manifested in the difficulty of finding good candidates. In the frank assessment of the procureur-général of Caen in 1868: "When one studies, with an open mind, the movement of electoral opinion, one is struck by the disadvantages that the government incurs because of the obscurity and mediocrity of its candidates. Not only do deficiencies in their reputation and merit limit their chances of success, but in the long run they damage the prestige of the cause they serve."[103]

At the very worst, the regime's local agents found it hard to find any local figures willing to serve on elective councils. The following rather desperate report from the subprefect of Ancenis in July 1852 reveals the scale of some imperial agents' problems:

> Generally the people to whom I offer municipal positions express the desire to accept them only when the municipal council is formed; they fear being perceived as having been imposed by the imperial authorities, especially if their name did not come out of the electoral urn. In any event, as I had anticipated, I find it very difficult to obtain a frank, clear, and definitive response to my openings. . . . Indifference, pusillanimity, and lack of initiative are the three major flaws of the political fabric of this locality.[104]

Above all, the local government system rested on a central contradiction between the principle of legitimation by universal suffrage and the imposition of imperial control by political and administrative fiat. The uncomfortable relationship between appointed mayors and elected municipal councillors went to the heart of this dilemma. Mayors found it increasingly difficult to establish their authority purely on the basis of their mode of appointment. A growing number of first magistrates accordingly sought to increase their legitimacy by running for election after being chosen by the authorities.[105] In the municipal elections of 1855, about thirty thousand mayors thus ran for election or reelection.[106] This, in turn, provoked a sharp reaction from authoritarian Bonapartist

---

[102] For an appreciation of the difficulties faced by a Bonapartist minister of the interior in striking a balance between central and local interests, see Noël Blayau, *Billault, ministre de Napoléon III* (Paris: Klincksieck, 1969), 274–75.

[103] Arch. Nat. BB30–389, report of 8 October 1868.

[104] Arch. Dépt. Loire-Atlantique, 1 M 188, report of the sub-prefect of Ancenis to the prefect of Loire Inférieure, 9 July 1852.

[105] The traditional practice was to appoint the mayors before municipal elections were held, so as to separate clearly the executive and deliberative functions of local councils.

[106] This information was given by Marquis d'Andelarre during the debate on the 1867 municipal law, in *Annales du Sénat et du Corps Législatif: Compte-rendu analytique des séances*, session of 12 April 1867 (Paris: Panckoucke, 1867), 86.

circles. In the following circular letter to prefects in June 1858, Minister of Interior Billault made clear his disapproval of such practices:

Mayors are integral members of the Municipal Councils over which they preside. They do not therefore have to seek from the ballot box a mandate that they hold from law and from the emperor himself. Their abstention will in any case have the advantage of giving the Municipal Council a more complete representation. In consequence, I invite you to urge these functionaries not to venture out personally as candidates in the electoral arena.[107]

As we will see, this injunction failed to stem the tide, and the Empire was eventually forced to reconsider its policy. By the late 1850s, accordingly, the regime was beginning to sense that all was not well in the management of its relations with the provinces. In April 1858 a commission of decentralization was established in the Senate, its report to the emperor acknowledging some of the administrative problems that overcentralization produced.

Centralization, under the slow but relentless influence of Parisian bureaucrats, has progressively overloaded local administrations with writings, exchanges of correspondence, consultations, or hierarchical referrals bringing with them a host of formalities, difficulties, and delays. With this incessant movement backward and forward from the periphery to the center and from the center to the periphery, political authorities are irritated and interests suffer. There is now a serious problem in the country, and all opponents of centralization find in it a limitless source of well-founded criticisms.[108]

The central problem, it was suggested, was inefficiency; no mention was made of the desirability of enhancing the administrative powers of local assemblies. By the early 1860s, however, the regime had woken up to the political dimension of the matter. In a letter to Rouher in June 1863, Napoleon III suggested that the Council of State's review of decentralization include measures that would enhance the powers of elected councils.

Our system of centralization, despite its advantages, has had the grave inconvenience of creating an excess of regulation. . . . Formerly the constant control of the administration over a host of matters could perhaps be justified, but today it has become a burden. To make the greatest possible number of citizens participate in the management and responsibility of affairs while preserving for central authorities those powers necessary to ensuring the

---

[107] Arch. Dépt. Loire-Atlantique, Papiers Billault, 20 J 20, Billault to prefects, 22 June 1858.
[108] Arch. Dépt. Loire-Atlantique, Papiers Billault, 20 J 26, report of the commission of decentralization to Napoleon III.

internal and external security of the state, to strengthen the autonomy of the department and the commune, to seek the new attributions that should be devolved to elected councils, this is the program we should pursue.[109]

This search for the promotion of greater local and departmental autonomy provided a stark contrast with the emperor's earlier assertions of the need for strong centralized power. This marked shift in emphasis can be explained by a number of factors, which made the move away from authoritarian centralism both desirable and necessary. The most significant development was the reemergence of adversarial politics in the late 1850s and early 1860s. The relative apathy that had given the Empire such peace and tranquillity during the early 1850s began to give way to a greater degree of opposition activism. Although the 1857 elections were a triumph for the government, five republican deputies were elected in Paris. The Italian question provoked a fierce clericalist backlash against the regime, with many priests taking up overtly hostile positions against the Empire's support for Italian reunification.[110] In 1862 a Bonapartist grandee noted the following in his diary: "Never perhaps since ten years has France faced such a worrying situation. The great party of order is disorganized, there is anxiety everywhere, and a sort of silent agitation is spreading across the country."[111]

The administration's reports on the 1863 elections attest to a growth of Orleanist and republican forces and a revival of legitimist participation in the electoral process (despite the hostility of the comte de Chambord). Overall, the situation remained well under control, and the regime's strength in the General Councils and in the overwhelming majority of municipalities was not seriously challenged. Nonetheless, the greater politicization of the early 1860s generated two trends that were a source of concern to the Empire. First, local electoral contests became more adversarial, requiring a greater and more vigorous display of administrative zeal to ensure the success of governmental candidates. Second, opposition forces (notably the republicans) began to gain ground in urban areas, confirming Persigny's admonitions against the political spirit of large agglomerations. In the immediate aftermath of the 1857 legislative elections, the emperor urged his minister of the interior to remain vigilant: "Far from lowering our guard, we must, on the contrary, look for ways in which we can fight the malicious spirit of large cities."[112]

---

[109] Arch. Nat., Papiers Rouher, 45 AP 11, Napoleon III to Rouher, 27 June 1863.

[110] A report was compiled by the minister of justice on the agitation of the clergy during the 1863 elections. See Arch. Nat. BB30-426.

[111] Comte Horace de Viel-Castel, *Mémoires sur le règne de Napoléon III* (Paris: Le Prat, 1979), 2:192.

[112] Arch. Dépt. Loire-Atlantique, Papiers Billault, 20 J 59; letter of the emperor to Billault, 29 June 1857.

By the late 1860s, however, the deterioration of the empire's position in heavily populated areas was apparent. A report from the procureur-général of Rouen noted the following: "Oppositional tendencies are enjoying notable and continuous progress. . . . The rebellious and dissatisfied spirit of the bourgeoisie has awakened with all its inconsistency; a muffled sense of discontent is spreading in the large centers of population where the bourgeoisie is dominant."[113] The procureur-général's colleague from Lyon (where, as in Paris, the entire municipal council was nominated by the emperor) underlined the same point: "It must be recognized that in cities, in county towns, and even in the smallest industrial centers oppositional tendencies have made considerable progress."[114] The effect of these developments was to polarize the cleavage between urban and rural politics and thus to increase the government's strategic dependence on its agrarian support. The problem, however, was that the institutions that played a key role in delivering this support came under increasing pressure precisely at the moment when the empire came to depend even more heavily on its rural base. This strain was caused by a number of factors. First, there was great public dissatisfaction with the formalism and obstructiveness that came to be seen as the hallmarks of bureaucratic behavior. Of particular significance were the administrative delays that rural communes suffered. Persigny noted the following in his introductory report on the decentralization decree of April 1861:

> The affairs of large towns, conducted with care and brought to general attention by their very importance, rarely suffer regrettable delays. It is the interests of small towns and rural communes, that is, the mass of the country, that remain in sufferance. In almost all communes of the Empire, municipalities have no other public works to execute than the creation of one or two local roads, the erection of a church, a presbytery, an asylum, and a school building that also houses the municipality. However, today, when a mayor has proposed and a municipal council has voted the construction of a presbytery, an asylum, or a school, their project has to be framed in a quadruple request for approval of plans and estimates, public assistance, taxes and loans, depending for the first two on the Ministry of Public Instruction, and for the latter two on the Ministry of the Interior; none of these requests can be finally approved anywhere except in Paris. These unexplained delays in the administration of affairs that concern them discourage local administrations and rightly irritate their populations.[115]

---

[113] Arch. Nat. BB30-389, report of 11 January 1869.

[114] Arch. Nat. BB30-389, report of 10 July 1869.

[115] Persigny, report to the emperor, 12 April 1861, in *Bulletin Officiel du Ministère de l'Intérieur* (1861), 96–97.

This tendency was noted in the emperor's 1863 letter to Rouher, and it inspired a determined campaign by the government to enhance the central bureaucracy's responsivess to public concerns. In a letter to all prefects in 1863, Béhic (Rouher's successor as minister for agriculture, commerce, and public works) commented as follows: "In the current state of legislation and the regulations that complete it, the processing of business, hampered by numerous formalities, suffers often regrettable delays." He ended with the plea "that matters in general, especially those which bear on private interests, should be examined, resolved, and treated with the greatest promptitude."[116] Some measures were taken to expedite affairs in the ensuing years, most notably the decree of April 1861, which transferred many of the powers exercised by central government to the prefects. But this merely compounded the general view of the bureaucracy as an unproductive and excessively rule-bound institution. In 1870 the secretary of the municipality of Laval complained that "administrative formalities are the curse of our time; under the pretext of respecting the law, they accustom the citizenry to apathy and ignorance; they hinder business without benefit to anyone."[117] Not only was this system ineffective, but the absence of local responsibility and accountability meant that the blame for all problems was laid squarely at the door of central government. The Empire's own strategists noted the following:

> Called upon to direct, watch over, and regulate everything, the state finds itself assuming so many diverse attributions and so many duties that it might absorb general, local, and even private interests in its sovereign authority. Its power is constantly called upon, for everything depends on it, since it decides, it helps and advises, authorizes or refuses. To all these prerogatives corresponds an immense responsibility. Everything seeming to emanate from the government, it is blamed for everything: for the good it cannot achieve, for the evil it cannot prevent. What authority would not become irritated in the accomplishment of such a role?[118]

These problems were compounded by the growing pressure the Empire's administrative agents faced in managing the centralized system of local government. The stability of the system depended critically on its perceived effectivess as well as in the regime's ability to maintain loyalty among its subordinates. From the early 1860s, however, the Empire found that both conditions were proving increasingly difficult to meet.

[116] Arch. Nat. F1a 49 (circulars of the minister of the interior, 1861–69); Béhic note to prefects, 2 July 1863.

[117] Arch. Nat., Papiers Odilon Barrot, 271 AP 29 (2), letter to Barrot, 1 March 1870.

[118] Arch. Nat., Papiers Eugène Rouher, 45 AP 11, from Projet de Loi sur les Conseils Généraux et les Conseils Municipaux, Corps Législatif, session 1865.

Criticism of the rule-bound character of the bureaucracy was often coupled with a denunciation of the role of the prefects, whose political and administrative functions were seen to typify the regime's authoritarian conception of local government. The electoral functions bestowed on the Bonapartists' local agents were a particular source of discontent, both within the administration and for the public more generally.

The difficulties of the regime were highlighted by the problems that mayors faced. As noted earlier, mayors were expected to play a critical role in rallying political support for the Second Empire during local and national elections. Their increasing unpopularity was reflected in the single statistic of the 1865 municipal elections: 4,444 of the 36,344 mayors who ran for reelection were rejected,[119] although the Empire's policy was often to reappoint loyal mayors who had suffered defeat.[120] However, this approach was invariably a source of further tension, as mayors with little local political support tended to be able to govern only by authoritarian means. If, however, the Empire gave in to communal opinion and appointed mayors who were known figures of the opposition, this naturally tended to reduce the regime's ability to influence local political outcomes. In 1859 the procureur-général of Riom warned as follows: "Many believe that the attitude of the legitimist party makes it dangerous to bestow influence upon it by admitting its members in the General Councils and especially by giving them the functions of mayor. There are a host of men from this party who occupy the latter position, but we cannot have any illusions about them."[121]

Indeed, the electoral arena became a source of concern for the Empire during the 1860s, as local populations showed increasing reluctance to accept the imposition of official candidates. By the late 1860s, the system of official candidacies was operating under severe constraints. Such candidates continued to be anointed for elections to the Legislative Corps. Even here, however, the system functioned satisfactorily only in some rural areas; by the mid 1860s, the Empire's political position in such large cities as Paris, Lyon, Marseille, Toulouse, Bordeaux, and Lille had become severely compromised. Furthermore, reports from procureurs-généraux warned against the political dangers of tying the fate of official candidates too closely to an administration that was gen-

---

[119] Information given by Segris on April 12 1867, during the debate on the 1867 municipal law. See *Annales du Sénat et du Corps Législatif: Compte-rendu analytique des séances*, session of 1867 (Paris: Panckoucke, 1867), 95.

[120] Jules Simon cites the case of a mayor who received only one vote in the municipal elections of 1863 but who was nonetheless reappointed. See Arch. Nat., Papiers Jules Simon, 87 AP 9 (carton 4). After the 1865 elections, however, only 692 of the defeated mayors were reappointed.

[121] Arch. Nat. BB30-368, report dated 11 July 1859.

erally regarded with resentment and suspicion. Noting the public hostility to official candidates in his area in 1869, the procureur-général of Toulouse went so far as to suggest that the party of "order" needed to constitute itself separately outside the administration, "to discipline itself and lead its own independent existence."[122]

This perception of growing public opposition to the administration provoked a contradictory response from the empire. On one hand, the regime accepted (and eventually encouraged) a greater degree of mayoral politicization, endorsing the actions of a large number of first magistrates who sought to enhance their legitimacy by running in the municipal elections of 1865. In the words of Rouher, "The nature of things forced mayors to seek a double baptism, that of nomination by the government and of election"; the government had to "leave mayors in the movement so that they could control it."[123] Even some authoritarian Bonapartists recognized that the Second Empire's commitment to universal suffrage made it necessary for mayors to run for office. Haussmann, although expressing opposition to this custom on grounds of principle, nonetheless conceded that "mayors and municipal councillors have always shown themselves more eager to please their electorate than to satisfy the government from which they derived their principal attributions. In any case, when there exists the possibility of holding both qualities, the mayor, if he holds only one, suffers a certain discredit as long as he is not invested in the other."[124]

On the other hand, this acknowledgment of the necessity and legitimacy of politics was accompanied—somewhat contradictorily—by continuing efforts to depoliticize local elections. From 1864 on, elections for municipal and general councils were increasingly conducted without extensive administrative interference, except in cases where known enemies of the Empire were running for election. As a circular from Minister of the Interior La Valette to prefects made clear in March 1864, "Every time an election assumes a political character, you should intervene clearly. But when, in light of the opinions of the contestants and the good spirit of local populations, the elections present no political significance, you should leave mayors and voters entirely free to choose the candidate who seems best suited to defend the interests of their locality."[125] There were nonetheless continuing complaints about

---

[122] Arch. Nat. BB30-389, report dated 7 July 1869.

[123] Cited by Lucien-Anatole Prévost-Paradol, *Quelques pages d'histoire contemporaine* (Paris: Michel Lévy, 1866), 279.

[124] Haussmann, *Mémoires*, 1:537–38.

[125] Arch. Nat., Papiers Eugène Rouher, 45 AP 5, circular to all prefects, 15 March 1864.

the intervention of the administration in local election campaigns. In a speech given at the Legislative Corps in July 1868, the marquis de Grammont denounced the intervention of the prefect Dubois de Jancigny in the recent election campaign for the General Council.[126] A member of the departmental assembly of the Gard protested that in the local elections of 1867,

> as soon as an official candidate is proclaimed, all the agents of the administration have but one thought, one goal, making his candidacy a success; subprefects, mayors, justices of the peace, commissioners of police, schoolteachers, tax collectors, employees of state companies, clerks, road menders, rural policemen, postmen, and tobacconists make this candidacy their constant preoccupation.[127]

Nonetheless, newspaper reports on local elections during this period confirm that this tactical withdrawal from the electoral arena was implemented in many areas by prefects.[128] This shift to a less active role for the administration was a source of some consternation to authoritarian Bonapartists such as Persigny, who asserted the following in typically scathing fashion: "Under the pretext of a bastardized liberalism that is merely the rationalization of weakness and the abdication of doctrines of authority, the Empire is being disorganized in all parts."[129] But this retreat was also made necessary by the Empire's frustrated acknowledgment that the political reliability of the administration left much to be desired. In the 1860s the files of the Ministry of the Interior and the Ministry of Justice abounded with directives urging officials to spare no effort to secure the election of official candidates.[130] Behind the strident calls for greater zeal lurked the realization that many officials at the lower rungs of the administrative ladder sympathized with opposition groups. In a confidential circular of 12 April 1866, the minister of the interior lamented the "insufficiency" of the political assistance functionaries gave in election campaigns, and there is evidence to suggest that

---

[126] Marquis de Grammont, *Discours sur les candidatures officielles* (Paris: Dupont, 1868), 10, 13.

[127] A. de la Borderie, *Les élections départementales de 1867: Lettres à un électeur* (Rennes: Catel, 1867), 14.

[128] See, for example, the approving article by Auguste Nefftzer in *Le Temps*, 16 July 1865.

[129] Bib. Nat., Papiers Persigny, nouvelles acquisitions françaises 23066, Persigny's letter to Napoleon III, 29 June 1865.

[130] For example, Arch. Nat. BB30-426 contains a letter dated 15 July 1864 from the secretary-general at the Ministry of Justice to the procureur-général of Nîmes, stressing the need for all officials of the ministry to support the official candidate in a by-election in the Ardèche.

public officials even actively campaigned for opposition candidates during some elections.[131]

By the 1860s, there was a general feeling within Bonapartist circles that centralization had been carried too far. A government-funded review ridiculed the minister of state responsible for fine arts for promulgating a decree that reduced the pitch of tuning forks by a quarter; although the purpose behind the decree was perhaps laudable (to prevent tenors from ruining their voices), the intrusion was evidence of the state's obsession with controlling all aspects of social life.[132] More seriously, the problems the Empire faced in its management of the provinces had now multiplied. The administration, which had helped consolidate the new imperial order in the aftermath of the 1851 coup, was universally decried for its abrasiveness and inefficiency. The key agents of the Empire in the departments and communes, the prefects and the mayors, found their authority challenged by the reemergence of electoral politics and by the growing local hostility to administrative authoritarianism. The centralization that the emperor had seen as an unlimited political benefit had become a clear liability, as the public blamed all the failings of their local administration on central government. The political opposition, which had bowed to the force of arms and the repression of the *commissions mixtes*,[133] was challenging the Empire strongly in many areas by the late 1860s, as the system of official candidacies proved increasingly ineffective and unpopular.

The regime's political base in the country as a whole was still broad, as shown by the 1869 elections (and even more spectacularly by the May 1870 plebiscite). But Bonapartist support in many parts of the country (especially urban areas) had declined significantly, and there was widespread disaffection with the centralist and authoritarian practices of the regime. As a report from the procureur-général of Rennes made clear after the 1869 elections, "Public opinion has not concealed its view that the moment had come to give back to the country a greater role in the management of its own affairs."[134] Imperial decentralization was thus born not primarily out of deference to the demands of the constitutional opposition but through an assessement of the internal failings and contradictions of the Second Empire's local government regime.

---

[131] Le Clère and Wright, *Les Préfets du Second Empire*, 84.

[132] F. Boilay, "Chronique," *Revue Européenne* 1 (1859): 687–88.

[133] The *comissions mixtes* were set up in the aftermath of the 1851 coup to judge all those who had taken part in acts of political resistance against the new order. Thousands were given prison sentences and deported, often on the basis of highly dubious evidence. For further discussion, see Georges Lassez, *La vérité sur le deux décembre* (Paris: Le Chevalier, 1874), 26–28.

[134] Arch. Nat. BB30-389, report dated 29 July 1869.

THE EMPIRE'S DECENTRALIST RESPONSE

The idea of decentralization was in many ways appealing to Napoleon III, partly as a result of his memories of the English system of local government and partly under the influence of close advisers such as Frédéric Le Play.[135] His response to the political and administrative crisis was to accelerate the pace of institutional liberalization, and in particular to promise significant reforms in local government. In 1865 the emperor asked the Council of State to produce a comparative study of decentralization.[136] In 1866 and 1867 there were modest increases in the competences of municipalities and General Councils (essentially in the budgetary powers of local government institutions),[137] although this gesture was offset by an extension of the powers of the prefects. In 1868 laws granting greater press freedom and the right to hold electoral meetings without prior administrative sanction were promulgated, and a step was taken in the direction of greater accountability by instituting the practice of ministerial interpellation in the Legislative Corps.[138]

This general trend toward liberalization was accentuated in 1870 with the establishment of the liberal Empire. The appointment of Emile Ollivier was accompanied by the promise of wide-ranging political and economic reforms. High on Ollivier's list of priorities was decentralization, for by 1870 many Bonapartists and liberals felt that a thorough reexamination of the local government regime was necessary. The liberal Empire established an extraparliamentary commission on decentralization as early as February. The minister of the interior Eugène Chevandier de Valdrôme recognized, in a letter to the emperor, that the promotion of further political liberalization had made the institution of greater decentralization all the more necessary: "One cannot, without a fundamental contradiction, give citizens a large and sincere measure of participation in the government of their country and yet continue to deny them the management of their most direct and intimate matters."[139]

The promise of further local liberties aroused interest and even enthu-

[135] Luc Gazeau, *L'évolution des libertés locales en France et en Belgique au cours du XIXeme siècle* (Paris: Pedone, 1905), 247–48.

[136] *L'Opinion Nationale*, 31 August 1865.

[137] Even these modest improvements were offset by an increase in the powers of the prefects. The 1867 law, for example, gave prefects the right to dissolve municipal councils and replace them with administrative commissions without even needing to set a date for fresh elections. This was one of the reasons the republicans strongly opposed the new law. See Emile Ollivier, *L'Empire libéral* (Paris: Garnier, 1904), 9:418.

[138] Alain Plessis, *Nouvelle Histoire de la France contemporaine, 1852–1871* (Paris: Editions du Seuil, 1979), 215.

[139] *Journal Officiel*, 22 February 1870, report of the minister of interior to the emperor on the formation of the 1870 commission of decentralization.

siasm in the immediate aftermath of the creation of the 1870 commission. In the words of the procureur-général of Agen, "[Emile Ollivier's] proposed reforms, which have aroused the greatest interest in our farthest provinces, are not those which bear on general political matters . . . but rather those which are intended to promote greater *communal liberties* and to develop individual initiative."[140]

Speaking in the Legislative Corps in June 1870, Clément Duvernois called for the "broadening of the role of provincial assemblies."[141] In the eyes of many liberal Bonapartists, the promotion of greater decentralization represented an intellectually coherent and politically effective response to the growing political and administrative problems the regime faced in the late 1860s. Presenting the 1867 law on municipalities to the Senate, the liberal Bonapartist Louis-Bernard Bonjean underlined the following numerous advantages of a moderate form of decentralization:

> If, indeed, it is indispensable that the government should retain firm control of the direct *management* of all parts of the administration concerned with state security and general prosperity, it could not take charge of the collective interests of local communities without getting bogged down in details and multiplying beyond reason the number of its agents: this would be a form of communism, that is, the most absolute and intolerable form of despotism. It is in the nature of things . . . to allow local communities to administer those affairs which are of exclusive concern to themselves. This system has, furthermore, considerable advantages: it forms the civic customs of the country and accustoms the citizenry to the management of public affairs; it lightens the burden of central government; and, just as important, it reduces the budget, by replacing salaried officials with the unremunerated efforts of the citizenry.[142]

But, as noted at the beginning of the chapter, the promotion of decentralization was not solely the concern of liberal Bonapartists. Many of their authoritarian counterparts also actively endorsed the principle. Former minister of the interior Ernest Pinard justified greater local freedom by an organic analogy: "For a nation to be strong and prosperous, there must be overabundance nowhere and some activity in all parts. The social organism is like the human body, which remains strong and healthy only if blood circulates freely in all its organs."[143] The Bonapartist "conspirator" Jules Amigues, who was strongly hostile to the liberal

---

[140] Arch. Nat. BB30-390, report from the procureur-général of Agen, April 1870; emphasis is in the text.

[141] *Journal Officiel*, 4 June 1870.

[142] Speech by Bonjean, 12 July 1867, in *Bulletin Officiel du Ministère de l'Intérieur* (1867): 472–73; emphasis is in the text.

[143] Ernest Pinard, *Mon Journal* (Paris, 1892), 1:223.

evolution of the Empire in the late 1860s, nonetheless advocated the adoption of substantive measures of decentralization.[144] His specific proposals included the "decapitalization" of Paris, the reform of universal suffrage, and the "emancipation" of the commune. All these measures were deemed to be entirely compatible with the principles of "authority," which were necessary for the continued health of the French polity.[145]

THE POLITICAL IMPERATIVES OF DECENTRALIZATION

There were also a number of political justifications for the pursuit of administrative decentralization. First, there was a need to provide a political response to the opposition groups' clamors for greater civil and political liberties. In a speech given to the Legislative Corps in 1864, Adolphe Thiers had criticized the Empire for denying the country its "necessary" freedoms: individual, press, and electoral freedom, as well as the right of interpellation and ministerial accountability in the Legislative Corps. Like most opposition politicians, Thiers regarded the Empire's promotion of administrative decentralization as a "distraction," aimed at diverting the gaze of public opinion from the necessity of political reforms.[146]

For many imperialists, however — indeed, for many authoritarian Bonapartists — the promotion of greater liberty through decentralization offered an ideal opportunity to meet the opposition on its own terrain and demonstrate the ideological superiority of imperialism over its rivals. As an anonymous Bonapartist pamphleteer suggested in 1866, the banner of liberty could be waved with equal if not greater vigor by the Empire. This could help to rally the support of the propertied classes and provide the regime with a bulwark against the subversive designs of its enemies. Granting broader political freedoms to the people was thus in the ultimate interests of the regime. The tract ended by quoting one of Napoleon III's aphorisms in his "Idées Napoléoniennes": "Above all, do not fear the people; they are far more conservative than you."[147] In this line of reasoning, the promotion of decentralization was a means of appealing to (and capitalizing on) the instinctive attachment of French society to order and social conservatism.

Following directly from this, the Empire's decentralization was also part of a deliberate strategy of playing rural populations off against urban centers. As noted earlier, the middle and late 1860s saw a steady

---

[144] Jules Amigues, "Restaurons les Parlements!" in *La politique d'un honnête homme* (Paris: Lachaud, 1869), 45–49.

[145] Jules Amigues, *Les aveux d'un conspirateur bonapartiste* (Paris: Lachaud, 1874), 8.

[146] Adolphe Thiers, *Discours sur les libertés politiques* (Paris: l'Heureux, 1865), 6.

[147] *Le tiers parti et les libertés intérieures* (Paris: Dentu, 1866), 13.

progression of support for opposition groups (notably republicans) in populated agglomerations. Faced with the prospect of political decline in these parts of the country, the Empire hoped that the offer of greater decentralization might consolidate and even broaden its support in rural France, hence countering the threat to the political base of Bonapartism. The establishment of the 1870 commission on decentralization was thus part of a strategic calculation. In particular, the regime believed that freeing local populations from the stifling burden of administrative conservatism would help regenerate the social and organizational fortunes of Bonapartism by attracting powerful local notables to the movement. The ambition of recruiting a political elite different in its ideological inclinations and political socialization had been one of the standard themes of Bonapartism since 1851. Immediately after the December coup, when Morny had sent a circular to all prefects describing the profile of the ideal Bonapartist candidate, he had stressed the importance of social criteria as opposed to ideological ones: "If a man has made his fortune by hard work in industry or agriculture, if he has taken care to improve the conditions of his workers, if he has made himself popular by a noble use of his fortune, he is preferable to what is generally termed a politician."[148]

In the late 1860s, as the political pressure on the Empire began to mount, administrative decentralization was seen as a valuable opportunity to reinvigorate local Bonapartist elites. The importance of enhancing the social base of Bonapartism was spelled out in a report of the procureur-général of Agen in early 1870. Writing about the local population's insistent demands for greater communal and departmental freedoms, he stressed the following: "These freedoms would have a no less favorable consequence: they would give back to those intelligent and devoted men, the rich landowners who devote their time and fortune to the public good, the legitimate influence they lose under the regime of bureaucracy and excessive centralization."[149] Interestingly, many authoritarian Bonapartists shared this opposition to the administrative despotism of local imperial potentates. These notables were often uncomfortable with the constitutional evolution of the regime in the late 1860s, but they sympathized with the idea of granting greater local liberty to the municipalities and especially the General Councils. There were even Bonapartist suggestions that provincial parliaments be restored; these measures were seen to have "the double advantage of giving greater satisfaction to liberal demands, and not weakening central authority by directing the pretensions of a single assembly at it."[150]

[148] Fond. Thiers, Papiers Baroche, 1132, Morny to prefects, 8 January 1852.
[149] Arch. Nat. BB30-390, report dated January 1870.
[150] Amigues, *Les aveux*, 8–9.

THE BONAPARTIST DEMOCRACY

From this perspective, many Bonapartists sympathized with some of the objectives expressed in the 1865 Nancy program,[151] even though their political and ideological instincts differed radically from those of the document's leading signatories.

Decentralization was also deployed as a means of building bridges with other opposition groups, particularly the monarchists. There was a precedent for such a move. During the campaign for the presidential elections of 1848, Louis Napoleon had proclaimed his adhesion to decentralization as a means of gaining the support of conservative elites.[152] In the early 1860s, as mentioned earlier, the Empire had sought to rally opposition politicians to the regime, stressing the achievements of Napoleon III in restoring order and promoting prosperity. In a circular to his prefects after the 1863 elections, Persigny had insisted as follows: "The government of the emperor does not reject anyone. Having recruited in its own ranks men from all parties and still continuing to do so, it remains true to its mission to rally everyone."[153] By the late 1860s, as the Empire's political position in urban centers became increasingly precarious, the prospect of rallying provincial royalists and Catholics to "the ranks of the great conservative army" seemed appealing to many Bonapartists.[154] The legitimists were a particularly worthy object of the Empire's attentions, for a number of reasons. The conflict over the Roman question had created a sharp antagonism between the regime and the ultramontane clergy and had rekindled the anticlerical component of popular Bonapartism.[155] But many imperialists did not lose hope of reestablishing close relations with the legitimists, who were believed to share a number of interests with the Empire. Like the Bonapartists, they regarded order as a supreme political virtue and firmly believed in hereditary authority. Also like the Bonapartists, they were attached to the principle of equal treatment of citizens by the law but rejected the revolutionary notion of social equality; similarly, they tended to regard freedom as a civil rather than a political attribute.

Thus, in a pamphlet written in 1864, the *légitimiste rallié* Charles Muller made the case for a rapprochement between Bonapartists and legitimists.[156] First, he made the tactical observation that legitimists were historically divided against the Orleanists, whereas they had no substan-

---

[151] For a broader analysis of the Nancy manifesto, see chap. 3.

[152] See Alfred de Falloux, *Le parti catholique: Ce qu'il a été, ce qu'il est devenu* (Paris: Ambroise Bray, 1856), 28.

[153] Arch. Nat. BB30-426, circular dated 21 June 1863.

[154] Fernand Giraudeau, *Nos moeurs politiques* (Paris: Dentu, 1868), 393.

[155] Bernard Ménager, *Les Napoléon du peuple* (Paris: Aubier, 1988), 206–7.

[156] On Muller's ideological evolution from legitimism to Bonapartism and his subsequent return to royalism after 1870, see Michel Denis, *Les royalistes de la Mayenne* (Paris: Klincksieck, 1977), 333–38.

tive quarrel with the Empire (although it was not clear on what basis the question of hereditary succession could be resolved). Then, he adduced three arguments to appeal to the legitimists: the emperor was popular throughout French society, being respected even by many who voted for legitimist candidates;[157] the Empire had restored order in the country, and this was well appreciated by the mass of the legitimist party, especially in the face of the reemergence of radical republicanism;[158] and the country could not afford to forsake the talents that the legitimists could bring to public office. "The upper classes have a useful function to perform in the state," he wrote.[159]

This attempt to bring closer two of the major forces of French conservatism bore some fruit in 1869–70. After the appointment of the Ollivier administration, attempts were made to effect a rapprochement between Bonapartist and legitimist groups. This was manifested in the formation of the commission of decentralization, which included a number of leading liberal legitimists such as Claude-Marie Raudot and Charles Garnier. It was also particularly evident in the stronger showing of Bonapartism in Catholic and legitimist heartlands in the elections of 1869, the plebiscite of May 1870, and the subsequent municipal and departmental elections.[160] In the department of the Loir-et-Cher, for example, the legitimist newspaper completely rallied to the Bonapartist cause during the campaign for the 1870 plebiscite, arguing for a common front against the threat of social revolution.[161] Similarly, in Nantes, the municipal elections of August 1870 saw the triumph of the republican list against an alliance of Bonapartists, legitimists, and clericalists.[162]

INSTITUTIONAL AND SOCIAL IMPERATIVES

The promotion of greater administrative decentralization was also seen as a means of enhancing the effectiveness of the bureaucracy. This again was an old liberal Bonapartist theme. In a circular to prefects in January 1852, Morny had stressed that the administration should avoid as far as possible "excuses, obstructions, and delays" and urged that the domi-

---

[157] Charles Muller, *L'Empire et les légitimistes* (Paris: Dentu, 1864), 64–65.

[158] Ibid., 83.

[159] Ibid., 94.

[160] For the elections of 1869, see Louis Girard, *Les élections de 1869* (Paris: Rivière, 1960), xv. See also Pierre de La Gorce, *Histoire du Second Empire* (Paris: Plon, 1903), 6:106–7, and Arch. Nat. BB30-390 for the reports of the procureurs-généraux of Angers (4 July 1870), Besançon (8 July 1870), Bordeaux (9 July 1870), Caen (11 July 1870), and Toulouse (7 July 1870).

[161] Georges Dupeux, *Aspects de l'histoire sociale et politique du Loir-et-Cher, 1848–1914* (Paris: Mouton, 1962), 400.

[162] *Le Temps*, 18 August 1870.

nant administrative mores should be comprehensively changed.[163] As noted earlier, there was growing public dissatisfaction with the failings of the administration in the 1860s. A Bonapartist pamphlet called for nothing less than a declaration of war against bureaucratic red tape and offered a number of practical solutions to the problem of administrative inefficiency.[164] In 1870 the imperial elite widely acknowledged these deficiencies. Thus General Favé, a Bonapartist member of the 1870 commission on decentralization, highlighted the conservative and procrastinating disposition of the bureaucracy and its tendency to assume decision-making powers that ought properly to have been taken by political authority.[165] But in such schemes there was no question of handing power over to locally elected bodies. Bonapartists believed that a reorganization of the relationship between the political center and the administrative periphery would sharpen and clarify the lines of responsibility between the executive and the bureaucracy, without introducing further mechanisms of democratic accountability at the local level. Distinctive to this conception of administrative decentralism was the view that better and more efficient decision making could be achieved without further devolution of power from the administration to local political elites. Indeed, there was a clear limit to the extent to which even liberal imperialists were prepared to countenance redefining the attributions of the administration. This, for example, was how Bonjean defined the proper limits of imperial decentralization:

> But if central government should, in general, abstain from all direct interference in local matters . . . it cannot, in the current state of the mores and habits of the French nation, avoid watching over the practices of local authorities. Indeed, although freely chosen by universal suffrage, these authorities are not infallible and impeccable; by their ignorance, their carelessness, their imprudence, without mentioning their lack of goodwill, they could seriously compromise not only those local interests with which they are entrusted but also the public interest and that of individuals.[166]

Finally, the pursuit of decentralization was intended to encourage the emergence of independent forms of associational activity and to strengthen the country's sense of social solidarity. The first of these objectives represented an extension of a consistent Bonapartist theme throughout the Second Empire. In a speech given at Limoges in 1858, for example, Prince Napoleon had warned against the dangers of allow-

---

[163] Fond. Thiers, Papiers Baroche, 1132, Morny to prefects, 8 January 1852.
[164] *Essai de décentralisation administrative pratique* (Paris: Lainé, 1861), 6.
[165] General Favé, *La décentralisation* (Paris: Dentu, 1870), 20, 97–98.
[166] Speech by Bonjean, in *Bulletin*, 472–73.

ing the state to occupy too prominent a position in the nexus of social and economic relations. "What we must fear, indeed," he said, "is the absorption of individual forces by collective powers; this would amount to the substitution of the state for the citizen in all matters pertaining to social life and would entail the weakening of all individual initiative under the tutelage of an excessive administrative centralization."[167] This reconstitution of an autonomous "civil society" was seen as a necessary condition for the cultivation of a genuine feeling of citizenship. But decentralization was also necessary to consolidate rural society, one of the key electoral pillars of Bonapartism. Ernest Pinard spelled out the point:

> If we make the province more attractive, there will be more settled families, a greater sense of morality, and a higher birth rate, and two of the plagues of our countryside will abate: the absenteeism of the rich and the migration of the poor. The landowner would remain with his farmers, the manager with his workers, the industrialist in his factories. There would be fewer marginals and many more men attached to their land. Patriotic sentiment, which is weakening today, would keep its deep roots in the native soil, which would no longer be abandoned. One loves one's great motherland only insofar as one remains attached to one's place of origin. Patriotism is the virtue of a sedentary, not nomadic, nation. In this population, which would work harder as it became more sedentary, some men would rise above others by their personal merits and by the services rendered to their communities; they would acquire a favorable influence through the healthy education of universal suffrage. They would become a guide for the weak and the fulcrum of the state.[168]

Decentralization could thus help bring about many of the key objectives of the Bonapartists: the rekindling of patriotism, the strengthening of the family, the defense of a form of social corporatism, the maintenance of its rural interests, and the promotion of social solidarity for conservative purposes. In a letter to the emperor in April 1868, the Alsatian Bonapartist Zorn de Bulach echoed these sentiments and underlined the antirevolutionary aspect of decentralization.

> By further introducing the peasant to political life, to the discussion of his local and communal interests, by decentralizing further[,] . . . we shall dig deeper Napoleonic roots in the soil. The government might seem less powerful, but only in appearance, for in reality it will be more solid and thus in a better position to resist surprises, especially those attacks which come

---

[167] Prince Jérôme Napoléon, *Economie politique: Discours et rapports du Prince Napoléon* (Paris, n.d.), 100–101. See also *Choix de discours et de publications du Prince Napoléon* (Paris, 1874).

[168] Pinard, *Mon Journal*, 1:223–24.

from big cities, which are too well organized, and which dominate the countryside by the excess of centralization.[169]

Yet this diversity in the Bonapartists' underlying objectives also pointed to the existence of serious contradictions in their approach to decentralization. It was not merely that the Empire was fundamentally divided between centralist and decentralist tendencies, as we will note in a moment, or that it never fully established whether the pursuit of decentralization was an end in itself or a means to a further set of objectives. The wider problem was that many of the specific objectives of the Bonapartist conception of decentralization were not fully consistent. During the first decade of the Empire, there was clear tension between criticism of the bureaucracy and the devolution of greater local power to the prefects — a set of practices that made the administration both the cause of the problem and its solution. During the liberal evolution of the regime, these contradictions became even more manifest. An attempt was made to preserve the apolitical nature of local government, which was one of the cardinal principles of Bonapartism. Yet at the same time the regime sought to use its local government reforms as a means of cultivating the support and cooperation of antirevolutionary opposition groups — a political objective, if ever there was one. Depoliticization also did not sit very comfortably with the encouragement given to mayors to confirm their legitimacy through universal suffrage.

Similarly, there was a genuine effort to promote decentralist solutions as a means of fostering a greater sense of citizenship and civic responsibility. However, there was a continuing tendency to emphasize the administrative and economic (as opposed to the political) aspects of individual citizenship. Bonapartists agreed that the burdensome presence of the state should be removed from the shoulders of individual citizens. But they appeared more interested in encouraging economic enterprise and social advancement than political autonomy and self-determination. There was also tension between seeking to maintain a fair and impartial system of administration and giving greater powers to local notables, who would inevitably use these resources to further their self-interested ends. All these contradictions were symptomatic of a broader strategic dilemma: how to promote a greater sense of citizenship without endangering the regime's social and political base in the country. The Second Empire's hesitations and contradictions over the promotion of decentralization were thus a manifestation of the fundamental problem with which it was confronted throughout the 1860s.

[169] Letter dated 22 April 1868, quoted in François Igersheim, *Politique et administration dans le Bas-Rhin, 1848–1870* (Strasbourg: Presses Universitaires, 1993), 343.

The Resistance of the Administrative Centralists

The promotion of greater decentralization was also hindered by the
fierce opposition of some authoritarian Bonapartists to any decentralist
measures that appeared to threaten the strength and cohesion of the
administration. In contrast with liberal Bonapartists such as Prince Napoleon and Bonjean, who sought to provide greater scope for autonomous associational activity in society, and those authoritarian Bonapartists who welcomed decentralization as a means of undermining the role
of local administrative agents, many doctrinaire imperialists were skeptical of the clamors for greater political liberty.[170] A Bonapartist administrator from Dijon aptly summarized their approach as follows: "In all
human institutions, as in man himself, independently of the organs that
help to carry out the different functions of existence, there is an internal
and invisible force, which is the very principle of life; such appears centralization to us."[171] In the analysis of a Bonapartist economist, local
government required "capacity, impartiality, public-spiritedness, and devotion"; these qualities could unerringly be found only in the administration, and certainly not (as the Nancy program had suggested) in elected local councils.[172] One Bonapartist notable even suggested creating
special administrative schools for training the mayors of rural communes.[173]

At best, the question of decentralization was seen as a purely administrative matter, which required no substantive alteration to the regime's
political and institutional practices. This conception of decentralization
was fully expressed in the decrees of March 1852 and April 1861,
which merely transferred powers held by central government to the prefects — an exercise in deconcentration rather than decentralization.[174] After his replacement at the Ministry of the Interior in June 1863, Persigny joined in the incipient debate over decentralization. In typically
robust fashion, he argued the case for a restricted conception of decentralization and strongly defended himself against accusations of authori-

[170] See, for example, Adolphe Granier de Cassagnac, *Souvenirs du Second Empire*
(Paris: Dentu, 1883), 3:165–68.
[171] V. Mouline, *Etude sur la centralisation, son origine et ses résultats* (Dijon: Lamarche,
1863), 49.
[172] R. Vignes, "A propos de la décentralisation," *Journal des Economistes* (October–
December 1865): 200–201.
[173] Baron Alfred de Turckheim, *Lettre à sa majesté l'Empereur Napoléon III sur une
application du principe des spécialités à l'organisation municipale* (Colmar: Hoffmann,
1856), 10–11.
[174] Léon Aucoc, "Les controverses sur la décentralisation administrative," part 1, *Revue
Politique et Parlementaire* (May 1895): 236.

tarian centralism. In a speech given at St. Etienne in August 1864, he claimed that he had always favored decentralization: "The decentralization that I have never ceased to favor is not the one that consists in delegating certain attributions of central government to local authorities, but rather the one that should emancipate the whole country."[175] However, his reaction to the tentative changes in the Empire's management of the local government regime in 1864 and 1865 suggested that his conception of the country's self-emancipation was still deeply colored by his authoritarian and centralist instincts. In three letters to the emperor in July and August 1865, Persigny denounced the drift toward greater liberalization in the regime's dealings with local government. Several trends were of particular concern.

First, he regretted the Empire's increasing willingness to expose mayors to the uncertainties of universal suffrage. As the sole representatives of political authority in the commune, mayors were functionaries, and therefore (in the authoritarian Bonapartist scheme of things) they could not be made accountable to the electorate. Any electoral defeat suffered by a mayor thus constituted an affront to the legitimacy of the administration.[176] Second, Persigny objected to the tactical withdrawal of administrative agents from the local electoral arena, arguing that such a move would compromise the "authority and independence" of mayors and thereby reduce their ability effectively to discharge their duties as agents of the state.[177] Third, the withdrawal of the administration from local politics could benefit only greedy and unscrupulous provincial elites, who would be allowed to enjoy unfettered control over local affairs. The public interest would thus be subverted, and private concerns would be given a free run. Persigny permitted himself a pun on the emperor's warning after his coup d'état: "One should not be surprised if good citizens are distressed and the bad ones rejoice."[178]

Fourth, the introduction of greater political autonomy in the departments and communes would weaken the powers of the prefects and thus further compromise the integrity of the administration.[179] Last, but not least, the decision to allow universal suffrage to express itself without administrative interference in local elections threatened the political

[175] Arch. Nat., Papiers Eugène Rouher, 45 AP 19, speech given on 24 August 1864.

[176] Bib. Nat., Papiers Persigny NAF 23066, Persigny to Napoleon III, 29 June 1865. In the words of Cormenin: "Every mayor is a functionary; all functionaries have a mandate from the government; all mandatees owe a good and loyal service to their superiors" (Le maire de village [Paris: Pagnerre, 1848], 44).

[177] Bib. Nat., Papiers Persigny NAF 23066, Persigny to Napoleon III, 5 August 1865.

[178] Ibid., 27 July 1865. After the 1851 coup Napoleon III had stated that good citizens should be reassured and wicked men should tremble.

[179] Ibid.

base of the Empire. Bereft of the clear guidance that the provincial administration traditionally provided, local populations would become entirely vulnerable to the sirens of false prophets and demagogues. Never known to understate his case, Persigny conjured up a dramatic vision of a country overcome by anarchy and subversion: "Disorder is being introduced in almost all the communes of France . . . the very foundations of the Empire, that is, the foundations of universal suffrage seem shaken."[180]

This fear of the political and administrative consequences of decentralization was widespread among authoritarian Bonapartists. Ernest Quentin-Bauchard expressed the typical view that most communes were effectively incapable of self-government:

Have those who demand that administrative decentralization should extend as far as communal *autonomy* considered the practical consequences of such a regime? To allow communes to govern themselves would be a very good thing, if they did so; but who does not have the sense of the thousands of interests that would suffer at the hands of incompetent municipalities?[181]

During the parliamentary debates on the 1855 municipal law, many participants argued that universal suffrage was not appropriate for communal elections, and in fact urged the government to revert to the First Empire's practice of appointing municipal commissions. Part of the fear was that universal suffrage could be exploited by revolutionary groups. In this spirit the prefect of Seine Haussmann vehemently denounced the Parisian populace in a letter to the emperor in July 1857:

Nothing good can be expected from this population without religious or moral principles, semiliterate, eager for pleasures, almost entirely relieved of medical and family obligations by charity. It huddles into Parisian factories, reads clandestine newspapers and pamphlets, signs up for secret societies that cannot be tracked by the police because of their number, and always votes to a man for revolutionary candidates.[182]

During the debate on the 1867 municipal law, the Bonapartist deputy Paul Pamard (the mayor of Avignon) stated the following to widespread assent from government benches:

I think we have forgotten too quickly the power of universal suffrage, and we must limit our recourse to it. Indeed, since 1848, and during eighteen

---

[180] Ibid., 5 August 1865.

[181] E. Quentin-Bauchard, *Etudes et Souvenirs* (Paris: Plon, 1902), 2:362.

[182] Arch. Dépt. Loire-Atlantique, Papiers Billault, 20 J 59, Haussmann to Napoleon III, 8 July 1857.

years, it has operated nineteen times. I do not think that any government, whatever its form, can function with such a frequent electoral regime.[183]

Many authoritarian Bonapartists believed that excessive recourse to universal suffrage would undermine the role of the administration. Indeed, in Persigny's view of the world, the only way to guarantee the unity and stability of the existing local government regime was further to concentrate local powers in the hands of the prefects. In his memoirs, he cited another letter written to the emperor in November 1866, in which he proposed to transfer the considerable patronage powers of the state from the ministries and central bureaucracy to the prefects. This measure, he argued, would constitute a true form of decentralization: "There is no greater service to render to the country than to decentralize the general solicitation; to withdraw it from Paris and to spread it among the eighty-nine departments; there could be no more moral action than to place it on a terrain where, all things and men being known, false virtues, false devotions, false talents, and false titles have no chance of success."[184]

In sum, the problem with the liberal Bonapartist conception of decentralization was that it would take away power from those who exercised it in the best interests of society and hand it over to groups whose concerns were self-regarding and often subversive. This conception highlighted the sharp division between centralist elites and decentralist local notables within the Bonapartist movement, both of whom subscribed to authoritarian values but nonetheless deeply resented each other's power and influence within the state.

THE CONCERNS OF THE PREFECTS

Persigny's fears were amplified by an authoritative group that added its voice to the debate over decentralization in the 1860s: the prefects. The pivotal role the prefects played within the imperial political and administrative system, the strength of their attachment to many aspects of centralism, and the fact that they expressed the views of many conservative imperialists gave particular significance to their contributions. Opposition to liberal reform was indeed widespread within the imperial administration.[185] Although some expressed sympathy with the objec-

---

[183] *Annales du Sénat et du Corps Législatif: Compte-rendu analytique des séances*, session of 8 April 1867 (Paris: Panckoucke, 1867), 255.

[184] Persigny, *Mémoires du duc de Persigny*, 317.

[185] See Charles Pouthas, *Histoire politique du Second Empire* (Paris: Sorbonne, 1956), 428.

Fig. 3. Jean Gilbert Victor Fialin, Duc de Persigny (1808–72), lithography
Bronemann, Bibliothèque Nationale, Paris. One of the oldest *compagnons de
route* of Napoleon III, Persigny was the principal ideologue of authoritarian
Bonapartism and a fervent advocate of centralization.

tives of the Nancy program of 1865, there was a general rejection of the claims and underlying assumptions of the decentralist camp.

The foundation of the prefects' institutional value system lay in their conception of the inherent superiority of the French administration over competing forms of social organization. In the words of former prefect Chévillard, "Administration consists in a collection of measures to enable the development of all the productive sources of a people, both in moral and material terms, and to ensure the distribution of all the wealth produced."[186] In short, he added grandly, "The administration carries the weight of great interests; it is entrusted with a civilizing mission."[187] A key feature of this function, to which all prefects were irrevocably attached, was the principle of political centralization, "one of the most precious conquests of 1790."[188] The unity and territorial integrity of France, the principle of equal application of laws, and the common association of every French citizen in a single political community were all immutable features of the political landscape. But the prefects' attachment to centralization extended not only to its political form but also to many of its administrative dimensions. Seven main arguments were adduced to support the main practices of administrative centralization.

First, it was claimed that centralized institutions acted as an effective shield against the dual threats of external invasion and internal subversion. This "powerful weapon" was particularly needed in the context of an increasingly volatile European situation and the growing menace of radical republicanism in France.[189] Mindful of the turbulence of France's recent history, and perhaps resigned to the likely recurrence of political upheavals in the near future, some prefects also saw administrative centralization as an important instrument for restoring order in the aftermath of revolution.[190]

Second, the administration was seen as the guarantor of impartiality and good order and the arbiter of social conflicts between competing class interests. Boyer de Sainte Suzanne thus argued against giving local authorities the unrestricted right to levy taxes, on the ground that such practices would rapidly foment class warfare, with landowners and

---

[186] Jules Chévillard, *De la division administrative de la France et de la centralisation* (Paris: Durand, 1862), 26.

[187] Ibid., 28.

[188] M. Fumeron d'Ardeuil [pseudonym for a group of imperial functionaries], *La décentralisation* (Paris: Plon, 1866), 5.

[189] *De la décentralisation: Objections au projet du Comité de Nancy par un ancien préfet* (Paris: Librairie Centrale, 1866), 18.

[190] Ibid., 58.

peasants turning local government institutions into instruments of mutual antagonism.[191]

Third, the benevolent functions of the administration were required in the exercise of the prefectoral *tutelle* (administrative supervision and control) of the communes. The Nancy manifesto had argued in favor of the emancipation of the commune, and particularly the reduction of administrative control, on the ground that local communities were entitled to manage their affairs without the state's interference. The prefects' typical response was that many communes were incapable of self-administration. As one of them argued, "It has happened that we have encountered communes where it was impossible to find a single literate man who could be made mayor."[192] During the debate over the 1867 municipal law, the minister presiding over the Council of State added:

> We have in our country 37,000 communes; there are 16,000 that have fewer than 500 inhabitants and in which it is difficult to find a municipal council that can offer all the guarantees of enlightenment, assiduity, and independence. It is especially the small communes that we should not abandon to the whims and fancies of hasty deliberations.[193]

Administrative decentralization was thus either undesirable or impossible. The immaturity of many (indeed, the majority of) communes made it undesirable to grant them greater political autonomy. At the same time, the principle of universal application of all laws made it impossible to grant greater autonomy only to those communes which had the capacity to exercise it.[194]

Fourth, the tutelle was necessary to prevent powerful local castes from exploiting their strength in relation to economically and socially underprivileged groups. As one prefect argued (echoing Persigny's fears), the withdrawal of the administration from the local political arena would leave the door open to the "big landowners," who would use their powers only to increase their fortunes. The prefect's presence, by contrast, was a guarantee of fairness. "The tutelle of the prefect will be

[191] Baron E. de Boyer de Sainte Suzanne, *La vérité sur la décentralisation* (Amiens: Jeunet, 1861), 15.

[192] *De la décentralisation*, 33; also Boyer de Sainte Suzanne, *La vérité sur la décentralisation*, 9.

[193] *Annales du Sénat et du Corps Législatif: Compte-rendu analytique des séances*, session of 9 April 1867 (Paris: Panckoucke, 1867), 299.

[194] Boyer de Sainte Suzanne, *La vérité sur la décentralisation*, 23. In any event, those communes which had the material and intellectual means of self-administration were most likely to be in opposition hands: from the perspective of authoritarian Bonapartism, they were politically incapable.

the best that can be chosen; it will be the most impartial, the most enlightened, the most active, and the most expeditious in its execution."[195]

As this quote suggests, the prefects saw their stewardship of the provinces as providing not only fairness but also competence in local goverment. They strongly resisted suggestions that many of the executive tasks currently fulfilled by the local administration be devolved to the General Council. In their view, deliberative assemblies were poorly equipped to provide leadership. Furthermore, only one individual could be responsible for implementing policy and discharging this responsibility effectively.[196] Two of the major criticisms leveled at the competence of the prefects were that they tended to have little knowledge of the departments in which they were posted and that their inclination to govern by authoritarian means offended local populations. This, in turn, reduced the administration's ability to interact fruitfully with the citizenry and thus compounded its ignorance of the provinces' real sentiments.

The prefects retorted that their knowledge of the local social and political terrain was acquired very rapidly after their arrival in the department, in large part due to the efficiency of the administration (notably the diligence of the subprefects). In any case, prefects could govern only with local support (whether tacit or explicit), and it was hardly in their interests to alienate those very groups with whom they needed to interact on a regular basis.[197] Sixth, there was a Saint-Simonian economic justification of administrative centralism. Local administrators could best oversee the economic development of departments, because they alone could act in the best interests of local populations.[198] They also exercised scrupulous control over the appropriation of public funds and provided much-needed restraint on the notorious tendency of communes toward financial profligacy.[199] In any event, the overwhelming majority of communes were not self-sufficient economically. According to the 1862 report on the financial situation of the communes, 33,454 of the 37,555 communes had an annual revenue of less than 10,000 francs.[200]

Finally, prefects recognized that some aspects of administrative centralization were inefficient but argued that the solution lay in transferring many of the central bureaucracy's powers to the local administration. For example, many of the administrative institutions of central government were unproductive and excessively formalistic. One prefect

---

[195] *De la décentralisation*, 125.
[196] Ibid., 41–42.
[197] Ibid., 52–53.
[198] Ibid., 64.
[199] Boyer de Sainte Suzanne, *La vérité sur la décentralisation*, 17.
[200] *Rapport sur la situation financière des communes de l'Empire* (1862).

cited the example of the grand corps, which were guilty of creating systems of rules that only they could interpret.[201] Persigny also denounced the powers of

> this expansionary, irksome, and all-powerful bureaucracy, which, by multiplying rules, formalities, and difficulties of all kinds, attracted to Paris, with the handling of all business, the distribution of all offices and favors and progressively undermined to its benefit the salutory influence of the prefects in the departments. By exaggerating, furthermore, all the excesses of centralization, it turned into a plague what had been of benefit to the whole country.[202]

Whereas many had claimed that administrative decentralization was the solution to these problems, prefects argued that the answer lay in transferring central powers to the local administration.[203] This solution had the advantage of reducing the political influence of the Parisian bureaucracy and giving further resources to the only true guardians of the interests of local populations. One prefect took this argument further by arguing for what would now be termed delocalization: the physical transfer of Parisian officials to the provinces.[204] There were also some proposals to reconstitute provincial territorial divisions as a means both of lightening the administrative burdens of prefects and of attending to problems that were of common interest to departments.[205]

From the elevated perspective of the imperial prefects, administrative decentralization was therefore a myth, and a dangerous one at that. Its proponents sought to weaken and divide the only institution that was capable of providing effective and impartial local government and replace it with alternatives that would do nothing but damage the fabric of provincial life. Indeed, prefects saw no advantage whatsoever to promoting greater political decentralization in the country. Centralization had helped to foster a sense of collective identity and purpose in France, and many prefects were concerned that its erosion would reduce citizens' identification with the broader community.[206] This, in turn, would make the country ungovernable: "France would become a simple aggregate of small provinces, of small cities that were half-federal and half-republican; such cities would be impossible to administer."[207] Imple-

[201] *De la décentralisation*, 68–69.
[202] Persigny, *Mémoires du duc de Persigny*, 307.
[203] *De la décentralisation*, 155–56.
[204] Ibid., 109–10.
[205] The case for the Nord is made by Alexandre Jonglez de Ligne, *Une province sans départements* (Paris: Dentu, 1868), esp. 23–28.
[206] Boyer de Sainte Suzanne, *La vérité sur la décentralisation*, 34.
[207] Fumeron d'Ardeuil, *La décentralisation*, 12.

menting the Nancy manifesto would serve only to disorganize local administration, and furthermore it would enhance "the power of local influences, this open wound of the province."[208]

The claim that greater local autonomy would have an educative function was also firmly rejected, on the ground that it would inevitably lead to the politicization of local government. In the words of the subprefect of Rambouillet, under a decentralized regime "local authority would naturally become an instrument in the hands of parties, a stepping-stone for personal ambitions. Similar considerations would naturally enter the deliberations of municipal councils. Local authorities would become political parties."[209] This reference to executive commissions was a response to the suggestion (voiced among others by the signatories of the Nancy program) that the General Councils be allowed to elect a permanent executive body, which would carry out the decisions of the council and represent the authority between plenary sessions. Predictably, prefects saw this proposal as an attempt to wrest power away from the local administration. Their objection to the notion of an executive commission was twofold. First, they argued that such an organization would confuse the chain of command and thus disrupt the smooth operation of local government. Second, and more important, a permanent executive commission would introduce an element of structural conflict between the prefect and the General Council.[210]

In short, the introduction of greater political decentralization would bring nothing but disaster to France. This perspective was summed up in the apocalyptic (and somewhat prophetic) vision of a Bonapartist prefect anticipating the consequences of the collapse of the centralized state: "Destroy this organization, and the first revolutionary tremor will bring all public services to a halt and suspend the administrative life of France; parties will take advantage of the weakening of authority to divide the country, civil strife will break out in favor of socialism, and the Foreigner will come to exploit our divisions and to try to capture France."[211]

THE FRUSTRATIONS OF THE 1870 COMMISSION

Centralist and decentralist undercurrents within Bonapartism were thus clearly divided over the question of extending municipal and departmental franchises. These divisions were sharply reflected in the work-

[208] Paul Cere, *La décentralisation administrative* (Paris: Dentu, 1865), 6; also *De la décentralisation*, 85.
[209] *De la décentralisation et des partis*, 30.
[210] *De la décentralisation*, 86.
[211] Boyer de Sainte Suzanne, *La vérité sur la décentralisation*, 29.

ings of the 1870 commission, which, as noted earlier, was set up under Ollivier to provide a wide-ranging discussion on the different aspects of the relationship between Paris and the provinces. The object of the commission, as spelled out rather optimistically by Minister of the Interior Chevandier de Valdrôme, was to examine "the problem of decentralization in all its aspects and to prepare its solution."[212]

To enable as broad a consultation as possible, representatives of all major constitutional groups were offered membership in the commission. In the end, only the republicans declined collectively, as an expression of general hostility to Ollivier and of skepticism about the sincerity of the Empire's commitment to local liberty. As the republican Ernest Picard remarked sarcastically, "The era of commissions is beginning; let us hope that it will not replace the era of liberty."[213] Nonetheless, the composition of the commission bore witness to the relative success of the liberal Empire in broadening the regime's appeal to other forces of "order." Ollivier was proud of the membership of the different commissions.[214] In his view, they were filled with "men of outstanding caliber: they were the elite, not only of France but also of the intellectual world."[215] The president of the commission was the Orleanist Odilon Barrot, a former adversary of the Empire whose *ralliement* was in itself a symbol of the regime's growing appeal to conservative liberals. Barrot's commitment to decentralization dated back to the 1840s, and under the Second Republic he had been an advocate of moderate change in the distribution of power between Paris and the provinces, contributing to the discussions of the 1851 parliamentary commission on local administration.[216] Although personally reviled by some conservatives for his narcissism and love of power,[217] Barrot was generally recognized as an eminent political personality. His acceptance of the presidency of the commission reflected the potential for a broad antirevolutionary alliance of imperialists, liberals, and conservatives. The fear of revolutionary socialism was very real in the early months of 1870, and many

[212] Report of the minister of the interior to the emperor on the formation of the 1870 commission of decentralization, in *Journal Officiel*, 22 February 1870.

[213] *L'électeur libre*, 10 February 1870.

[214] Three commissions were set up in early 1870: on administrative decentralization, on the administration of Paris and the department of the Seine (presided over by the minister of the interior), and on higher education (chaired by Guizot).

[215] Ollivier, *L'Empire libéral*, 12:538.

[216] For a sample of his views during this period, see Arch. Nat., Papiers Odilon Barrot, 271 AP1 A6, letters to an Englishwoman.

[217] In the scathing words of Maxime du Camp, Barrot was "bloated, swollen, puffy, believing himself a statesman because he was bursting with vanity, and confident in his importance because he was hollow" (Maxime du Camp, *Souvenirs d'un demi-siècle, 1830–1870* [Paris: Hachette, 1949], 76).

radical republicans saw the issue of decentralization as an attempt to cement an alliance of conservative forces resisting political change. In *L'Espérance du Peuple* La Rochette mocked the appearance of a number of "officious sheets," which seemed

> more and more frightened by the febrile activity that has seized Paris and the revolutionary impetus that is driving the capital into the hands of the Revolution. What can be done to arrest this accelerated movement? How to prevent the Parisian volcano from igniting France again? They can find, these officious sheets that tremble with fear, only one means: decentralization.[218]

Thus common interests transcended the political diversity of the commission's membership. But this broader convergence of interests was not translated into a common approach to the question of decentralization. Alongside such members of the Council of State as Léon Aucoc, Edmond Blanc, and Joseph Boulatigner, who were naturally skeptical of any measure that challenged the powers of the state, the Bonapartist representatives were divided in their approach to decentralization. General Favé, the author of a pamphlet on the question,[219] was a positive advocate of greater local liberty, as were the senators Bonjean and Le Play; but the comte Joachim Murat and especially the vice-president of the commission Baron Benoist d'Azy were traditional Bonapartist centralists.[220] These divisions were mirrored among the conservative liberal members of the commission, which included instinctive centralists such as Maxime du Camp,[221] cerebral advocates of state power such as Dupont-White,[222] but also convinced decentralists such as Prévost-Paradol, Metz de Noblat, Charles Garnier, and Freycinet.[223] The liberal monarchist view was represented by Andelarre and especially Raudot, the most prominent legitimist pamphleteer on decentralization.[224] In sum,

---

[218] Quoted in Pierre Guiral, *Prévost-Paradol, 1829–1870: Pensée et action d'un libéral sous le Second Empire* (Paris: Presses Universitaires de France, 1955), 681.

[219] See n. 165.

[220] Baroche, *Second Empire*, 608.

[221] "I am a centralist by temperament, and I was apprehensive that the commission would be concerned mainly with political questions, about which I am incompetent" (Maxime du Camp, *Souvenirs littéraires* [Paris: Hachette, 1883], 2:486).

[222] Charles Dupont-White was the celebrated defender of centralism; his works include *L'Individu et L'Etat* (1856), *La Centralisation* (1860), and *La liberté politique considérée dans ses rapports avec l'administration locale* (1864).

[223] For an account of Freycinet's experiences as a member of the 1870 commission, see his *Souvenirs, 1848–1878* (Paris: Delagrave, 1914), 89–98.

[224] See Jean Pierre Rochet, "Un opposant légitimiste libéral, Raudot," in *Les républicains sous le Second Empire*, ed. Léo Hamon (Paris: Editions de la Maison des Sciences de l'Homme, 1993).

the range of opinions on decentralization within the commission mirrored the heterogeneity of views on the subject within the Bonapartist camp.

Under these circumstances, it came as little surprise that the workings of the commission yielded few concrete results.[225] There was agreement to divide the work into three functional groups, focusing on the attributions of the commune, canton, and department respectively.[226] Two of the questions that provoked the most passionate discussions were the mayors' mode of appointment and the extension of the General Council's attributes. The latter issue aroused as much public interest as the appointment of mayors. As a report from the procureur-général of Besançon made clear in early July 1870,

> Public opinion is still impatient; it is now concerned about the delay in the promulgation of the law on the General Councils. It would be regrettable if the discussion . . . did not take place in time for the proclamation of the law before the next session of the General Councils, so that the councillors would therefore not be able to appoint their presidents and secretaries.[227]

There were indeed a number of areas of discussion: the mode of designation of the leading members of the council, but also the broadening of the attributions of the assemblies (following the trend set by the 1866 law) and the limitation of the role of the prefect; the publicizing of the debates of the council; and the creation of a permanent body that would represent the council between sessions. The departmental subcommission came up with a radical scheme that included the establishment of a permanent executive commission of the General Council, which would be given wide-ranging powers of execution and control. Had this scheme been implemented, it would have transformed the prefect into a subordinate of the departmental notables, effectively making the latter the dominant political figures of the locality.[228] Although the deliberations of the commission were interrupted by the Franco-Prussian War, it was unlikely that the Empire would have accepted such a drastic reorganization of local government. In the law of 23 July 1870 — one of the final pieces of local government legislation the regime adopted before its collapse — the Legislative Corps agreed that the election of its president and secretary should be left to the General Council. A few weeks earlier, on 14 June, it had also been agreed to give departmental assemblies the right to choose which newspapers could carry

---

[225] For a detailed examination of the discussions, see Brigitte Basdevant-Gaudemet, *La commission de décentralisation de 1870* (Paris: Presses Universitaires de France, 1973).

[226] Ibid., 49–51.

[227] Arch. Nat. BB30-390, report dated 8 July 1870.

[228] Basdevant-Gaudemet, *La commission de décentralisation*, 87.

official legal announcements (a power hitherto exercised by the prefects).[229]

However, more substantial reforms were rejected. Thus, the proposal to allow the council's debates to be made public was not approved. Furthermore, the suggestion that General Councils be allowed to express political views was endorsed by the Legislative Corps but rejected by the Senate.[230] In the end, the Empire shied away from any reform that substantively altered the distribution of power within the department. In particular, there was a clear commitment to reject any proposal that transferred significant powers from the administration to locally elected bodies. Despite finding support among Bonapartist advocates of decentralization,[231] the question of giving departmental assemblies some of the powers of tutelle exercised by prefects over the communes was not considered further. In the Empire's view, an issue of principle was at stake: only the central government had the capacity to determine the general interest. In the words of Minister of State Adolphe Vuitry:

> General Councils are departmental bodies; they administer departmental resources; they can, if need be, enlighten the government on certain questions of public interest. But when an issue of public interest bears directly on the interest of communes, public authority itself, with all the guarantees it offers, is entrusted with the responsibility of defending this interest.[232]

This centralist principle also prevailed in discussions of the mayor's role. This question would provide one of the dominant campaigning themes of decentralists during the 1860s, as we will note in the following chapters. There was widespread resentment of the Empire's conception of the mayor as an exclusive servant of the regime's political and administrative interests. Echoing Thiers, a local politician described mayors as sub-subprefects and denounced the regime's tendency to rely on these officials during election campaigns as a "deplorable and vicious" practice.[233] The 1865 Nancy manifesto advocated the retention of the executive's nominating prerogative but proposed that its choice be made from the municipal council.[234] Republicans also consistently

[229] Emilien Constant, "Emile Ollivier et la décentralisation sous le Second Empire," in *Regards sur Emile Ollivier*, ed. Anne Troisier de Diaz (Paris: Sorbonne, 1985), 188.

[230] Basdevant-Gaudemet, *La commission de décentralisation*, 89.

[231] For example, Félix Lebon, *La Décentralisation* (Cannes, 1870).

[232] Vuitry's intervention during the debate on the 1867 municipal law, in *Annales du Sénat et du Corps Législatif*: compte-rendu analytique des séances, session of 9 April 1867 (Paris: Panckoucke, 1867), 283.

[233] E. Marion, *Les maires de village aux prochaines élections* (Paris: Le Chevalier, 1869), 5.

[234] *Un projet de décentralisation* (Nancy: Vagner, 1865), 41.

argued for the abolition of the state's practice of appointing mayors, and most called for this prerogative to be restored to the municipal council.[235] In the debate in the Legislative Corps in late May and early June 1870, some republicans such as Jules Favre also argued for the election of the mayor by the municipal council.[236] Within imperial circles the matter gave rise to much debate. Liberal Bonapartists argued that a reform of the mode of appointment of mayors would constitute a step in the right direction by promoting the cause of greater self-government. The procureur-général of Agen put it thus in January 1870:

> The establishment of communal and departmental franchises would not pose a serious threat to public order and would appear to be endorsed here even by the most timorous conservatives. The appointment of mayors from municipal councils, a less minutious surveillance over communal affairs on the part of administrative bodies, would accustom local populations to watch over their own affairs, without turning to the state for trifling matters.[237]

By April 1870 the reports of the procureurs-généraux suggested that Bonapartist opinion on the issue was somewhat divided, but with a clear trend toward moderate reform. In some areas, it was reported that the question of how mayors were chosen was not a matter of great public concern,[238] or that the majority view favored a retention of the status quo.[239] But in most areas, there was support for cautious change: the continuing appointment of mayors by the state, but with the choice being restricted to elected members of the municipal council[240] — in short, the proposal advocated by the Nancy manifesto. The commission debated the question, and under the influence of Prévost-Paradol agreed (by a single-vote majority) that mayors should be elected by their municipal councils (with the exception of Paris and Lyon, whose first magistrates would continue to be chosen by the government).[241] But this proposal was furiously rejected by the minister of the interior, and the matter brought the commission into open conflict with the government. When the question was brought to the Legislative Corps in late May 1870, the government made it clear that its conception of municipal

---

See Maurice Reclus, *Ernest Picard, 1821–1877* (Paris: Hachette, 1912), 178.

[236] *Annales du Sénat et du Corps Législatif*, session of 24 June 1870 (Paris: Journal Officiel, 1870), 131–40.

[237] Arch. Nat. BB30-390, report of January 1870.

[238] Arch. Nat. BB30-390, report from the procureur-général of Bourges, 4 April 1870.

[239] Ibid., report from the procureur-général of Angers, 8 April 1870.

[240] Arch. Nat. BB30-390 shows these views outlined in the reports of the procureurs-généraux of Agen (8 April 1870) and Besançon (12 April 1870).

[241] Guiral, *Prévost-Paradol*, 682–83.

reform was much more limited than that proposed by the commission. In the end, the law of 23 July 1870 adopted the Nancy proposal: it retained the state's prerogative to appoint mayors while conceding that they would be chosen from the municipal council.[242]

Why did the Empire reject the commission's proposal? It was widely believed that the government had decided to use the issue of the mode of appointment of mayors to demonstrate its strength, and particularly its ability to resist internal and external pressures for greater political liberalization.[243] In a speech justifying the government's position in the Legislative Corps, Ollivier rejected opposition claims that the Empire's main reason for retaining control of the appointment of mayors had been to preserve its electoral influence in the provinces. "However great our desire to grant the greatest degree of autonomy possible to communes, we do not believe that this autonomy should go as far as destroying the principle of the nomination of mayors by the executive."[244] The principle that Ollivier invoked was based on three considerations. First, because the mayor was responsible for discharging functions that were in the general interest, it was the government's duty to ensure that an appropriate figure was chosen. Second, the mayor was a public servant and could not therefore (in the Bonapartist scheme of things) be appointed by direct or even indirect election.[245] This position had been made clear by the emperor in a letter to Ollivier in February 1870 (even before the first meeting of the commission).[246] In this sense, the government's position over the issue simply reflected the emperor's own views, which were also widely held in Bonapartist circles. In the words of Senator Maupas:

"A government that wishes, as it must, to remain in control of all political activity in the state has the right to reserve for itself a number of essential prerogatives: among these, in the administrative order, the nomination of mayors in all communes."[247]

Third, the refusal to accept the elective principle for mayors was also based on the Empire's appreciation of the current political context. As already noted, the republican opposition had made consistent progress

[242] Basdevant-Gaudemet, *La Commission de Décentralisation*, 60.
[243] Ibid., 61.
[244] Ollivier, *L'Empire libéral*, 12:512.
[245] This is not to say that they could not run for election. Universal suffrage could give mayors the stamp of public approval, but the source of their legitimacy could come only from the Empire.
[246] Ollivier, *L'Empire libéral*, 12:549.
[247] Charlemagne Emile de Maupas, *Mémoires sur le Second Empire* (Paris: Dentu, 1885), 2:554.

in urban areas during the 1860s, so that by 1870 the political position of the Empire in many cities was extremely precarious. This was to be confirmed in the municipal elections of early August 1870, which were held after the declaration of war against Prussia. Republican lists triumphed in Lyon, Marseille, le Havre, Saint-Etienne, Bordeaux, Toulouse, as well as in numerous smaller towns such as Nîmes, Orléans, and Carcassonne.[248] Under these circumstances, granting urban municipal councils the freedom to elect their mayors would have been tantamount to handing over complete control of many cities to the forces of subversion — a prospect that provoked violent reactions from the authoritarian Bonapartist press.[249] The dangers of this situation were also forcibly underlined by many procureurs-généraux in their reports during this period.[250] But the problem was not limited to cities. Surveying the deliberations of rural municipal councils, one Bonapartist concluded that they were "incapable of conducting a serious discussion";[251] another lamented the inefficiency of many mayors, especially those who combined their functions with a professional occupation.[252] During the debate on the 1870 law on the nomination of mayors, the Alsatian deputy Zorn de Bulach, who was also a rural mayor, expressed the conservative Bonapartist notables' sense of unease about the institution of universal suffrage in rural communes:

> I know the countryside, I hear what goes on there, because I live among rural populations; I am happy to do so, because it is still there that we find the true vitality of the country; this is where we find the soldier, the worker, the French laborer; this is where we still find the most honesty, the greatest sense of morality and religiosity. Do you know what would happen in many a commune if mayors were designated by universal suffrage or appointed by their municipal councils? In many communes, some would be appointed for considerations of personal ambition, others for family reasons; others still because of the need to build roads, or divide communal property, or clear the forest for cultivation; mayors would no longer be chosen on grounds of merit.[253]

[248] See an analysis of the elections in *Le Temps*, 9 August 1870.

[249] See, for example, *Le Pays*, 4 January 1870.

[250] For example, Arch. Nat. BB30-390, report dated 9 July 1870 from the procureur-général of Bordeaux.

[251] Paul David, *La commune rurale au point de vue administratif et social* (Toulouse: Paul Savy, 1858), 29.

[252] Durand, *Projet de réorganisation des mairies des grandes villes* (Bordeaux, n.d.).

[253] Baron Zorn de Bulach, intervention during the debate on the 1870 law on the nomination of mayors, 22 June 1870, in *Annales du Sénat et du Corps Législatif: Compte-rendu analytique des séances* (Paris: Journal Officiel, 1870), 81.

Bonapartist opinion in the countryside was also deeply hostile to the notion of subjecting the "lieutenants of the army of order"[254] to the vagaries of universal suffrage. In the words of a former imperialist parliamentarian from Nîmes: "I appreciate the utility and the necessity of universal suffrage as the basis of our institutions; I only wish it were better regulated and moralized, which I believe is not altogether impossible. For I cannot accept that universal suffrage *cannot go astray in the choice of a mayor*, and that it is in consequence the best way to safeguard communal interests."[255]

In the final analysis, the Empire's responses over the issue were symptomatic of the cross pressures faced by the regime in 1870. Liberal Bonapartists presented the decision to change the mode of designation of mayors as a victory for the forces of "movement," even though its scope was considerably more limited than the reform the commission had advocated. It was undeniable that the law of July 1870 represented an acknowledgment of the importance of universal suffrage. It could even be argued that the legislative change represented a substantial departure from the classical Bonapartist conception of the mayor as an executive agent of the state. However, the significance of the change was rather limited by the fact that the proportion of mayors chosen from outside the municipal council never exceeded 2 percent.[256] For example, in a letter to the emperor after the 1865 municipal elections, Persigny noted that only approximately 300 mayors (out of more than 37,000) had been chosen from outside the municipal council.[257] The reform of July 1870 was thus not so much an expression of the desirability of change as a recognition of an existing set of practices.

Ultimately, the commission's short-term failure could be attributed to a number of factors. First, its size and ideological heterogeneity made it a somewhat unwieldy instrument for exploring the issue of decentralization in a coherent and efficient manner. Many of the members of the commission felt that proceedings had lacked a clear focus. The most scathing indictment was typically offered by Maxime Du Camp, who asserted that its discussions had been pointless: "This commission of decentralization has not left an indelible imprint on my mind . . . we left each other without any sense of what we had achieved."[258] Furthermore, as already noted, the government kept a watchful eye over the commission and frustrated its efforts to promote greater political decen-

---

[254] Baron de Sède, *Le choix des maires* (Arras: De Sède, 1870), 2.

[255] *De la nomination des maires, par un ancien député* (Nîmes: Clavel-Ballivet, 1870), 13–14; emphasis is in the text.

[256] Pinard, *Mon Journal*, 1:30.

[257] Bib. Nat., Papiers Persigny NAF 23066, Persigny to Napoleon III, 5 August 1865.

[258] Du Camp, *Souvenirs littéraires*, 487.

tralization. This was exemplified by the outcome of the debate on the question of mayors, where all the political and administrative representatives of the Bonapartist state voted en bloc against proposals for substantive reform.[259] The government also had to contend with the prefects, who reacted to the creation of the commission by voicing strong opposition to any measures that might further weaken their hold on the local administrative system.[260]

These forms of institutional conservatism were abetted by the Legislative Corps and particularly the Senate, whose discussions of local government reform in the summer of 1870 revealed the continuing strength of centralist feeling within the Bonapartist movement. Above all, the commission was seen as a consultative rather than a policy-making body, especially after its views began to diverge from those of the government. Initially proposed by the minister of the interior as a body that would provide the final and comprehensive solution to the problem of centralization, the commission ended its days being dismissed by Ollivier as "a preparatory commission without any kind of legal authority."[261] To add insult to injury, the government even dragged its feet about publishing the conclusions of the commission.[262]

THE BALANCE-SHEET OF BONAPARTIST DECENTRALISM

Like the Second Empire as a whole, Bonapartist decentralization was a diverse and often contradictory phenomenon. However, it has been sufficiently analyzed in these pages to dispel the notion that it was a mere tactical or rhetorical device. This is my first general conclusion: underlying the Bonapartist conception of local liberty was a distinct civic project, which was articulated by imperial ideologues and pamphleteers and widely discussed among the different branches of the Bonapartist state. My appraisal of this debate also definitively puts to rest the conventional notion that there were no precise conceptual or theoretical underpinnings to the Bonapartist administrative system.

At the same time — and this is the third point — we have seen that there were strong elements of tension in the imperial civic project. The

[259] See the breakdown of the commission vote on the question of the election of mayors in *Journal de Paris*, 3 April 1870. No Bonapartist voted in favor of the proposal; only a small number abstained (including Parieu, the president of the Council of State).

[260] *Le Temps*, 12 April 1870.

[261] Ollivier's intervention during the Legislative Corps session of 27 June 1870, in *Annales du Sénat et du Corps Législatif: Compte-rendu analytique des séances* (Paris: Journal Officiel, 1870), 210.

[262] See the complaining letter by Odilon Barrot, in *Le Temps*, 27 June 1870, and the sarcastic comment by Hector Pessard in the *Journal de Paris*, 1 July 1870.

problem was not that the Second Empire lacked a positive vision of citizenship but that its elaboration failed to reconcile the conflicting imperatives of Bonapartist elites: depoliticization and the practice of universal suffrage, administrative omniscience and citizen involvement in local life, the maintenance of social order and preservation of the Revolutionary heritage of civil equality, the cultivation of a traditional and deferential polity and the modernization of political life. There is no doubt that the Second Empire genuinely desired to see greater civic participation in public affairs, and indeed that it greatly contributed to the development of the modern conception of citizenship in France. But the imperial regime never really decided on what precise terms this involvement should occur, nor indeed what ultimate purpose it might serve. This inconclusiveness was a hallmark of the Second Empire, as even a sympathetic historian noted: "Napoleon III knows only how to begin things."[263] Sadly for him, the nephew was not in this respect a true disciple of his prodigious uncle.

One might infer from the aforegoing that the balance sheet of the Empire with regard to decentralization was essentially negative. The circumstances in which the regime collapsed in the wake of Sedan, the frustration of many leading commission members with the obstructionism of the government, the abrasive and reactionary character of Bonapartism under the Third Republic, and the republican demonology of imperial authoritarianism all helped to create the impression that the Empire's efforts at promoting a more positive and open conception of citizenship had faltered completely.[264] Republican administrative historians added the final nail to the imperial coffin by subsequently establishing the image — "myth" is a more appropriate term[265] — of the Second Empire as a regime in which municipal and departmental liberties had been completely extinguished.[266]

However, this case should not be overstated. As we have seen, the Bonapartist regime made discrete attempts to alter the conditions under which local government institutions operated throughout the 1860s. Many of these efforts yielded concrete changes, whose impact was by no means insignificant. This was particularly the case at the departmental level, where the July 1866 law widened the budgetary attributions of

---

[263] Lamy, *Etudes sur le Second Empire*, 445.

[264] On the fate of the Bonapartist movement after 1870, see Rothney, *Bonapartism After Sedan*.

[265] Le Clère and Wright, *Les Préfets du Second Empire*, 158–60.

[266] See, for example, Alexandre Hesse, *L'administration provinciale et communale en France et en Europe, 1785–1870* (Amiens: Caron, 1870), 481, and Emile Monnet, *Histoire de l'administration provinciale, départementale et communale en France* (Paris: Rousseau, 1885), 446–47.

the General Councils and reduced the role of the prefects to one of a posteriori control in a large number of areas concerned with departmental matters (such as road construction and maintenance). The cause of economic decentralization was thus substantively advanced during the 1860s, and this as a direct result of the Empire's legislation.[267] At the same time, the particular civic project underlying the regime's approach to local politics was far less successful. As I noted at the beginning of this chapter, the Second Empire attempted to use its local government system to promote a distinct type of citizenship, which respected established order, concerned itself with material and technical matters rather than political ones, and identified with the Bonapartist values of consensus and order. However, this depoliticized conception of citizenship was constantly undermined by a number of factors.

First, it came up against the continuing social and economic powers of local notables, whose entrenched authority was often difficult to circumvent. A subprefect who had just arrived in a locality could find himself dealing with the likes of the count of Fourmestraulx-Saint-Denis, a local castellan who functioned as deputy mayor and mayor of Gussignies (Nord) from 1815 to 1867.[268] Arriving to work on a property owned by Baron Rothschild in the Brie region in October 1856, the revolutionary republican Gustave Lefrançais noted contemptuously that "the mayors and municipal councillors of all the neighboring communes are men of the baron. All of them speak, move, quarrel, and are entranced by the name of Monsieur le Baron."[269] An opposite but equally frustrating problem was the rise of adversarial politics in the communes, especially after 1860. Ironically, these political conflicts were exacerbated by the Empire's own attachment to (and repeated practice of) universal suffrage, which created lines of fracture within the community and even within the administration—as the ambiguous position of the Bonapartist mayor demonstrated all too well. Frequent elections, as the Bonapartists found to their chagrin, were hardly a recipe for creating a depoliticized community.

The Empire's record on decentralization can also be judged on the basis of the evolution of the regime's local political and administrative practices. In this respect, the picture in 1870 differed considerably from the regime's early days. For example, the political and administrative

[267] Bodineau and Verpeaux, *Histoire de la décentralisation*, 53.

[268] Jules Prignet, *Souvenirs: Le Comte de Fourmestraulx-Saint-Denis* (Valenciennes, 1867), 6.

[269] Gustave Lefrançais, *Souvenirs d'un révolutionnaire* (Brussels: Hautstont, 1902), 235.

relationship between Paris and its provinces became progressively less centralist during the two decades of imperial government. The prefects' centralized control over local political and administrative life, which the regime had intended in the early days of the Empire, was effectively replaced by a much more fluid and complex set of interactions between center and periphery (as well as within the periphery). The prefects' powers were progressively challenged by three (sometimes rival, often collusive) sets of local actors: the mayors, the general councillors, and the elected representatives in the Legislative Corps. Mayors of large towns or cities and leading members of the General Council were almost invariably figures with strong local prestige, many of whom also enjoyed powerful positions in Paris. One wag noted in 1869: "The race of multiple office-holders has always existed, but it has never been as flourishing as it is today."[270]

Indeed, it has been estimated that for the duration of the Empire, two-thirds of all ministers, three-fifths of the Council of State, and more than four-fifths of all members of the Legislative Corps also served on the General Council.[271] The presidency of the latter body was often held by a highly influential figure in the Parisian hierarchy of Bonapartism. These individuals could sidestep the machinations of the local administration with relative ease, and indeed it was often they who set the standards and norms that the prefects had to follow. In departments where the presidency of the departmental assembly was held by the likes of Persigny, Morny, Rouher, Baroche, Billault, and Fould, it was clearly these elected notables who held sway over local affairs, not the representatives of the state. The same was true of a large number of powerful members of the Legislative Corps, whose networks allowed them to circumvent and often subvert the position of the administration in their department.

Already in 1866 Persigny had deplored the political consequences of the drift toward parliamentary government: "The deputy is tending to become a figure of disproportionate importance in his locality, for he is the source of all favors and disposes of the patronage of the state over the whole administration. Moral influence is thus slipping away from the administration into his hands."[272] At a lower level of the administrative hierarchy, Bonapartist bureaucrats watched helplessly as power seeped away from administrative to elective bodies. The subprefect of Tournon noted rather plaintively in 1865:

---

[270] Aurélien Scholl, in Le Lorgnon, 11 December 1869.
[271] Le Clère and Wright, Les Préfets du Second Empire, 136.
[272] Speech in the Senate, 14 February 1866; quoted in Farat, Persigny, 293.

By a singular anomaly in our administrative organization, [the subprefects] witness the arrival, through the prefects, of precise daily orders that have to be executed within specific times; but when they look around them to en- sure that these injunctions have been followed, they come face-to-face with mayors, whose various and important attributions have given them greater effective powers than their own and whose failings cannot be remedied by administrative action.[273]

The same remark, incidentally, could have been made by prefects in relation to the role of mayors of larger towns and cities. These periph- eral forms of power increasingly undermined the centralist thrust of the Empire's political management of its provinces and forced the govern- ment to take local opinions, preferences, and interests into account. A similar change could be noted in the electoral arena. In the early days of the Empire, as seen earlier, the regime spared no effort to line up the administration behind official candidates in legislative and local elec- tions. By 1870, as a result of a number of factors (most notably the parliamentary evolution of the regime, the internal political fragmenta- tion of the administration, the unpopularity of official candidacies, the growing ineffectiveness of the system in many areas, and the social and political entrenchment of local notables), this practice was no longer considered feasible or even desirable in many constituencies.[274] In the Limousin, for example, the 1869 elections were conducted with little prefectoral direction, largely because many local administrative officials politely but firmly refused to rally behind the official candidate.[275]

Local political factors were therefore allowed to play a much more significant role in determining electoral outcomes, as was symbolized by the growing proportion of mayors who ran for election.[276] In municipal and cantonal elections, there was also a clear reduction in overt admin- istrative interference after the mid-1860s. Official candidates continued to be anointed for legislative elections, but even here the regime recog- nized that the heavy-handed intervention of the local administration could often be counterproductive. In his memoirs, Ollivier noted with satisfaction that the Empire's support in the May 1870 plebiscite had increased substantially compared with the 1869 vote. He ascribed this growth in support to the relative neutrality of the administration during

---

[273] Marquis Tristan de l'Angle-Beaumanoir, *Etude administrative* (Paris: Dupont, 1865), 12.

[274] Girard, *Les élections de 1869*, viii–ix.

[275] See Corbin, *Archaïsme et modernité*, 893–94.

[276] See Jean Goueffon, "La candidature officielle sous le Second Empire: Le rôle des considérations locales," in *Les facteurs locaux de la vie politique nationale: Colloque*, ed. Mabileau (Paris: Pedone, 1972), 379.

the campaign, quoting reports from procureurs-généraux who corroborated this view.[277] As I argued in the introduction, the Second Empire's practice of universal suffrage thus directly contributed to the development and consolidation of democratic practices in France.

Equally significant was the Second Empire's role in the emergence of modern municipal politics. The reemergence of adversarial politics and the challenge of opposition groups in electoral contests in the early 1860s rapidly demonstrated the limits of a centralist system that had to operate through universal suffrage. This was brought home most vividly in the government's policy over the appointment of mayors. In the early days of the Empire, the regime made clear that it expected the absolute subordination of the mayor to central government. Mayors who failed to give effective support to official candidates, for example, could expect little sympathy from the government. A circular letter from Minister of the Interior Billault to all prefects in 1857 sounded a typically sharp warning: "You must take all measures to bring home to those mayors whose opposition becomes known to you that their refusal to support governmental candidates is incompatible with their duties as functionaries, and if they persist in this vein, the most elementary considerations of loyalty would require them to resign."[278]

By the early 1860s, however, the regime was forced to adopt a much more flexible posture. Dismissing a mayor who exhibited sympathies for republican or legitimist candidates was recognized as counterproductive in areas of local opposition strength.[279] Similarly, it made little sense to appoint a mayor from outside the municipal council if the vast majority of elected councillors were from the opposition. Thus, although the government retained the power to appoint mayors and reaffirmed this prerogative in its confrontation with the 1870 commission, its choices were increasingly influenced by a recognition of local correlations of power. By the late 1860s, accordingly, the regime appointed republican mayors in urban areas with large republican support, and this represented a further recognition of the regime's departure from centralist practices.[280]

The number of dismissals of mayors also declined significantly in the regime's liberal evolution. Thus, for example, only a handful of mayors were suspended for political reasons during the 1869 legislative election

[277] Ollivier, L'Empire libéral, 12:399.

[278] Fond. Thiers, Papiers Baroche, 1132, Billault to prefects, circular letter dated 11 June 1857.

[279] Thus, after the 1863 elections, only thirty-one mayors were dismissed for political reasons. See Le Clère and Wright, Les Préfets du Second Empire, 145.

[280] See, for example, the reports on the 1870 municipal elections in Le Temps, 24 August 1870.

campaign, after the minister of the interior gave clear instructions to this effect to the prefects.[281] Even with respect to such a hallowed principle as the appointment of mayors, therefore, the evidence clearly suggests a trend toward what might be termed creeping (or incremental) democratization. As a defender of the Bonapartist record stated, "The choices of mayor made by the Empire were fitting and based much less on partisan considerations than is generally believed."[282] I thus conclude that both the debates of the 1860s on centralization and the municipal practices of the Second Empire constituted a turning point in defining a new civic consensus in France about the status and functions of the mayor.[283]

For all its achievements, however, the Second Empire never fully squared the circle between authority and liberty. It is certainly conceivable that without the Franco-Prussian War the regime would have evolved into a neorepublican and decentralized parliamentary democracy, and many of its liberal supporters in the late 1860s were pushing it in this very direction.[284] But the cross pressures were extremely powerful, and these forces eventually triumphed. Thus, the abiding image of the Second Empire toward the end of its reign is that of a regime that pulled in many different directions. This was fully reflected in the local political situation in the late 1860s. A government that prided itself on its depoliticized vision of local communal life had witnessed the development of widespread political competition at the local level through universal suffrage. A regime committed to order, authority, and centralized power was faced with a system of territorial administration that was often (particularly in heavily populated communes) disorderly and anarchic. Even more frustrating was the disparity between the significant success of the Empire's modernization and urbanization policies and its dramatic failure to retain political support in France's cities and large towns by the late 1860s.

To make matters even worse, the political loyalty of the provinces to the Bonapartist cause proved somewhat ephemeral. Indeed, after 1870 the regime rapidly lost the support it had done so much to cultivate during the triumphant years of the imperial reign. Writing shortly after

---

[281] Circular letter of Forcade to prefects, 3 May 1869; quoted by Forcade during the Legislative Corps session of 24 June 1870; in *Annales du Sénat et du Corps Législatif: Compte-rendu analytique des séances* (Paris: Journal Officiel, 1870), 148.

[282] Fernand Giraudeau, *Vingt ans de despotisme et quatre ans de liberté* (Paris: Lachaud, 1874), 79. The title is, of course, ironic.

[283] Maurice Agulhon et al., *Les maires en France du Consulat à nos jours* (Paris: Publications de la Sorbonne, 1986), 14.

[284] See, for example, Etienne Lamy, *Le tiers parti* (Paris: Librairie Internationale, 1868), 86–87.

the plebiscite of May 1870, the Catholic journalist Louis Veuillot could not help savor the irony: "The Empire has done everything for the cities, and they are ungrateful; it will continue to do so, only to make the cities even more ungrateful. And when it will come to defending the regime other than by the ballot, the rural populations that cast so many votes in its favor will not lift a finger."[285]

[285] Louis Veuillot, *Mélanges religieux, historiques, politiques et littéraires*, 3d ser. (Paris: Vivès, 1876), 4:517.

Chapter 2

TRADITION AND CHANGE: LEGITIMIST
CONCEPTIONS OF DECENTRALIZATION

IN A LETTER written to Alexis de Tocqueville in 1856, the legitimist Arthur de Gobineau was particularly scathing about his fellow countrymen. In his view, the French were "a people who, whether under a republic, a representative government, or an empire, always piously manifest an excessive enthusiasm for the intervention of the state in all its affairs." He concluded: "Not only will such a people never possess free institutions, but it will never even apprehend what they are. In essence, it will always have the same government under different names."[1]

No account of the intellectual opposition to centralization under the Second Empire could claim to be complete without a thorough exploration of the legitimist view. Legitimists were among the first to launch the campaign for decentralization in the early 1860s;[2] indeed, if any political group could rightly claim antecedence in its unrelenting hostility toward centralization, it was the legitimists. Under the Second Empire, royalist opinion was mainly articulated by this political group, which proclaimed its belief in the hereditary principle and thus its fidelity to the elder branch of the Bourbon monarchy. The legitimist association with the theme of local liberty is commonly recognized in broader studies of the period, as well as in histories of public institutions or decentralization.[3] Yet the significance of the phenomenon is often downplayed, in a number of ways.

First, the relevance of legitimism is generally undervalued. Thus, there is as yet no monograph on its political and intellectual development during the Second Empire.[4] Defeated and marginalized after the 1830 revolution, legitimists are typically seen as "entirely passive";[5] one modern historian, in a furious admixture of metaphors, compares them to

---

[1] Gobineau to Tocqueville, 29 November 1856, in *Ce qui est arrivé à la France en 1870*, by Arthur de Gobineau (Paris: Klincksieck, 1970), 55.

[2] See, for example, *Journal de la Ville et des Campagnes*, 13 May 1863.

[3] Ohnet, *Histoire de la décentralisation*.

[4] For a short general introduction to nineteenth-century legitimism, see Stéphane Rials, *Le légitimisme* (Paris: Presses Universitaires de France, 1983). The most comprehensive study is by Steven Kale, *Legitimism and the Reconstruction of French Society, 1852–1883* (Baton Rouge: Louisiana State University Press, 1992).

[5] Charlotte Muret, *French Royalist Doctrines Since the Revolution* (New York: Columbia University Press, 1933), 138.

"a withered old trunk" afflicted by "senile lethargy."[6] It is true that in their own writings they often present themselves as a retreating force,[7] contemplating the "smell of decay"[8] around them before their final exit from the political stage in the 1870s. It is also frequently assumed that legitimist conceptions of decentralization formed a coherent and unchanging whole, which was subject to little variation in the nineteenth century.[9] In other words, decentralization is seen as a reified concept, a nostalgic homage to a former (and imagined) condition rather than a dynamic doctrine that was forged as a response to a precise range of problems.

There is but a small step from such accounts to the view that the legitimist notion of decentralization was purely instrumental. This view is commonly expressed in the claim that legitimism was not so much a political doctrine as a representation of the specific interests of the nobility. During the Second Empire, Bonapartists, liberals, and republicans often offered this standard criticism, and we will see that it contains an element of truth. But it is simply insufficient to reduce all legitimist views to this dimension, as does an authoritative analysis of the General Council under the Second Empire: "Largely at one with the nobility, legitimism is much more the opinion of a homogeneous and precise social group than a political ideology with a broad appeal."[10] Equally dismissive is the historian of the French nobility who after noting the legitimist nobles' "vociferous" advocacy of decentralization during the nineteenth century, casually adds that "too much should not be made of this. . . . Just as the speeches made to the agricultural societies often expressed wishful thinking for a seigneurial past, so these tirades praising localism, far from being a genuine exercise of power, were an indirect discourse on family distinction."[11] The ideational dimension is again rejected here, this time in favor of subjective and particularist narratives.

My account of decentralization takes legitimist views seriously, as indeed befits a political force that was still deeply entrenched in local communities between 1852 and 1870. Nor is it the case, as is too often thought, that legitimists were completely alienated from the centers of power. Throughout the Second Empire, they occupied positions of strength in local assemblies situated in their heartlands, both at municipal and cantonal levels. In the Loire-Inférieure, for example, the Gen-

---

[6] André Jardin, *Histoire du libéralisme politique* (Paris: Hachette, 1985), 380.

[7] Duc de La Rochefoucauld Doudeauville, *La vérité au peuple* (Paris: Poussielgue, 1851), 29.

[8] Armand de Pontmartin, *Lettres d'un intercepté* (Paris: Hachette, 1871), 262.

[9] Rémond, *Les droites en France*, 57–58.

[10] Girard et al., *Les conseillers généraux en 1870*, 139.

[11] David Higgs, *Nobles in Nineteenth-Century France* (Baltimore: Johns Hopkins University Press, 1987), 142.

eral Council was effectively controlled by the legitimist aristocracy.[12] More generally, it has been noted that legitimists were by far the most important single political group in the departmental councils by 1870;[13] many contemporaries also observed this preponderance of conservative monarchists.[14]

Legitimists were therefore hardly a marginal force, especially if one considers their entrenched positions in prestigious institutions such as the army,[15] the role that many legitimist landowners played in the development of agriculture,[16] and the broader social authority that their elites continued to wield (especially in rural parts of France).[17] In addition to all of this, legitimist candidates could often depend on the support of the clergy, who were a powerful force in the countryside;[18] this mobilization often made a decisive contribution to their political success in elections, as was freely acknowledged by legitimists (and deplored by their adversaries).[19] These forms of social authority often had direct political consequences; thus, the equation of legitimism with the nobility was often a source of the party's distinct appeal. The public prosecutor of Bordeaux complained: "Vanity still acts as a recruiting force for this party; to let it be known that one identifies with the legitimist cause is to elevate one's name; a nobleman, it is said, can be only a legitimist, and the distance from this appreciation to the converse notion is small. In the Périgord, especially, there is this general weakness: everyone wants to be noble."[20]

Politically and socially significant as a group, the legitimists were also active in the intellectual field during the Second Empire; it was far from the case that their conception of decentralization was simply a regurgitation of Bonaldian counterrevolutionary doctrines.[21] Indeed, the Sec-

---

[12] Blayau, *Billault*, 224.

[13] Girard et al., *Les conseillers généraux en 1870*, 138.

[14] Henry Moreau, *Les élections des conseils généraux* (Paris, 1861), 8.

[15] See William Serman, "La Noblesse dans l'Armée Française au XIXeme siècle," in *Les noblesses européennes au XIXeme siècle* (Rome: Ecole Française, 1988), 555.

[16] Adeline Daumard, "Noblesse et aristocratie en France au XIXeme siècle," in ibid., 93.

[17] See Denis, *Les royalistes dans la Mayenne*, 248.

[18] Gabriel Vanel, *Le Second Empire* (Paris: Marigny, 1936), 48.

[19] See, for example, Louis de Kergorlay, quoted in Nassau William Senior, *Conversations with Distinguished Persons during the Second Empire, 1860–1863* (London: Hurst, 1880), 1:8–9.

[20] Arch. Nat. BB30-368, report dated 6 July 1859.

[21] On this period, see J. J. Oechslin, *Le mouvement ultra-royaliste sous la Restauration, son idéologie et son action politique* (Paris, 1960). On Bonald, see Martin Ferraz, *Histoire de la philosophie en France au XIXeme siecle: Spiritualisme et Libéralisme* (Paris: Perrin, 1887), 85–164, and Charlotte Muret, *French Royalist Doctrines*, 10–34.

ond Empire brought many new features to legitimist conceptions of local liberty, most notably an attempt to come to terms with its liberal political dimensions.[22] The neglect of this feature of legitimist discourse is partly attributable to the absence of detailed studies of the period between 1852 and 1870. The first part of this chapter therefore offers an account of the key principles and values of legitimism. The views of their leaders, parliamentarians, local representatives, journalists, and writers thus provide the principal basis for examining the evolution of Bourbon royalist political attitudes. After noting some elements of diversity and tension within legitimism, I identify a number of core features of its ideology: the defense of the monarchy, the promotion of religious institutions and values, and the celebration of the virtues of the aristocracy — all of which were informed by an organic conception of society and a pessimistic view of human nature.

These key components of legitimist thought are seen to inspire both the legitimists' critique of centralization and their distinct solutions to its problems. In the case of the critique of centralized institutions, a number of specific features of the legitimist approach become apparent: a condemnation of the noxious role of Paris, which was seen as a haven of material and spiritual decadence; a complaint against the effects of centralization on the rural world, particularly the problem of rural depopulation; and a radical objection to the activities of the administration, whose despotism seemed matched only by its lack of political accountability. These criticisms served as the basis for the legitimists' positive project for local liberty, which is subjected to critical scrutiny in later sections of this chapter.

I conclude that the legitimists did indeed have a particular — and in some sense unique — blueprint for redefining citizenship in France, based on a reorganization of local government, politics, and administration. This vision was entirely consistent with the core ideological principles of legitimism and provided clear alternatives both to the existing local government system of the Second Empire and to the republican paradigm of citizenship. However, the project was seriously weakened by a number of central contradictions. At the heart of these tensions was an unreconciled opposition between incompatible conceptions on the nature of freedom. This tension was expressed in two different types of discourse: on one hand, a set of claims about the rights of citizens, which stressed the importance of individual freedoms, and on the other, an argument about the duties of subjects, where emphasis was predominantly placed on the necessary social and moral constraints on individual liberty.

---

[22] In this respect my analysis diverges from Kale's excellent account of legitimist decentralization. See *Legitimism and the Reconstruction*, 89–134.

The Identity and Variety of Legitimism

Finding a common thread among the different and often fractious con-
stitutive elements of the legitimist movement is not always an easy matter. Indeed, such was the diversity of its manifestations under the Second Empire that doubts were frequently expressed about the very
existence of a legitimist party. Here, for example, is the condescending
view of the Bonapartist Jules Amigues in 1869:

> I see, among these so-called legitimists, absolutists, liberals, clericalists, ec-
> centrics, proud upholders of divine right, credulous theoreticians of divine
> right combined with universal suffrage. Where is the community of inter-
> ests? I see a divided and scattered caste, destroyed by the storms of revolu-
> tion and the failings of its own history; lacking any cohesion; without any
> community of spirit or solidarity; and dispersed among the countless vag-
> aries of individual fortune. I know barons who work as shoemakers, a
> marquess who is a porter, others who are even less; when a social class
> abandons its underprivileged in this way, one can say with certainty that its
> historical role has ended.[23]

Although Amigues may well have been justified in his final affirmation, his assertion of the political demise of legitimism was premature.
Legitimism — albeit in a somewhat modified form — was to survive as a
significant political force for much longer than Bonapartism. Amigues
was also guilty of the not uncommon conflation of legitimism with an
exclusive social class. The nobility did indeed occupy a central position
in the political and ideological structures of the legitimist movement,
but legitimists were defined principally by their attachment to a number
of core institutions and norms: the monarchy, the Catholic Church, the
family, a hierarchical conception of social order, a measured degree of
decentralization, and a traditional system of values. Contrary to the
accepted view, the force and directness of these basic principles (rather
than the aristocratic origins of its elites) gave legitimism its distinct
identity in nineteenth-century French politics.

Yet behind this apparent simplicity lurked a complex maze of internal
tensions and contradictions, which remained integral to the identity of
French legitimism during the Second Empire. These paradoxes were numerous and often striking. In line with the canons of conservatism, legitimists attacked all forms of rationalist thought, priding themselves on
their attachment to common sense, experience, and intuition rather
than to the abstract and general categories of "systematic thinking."[24]

---

[23] Amigues, *La politique d'un honnête homme*, 130–31.

[24] Duc de Sabran-Pontèves, *A travers les champs de la pensée* (Paris: Librairie Catholique, 1869), 235.

Yet their own system of values was based on moral and political precepts that were both formalistic and metaphysical. They deplored the emergence of individualism, which they equated with the corruptive influence of Protestantism, one of the scourges of the modern age.[25] But for all their rhetoric, they were often fiercely individualistic in their political demeanor. This individualism often bordered on eccentricity, as in the case of the chevalier de Fréminville, an outstanding seafarer, distinguished botanist, and fierce legitimist who used to parade around his castle dressed alternatively in medieval armor and women's clothes.[26]

Legitimists also proclaimed the immutability of their core principles and constantly invoked the weight of tradition as the justifying ground of their beliefs. But they held changing and often conflicting views over such key questions as the specific political attributions of the monarchy, the interpretation of 1789, the role of universal suffrage, the definition of freedom, the rights and duties of citizens, and the proper relationship between church and state. Indeed, even the identification of core principles could be problematic. Legitimists could be dogmatic in their attachment to apparently insignificant symbols (such as the royalist flag) and obtusely uncompromising on certain social questions (notably in civil and religious controversies). But in politics they were generally flexible, sometimes accommodating, and often—as we will see—opportunistic.

The replacement of Charles X by the July Monarchy in 1830 had been met with dignified but uncompromising hostility.[27] But many legitimists rallied to the Republic in 1848, later switched to the Empire in 1852, and through its duration maintained an ambivalent and often collusive relationship with the Bonapartist regime. There was also profound tension between the conservative and counterrevolutionary dimensions of their political creed. As conservatives, legitimists were indefectibly attached to all social and political institutions that promoted order and stability. Hence their emphasis on the monarchy, religion, private property, and the family; hence also their equivocal relationship with the Second Empire, whose aspiration to "make the wicked tremble" they endorsed wholeheartedly. But as counterrevolutionaries they were often committed to goals that were subversive of the social and political order that had evolved since 1789. This placed many legitimists in philosophical opposition to the Bonapartist regime, whose constitution proclaimed (in its first article) an unqualified adhesion to the civil and political legacy of the Revolution.[28] This dichotomy between

[25] Guillaume Véran, *La question du dix-neuvième siècle* (Paris: Dentu, 1866), 98.
[26] Christian de Bartillat, *Histoire de la noblesse française* (Paris: Albin Michel, 1988), 1:441.
[27] For a strong critique of the 1830 revolution, see Jules de Polignac, *Considérations politiques sur l'époque actuelle* (Paris: Pinard, 1832).
[28] "The constitution recognizes, confirms, and guarantees the great principles pro-

conservation and change was reflected in equally contradictory appreciations of the ultimate destiny of humanity. Their conservative instincts were driven by an abiding sense of pessimism about human nature, typically expressed in virulent denunciations of the decadence of modern society. But this gloom was at times displaced by an optimism that affirmed — even and perhaps especially in the absence of supporting evidence — their resolute belief in a better future for humankind.

It is arguable that all these elements of contradiction were expressions of a clash between the realist and romantic undercurrents coexisting within French legitimism. The realist aspect of legitimism was partly a product of its consistent alienation from the centers of political and administrative power after 1830.[29] Lacking responsibility for the management of public affairs, legitimists could afford to cast a dispassionate eye on society. But this capacity for social observation and trenchant political analysis was often subverted by countervailing historical and ideological influences that stressed the importance of sentiment, instinct, and passion.[30] This constant dialectic between reason and emotion produced contrasting political assessments. Reason (based on experience) enabled the legitimists to apprehend the decline of rural France, the plight of its agricultural workers, and the shameless exploitation of the industrial proletariat. But a realistic appreciation of their material interests led many legitimists to denounce the political threat the lower orders posed. Emotion (and religious duty) dictated their presence on the side of the suffering and the display of Christian acts of charity and compassion. But reason almost invariably required lending support to those who saw in the "vile multitude" nothing but a potential source of social disintegration and political chaos. Reason (and shared memories of the cells of Sainte-Pelagie)[31] suggested that many republicans were men of honor, with whom legitimists could fruitfully cooperate in the pursuit of common goals. Emotion, however, reminded them that these same republicans were the descendants of the Revolution, who believed

claimed in 1789, which are the foundation of the public law of France" (quoted in *Les Constitutions de la France*, ed. Debbasch and Pontier, 165).

[29] On the events of 1830–32, see Hugues de Changy, *Le soulèvement de la Duchesse de Berry, 1830–1832* (Paris: Albatross, 1986).

[30] On the link between romanticism and legitimism, see André-Jean Tudesq, "L'influence du romantisme sur le légitimisme sous la Monarchie de Juillet," in *Romantisme et Politique, 1815–1851* (Paris: Armand Colin, 1969), 26–36.

[31] On the good relations between republicans and legitimists at Sainte-Pelagie after the 1851 coup, see Martin Nadaud, *Mémoires de Léonard ancien garçon maçon*, ed. Maurice Agulhon (Paris: Hachette, 1976), 404–5; see also Maurice Joly, *Maurice Joly par lui-même* (Paris: Lacroix, 1870), 10–12. For a history of this institution, see Emile Couret, *Le pavillon des princes: Histoire complète de la prison politique de Sainte-Pelagie* (Paris: Flammarion, 1891).

in secular education, free love, and divorce and also celebrated both the act of regicide and the atrocities in the Vendée.

Legitimism was thus dualistic and ambivalent: ostensibly united in its core principles, it was often uncertain about their precise definition and scope and further troubled about their relationship with its adjacent and peripheral concerns. A legitimist journalist explained the problem in the following terms: "Principles are immutable, but their application varies infinitely according to space, time, men, and circumstances."[32] The epitaph of a royalist journalist for a colleague summed up this legitimist paradox: "Man is the union of soul and body: a wonderful union whose acts are incomprehensible."[33] This fundamental dualism will emerge in the legitimist approaches to local liberty and the redefinition of the principles of citizenship.

THE HEREDITARY MONARCHY

The defining principle of legitimism was its attachment to the monarchy and the principle of heredity. "Legitimist doctrine," asserted the pamphleteer A. Clozel de Boyer in 1851, "is all in the absolute principle of royal inviolability."[34]

Acceptance of the superiority of the hereditary principle presupposed a general theory of the nature of government. A hereditary monarchy was appropriate first and foremost because it was part of the chain of being. For Charles Muller the legitimist principle represented "the application of divine law."[35] Antoine Blanc de Saint-Bonnet added: "The state represents a divine power; otherwise it could not command the human will."[36] The Catholic legitimist Louis Veuillot invited his legitimist friends to celebrate the divine character of the monarchy: "This consecration given by Heaven and time to a race chosen to govern the people and to stand eternally in the midst of the family as the hand, the heart, and the equity of the father."[37] Second, heredity was a superior principle of social and political order because it was based on historical continuity. Tradition occupied a central position in the value system of legitimism. The passage of time represented a consecration that transcended the actions of any individual ruler: "Society revolves around heredity, which rests precisely on the principle of the immutability of

[32] J. Bourgeois, *Le catholicisme et les questions sociales* (Paris: Poussielgue, 1867), 12.
[33] Jean-Joseph-François Poujoulat, *Etudes et portraits* (Paris: Lefort, 1868), 180.
[34] A. Clozel de Boyer, *Monarchie ou anarchie* (Paris: Garnier, 1851), 23.
[35] Charles Muller, *La légitimité* (Paris: Dentu, 1857), 24.
[36] Antoine Blanc de Saint-Bonnet, *De la restauration française* (Paris: Hervé, 1851), 368.
[37] Veuillot, *Mélanges religieux*, 1st ser., 6:292.

order. With heredity, it is not man who governs but the king, and the
king does not die."[38] Despite appearances, ultimate power was therefore
vested not in an individual but in a principle: "Power is and must be an
abstraction. The man in whom it is vested is not an individual but an
incarnation."[39] Human intervention was thus powerless against the
mysteries of social order.

> The constitution of a people is not a plan drawn by an architect or the
> program of an organization; it is its very nature, its moral and political life;
> it is not an improvisation but a succession of ideas that are unseen but that
> are like the sap and foliage of a tree. The constitution of a nation such as
> France does not lie on a page written by man; it is all in its traditions.[40]

This neo-Burkean invocation of the weight of traditions was often
deployed in arguments against the elective principle that liberals and
republicans favored: "You rely on the verdict of random majorities; we
rely on the verdict of time. There is in the life of all societies a solidarity
more respectable than that of its current generation; it is that of all
generations, which will succeed each other under the same roofs and in
the same fields."[41] From this perspective, the search for alternative constitutional forms was at best superfluous and at worst dangerous: "Let
us not look therefore for new constitutions for states: the ones they
have are theirs, and, accordingly, they are the ones that suit them."[42]
But even though legitimists were careful to separate the justification
of the hereditary principle from any utilitarian considerations, their arguments often insisted on the valuable purpose of monarchical institutions. A hereditary monarchy was useful because it was a reflection of
excellence and a model for the rest of society; it was, in the words of an
advocate of legitimism, an "element of emulation."[43] Furthermore, this
institution was seen as a source of political regeneration for a country
wearied by decades of turmoil and instability: "Only the monarchy can
awaken us from the political indifference that is the necessary consequence of the countless changes we have witnessed since the beginning
of the century."[44] At the same time, the hereditary monarchy was seen
as the only institution that could contain the power of central govern-

---

[38] Alexandre Weill, *Génie de la monarchie* (Paris: Dentu, 1850), 82–83. See also *Questions brûlantes: République et monarchie* (Paris: Dentu, 1848).

[39] Alexandre Weill, *De l'hérédité du pouvoir* (Paris: Dentu, 1849), 29–30.

[40] Eugène de Genoude and Henri de Lourdoueix, *La raison monarchique* (Paris: Sapia,
1838), vi.

[41] Muller, *La légitimité*, 56.

[42] Antoine Blanc de Saint-Bonnet, *Politique réelle* (Paris: Bailly, 1858), 63.

[43] Jules Benoid, *Des avantages de l'hérédité: Etude politique* (Paris, 1870), 13.

[44] Henri de la Broise, *Le vrai et le faux libéralisme* (Paris: Lethielleux, 1866), 66.

ment within just and acceptable limits[45] and also prevent the passions of the multitude from degenerating into despotism: "By its permanence, which is not even interrupted by death, power is an eternal obstacle against the efforts of turbulent passions, the more solid in that it has been constructed over centuries."[46] This conception of the monarchy as a restraining influence on the state was one of the mainstays of the legitimist view that only a hereditary monarchy could guarantee a genuine form of decentralization and political liberty in France: "If liberty, instead of being a rival power to royal authority, as in constitutional systems, was a right expressed in civil, communal, departmental, and national freedoms, it would find in royal power a protector interested in maintaining its existence."[47]

Appreciating that attack was often the best form of defense, legitimist writers also attempted to justify the monarchical principle by denying the validity of alternative conceptions of social and political order. First in this counteroffensive was a strenuous rejection of the Bonapartists' "hermaphrodite" notion that "a monarch could owe his throne to the votes of his subjects."[48] Equally worthy of derision was the Machiavellian notion that the art of governing could be formally transcribed and inculcated: "The capacity to govern is not visible and never has been. The external gifts that we hold from nature or from work are unrelated to the art of government."[49] But most important, there was a categorical rejection of the Jacobin principle of popular sovereignty. The concept seemed incoherent to many legitimists: "Any sovereignty presupposes subjects: where would be the subjects of a sovereign people?"[50] Legitimist writers mounted a formidable barrage against this contemptible notion. Jules de Polignac declared that the principle of popular sovereignty "serves only to prepare and carry out political upheavals."[51] A society founded on such a principle, warned the ultramontane Louis de Ségur in 1861, could have only one destiny: "the total destruction of divine order on earth, and the perfect reign of Satan in the world."[52] For another Catholic pamphleteer the doctrine of popular sovereignty represented a revolt of man against God: "It is the negation of all moral and religious forms of order; it is the reign of atheism."[53] A monarchist com-

---

[45] Eugène Véron, *Lettres Parisiennes* (Grenoble, 1866), 20.

[46] Baron de Fontarèches, *Monarchie et liberté*, 2d ed. (Paris: Dentu, 1861), 21.

[47] Ibid., 22.

[48] Auguste Bouchage, *Sauvons la France* (Toulouse: Delboy, 1871), 49.

[49] Jean-Baptiste-Victor Coquille, *La royauté française* (Paris: Lecoffre, 1874), 52.

[50] Baron de Fontarèches, *Révolution et despotisme* (Paris: Dentu, 1861), 17.

[51] Jules de Polignac, *Réponse à mes adversaires* (Paris: Dentu, 1845), 18.

[52] Mgr. de Ségur, *La révolution* (Paris: Tolra et Haton, 1861), 10–11.

[53] Jean-Baptiste-Victor Coquille, *Politique chrétienne* (Paris: Palmé, 1868), 15.

pleted the unholy trinity by dismissing the doctrine of popular sovereignty as a form of "political Protestantism."[54]

What above all made legitimists object to the doctrine was its Jacobin assumption (rooted in Protestant individualism) that man possessed the power to emancipate himself from the greater order from which he had emerged.[55] This belief, legitimists argued, was not only wrong but dangerous, for the myth of human independence was the breeding ground for political tyranny and social subversion. "When children call themselves the heads of the family, when subjects believe themselves to be sovereign and pretend to govern the state, we will have anarchy, the dissolution of the family or the state."[56]

THE COMTE DE CHAMBORD

Monarchism was not only an ontological principle. At all moments, it was also an expression of the values and aspirations of an individual. After 1830, when Louis-Philippe deposed the Bourbon monarchy, the legitimist pretender to the throne was the comte de Chambord, grandson of Charles X. Watching over the affairs of his people from his dignified exile in Venice and in the Austrian village of Frohsdorf,[57] Chambord maintained an inexorable presence in the legitimist imagination. The relationship between the legitimist subjects and their monarch took a variety of forms, which reflected the political and ideological diversity of French legitimism under the Second Empire.

After 1852 a small minority of legitimists rallied publicly and wholeheartedly to the Bonapartist regime. For these pragmatic monarchists — Pastoret, Dupin, La Rochejaquelin, Larochefoucauld — the Empire had earned its legitimacy by its "providential"[58] defeat of republicanism and Orleanism and its guarantee of public order and economic prosperity. Their reasoning was summed up by an anonymous pamphleteer whose agitated syntax revealed the depth of his irritation against his former legitimist colleagues: "It is already ungrateful to turn against the one who saved us and gave us tranquillity, peace at home, and the enjoyment of our fortunes; but to try and bring down the same man, at the evident risk, if he falls, of being ruined and collectively led to catastro-

---

[54] Baron de Fontarèches, *La souveraineté du peuple* (Paris: Dentu, 1865), 21.

[55] Sébastien Laurentie, *L'athéisme social et l'Eglise* (Paris: Plon, 1869), 75–76.

[56] Fontarèches, *La souveraineté du peuple*, 25.

[57] For vivid accounts of life in Chambord's court, see Marquis René de Belleval, *De Venise à Frohsdorf: Souvenirs et récits* (Paris: Dentu, 1880); René Monti de Rézé, *Souvenirs sur le comte de Chambord* (Paris: Emile-Paul, 1931); and Jean-Paul Bled, *Les lys en exil* (Paris: Fayard, 1992).

[58] Duc de La Rochefoucauld Doudeauville, in *La Patrie*, 19 April 1856.

phe, is sheer irresponsible folly."[59] Close in spirit to these Napoleonic royalists were those who could be described as satisfied legitimists: platonic followers of an absent monarch, yet in truth the contented subjects of the newly proclaimed imperial dynasty. Unlike the first group, they did not publicly trumpet their allegiance to the new order. Nonetheless, they remained broadly supportive of the Bonapartist regime — often voting for its candidates in national and local elections — while claiming to honor the person of Chambord.[60] The practical value of such pledges was often negligible; when it came to giving concrete support to a legitimist candidate or subscribing to a legitimist newspaper, for instance, most of them looked the other way.[61]

A third group was more explicitly political than the second and was centered around a small group of notable parliamentarians such as Antoine Berryer, Alfred de Falloux, Ferdinand Béchard, and Claude-Marie Raudot. These liberal legitimists envisaged a restoration of the Bourbon monarchy in the form of a constitutional rather than an executive monarchy, because they regarded the notion of divine right as a useless fiction. The monarchy was valuable only to the extent that it enabled the attainment of a set of desirable political and social ends: constitutional government, civil equality, and administrative accountability. These "reflective"[62] royalists saw their prime task as negotiating the return to power of Chambord through a coalition of all monarchist groups. Hence their repeated (but unsuccessful) efforts to secure an agreement between Chambord and the Orleans pretenders over the principle of monarchical "fusion."[63]

These attempts at compromise were furiously rejected by a fourth category of legitimists, who saw themselves as "irreconcilable." Based in large part in the Catholic territories of the West, parts of the Midi, and the South,[64] these legitimists constantly warned against the "flatteries of liberalism."[65] They appreciated the comte de Chambord precisely because he was a pure symbol of counterrevolution. This form of legitimism was politically authoritarian, socially reactionary, religiously

[59] *Comment d'après la religion et la morale doit-on comprendre la légitimité?* (Paris: Montdidier, 1858), 25.

[60] Claude-Noël Desjoyeaux, *La fusion monarchique, 1848–1873* (Paris: Plon, 1913), 112.

[61] The legitimist journalist Théodore Muret thus wrote of the "egoism and indifference" of many legitimist nobles during the July Monarchy. See his memoirs, *A travers les champs* (Paris: Garnier, 1858), 1:209.

[62] Daniel Halévy, *La fin des notables*, 13.

[63] Duc de Castries, *La monarchie interrompue* (Paris: Taillandier, 1983), 2:169.

[64] On the Gard, see Brian Fitzpatrick, *Catholic Royalism in the Department of the Gard, 1814–1852* (Cambridge: Cambridge University Press, 1982).

[65] Sébastien Laurentie, *Souvenirs inédités* (Paris: Ploud, 1892), 302.

Fig. 4. Photograph of Louis Veuillot (1813–83), Bibliothèque Nationale, Paris. The most talented journalist in the intransigent Catholic camp, Veuillot was a virulent critic of the Revolutionary tradition.

devout, and adamantly hostile to any form of reconciliation with the legacy of 1789. The intransigence of their spirit was summed up by Louis Veuillot: "The comte de Chambord must not go to the Revolution; the Revolution must come, or rather must lead us, to him."[66] Finally, for a large part of the *peuple légitimiste*, the comte de Chambord was an object of veneration simply because he was the incarnation of legitimate royalty (as opposed to any broader social and political program). The quasi-religious fervor with which he was sometimes regarded is well captured in the following account of a visit to Frohsdorf by a group of workers from Lyon:

> At the moment when the doors of the prince's apartment opened, I felt my heart pound. . . . We were at last with the one we had traveled so far to see. One of us had been entrusted with making a speech; but at the sight of this great and noble figure, under the powerful influence of his grand and majestic gaze, he remained silent for a moment. At last, encouraged by a graceful smile, he overcame his emotion, and with eyes full of tears he said to the prince: "Sire, I would like to embrace you." "Why not?" replied the comte de Chambord, and advancing forward he took him in his arms and embraced him.[67]

THE UNITY OF LEGITIMISM WITH CATHOLICISM

Religion occupied a central position in the social and political value system of legitimists, especially those who were devout Catholics. In the Catholic conception of territoriality, membership in the parish was often just as important as association with a particular local collectivity such as the commune.[68] "Legitimist opinion is a creed, better still, a religion,"[69] noted the legitimist publicist Alexandre d'Adhémar in 1843. The Catholic legitimist Sébastien Laurentie declared that no society could be conceived without a true religion: "The idea of society is identical with that of religion, and as there is only one true religion, there can be only one true society, which is the society linking man to God and bringing men together in the same worship, the same love, and the same duties."[70]

Catholicism represented this "true" religion, and although not every

---

[66] Veuillot, *Mélanges*, 292.

[67] *Gazette de Lyon*, 28 May 1850, quoted in Emmanuel de Curzon, *Documents contemporains pour servir à la restauration des principes sociaux* (Poitiers, 1851), 107.

[68] In the words of Philippe Boutry, "The parish remains between 1815 and 1880, and sometimes even beyond, the significant space of French Catholicism" (*Prêtres et paroisses au pays du curé d'Ars* [Paris: Cerf, 1986], 17).

[69] Comte Alexandre d'Adhémar, *Du parti légitimiste en France* (Paris: Dentu, 1843), 51.

[70] Laurentie, *L'athéisme social et l'Eglise*, 63–64.

single legitimist was devout (or even Catholic), during the Second Empire the overwhelming majority of legitimists defined themselves as members of the Roman Catholic Church. But if most legitimists were Catholic, most Catholics were by no means devotees of the legitimist cause. As Stéphane Rials has noted, Catholicism in the 1840s and 1850s was divided into two cross-cutting cleavages: liberal and intransigent, Gallican and ultramontane.[71] The first was a division about temporal matters, but also about the proper relationship between religion and politics. The second cleavage bore on whether the Vatican should constitute the primary source of spiritual leadership for French Catholicism. During most of the 1850s legitimist elites tended to argue for a separation of politics from religion and for a benevolent but not subservient relationship with the Vatican. This view was often the object of violent attacks from ultramontane quarters.[72] Another factor preventing a close identification of Catholics with legitimist politics during the 1850s was the excellent relationship intially forged between the Second Empire and the church. "The emperor has realized its most cherished goals in granting Catholicism the most complete freedom of expression it has enjoyed in centuries,"[73] rejoiced a legitimist convert to the Bonapartist regime shortly after the proclamation of the Empire.

This honeymoon, however, ended when Napoleon III supported the principle of Italian unification in 1859, thus endorsing the attack on the temporal powers of the pope. This turning point had three important consequences for legitimism: it alienated many Catholics from the Bonapartist regime; it united them in the defense of the Vatican (thus weakening the position of Gallicanism); and it brought the political and religious branches of French Catholicism into close alliance. The comte de Chambord underlined the latter point strongly: "No, the cause of the temporal sovereignty of the pope is not isolated; it is that of all religion, of society, of freedom."[74] Thus, even though the Bonapartist regime was able to repair some of the damage caused by its Italian policy, the 1860s saw a growing convergence between legitimism and Catholicism, a trend that continued well into the following decade.[75] But even at the

<hr/>

[71] Stéphane Rials, "Légitimisme et Catholicisme, 1830–1883," in *Révolution et contre-révolution au XIXeme siècle* (Paris: Albatros, 1987), 194–95.

[72] For an example of such polemics, see Falloux, *Le parti catholique*, and the reply by Louis Veuillot, *Le parti catholique: Réponse à M. le Comte de Falloux* (Paris: Vivès, 1856).

[73] Marquis de La Rochejaquelin, *La France en 1853* (Paris: Simon, 1853), 125.

[74] Letter to Vicomte de Saint-Priest, 9 December 1866, in *Manifestes et programmes politiques de M. le Comte de Chambord*, by Comte Henri de Chambord (Paris: Sauton, 1873), 14.

[75] This did not mean that old divisions were forgotten. The Gallican legitimist press (for

height of this political convergence, the interests of legitimists and intransigent Catholics remained separate; the latter could be distinguished by the intensity of their professions of faith in the divine principle and in the priority given to the religious struggle over all other forms of political activity. In the words of the public prosecutor of Angers:

> There exists an enthusiastic party, recruiting mostly among legitimists, disciplined by the Saint Vincent of Paul Society, subject to the inspirations of the ultra-Catholic press, which dreams only of religious absolutism and theocracy, which speaks with contempt of the Gallican Church, the Concordat, and all the laws that govern relations between church and state . . . and which demands a return to the monastical orders of the Middle Ages.[76]

How did this progressive penetration of religion into its political struggles influence the ideological structure of legitimism? Three broad themes may be noted. First, a strong emphasis on the fallen condition of man appeared in legitimist literature during this period. Laurentie lamented the decline of the moral and political certainties of old: "The world is deeply unsettled. Everything is wavering: ideas, opinions, rights, powers, all is uncertain, and all is in decline; all bonds are broken; there is no longer any family, dynasty, or nation; the people are like a herd scattered by diplomacy or enslaved by conquest."[77] Blanc de Saint-Bonnet was equally morose: "Respect, this love of what is greater, no longer cements the wonderful spiral of hierarchy. Pride is now taking apart the bricks that have been softened by error . . . the fall is continuing every day."[78]

Second, there emerged a marked tendency toward mysticism, which could take a variety of forms. This was the era of Mariology, of holy processions to Lourdes, and of celebrations of the miraculousness of social life.[79] Many times it was simply articulated as wonder at the complex ways of God. This providentialism at times pulled the legitimist party away from the notion that politics was an entirely rational process based on agency, calculation of interest, and compromise. Instead,

---

example, *La Gazette de France*) never missed an opportunity to taunt the intransigent ultramontanism of the likes of Louis Veuillot. The latter, in turn, carefully explained his relations with legitimism in an article in *l'Univers* on 12 December 1868: "The legitimists, the legitimist party, and the legitimist press are for us three very distinct things. Among the legitimists, we are happy to have a number of people with whom we are in complete agreement . . . in the legitimist party, we have more or less open adversaries. In the legitimist press, we have only fierce enemies" (Veuillot, *Mélanges religieux*, no. 3, 2:206–7).

[76] Arch. Nat. BB30-368, report dated August 1858.

[77] Laurentie, *L'athéisme social et l'Eglise*, 141.

[78] Blanc de Saint-Bonnet, *Politique réelle*, 2–3.

[79] Duc de La Rochefoucauld Doudeauville, *La fontaine miraculeuse de Lourdes* (Paris: Raçon, 1964).

the mystery of the divine will was stressed, accompanied by a belief that everything would turn out favorably in the end. A pessimistic alternative to this view was the notion that history was a cyclical process, from which man could not—and should not—break out.[80] There was a short step from fatalism of this kind to complacency, and not surprisingly legitimist elites were often accused of leaving too much in the hands of destiny or the almighty. A loyal but lucid observer noted: "During the entire duration of the Empire, insofar as it had any strength at all, the royalist party was driven by the force of inertia."[81]

Finally, the critique of the type of society created by the French Revolution was increasingly articulated through religious concepts and categories. A distinction should be made here between the administrative, social, and political legacies of 1789. As we will note later, the administrative structure created by the Revolution was universally regarded as a calamity in legitimist circles. The political heritage of liberal republicanism (civil equality, freedom of religion, and representative government) was also decried en bloc by intransigent legitimists and clericalists, who saw no possibility of compromise with the Revolution.[82] But most liberal legitimists accepted and even embraced this heritage; after all, these very same principles had been proclaimed by the royal charter of 1814. Falloux could thus declare in all equanimity that "not only does '89, defined as it ought to be by the discerning minds of all parties, contain nothing anti-Christian, it is not even an antimonarchical event. Seen with a dispassionate eye, it appears more as a date than an origin."[83] Similarly, Muller spoke of the "salutary action of the Revolution in France and in the world."[84] A legitimist pamphleteer even went so far as to represent the Revolution as "one of the most beautiful moments in our history."[85]

But the social legacy of the Revolution was the object of universal reprobation in legitimist circles. The destructive consequences of these social changes on the family were noted as follows:

> The French Revolution had a noxious influence on private mores: social disorders always have their repercussions in the domestic sphere. It further

---

[80] Jules de Polignac, *Etudes historiques, politiques et morales* (Paris: Dentu, 1844), 354–55.

[81] Marquis René de Belleval, *Souvenirs de ma jeunesse* (Paris: Lechevalier, 1895), 132.

[82] See, for example, Ségur: "Fighting the revolution is therefore an act of faith, a religious duty. It is furthermore an act of good citizenship and honesty, for it is a defense of the fatherland and the family" (*La révolution*, 12).

[83] Falloux, *Le parti catholique*, 131. See also Joseph de Rainneville, *Catholiques tolérants et légitimistes libéraux* (Paris: Michel Lévy, 1862), 147–49.

[84] Denis, *Les royalistes de la Mayenne*, 271.

[85] Louis d'Armailhac, *La légitimité et le progrès* (Poitiers: Oudin, 1871), 78.

Fig. 5. Comte Alfred de Falloux (1818–86), lithography, Bibli-othèque Nationale, Paris. The most oustanding intellect in the liberal legitimist camp, Falloux attempted throughout the Second Empire to modernize the political principles of Bourbon royalism.

attempted, in a much more direct manner, to loosen family ties, to limit the powers of fathers[,] . . . and to destroy the saintly nature of marriage, by transforming it into a precarious lease that can be renewed or broken at the whim of its contractants."[86]

Ségur summed up the pernicious products of the Revolution in a lapidary formula: "Incredulity, Protestantism, Caesarism, Gallicanism, rationalism, naturalism, false science, false education."[87]

In sum, the Revolution (in both its historical and its contemporaneous manifestations) was seen to pose a growing threat to the three sacred principles of legitimism: private property, the family, and religion.[88] The infusion of religious themes into legitimist thinking thus gave it a distinctly devout coloring during this period. This trend would reach its climax after 1871, with the emergence of the themes of atonement and penitence. But during the 1860s the main effect of these religious themes was to give a greater sense of political and ideological cohesion to the legitimist cause. In certain regions, the leadership of the legitimist party was recruited directly from the local clergy.[89] Even where this was not the case, there was a strong equation of the religious cause with that of the monarchy: "Under the cover of the pope the cause of the king is furthered."[90]

Secular legitimists were no different. "We rely on the Catholic spirit of France," asserted Muller.[91] A legitimist journalist echoed in 1870: "French by the grace of God, it is also by his grace that we are royalists and Catholics. We have never separated our faith from our political convictions: what the one advises we wish the other to approve."[92] The sense of moral certainty that religion provided also underpinned the messianic dimension of legitimism, which was most visible in its support for colonization and the idea of a civilizing mission for France outside Europe.[93] More important, perhaps, this focus on moral and social concerns served to remind many legitimists that, the vagaries of

---

[86] Albert Du Boys, *Des principes de la révolution française considérés comme principes générateurs du socialisme et du communisme* (Lyon, 1851), 193.

[87] Ségur, *La Révolution*, 119. See also Un Français d'Alsace, *Le libéralisme catholique* (Paris: Douniol, 1874), 48.

[88] Gabriel de Belcastel, *La citadelle de la liberté* (Toulouse, 1867), 27.

[89] See, for example, the procureur-général's report on the activities of the bishop of Moulins, in Arch. Nat. BB30-368, 10 April 1859.

[90] Arch. Nat. BB30-368, report from Agen, 7 July 1859.

[91] Muller, *La légitimité*, 193.

[92] Article by Mayol de Lupé, in *L'Union*, 9 May 1870.

[93] For a celebration of the conquest of Algiers by Charles X, see Comte Henri de Chambord, "Manifeste de 1852," in *Manifestes et programmes politiques de M. le Comte de Chambord*, 10. On the Algerian question, see Claude-Marie Raudot, "L'avenir des nations," in *Mes oisivetés* (Avallon, 1862), 465–504.

politics notwithstanding, a wide gulf remained between their conception of citizenship and that of the rest of the French polity. This chasm will become manifest in the evocation of their conception of decentralization.

The Elements of an Organic Society

The legitimist social order was the antithesis of liberal individualism. Society was an organic entity, in which each part existed only in relation to a greater whole: "A society is not a mere assemblage of heterogeneous parts; all its components are connected and linked to form a whole."[94] This spiritual dimension in the collective existence of a people was also necessary for forging the characteristics of a nation: "The nation is not the crowd that passes and is replaced by another; it is an organized people; it is a society in the totality of its existence."[95] The nobility provided the beneficial and necessary link between different social groups. Legitimist writers painted a grim picture of a society deprived of its aristocracy: "When there exist neither distinctions of rank nor associational links, when individualism has become the only moral and institutional principle, the torch of honor is extinguished, and rampant selfishness spreads like a cancer throughout the social organism."[96]

The distinct social virtues that the good legitimist citizen espoused were thus easily defined: "Courage, hard work, perseverance, economy, temperance, honest and sincere affections, respect of others and of oneself."[97] Fidelity was also highly appreciated, particularly because it was applicable in public as well as in private life.[98] Ideally, the nobility practiced all these virtues. Blanc de Saint-Bonnet's list of characteristic noble values included piety, honesty, honor, selflessness, bravery, compassion, humility, and sainthood. More controversially (although representing a strong undercurrent among legitimists), he also saw the virtuous nobleman as somewhat removed from the affairs of the public world: "Unless summoned by his king, the nobleman cultivates his field; he acquires honorability and not popularity."[99] Honorability was based on reputation and social standing, which could not be determined by popular

---

[94] Coquille, *Politique chrétienne*, vi.

[95] Muller, *La légitimité*, 61.

[96] Ferdinand Béchard, *Essai sur la centralisation administrative* (Paris: Hivert, 1836), 57–58.

[97] E.S., *Causeries avec mes concitoyens des villes et des campagnes* (Compiègne, 1869), 6.

[98] Sébastien Laurentie, *Mélanges: Religion, philosophie, morale* (Paris: Vivès, 1865), 542; see also Muller, *La légitimité*, 8.

[99] Blanc de Saint-Bonnet, *De la restauration française*, 259.

suffrage. Indeed, the idea of politics as a sphere of public activity based on general principles was instinctively repulsive to many legitimists — hence their attachment to the notion of decentralization, which restricted public life to the familiar and comfortable boundaries of the *pays*. The rejection of high politics was also frequently expressed in a reformulation of all political questions in ethical terms: "There are no political questions, only moral ones."[100]

Legitimism possessed a distinct conception of social order, at the center of which rested the family. Although generally appearing in third place in legitimist writings (after the monarchy and the church), the family was in a sense the primary social institution in legitimist ideology. Jean-Baptiste Coquille defined legitimism as the simple extension of family norms and values to the public sphere: "Legitimism is only the extension of the family principle to the state."[101] Laurentie clarified the intuition: "Political laws must tend to conform with laws of the family; not that political society can be led with the same simplicity as the domestic home, but its leadership must be similarly paternal and respectful of freedom, and obedience must be based on love; it is in this respect that the family remains a model for political society."[102]

The family was a model in a triple sense: it symbolized the principles of patriarchy, hierarchy, and social inequality, the absence of which would threaten all societies with disintegration. In the words of Muller, "Inequality is both the inevitable result and the ground for the existence of labor and family, these great laws of all civilizations and societies."[103] Rousseau's notion of social equality, which laid the philosophical foundation of modern republicanism, was thus dismissed as dangerous sophistry: "Instituted by God himself to spur honor and promote charity and self-sacrifice, the inequality of conditions has always been and will always be, despite the eloquent paradoxes of the sophist of Geneva, one of the providential elements of human destiny on earth."[104] Hierarchy was also seen as an invaluable means of sustaining and reinforcing social relations: "A hierarchy is necessary, because the more there are classes in society, the more the transition will be limited from the highest to the lowest rung of the social ladder and the greater will be the bonds of subordination that will tie men to each other."[105]

If the family was the symbol of the hierarchical structure of society, its natural paradigm was the aristocracy. Conservatives of all ilks (in-

---

[100] Ibid., 169.
[101] Coquille, *La royauté française*, 88.
[102] Laurentie, *Mélanges*, 329–30.
[103] Muller, *La légitimité*, 223.
[104] Béchard, *Essai sur la centralisation administrative*, 1:8.
[105] Du Boys, *Des principes de la révolution française*, 10.

cluding conservative republicans) believed in the functional virtues of hierarchy. But legitimists were distinctive in the particular vocation they ascribed to the noble element in the social hierarchy. The most important duty of the aristocracy was to govern.

> Taken in its broadest sense, aristocracy is the most indispensable element in any society. It cannot seriously be maintained that in any community of men the most intelligent, the bravest, the most honest and public-spirited elements should have a lesser say in the administration of common matters than the stupid, lazy, cowardly, and unknown elements. . . . The more a government is in the hands of the elite, the better the ship of state will be governed.[106]

Although the legitimist party was not exclusively aristocratic—Berryer was of middle-class origin, and Veuillot's father was working-class[107]—the overwhelming majority of legitimist leaders were scions of the nobility. As noted at the beginning of this chapter, this social predominance was both politically and ideologically significant. The beneficial role of the aristocracy was celebrated in legitimist writings. Coquille represented the nobility as the bearer of the nation's best values of continuity: "If the bourgeoisie represents movement and variety, it befalls to the nobility to represent consistency and perpetuity. Only territorial property offers guarantees of duration: personal fortunes provoke envy, whereas territorial fortunes generally meet with public consideration."[108] Blanc de Saint-Bonnet stressed the social and moral virtues embedded in the aristocracy: "In the midst of the social field, the nobility is an upright sheaf that continues to produce and provide its grain."[109]

MAN AS A FALLEN BEING

Running through all aspects of legitimist political and social thought was a deeply pessimistic philosophical anthropology: "Evil is in human nature."[110] This negative approach was a direct consequence of the legitimist rejection of rationalist doctrines, which construed man as a Promethean being. Legitimist writers regarded rationalism as a negation of the true principles of human nature: "Instead of attaching itself by tradition to past times and seeking solace in the humble adoration of the hand that guides us without enslavement, rationalism takes pleasure in proclaiming an absolute antagonism between past and present and in

[106] Marquis de Mailly-Nesle, *La révolution est-elle finie?* (Paris: Dentu, 1853), 69–70.
[107] Charlotte Muret, *French Royalist Doctrines*, 123, 159.
[108] Coquille, *Politique chrétienne*, 133.
[109] Blanc de Saint-Bonnet, *Politique réelle*, 65–66.
[110] Blanc de Saint-Bonnet, *De la restauration française*, 109.

isolating man in an apparent omnipotence."[111] Rationalism was responsible for three fundamentally flawed propositions about the essence of
man. The first was the view that man was a predominantly physical
being, whose primary needs could be met by material means. The out-
raged Blanc de Saint-Bonnet asserted in response: "Man is not placed in
this world to meet his needs but to develop according to the efforts it
awakens in his soul. For it is thus that he elevates himself from nature.
What a lamentable way to form man than to turn him away from his
saintly aspirations!"[112] The second error consisted in the postulate that
man was essentially good. Blanc de Saint-Bonnet fiercely rejected Rousseau's view that man was a natural innocent who was perverted by
society: "Man is born evil, and society brings him back. Or rather, he is
born in evil, and the church restores him."[113]

The final fallacy lay in the belief — again articulated by Rousseau and
emblazoned in the first article of the 1789 Declaration — that man was
born free and that all men were in a primordial sense equal. Legitimists
often quoted freedom as a desirable social and political goal. But liberty
was not to be confused with liberal notions, which smacked rather of
license. One indignant legitimist declared: "The epithet *liberal* signifies
that liberty is the right not to distinguish between right and wrong,
between what should remain protected by law and what should be explicitly forbidden by it."[114] Indeed, at a philosophical level the legitimist
conception of liberty was circumscribed by a recognition of the hierarchical nature of the universe. Man could enjoy a range of "external"
freedoms, but only on the condition that he recognized the greater dependence between his inner self and his creator: "One cannot be free
and without faith."[115] The same was true of the principle of equality:
"True equality can exist only before God."[116] This dependence was an
incontrovertible part of man's nature and had been established with
divine intent: "It is in man that this humiliating and profound dependence is most developed. It seems that providence wished at the dawn
of our lives to inflict a lesson upon our vanity, in order to bend us to the
yoke of subordination, from which we can never be totally emanci-
pated."[117]

The essence of human nature was therefore not to be found in the

[111] Marquis de Dreux-Brézé, *Quelques mots sur les tendances du temps présent* (Paris: Vaton, 1860), 5.
[112] Blanc de Saint-Bonnet, *De la restauration française*, 5.
[113] Blanc de Saint-Bonnet, *Politique réelle*, 49.
[114] Bernardi, *La Révolution*, 58.
[115] Blanc de Saint-Bonnet, *De la restauration française*, 7.
[116] Duc de La Rochefoucauld Doudeauville, *Cri d'alarme* (Paris, 1861), 15.
[117] Du Boys, *Des principes de la révolution française*, 2.

mindless abstractions of rationalist thought. "Human nature has only one origin," noted Abbé Léon Godard;[118] no further philosophical elucidations were necessary. Blanc de Saint-Bonnet accordingly deduced that the nature of man was centered around divine love: "Man is a being in quest of happiness; and since happiness can come only from the possession of an infinite being, man is in pursuit of the infinite being; and since the movement necessary from one being to the other is love, *Man is nothing but a being endowed with love.*"[119] Those who derived their conception of man from any other philosophical premise were not so much wrong as incoherent, for man could exist only in relation to a greater being: "To deny God is to deny being and the very reason for its existence; it is to deny the real world, to deny all that is the object of knowledge, it is to deny man, to deny life; the assumption of atheism is in one word an empty hypothesis."[120] Precisely the preponderance of this philosophical nihilism in modern society lay at the heart of the despairing tone that many legitimist thinkers adopted. The future offered little hope to Veuillot: "Weakened by sin, humanity inclines gradually toward error, and the road to error leads on to death; or rather, error itself is death."[121] Given these circumstances, many legitimist commentators concluded that man's state of decay was so advanced that the species as a whole was doomed.

> Unfortunately, all that man does, he does in the order of evil. . . . So our civilization today is mired in evil. It is generally declining ever since Christianity is no longer its government. Even the methods furnished by Christianity have only accelerated this decline. Its delicacy of thought, the capital that it prepared, have merely offered an even greater lever for human dissolution.[122]

THE CRITIQUE OF CENTRALIZATION

In the legitimist mind, the theme of degeneration was commonly associated with the blight of centralization. If rationalism represented the perversion of the individual, centralization was the symbol (as well as one of the principal causes) of the decadence of the collectivity.

The critique of Jacobin centralism was one of the oldest and most constant features of royalist ideology. During the Restoration, ultra-

[118] Abbé Léon Godard, *Les principes de 89 et la doctrine catholique* (Paris: Lecoffre, 1863), 12.
[119] Blanc de Saint-Bonnet, *Notion de l'Homme tirée de la notion de Dieu* (Paris: Pitois-Levrault, 1839), 27; emphasis is in the text.
[120] Laurentie, *L'athéisme social et l'Eglise*, 15.
[121] Louis Veuillot, *L'illusion libérale* (Paris: Palmé, 1866), 18.
[122] Blanc de Saint-Bonnet, *De la restauration française*, 347.

royalists such as Villèle, Bonald, and Castelbajac repeatedly demanded the return to prerevolutionary forms of local liberty, involving communal emancipation and the revival of provincial territorial divisions.[123] Their successors after 1830 appropriated this theme with relish: "Today a monopoly disposes of all material power in France," complained the comte d'Adhémar under the July Monarchy. "It has extinguished provincial independence under the burden of a formidable centralization." [124] "Centralization and political absolutism are two branches of the same tree," asserted Gobineau during the Second Republic.[125] During the Second Empire, legitimists denounced the "exaggerations" of centralism with a greater degree of forcefulness and consistency than any other political movement. At the heart of the legitimist critique was the attempt to locate centralization in both the theory and the practices of the French Revolution.

At a theoretical level, centralization was seen as a direct consequence of the Jacobin doctrine of popular sovereignty, which provided the ideological justification of republican despotism.[126] Legitimists also strongly opposed the republican idea that the state should concern itself with the good life—a doctrine whose execution necessitated strong centralized power. Béchard disparaged the ungodly character of such notions: "The theory that makes the state a providential institution to lead men toward happiness and virtue and to force them into the yoke of public happiness is an essentially pagan and pantheistic theory."[127] Centralization was thus not a contingent occurrence but a direct and necessary consequence of the application of revolutionary doctrines in France.

From a historical perspective, legitimist writers tended to play down the significance of monarchical absolutism in the development of centralized state power in France. The prerevolutionary era was generally presented as the golden age of local liberty in France;[128] insofar as it was acknowledged, monarchical centralization was seen as a contingent feature of the royal polity.[129] A legitimist journalist went so far as to blame Protestantism for the origins of French absolutism: "Centralization was

[123] Rémond, *Les droites en France*, 57.

[124] D'Adhémar, *Du parti légitimiste*, 35.

[125] Arthur de Gobineau, "La centralisation devant l'Assemblée Nationale," *Revue Provinciale* 1 (1848): 174.

[126] Véron, *Lettres Parisiennes*, 21–22.

[127] Ferdinand Béchard, *Du projet de décentralisation administrative annoncé par l'Empereur* (Paris: Gazette de France, 1864), 17.

[128] Alfred Chavane, *Les assemblées de province et les conseils généraux* (Paris: Wittersheim, 1870), 7–23.

[129] See, for example, Claude-Marie Raudot, *La décentralisation* (Paris: Douniol, 1858), 9–29.

like a universal precaution against the seditious spirit engendered by Protestantism."[130] But this glowing view of the old order faced some formidable opposition. Published in 1856, Tocqueville's *L'ancien régime et la révolution* had popularized the notion that modern centralization was less a product of the Revolution than a continuation of established monarchical practices. Despite their respect and admiration for Tocqueville, legitimist writers generally tended to reject this notion of historical continuity between the old order and the new.[131] For one thing, there was no comparable doctrinal base to popular sovereignty before 1789, even in the practices of the absolute monarchs.[132] Furthermore, monarchical centralization was in their view largely beneficial to the interests of the country, because it helped forge a sense of social and political unity while respecting the territorial and cultural diversity of the kingdom.[133] It was precisely this element of diversity that had been senselessly destroyed by the administrative reorganization promulgated by the Revolution:

> Provinces were natural aggregations, formed by affinities of race, traditions, and customs. They had their capitals, their assemblies, their universities, their individual genius, all of which could to a certain extent counterbalance the exaggerations of the principle of centralization. In the place of these great territorial divisions, which had their own grounds for existence, the Revolution created the arbitrary divisions of its departmental system.[134]

Another historical explanation of centralization that legitimist writers firmly rejected was the claim that the French were culturally unfit for self-government. Often presented in the form of a casual intuition by many advocates of centralization, this anthropological claim was given its most rigorous exposition in the sociological determinism of Charles Dupont-White.[135] Claude-Marie Raudot dismissed his conclusion that France could be governed only by a strong administration by a *reductio ad absurdum*: "We are, you claim, a race that is incapable of self-administration; but since all our functionaries come from the same race, they must therefore be incapable of directing the others."[136] The core of

---

[130] Article by Poujoulat in *L'Union,* 7 March 1870.
[131] Roger de Larcy, "La décentralisation de 1789 à 1870," *Le Correspondant* 46 (1870): 5–6.
[132] Fontarèches, *Monarchie et liberté,* 57–63.
[133] Rainneville, *Catholiques tolérants,* 101–2; see also Béchard, *Essai sur la centralisation administrative,* 2:xvi.
[134] Muller, *La légitimité,* 175.
[135] See chap. 1, n. 222.
[136] Claude-Marie Raudot, *L'administration locale en France et en Angleterre* (Paris: Douniol, 1863), 5.

Dupont-White's thesis was that Saxon peoples were historically and culturally conditioned to rule themselves without centralized institutions, whereas Latin races had been driven in the opposite direction by the lasting heritage of the Roman conquest. Raudot also ridiculed this antithesis:

> Indeed, the English are a mixture of ancient Celts with Germans, Normans, and Scandinavians. But is the French stock not also a mixture of Celts, Germans, and Normans? Because the Romans have left a slightly deeper imprint on the Gauls, can one deduce that the English are a superior race, completely capable of self-government, whereas we are some sort of Hindus who have to be led by the nose?[137]

A pure creation of the Revolution, the centralized administrative structure had been preserved by Napoleon and maintained by all successive regimes thereafter. In their critique of centralization during the Second Empire, legitimists rounded on the dysfunctions of the administration with particular venom. In an article directed against what he called administrative tyranny, Louis Veuillot complained that "at the lower levels [of the bureaucracy] one encounters all sorts of petty tyrants, impassive, formalistic, incapable of any good grace, and who know only too well how to make their petty power count."[138] The pernicious role of the prefect was denounced with equal vigor: "A stranger to the department, which he only crosses at a rapid pace on his way up the rungs of the prefectoral ladder, the prefect becomes an instrument of ministerial intrigues, and in administration a mere signing machine. It is impossible for him to fulfill with intelligence any of the numerous attributions with which he is overburdened."[139] As with all opposition groups, recriminations against the role of the administration were particularly vehement during elections. Legitimist writers deplored the Empire's consistent use of administrative agents for partisan purposes. In the following diatribe, the author denounced the coercive role mayors played, and particularly the leverage they enjoyed against vulnerable and dependent peasant communities:

> The deputy mayor, the schoolteacher, the tax collector, the director of the post office, the rural policeman, the tobacconist, the innkeeper, the road mender, how many lives depend on the administration, ready to be thrown into the political struggle on the impulsion of the mayor, invested with the authority of the prefect! The fate of the peasant can be guessed in this

---

[137] Ibid., 4.

[138] Veuillot, *Mélanges religieux*, no. 2, 4:298.

[139] Béchard, *Essai sur la centralisation administrative*, 2:3. See also his pamphlet *Les élections en 1869: Lettre aux Nîmois* (Nîmes, 1869), ix.

scramble. It is the duty of all these agents to push him to vote, and he himself is too dependent on their goodwill and is too accustomed to revere in them the prestige of authority to resist their influence.[140]

Finally, and perhaps most critically for legitimist writers, centralization was deeply problematic because of the following damaging social and political effects: "The loss of authentic social forces and the unleashing of evil and subversive passions."[141] Observing French society in 1865, a legitimist publicist noted the same two contradictory tendencies: "On one hand, energetic and long-contained aspirations are beginning to appear; on the other hand, we have the continuing spectacle of languid irritation and flaccid vice."[142] The most troubling manifestation of social passions was the French predilection for revolutionary change, which was greatly facilitated by the existence of centralized institutions. Blanc de Saint-Bonnet lamented the dissolution of all autonomous forms of social activity, which left the population perpetually exposed to the threat of tyranny: "Centralization makes us fear that there may no longer be any moral aristocracy, and that these aristocracies only exert their influence on an individual basis, and that all useful social actions come exclusively from the state. Our vices and follies have speedily led us to this extreme situation, which leaves us exposed to despotism."[143]

The most invidious political consequence of this social degeneration was the erosion of all sense of civic responsibility — a conclusion underlined by Raudot: "Not only is a nation great by its wealth and the number of its inhabitants, but its greatness comes especially from the spirit that guides its citizens, by their moral qualities. Alas! With a few exceptions, we no longer have any ardent passions for public life, no social energies, no dignity of character."[144] Legitimists viewed decentralization as the only means of reviving the civic spirit of the French nation.

THE CITY OF BARBARIANS

Many features of the general critique of centralization outlined in the previous section were shared by other political traditions. The damaging legacy of the French Revolution, the pernicious role of the adminis-

---

[140] Charles de Lacombe, *De l'arbitraire dans le gouvernement et dans les partis* (Paris: Douniol, 1864), 15–16.

[141] Béchard, *Essai sur la centralisation administrative*, 2:iii.

[142] Armand Foucher de Careil, *De la centralisation politique* (Paris: Lainé et Havard, 1865), 25.

[143] Blanc de Saint-Bonnet, *Politique réelle*, 62.

[144] Raudot, *L'administration locale*, 22.

tration, the social atrophy and moral corruption produced by a combination of excessive regulation and relentless political individualism — all these traits were also denounced by republican, liberal, and even Bonapartist decentralists, even though legitimists were undoubtedly distinct in their emphasis both on the revolutionary origins and the corruptive social consequences of administrative centralization.

However, a number of other elements of the legitimist critique were more exclusive. Of these, the most dramatic was legitimists' condemnation of Paris, the fallen city that in their eyes symbolized the degeneracy of French society. There were, of course, legitimists who lived in the city and appreciated its character; a somewhat optimistic royalist even went so far as to suggest that "Paris exudes royalism from its every pore."[145] But this was a minority view. Blanc de Saint-Bonnet denounced "the industry of luxury," which had its heart in France's capital city.[146] "Paris is beautiful, Paris is splendid, Paris is full of animation and life; yes, Paris is all these things," added Muller, remarking, however, "but France is sad, colorless, and without movement."[147] Many legitimists did not even partake in the positive element of his appreciation. Upon leaving his native region to be educated in the capital, Falloux remembered: "Paris provoked no dazzlement in my mind. I deeply regretted Angers and the Anjou and remained apprehensive and distrustful of Parisians."[148] A legitimist advocate of decentralization went further in his negative assessment: "It has been established that a prolonged stay in Paris is detrimental to health: the air is insalubrious and the activity ceaseless; even the food is poisonous; it causes the most serious disturbances to the health of individuals."[149]

This ingrained sense of suspicion, which legitimists instinctively experienced at the mere mention of the capital city, was based on a plurality of considerations. First and foremost, Paris was the historical seat of social and political revolution, with all the unpleasant connotations that this term evoked in the legitimist imagination: regicide, persecution of the nobility, expropriation of the church, incessant political turmoil, and mob rule.[150] Raudot welcomed the suppression of the central municipality of Paris and suggested that the Hôtel de Ville be converted into a museum, so as to deny the rioting masses their natural political symbol.[151] This consistent aspiration to radical change was embedded in

[145] Louis Lazare, *La France et Paris* (Paris: Bibliothèque Municipale, 1872), 257.
[146] Blanc de Saint-Bonnet, *La restauration française*, 57–59.
[147] Muller, *La légitimité*, 173.
[148] Alfred de Falloux, *Mémoires d'un royaliste* (Paris: Perrin, 1888), 1:23.
[149] Kuntz de Rouvaire, *La décentralisation* (Paris, 1859), 73.
[150] See, for example, Véron, *Lettres Parisiennes*, 29–30.
[151] Claude-Marie Raudot, "La Décentralisation," *Le Correspondant* (1861): 263–64.

the city's working population and represented nothing less than the victory of nihilism over social order.

> This city, which calls itself the brilliant metropolis of the universe[,] . . . contains in its midst thousands of men invested with political rights, whose unique and sole purpose is to destroy. It is not for them a question of promoting principles or obtaining such and such a form of government that might be more favorable to liberty . . . no, all the words and deeds of these men represent absolute ignorance and pure brutality. We have often spoken of the barbarians of the interior: they are already here.[152]

The general attributes of the lower orders indeed seemed open to considerable improvement. One legitimist could find in Paris only "religious ignorance, and with it lack of faith and piety, brutal vices, greed, inebriation, immorality, corruption, shamelessness, adultery, and the most heinous crimes of our civilization."[153] But the danger was not restricted to the working class. Equally potent was the problem posed by the intellectual life of the city, and especially its political press: "Atheism, lack of faith, and ungodly and ridiculous religions have always found their home in this city, and excessive centralization gives them every opportunity to spread their impure and corruptive influence everywhere," noted Comte Jules de Cosnac indignantly.[154] Blanc de Saint-Bonnet was no less categorical: "Woe is the country that is led by its literary men, inconsistent spirits who are moved by appearances and easily unsettled by the winds of opinion. They are as incapable of connecting to reality as of understanding true greatness."[155]

To others the situation was better captured in an avian metaphor: "All those afflicted by ambition, misery, anger, and temerity of fortune soon discover that there is only one place in the world to meet: in Paris; all the hotheads, all the windbags . . . descend upon Paris cawing like a swarm of crows."[156] For many legitimists Paris was therefore a metaphor for a type of social and intellectual corruption that was produced by the urban way of life in particular. Inherent in the legitimist perspective on centralization was thus a critique of urbanization, a notable feature of the Second Empire's social policy. In this context, Baron

---

[152] Article by Poujoulat, in *L'Union*, 12 February 1870.

[153] M. Veyland, *Moralisation des classes indigentes* (Metz, 1854), 1. For an equally morose view, see Antonin Rondelet, *Les mémoires d'Antoine* (Paris: Didier, 1860), 190–94.

[154] Comte Gabriel-Jules de Cosnac, *De la décentralisation administrative* (Paris: Dentu, 1844), 18–19.

[155] Blanc de Saint-Bonnet, *Politique réelle*, 79 n. 3.

[156] Arthur de Gobineau and Louis de Kergorlay, "Introduction," *Revue Provinciale* (1848): 6.

Haussmann's grandiose plans for urban renovation in Paris were a natural focus of legitimist concern.

As part of its wider program of infrastructural development, the Second Empire's transformation of Paris during the 1850s and 1860s seemed to many legitimists a violation of the fundamental laws of social order.[157] As the defender of the principles of tradition and familiarity, Veuillot deplored the destruction of the house in which his father had been born: "I have been chased away; another has come to settle there, then my house has been razed to the ground, and the sordid pavement has covered everything. City without a past, full of spirits without memories, of hearts without tears, of souls without love! City of uprooted multitudes, movable heap of human rubble, you can grow and even become the capital of the world, but you will never have any citizens!"[158] Veuillot also objected vehemently to Haussmann's insistence on continuing construction work on Sundays, the sacred day of rest for all Catholics: "Christians regard the systematic violation of Sunday rest as an act of pure savagery, a gratuitous insult to their sentiments, an outrage against God himself, which God will avenge."[159]

Haussmann believed that the reconstruction of Paris was an essential means of containing the threat of social revolution. The legitimist journalist Poujoulat rejected this assumption, warning against the political consequences of such a great influx of migrant workers into the city: "So many workers to rebuild Paris make as many socialists to destroy society."[160] The duchesse de Dino feared — somewhat prophetically — that the transformation of the city into a haven of sensuous pleasures would ultimately undermine the very foundations of social order: "These gigantic efforts . . . to stimulate pleasures of all types seem indicative of a deplorable social condition; I can barely articulate the horror that seizes me at the sight of this agitated and fevered population, relentlessly trailing around its curiosity and passions from one arena to another. It is evident that the precipice lined with gold and flowers is nigh, and that it will soon devour, in a blaze of fire, blood, and filth, all those who sing, dance, and make merry at the edge of the crater."[161]

The legitimist approach to urbanization was not limited to a condemnation of moral corruption and political turmoil. More interesting was a critique of the social consequences of the destruction of traditional neighborhoods. For Laurentie, one of the most worrying aspects of

---

[157] On the program, see Girard, *La politique des travaux publics du Second Empire*.
[158] Louis Veuillot, *Les odeurs de Paris* (Paris: Palmé, 1867), ix.
[159] Veuillot, *Mélanges religieux*, no. 3, 2:213.
[160] *L'Union*, 4 October 1869.
[161] Duchesse de Dino, *Chronique de 1830 à 1862* (Paris: Plon, 1910), 4:213.

Haussmann's project was the physical separation of the more affluent sections of the city from the poor sections:

> "This separation, if consummated, would overturn all that is good, humane, and fraternal in Christianity. A city whose neighborhoods would be divided between, on the one hand, those blessed with good fortune, wealth, and elegance, and on the other, the population condemned to work for its livelihood, such a city would not long be a Christian city; it would become a city of barbarians.[162]

The logical implications of this separation were further outlined in a vivid contrast, which ended with an ominous warning: "Assuming it were possible to separate the inhabitants of a city into these two parts . . . you would have two populations unknown to each other, fearing and detesting each other, two hostile populations, whose interactions would only underline their contrasting fortunes. Assume that this were the case, and consider whether such a city could maintain its security for very long."[163] Here again one cannot but notice the dualism in the legitimist view of postrevolutionary society. On one hand, the working population of Paris was seen as the embodiment of barbarity, for both its political and its moral proclivities. On the other hand, it was recognized that the workers were victims of social injustice. They faced material conditions produced by political manipulation and social engineering for which they were in no way responsible. In this sense, no matter how dangerous the threat posed to social order, legitimists were capable of expressing compassion and sympathy for the human plight of the city's impoverished working population. And, consistent with their Christian beliefs, they were even prepared to contemplate the prospect of redemption: "These crowds are less perverted than misled. One can find in their midst many souls who aspire to justice, order, freedom, and especially charity, in a word, to Christianity."[164]

THE MENACE TO RURAL SOCIETY

As an integral part of their critique of the urban way of life, legitimists constantly voiced their concern about the pernicious effects of centralization on the rural world. This particular preoccupation was evidence of the key role assigned in the social and political value system of legitimism to the provinces, the "embodiment of our cherished freedoms."[165]

Many legitimist figures were wealthy landowners; others, such as

[162] Laurentie, *Mélanges*, 466.
[163] Ibid., 469.
[164] Veuillot, in *L'Univers*, 6 November 1868; Veuillot, *Mélanges religieux*, no. 3, 3:77.
[165] André Barbès, *Les traditions nationales autrefois et aujourd'hui dans la nation française* (Paris: Douniol, 1873), 288.

Raudot, involved themselves closely in the defense of agricultural interests in their department throughout the Second Empire.[166] From the
1830s and 1840s on, one could also note the emergence of a distinct
type of intellectual in the provinces: the legitimist man of letters, who
devoted much of his time to regional history and genealogical research.
In this respect the case of Arthur de la Borderie is illuminating.[167] These
legitimists (or Catholics) frequently equated the legitimist cause with the
protection of the provincial world's interests.[168] Whenever their elites
seemed tempted to follow a different path, warnings were at hand urging a return to the natural interests of legitimism. Thus, in 1852 Veuillot urged the legitimists "to make themselves not 'people' but peasants; to be the first of peasants, men of the earth first and foremost,
promoters and guides of agricultural progress, founders and patrons of
all charitable associations."[169]

There was no doubt that many features of rural life represented cherished symbols and values in the legitimist imagination. First, the provinces were a repository of the historical traditions and social identities
of particular localities; they characterized the diversity that was an essential component of the cultural identity of the French nation. But
identification with the provinces was also a political act, a way of reaf-
firming the survival of modes of thought, habits, and customs which the
Revolution had consciously attempted to eradicate. Hence the frequent
legitimist demands for the protection of local dialects and provincial
identities,[170] most notably in the petition Charency, Gaidoz, and de
Gaulle sent to the Legislative corps in 1870.[171] Hence also the insistence
with which many legitimist publicists called for the restoration of the
former provinces.[172] Coquille underlined the point: "And what is still
more popular than these names of provinces which link the present to
the past? The French are still proud to be Bretons, Normans, and Burgundians. No one seriously takes pride in belonging to such and such a

---

[166] J.-P. Rocher, "Un opposant légitimiste libéral, Raudot," in *Les républicains sous le
Second Empire*, ed. Hamon, 165.

[167] See "Arthur de la Borderie," in *Le Bretonisme: Les historiens bretons au XIXeme
siècle*, by Jean-Yves Guiomar (Rennes: Société d'Histoire et d'Archéologie de Bretagne,
1987), 184–89.

[168] See, for example, N. G. Victor Vaillant, *Décentralisation et régime représentatif*
(Metz, 1863), 12.

[169] Veuillot, *Mélanges religieux*, no. 3, 3:215.

[170] Charles des Moulins, *Du provincialisme et de ses inconséquents* (Bordeaux:
Gounouilhou, 1864).

[171] Comte de Charency, H. Gaidoz, and Charles de Gaulle, *Pétition pour les langues
provinciales au Corps Législatif de 1870* (Paris: Picard, 1903).

[172] See, for example, *Varia: Les départements et les provinces* (Nancy: Vagner, 1860),
36–37; Comte d'Osmond, *L'Etat par la province* (Nevers: Michot, 1871), 24–25.

department."[173] The province was also the primary location of the commune, which legitimists represented as the fulcrum of the social, political, and religious identity of each citizen.

> Before being an independent businessman, entrepreneur, farmer, or man of letters, you are a citizen; you belong to this primary association we call the commune. You live among men to whom you are attached by common bonds of memory, affection, and experience; the church where you kneel with them to pray to the Lord, the cemetery where your fathers rest next to theirs. It is in the commune that the fatherland has its roots.[174]

For many legitimists, the provinces also typified the principle of productive labor.[175] Contrasts were frequently drawn in legitimist literature between the precariousness of urban existence and the dependable and reassuring occupations of rural life. Workers who migrated to towns and cities often found nothing but unemployment, misery, and hunger.[176] Agricultural life, however, could offer firmer guarantees: "It is only in the countryside that the population can grow, because tilling the land requires many hands and offers a guaranteed income."[177] Over and above these political and industrial concerns, legitimists identified the rural world with values they saw as essential to a civilized society. Returning to her beloved locality of Sagan after a frantic and unsettling visit to Paris, the duchesse de Dino was relieved to find herself back in an atmosphere of "calm, meditation, and contemplation."[178]

For some legitimists, however, life outside urban centers was not simply a succession of tranquil moments. Falloux warned against equating provincial life with hedonism: "It would be unfair to the countryside if those who did not know it imagine that it is only a place for simple pastoral pleasures. Everything there is in a state of concentration and perfectibility. One can read there with greater concentration, discuss matters with greater intimacy, and also make lasting friendships."[179] Above all, life among rural communities offered the guarantee of a healthy social and moral framework. In Veuillot's idealized narrative, his native village was represented as the embodiment of all the best Christian virtues: natural hierarchy and patriarchy, honesty, thrift, in-

---

[173] Coquille, *La royauté française*, 349.

[174] Muller, *La légitimité*, 147.

[175] Comte Henri de Chambord, "Lettre sur l'agriculture," dated 12 March 1866, in *Correspondance de 1841 à 1871* (Geneva: Grosset et Trembley, 1871), 246–48.

[176] Georges de Cadoudal, *Esquisses morales, historiques et littéraires* (Paris: Sarlit, 1861), 338–39.

[177] Coquille, *Politique chrétienne*, 59.

[178] Dino, *Chronique*, 46.

[179] Falloux, *Mémoires d'un royaliste*, 2:241–42.

dustry, and sexual probity. No unseemly passions came to trouble the felicity of this bucolic existence: "There was no envy or hatred. No one considered himself enslaved or accursed. Everyone had their Sunday, their place at church, and even in society; and all could count on their place in Heaven. Everyone joyously watched their beautiful children grow into strong men and affectionate sons. In short, one lived happily and died in peace."[180]

For many legitimists, the practices of centralization seemed to threaten this entire system of social and political values. Armand Foucher de Careil remarked the following in a pamphlet: "Under a decentralized system, the general movement is favorable to the countryside and to agriculture, whereas in a centralized system, it is disastrous for agriculture and exclusively favorable to towns, and to big towns at that."[181] The most telling symptom of this "unfavorable movement" was the phenomenon of rural depopulation, which was noted with alarm in many legitimist and Catholic writings during this period. The Abbé Bernaret, giving an account of his diocese in 1863, warned that landowning families were increasingly falling prey to "the miserable habit of living in towns at the expense of the countryside."[182] The migration of the peasantry from the land was not a particularly new phenomenon, but the Second Empire's urbanization policies served to accentuate the unfavorable contrast between town and country life.[183]

At the same time, legitimists suggested that there was also a distinct trend toward pauperization in peasant communities, which forced local populations to seek a better fate elsewhere. Thus, the marquis de Dreux-Brézé identified the main causes of rural depopulation as solitude, poverty, and the inequality of conditions faced by agricultural workers.[184] Some regarded the phenomenon of rural depopulation as a symptom of an even worse problem: the degeneration of the French race. Raudot lamented the decadence of society, visible first and foremost in the country's calamitous birth rate: "Of all the states in Europe, France is the one where the birth rate has grown least over the last century, and even this sluggish growth is slowing down."[185] Decadence

---

[180] Veuillot, *Mélanges religieux*, no. 3, 3:697–98.

[181] Armand Foucher de Careil, *La dépopulation des campagnes* (Paris: Lainé, 1867), 13.

[182] Quoted in "The French Nobility in the Nineteenth Century," by Ralph Gibson, in *Elites in France*, by Jolyon Howorth and Philip Cerny (London: Pinter, 1981), 21.

[183] For an analysis of landowner concerns over depopulation during this period, see Pierre Féral, *La Société d'Agriculture du Gers sous le Second Empire* (Auch, 1973), 20–23.

[184] Dreux-Brézé, *Quelques mots*, 48.

[185] Claude-Marie Raudot, "La décentralisation en 1870," *Le Correspondant* (1870): 190.

was also directly associated with the development of industry: "Premature debauchery has so degraded our race that it is with the greatest difficulty that the necessary number of military recruits can be found each year."[186] Foucher de Careil denounced "vice, drunkenness, and the need for unseemly pleasures, which bring rural populations into the cities and create immorality in the countryside, so that the depopulation of the countryside is both the cause and the effect of our racial degeneration."[187]

Similar considerations inspired Gobineau's shift from the problematic of provincial autonomy to the question of race after 1850. In his unfinished work on the origins and consequences of the Franco-Prussian War, he emphasized the physical degeneration of the French peasantry and criticized those who idealized the social and moral virtues of this decadent class.[188]

THE TYRANNY OF ADMINISTRATIVE POWER

A third distinct focus in the legitimist critique of centralization was the role of the administration. Again, this theme was common to all decentralists; it was scarcely possible to object to the overbearing presence of the state in French public and private life without at the same time expressing some opposition to the administration's functions. The legitimists occupied a particular position in this debate in two respects.

First, they could claim the privilege of antecedence. As noted earlier, the legitimist critique of the principles and purposes of the Jacobin state sprang from a counterrevolutionary tradition that had rarely wavered in its hostility to the idea of extensive state power.[189] Second, the legitimists were distinct in the sheer scope of their ideological opposition to the functions of the administrative machinery of the state. The extreme and categorical nature of their hostility is well captured in the following lament by Roger de Larcy in April 1870 — at a time when many liberals were expressing cautious optimism at the prospect of the decentralist reforms promised by Ollivier:

> The spirit of the old administration still rules over all of France. We are surprised and annoyed by this; but a change in personnel would do nothing to alter the situation. The very spirit of our administrative institutions

---

[186] Claude-Marie Raudot, *De la décadence de la France*, 3d ed. (Paris: Amyot, 1850), 122.

[187] Foucher de Careil, *La dépopulation des campagnes*, 15.

[188] Gobineau, *Ce qui est arrivé à la France en 1870*, esp. 100–102.

[189] For an account of the question of decentralization during this period, see A. Rousseau, *L'idée décentralisatrice et les partis politiques sous la restauration* (Vannes: Lafolye, 1904).

needs reforming. . . . Over the last sixty years we have succeeded in carrying out many political revolutions, both violent and peaceful. Kings, ministers, and heads of Empire have changed or yielded; but the offices remain,
prefects succeed and indeed resemble each other, and it is they who in reality govern. If we really want freedom, this is the power we must destroy.[190]

Legitimists were therefore concerned not only with the consequences
of state actions on the public spirit but also (and perhaps especially)
with the recruitment of administrative elites, the type of institutions
they controlled, the scope of the powers they exercised, and the ultimate
purposes of state power itself. The mediocrity of the higher civil service
was generally decried in legitimist circles. Gobineau sneeringly contrasted the bureaucratic pretensions to "omniscience" with the chaos of
decision making in the French state.[191] Even more than its incompetence
and arrogance, the qualities that marked the higher civil service for es-
pecial damnation were its servility and political corruption. A commonly advocated solution was believed to lie in making a number of
senior administrative offices nonremunerative. Muller thus argued that
if prefects and subprefects did not receive public salaries, the general
interest could be served in two ways: the budget would be reduced, and
these offices would be filled by men of independent means who could
provide all the necessary guarantees of competence, dignity, and honor.[192]
The problem of personnel quality, in other words, was partly a reflection of the decline of aristocratic recruitment into state offices. Conversely, this analysis also suggested that the social classes that occupied
prominent positions in the bureaucratic hierarchy were unfit to play a
leading role in society. The main target of this criticism was the bourgeoisie, which seemed to regard the occupation of administrative positions almost as a natural right: "One of the great scourges of our time is
the obsession with offices, the sheer frenzy with which public employment is sought, all based on the disastrous bourgeois notion that the
state should be responsible for finding positions for their sons."[193]
This attack on the privileged position of the bourgeoisie within the
state — a neat inversion of the prerevolutionary complaints against the
appropriation of public offices by the aristocracy — dovetailed with a
broader theme: the inflated growth of administrative personnel during
the Second Empire. The unnecessary expansion of the bureaucracy appeared as a leitmotiv in legitimist writings even before this period. Writing during the Second Republic, Béchard found the situation so alarm-

[190] Larcy, "La décentralisation," 26.
[191] Gobineau, *Ce qui est arrivé à la France*, 75.
[192] Muller, *La légitimité*, 227.
[193] Ibid., 241.

ing as to justify a (somewhat barbarous) neologism: France, in his view, was governed by a "functionocracy."[194] Two decades later circumstances were no better; indeed, they appeared worse to many legitimist observers. Raudot summed up their view with some telling statistics:

> Since 1849 our army of bureaucrats has grown like our army of soldiers; taken together, it amounts to more than twelve hundred thousand men, who devour not only the finances but the vital energies of France. If we leave women out, we have barely nineteen million men in France; there are hardly nine and a half million adults, so that one Frenchman in every eight is a bureaucrat . . . and of the seven others one or two at least solicit the favor of becoming bureaucrats.[195]

Another aspect of the same problem was a division of the bureaucracy into separate administrative corps, many of which were regarded as entirely superfluous by legitimist writers. One legitimist journalist likened prefects to "old and outdated material, sounding like rusty metal." He demanded that they all be dispatched to golden retirement in the Senate.[196] The Council of State, in the eyes of another, was nothing but "a generously salaried piece of inconsequence."[197] Not surprisingly, there were constant legitimist calls for the abolition of these separate administrative institutions.

Underlying the corrupt social and political purposes of bureaucratic expansion, legitimists also detected a more sinister project: the destruction of individual autonomy, with all citizens being cast in a mold of social and cultural uniformity. Gabriel de Belcastel presented this trend in a typically apocalyptic metaphor: "The most terrible instrument of tyranny ever seen since paganism is the omnipotence of the state, this abstract, irresponsible, and intrusive force that destroys the individual and pulverizes the living members of the human race in order to reduce them to ashes."[198] The problem ultimately stemmed from the state's desire to assume the role of Providence and thus to satisfy all the material and spiritual needs of the population. As noted earlier, legitimists violently condemned this objective, not only because they regarded it as an unwarranted intrusion into the private concerns of the citizenry but also because of the real threat it posed to public liberties. More than any other political group in France, perhaps, legitimists did not need re-

---

[194] "Une fonctionnocratie" (Ferdinand Béchard, *La commune, l'Eglise et l'Etat dans leurs rapports avec les classes laborieuses* [Paris: Giraud, 1849], 1:xiii).

[195] Raudot, "La décentralisation en 1870," 196.

[196] Raoul Calary, in *La liberté électorale, organe de l'émancipation provinciale*, 24 February 1870.

[197] A. Escande, in *Gazette de France*, 29 May 1870.

[198] Belcastel, *La citadelle de la liberté*, 17–18.

minding of the unfortunate lapses that could occur when the French
state took it upon itself to promote universal happiness for its citizens.

At the same time, there was a profound contradiction in the legitimist
position about the state's social purposes. Unlike the liberals, who believed that very few justifiable grounds existed for extensive state intrusion in both economic and social questions, legitimists did not reject
outright the notion that the state should have a moral purpose. On the
contrary, they believed that it was the duty of public institutions to
promote proper norms and values in society: "To govern is, in sum, the
art of guiding men toward virtue."[199] Indeed, for some legitimists this
ethical purpose took priority over the public-order functions of the
state: "It is true that the state has a mission to preserve order and peace;
but this is a secondary mission, subordinated to its moral and religious
principles. The state is an armed missionary."[200]

This ethical "mission" clearly required a state that sought to define
the good life for the citizenry. The legitimist objection to the idea of a
providential state was therefore not so much a matter of principle as of
substance: what were rejected were the particular values disseminated
by the modern state. A more critical way of making the same point is to
suggest that legitimists would have been much less critical of administrative tyranny if the underlying principles and social purposes of the
state had been legitimist.

DECENTRALIZATION AS A POLITICAL IMPERATIVE

As with its critique of the Jacobin state, the legitimist advocacy of decentralization was based on considerations and preoccupations that
were often exclusive to the legitimist movement. However, there were
some common themes with republican and liberal decentralists. As we
will note, legitimists were essentially united in the view that mayors
should be elected by the municipal council and that the General Councils should be given greater latitude to make policy in areas pertaining
exclusively to local interests. Legitimists also shared with all opposition
groups a visceral hostility to the prefects, whose administrative powers
they sought to curb drastically. These joint goals enabled the legitimists
to share a political platform with individuals and political groups from
markedly different ideological horizons during the 1860s. But behind
this apparently ecumenical discourse—typified in many senses by the
1865 Nancy manifesto—there remained a core decentralist project that
was unique to legitimism. As we will see, this project was in places

---

[199] Blanc de Saint-Bonnet, *La restauration française*, 102.
[200] Coquille, *La royauté française*, 135.

fundamentally incompatible with the principles and values of other political movements. This divergence raised a number of problems that
divided the legitimist movement throughout the Second Empire. How
far should legitimists make common cause with groups whose conceptions of decentralization and political citizenship were radically different from theirs? Was purity in isolation preferable to compromises that
would bring legitimists back into the political mainstream? And, most
fundamentally, under what circumstances should the priority given to
decentralization be modified in the name of higher-order principles?

The political imperative behind the legitimist advocacy of decentralization should first be understood in the context of the debate between
abstentionists and participationists in the aftermath of 1851. After the
proclamation of the Second Empire, a dominant section of the legitimist
movement—led by the comte de Chambord—advocated a complete
withdrawal from public life. No legitimist was to swear an oath of allegiance to the new regime; any deviation from this rule would compromise the integrity of legitimism. The act of political abstention would
constitute a dignified protest against the iniquity of the Bonapartist
coup and allow the legitimist party to safeguard its distinct ideological
identity around its exiled monarch.[201] In the words of one legitimist,
"The traditional monarchy has to present itself to France untouched by
any contamination with values that could pervert the moral sense of the
nation and make it lose the prestige that is so essential to its authority."[202]
Although about 450 legitimists were elected to the General Council in
1852, the mass of legitimist cadres intially followed their leader's injunction and stayed away from the public arena.[203] But this position
rapidly came under fire from different quarters within the legitimist
movement. Pragmatists such as Muller argued that political participation and public office were essential for the defense of local interests.

> It is not a matter of indifference that interests, gathered together by the
> Lord under the shade of the same church, should be wisely administered,
> that peace and justice should reign in the village, and that the rising genera-
> tions should be inspired by examples of civic virtue. The happiness of a
> community can depend on the choice of a mayor or of the composition of a
> municipal council.[204]

Others used much stronger language. The normally urbane Falloux
described Chambord's injunction against political participation as noth-

---

[201] For an account of this debate within the legitimist party, see Falloux, *Mémoires d'un
royaliste*, 2:195–207.
[202] La Rochejaquelin, *La France en 1853*, 97.
[203] Rials, *Le légitimisme*, 77.
[204] Muller, *La légitimité*, 285.

ing less than an act of desertion, given the enormity (and urgency) of the tasks the party faced: "We have to moralize the communes and towns, fight against revolutionary influences, and found religious institutions in these places. All the strength and reputation of the old royalist party could be devoted to this task, with great honor to itself and great profit for France."[205] From the opposite wing of the legitimist movement, Ségur asserted with equal vigor that no good legitimist citizen could look the other way while society was being exposed to the menace of radical republicanism: "To fight the Revolution is an act of faith, a religious duty of the first magnitude. It is, in addition, the act of a good citizen and honest man, for it represents a defense of the fatherland and the family."[206]

In most improbable fashion, the middle position was occupied on this particular occasion by Veuillot, who encouraged a deliberate but restrained form of participation in public life: "We find ourselves in certain respects as in a foreign country, observing the general norms that rule public life, appealing to those rights whose corresponding duties we are happy to fulfill; but we refuse to enter into the temples and burn incense."[207] Stated differently, this view contended that the public arena should be exploited at every available opportunity to propagate the legitimist message, but that the party should eschew all association with the political ends of Bonapartism—a position that, arguably, Veuillot himself failed to uphold on a number of critical occasions.[208]

It is important to note how deeply the participationist view was embedded in a belief in the essential value of local political life. By the early 1860s, the abstentionist line was being given much less prominence, as there emerged a growing appreciation of the pitfalls of political isolation. In his manifesto of November 1862, Chambord invited legitimists to make their views on decentralization known to the wider public. At the same time, he gave his blessing to legitimist efforts to reach out toward representatives of other political groups: "Get to work energetically, bring together, even from outside our ranks, all those who can offer the wisdom of their experience."[209] But the concretization of this exhortation was problematic on three counts.

First, the absence of clear directives made it possible for different groups of legitimists to make contradictory political alliances. In 1863 liberal legitimists such as Berryer and Falloux joined the Union Libérale,

[205] Falloux, *Mémoires d'un royaliste*, 2:219.
[206] Ségur, *La Révolution*, 12.
[207] Veuillot, *L'illusion libérale*, 128.
[208] Most notably—and notoriously—in his cravenly endorsement of the 1851 coup. See his "Appel en faveur du Président," *L'Univers*, 6 December 1851.
[209] Chambord, *Manifestes et programmes*, 214.

an interparty electoral grouping of moderate opponents to the Empire. Other legitimists, however, preferred a rapprochement with the Empire, which seemed a better guarantor of social order and political stability. In this respect the regime's evolution toward the liberal Empire created even more uncertainty and confusion within legitimist ranks.

Second, alliances could be reached only on the basis of compromise. Many legitimists expressed their apprehension that too many exercises in tactical accommodation would undermine the political force and ideological coherence of their principles. The question of decentralization was a case in point. The publication of a program on local government by a congress of liberal and legitimist provincial newspapers in September 1869 was a source of much anguish to Laurentie: "It is indeed the case that decentralization is in great public demand; but this demand would become a utopia if it were separated from the natural conditions of morality and social order which are the first laws of collective life. It would also be a utopia if its search were conducted by the fanciful assemblage of disparate and often hostile forces."[210]

Finally, and at a most fundamental level, there was a continuing ambivalence in legitimist discourse about the character and purpose of local political activity. In much legitimist literature, local public life was associated with goals that were eminently ideological: the defense of religion, the promotion of aristocratic leadership, and the struggle against republican political subversion. In this sense, local politics was seen as a partisan instrument, the privileged vehicle for extending the sectional appeal of legitimism in society. This proselytizing approach cut across the legitimist ideological spectrum; it was the underlying source both of Falloux's sense of urgency and of Veuillot's exhortations to the legitimists. But, somewhat paradoxically, legitimists also frequently stressed the importance of depoliticizing local government institutions. From this perspective, they believed that many of the problems faced by communes could be resolved easily if partisan divisions were transcended.

This logic dictated the opposition of many legitimists to the idea of publicizing the sessions of local assemblies:[211] "Neither the General Council nor its lower counterparts should be subjected to external pressures, be exposed to the violences of turbulent groups, or deliberate under adverse conditions and especially under insults."[212] Many legiti-

---

[210] *L'Union*, 28 September 1869.

[211] Both in the sense of admitting the public and allowing greater public information through press reports and discussions.

[212] N. G. Victor Vaillant, *Congrès décentralisateur de Lyon: Nos réserves* (Metz, 1870), 89.

mists believed that political questions should be completely banned from local assemblies.[213] In an article appropriately entitled "No Politics in the Nomination of Municipal Councillors," Jean de Mayenne presented a glowing picture of this nonantagonistic conception of local politics: "If we wish seriously to constitute our communal administration, it is necessary that men who can be of service to the community should be elected irrespective of political inclination or affiliation. . . . Indeed, it is when honest folk come to discuss their common interests independently of politics that they discover that, on many points, they can easily come to agree."[214]

Ultimately, this unresolved opposition between the sectional interests of legitimism and the ideal of an apolitical sphere of local government symbolized the problematic nature of the local political process for the legitimist movement. By the end of the 1860s, there was a general recognition that the revival of the fortunes of the legitimist party depended to a significant extent on the reconstitution of its local political networks. But this was where the consensus ended. Until the fall of the Second Empire, legitimists remained unsure as to whether they wanted an alliance with the regime or with the constitutional opposition; in Lyon, for example, the legitimist newspaper *La Décentralisation* campaigned strongly with republicans on a platform of communal and departmental reforms.[215] But even when such alliances were formed, there was a further lack of clarity as to whether (and on what terms) legitimists should compromise on their principles, and indeed whether they wanted to create a local political sphere in which ideological passions were excluded, or alternatively to use local politics precisely as a means of reviving the ideological appeal of legitimism.

A DISTINCT INSTITUTIONAL FRAMEWORK

More than the internal contradictions that characterized its approach to the question of decentralization, the distinct imprint of the legitimist project could be recognized in its conception of the institutional underpinnings of territorial government. Again, this particularism was not immediately apparent; legitimists, Catholics, and liberals alike spoke of the need to emancipate localities from the burden of centralism. The Alsatian Catholic Emile Keller thus stressed that "it is time to associate the country more substantively with the administration of its own af-

---

[213] See, for example, François Lallier, *L'élection municipale et le suffrage universel* (Paris: Le Clère, 1873), 14.
[214] Jean de Mayenne, article in *La liberté électorale*, 16 June 1870.
[215] *La Décentralisation*, 26 August 1869, 26 March 1870.

fairs and to establish our political freedoms on a genuine decentraliza-tion."[216]

Although there was a common directive principle informing all refor-mist approaches to local government — the greater involvement of the citizenry in the administration of their affairs — considerable differences existed among political groups about the manner in which this principle should be interpreted. Indeed, a close examination of legitimist ideas about the reform of local government reveals a number of concerns that were specifically legitimist. Three areas are particularly worthy of atten-tion: the emphasis on the link between religion, the monarchy, and de-centralized institutions; the overhaul of the system of territorial admin-istration; and the changes envisaged in the powers of elected assemblies. Some of these proposals did not meet with unanimous approval within the legitimist fold — a measure of the extent to which the debate about decentralization took place not only among political traditions but also within them.

The first distinctive trait of the legitimist theory of decentralized insti-tutions was its conception of the identity of the commune. Other politi-cal traditions saw the commune as a sphere of citizenship, cultural sociability, and administrative excellence; legitimists defined it primarily as the focus of moral and religious activity. For former prefect Jules Chévillard, the moral personality of the commune was founded above all on its Christian institutions.

> The commune is the parish; the parish is Christianity, and Christianity is the civilization of Gaul: hence its strength in all struggles and its resistance against the fiercest attacks. . . . The strength of the commune is entirely moral; it resides in the hearts and beliefs of its inhabitants: far from under-mining them, the passage of time renews these sentiments with every gener-ation.[217]

All the communes of France had joined together in an indissociable affiliation with the hereditary monarchy. In the organic conception of society that legitimists favored, there was an unbroken chain linking the individual to the family, the family to the commune, the commune to the province, and all provinces to the monarch. Local institutions were therefore part of a greater whole, whose existence was a condition of their freedom and integrity. In the absence of this greater social and political entity, local institutions were condemned to languish. A politi-cal system founded on the principle of popular sovereignty, for example,

---

[216] Emile Keller, *Aux électeurs de Vendée* (1869).

[217] Jules Chévillard, *Etudes d'administration: De la division administrative de la France et de la centralisation* (Paris: Durand, 1862), 75–76.

could never be expected to promote a genuine measure of local liberty. Baron de Fontarèches underlined the point in a discussion of the Second Empire's attempts to promote its particular form of decentralization: "The imperial monarchy is founded on the principle of popular sovereignty, which expresses a strong sense of unity and dominates all of society, crushing everything in its omnipotence. It cannot allow any group of separate and distinct interests to survive under a free and independent administration."[218]

The case for affirming the centrality of the monarchy in decentralized local government institutions was based on historical and ideological considerations. Historically, legitimists argued that French monarchs had been effective and dedicated guardians of local liberties: "It is under the auspices and with the help of our royalty that the municipal system developed. The city, like royalty, is a perpetual family; they are both united by the same perpetual interests."[219] It naturally followed that only the monarchy had the necessary moral and political qualities to guarantee the integrity of local institutions.

> Decentralization is essentially a monarchical doctrine. It can be sincerely and effectively introduced only with the monarchy, the guarantor and guardian of all rights. Only the monarchy is not fearful of dignity and independence. Only the monarchy, which embodies the unity of the nation, can be sufficiently strong to bind together the free institutions of the commune, the department, and the province. Only the monarchy can be strong enough to be the axis around which revolve the representative institutions of a free and Christian society.[220]

The question of administrative reform also elicited a distinct (albeit not always harmonious) set of responses from the legitimists. There was unanimous agreement on the necessity of overhauling the judicial system; thus Raudot proposed to suppress the immunity from prosecution that public functionaries enjoyed, to abolish the separate system of administrative justice operated through the prefectoral councils and the Council of State, and to nominate all magistrates from a list of candidates submitted by the General Council.[221] Also widespread was the idea that administrative procedures could be greatly simplified by reducing and streamlining the existing body of regulations. Furthermore, there was ardent support for proposals to abolish the function of the subprefect. However, the fate of the prefectoral corps provoked a greater

---

[218] Fontarèches, *La souveraineté du peuple*, 58.
[219] Coquille, *La royauté française*, 61.
[220] Henry de Riancey, in *L'Union*, 23 September 1869.
[221] Raudot, "La décentralisation en 1870," 199.

degree of discussion. It was generally agreed that these despised agents of centralized power had to relinquish many of their prerogatives to the General Council, but there were different views as to how far this process of emasculation was to be carried out. Some legitimists argued that prefects should be made to retain certain public-interest functions, especially in relation to smaller communes, which often lacked the knowledge, means, or personnel to administer themselves adequately.[222] Some also proposed that prefects no longer be appointed by the government but rather be chosen by the departmental assemblies—a measure destined to ensure the selection of men with local roots and attachments.[223]

Others, however, argued that all prefectoral functions should simply be transferred to elective bodies at communal, cantonal, and departmental levels. Under these circumstances, the prefectorate no longer served any useful purpose and could thus be abolished.[224] The last proposal was sometimes coupled with another cherished legitimist aspiration: the restoration of the territorial division of the country into provinces. Raudot proposed to replace the eighty-nine prefects with about thirty governors, whose tasks would be to control and regulate the activities of local assemblies and to coordinate common projects among departments.[225] Some legitimists even advocated the establishment of regional governments, consisting of provincial governors and executive agents of the General Council. These institutions could exercise a wide range of financial and executive powers, including raising revenue through taxation: "The department should be allowed to determine not only local levels of taxation but also how to spend all revenues raised in this way."[226]

Finally, legitimists envisaged a considerably stronger role for locally elected assemblies. First, they proposed to ban multiple office-holding, a practice that frequently enabled local councillors to double up as members of national legislative bodies. They viewed these practices as leading to corruption and inefficiency: "Multiple office-holding frustrates unemployed abilities by favoring probable incompetence."[227] The powers

---

[222] A. Bailleux de Marisy, *Transformation des grandes villes de France* (Paris: Hachette, 1867), 241.

[223] Alphonse de Calonne, "Les partis dans la nouvelle Chambre," *Revue Contemporaine* 72 (November–December 1869): 549.

[224] Alphonse de Calonne, "De la décentralisation," *Revue Contemporaine* 74 (March–April 1870): 57.

[225] Raudot, "La décentralisation en 1870," 200.

[226] Calonne, "Les partis dans la nouvelle Chambre," 550. See also the vigorous plea for departmental emancipation in *Association Normande. Comité de décentralisation: Organisation cantonale* (Caen: Le Blanc, 1871).

[227] Louis Revelière, *De la vanité des institutions* (Paris: Lecoffre, 1880), 333. See also Gustave Lambert, *Rénovation administrative* (Bayonne: André, 1863), 21.

taken away from the central and provincial administrations were to be exercised by municipal, cantonal, and departmental councils within the regulatory framework of a unitary state. The principal instrument of provincial emancipation in the eyes of the legitimists was the General Council, whose attachment to order and social conservatism was highly appreciated. In the words of an admirer:

> The General Council, even in the petty and skimpy form it has been given in earlier laws, is clearly the association of some of the best minds of every department. In this assembly sit men of experience, and troublemakers, even well-meaning ones, find themselves in an even smaller minority there than in political assemblies of a higher order.[228]

The attributions of the council were to be widened considerably to include most of the prefects' executive powers.[229] There were also frequent proposals to increase the funds available to departments by reducing the military budget. For example, Alphonse de Calonne suggested that the network of local roads be completed by transferring one hundred million francs from the ministries of war and navy.[230] These new powers and attributions would be wielded by a newly created permanent commission, which would remain active throughout the year and assume executive power in the name of the General Council between its sessions. Legitimists also proposed to increase the nominating powers of the departmental assembly to include not only the designation of its own president and secretary but also the appointment of all major departmental functionaries. Last, the General Council was to be allowed to express its views on all matters of public interest, including political questions.[231] More troubling was the question of municipal emancipation. Raudot underlined that legitimists were no advocates of unfettered communal liberty.

> We ask for communes that are not sovereign but merely free under the law; they should not have the power to irritate citizens and violate laws; but, independently of the tribunals, the necessary control over their decisions should be carried out not by the agents of central government but to a considerable extent by the local representatives themselves.[232]

---

[228] Vicomte de Sarcus, *Lettre d'un provincial à propos du vote du Conseil Général de l'Oise sur la décentralisation* (Dijon, 1864), 10.

[229] Edouard de Ventavon, *Essai sur la décentralisation* (Paris: Dentu, 1870).

[230] Alphonse de Calonne, "Le projet de loi sur les chemins vicinaux," *Revue Contemporaine* 62 (March–April 1868): 766.

[231] Raudot, "La décentralisation en 1870," 200.

[232] Raudot, *L'administration locale*, 14.

Although most legitimists agreed that mayors should be elected by the municipal council and should be entrusted with selecting the communal schoolteacher, they were divided about how much power municipal delegates could wield. Leading the party of those who took a cautious view of communal emancipation was the comte de Chambord, who spoke of the need to "decentralize the administration broadly but progressively and with prudence, without taking away the initiative and security that it enjoys from the tutelage of the state."[233] A legitimist journalist agreed emphatically with the retention of the tutelle: "Let us frankly agree that it would be foolhardy to emancipate completely what we call communal government, and that it would be better to leave it in the hands of central government than to abandon it without guarantees to its own devices."[234] In his speech at the plenary session of the 1870 commission of decentralization, Jules de Cosnac (who had rallied to the Empire in the 1869 elections)[235] also agreed: "In establishing decentralization, we must be careful not to replace the absolutism of the administration with the despotism of mayors."[236] Behind these expressions of caution one could clearly detect the traditional legitimist fear of urban political radicalism, which was heightened in the late 1860s by the eruption of working-class militancy. The pernicious doctrines of the First International concerning local autonomy were accordingly denounced vigorously: "Under the title of solidarized communes, an iron-fisted despotism would weigh on the countryside, reducing its inhabitants to slavery."[237]

Although equally categorical in their condemnation of radical republicanism, other legitimists refused to use its menace as a pretext for denying communes the greater autonomy they demanded and indeed had enjoyed before the Revolution.[238] Calonne argued that the "despotism" of the mayor was a consequence of his system of nomination, coupled with a number of unnecessary powers he had acquired through his status as an agent of the state. If these provisions were changed, there would be nothing to fear from the empowerment of communes.[239] More important, it was suggested that the necessary administrative control of communes could be achieved by more effective methods than the discredited practice of tutelle.

[233] Chambord, *Manifestes et programmes*, 214.
[234] Vaillant, *Congrès décentralisateur de Lyon*, 83.
[235] Corbin, *Archaïsme et modernité*, 896.
[236] Comte Gabriel-Jules de Cosnac, *Discours à la Commission de décentralisation* (Paris: Dentu, 1870), 34.
[237] Vaillant, *Congrès décentralisateur de Lyon*, 18.
[238] Edouard Quesnet, *Les élections municipales depuis 1763 jusqu'à nos jours* (Rennes, 1870).
[239] Calonne, "De la décentralisation," 55.

It is essential, beyond doubt, to safeguard individual rights, to prevent majorities from becoming oppressive, and to stop particularist tendencies from replacing the general interest; but to achieve this result, there is no need to maintain a system of controls that would always be ineffective or arbitrary; the result can be achieved by ensuring the proper representation of interests in the commune, and in granting each individual the right to appeal in the courts against any decision that violated the law.[240]

The euphemism about the "proper representation of interests" in fact referred to another core feature of the legitimist conception of local government, which is detailed in the following section: the central role assigned to propertied classes, particularly the aristocracy.

The Government of Natural Elites

Legitimist writers invoked three principal arguments to support the preponderance of the aristocracy in local government: the preservation of social order, the inspiration to other social classes, and the interests of the nobility itself.

In his letter on decentralization of November 1862, the comte de Chambord highlighted the main purpose of local government as the defense of social order and the prevention of revolution: "The more the democratic spirit gains ground, the greater is the urgency to regulate and organize it so as to preserve the social order from the perils to which it might be exposed."[241] Chambord hoped that a proper system of decentralization would help to reestablish France's "natural hierarchy"; hence the need to "multiply and bring within collective reach opportunities to be of service through the devotion, according to individual talents, to the administration of common interests, by also ensuring that the ranks of society are ordered in accordance with ability and merit."[242] From this perspective, it seemed obvious that a privileged position in the administration of local affairs should be reserved for the nobility, the natural defenders of propertied interests in society. Coquille spelled out this thought in full: "*Self-government* requires men of leisure, and in consequence of fortune and independence of means. All this is given by real estate, and only by it. Patrimonies have been fragmented by the Civil Code; even industrial and commercial fortunes have succumbed to liquidations and forcible redistributions. Every Frenchman has his for-

---

[240] J. Bourgeois, article in *Gazette de France*, 22 February 1870.
[241] Chambord, *Manifestes et programmes*, 216.
[242] Ibid., 214.

tune to make, and *self-government* requires fortunes that are already established."[243]

In addition to offering the best guarantee of social order, the aristocracy was ideally suited to local office because it provided an example of social and moral excellence to the rest of society. The marquis de Belleval nostalgically recalled the medieval municipal system, in which a dominant role was reserved for the nobility: "Our ancestors . . . understood that the indisputable means of endowing a function with esteem was to give it a high importance in the eyes of the vulgar, not only by means of the elites chosen to exercise them, but also by the ceremonial that accompanied their election and inauguration."[244]

What was done for the *vulgus* in the Middle Ages could be repeated in modern times; in any event, the practice of empowering the aristocracy was seen as a valuable means of educating the lower orders in the virtues of tradition and social conservatism. In opposition to the tide of opinion favoring social egalitarianism, Victor Vaillant stoutly defended the practice of transmitting political influence on the basis of inherited wealth: "Is it not a good thing to give popular elements a sense of the habits and customs of tradition? The transmission of influence is in keeping with natural law, and it is right that in our country — more than in any other — we have the tendency to put children in the same positions occupied by their fathers."[245] In sum, society would benefit from the presence of the aristocracy in local government in two ways: its communes and departments would be well administered, and its "popular elements" would learn to appreciate the social and administrative virtues of the nobility.

However — and rather paradoxically in light of the above arguments — aristocratic local government was also justified in legitimist writings on the grounds of the particular interests of the nobility. As France moved into the second half of the nineteenth century, many legitimists drew attention to the profound social and moral crisis that afflicted the nobility; in the eyes of one pamphleteer, the aristocracy seemed to have "abdicated all sense of initiative."[246] In his *Mémoires d'outre-tombe*, Chateaubriand had succinctly formulated the problem: "The aristocracy has three successive ages: the age of superiority, the age of privileges, and the age of vanities: starting with the first, it degen-

---

[243] Coquille, *Politique chrétienne*, 114–15.
[244] Belleval, *Souvenirs de ma jeunesse*, 13.
[245] Vaillant, *Décentralisation et régime représentatif*, 83.
[246] Gustave de Bernardi, *La vérité divine et l'idée humaine* (Paris: Sarlit, 1870), 351.

erates into the second before disappearing in the last."[247] Although this predicament ultimately resulted from the Revolution's destruction of aristocratic privileges, its proximate causes were thought to be social as well as political. Some explained this decadence by the declining social homogeneity of the nobility. Here is the typically forthright view of Blanc de Saint-Bonnet:

> In France the nobility has destroyed its line of demarcation with the bourgeoisie by taking its values; and the bourgeoisie has blurred what distinguished it from the people by appropriating its instincts. If this is democratization, so be it; but the fact remains that the aristocracy has become soiled by the people, and this stain has fallen upon it, leaving it in the condition in which we find it today. . . . In the old days, in the great houses, children were toughened, and they later became men. Today, as they are brought up in all classes, children are good only for devouring the resources of their fathers or for stealing.[248]

Others explained the crisis as a symptom of the growing moral corruption of aristocratic elites. Reviewing the history of the first half of the nineteenth century, the marquis de Mailly-Nesle chronicled the emergence of a new form of decadence among the nobility.

> The traditional lord of the land, of simple and easily satisfied tastes, a lover of the soil and of the pleasures it offers naturally, disappeared to make way for the well-known type that can be recognized everywhere in the display of every manner of pomposity and incompetence. . . . [E]namored with luxury and comfort, unknown to the country, whose existence is revealed only by his slovenly dress and eccentric speech, he remains totally ignorant of the spirit of the populations in whose midst he lives.[249]

Falloux warned that the continuation of such trends would ineluctably lead to the demise of the aristocracy: "Another few years of this situation of inertia, of hopelessness, and of ignorance, and [the French aristocracy] will no longer be political or chivalrous; it will be nothing, support nothing, be of use to no one, and contribute nothing!"[250] Those who sought to preserve the purity of the nobility by insulating it from the passions of public life were in his view greatly mistaken: "You think to save the morality of the French aristocracy by preserving it from daily contact with revolutions, but I think that only by this contact can it be prepared to understand them and capable and worthy of control-

---

[247] Alphonse de Chateaubriand, *Mémoires d'outre-tombe* (Paris: Librairie Générale, 1973), 1:41.

[248] Blanc de Saint-Bonnet, *De la restauration française*, 255–56.

[249] Mailly-Nesle, *La révolution est-elle finie?*, 33–34.

[250] Falloux, *Mémoires d'un royaliste*, 2:215.

ling them."[251] The only solution was therefore to bring the nobility back into public office. In the words of Muller, "It is necessary to open other careers and avenues than mere pleasures to those we call the blessed of the earth; it is imperative to struggle against the habits of idleness that are destroying them, to give them a function in the state, and to occupy their leisure by offices whose sole remuneration would be honor."[252] Thus, from this perspective, the road to social and moral salvation went through politics.

In short, the legitimist justification of the nobility's leading role in local institutions was all at once political, ideological, and pragmatic. But it was hard not to notice that the sum of the arguments advanced was profoundly contradictory. Legitimists spoke of the need to open local office to all talents. In the words of Blanc de Saint-Bonnet, "From all classes, free rein should be given to virtue, merit and loyalty, honors, and social advantages; here are, in the eyes of the king, the guarantees of happiness and peace."[253] But, at the same time, legitimist writers maintained that wealth and social influence should be decisive factors in the recruitment of local political elites. Chambord was at pains to defend the legitimist party from accusations of exclusive service to the cause of aristocratic interests: "I will not be the king of an exclusive class, but the monarch or rather the father of all."[254] Yet, as we have just seen, legitimists freely contended that no social class was more apt to provide social and moral leadership in the localities than the nobility.

However, the deepest incongruity lay in the contrast between the sociological reality of the aristocracy and its ideological representation by legitimist intellectuals. As an ideal, the nobility was presented as a valuable model for the rest of society; hence the justification of its dominant presence in local government. But the same writers recognized the real aristocracy of the 1850s and 1860s as morally corrupt and politically incompetent — in effect, possessing the very opposite qualities of those required for successful leadership. Even by legitimist standards, this was a particularly difficult circle to square.

THE PRECONDITIONS OF SOCIAL LIBERTY

The promotion of greater liberty lay at the heart of legitimist schemes for redefining the notion of citizenship in France. However, a closer scrutiny of legitimist conceptions of social liberty unearthed a further

[251] Ibid., 214.

[252] Muller, *La légitimité*, 225.

[253] Blanc de Saint-Bonnet, *Politique réelle*, 77.

[254] Letter to Duc de Noailles, 22 December 1850, in *Correspondance*, by Chambord, 108.

set of contradictions. In common with all political movements, legitimists proclaimed their strong attachment to the principle of freedom, and indeed they often presented their own doctrine of decentralization as a vindication of the idea of liberty. Chambord wrote of individual and collective liberties as being "inalienable and sacred."[255] Béchard argued that the structures of local government should consist of "a system of free expansion of human conscience, intelligence, and activity."[256] Calonne even went so far as to reduce the whole issue of decentralization to a question of individual liberty.

> Individual liberty, this is the true foundation of decentralization . . . the task of decentralization does not reside in a reform of the departmental and communal system, as our experts seem to think; it requires above all a revision of our civil legislation, so as to make free men of all us serfs who are presently enchained by the state.[257]

The list of freedoms to be restored was extensive; it included freedom of expression and association but also that of education, as well as the freedom to own property and to construct houses, bridges, roads, and churches.[258] In this approach, therefore, legitimist writers viewed freedom as a set of rights that needed to be claimed against the state. These rights were restricted only by the harm principle (they were valid insofar as they did not impinge on the essential freedoms of others). They could be exercised by collective groups and associations but also by territorial entities such as communes and departments. Their ultimate fulfillment, however, lay in their enjoyment by the individual citizen. In short, this notion of freedom was rights-based, individualistic, and nonrestrictive.

Yet this open conception of freedom proclaimed in some legitimist writings was subverted by an altogether different approach, in which the emphasis was placed on almost the opposite values. Against those legitimists who defined liberty as a right, it was stressed that freedom was above all a duty. In the words of Ségur, liberty was "the power to fulfill without obstacles the true *duties* of the citizen."[259] Against those who demanded the extension of political liberties, it was underlined that freedom was a good that should be offered only in measured doses: "Giving too much power to the people is often detrimental to its free-

---

[255] Letter to Duc de Lévis, 12 March 1856, in *Manifestes et programmes politiques*, by Chambord, 11.

[256] Béchard, *La commune, l'Eglise et l'Etat*, 1:xi.

[257] Calonne, "De la décentralisation," 52.

[258] Ibid., 53.

[259] Ségur, *La Révolution*, 90; emphasis added.

dom."[260] Against those who regarded political freedom as an essential component of a liberal society, it was argued that "political liberty is of a very low order; indeed, it does not represent true liberty."[261] And most fundamentally, against those who believed that liberty could serve as one of the foundations of political order, it was emphasized that freedom was in fact a highly subversive principle: "When there is somewhere a great state of political agitation, it is a strange idea to try to appease or destroy it by raising the banner of liberty; one might just as well try to put out a fire with combustible elements."[262]

These two conflicting discourses were ultimately the expression of a contingent view of freedom. In effect, legitimists regarded liberty as a conditional good, whose realization depended on a prior set of specifications. Blanc de Saint-Bonnet spelled out the necessary qualifications for the exercise of liberty: "Everyone agrees that Christian nations have to be left a judicious amount of freedom. But this prudent limit is easy to determine: it is to give the freedom to do good, and to deny the freedom to do evil and to destroy oneself."[263] Vaillant was in full agreement: "A judicious degree of freedom is that which never veers away from its legitimate goal and remains practical so as not to encourage agitation."[264] An example of a "harmful" type of liberty that legitimists (and especially intransigent Catholics) often mentioned was the freedom of the press. Thus Muller rejected the notion that such a freedom was a desirable goal: no individual or group could claim an inalienable right to excite public opinion and preach insurrection.[265] A retired priest from Besançon was even more forthright:

> The true means of supporting genuine freedom is to proscribe its evil aspect, which leads fatally to anarchy or despotism. The church has always agreed to this denial of malevolent liberty and will always agree to it; she cannot do otherwise, for tolerance, in this case, would only lead to a confusion of good and evil and drive communities toward indifference and skepticism.[266]

The legitimist conception of liberty was therefore deontological, in that it presupposed a theory of the good life. This philosophical underpinning enabled legitimists to make a clear distinction between good

---

[260] Rainneville, *Catholiques tolérants*, 8.

[261] Jean Loyseau, *Pouvoir et liberté* (Paris: Dillet, 1872), 360.

[262] Du Boys, *Des principes de la révolution française*, 7.

[263] Blanc de Saint-Bonnet, *Politique réelle*, 74.

[264] Vaillant, *Décentralisation et régime représentatif*, 30.

[265] Muller, *La légitimité*, 158.

[266] Abbé Boisson, *Essai sur le libéralisme en réponse aux libéraux catholiques* (Besançon: Tubergue, 1869), 12.

and harmful liberty. In this context, most definitions of valid liberties offered in legitimist writings stressed the essential link between freedom and religion. Belcastel asserted that the true basis of freedom could be found only in the principle of "divine sovereignty."[267] Veuillot noted that "religious freedom contains within it all true freedoms"[268] and that all other conceptions of liberty were chimerical: "For us Catholics, freedom can be only a means of gaining or preserving order and freedom. And order and freedom are above all the respect of God's law."[269] All conceptions of freedom, both public and private, were therefore derived from this axiom.

This perspective also colored the legitimist delineation of the specific range of freedoms that should obtain in an effective system of local liberty. In this respect the key premise was that man needed to be internally free before he could be entrusted with the liberty to administer his external acts. Coquille underlined the point: "All forms of *self-government* are founded on the Catholic principle. Despotism is born from the weakening of the church."[270] Hence the paradox of freedom: man could achieve civic liberty only if he recognized his subordination to a higher set of moral and religious laws. In the words of Coquille again: "To govern and administer oneself, and to be judged by one's peers, is all that political freedom amounts to. This freedom has as its necessary foundation customs and traditions, as well as the religious principle."[271] In 1838 Berryer had taken this point to its extreme (but logical) conclusion by arguing that the emancipation of slaves was a worse condition than slavery itself unless it was preceded by their religious and moral education: "Freedom without morality, without work, is slavery; indeed, it is a hundred times worse than slavery!"[272]

This traditionalist notion of freedom also explained the emphasis legitimists placed on issues of social morality, particularly religious education. An important element in the legitimist program for local government was to enable communes to establish religious associations that could operate without state interference in areas such as charity, public works, and education.[273] A legitimist journalist explained the essential

[267] Belcastel, *La citadelle de la liberté*, 14.

[268] Veuillot, *Mélanges religieux*, no. 3, 2:215.

[269] Veuillot, *Les odeurs de Paris*, 13. See also Ed. de Gavardie, *Etudes sur les vraies doctrines sociales et politiques* (Pau: Veronese, 1862), 296.

[270] Coquille, *Politique chrétienne*, 114.

[271] Ibid., 113.

[272] Antoine Berryer, "Discours sur l'abolition de l'esclavage," 15 February 1838, in *Oeuvres de Berryer* (Paris: Didier, 1872), 2:331.

[273] Sébastien Laurentie, in *L'Union*, 6 January 1870.

connection between decentralization and the development of religious associational activity.

> Communes, towns, and departments have the right to partake in the found-ing of free associations, whatever title they may be given, or to attribute educational functions to already founded organizations that are deemed worthy of exercising them. In this way, freedom of education is linked to municipal and provincial freedom; it is an essential aspect of decentraliza-tion.[274]

The hesitations and frequent contortions of the legitimists on the question of determining the limits of local liberty ultimately stemmed from the ambiguities inherent in their conceptions of freedom. At one level legitimists (especially those of a liberal disposition) tended to see civil and political freedom as inalienable rights, which had been sancti-fied by the French Revolution. Their discourse on civic liberty was in this sense often indistinguishable from that of Orleanist liberals, moder-ate republicans, and liberal Bonapartists: there was a common emphasis on the protection of the individual, the definition of positive political and associative rights, and the preservation of human conscience from the dictates of coercive norms. Other legitimists (notably those of a mil-itantly religious disposition) rejected this framework in its entirety. Free-dom was for them not a right but a duty, not an individual entitlement but a collective goal, and, most essentially, not a privilege of private consciences but a commandment of moral law: "Freedom is everything that makes the individual abstract from himself and his own interests in view of the general interest."[275]

The application of this contradictory conceptual framework to com-munal and departmental government and politics could produce only striking contradictions. Legitimists were in favor of freedom of con-science, but they also advocated banning corruptive newspapers and journals. They supported the principle of freedom of religion but often attempted to deny non-Catholics the rights of burial in the communal cemetery. They celebrated the temperamental and cultural diversity of France, thereby accepting and even encouraging the free expression of its social diversity, but allowed no such discretion in the moral and religious sphere. Finally, they aspired to liberate the individual citizen from the oppressive norms of the Jacobin administration and the Civil

---

[274] Rouyé, in *L'Union*, 15 March 1870.
[275] Broise, *Le vrai et le faux libéralisme*, 124. The similarity with certain forms of Jac-obinism is compelling.

Code, but they also argued that his ultimate freedom lay in an unquestioning affirmation of his allegiance to custom, tradition, and religion.

The Limits of Universal Suffrage

This philosophical ambiguity about the notion of freedom was also apparent in the sphere of political liberty, particularly over the question of universal suffrage.

Even before the Second Empire, it is fair to note, legitimist writers were somewhat perplexed by the matter. At certain times liberal legitimists had sought to reconcile the monarchy with political modernity by embracing the principle of the (male) universal vote, whereas traditionalists had objected that the latter represented an unacceptable dilution of the monarchical principle. At other moments the debate was further complicated by the intrusion of tactical considerations. For much of the July Monarchy many traditionalist legitimists, conscious of the appeal of Bourbon royalism in rural constituencies, advocated universal suffrage as a means of countering the privileged electoral rights of the urban bourgeoisie.[276] Conversely, in 1850 the majority of liberal legitimists, terrified by the swelling tide of popular radicalism, endorsed an electoral law that severely restricted the voting rights of the working population.[277] In broad terms, the legitimist view of universal suffrage during the Second Empire was characterized by similar divisions over questions of principle and tactics. But the general trend was inimical to the principle of universal voting rights; this hostility was mingled with a great deal of intellectual uncertainty about its application to local politics.

The confusion about the role and limits of universal suffrage ran so deep within the legitimist tradition that frequently it was encountered in the writings of the same individual. Muller, for example, noted approvingly that universal suffrage was an excellent instrument for protecting conservative interests.[278] But at another juncture he appeared skeptical of the value of majority rule: "It is not a people with a rebellious spirit and advanced civilization such as ours who will ever appreciate that one or two additional votes can legitimately give an advantage to one party rather than another."[279]

Veuillot was equally incoherent about the political consequences of universal suffrage. At one moment he asserted most emphatically that

---

[276] Denis, *Les royalistes de la Mayenne*, 268.

[277] Stéphane Rials, "Les royalistes français et le suffrage universel au XIXeme siècle," in *Révolution et contre-révolution*, 155.

[278] Muller, *La légitimité*, 143.

[279] Ibid., 15.

the popular vote, lacking all coherence or sense of purpose, could only degenerate into anarchy and violence: "The destiny of the multitude is to be lifted by the winds, to scatter, to be blinded, to stain, to fall, and to allow power to guide it wherever it wants."[280] Yet elsewhere he also maintained that the most subversive social category in France was not the proletariat or the peasantry but the middle classes. Indeed, left to its own devices, universal suffrage appeared as an inherently counter-revolutionary political instrument: "Since the last fifty years the assem-blies emanating from bourgeois suffrage have been revolutionary; they were the ones which made 1830 and 1848. Left to themselves, the peo-ple have always opposed the Revolution; all the great exercises in uni-versal suffrage attest to this; all the titles that the Napoleonic dynasty holds from it, from the first to the last, are counterrevolutionary."[281] Not only did the people not lack a sense of political purpose, it seemed their primary instincts were in fact highly favorable to order and social conservation.

A clearer sense of the legitimists' ambivalence may be obtained by examining their specific objections to universal suffrage. First, as men-tioned earlier, many traditionalists felt that such a system constituted an affront to the hierarchical principle inherent in the hereditary monarchy. In the words of Blanc de Saint-Bonnet, "The displacement of social power by universal suffrage represents the overthrow of hierarchy, the degradation of man, the destruction of the achievements of history, and the dissolution of peoples."[282] A second common objection was that uni-versal suffrage, by giving equal weight to every vote, in effect rewarded ignorance at the expense of intelligence: "Is there anything more con-trary to the truth than to place at the same level the highest and lowest forms of intelligence and to hold them as equivalent; to hold as equal the deepest form of learning and the crassest form of stupidity; to hold as equal the fortune that procures independence to man and the sense of need that makes him dependent upon others?"[283]

Third, great concern was expressed about the unpredictable nature of electoral outcomes. Joseph de Rainneville, although politically inclined toward liberalism, rejected universal suffrage because "we fear the in-consistency of the multitude."[284] Falloux viewed the electorate as "a vast assemblage of secondary prejudices and permanent interests"; it was impossible for such an uncoordinated mass to identify the general inter-

---

[280] Veuillot, *Les odeurs de Paris*, x–xi.

[281] Veuillot, *Mélanges religieux*, no. 3, 2:421–22.

[282] Antoine Blanc de Saint-Bonnet, *La loi électorale* (Paris: Casterman, 1875), 14.

[283] Comte de Gardane, *De la souveraineté nationale* (Paris: Le Chevalier, 1868), 28.

[284] Rainneville, *Catholiques tolérants*, 9.

est, let alone to respond to it.[285] More particularly, the practice of the mass vote was suspected because of the malleability of the electorate and its predisposition to accept the impositions of centralized authority. A legitimist journalist stated in 1870: "We regard universal suffrage as the most effective auxiliary of centralization. For eighteen years, have we not seen it be humbly subservient to the wishes of those in power? We fear its complacency as much as its anger; enthusiasm that comes too easily can lead to prolonged failures."[286]

Finally, universal suffrage was also inadequate for the type of political elite it produced. Coquille drew an analogy between the instrument and its outcome: "The election from below only produces lowly men, whose sentiments and ideas are a common reflection of those of the collectivity."[287] Commenting on the 1865 municipal elections, a legitimist journalist asserted: "If there is one word that can be applied to the current municipal elections, it is the term 'revolutionary' . . . the functions of councillor fall at every election into the hands of a lower class."[288] The systematic exclusion of "honest" virtues from the electoral system drew the following tirade from Veuillot:

> Universal suffrage has given us many false figures. We have seen at the rostrum professional comedians, irregulars of all kinds, even Negroes; but the true man of the people, the true peasant, the indisputable worker, the man of open heart and common sense upon whom rests all the burdens of social life . . . who has seen him since 1789?[289]

Given this broad range of objections to the principle and practice of universal suffrage, legitimists were naturally guarded about its application to local politics. There were some cautious expressions of support. Despite his reservations about its principle, Falloux maintained that the universal vote in its current form was desirable at the communal level, because it generally produced conservative majorities.[290] Fontarèches argued that voters would be able to make reasoned choices in communal and cantonal elections but not in legislative ones: "The electoral mass is necessarily blind and ignorant when it comes to the nomination of deputies."[291] The reason for this distinction was not entirely clear in legitimist writings. Was the electorate better placed to make the appropriate

[285] Falloux, *Mémoires d'un royaliste*, 2:153.
[286] Mayol de Lupé, in *L'Union*, 16 April 1870. Note the "personalization" of universal suffrage.
[287] Coquille, *La royauté française*, 52.
[288] Quoted in Broise, *Le vrai et le faux libéralisme*, 80–81.
[289] Veuillot, *Mélanges religieux*, no. 3, 3:412.
[290] Falloux, *Mémoires d'un royaliste*, 2:409.
[291] Fontarèches, *La décentralisation*, 118.

choices at the local level because it was more likely to know the candidates? Or was it rather that the mass of voters could perfectly well understand local issues but were incapable of grasping great matters of state?

Even more worrisome were the actual and potential political consequences of the system. Most legitimists were concerned that universal suffrage would give too much power to the populations of the communes, a fear that largely inspired legitimist opposition to the election of mayors by universal suffrage.[292] Clozel de Boyer deplored the handing over of power to the "beardless tramps" of society;[293] Laurentie similarly warned that communal elections organized under universal suffrage would simply deliver the communes and departments "to the demented utopians."[294] Last, many thought the mass vote was unsuitable for local elections because it excluded an important range of legitimate interests. In an article published the day before his death in January 1870, Béchard condemned universal suffrage in local elections as contrary to the interests of the propertied classes.

> Individual and direct universal suffrage . . . without any conditions other than a residence requirement of six months in the department or canton exclusively represents the interests of the classes that are little taxed and leaves without defense the interests of property. Unless reformed, such an electoral system will invariably hand over the administration of communes to those with little interest in preventing the dilapidation of our finances.[295]

There were two possible solutions to this problem of underrepresentation: special provisions could be made to ensure the presence of propertied interests on local councils through some form of corporate representation, or—more radically—the electorate could be restricted to those with a direct stake in local administration, "those men, heads of household or landowners, who have to bear the costs of the contributions voted by the general and municipal councils."[296] This proposal to restore the limited suffrage brought into the open what had been implicit in much of the earlier discussions about the universal vote: for legitimists, political liberty could not be entirely divorced from social privilege. Political institutions were free to the extent that they defended or promoted the interests of certain sections of society. More broadly, political freedom depended not on the citizen's capacity to make ratio-

---

[292] Cosnac, *Discours à la Commission de décentralisation*, 30.

[293] Clozel de Boyer, *Monarchie ou anarchie*, 23–24.

[294] *L'Union*, 16 March 1870.

[295] Ferdinand Béchard, "Garanties contre le socialisme dans les élections locales," *L'Union*, 6 January 1870.

[296] Ibid.

nal decisions but on the prior existence of a healthy social and moral framework.

Although on the liberal wing of the legitimist party, Albert Du Boys expressed his skepticism toward political change by an organic metaphor: "Should social reform not in all circumstances precede and take primacy over political reform? Should one not heal a sick patient before asking him to carry out actions that presuppose health and strength?"[297] Clearly, an unhealthy society could not be entrusted with as dangerous and unpredictable an instrument as universal suffrage.

THE CONTRADICTIONS OF THE LEGITIMIST PROJECT

Redefining the principles of citizenship through territorial reform placed the French legitimist movement in a curious and somewhat paradoxical position at the end of the Second Empire. On one level, legitimists could take pride in the apparent conversion of all major political forces to the idea of greater communal and departmental autonomy. Once the ideological preserve of marginal and embittered relics of the ancien régime, the doctrine of decentralization had become a universally recognized political principle by 1870. As we will note in the following chapter, the liberals also played an important role in shifting public attitudes on the matter (especially during the 1860s). But it was the legitimists who kept the torch of local liberty burning throughout the July Monarchy, the Second Republic, and the Second Empire. The triumph of decentralist ideas in the final years of the Bonapartist regime was in no small way a tribute to the selflessness and dedication with which two generations of legitimists defended the doctrine of local liberty between 1830 and 1870.

The paradox, however, was that — unlike the republican movement — this intellectual success was of little discernible benefit to the legitimist party. Its parliamentary representation remained comparatively modest; its autonomous political networks, controlled in principle from Frohsdorf, were generally somnolent; even its impressive cohort of communal and departmental elected representatives remained relatively passive. These limitations were symptoms of more general weaknesses of the legitimist movement: a tendency toward internal fragmentation and petty division; a political leadership that (with a few notable exceptions) lacked both strategic vision and tactical acumen; and above all a monarch who, for all his honor and integrity, was a monument to atavism and political ineptitude.[298]

---

[297] Albert Du Boys, *Mémoires*, quoted in *Le légitimisme dauphinois, 1830–1870*, by Bernard Jacquier (Paris: CRHESI, 1976), 107.

[298] Léonce de Brotonne, "Les partis monarchistes sous le Second Empire," *La Nouvelle Revue* (November–December 1885): 256.

Assessed on its own terms, the legitimist doctrine of decentralization represented a significant contribution to the debate about the reform of local social and political life in France. As we have seen throughout this chapter, the legitimist project contained a number of highly distinctive features: the stipulation of a necessary link between decentralization and monarchical institutions; the key role assigned to religious institutions and aristocratic government; the severe condemnation of Paris (which was amplified after the Paris Commune and led to legitimist and Catholic calls for a "decapitalization" of the city);[299] the preference for a departmental as opposed to a communal system of decentralization; proposals for a radical overhaul of the administrative structure; and a conception of freedom that was conditioned by the imperatives of social and moral norms.

I offer three brief remarks about the project as a whole. First, the congruence of these proposals with the social and political interests of the legitimists is obvious. The political and administrative structures envisaged in the proposed reforms were legitimist in character and purpose; similarly, the personnel of local assemblies was to be recruited from a social class that was overwhelmingly favorable to the legitimist cause. Furthermore, the locus of power in the legitimist local government system was not the commune, where legitimists were sometimes weak, but the department, where their political representation was considerable.

Second, the legitimist evaluation of centralization was in many respects trenchant, even though legitimist writers showed a marked tendency to exaggerate the significance of administrative dysfunctions. Their analysis was most telling in areas with which they were most familiar: the social and moral atrophy of provincial life and the devastating effects of urbanization on rural communities. In this sense, the legitimist critique can be read as a final, anguished farewell to a form of sociability that was on the verge of extinction: a world of gentility and simplicity, of local concerns and innocent pleasures, in which every member of the community knew his station and his overall purpose in life. Of the specific solutions the legitimists advanced, the most radical was the reestablishment of provincial territorial divisions and regional governments, an interesting (although not necessarily decentralizing) idea that had to wait more than a century to be executed — ironically by a Socialist administration.

Finally, the organic character of the legitimist proposals is striking. The project could not be implemented piecemeal, because its core components depended on and reinforced each other. The monarchy guaran-

---

[299] See, for example, Comte de Galembert's pamphlet *De la décentralisation et du transfert en province de la capitale politique de la France* (Tours: Mame, 1871).

teed the constitutional freedoms of the localities; the latter, in turn, could enjoy their autonomous privileges only because they all partook in a common identification with the sovereign. It was in the best interests of communes and departments to be led by the aristocracy; at the same time, the aristocracy needed public office in order to affirm and realize its social and political vocation. The liberation of communes entailed the promotion of religious and moral institutions at the local level; these institutions could thrive only in a political culture that welcomed and guaranteed the sacred principles of the Catholic faith.

There were, however, two overarching problems with this legitimist project: it was unclear under what circumstances it could be achieved, and many of its internal provisions were not entirely consistent. The achievement of the legitimist program for local government was problematic because it was difficult to foresee the circumstances that would make possible its implementation. If their critique of the atrophy of social institutions was correct, it seemed impossible that the desired political order could emerge spontaneously through the activities of local groups and associations. In any event, as previously noted, a piecemeal approach was not practicable: only a change at the apex of the political system could bring about the new decentralized order in the departments and communes. But for such a legislative reform to occur, all other parties would have to be convinced that the legitimist scheme for local government reform was superior to their own — a highly unlikely eventuality. The only possible scope for influencing policy, therefore, was through an alliance with other parties. But alliances necessarily required ideological compromises, and compromises would undoubtedly have eroded the distinctive features of the legitimist project — as many anxious legitimist writers noted during the 1860s.

The greater problem, however, lay in the internal coherence of the scheme. The legitimists' aspirations to redefine the principles of citizenship along decentralist lines were afflicted by a number of essential contradictions. The first concerned the nature of political activity. One strand of legitimism was — rather like the conservative and authoritarian undercurrent within Bonapartism — instinctively suspicious of "high" politics and accordingly devoted itself to creating a system of local government that excluded political passions as much as possible. Hence legitimist proposals to depoliticize communal and departmental elections, ban multiple office-holding, and prevent the publicity of discussions of local assemblies; hence also their hostility to the election of mayors by universal suffrage. Yet this logic of depoliticization was undermined by a profoundly ideological vision of the purposes of local government, which remained defined in highly political (and partisan) terms. The advocacy of aristocratic rule and religious education was nothing if not a political goal. To believe that an apolitical and consensual form of local government could be constructed on the basis of such principles was quite simply to indulge in wishful thinking.

The second element of tension was no less striking. Legitimist theorists spared no effort to highlight the social and moral excellence of the aristocracy, which was represented as the repository of all the best social virtues: the nobility was (among other things) pious, honest, selfless, and compassionate. It seemed therefore quite natural that this exemplary class should be given a privileged role in the refurbished structures of local government. But this assignment was inconsistent with two other claims made by the legitimists. It was incompatible with the proposition that they favored the equal access of all groups of citizens to positions of honor and influence: how could the appointment of aristocrats to key positions in the national and provincial bureaucracies, for example, be reconciled with the principle of equality of opportunity? Even more paradoxically, it was also inconsistent with the legitimists' severe critique of the social mores of the aristocracy. For there were few more severe strictures against the perversion and depravity of the nobility during the Second Empire than the fiery lines written by Falloux and Blanc de Saint-Bonnet. But if their class was so degenerate, how plausible could be its claim to represent the natural government of the provinces?

The third contradiction lay in the legitimists' general conception of the state, from which their particular notion of decentralization was derived. In their criticism of the republican and Bonapartist views of public authority, legitimists roundly condemned the idea of the providential state. In their eyes, the state had a duty to defend the community against external threats, to maintain public security, and to administer general utilities. It had no distinct vocation beyond these essential functions, and especially not that of legislating for the political and material welfare of its citizens. The implication of this position was that the state should remain neutral with respect to different conceptions of the good life; happiness was a matter for the private concerns of the citizenry. But this rejection of public intervention was apparently forgotten when the legitimists aspired to promote their own ideological objectives. In the communal and departmental life, for example, legitimists were committed to defending highly normative forms of existence: an aristocratic code of values, a strict set of moral principles, and a religious conception of social life. Under such circumstances, there was not a great deal of scope left for the concept of public neutrality.

Finally, and perhaps most important, there were incoherences in the notion of local liberty that legitimists advocated. Two inconsistencies are particularly revealing. An important legitimist objection to Bonapartist practice was the deprivation of local communities' political rights. Until the late 1860s, individual citizens were denied basic rights of association and expression; throughout the Second Empire, the integrity of universal suffrage was compromised by the direction, manipulation, and frequent intimidation of voters. Legitimist demands for the emancipation of the provinces were therefore partly couched in terms of restoring the exercise of these basic political freedoms to the individual citizen. But although there is no reason to doubt the sincerity of its expression, this project of individual liberation was subverted by an alternative and conflicting set of priorities. It was weakened first by a program of social, moral, and religious reconstruction which was both hierarchical and anti-individualistic. Legitimist social theory rejected rationalist notions of human independence and moral autonomy; it also condemned as anti-Christian any radical conception of social equality. Instead, it offered a conception of freedom that lay particular emphasis on duty, responsibility, and the recognition of superior and unquestionable social and moral norms. Legitimists were therefore favorable to breaking the imperial stranglehold on civil and political liberties, but only to replace it with an equally burdensome set of social and moral restrictions on the citizenry.

The legitimist project of liberation was also undermined by a marked reluctance to concede full political rights in the electoral sphere. Decentralization was meant to enable a greater degree of public participation and involvement in local affairs. Indeed, one of the most telling legitimist criticisms of Bonapartist paternalism was its failure to grant local communities their legitimate influence in the political and administrative systems. However, the legitimist conception of political freedom was also highly restrictive. As we have noted, universal suffrage was generally regarded with suspicion and hostility by legitimists, many of whom sought to qualify its application by introducing restrictions based on property and residence. Withdrawing the vote from entire groups on the grounds of their social and material conditions was not exactly compatible with the project of individual emancipation. To repeat, the problem here was not dissemblance but conflicting priorities. Legitimists genuinely aspired to enhance the political freedoms of the communes' inhabitants, but they doubted that the mass of citizens had the necessary capacities to make adequate use of these liberties. Furthermore, legitimists attached an even greater importance to the defense of propertied interests. When these interests appeared to be under threat by the exercise of collective political rights, then the latter clearly had to be sacrificed.

The most common explanation of the failure of the legitimist party after 1870 is its "anachronism."[300] Legitimists are typically presented as bearers of an outmoded way of life; advocates of retrograde moral customs and deeply reactionary political values that were singularly unsuited to the realities of a mass democracy and a rapidly industrializing society. Chambord's instransigence over the white flag, which sealed the fate of the legitimist party in the early 1870s, is thus typically seen to express an ideological repudiation of "the entire cultural, political, and social legacy of the Revolution."[301] But this dichotomy between tradition and modernity is somewhat too simplistic. As we have seen in this chapter, many liberal legitimists ardently desired to adapt their movement to the exigencies of modern times; in the writings of Falloux, for example, this adaptation was a condition of the party's survival. Furthermore, many legitimists (and indeed often the least liberal ones in political terms) had an acute perception of the causes and manifestations of the social ills of modern industrialized society. The problem, however, was that a clear solution was never found to the conflicting imperatives of liberty and authority. This duality ran not merely among different groups but often within the same individual.

The question of decentralization illustrated the pervasive nature of this dualism among legitimists. For the contradictions we have identified throughout this chapter ultimately stemmed from two radically different types of discourse that coexisted in legitimist writings. The first was a modern discourse on citizenship, in which legitimists spoke the language of freedom, participation, choice, and inalienable rights — all of this clear evidence of an attempt to come to terms with modern politics. However, this language was subverted by a second type of discourse, in which the individual was represented not as a citizen but as a subject: hence the emphasis on allegiance, hierarchy and patriarchy, religious obligation, and moral duty. By the end of the Second Empire, the legitimists were still fundamentally unclear about how to manage the transition from their traditional notion of a community of subjects to the modern concept of a society of citizens. This lack of ideological clarity, together with the inflexibility of the comte de Chambord in the early 1870s, eventually ended the political dreams of French legitimism in the early Third Republic.

[300] Robert R. Locke, *French Legitimists and the Politics of Moral Order in the Early Third Republic* (Princeton: Princeton University Press, 1974), 270.
[301] Steven Kale, "The Monarchy According to the King: The Ideological Context of the *drapeau blanc*, 1871–1873," *French History* 2, no. 4 (December 1988): 423.

Chapter 3

BETWEEN HOPE AND FEAR: THE LIMITS OF LIBERAL CONCEPTIONS OF DECENTRALIZATION

TRAVELING through provincial France in 1863, Hippolyte Taine mused that his countrymen seemed to have an inordinate capacity to suffer "without difficulty, and even willingly, being organized and regimented."[1] He concluded despondently: "The state of France resembles a state of siege: at every instant the freedom of the individual is sacrificed to the state."[2] Writing in the *Revue des Deux Mondes* one year later, Charles de Rémusat complained that "France is trapped in the tightly meshed nets of an administration that is accountable to no one."[3]

Opposition to political absolutism and administrative tyranny is the essential hallmark of liberal thinking, and this chapter will show that liberal intellectuals and politicians played an important role in the debate on local liberty and citizenship during the Second Empire. A minority of thinkers and public figures, inspired by the Jacobin tradition, continued to see political and administrative centralization as an incontrovertible benefit.[4] For such men — most notably Adolphe Thiers and Charles Dupont-White[5] — the state provided a set of goods that were invaluable for promoting the general interest and the values of good citizenship.[6]

Most liberals, however, agreed that the state was a "predatory universal administrator" whose expansionary instincts needed to be curbed to

---

[1] Hippolyte Taine, *Carnets de voyage: Notes sur la province, 1863–1865* (Paris: Hachette, 1897), 190.

[2] Ibid., 234.

[3] Charles de Rémusat, "Situation politique de la France," *Revue des Deux Mondes*, 15 October 1864, 917.

[4] See, for example, Virgile Mouline, *Etude sur la centralisation, son origine et ses résultats* (Dijon: Lamarche, 1863), and Alfred Legoyt, *De la centralisation administrative* (Paris: Revue Administrative, 1849). The latter being a head of division at the Ministry of the Interior, his defense of centralism was perhaps not too surprising.

[5] The best biographical study is by Henri Malo, *Thiers, 1797–1877* (Paris: Payot, 1932); for an overview of Dupont-White's life and career, see Emile de Laveleye, *Un précurseur: Charles Dupont-White* (Paris: Imprimerie Nationale, 1888).

[6] For an analysis of the life and political philosophy of Dupont-White, see my article "A Jacobin, Liberal, Socialist, and Republican Synthesis: The Original Political Thought of Charles Dupont-White (1807–1878)," *History of European Ideas* (1998).

enable the flourishing of greater political liberty and civic virtue.[7] A liberal grandee recorded in his memoirs: "An energetic campaign had been mounted throughout the Empire by liberals of all persuasion against the excessive centralization of public administration and the absorption of all social activity by the domination of the state. It was our favorite theme."[8]

But, as during much of the nineteenth and early twentieth centuries, there was an enigmatic and even mysterious quality to the liberal phenomenon in France during this period.[9] On one hand, French political history in these years can be read in terms of a progressive development of liberal ideas and liberal institutions. Albert Thibaudet had this very point in mind when he declared that "there is in France an undercurrent of liberalism and liberal ideas which is much more robust than is generally believed."[10] Perhaps so, and in a sense this chapter is making the same point. On the other hand — and this is where the problem begins — this strength is often difficult to isolate with precision. For one thing, it is obscured by the apparent inability of liberals to recognize the central elements of their own doctrine, or indeed even each other. Writing at the turn of the century, at the height of the liberal regime of the Third Republic, the republican sociologist Emile Faguet paradoxically confessed: "I do not think I have ever, in all my life, met a Frenchman who was a liberal."[11] A generation later, Emmanuel Beau de Loménie lambasted the use of the term, "the source of so many absurd and dishonest confusions."[12]

An evocation of the great liberal figures of nineteenth-century French political thought brings further mystification. Benjamin Constant and Alexis de Tocqueville immediately spring to mind,[13] yet the latter never

---

[7] Eugène Poitou, *La liberté civile et le pouvoir administratif en France* (Paris: Charpentier, 1869), 86.

[8] Albert de Broglie, *Mémoires du Duc de Broglie* (Paris: Calmann Lévy, 1938), 1:348.

[9] On the early history of liberal institutions and ideas, see Paul Thureau-Dangin, *Le parti libéral sous la Restauration* (Paris: Plon, 1876); on Say's attitudes toward colonialism, see H. Oppenheimer, *Le libéralisme français au début du XIXeme siècle* (Paris: Sirey, 1930); on the post-Revolutionary generation of French liberals, see Cheryl B. Welch, *Liberty and Utility: The French Idéologues and the Transformation of Liberalism* (New York: Columbia University Press, 1984).

[10] Albert Thibaudet, *Les idées politiques de la France* (Paris: Stock, 1932), 49.

[11] Emile Faguet, *Le libéralisme* (Poitiers: Société Française, 1902), 307. On the ideological evolution of liberalism after 1870, see William Logue, *From Philosophy to Sociology: The Evolution of French Liberalism, 1870–1914* (Dekalb: Northern Illinois University Press, 1983).

[12] Emmanuel Beau de Loménie, *Les responsabilités des dynasties bourgeoises* (Paris: Denoël, 1943), 1:20.

[13] On Constant, see Stephen Holmes, *Benjamin Constant and the Making of Modern Liberalism* (New Haven: Yale University Press, 1984); for a comparison of the two men,

seriously read the works of the former.[14] Indeed, Constant's works seem
to have been more appreciated by legitimists than by his fellow liberals.[15]
Later in the century came Ernest Renan, a towering figure by any standards, who subscribed to decentralization yet remained deeply suspicious of the political freedoms demanded by his liberal colleagues during the 1860s;[16] he even wrote that "the latter half of the Second Empire
perhaps gave the greatest amount of freedom realizable in France without provoking excesses."[17]

Most intriguing of all is the position of Tocqueville, whose genius was
recognized by his admirers as much as by those who disagreed fundamentally with his views.[18] However, his intellectual influence on liberal
thought after 1860 was minimal; publicists such as Edouard Laboulaye,[19]
Paul Leroy-Beaulieu, and Lucien-Anatole Prévost-Paradol were much
more often read, discussed, and quoted than the elegant author of *L'Ancien Régime et la Révolution*.[20] This no doubt attests to the relative
weakness of liberalism in France during this period, but it is also perhaps a comment on the intricacy and complexity of Tocqueville's liberalism, which did not lend itself easily to appropriation by political
groups and intellectual currents.

---

see George Armstrong Kelly, *The Humane Comedy: Constant, Tocqueville, and French
Liberalism* (Cambridge: Cambridge University Press, 1992).

[14] This was not so much a slight on Constant as something of a general intellectual
method. Tocqueville confessed that he was incapable of reading the work of others, for
reasons that many will find familiar: "When I have to treat any subject, I find it almost
impossible to read any of the books that have been written on the same question. The
encounter with the ideas of others sends me into a state of such agitation that reading
these books becomes physically painful" (quoted in "Tocqueville," by Emile Faguet, *Revue des Deux Mondes*, 1 February 1894, 645).

[15] For positive references to his work, see, for example, Ferdinand Béchard, *De l'administration de la France: Essai sur les abus de la centralisation* (Paris: Perrodil, 1845), 1:56–
57.

[16] "The cause of administrative decentralization is too popular for us to have to insist
on it any further" (*La réforme intellectuelle et morale* [1871], in *Oeuvres complètes de
Ernest Renan* [Paris: Calmann Lévy, 1947], 1:389–90).

[17] Quoted in Roger Soltau, *French Political Thought in the Nineteenth Century* (London: Ernest Benn, 1931), 225.

[18] For some contemporary views, see Louis de Kergorlay, *Etude littéraire sur Alexis de
Tocqueville* (Paris: Douniol, 1861); Léon Arbaud, "Tocqueville," *Le Correspondant* 31
(January 1866): 5–25; Edouard Laboulaye, "Alexis de Tocqueville," in *L'Etat et ses lim-
ites* (Paris: Charpentier, 1863), 138–201; and Charles Savary, *Alexis de Tocqueville* (Paris:
Retaux, 1870).

[19] For a sharp analysis of Laboulaye's life and intellectual evolution, see Jean de Soto,
"Edouard de Laboulaye," *Revue Internationale d'Histoire Politique et Constitutionnelle*
(1955): 114–50.

[20] On the life and works of Leroy-Beaulieu, see Dan Warshaw, *Paul Leroy-Beaulieu and
Established Liberalism in France* (Dekalb: Northern Illinois University Press, 1991).

To make matters even worse, nineteenth-century French liberalism also has a somewhat protean quality. The elusiveness of the liberal phenomenon emerges immediately in attempts to delineate its precise shape under the Second Empire. For some hostile contemporary observers, this was a thankless task: liberalism was merely a "political chameleon" that "changes color depending on where it finds itself; it lacks a clear banner that can enable its immediate identification."[21] Later historians were often even harsher. Although not at all unsympathetic to its cause, Pierre de la Gorce noted sarcastically that the liberal party of the Second Empire "seemed to reside everywhere without being attached anywhere."[22]

Perhaps as a response to such doubts about their existence, some observers have fallen prey to the opposite affliction: the tendency to see liberals everywhere. In some modern analyses of liberalism in nineteenth-century France, there is indeed a regrettable tendency to conflate liberal ideas and values with those of the liberal movement. As we will note shortly, the 1860s witnessed a remarkable proliferation of liberal tendencies within mainstream political movements. But the existence of these liberal republicans, Bonapartists, and legitimists does not justify the extension of the banner of liberalism to all these individuals and groups, irrespective of their degree of attachment to and entrenchment within their respective political cultures.[23] Defining *any* person who believes in civil and political freedom as a liberal — including notable republicans such as Ferry, Gambetta, Simon, Waldeck-Rousseau, and Vacherot[24] — may at some high level of generality be useful, but it does little to advance a proper philosophical understanding of the specific problems confronting liberals during the Second Empire.

This is not merely a matter of taxonomical convenience. An unduly elastic definition of liberalism greatly obscures the fact that its political representatives shared an unmistakable liberal ethos, which was markedly different from that of the republican, legitimist, and Bonapartist movements. Although operating in different networks and through diverse social and political institutions, there remained a number of common features to this liberal creed: a clear sense of social identity and economic purpose, centering around the defense of bourgeois interests; a cautious and flexible approach to political practice, based on the ad-

---

[21] Baron de Fontarèches, *Libéralisme et révolution* (Paris: Dentu, 1862), 7. See also Alexandre Rémy, *La faction orléaniste* (Paris: Desloges, 1852), 164.

[22] La Gorce, *Histoire du Second Empire*, 4:193.

[23] For instances of the conflation of liberalism with liberal republicanism, see Louis Girard, *Les libéraux français* (Paris: Aubier, 1985), 183; Jardin, *Histoire du libéralisme politique*, 382–91.

[24] For example, Georges Burdeau, *Le libéralisme* (Paris: Editions du Seuil, 1979), 115.

vocacy of moderate change and a rejection of deductive reasoning; an insistence on the unconditional validity of such key values as liberty and the rule of law; a particular conception of the state, derived in large part from this view of liberty; and a specific political and institutional lineage, based on an interpretation of French history since 1789. These principles were enunciated with great vigor (and often equal talent) in liberal writings, most particularly in the liberal press, where publications such as the *Journal des Débats*, the *Temps*, the *Revue des Deux Mondes*, the *Correspondant* (a liberal Catholic publication), and the *Journal de Paris* often set the tone for public discussion in France during the 1860s.[25]

But this is not the sum of the liberal enigma. Mysterious and elusive, nineteenth-century French liberalism is also an intrinsically contradictory phenomenon. This contradiction appears in two dimensions. First, there was a remarkable contrast between the increasing inclusiveness of liberal concepts in the political discourse of the later Second Empire and the actual fortunes of the liberal party. Sympathetic observers at the time noted with pleasure the ideological appeal of liberalism; as one of them stated, "Time passes, and liberal ideas are making progress, spreading, and rallying ever greater numbers."[26] During the 1863 elections, when republican and monarchist opposition groups developed an anti-imperial forum for interparty cooperation against official candidates, it was given the evocative title of Union Libérale. In the 1860s self-styled liberals emerged within the republican party, where even many hitherto Jacobins publicly declared their conversion to liberal values; within the Bonapartist movement, where the so-called *tiers parti* advocated a wide range of political and constitutional changes, many of which were eventually realized in the liberal Empire in 1869–70;[27] and (as we saw in the previous chapter) even among an influential fraction of the legitimist and Catholic party.[28] As a leading liberal pamphleteer noted wryly, "The Empire has produced as many liberals as the republic has conservatives."[29]

Yet this profusion of liberals proved of little value to the liberal party. Indeed, when the imperial regime collapsed in 1870, it was not the lib-

---

[25] Gustave Claudin, *Mes souvenirs, 1840–1870* (Paris: Calmann Lévy, 1884), 201. Other national liberal publications included *La Presse*, *La Revue Nationale*, and the *Courrier du Dimanche*.

[26] Etienne Coquerel, "1868–1869," *Le Lien*, 2 January 1869.

[27] For an example of the program of this grouping, see *Le tiers parti et les libertés intérieures* (Paris: Dentu, 1866), 13–14.

[28] See Charles de Mazade, *L'opposition royaliste: Berryer, de Villèle, de Falloux* (Paris: Plon, 1874), esp. 1–60.

[29] Prévost-Paradol, *Quelques pages d'histoire contemporaine*, 3:287, 290.

erals but the republicans who eventually emerged as the dominant political group in France. The argument of this chapter is that the main explanation for this political failure resided in the lack of intellectual coherence of the liberal project. As we will see, there were profound ideological contradictions in the liberal conceptions of local liberty and citizenship. Critics of the liberals' approach have tended to focus on their political motivations, viewing their espousal of local liberty merely as a convenient means of challenging the power and authority of the Second Empire. For example, Louis Girard sees liberal decentralization as merely a "means of political and social reaction to imperial democracy."[30]

The approach I take here is somewhat different. I agree that liberals were indeed ambivalent about the scope of the decentralist reforms they wished to promote. But this uncertainty was less the product of opportunism or cynicism than the necessary consequence of an attachment to a set of inherently contradictory political values. As the second decade of the Empire unfolded, many liberals became apprehensive about the rise of radical republicanism. They increasingly wondered whether the introduction of wider municipal franchises might unduly weaken the state and unleash destructive passions within the political system and the social order. These interrogations triggered a number of recurring tensions among different liberal goals and principles: preserving social order and promoting political and economic change; advocating greater mass involvement in public life and responding to the paternalistic impulsions of liberal elites; according sanctity to individual and group rights and upholding the general interest; liberating the individual from institutional dependency and maintaining a stable framework for social order; responding to the demands for greater local autonomy and sustaining a sense of national unity; limiting the role of the state and maintaining the unitary structure of the polity; and articulating the interests of the bourgeoisie while proclaiming the transcendence of class conflict in society.

These clashes in many senses reflected tensions among the different ideological principles to which liberals subscribed. The core values on which these principles rested are identified in the next section.

THE UNIVERSALITY OF THE BOURGEOISIE

The social identity of Second Empire liberals centered inexorably around the bourgeoisie and its values. The definition of a bourgeois was elastic; as seen by a liberal daily in 1849, it included small- and large-scale

---

[30] Louis Girard, *Les libéraux français* (Paris: Aubier, 1985), 193.

property owners, industrialists, small business owners, artisans and shopkeepers, functionaries, men of independent means, and even members of the national guard.[31] More than by a set of occupations, the bourgeoisie was identified by a particular way of living and thinking and an attachment to a distinct set of attitudes: a respect for political order, the defense of economic stability, a belief in the necessity of education, a propensity toward moderation in all things, and above all a worship of prudence, which was the cardinal virtue of all good nineteenth-century French liberals.

The interests of these social groups were most prominently articulated by Orleanist liberals, who discreetly assumed the political heritage of the July Monarchy.[32] For those hostile to this tradition, this heritage was simply one of self-interest, corruption, and greed.[33] A legitimist journalist dismissed Orleanism as "the attitude of monopoly and exploitation, the mentality of centralizing tyranny and exclusivism, the spirit of arbitrariness that is hostile to any sort of principle, and finally the tendency toward usurpation which constantly seeks to establish governments that pursue their own interests."[34] In his report to the prefect of Cahors, the police commissioner of Cajarc (Lot) offered the stereotypical Bonapartist view: "The attitude of the public would be good were it not facing the pressure and intrigues of the rich and influential bourgeoisie, which misses the July Monarchy and wishes for its return, in the hope of recapturing power and influence exclusively for themselves."[35]

There was no denying that Orleanist liberalism was a social creed as much as a political ideology. Laboulaye identified middle-class groups as the principal bearers of liberal values: "The strength of any community resides in its middle classes."[36] Many liberals, although noting the universality of the values of the middle classes, denied the existence of a distinct bourgeoisie: "There is no longer in France either a working class or a bourgeoisie. There are parties, sects, and clans; there are no longer any classes, tribes, or castes. In a nation in which there is no nobility, there can be neither bourgeoisie nor working class."[37] A differ-

---

[31] *La Bourgeoisie, Journal des Amis de l'Ordre*, May 1849.

[32] See A. Bardoux, *La bourgeoisie française, 1789–1848* (Paris: Calmann Lévy, 1886).

[33] For example, the liberal Bonapartist Adolphe Guéroult's uncharitable definition of Orleanism in *L'Opinion Nationale*, 7 February 1870: "It is in all things the bourgeois regime and spirit, not as an emanation of the most enlightened part of the nation but as the expression of a system of privileges without roots, without endurance, and without greatness."

[34] H. de Lourdoueix, *La révolution c'est l'orléanisme* (Paris: Dentu, 1852), 214.

[35] Report of November 1864, in Arch. Dépt. Lot, 4 M 28.

[36] Edouard Laboulaye, *Le parti libéral, son programme et son avenir* (Paris: Charpentier, 1864), 29.

[37] Saint-Marc Girardin, *Souvenirs et réflexions politiques d'un journaliste* (Paris: Michel Lévy, 1859), 122.

ent way of making the same point was to claim that the entire society was bourgeois. In the words of the exiled duc d'Aumale, "Let us be serious . . . we are all, whether we like it or not, bourgeois men, and that is indeed all we are." In Aumale's view, the bourgeois spirit was gradually pervading all of society.

> Its habits and its attitudes are slowly but surely seeping into rural France; what the bourgeoisie wants today almost all of France will desire tomorrow. One cannot therefore conduct politics seriously by pretending to ignore or despise the middle classes; it is easy to defy them, for they are not revolutionary. It is not as easy to last without their esteem and support.[38]

Naturally, not all members of the bourgeoisie were liberals between 1852 and 1870; conversely, important figures within the liberal elite such as the Broglie dynasty were of aristocratic origin; some, like Thiers and Prévost-Paradol, even came from lower-middle-class backgrounds.[39] But these exceptions largely confirmed the rule, which was reinforced by a sense of negative identity. Throughout the first half of the nineteenth century, and well into the Second Empire, liberals also defined themselves by a common aversion to the aristocracy, at whose hands they had historically suffered many political humiliations. By the middle of the century, the main threat seemed to emanate from the working class; Adolphe Thiers denounced the "vile multitude,"[40] whose illiteracy and amoralism were deemed to pose a persistent threat to the orderly way of life that the bourgeoisie cherished. This degeneration was often contrasted with the ideal virtues of the masses. "The people," in the words of a liberal publication, "are the noble and honest throng that reasons and works and that, child, husband, brother, and father, forms the productive hive of bees that is France."[41]

This distinct identity of liberal elites was also a function of shared sociological attributes: in cultural dispositions, a positive bias toward education and learning, reflected in the significant number of Orleanist and liberal Catholic grandees elected to the Academie Française during the Second Empire (Montalembert, Silvestre de Sacy, Victor and Albert de Broglie, Dufaure, Prévost-Paradol, d'Haussonville);[42] in occupational terms, an overrepresentation of liberal professions among its po-

[38] Duc d'Aumale, "Lettres de Vérax," in *Ecrits politiques, 1861–1868* (Brussels: Briard, 1869) 164.

[39] Malo, *Thiers*, 7–20; Guiral, *Prévost-Paradol*, 16–21.

[40] An expression used in a speech on 24 May 1850, in *Discours parlementaires de M. Thiers* (Paris: Calmann Lévy, 1880–81), 9:40.

[41] *Le Libéral*, August 1849.

[42] For a scintillating portrait of this generation of *immortels*, see Jules Barbey d'Aurevilly, *Les quarante médaillons de l'Académie* (1863; reprint, Paris: Armand Colin, 1993).

Fig. 6. Duc Victor de Broglie (1785–1870), lithography Grégoire et Deneux, Bibliothèque Nationale, Paris. A leading Orleanist under Louis Philippe, de Broglie was one of the main liberal pamphleteers during the Second Empire and a member of the Académie Française. His son Albert de
Broglie was a leading figure in conservative circles during the 1870s.

litical elites; in economic attitudes, a tendency to regard property ownership rather than political rights as the defining attribute of citizenship;[43] in the philosophical sphere, an individualist, skeptical, and rationalist approach to moral and political issues; in religious matters, a temperamental preference for Gallicanism and an instinctive dislike of ultramontanism, which could sometimes degenerate into anticlericalism;[44] and finally, in geographical terms, a heavy concentration in urban and semiurban areas and a frequent lack of understanding of (and sympathy for) the traditionalist concerns and practices of rural France.

Taine expressed this intellectual disdain in a horticultural metaphor: "A society is like a garden: it can be laid out to produce peaches and oranges, or else carrots and cabbages. Ours is entirely laid out for carrots and cabbages."[45] Prévost-Paradol deplored the Second Empire's continuing electoral dependence on "the most ignorant and lifeless parts of French society."[46] Dupont-White's formula was even less subtle: "Land of mountains, land of idiots."[47]

THE VIRTUES OF PRUDENCE AND FLEXIBILITY

The ability to adapt to circumstances was seen as a hallmark of French liberalism throughout the nineteenth century. A popular ditty of the Second Empire underlined this perception in its depiction of the liberal politician:

> Applaud his every sentence, his word is certitude
> He cannot err, even all alone against a multitude.

---

[43] "The property owner is the citizen by excellence" (Albert de Broglie, "Un réveil libéral en province," *Revue des Deux Mondes* 33 [October 1863]: 540.
[44] Edouard Laboulaye's indictment of ultramontanism was typical:

When one reads the modern defenders of Catholicism, one is struck by their indecision and timidity; they move forward only by looking backward. It seems their religion consists only in never deviating from Roman ideas even when questions of dogma are not at stake; for them, what establishes the limit between reason and faith is not the symbol but the decree of the Index. It was not thus in our Gallican church, which ought not to be forgotten so quickly. ("Le rationalisme chrétien," in *Etudes morales et politiques* [Paris: Charpentier, 1862], 89).

Also worthy of note were Charles Dupont-White's scathing views on clericalism, as, for example, in *Des candidatures officielles* (Paris: Guillaumin, 1868), 31.
[45] Taine, *Carnets de Voyage*, 33.
[46] Lucien-Anatole Prévost-Paradol, *Lettres posthumes de Prévost-Paradol* (Brussels, 1871), 34.
[47] Dupont-White, *La centralisation*, 270.

> Yet he is prudent and flexible, when required,
> Even if he later sounds purposeful and decided.[48]

Political prudence and intellectual flexibility were certainly plentiful among Second Empire liberals. Their sense of caution was partly born out of fear, a primordial emotion that (especially in times of turbulence) was the dominant impetus for liberal action and, perhaps more often, inaction. This was how a sympathetic observer described her languid liberal contemporaries under the Empire:

> The most numerous party enjoying above all a quiet time, having Orleanist constitutional opinions, but fearing revolutions, and never taking advantage of its strength to force the government to take the appropriate path. The constitutional elites of this party thus have a considerable army behind them, but the soldiers are paralyzed by fear and inertia, so that the leaders end up facing enemy fire alone. Indeed, if they enjoined their supporters to follow them, they would find very few who would.[49]

Prudence was not merely dictated by fear. It also sprang from the firm rejection of positive anthropological assumptions concerning human nature. Distinguishing himself from the revolutionary heritage, François Guizot flatly declared: "I do not believe in the essential goodness of man."[50] A liberal publicist echoed: "Man has been created to struggle, and he lives only on condition that he fights."[51] Also widespread was the belief that there were natural limits to the effectiveness of political intervention in society. Dupont-White typically believed that political action could be expected merely to minimize social friction, not eliminate it.

Even the search for common interests — the cornerstone of classical liberal ideology — could not be guaranteed to produce a positive outcome: "Men cannot come into contact with each other without competing, and there can be no competition without hatred."[52] In 1861 a provincial liberal pamphlet, although pleading for a reconciliation of the upper and lower classes, noted soberly: "Our egoistic instincts have a free rein; their cupidity grows with our successes, and they know only external constraints as their limits."[53] Two years later another pamphlet

---

[48] "Un libéral, chanson nouvelle" (1867), Bib. Nat. Ye. 53297.

[49] Madame Elise Dosne, *Mémoires de Madame Dosne, l'égerie de M. Thiers* (Paris: Plon, 1928), 2:322.

[50] François Guizot, "La génération de 1789," *Revue des Deux Mondes*, February 1863, 871.

[51] H. Mille-Noé, "La Paix Perpétuelle," *Revue Libérale* 10–25 August 1867, 247.

[52] Dupont-White, *La centralisation*, 14.

[53] "Aristocratie et démocratie," in *Varia: Aristocratie et democratie* (Nancy: Vagner, 1861), 36.

developed the same point: "Our instincts of vanity, of cupidity, of envy, of hatred, and of sensuality are indestructible. To eliminate them is beyond our power; moderating them is all that we can achieve, and this is all that, in the political sphere, has been accomplished by our most successful governments."[54]

Political practice was regarded as an open-ended exercise, in which rules and procedures needed to be constantly adapted to the exigencies of the moment: "No principle is absolute."[55] This flexible and experimental conception of politics tended to be contrasted with the legitimist view, which liberals often saw (not always fairly) as the rigid application of immutable principles.[56] Liberal practice was also frequently counterposed to the Jacobin republican approach to politics, which was perceived as a paradigm of intellectual dogmatism. Ollivier, a republican convert to political liberalism in the 1860s, spelled out this opposition between liberal empiricism and Jacobin inflexibility.

> The Jacobin school starts from two or three premises, from which it draws a number of conclusions that appear irrefutable. This is not the way to proceed in politics. Politics is not, any more than philosophy, an abstract science in which one proceeds a priori; politics, just as and even more than philosophy, is an experimental science.[57]

From the vantage point of the 1860s, examining the recent past and contemplating the present only underlined the necessity of this positivist approach. Since Bonaparte's second abdication in 1815, France had experimented with monarchical, republican, and imperial constitutions, none of which seemed able to provide political stability and institutional continuity. This predicament was the source of the liberals' practical empiricism, which found expression in their refusal to subscribe to any "metaphysical" position on France's constitutional future. Despite the Empire's institution of an oath of allegiance to its constitution, which was a precondition of holding any elective office, many legitimist and republican politicians continued to regard the promotion of their respective constitutional alternatives as the best guarantee for France's political future. Most liberals, by contrast, were regime agnostics; they

---

[54] "De l'éducation politique de la France," in *Varia: De l'éducation politique de la France* (Nancy: Vagner, 1863), 45.

[55] Albert de Broglie, *Mémoires du Duc de Broglie*, 280.

[56] See, for example, A. Siguier, *Les légitimistes et les orléanistes* (Paris: Philippe, 1837), 94–95.

[57] Ollivier's speech at the Legislative Corps, in *Annales du Sénat et du Corps Législatif: Compte-rendu analytique des séances*, session of 5 April 1870 (Paris: Journal Officiel, 1870), 595.

believed that the substance of a constitution was much more important than its form.

> Let us no longer quarrel, as we have done over twenty-five years, over political and dynastic forms or over which monarch might be worthy of our preferences; let us first agree on one point: the best and most durable government will be the one that succeeds in granting the greatest number of citizens the largest number of their legitimate aspirations, in other words, of freedoms.[58]

In practical terms, this signified a willingness loyally to support any constitutional order that offered to guarantee the basic principles of political liberalism. From this perspective, Rémusat declared his indifference to either monarchy or republic.[59] Albert de Broglie added: "Freedom has, in the final analysis, only three indispensable and *sine qua non* demands to make of a constitution: sincerity in elections, right of discussion in the press and on the floor of the House, and proper accountability of those in power."[60] Instead of advocating a new political order as a condition of acquiring valid constitutional principles, many liberals thus preferred to support and promote these principles from within the Empire; after 1870, a similar approach would be adopted toward the Republic.[61] Although elastic, this liberal approach was not necessarily opportunistic. Indeed, it could be as uncompromising as that of other opposition groups on basic questions of principle. But it sought to achieve its ends by distinctive methods: an inclusive rather than an exclusive approach to existing constitutional norms; gradualist means rather than a major political upheaval; and discussion and intellectual exchange as opposed to ideological confrontation.

As will be underlined throughout this chapter, these methods were the hallmarks of political liberalism under the Second Empire.

LIBERTY AND THE RULE OF LAW

Central to the pursuits of Second Empire liberals was the promotion of greater civil and political liberty and the defense of the rule of law. In the aftermath of Louis Napoleon's coup, the Orleanist comte d'Haussonville defined the core values of the liberal opposition in these terms: "It has too often been said that men of moderate opinions had no solid

---

[58] Maurice de Foblant, "L'Union Libérale," *Le Correspondant* 77 (1869): 449.

[59] Charles de Rémusat, *Mémoires de ma vie*, ed. C.-H. Pouthas (Paris: Plon, 1958), 80.

[60] Broglie, "Un réveil libéral," 550.

[61] The opening sentence of Charles Dupont-White's *La République conservatrice* (Paris: Guillaumin, 1872) reads: "It seems to me that undue importance is given to the form of a government" (3).

beliefs and that revolutions simply tossed them to each other as a sort of ballast. . . . Let us at last hold on to something; let us defend our rights, our civil and political rights, all equally violated by imperial utopias."[62]

Upholding the rule of law was the first step toward a liberal polity. The broad program of Second Empire liberals was delineated by Laboulaye, who identified a range of essential freedoms to which all liberals subscribed. He distinguished between individual and social freedoms, as well as between private and political liberties. The latter were ultimately dependent on the former: no society could be free unless it respected a wide range of personal liberties. In this context, one of the key freedoms identified was property ownership: "Property is the fruit of our activity, and it is because this fruit belongs to us that we are hardworking, frugal, and ethical . . . property is the fruit of liberty; it is the realization of freedom."[63] Thus in a free society individuals and groups were allowed to express their economic, social, and political preferences to the full extent of their desires, and with the only caveat that these preferences did not harm their fellow citizens.

In 1863 Ollivier eloquently expressed this general conception of liberty in a speech that in some respects foreshadowed his later conversion to the liberal Empire.

> Full responsibility of the agents of the state, a press subject to the common law; free elections, an active municipal life, the initiative of government contained within reasonable limits; a government having the right to do good but not preventing others from doing so as well . . . in a word, political freedom, religious freedom, civil freedom, freedom of education, or better still, freedom without qualification, this is what we need.[64]

Liberty without anarchy, order without despotism: this motto summed up the distinct yet ambivalent character of the liberal notion of freedom. Liberty was a multidimensional phenomenon, comprising economic and social facets, as well as political ones. Furthermore, liberty was intimately linked to the conservative notion of order. In a minimalist interpretation, this simply meant that liberty could be enjoyed only under the rule of law; this position was standard among liberals and conservatives. But there was also the implication that the enjoyment of freedom depended on the extent to which the existing social order could

---

[62] Comte Othenin d'Haussonville, "Qui nous sommes," in *Souvenirs et mélanges* (Paris: Calmann Lévy, 1878), 89.

[63] Laboulaye, *Le parti libéral*, 29, 34. See also Adolphe Thiers's earlier work, *De la propriété* (Paris: Paulin, 1848).

[64] Speech at the Legislative Corps, 1863, in *Annales du Sénat et du Corps Législatif: Compte-rendu analytique des séances* (Paris: Corps Législatif, 1863), 55–56.

be maintained. As a liberal publicist had once stated, "We do not like the power of the sword, but an honest and intelligent sword is preferable to a savage and bloody pike."[65]

This remained the position of most liberals; as we will note later, it came to play an important role in defining the priority that liberals were prepared to give to reformulating the principles of good citizenship. In addition, liberty was seen as a good in itself but also a means of achieving a further set of desirable ends: ending the era of political conflicts and improving the moral and material conditions of society. Finally, the liberal notion of freedom was pluralistic: it recognized that well-meaning individuals could follow different paths toward promoting the common good, and indeed that such ideological diversity was a prerequisite for a free society. In the words of Montalembert, "Uniformity is of all forms of servitude one of the most inadmissible."[66] Yet this approach was not relativistic; there was no suggestion that different conceptions of the good were equally valid. Indeed, this rejection of relativism would later be invoked in qualifying the degree of liberal enthusiasm for local liberty.

THE FRUGAL STATE

Second Empire liberals inherited from the classical liberal tradition a strong suspicion toward the intrusion of the state into the public and especially the private domain.[67] This concern was heightened by the political and administrative practices of the imperial regime, particularly during its authoritarian phase. "It is a mistake to believe that the state should always have the last word in all matters," asserted Laboulaye.[68] Albert de Broglie expressed feelings of frustration, which were common to his fellow liberals.

> Common sense tells us that the state is of necessity policeman, soldier, and legislator; but does it also have to be a banker, an industrialist, a priest, a schoolteacher, a chaplain, who assumes the burden of satisfying all the moral and material needs of the nation, from road building, the supply of water, the development of forestry, the regulation of credit and arts to private matters of charity and religion?[69]

[65] Saint-Marc Girardin, "Chronique," *Revue des Deux Mondes*, 15 May 1849, 704.
[66] Charles de Montalembert, "La Décentralisation," *Le Correspondant* 24 (1865): 1011.
[67] On early liberal doctrines of the state in France, see Henry Michel, *L'idée de l'Etat en France* (Paris: Hachette, 1898), 307–16.
[68] Edouard Laboulaye, *Histoire politique des Etats-Unis* (Paris: Durand, 1866), 3:113.
[69] Broglie, "Un réveil libéral," 536.

In particular, there was a sense that French public and private life was overregulated. Professionals could no longer apply their skills without the active intercession of the state.[70] There were different nuances among liberals over the proper limits of state intervention. The debate between free trade and protectionism, for example, created a sharp and irreconcilable division during the 1860s, after the Empire's partial conversion to free trade.[71] However, there was a broad measure of agreement over the essential attributes of public authority. The ideal state had to be sovereign, of course, in order to defend and promote French national interests abroad, but not aggressive or militaristic, and certainly not adventurist.[72] The Empire's Syrian, Chinese, and Mexican expeditions were thus roundly condemned in liberal circles.[73]

The state had to be scrupulously impartial in upholding the general interest and administering the law. As Dupont-White stated succinctly, "What constitutes a nation is the quality of its government; it is the rule of law in society."[74] In the religious sphere, most liberals advocated a separation between church and state (a measure deemed to be in the best interests of both institutions) and the equal treatment of all religious faiths. In this context, the Empire's attitude toward the Roman question was a source of division among liberals: some joined the church in demanding French support for the Vatican, and others applauded the campaign for Italian unification.[75] The ideal liberal state was also frugal, keeping a tight rein on public expenditure; from this perspective, liberals were fiercely critical of what they perceived as the extravagant increase in taxation and public borrowing needed to finance the Empire's vast infrastructural projects throughout France.[76]

A virtuous state was also modest in size, keeping only the minimum number of public functionaries necessary to maintain essential public services. Throughout the Empire, liberals (in the same way as legitimists) denounced the spectacular increase in the number of state officials, at both the national and the local level; this increase was seen to contribute to the decline in public standards of integrity.

---

[70] Ibid., 540.

[71] For a strong expression of the case for free trade, see Michel Chevalier, *Examen du système commercial connu sous le nom de système protecteur* (Paris: Guillaumin, 1852).

[72] Auguste Victor Laurent Casimir Perier, *Les finances et la politique* (Paris: Michel Lévy, 1863), 332; see also Taxile Delord, *Histoire illustrée du Second Empire* (Paris, 1880–83), 3:384, 4:428–29.

[73] Thiers's views are quoted in *Conversations with Distinguished Persons*, by Senior, 176.

[74] Dupont-White, *La centralisation*, 10.

[75] Lucien-Anatole Prévost-Paradol, *Les anciens partis* (Paris: Dumineray, 1860), 32–33.

[76] Prévost-Paradol, *Quelques pages d'histoire contemporaine*, 3:37–39.

The social thought of French liberals during the Second Empire was relatively underdeveloped; only in the somewhat specialized publications on political economy were much time and energy devoted to the role the state could perform in raising the economic and cultural standards of the nation.[77] But Second Empire liberals did make some efforts to come to terms with new social realities. A few progressive liberals not only accepted but stipulated that the state had a duty to protect the weaker members of the national community from absolute deprivation. For Dupont-White, the state was needed for redistributive purposes, to increase the well-being of "the most numerous and least fortunate classes."[78] Fellow liberal Rémusat added: "Civilization has demands and democracy has needs, which do not permit us to abandon to voluntary or charitable activities certain moral interests that require oversight and direction. The principle of equality necessitates a measure of uniformity in the distribution of goods and social benefits."[79]

Most of all, the liberal state had a duty to preserve the social and moral unity of the nation and to refrain from any practice that might impair or undermine this sense of collective cohesion. In this context, Rémusat's expression of attachment to the social aspect of state action was part of a broader argument against federalism. This attachment to national unity, which to an important extent acted as a foil to the liberal conception of local liberty, was part of the ideological legacy of 1789.

The French Revolution through Liberal Eyes

Second Empire liberals were also characteristically possessed of a particular sense of their historical lineage. They viewed the 1789 Revolution as a key stage in the development of liberal principles in France but as somewhat distinct from the event celebrated by Jacobins, moderate republicans, and Bonapartists. There was some measure of common ground. In particular, liberals welcomed 1789 as the source of the nation's political and administrative unity. Ollivier waxed lyrical about "these principles of '89 which have given unity to our fragmented coun-

[77] See, for example, the works of Michel Chevalier, notably *Lettres sur l'organisation du travail* (Paris: Capelle, 1848) and *Les questions politiques et sociales* (Paris: Revue des Deux Mondes, 1850). See also Joseph Garnier, *Tableau des causes de la misère et des remèdes qu'on peut y apporter* (Paris: Garnier, 1858); Clémence Royer, "Moyens d'améliorer le sort des classes ouvrières," *Journal des Economistes* (January–March 1869): 404–29; Jules Duval, "Les fonctions économiques de l'Etat," *Journal des Economistes* (January–March 1870): 382–96.

[78] Dupont-White, *L'individu et l'état.*

[79] Charles de Rémusat, *Politique libérale, ou fragments pour servir à la défense de la Révolution française* (Paris: Michel Lévy, 1860), 426.

try and which have transformed a community divided by castes into a nation of equals."[80] Likewise, Thiers highlighted the importance of the Bonapartist legacy, which had given the country "an admirable administration."[81]

Liberals also shared with republicans the sense that the political thrust of the Revolution was not yet fully completed. Prévost-Paradol expressed this thought concisely: "The French Revolution has founded a society, but it has yet to find its government."[82] In addition, as we will note later, memories of the 1790s lingered to create a strong antipathy among liberals toward any form of federalism. There was also an identification with three of the key principles of 1789: "Equality, liberty, and sovereignty of the nation."[83]

But the liberal definition of these concepts was quite distinct. Equality was regarded as a civil rather than a political concept, which guaranteed all citizens equal rights and equal treatment by law. Social equality tended to be given a restricted definition, being seen as the right of the middle classes to be granted equal access to the privileges the aristocracy enjoyed; any more comprehensive conception of equality between classes was dismissed as chimerical.[84]

There were other differences. The republicans saw the events of 1789 as the stage on which the people became the subjects of history; in Michelet's account of the Revolution, "The principal actor is the people."[85] For liberals, by contrast, the true heroes of 1789 were the middle classes; in Thiers's evocation (following Guizot's), the "bourgeois, lawyers, doctors, and businessmen" were the principal protagonists of the drama, and it was their rights that the new political order had sanctified.[86] Indeed, liberals defined the freedoms granted by 1789 in negative rather than positive terms, placing a strong emphasis on individualism and particularly the inalienable right to own property.

Sovereignty of the nation, finally, was quite different from the republican conception of popular sovereignty. Liberals deemed a nation to be sovereign if it was governed by a constitutional government that was

---

[80] Emile Ollivier, "Sur la Révolution" (10 June 1861), in *Démocratie et liberté* (Paris: Librairie Internationale, 1867), 24.

[81] Thiers, *Discours sur les libertés politiques*, 47.

[82] Lucien-Anatole Prévost-Paradol, *La France nouvelle* (Paris: Calmann Lévy, 1868), 296.

[83] Duc Decazes, *La liberté et les conservateurs* (Paris: Schiller, 1868), 18.

[84] See Adolphe Thiers, "Discours sur les principes de 1789" (Legislative Corps, 26 February 1866), in *Discours parlementaires de M. Thiers*, 10:341.

[85] Jules Michelet, *Histoire de la Révolution Française* (Paris: Robert Laffont, 1979), 1:37.

[86] Thiers, *Discours sur les libertés politiques*, 47.

Fig. 7. Lucien-Anatole Prévost-Paradol (1829–70), lithography Lemoine, Bibliothèque Nationale, Paris. A highly acclaimed liberal pamphleteer, Prévost-Paradol rallied to the Empire in January 1870. He committed suicide after learning of the outbreak of the Franco-Prussian War.

responsible to parliament. Popular sovereignty in this sense did not necessarily signify (as it did for all republicans) the abolition of the monarchy; nor was it in any logical sense connected to male universal suffrage.[87]

Liberals thus shared with republicans (and to some extent the Bonapartists) the sense that the Revolution was a defining moment in shaping their political destiny. But there were important differences — both of style and substance — in their conception of the significance of 1789. However much they disagreed about its particular acts, both Jacobin and moderate republicans tended to regard the revolutionary drama as an almost mythological process, in which the sacred principles of their desired political order were first enacted. Liberals, for their part, adopted a much less reverential and more critical view of the Revolution. They were inclined to restrict its positive nature to a particular phase; Louis de Carné thus distinguished three different revolutions within the totality of events between 1789 and 1799, with only the first (the experiment of the constitutional monarchy) being seen as liberal.[88] Above all, they harbored grave reservations about the process of revolution itself, presenting it as a weapon to be wielded only in extreme circumstances.

Discussing his own attitude during the prelude to the 1830 events, the Orleanist Victor de Broglie typified the conservative liberal view of revolution: "For my part, I thought that in 1830 France should wisely follow the example given by England in 1688: to accept the idea of a revolution only under real and pressing circumstances, and to accept of the revolution only what was strictly necessary; finally, to graft as much as possible of the new order of things upon the old."[89]

Another Orleanist described the events of 1848 as "a frenzied storm originating in the spirit of evil . . . and hurling France into an unknown abyss."[90] Revolutions were thoroughly disagreeable events and were therefore to be eschewed if at all possible. If, regretfully, they proved to be unavoidable, their effects had to be contained at all costs.

This cautious approach was expressed in the liberals' critical appreciation of the negative aspects of 1789. First, there was a scathing denunciation of Jacobinism. "All Jacobinisms are brothers," mused the journalist Hector Pessard, denounced as a bourgeois liberal both by radical republicans and by moderate Bonapartists.[91] For Ollivier, Jacobinism was not so much a doctrine as a method, which still posed a

[87] M., *Qu'est-ce que l'orléanisme?* (Paris: Dentu, 1870), 17–18.

[88] Louis de Carné, "Le problème de 89," *Revue des Deux Mondes* (October 1852): 91.

[89] Victor de Broglie, *Souvenirs, 1785–1870* (Paris: Calmann Lévy, 1886), 3:393.

[90] Claremont-Weybridge, *Notes et souvenirs, 1848–1866* (Dinan: Peigné, 1871), 1.

[91] Hector Pessard, *Mes petits papiers, 1860–1870* (Paris: Calmann Lévy, 1887), 139.

menace to contemporary society. This pernicious system was vividly
contrasted with the liberal method in politics:

> Some attempt to convince their opponents, and not to impose their views,
> operating only by consent. . . . In their eyes no success is worth being pur-
> chased by violence, by duplicitousness, or even by a sleight of hand. They
> respect and even defend the freedom of their opponents; they believe that it
> is a necessary condition of their own liberty. Others, by contrast, seek only
> to gather the necessary strength to carry the waverers and subjugate their
> opponents. . . . The first are liberals, whatever their party; the second are
> Jacobins, whatever their emblem.[92]

Second, although homage continued to be paid to some of its ideals,
there was little idealization of the practical achievements of the Revolution. Given the way it ended, the experiment of constitutional monarchy between 1789 and 1792 was hardly the stuff of which founding
myths were made. This paucity of endogenous material therefore tended
to make liberals more eclectic in their selection of suitable political
models. Not infrequently they could be found pointing approvingly to
the political and constitutional arrangements of other countries—a
measure of their erudition, no doubt, but also perhaps of their lack of
secure ideological moorings in recent French historical experience.

After Tocqueville introduced French liberals to the spirit of the New
World, Laboulaye produced a history of the United States that went
through four successive editions by 1870.[93] Many liberal pamphleteers
pointed to the American system of local government as a model for
French (and indeed European) emulation.[94] Others found solace in Britain, whose system of local government Leroy-Beaulieu praised;[95] the duc
de Noailles was particularly pleased to find in the United Kingdom a
"judicious decentralization";[96] Taine traveled to England in 1860 and
1862 to confirm his preconceived ideas about the cultural differences

---

[92] "Lettres sur 'La Révolution Française' par E. Quinet" (January 1866), in *Démocratie et liberté*, by Ollivier, 346–47.

[93] Edouard Laboulaye, *Histoire politique des Etats-Unis*, 3 vols. (Paris: Durand, 1855–1866).

[94] See, for example, Cornelius de Boom, *Une solution politique et sociale: Confédéra-tion, décentralisation, émigration* (Paris: Michel Lévy, 1864), 106–8. The same themes are canvassed in his later work *Unité Européenne* (Paris: Toinon, 1867). See also Edouard Portalis, *Les Etats Unis, le self-government et le césarisme* (Paris: Le Chevalier, 1869), 137–39.

[95] Paul Leroy-Beaulieu, *L'administration locale en France et en Angleterre* (Paris: Guillemin, 1872).

[96] J. de Noailles, "De la décentralisation en Angleterre," in *Essais de politique contem-poraine* (Paris: Amyot, 1869), 152.

between the English and the French;[97] and Montégut noted that "the Anglo-Saxon race is one of the most important cogs in the great political machine of the universe."[98] Dupont-White, who was perhaps also celebrating his partly Anglo-Saxon origins, gave this liberal Anglophilia its highest expression when he declared the following: "After God, freedom comes from England."[99]

The most significant manifestation of the refusal to idealize the revolutionary period was expressed in a critical attitude toward its shortcomings. There was a general disparagement of the sanguinary excesses and the administrative chaos generated by the Revolution. At a deeper level, the political and cultural failings of its principal actors were singled out.[100] The 1789 Revolution, as seen through liberal eyes, thus illustrated both the necessity and the limits of political change. Necessity, because certain injustices and dysfunctions had to be remedied in order to protect the social order from corrosion and degeneration. This was the sense in which liberals (even those of a conservative disposition) were distinct from reactionaries and counterrevolutionaries: they recognized the paradox that substantial political change was sometimes an inescapable means of maintaining order. The Orleanist Decazes acknowledged this fully: "Only by perfecting and even innovating is conservatism possible."[101] A liberal pamphleteer from Dijon added: "The true art of liberal government does not consist in the absolute leveling of society, any more than true conservatism consists in stagnation; both require the gradual and progressive adaptation of institutions to the ever changing spirit of the times."[102]

This change, however, had to be carried out with moderation and care, and with a heavy dose of that cardinal of liberal virtues, prudence. This was how a consummate practician summed up the liberal approach to political change:

[97] On this period of Taine's life, see J. Wright, *Un intermédiaire entre l'esprit Germanique et l'esprit français sous le Second Empire: Camille Selden* (Paris: Champion, 1931), 76–78.

[98] Emile Montégut, "Du génie de la race anglo-saxonne," *Revue des Deux Mondes* (September 1859): 1029.

[99] Charles Dupont-White, *Le progrès politique en France* (Paris: Guillaumin, 1868), 229. See also his article "L'administration locale en France et en Angleterre," *Revue des Deux Mondes* (February 1863): 568–94.

[100] For a critique of the Revolution that anticipated many of Taine's later attacks, see Ernest Renan, "L'école libérale et ses principes," *Revue des Deux Mondes* (August 1858): 684.

[101] Decazes, *La liberté et les conservateurs*, 78.

[102] *Décentralisation, par un bourguignon* (Dijon: Lamarche, 1863), 33–34.

The liberal does not trumpet his achievements. He is modest and does not announce any grandiose plans; he is in no hurry; he takes each object one after the other and touches it only with infinite prudence, like craftsmen who focus on delicate objects and who are seen, magnifying glass in hand, working with delicate instruments in a state of deep concentration.[103]

Unity, Diversity, and the Two Liberalisms

Liberals were thus united by a common attachment to a distinct political tradition. All liberals proclaimed the political centrality of the middle classes; the virtues of prudence and flexibility; the irrevocable nature of liberty, the rule of law, and constitutional government; the institutional advantages of a well-tempered and frugal state; and the irreversibility of certain key principles of the French Revolution. Leroy-Beaulieu's definition of the purposes of political economy aptly summed up the consensual goals that most liberals espoused: "What it teaches is the harmony of classes and the solidarity of interests; what it recommends is work, order, and frugality. It dispels all the prejudices that interfere with the production or the distribution of goods; it puts justice in the place of violence; it teaches respect for natural laws, which are futile to oppose."[104] These objectives were seen to be in the interests of all social groups; indeed, it was an article of faith among liberals that "what liberals ask is for the common profit of all."[105]

Another common trait was the tendency to dismiss the significance of "high" politics. In May 1870 the Ligue de la Décentralisation was founded. The Ligue was a Parisian organization bringing together "all shades of liberal opinion" to promote the practice of self-government.[106] Its newly elected president began his acceptance speech by claiming — no doubt somewhat disingenuously — that "we do not have to be concerned with the theories and systems of political parties, for in politics we shall not become involved."[107] In opposition to politics, which was a source of unnecessary divisions and sterile conflicts, French liberals (like their peers elsewhere) claimed to prefer the search for common interests and the identification of practical goals.

Furthermore, liberals were defined by an instinctive sense of opposi-

---

[103] Adolphe Thiers, "Discours sur les principes de 1789," 379.

[104] Paul Leroy-Beaulieu, *De l'état moral et intellectuel des populations ouvrières* (Paris: Guillaumin, 1868), 289–90.

[105] Laboulaye, *Le parti libéral*, 5.

[106] On the founding of the organization, see *Le Temps*, 30 May 1870.

[107] Speech by M. Renouard, 27 May 1870, in *Ligue de la Décentralisation* (Paris: Dubuisson, 1870), 16.

tion to tyranny and arbitrariness in all its manifestations, as captured in the following diatribe by Prévost-Paradol:

> There are not two despotisms in the world, but only one: the one that comes full of its own self-infatuation, armed with its arrogant pretense to certainty, its resolve to oppress its subjects for their own good and to save them despite themselves. This despotism often changes its name and shape; it can be richly brocaded in gold and silver or humbly attired in a frock, purple robe, or threadbare coat, wearing a tiara, a crown, or a revolutionary cap; but it is always the same and cannot open its mouth without being instantly recognized and detested by all those who have at heart the dignity of man.[108]

This opposition to despotism called for a firm stance against the dictatorial government of the Second Empire. But, in keeping with the liberal temperament, this opposition was not unconditional. Shortly after Louis Napoleon's coup, Louis de Saint-Aulaire made clear that certain alternatives were even worse than Bonapartist tyranny: "It is unlikely that the most abominable and most absurd government we have ever had in France will last any longer than the others; but as long as the *reds* seem to be their probable inheritors, I shall not work toward its immediate replacement."[109] Similar feelings prompted Montalembert to offer his adhesion to the Bonapartist coup in December 1851 — an endorsement that he soon repudiated but that haunted him for the rest of his life.[110]

Despite these common features, there was also much diversity among Second Empire liberals. They were much less of a party (even in the limited sense of the term in mid-nineteenth-century France) than their political counterparts. Throughout the Second Empire, personal, temperamental, and ideological differences persisted among different liberal groups, resulting in what one historian somewhat uncharitably characterized as a "chaotic mixture."[111] These variations were perceptible in contrasting and sometimes crosscutting dimensions. At the individual level, there were damaging conflicts of rivalry and ambition, as, for example, between older and more experienced leaders such as Thiers and the new generation of men such as Ollivier; feelings of personal and temperamental distaste among rival clans, such as between the Broglie

---

[108] Prévost-Paradol, *Quelques pages d'histoire contemporaine*, 3:273–74.

[109] Letter to Barante, 24 March 1852, in *Souvenirs du Baron de Barante, 1782–1866*, by Prosper de Barante (Paris: Calmann Lévy, 1901), 8:27; emphasis is in the text.

[110] For a selection of his letters during this period, see André Trannoy, "Notes et lettres de Montalembert, 1848–1852," *Revue Historique* (October–December 1946): 408–42.

[111] Guido de Ruggiero, *The History of European Liberalism* (London: Oxford University Press, 1927), 203.

and Rémusat dynasties. Some of these individual differences stemmed from contrasting historical experiences. Between generations, there was a subtle but distinct difference between the Orleanist elites who were socialized into politics under the July Monarchy and the political generation that came of age in the 1860s. The latter tended to be less socially exclusive than the former and less suspicious of republicanism. They were more resigned to the ineluctability of mass politics, which did not inspire in them the "religious terror" it had provoked in Tocqueville.[112] Prévost-Paradol was in many respects their mouthpiece: "No one is less willing than us to contest or even complain about the progress of democratic opinion, for we have to accept inevitable occurrences, and no human hand seems able to reverse the more or less rapid tide that is sweeping all modern societies toward democracy."[113]

There were also significant differences between economic and political conceptions of liberalism, which found their most graphic illustration in the clash between free trade and protectionism but which were also reflected in contrasting assumptions about human nature. For the economists, man was by essence a bearer of capitalist values. His ultimate fulfillment as an individual could therefore be found only in the sphere of production: "Intelligence has been given to man to dominate the material world. By this intelligence, he can penetrate the laws of nature and discover its secrets. He can identify natural forces, subjugate them to his will, and indeed make them work in his place and at his behest."[114] For this reason, many liberals such as Michel Chevalier found no incompatibility between their core economic values and their political allegiance to the Empire.[115] For political liberals, by contrast, the true nature of man was social, and his destiny lay in reconciling his subjectivity with the practices of good citizenship — in which sphere the Empire's record was by general consensus considerably less flattering.

A temperamental divide between Parisian and provincial liberals was also apparent. The Parisians were often notables of an intellectual disposition, elitist, prosperous, politically well connected, statists (and often centralists), and at the same time rather detached from the vagaries of ordinary life. Provincial liberals, however, tended to be involved in industrial or agricultural concerns and were thus closer to the economic and social realities of life under the Second Empire. They believed in the

---

[112] Alexis de Tocqueville, *De la démocratie en Amérique* (Paris: Gallimard, 1961), 1:4.

[113] Prévost-Paradol, *Quelques pages d'histoire contemporaine*, 2:166–67.

[114] Michel Chevalier, *Le progrès dans la société et dans l'état par les libertés économiques* (Paris: Guillaumin, 1867), 6.

[115] Conversely, this dichotomy also explained how politically conservative Bonapartists such as Rouher and Baroche could nonetheless be ardent exponents of the principles of free trade.

virtues of associational life and in the pleasures of shared customs and local traditions. As such, as we will note later, they were often deeply suspicious of Paris—of its political, economic, and administrative might but also of its sedate, complacent, and often arrogant elites (not excluding for these purposes their Parisian liberal colleagues, often accused of gliding too easily into the comfortable antechambers of central government).[116] These liberals often railed against the vacuousness and frivolity of the Parisian lifestyle, even if they often could not help partaking in its excesses.[117]

Equally sharp was the cleavage between secular and religious conceptions of liberalism. Secular liberal opinion was often suspicious of Roman Catholicism, particularly of the Vatican.[118] Many found an acceptable compromise in the sobriety and pragmatism of Gallicanism, but some figures such as Charles Sainte-Beuve were so compelled by their detestation of the church that they lurched toward an almost Jacobin form of anticlericalism.[119] Furthermore, secular liberals were rationalist and individualist by intellectual disposition (a tendency reinforced by the presence of liberal Protestants in their midst),[120] whereas liberal Catholics—typified in many respects by Laboulaye—remained instinctively committed to the mysticism of their faith and to the comforting solidarity of their elective community. In short, many secular liberals were agnostics and sometimes even cynics, whereas their Catholic counterparts were moralists, who believed in the redemptive potential of religion for all humankind.[121]

One can summarize these contrasts by concluding that alongside a core ideology there subsisted a number of overlapping liberal undercurrents during the Second Empire: political and economic, Parisian and provincial, centralist and decentralist, and secular and religious. However, within this diversity it is possible to identify two distinct clusters. On one side were the optimistic liberals, who saw themselves as the inheritors of the Enlightenment values of reason and progress: "Liberalism has a faith, the belief in progress, as well as the conviction that

---

[116] Edouard Descola, *L'émancipation départementale* (Paris: Maillet, 1869), 11.

[117] Charles de Rémusat, *Mémoires de ma vie*, 50.

[118] For the example of the liberal *Revue de l'Instruction Publique* during this period, see Charles Dejob, *Le réveil de l'opinion dans l'Université sous le Second Empire* (Saint-Cloud, 1914).

[119] See Sainte-Beuve's vehement denunciation of clericalism in the Senate in May 1868, quoted in René Rémond, *L'anticléricalisme en France de 1815 à nos jours* (Brussels: Complexe, 1985), 164–66.

[120] See Ferdinand Buisson, *Le christianisme libéral* (Paris: Cherbuliez, 1865).

[121] For a definition of the principles of liberal Catholicism, see J. H. Serment, *Le libéralisme* (Paris: Cherbuliez, 1860).

freedom is valuable and beneficial, that truth can emerge from discussion, and that infinite perfectibility is the natural trend of humanity."[122] This progressive liberalism was open, tolerant, trusting, and humane; it was a "liberalism of hope." Its practitioners were men such as Prévost-Paradol, Laboulaye, and Ollivier, who were often not far removed from the values espoused by moderate republicans; like them, in particular, they rejected conservatism and believed in the possibility of incremental change and political accommodation.[123]

Standing against this benign view of the world was a more conservative strand of liberalism, typified by Thiers and (broadly) by the older generation of Orleanist figures such as Odilon Barrot and Jules Dufaure. This "liberalism of fear" was paternalistic by instinct, deeply distrustful of mass opinion, and deadened by the fear of social anarchy and radical republicanism. At heart it was deeply suspicious of human nature and afflicted by an almost pathological feeling of pessimism. Part of this sense of gloom came from a recognition that a new age of mass politics was about to dawn, in which the traditional certainties of classical liberalism would be of little value. Tocqueville—who (consummate liberal to the last) had a foot in both camps—expressed something of this anxiety when he noted that he found himself "in vain pursuit of a shadow that eludes me every day."[124]

This sense of uncertainty placed a heavy strain on these liberals' attachment to public reason. It was an article of faith of the liberal tradition that social and political differences had to be reconciled through an appeal to common interests: "What do differences of origin matter if we can reach a common understanding, from which unity of action is possible?"[125] But this intellectual belief in the possibility of a "reasonable" politics clashed fundamentally with deeply held intuitions about the inherent unreasonableness of human nature. It also clashed with a growing appreciation of the realities of mass politics, particularly the malleability of an ill-educated and volatile public opinion. Hence the increasingly frantic tone of many conservative liberal utterances after 1848, especially at times of crisis. Indeed, my analysis of the debates over decentralization and citizenship during the 1860s shows that the

[122] Auguste Nefftzer, "Libéralisme" (1863), in *Oeuvres de A. Nefftzer* (Paris: Librairie du Temps, 1886), 113–14.

[123] On the distinction between liberalism and conservatism, see Edouard Laboulaye, "Les Deux Politiques," *Revue Nationale* 2 (1867): 3–4.

[124] Letter to Royer-Collard, 6 April 1838, quoted in "L'amitié de Tocqueville et de Royer-Collard," by De Lanzac de Laborie, *Revue des Deux Mondes* (July 1930): 883.

[125] Count Daru, speech at the Legislative Corps, 22 February 1870, in *Journal Officiel*, February 1870.

optimistic vision of progressive liberalism eventually came to be crowded out by the liberalism of fear.

LOCAL LIFE AS A CORE LIBERAL VALUE

Local social and political institutions occupied a prominent position in the minds of French liberals during the Second Empire, especially from the early 1860s on.[126] For Prévost-Paradol, the reform of local institutions was a matter of life and death: "What is at stake is nothing less than our greatness or our decadence."[127] Saint-Marc Girardin opined that decentralization was "the most serious question of our political and social condition."[128]

It was largely through its decentralist literature that liberal ideas were disseminated in the 1860s. By 1871, for example, Laboulaye's *Le parti libéral* had been through eight editions; his *Paris en Amérique* (a political fable on the virtues of American democracy) had been through no less than twenty-six.[129] Whereas during the first half of the century liberals had tended to construct their vision of the polity from the top down, during the 1850s and 1860s their emphasis shifted perceptibly toward identifying the proper social, cultural, and even moral conditions for good government, in short, the definition of a civil society. The reasons for this ideological shift were partly political, as we will note later; the liberal rediscovery of the provinces was to some extent a reaction against the perceived political and administrative authoritarianism of the Second Empire. But this political reaction in fact enabled French liberals to realign their principles with some of the values of the classical liberal tradition and rediscover the writings of earlier figures in the history of liberal thought in France.[130]

In particular, this realignment heightened the perception that it made little sense to construct a political order without also giving considerable thought to the type of society it would eventually come to govern. In this sense, the liberals' espousal of decentralization was not a mere

---

[126] See H. Bosselet, *Lettres de Monsieur Journal* (Paris: Dentu, 1860); J. Notaras, *De la centralisation* (Paris: Mocquet, 1861); *Essai de décentralisation*; A. Simiot, *Centralisation et démocratie* (Paris: Dentu, 1861); Ferdinand Cavenne, *Un mot sur la décentralisation* (Paris: Dentu, 1863); and *Liberté municipale: Nomination des maires par les électeurs* (Saint-Germain, 1866).

[127] Prévost-Paradol, *Quelques pages d'histoire contemporaine*, 3:289.

[128] In *Journal des Débats*, 24 February 1870.

[129] The first edition was published under the pseudonym "Dr. René Lefebvre, Parisien," in 1863.

[130] David de Penanrun, *Décentralisation: Le passé, le présent, l'avenir* (Caen: Le Blanc, 1870).

tactical instrument for attacking the Empire, as is so often suggested. It was also a means of rethinking their fundamental approach to politics, especially the relationship between state and society. From this perspective, local institutions were assigned a critical role. They were seen to provide an essential range of social, moral, political, and administrative benefits: they served as a fulcrum of sociability, a method of elite recruitment and mass political education, an instrument of bourgeois emancipation and self-government, a purveyor of collective moral values, a more frugal and efficient means of administering local affairs, and an effective counterweight to the threat of social revolution. In short, liberals believed that a strong sense of citizenship could be nurtured in France through the reform of territorial institutions.

The principal symbol of local political life, in its institutional and territorial dimensions, was the commune. Liberals saw the commune as the natural source of sociability in society, based as it was on a set of associational and historical affinities that predated centralized state institutions. A liberal pamphlet explained its significance:

> The association of individuals in the same commune creates not only common interests but also common sentiments. The need to see each other, to communicate, to agree on matters of business or even pleasure, to look after one another, to give each other the spectacle of life . . . produces a community of feelings which generates a real affection among those who partake in it. People from the same town and village are fond of each other because in others they find a part, and indeed a great deal, of themselves.[131]

Living together was thus not just about self-protection or even a search for common interests. It was an expression of sociability in its widest possible sense: the creation of a sense of social solidarity, the pursuit of common pleasures, the acquisition of cultural values, and the affirmation of a sense of historical identity. In short, membership in the commune was a prerequisite for developing a positive sense of citizenship; it was in the commune that the individual reconciled his subjective nature with his social being.

This sense of citizenship could develop only with freedom, as all liberals noted.[132] At the same time, this development required a distinct social space: the commune, which represented the meeting point between local and national sociability. Indeed, liberals claimed that there was complete complementarity between fostering local affiliations and cultivating wider patriotic interests: "Because one is a Breton or a Nor-

---

[131] "De la décentralisation," in *Varia: Morale, Politique, Littérature* (Paris, 1860), 77–78.

[132] Martin Ferraz, "Charles de Rémusat," in *Histoire de la philosophie en France*, 405.

man, and one loves one's locality, one is not any less a good Frenchman; perhaps this makes one an even better patriot."[133] The commune was thus the privileged space within which individual and group socialization occurred.

The commune was an institution for promoting sociability but also for providing a range of civic functions. There was a strong emphasis on the importance of the commune for the political education of the citizenry. A liberal pamphleteer from Bordeaux explained:

> If freedom is the condition of modern states (and who says freedom says struggle, competition, discussion), men have to be prepared for it. And what could better prepare them than local institutions, charitable associations, municipal councils, and local powers, where a great mass of men have to enter, act, and learn how to tolerate each other, to appreciate one another, and thus to live together?[134]

More important, an increase in public involvement in politics would have the effect of flattering the political ambitions of local notables. In the eyes of Prévost-Paradol, this practice would allow for a significant number of valuable transformations:

> Changing the commune, the canton, the department, into as many practical schools of public life; to give local satisfaction by useful activities to legitimate ambitions that today are consumed in dissatisfaction and obscurity, or that uselessly lay siege to the congested avenues of central government; finally, to interest a great number of citizens in the good administration of public affairs, and to disseminate, by practice and good example, the salutary habits of free discussion and individual responsibility into the most humble ranks of the nation.[135]

In addition to bringing different social groups together, promoting a sense of civic responsibility, and helping to satisfy the rightful ambitions of aspiring political elites, an independent and vibrant local political life could help to induct the citizenry into the practice of universal suffrage. As noted earlier, many liberals were ambivalent about not only the principle of universal suffrage but also the manner in which it was practiced by the Second Empire. Some liberals viewed regular and frequent electoral consultations as a means of giving citizens the opportunity to appreciate the value of political autonomy.

One particularly important benefit was the defense of local interests. Elections were a privileged instrument for influencing local political out-

---

[133] Laboulaye, *Le parti libéral*, 117.
[134] Ernest Fournier, *Les réformes nécéssaires* (Paris: Guillaumin, 1869), 113.
[135] Prévost-Paradol, *La France nouvelle*, 83–84.

comes, as they enabled communities to choose their local councillors and exercise some measure of control over the designation of their mayor. Using one's vote with discernment was in this sense not only of intrinsic value but also a matter of great practical consequence.

During the campaign for the 1865 municipal elections, Prévost-Paradol went so far as to urge all his fellow liberals to vote as a matter of "patriotic duty."[136] Regular electoral activity at a local level was indeed a measure of civic maturity: "The zeal of the citizen for the interests of his commune is the sign and guarantee of his devotion to the general interest of his country."[137] Particularly valuable here was the potential socializing effect of regular electoral participation on the working class. Pleading for Paris to be given back the right to elect its municipal council, the liberal Catholic Augustin Cochin also argued that a properly representative communal regime could have substantive moralizing effects on the city's working population.

> There are only two places where workers meet: they cross paths in nightclubs, and their opinions come together in newspapers. Coming out of these places of agitation and not reflection, they return from their workshops, which adjoin our palaces, into their lofts, which are adjacent to our most beautiful homes. Subjected to this lifestyle for five years, they are suddenly tossed, like a torrent without ditches, into the storm of general elections. Is it unreasonable to think that if these intelligent workers had had to try out their views (in a manner of speaking) in municipal elections, if these elections had returned a number of councillors of their choice, if these councillors had kept in close touch with those they represented, this natural organization of the popular vote would make workers more enlightened and more inoffensive?[138]

Although liberals shared with republicans an ambition to involve the citizenry in local public life, the sense of social purpose that underlay their aspiration was somewhat distinct. While inviting all classes to participate in the life of the city, liberals expressly reserved the leading role in local politics for their privileged social constituency: the middle classes. The recruitment of political elites had, in the interests of the nation as a whole, to favor the privileged sections of society; hence Victor de Broglie's claim that effective leadership was best found "wherever there is wealth, independence, and in their wake, leisure, education, and enlightenment."[139]

[136] Prévost-Paradol, *Quelques pages d'histoire contemporaine*, 3:226–27.
[137] Pougnet, *Hiérarchie et décentralisation*, 130.
[138] Augustin Cochin, *La ville de Paris et le corps Législatif* (Paris: Douniol, 1869), 82.
[139] Victor de Broglie, *Vues sur le gouvernement de la France*, 2d ed. (Paris: Michel Lévy, 1872), xxxix.

In his speech at the opening session of the commission of decentralization in March 1870, Barrot defined decentralization as a means of
allowing "the middle class to take up the accomplishment of its duties."[140]
In a letter to the minister of the interior at the conclusion of the commission's work in June 1870, he again highlighted the social dimension
of his conception of decentralization: "Greater local liberty would provide useful employment and activity to landowners and industrialists,
who are sometimes called men of leisure because our laws often con-
demn them to enforced inactivity."[141]

Liberal members of the 1870 commission constantly evoked the
theme of reviving local power as a means of countering the enforced
idleness of the middle classes.[142] This idea was often blended with the
classical liberal proposition that the middle classes had a historical vocation (and even duty) to exercise power and influence in the best interests of society. A liberal Catholic pamphleteer described this "mission"
of the provincial bourgeoisie in extensive terms:

> Our desire would be that the great landowner should be the friend and
> councillor of the inhabitants of his commune, and that by his good advice,
> by his influence, and even when necessary by his money, he should attempt
> to support workers and smallholders who face temporary difficulties
> through no fault of their own; he should prevent, by a timely intervention,
> the ruin and dispersal of families, this plague of the modern age.[143]

It is worth noting two contradictions in the liberal posture here.
There was tension between the appeal to supersede social divisions by
raising the banner of common interests and the advocacy of a leading
role for one particular section of society. It was also somewhat inconsistent to view decentralization as a means of promoting individual liberation and, at the same time, as an instrument of reinforcing traditional
social institutions.

Part of the reason liberal thinkers and politicians felt impelled to
make such contradictory claims was their belief that a dynamic local
government regime also needed to serve broader social functions. In
particular, they felt that a vibrant political life at a local level could act
as a mechanism for preserving and even regenerating the social order.
The authors of *Varia* expressed this view in 1860: "The autonomy of
the provinces and the communes, indispensable for the satisfaction of
certain special needs, is not merely a necessary condition for the devel-

[140] Quoted in *La Décentralisation*, 5 March 1870.
[141] Barrot to Chevandier de Valdrôme, in *Le Temps*, 1 July 1870.
[142] For example, Waddington, quoted in *Le Français*, 20 March 1870.
[143] Justin Fèvre, *Mission de la bourgeoisie* (Paris: Douniol, 1864), 111.

opment of the human personality and the general exercise of freedom but also one of the foundations of public order and social discipline."[144]

The ethically regenerative potential of local liberty was identified forcefully in an editorial of the liberal monarchist *Revue de la Décentralisation*.

> The best means of raising the young generation to the height of its mission, indeed, the only way to complete its political education, is to develop local liberties . . . this will give our youth the habits of activity, courage, and finally life itself. For, as we never cease to repeat, the aim of decentralization is mainly moral. . . . It is a matter of managing the moral and intellectual interests of local communities; it is a question of finding out whether France will continue to be cowardly, fainthearted, downcast, inert, ignorant, and incapable, or whether she will become strong, courageous, active, and capable.[145]

Although it shared some features with other traditions, the liberal conception of the commune was thus distinct from Bonapartist, republican, and legitimist views of local life. As noted in chapter 1, Bonapartists viewed the commune as a depoliticized entity, a loyal and subordinate unit in an omniscient hierarchy that governed society in the best interests of all. While rejecting the notion of local depoliticization, legitimists were also inclined to use the family metaphor when describing the commune. But their hierarchy tended to be based on the power and authority of traditional social forces—the nobility and the clergy—rather than administrative institutions. In contrast to both of these approaches (as we will note in chapter 4), republican elites emphasized the civic and egalitarian character of the commune. Even though part of a more elaborate system of territorial organization, the commune was an autonomous entity, which was mature enough to exercise a specified range of political attributes. But it was also presented by republicans as a sphere of social equality, in which all citizens (irrespective of class, education, income, or occupation) could exercise equal rights and aspire equally to public office.

The liberals, for their part, claimed to reject the social and administrative hierarchies of the monarchists. Yet at the same time they were suspicious of the leveling tendencies they claimed to detect in the republicans' approach. Despite their egalitarian rhetoric, indeed, liberals tended to regard the local government system as an instrument for the promotion of order, as well as the pursuit of notabilist ambitions.[146]

---

[144] *Varia: Morale, Politique, Littérature*, 118–19.

[145] *Revue de la Décentralisation*, 16 May 1870.

[146] Charles de Ribbes, *La nouvelle école libérale et la décentralisation* (Marseille: Olive, 1859), 24–25.

The Liberal Critique of Centralization

The liberal advocacy of local liberties was not merely an abstract expression of preference for a range of cherished political values. The call for decentralization was also a response to the perceived social, political, and administrative deficiencies of the Second Empire, most of which were believed to be caused by excessive administrative centralization. Again, the liberal critique of centralism shared many features with other political traditions. In particular, there was a strong belief that the Empire's practice of centralization was not an instrument for delivering effective local administration. The deficiencies in the Empire's local government regime were characterized by three principal features: a denial of autonomy to local actors, an excessive and arbitrary exercise of administrative power, and an overt politicization of local government institutions.

As noted earlier, liberals objected vehemently to the Bonapartists' paternalistic view of local communities. The notion that communes were intrinsically unfit for self-government and were to be ruled only by an agent of central authority was singled out for special criticism by the liberal authors of the Nancy program in 1865.

> The inhabitants of a commune possess a heritage: a public road, fountains, a washhouse, a school, a communal building, a church, a charitable association, and, in certain points, a market, a slaughterhouse, a home, and a college. They have to decide on collective expenditure and also determine appropriate levels of taxation to supplement their income. Are these various objects beyond their intelligence, and does their achievement require their direction, enlightenment, and guidance by an agent of central government, placed far away from them, whom they do not know and who knows nothing of them?[147]

The paternalism of the Empire might conceivably have been more tolerable had it brought effective local government in its wake. But in the eyes of the liberals the system represented the worst of all possible worlds: it was inefficient, wasteful, and authoritarian; at the same time it denied local actors their rightful say in matters affecting their vital interests.[148] This denial took different forms. As we saw in chapter 1, mayors were appointed by the state rather than chosen by their respective municipal councils throughout the Second Empire; according to the law of 1855, mayors could be chosen even from outside the municipal

---

[147] *Un projet de décentralisation*, 27–28.

[148] For a typical liberal view of the corruption of local government, see Edouard de Sonnier, *Un Conseil Général sous l'Empire* (Blois: Marchand, 1871).

council, a fact that was deplored by most liberals.[149] In the most extreme manifestation of centralized control, however, local communities were deprived even of the right to elect their own councillors. Paris and Lyon were placed under a special administrative regime, in which the entire municipal council was nominated by the emperor. Liberals (and republicans) were infuriated by the reign of Baron Georges Haussmann in Paris and condemned the apparent absence of any mechanism of accountability for the actions of the administration. Laboulaye articulated the sense of helplessness that many fellow Parisians felt:

> The expenses on primary instruction, on homes, on charitable associations, on the national guard, the maintenance of roads and sewers . . . are these all matters that do not concern me? Am I not to be consulted on any of these questions, and to be denied the right to elect my representatives who could vote and control these forms of expenditure? What is a Parisian in Paris? A stranger. In fact, I am mistaken, the condition of the stranger is infinitely preferable: everything is geared toward his pleasures, and he pays no taxes.[150]

A central part of Laboulaye's objection to the absence of representation was couched in terms of a defense of propertied interests against the financial unaccountability and arbitrary practices of the administration. This was an important feature of the liberal objection to the Empire's conception of local government, and it reflected a key social purpose of the liberal conception of citizenship.

Another source of concern was that the state had the power to suspend and dissolve municipal councils deemed to be irredeemably divided or believed to have overstepped their statutory limits of action. A suspended municipal council was replaced by an administrative commission appointed by the prefect. Many liberals considered the powers of suspension a threat against the political integrity of municipal councils.

Dissolutions were a modest but regular feature of the local government order of the Second Empire, and they generally tended to be carried out as a sanction against councils that displayed unrelenting hostility to the regime. In Toulouse, for example, the municipal council was dissolved in 1867, two years after the victory of the liberal and republican opposition list led by Paul de Rémusat.[151] In this respect, the state's practice of appointing mayors was seen as fundamentally inconsistent

[149] Albert Desjardins, *La nomination des maires dans l'ancienne France* (Paris: Douniol, 1870), 57–59.

[150] Edouard Laboulaye, *Le parti libéral*, 112–13.

[151] Paul de Rémusat's account of the events was given in *De la dissolution du Conseil Municipal de la Ville de Toulouse*, by Paul de Rémusat (Paris, 1867).

with the principles of decentralism. In the words of Auguste Nefftzer, "A complete system of decentralization necessarily implies the election of mayors."[152] It was particularly insensitive, from this point of view, that mayors were chosen even before municipal elections were held.

> Is it really sensible to offer a commune the miserable alternative of electing, whether it likes it or not, a municipal council in which the mayor, appointed in advance, can find himself at ease; or else to surround this mayor with hostile councillors, so that a dissolution of the municipal council becomes indispensable?[153]

These types of actions produced the strong sense that the powers of the administration were wielded arbitrarily and without sufficient regard for the public interest. The symbol of this provincial despotism was the prefect, portrayed in the 1865 Nancy program as the supreme instrument of imperial malevolence.

> The one who occupies the place of honor in all ceremonies and public gatherings, in all agricultural shows, in all assemblies where prizes are given out; the one who, in fact, appoints and dismisses all the mayors and deputy mayors; who controls all the schoolteachers; who directs the activities of police commissioners and rural policemen; who watches over all the newspapers, as well as the printing presses and tobacconists; who authorizes the opening and closing of nightclubs[;] . . . and who above all points out to the voters of his department all the candidates he would like to see elected as members of the Legislative Corps, General Council, and municipal council.[154]

THE POLITICIZATION OF LOCAL GOVERNMENT

Although the earlier portrayal undervalued the national and local constraints under which prefectoral power was exercised throughout the Second Empire,[155] it also highlighted a further grievance against the administrative agents of the state: excessive politicization.

All opposition parties denounced the political functions that prefects and their subordinates performed. They particularly resented the practice of anointing "official" candidates at national and local elections, for a number of reasons. They regarded official candidacies as a violation of the spirit of universal suffrage. These appeared to pervert the

---

[152] *Le Temps*, 17 January 1870.

[153] Comte Othenin d'Haussonville, *Lettre au Sénat* (Paris: Dumineray, 1860), 24.

[154] Ibid., 13–14.

[155] For a reassessment of the role of the prefects, see Le Clère and Wright, *Les Préfets du Second Empire*.

principle of representation, in that successful candidates were deemed to represent the interests of the government rather than those of the nation as a whole.[156] Official candidates benefited from the patronage of the state and its local representatives (including, for these purposes, the mayors). As noted in chapter 1, this administrative intervention was always much more effective in rural areas than in urban ones, and it was greater in the early Empire than in its later years.

Nonetheless, official candidates enjoyed significant triumphs over the liberal opposition. Most leading Orleanist figures (with the notable exception of Thiers) were defeated in the legislative elections of 1863 and 1869; the list of casualties included the Rémusats (the father in 1863, his son Paul in 1869), Casimir Perier, Dufaure, and (as we will see later) Prévost-Paradol;[157] Laboulaye ran for election in 1857, 1864, and 1866 and each time was defeated by the official candidate.[158] Liberal politicians also denounced the use of the administration's agents for partisan ends as a corruption of the state's functions.[159] As Barrot argued in relation to the electoral dimension of centralization, "This practice . . . perverts the operation of our institutions and indeed perverts itself. The administration ceases to be a means of distributing the resources of the state with justice and discernment; it becomes a means of conquering and preserving a majority in parliament."[160]

In this context, the role of mayors was a particular source of concern to liberals.[161] Given their strategic location in each commune, mayors were key agents in the operation of the Second Empire's local government regime. Many liberals denounced the regime's growing practice of selecting mayors as official candidates; this apparent encouragement of multiple office-holding was seen as a further distortion of the principle of representation.[162]

The mayors' role during elections was also a constant source of irritation to the opposition, particularly in rural communes where mayors often used their authority to influence the electoral turnout and mobilize support for the official candidate. During the 1869 legislative elections, Prévost-Paradol reminded mayors of their material and moral responsibilities and exhorted them to adopt a less overtly partisan role in the campaign.

---

[156] Albert de Broglie, "Les candidatures officielles," *Le Correspondant* (1868).
[157] Ménager, "1848–1871: Autorité ou Liberté," 139.
[158] Soto, "Edouard Laboulaye," 116.
[159] See Charles Dunoyer, *Le Second Empire et une nouvelle restauration* (London: Tafery, 1864), 2:48.
[160] Odilon Barrot, *De la centralisation et de ses effets* (Paris: Dumineray, 1861), 188.
[161] See Charles Perint, *De la nomination des maires* (Paris: Dentu, 1870).
[162] Prévost-Paradol, *Quelques pages d'histoire contemporaine*, 2:64–65.

The abusive practice that consists of asking communal officials to hand over to the rural voter not only his voting card but also the official candidate's ballot paper should be regarded as a violation of the sincerity of the election. The simultaneous handing over of an official document with the ballot paper of a particular candidate appears too much as an injunction of the authorities not overly to influence the attitude of many voters.[163]

SOCIAL APATHY AND THE LACK OF CIVIC CULTURE

If an important aspect of centralization was the manner in which it was practiced by the Empire, this was only the beginning of the problem. As the admonition of Prévost-Paradol made clear, the ills of centralism were compounded by the traditionalism and backwardness of rural communities, as well as the absence of intermediate institutions in society. It was a commonly held view in the 1860s that French society suffered from apathy, which was deemed to stem from the Revolution's historical destruction of traditional social and political institutions. As the authors of *Varia* put it, "By its intrusion in all matters that seemed to concern the general interest, centralization has severely hindered individual initiative and attempts to form collective associations. It has substituted itself to the citizenry in a multitude of actions and operations that formerly required of those who executed them the will and capacity to organize themselves freely."[164]

During the Second Empire, liberals bemoaned the absence of civic virtues in society. Prévost-Paradol brooded on the fate of a nation apparently gripped by discouragement and lassitude: "Appearing henceforth incapable of love or hatred, having overcome its passions and lost all sense of hope, France regards its governments and their various efforts to cure her condition as a dejected patient who listens to his doctor with quiet indifference."[165] In Barrot's view, the omnipresence and omnipotence of the state forced individuals to retreat from the public sphere and seek fulfillment in private and self-interested concerns. This "rampant search for material pleasures and puerile vanities"[166] was profoundly damaging to the civic health of the nation. A pamphleteer from Bordeaux also noted that centralization had created a culture of dependency on the state and broken all habits of self-sufficiency and individual initiative. Worse still, it had brought about a "spirit of vanity that

---

[163] Lucien-Anatole Prévost-Paradol, *Aux maires des 38000 communes de France: Lettre circulaire* (Paris: Le Chevalier, 1869), 6–7. For a Bonapartist reply, see *Un maire à M. Prévost-Paradol: Réponse à sa lettre circulaire* (Paris: Dentu, 1869).

[164] "De l'éducation politique de la France," 57.

[165] Prévost-Paradol, *La France Nouvelle*, 336–37.

[166] Barrot, *De la centralisation*, 72.

... views frivolities with honor and esteem, rather than rewarding deeds that demonstrate the value and strength of man."[167]

Indeed, the denunciation of materialism and other forms of immorality was a constant theme in opposition writings during this period. A liberal writer from Dijon highlighted the corruptive influence of centralized institutions thus:

> By dint of being governed, administered, and regimented, the citizens have lost the use of their limbs; someone is always speaking and acting on their behalf, thus alienating them from public life and making them lose interest in their civic duties; so they look instead for different avenues, and they sign up with the brigade of simple, light, and scurrilous moral values.[168]

Centralization was thus held responsible for a wide range of social ills. Charles de Rémusat blamed it for turning the French into a servile nation: "I understand by servility not only the attitude of adulatory courtesanship which has in all times lowered so many characters but a disposition that seems more excusable, a taste for protection, which is itself the product of a long habit of incapacity to answer for oneself."[169] Prévost-Paradol denounced the existing local government system, "which transforms, by the nature of things, a whole neighborhood into either an anxious seeker of favors or a grateful and subservient ward."[170]

Yet this servile nation, which seemed to revel in feelings of social subordination and institutional dependency, was also capable of regularly overthrowing its governments. Ernest Fournier attempted to explain the paradox: "One can identify two contradictory tendencies in France: a rebellious spirit and a disposition toward servile submission. In no other country, with the possible exception of Russia, is there such a contrast. . . . This state of affairs has its source in centralization, which crushes the masses while overstimulating powerful personalities."[171]

The belief that centralization was a cause of revolution in France was another common theme in the decentralist literature, particularly among liberals and legitimists. Tocqueville's *L'Ancien Régime et la Révolution* (1856) had done much to popularize the view that centralization was intimately linked to the incidence of revolution in France. His study of the French Revolution described the emergence of a new type of administrative power, "emerging in its own right from the ruins created by the

[167] Fournier, *Les réformes nécéssaires*, 118.
[168] Edouard Langeron, *La question communale* (Dijon, 1865), 24.
[169] Charles de Rémusat, *Politique libérale*, 423. See also *Souvenirs et impressions de 1851 à 1870* (Paris, 1879), 21.
[170] Prévost-Paradol, *Quelques pages d'histoire contemporaine*, 2:184.
[171] Fournier, *Les réformes nécéssaires*, 102.

Fig. 8. Charles de Rémusat (1797–1875), lithography Auguste Bry, Bibliothèque Nationale, Paris. A progressive liberal and the author of perceptive political and historical commentaries during the Second Empire, Rémusat rallied
to the Republic after 1870. He served as minister of foreign affairs between
August 1871 and May 1873.

Revolution."[172] The political generations of the 1850s and 1860s were particularly receptive to the problematic of revolution. By the early 1870s, especially after the experience of the war and the Paris Commune, there was a general feeling that the existence of strong state institutions was intimately linked to the cycle of revolution and counterrevolution which France had experienced continuously since 1789.[173] As the Parliamentary Commission of Inquiry on the causes of the 1871 Commune noted rather dolefully, "The revolutionary spirit has become an integral part of our national character . . . unrelenting in our obsession with change, we accept any government that is imposed upon us by a riot. We are afflicted with a superstition of power, but of revolutionary power; we ask everything of the state, it is for us the *deus ex machina*, and every time we are unhappy we want a different God."[174]

For Barrot, writing in the early 1860s, the frequency of revolutionary upheavals in France since 1789 was to be explained not in terms of the French national temperament or political culture but in terms of the "excessive concentration of power and the complete disintegration of society."[175] This concentration naturally turned the attention of liberals toward Paris.

THE CITY OF PARIS

Revolution was thus produced by a plurality of factors, all attributable in some way to the pressures of centralization. But if the deep sociological causes of revolution were important, the role of Paris seemed even more critical.

The theme of the two Frances, one Parisian and the other provincial, was old in French political and literary discourse.[176] The capital city inspired many different (and often contradictory) intellectual representations in liberal writings throughout the nineteenth century.[177] Most paradoxical was perhaps a little book by a provincial author, whose argument was summarized in a title as audacious as it was mystifying: *Paris n'existe pas* (Paris does not exist).[178] Some Parisian liberals can-

[172] Alexis de Tocqueville, *L'Ancien régime et la révolution*, ed. J.-P. Mayer (Paris: Gallimard, 1967), 66.

[173] See, for example, S. Mony, *De la décentralisation* (Paris: Dupont, 1871), 108.

[174] *Enquête Parlementaire sur l'Insurrection du 18 Mars 1871* (Paris: Librairie Législative-Wittersheim, 1872), 40.

[175] Barrot, *De la centralisation*, 153.

[176] Alain Corbin, "Paris-province," in *Les lieux de mémoire*, ed. Nora, part 1, 3:802.

[177] See, for example, Mme. Emile de Girardin, *Lettres Parisiennes* (Paris: Charpentier, 1843), 285.

[178] Paul-Ernest de Rattier, *Paris n'existe pas* (Bordeaux: Balarac, 1857).

didly confessed that the whole question of decentralization was su-
premely boring, or at best a conspiracy of second-rate provincial intellectuals to gain greater power and influence.[179] In reply, the authors of
the Nancy program denounced the "omnipotence" of Paris and expressed the hope that "the province, where fourteen out of every fifteen
inhabitants of the Empire reside, should not always and in all things be
the most humble tributary of Paris."[180] Cochin noted that the administration and the population of Paris were equally detested in the provinces: "They are seen, the one as much as the other, as dangerous forces,
inclined by their very nature and in systematic fashion the first to de-
molish buildings and the second to bring down governments."[181]

At the same time, for the political opponents of the Empire, Paris was
the seat of a corrupt and frivolous regime, whose ostentatious rituals
bore witness to the decadence of the Bonapartist elites. For the Goncourt brothers, the luxury and opulence of Paris under the Empire had
also corrupted the working class, depriving it of its virile and martial
qualities.[182]

Some believed that the Empire had ruined French intellectual life,
having produced a distinct Parisian spirit that had little to offer except
trifling values: "Much boldness, talent, and spirit but no philosophy, no
method, and no deductive power."[183] For many provincials, Paris was
also the principal source of bureaucratic waste and financial profligacy;
one commentator typically denounced "the poor distribution of state
resources and the accumulation of wealth in Paris."[184] Above all, for
conservatives of all dispositions, Paris was the abode of social revolutionaries, "this gang of ferocious savages in whose midst we happen to
live," as Barrot asserted rather frantically in 1848.[185]

But not all was ruin and desolation; there were also positive images
of the city. For some liberal intellectuals, the capital represented the
superiority of reason, and it was often unfavorably contrasted with the
ignorance and superstition of the provinces. For its artistic and cultural
elites, in particular, Paris was not just "a seat of ideas, a workshop of
progress, a meeting place of peoples, the heart of Europe. . . . Paris is

---

[179] Etienne Maurice, *Décentralisation et décentralisateurs* (Paris: Librairie Nouvelle,
1859), 15.

[180] *Un projet de décentralisation*, 12.

[181] Cochin, *La ville de Paris*, 7.

[182] Edmond de Goncourt and Jules de Goncourt, *Journal* (Paris: Flammarion, 1935),
4:136.

[183] Emile Leclercq, *La guerre de 1870: L'esprit Parisien, produit du régime impérial*
(Brussels: Claasen, 1871), xi.

[184] Fournier, *Les réformes nécéssaires*, 117.

[185] "Lettre à une anglaise," 1 July 1848, in Arch. Nat. 271 AP 1, Papiers Odilon Barrot.

also an immense museum, a mass of libraries, the recipient of the masterpieces of the human hand and mind."[186] For centralist liberals such as Dupont-White, the capital was the source of every positive feature of public life: "In France the path of progress resides in centralization. . . . The country is the soul, the government is the organ, progress is the result. France can effectively gather its thoughts only in the capital, and its strength only in government."[187]

Liberals also very much shared the sense that the city was a center of artistic and cultural excellence. After all, many of their leading political and intellectual figures were based in the city, often occupying key positions in elite Parisian institutions such as the Académie Française and the Institut and in liberal newspapers and journals. At the same time, there was agreement that the concentration of resources in the capital was somewhat excessive. Victor de Broglie noted: "Paris is both the head and the heart of this vast empire, the head, where all the intellectual activity of the nation is concentrated; the heart, toward which flows, by a thousand channels, all that she possesses of blood, of life, and of substance."[188]

In the decentralist literature this acknowledgment was often the prelude to suggestions that Paris should be deprived of many of its instruments of political and intellectual dominance. This deprivation could take two forms: for the clericalists, it involved the wholesale destruction of the licentious (not to say blasphemous) art and literature that flourished in the city; for more moderate advocates of change, it necessitated a transfer of artistic and cultural resources away from Paris to the provinces.[189]

However, liberals were generally disinclined to follow either approach, preferring instead to support the promotion of greater artistic and cultural excellence in the provinces: "It is not, indeed, a matter of asking for the decapitation of Paris; it is not a question of disputing this metropolis its birthright and its intellectual supremacy over other cities; it is merely a matter of recognizing that the province—having now reached its maturity—knows how to think, speak, and act and can therefore free itself from the domination of Paris."[190] For most liberals, a distinction had to be drawn between the symptom and the disease:

---

[186] Paul de Saint-Victor, *Barbares et Bandits* (Paris: Michel Lévy, 1871), 42.

[187] Dupont-White, *La centralisation*, 347.

[188] Victor de Broglie, *Vues sur le gouvernement*, xxv.

[189] See, for example, Dupray de la Mahérie, "Notre profession de foi en matière de décentralisation littéraire et scientifique," *La décentralisation littéraire et scientifique* 1 (October 1863): 1–7.

[190] Arsène Thévenot, *De la décentralisation intellectuelle et des progrès des arts, des sciences, et des lettres en province* (Paris: Dentu, 1864), 6–7.

"Paris suffers as much and perhaps even more of these plagues that it disseminates. It is the seat of the disease but not the disease itself."[191]

Indeed, despite their reservations about the excessive concentration of administrative power in the city, liberals were inclined to retain a distinct attachment to the political and intellectual spirit of Paris.[192] Renan summed up the duality of the capital in these terms: "Paris is the reason for the existence of all of France. It is its source of light and heat, which might well be called a source of moral corruption, provided it is granted that charming flowers can grow on this manure, some of them rare in their beauty."[193]

Others offered a negative contrast between the independent spirit the capital displayed and the servility of the provinces. A typical example was Montalembert's gloomy estimate of the public spirit outside Paris during the early 1860s.

> The public spirit in the provinces is truly deplorable. . . . Everyone has sold his honor cheaply and is now pliantly submissive to tyranny; there are no thoughts of resistance. Those who try to fight the authority of prefects and administrative authorities are seen as demented. Cowardice and corruption have invaded all layers of society.[194]

Especially for progressive liberals, Paris was the symbol of resistance to the oppressive order of the Empire, but also a place where the true values of integrity and moral rectitude continued to survive. But this image was particularly ambivalent. When this oppositional spirit swung too far in the direction of turbulent or violent political unrest, liberals became extremely apprehensive about the influence of Paris. They were keenly aware that the capital city was also the home of the forces of movement, of those radical republicans who threatened to overhaul not only the political order but also the social and economic fabric that underlay it. Indeed, faced with the growing threat of radical republicanism during the 1860s, liberals increasingly came to see Paris less as an expression of the nation's cultural and artistic excellence than as a repository of political instability and social anarchy. The advocacy of decentralization, from this perspective, was seen as a means of fortifying the provinces in order to counterbalance the revolutionary threat posed by Paris. Hence Barrot's belief in 1870 that it was essential to "revive the old France, to make it live again, in order to create provincial cen-

[191] Augustin Cochin, *Paris et la France* (Nantes: Forest et Grimaud, 1870), 20.

[192] L. Dagail, *De la décentralisation administrative* (Paris: Dentu, 1871), 217–22.

[193] Ernest Renan, "La monarchie constitutionnelle en France," *Revue des Deux Mondes*, 1 November 1869, 100.

[194] Quoted in Alfred Darimon, *L'opposition libérale sous l'Empire, 1861–1863* (Paris: Dentu, 1886), 41.

ters that can resist the destructive and revolutionary tendencies of Paris."[195]

In this context, liberals parted company with republicans on the question of the reform of municipal institutions in Paris. As noted in chapter 1, all republicans demanded the return of elected municipalities in Paris and Lyon. Liberals, however, were much more guarded. Prévost-Paradol articulated their concerns in February 1870: "Who would not be alarmed at the prospect of the election and the legal existence of a Parisian municipal council in which the candidates of the Folies-Belleville might have a majority?"[196] In a letter to a newspaper one month later, he added that it was also probably better under present circumstances for the mayors of Paris and Lyon to be chosen by the government.[197] Order, in sum, was clearly a more important political value than communal democracy. This prioritization, as we will see, increasingly came to dominate liberal thought and action after 1865.

THE DILEMMAS OF DECENTRALIZATION: THE LIBERAL PROGRAM AND ITS LIMITS

The liberal advocacy of decentralization was a direct response to a diagnosis of the social and political ills provoked by centralization. The proposals aimed to enhance the role of individuals and representative groups within the territorial government system and thus to create favorable conditions for the development of good citizenship. Liberals hoped that these objectives could be met by a number of measures, most notably by enhancing the powers of municipal and departmental administrations; partly abolishing the special regime under which Paris and Lyon were governed; insisting on the representative (as opposed to the administrative) functions of the mayor; and decreasing the powers of the central and provincial administrations, particularly those of the prefects. There were also occasional demands for the reestablishment of a territorial division above the departments, designated as either regions or provinces.[198]

Yet, in keeping with the prudence and incrementalism that were the hallmarks of liberal practice, there were also clear limits to many of these objectives and indeed a considerable degree of ambivalence about

---

[195] Letter to E. Adam, 1870, quoted in *Mes sentiments et nos idées avant 1870*, by Juliette Adam (Paris: Lemerre, 1905), 434.

[196] *Journal des Débats*, 17 February 1870.

[197] Letter to *La France*, 24 March 1870.

[198] For example, *Varia: Les départements et les provinces*, 31–68. Prévost-Paradol also advocated the creation of a regional council, which would discuss matters of common interest to contiguous departments. See *La France Nouvelle*, 82–83.

the scope of the intended reforms. This ambivalence was symbolized most tellingly in the liberal view of the administration, for which a more modest role was sought, whereas its structure and fundamental purposes remained the object of continuing respect and even veneration. At the root of this uncertainty was a clash between two basically contradictory principles in the liberal value system: the attachment to national unity on one hand and the promotion of local liberty on the other.

Further conflicts of principle only added to the liberal sense of ambivalence; for example, there were continuing tensions between preserving social order and implementing political change, liberating individuals from institutional dependency and maintaining traditional forms of social cohesion, and, last but not least, following paternalistic instincts and deferring to mass opinion. These contradictions considerably undermined liberal professions of faith in the practice of local liberty, especially as the political situation became more alarming in the second half of the 1860s.

The Rejection of Federalism

Although often hesitant about the proper alternatives to the present order, liberals were of one mind about the Bonapartist system's attempts to reform itself in the 1850s and 1860s. In particular, they contemptibly rejected the imperial conception of decentralization as expressed in the administrative decrees of 1852 and 1861.[199] These measures, in their eyes, merely transferred a broad range of powers exercised by central government to the prefectoral administration, without in any way increasing the attributions of local representative institutions. A liberal publicist from Arras firmly denounced this Bonapartist conception of decentralization:

> To decentralize is to take away the omnipotence of the state in order to allow communes and departments some independence in the management of their interests; but when, instead of this, the powers invested in ministers are simply transferred to prefects, the surveillance of the state is reinforced and aggravated, not reduced.[200]

These remarks highlighted key features of the liberal critique of the Bonapartist state: its apparent absence of impartiality and its tendency to subvert the rule of law for partisan purposes. However, many liberals

---

[199] See chap. 1.

[200] Henri-Auguste Billet, *De la décentralisation administrative* (Arras: Courtin, 1866), 8–9.

had a dichotomous view of the central and provincial administrations: the former was seen as the upholder of the public interest, and the latter seemed too often to act merely as the repository of local passions and petty influences. Faced with such a choice, liberals had no hesitation about which regime they preferred to be governed by: "Men are more willing to accept the tyranny of government than the tyranny of a neighboring authority."[201] But, as noted earlier, the liberal conception of decentralization was primarily concerned not with good administration but with social and moral purposes: increasing mass involvement in public life and establishing the conditions for effective citizenship. Victor de Broglie believed that the former was a prerequisite of the latter: "If in the future we want anyone to become involved in politics, small or great, general or local[,] . . . if we want our aggressive and petulant children to become true citizens, we must at all costs initiate them into the active art of public administration."[202]

Indeed, at the heart of liberals' solution to the various problems posed by centralization was the invention of a new intellectual paradigm for the relationship between the individual and the state. It was widely believed that the scope for the expansion of state activities in France had been limitless; hence the tyrannical character that public authority had assumed for too long. How was this tendency to be curbed and even reversed? To Laboulaye the solution appeared simple:

> There is but one way: it is to limit the state, to determine the sphere in which it exercises absolute authority but which it must not overstep; in other words, centralization, which is good and legitimate when it defends our national independence and peace but despotic and revolutionary when it exceeds its role, has to be replaced by the free government of the individual by himself, *self-government*; we lack the word because we do not possess its substance.[203]

This notion of self-government was, however, circumscribed by a conception of the national interest which continued to be given an extensive functional definition by most liberals. There was in this sense a fundamental contradiction between the liberals' philosophical preference for a minimalist state and their instinctive attachment to political unity. Indeed, French liberals typically defined the functional purposes of the state in broad terms to include not only public order, justice, finance, and defense but also local taxation, education, and health, most

[201] Ernest Bersot, "La Décentralisation," in *Questions Actuelles* (Paris: Didier, 1862), 221.
[202] Victor de Broglie, *Vues sur le gouvernement*, 12.
[203] Laboulaye, *L'Etat et ses limites*, 72.

key aspects of which were deemed too important to be left entirely in the hands of local elites. This sense of priority accorded to the concerns of the center was typified in the definite bias against federalism in liberal circles. This prejudice was based on cultural, ideological, and political considerations.

Liberal hostility to federalism was a legacy of tradition: "The unity of France comes from the crucible of history."[204] Since the Revolution, liberals had always stood for the preservation of the center's powers against autonomist and secessionist claims from the periphery.[205] Furthermore, liberals could not forget that the most ardent advocacy of federal (or quasi-federal) solutions came from either revolutionary socialist or counterrevolutionary quarters. In the case of the latter, they formed part of a broader political project with which liberals were in fundamental disagreement: the dismantling of the social, political, and administrative legacy of the French Revolution. In addition, however great its success under different climes, federalism was deemed to be inapplicable to France, where social relations were seen to be historically more antagonistic than elsewhere. This was the essence of Dupont-White's historical case against the importation of federalist ideas into France.[206]

But, perhaps most important, federalism was also believed to be inconsistent with the preservation of national unity, which to liberals remained a much more valuable asset than even the most optimal system of local government. An article in the liberal *Journal des Débats* thus argued that promoting local liberty and self-government was possible only to the extent that they did not "undermine the principle of centralization, which seems to us important to defend as the consequence, the true form, and guarantee of national unity."[207] Unity was defined legally (the institution of the same legal regime across the entire country); politically (the attachment of all parts of the nation to a particular political community); bureaucratically (the application of the same set of administrative standards across the territory); culturally (the definition of a national cultural idiom, distinct from the discourse and practices of local communities); and socially (respect for civil equality and the rejection of the influences of traditional social corporations such as the nobility and the clergy). In all these spheres most liberals judged the presence of the centralized state to be vital; they regarded

---

[204] Ernest Desmarest, *Les Etats provinciaux: Essai sur la décentralisation* (Paris: Librairie Internationale, 1868), 77.

[205] Alan Forrest, "Regionalism and Counter-Revolution," in *Rewriting the French Revolution*, ed. Colin Lucas (Oxford: Clarendon Press, 1991), 152–53.

[206] Dupont-White, *La liberté politique*, 73.

[207] L. Alloury, in *Journal des Débats*, 5 January 1870.

any qualification to its role as a threat to the essential interests of the community.[208]

National unity and local liberty were both important but not of equal value. Indeed, any substantive threat to the former made it entirely justifiable to jettison the pursuit of the latter. Thus, for all the declamations of the liberals during the 1860s, the pursuit of decentralization was a conditional rather than a categorical imperative. A liberal Bonapartist politician summed up the liberals' priorities succinctly: "Order first, freedom later."[209] The degree of priority that could be attached to the enactment of a self-governing local government regime was in fact contingent upon the attainment (or maintenance) of a set of propitious political circumstances at the center. This rank ordering was clearly demonstrated in the evolution of the liberal position on the reform of communal institutions.

THE REFORM OF COMMUNAL INSTITUTIONS

The ambivalence inherent in the liberal notion of self-government was graphically illustrated during the much-debated question of the reform of communal institutions. At the rhetorical level, there was again a strong emphasis on liberating territorial institutions and their "natural representatives" from the crushing oppression of administrative centralism.[210] The authors of *Varia* trumpeted that "it was high time to end the long usurpation that has deprived the communes and departments of the management of their own affairs."[211] Prévost-Paradol stressed the importance of providing each commune with a mayor who was not beholden to the administration: "*Self-government* must penetrate deep into our rural communes, which must learn to govern themselves at their own risk and peril by means of freely chosen councils."[212] The Nancy program further noted that the Second Empire's practice of local government was inconsistent with its proclaimed commitment to universal suffrage. It was fundamentally contradictory to give citizens the right to elect their members of parliament every six years but to deny them the right to choose their mayors: "Universal suffrage reigns above; it is only natural that we should ask that it also rule from below."[213]

During the debate on the 1870 municipal law, the deputy Antonin

[208] On this question, see, for example, Thiers's speech to the Legislative Corps, 3 July 1868, in *Discours parlementaires*, by Thiers, 12:89–90.

[209] Victor Duruy, *Notes et souvenirs* (Paris: Hachette, 1901), 1:194.

[210] A. Gaulier, in *Le Temps*, 27 June 1870.

[211] "De l'éducation politique de la France," 76.

[212] Prévost-Paradol, *La France nouvelle*, 79.

[213] *Un projet de décentralisation*, 18–19.

Lefèvre-Pontalis completed the liberal program by rejecting the Bonapartist conception of the mayor as an agent of central government.

> The attributions of the mayor as an agent of central government are sec-
> ondary; his specifically communal attributions are on the other hand of the
> utmost importance. . . . Municipal liberty is the training school for political
> liberty. It must be given not in measured doses but in large portions. Only
> when we will have nothing to demand in terms of liberty will we have
> nothing to fear by way of revolution.[214]

In theory, accordingly, the demand for communal emancipation was
extensive: liberals expressed the hope that communes would be freed
from the tutelage of the state and that mayors would be released from
that of the administration. Furthermore, the Nancy program demanded
that the institution of universal suffrage be applied to the selection of
mayors. Yet these claims were not quite as radical as they appeared. For
instance, the expression of preference for universal suffrage was strictly
circumscribed. The republicans (particularly their radical wing) advocated the election of mayors by universal suffrage — a view that was
entirely consistent with their belief in the validity of the principle. Even
progressive liberals, however, regarded the use of universal suffrage as
an instrument for choosing the mayor as a mistake.[215] When they campaigned for the involvement of universal suffrage in the designation of
mayors, therefore, liberals tended to mean only that first magistrates
ought to be chosen from within the municipal council. In other words,
they preferred an indirect method of election.

However, even this modest proposal was the source of further division. For the question remained: who was entitled to appoint the
mayor? By the late 1860s, the Center-Left (consisting mainly of former
Orleanists) argued that this choice should be made by municipal councils, and the Center-Right (former official candidates who had converted
to liberalism) suggested that it be exercised by the state.[216] The Nancy
program had fully reflected this ambivalence.

> The mayor is the agent of the commune. It would therefore seem natural
> that this figure be chosen either directly by his voters or indirectly by their
> representatives, that is, by the municipal council. So many of us naturally
> expressed the wish that this line of policy be recommended, but the major-
> ity were of the view that since the mayor was both the representative of the
> commune and the delegate of the state, he should continue to be chosen by

---

[214] Speech of 22 June 1870, in *Annales du Sénat et du Corps Législatif: Compte-rendu
analytique des séances* (Paris: Journal Officiel, 1870), 2:136–37.

[215] Prévost-Paradol, *Lettres posthumes*, 19.

[216] *Le Temps*, 4 January 1870.

the government, on condition that he was picked from the elected members of the municipal council.[217]

For all their apparent commitment to municipal emancipation, accordingly, liberals were deeply divided over their conception of the mayor's role. Part of the reason for their hesitation stemmed from a deep-seated suspicion of universal suffrage, which was deemed incompatible with fulfilling the public-interest functions of the mayor. Underlying this ambivalence was a continuing belief in the virtues of enlightened paternalism, which was believed to offer a more reliable basis for selecting the executive agent of the commune than the electorate. A concrete example of this dualism can be seen in the evolution of Ollivier's position. During the 1860s, as he progressively moved closer to the Empire, Ollivier continued to proclaim (both publicly and in his private diary) his attachment to the principle of decentralization. As noted in chapter 1, after the advent of the liberal Empire in January 1870, he set up an extraparliamentary commission of inquiry into local government.

Speaking at the Legislative Corps in February 1870, Ollivier spelled out the need to restore the integrity of mayors: "We have regretted that mayors, unduly engaged in electoral battles, have accordingly compromised their integrity as communal magistrates." The aim of the 1870 commission, in his view, was thus to prepare "a project of decentralization that will have as its goal precisely to take away from all governments that succeed each other in France the temptation to use the immense powers with which centralization provides them."[218] One of the principal instruments of this "temptation" was the power to nominate mayors, and it was being clearly suggested that a significant reform was in the offing. However, this implicit pledge to release mayors from their dependency on the administration was not fully honored. Despite the recommendations of the commission, inspired by the intervention of Prévost-Paradol,[219] the municipal law of June 1870 firmly retained the prerogative to appoint mayors in the hands of the state.

Ollivier's position on the question of mayors was principally inspired by a fear that was common to all liberals in the final years of the Second Empire: the rise of radical republicanism. After the mid-1860s, indeed, the specter of municipal socialism had begun to haunt liberals across France. In a letter to Baron de Barante in February 1863, Victor de Broglie remarked the following with some acidity: "The red republicans

[217] *Un projet de décentralisation*, 41.
[218] *Corps Législatif: Compte-rendu analytique des séances* (Paris: Journal Officiel, 1870), 2:416.
[219] Guiral, *Prévost-Paradol*, 682–83.

are looking forward to many successes in the forthcoming city elections and will no doubt come up with individuals who are heavily compromised in socialism. There has never been any less hope for the defenders of an honest freedom, and even if we still pray for it, we feel like a tribe of Red Indians among the white populations of America."[220]

In October 1869 Ollivier expressed a similar sense of apprehension: "I cannot go so far as to grant municipal councils the right to elect their mayors. . . . If we agree to this proposal, the revolutionaries will demand that mayors be chosen by universal suffrage; and if we accede to this demand, they will ask for the suppression of mayors."[221] This was again an expression of the principle of conditionality: a liberal local government regime could not be enacted under conditions deemed politically inimical to central government. This menace seemed particularly potent in France's cities and large towns. A liberal pamphleteer noted in 1870: "Eight or ten big cities are capable of producing on a smaller scale the agitations of Paris; they all contain masses that can carry out their own little riots."[222]

Although perhaps not entirely unreasonable, this view clashed with the earlier liberal postulate that granting a greater measure of local liberty would serve the prophylactic purpose of containing and even *preventing* the spread of social and political revolution. In 1860, as part of his advocacy of decentralization, Léonce de Lavergne had declared:

> Elective councils of the commune and the department are not given to excesses and follies. . . . If we have time and again despaired of a free government, it is because we have not been sufficiently prepared for it by a proper experience of local franchises. Essentially positive, local interests do not really lend themselves to fashionable theories and sweeping passions.[223]

By the late 1860s this sanguine approach was no longer considered tenable by most liberals. Some starry-eyed individuals continued to harbor the illusion that communal liberties could be extended without raising the political temperature of the country.[224] Even as late as June 1870, an article in *L'Opinion Nationale* could claim that "the communes are too deferential and loyal for central government ever to have to fear

---

[220] Broglie to Barante, 8 February 1863, in *Souvenirs du Baron de Barante*, by Barante, 362–63.

[221] Emile Ollivier, *Journal, 1846–1869* (Paris: Julliard, 1961), 2:384, 386.

[222] Lebon, *La décentralisation*, 11.

[223] Léonce de Lavergne, *La constitution de 1852 et le décret du 24 novembre 1860* (Paris: Dumineray, 1860), 42–43.

[224] See, for example, Lebon's view that "all political freedoms do not pose a threat provided strong local government exists, as in the United States or England" (*La décentralisation*, 35).

their hostility."[225] But most liberals did not share this benevolent optimism. After 1868 many cities and large towns were agitated by waves of strikes, often accompanied by violent expressions of political protest. Radical republican groups took advantage of the more tolerant legislation the Empire introduced in 1868 to inflame public opinion; in some cities these groups benefited from the tacit and even active support of the regime.[226] The passions of local political life in urban areas, far from being a potential source of regeneration, came to be seen by most liberals as a grave threat to social order. In 1870 the *Revue des Deux Mondes* described society as facing a "state of siege";[227] another liberal pamphleteer compared striking workers to "an army that is organizing itself for the Revolution."[228]

Under these circumstances, according greater priority to local liberty over the defense of the social good became increasingly problematic. The menace of social revolution thus placed increasingly heavy strains on one of the central premises of the liberal case for decentralization.

THE ROLE OF THE ADMINISTRATION

As we noted earlier, the denunciation of the pernicious role of the administration was commonplace among liberals throughout the Second Empire. Given their express commitment to the principle of self-government, it might have been expected that this hostility would be translated into substantive proposals for administrative reform. Yet those concrete suggestions for change which emerged were limited in number, modest in their ambitions, and indeed ambivalent about their ultimate purpose. I will argue here that this restraint was caused by a number of factors, of which probably the most important was a lingering attachment to the structural principles of French administration. In other words, beneath the rhetorical commitment to local liberty and decentralization continued to lurk a powerful (and not fully resolved) identification with the centralist institutional purposes of the French state.

Several features of the French bureaucratic machine were a source of concern to liberals. They generally believed that the growth of the bureaucracy had contributed to the collapse of standards of public integrity. Thus, a local pamphlet railed against "the bureaucratic spirit with its arrogance, its caste prejudices, its political nullity, its disdain for the

---

[225] B. de la Cadière, in *L'Opinion Nationale*, 26 June 1870.

[226] This was noted by Ernest Duvergier de Hauranne, in *La coalition libérale* (Paris: Le Chevalier, 1869), 23–25.

[227] Charles de Mazade, "Chronique de la Quinzaine," *Revue des Deux Mondes*, 1 April 1870, 757–58.

[228] Abel Joire, *Questions industrielles et questions sociales* (Paris: Masson, 1870).

public, and its humility toward the governing powers, whoever they are and whatever they do."[229]

The symbol of this institutional perversion was the prefect, who was the target of considerable abuse from decentralist publications in general. Although liberals rhetorically echoed this vituperation, they signally refused to follow the lead of republican and legitimist pamphleteers who called for the complete abolition of the prefectoral corps. At best, they joined in opposition calls for a purge of the administration[230] but did not advocate significant structural reforms. They rejected out of hand proposals to elect subprefects by universal suffrage or to have prefects appointed by the General Council: "Political unity would be threatened, and the heart of the administration would move from the center to the extremities."[231] Instead, the liberal solution to the problem of prefectoral power was seen to lie in scaling down the prerogatives of the institution.

It was also suggested that a greater number of executive (and supervisory) functions should be assigned to the General Council, notably in the budgetary sphere. Finally, to assist the departmental assembly with these tasks, the creation of a permanent executive commission of the departmental assembly was mooted by the Nancy program and subsequently taken up by liberal publicists.[232]

Three further features of the administrative system were also causes of preoccupation to Second Empire liberals: the political role of the Council of State, the system of administrative justice, and the legal irresponsibility of public servants. The Council of State played a dual role in the legislative process. On one hand, it was responsible for drafting legislation prior to its discussion and adoption by the Legislative Corps. On the other hand, for most of the Second Empire the council was entrusted with defending government legislation in the chamber. Ministers were responsible not to the legislature but directly to the emperor.[233]

The opposition deplored this state of affairs. The institution of a ministry that was truly responsible to the Legislative Corps was one of the

---

[229] "De l'éducation politique de la France," 57.

[230] Charles de Rémusat, *Mémoires de ma vie*, 258; see also the articles by Ulysse Ladet in *Le Temps*, 16 January 1870, and by Prévost-Paradol in *Journal des Débats*, 22 and 26 January 1870. In the latter article, Prévost-Paradol went to great lengths to minimize the extent of the purge required.

[231] Billet, *De la décentralisation administrative*, 12.

[232] *Un projet de décentralisation*, 58–61.

[233] As Napoleon explained in a letter to Persigny (9 February 1863), "Ministers must internalize the spirit of the constitution, which makes them responsible to me alone, which makes me responsible for their actions. They must therefore do nothing important without my assent" (quoted in *L'Empire libéral*, by Ollivier, 3:81–82).

most consistent demands of the liberal opposition (as well as the constitutionalist minority within the Bonapartist movement).[234] But the prelegislative role of the Council of State was also sharply criticized. Prévost-Paradol deplored the central role accorded to the council, which
often seemed to become the principal agent of legislative codification
rather than its instrument.[235] Laboulaye argued that the monopoly given
to the Council of State in legislative initiation and preparation created a
body of laws that were often ill suited to the needs and aspirations of
the public.

> In a democracy the laws, as all else, have to be the expression of popular
> will; how can this will be known if it is not consulted? A Council of State
> may be wiser and more intelligent than the majority of the nation, but the
> best laws for a people are not an absolute matter; they are those which,
> within reasonable limits, best respond to its needs and its desires. This is
> why, on the question of the purposes of law, public opinion is more knowl-
> edgeable than the Council of State.[236]

Two other features of the administrative system that worried liberals
were local administrative justice and the legal irresponsibility of public
servants. In the latter case, the problem was simple: no member of the
bureaucracy could be held accountable for his actions before a court of
law. Criminal proceedings could not be instituted in a civil court against
a prefect who abused his legal powers or a magistrate who was guilty of
corruption. Most liberals thus demanded the suppression of the legal
provision that guaranteed immunity from public prosecution to all state
functionaries. In the stern opinion of Casimir Perier, "Article 75 of the
constitution has become, under the present regime, the most powerful
instrument of arbitrary and oppressive rule which could be imagined by
an ardent champion of absolutism."[237]

Many also viewed the system of administrative justice as grossly partial. Most local complaints against the administration were brought to
the prefectoral council, a judicial body entrusted with interpreting administrative law. Its decisions were final, and there was no provision for
appeal. Some liberals argued that this institution merely created a parallel and arbitrary system of justice. The Nancy program thus campaigned for the abolition of these prefectoral councils and the transfer
of all administrative litigation to civil tribunals. The reason for propos-

[234] See, for example, the January 1864 speech by Latour du Moulin on ministerial responsibility, in *Autorité et liberté*, by Pierre-Célestin Latour du Moulin (Paris: Hachette,
1874), 2:48–49.
[235] *Journal des Débats*, 16 February 1870.
[236] Laboulaye, *Le parti libéral*, 214–16.
[237] Auguste Victor Laurent Casimir Perier, *L'article 75 de la Constitution de l'an VIII
sous le régime de la Constitution de 1852* (Paris: Le Chevalier, 1867), 32.

ing such a reform was unambiguous: "It is contrary to sound principle to grant judicial power to movable functionaries in matters where the state is both judge and party."[238]

Yet these criticisms were not universal. Some liberals were opposed to the political and legislative functions of the Council of State and deplored its inherent bias against the provinces: "We know by experience to what extent the Council of State is attached to the prerogatives of central government at the expense of the interests of the communes and departments."[239] But other liberals took a more benign view of the institution and indeed often welcomed its not-insignificant role in bringing to book the excesses of the imperial administration.[240] Some liberal pamphleteers also argued that there was nothing wrong with the principle of a separate regime for local administrative justice: "The prefectoral council is an impartial intermediary among the commune, the department, the state, and private persons. This role is presently discharged inadequately, in appalling conditions; however, the principle of the institution is excellent; it is merely a question of knowing how to use it."[241]

Indeed, the overall impression of the administration that emerged from the liberal critique was ambivalent in a number of respects. First, as previously noted, there was a striking contrast between central and territorial administrative institutions. The former were generally seen as reliable and devoted to the public interest, whereas the latter appeared as inefficient and partisan.[242] But even this negative view was often qualified by the proposition that it was not the institutions that were flawed but rather the manner in which they were used by the Second Empire.

Alternatively, the problem was identified in terms of personnel recruitment. The regime was blamed for the way in which particular members of the various local administrations were appointed and promoted, but the institutions themselves were exempt of criticism; in some liberal writings, they were often portrayed in a highly favorable light. Victor de Broglie, for example, noted that "the institution of prefectures, an achievement of the consulate at its best, is sensible and well planned. The prefect is above all the government's representative, responsible for executive power throughout the department; he represents the rights and general interests of the state; he is the voice that commands, the eye that supervises, the hand that acts."[243]

---

[238] Un projet de décentralisation, 63.

[239] Charles Tassin, Un mot à l'enquête ouverte sur la question de décentralisation (Troyes: Dufey-Robert, 1866), 26.

[240] Wright, Le Conseil d'Etat, 165.

[241] Fournier, Les réformes nécéssaires, 168.

[242] Saint-Marc Girardin, "La Décentralisation," Journal des Débats, 24 February 1870.

[243] Victor de Broglie, Vues sur le gouvernement, 173.

Even more ebullient was Thiers's assessment in the final volume of his history of the First Empire: "This firm, active, and trustworthy administration, which makes our accounting system the most effective in existence, our power the most operational of all Europe, and which remains steady when our governments are panicked by the influence of revolutions . . . it maintains France upright even when its head vacillates."[244]

Although expressed in his characteristically hyperbolic style, Thiers's view of the administration was in the final analysis broadly representative of liberal opinion. Although its political functions were deplored, the bureaucracy continued to be perceived as an instrument of administrative excellence, which maintained public (and especially financial) order irrespective of the political turbulences that swept the center. Therefore, in the name of two core liberal values — the preservation of national unity and the maintenance of social order — a unitary and centralized administrative system needed to be maintained, even if the behavior of its individual agents sometimes left a great deal to be desired. Liberals thus often ended up with a schizophrenic position on the role of the administration, seeing it both as a source of unlimited public virtue and as an agent of undesirable political passions.

Again, Ollivier most strikingly typified this contradictory approach. On one hand, his positive appraisal of the administration was not far removed from the encomium Thiers offered. Speaking of the administrative institutions he inherited when he took office in January 1870, Ollivier declared that the French bureaucracy was

> superior to everything that has existed and will exist at all times and in all countries: it contained honest, educated, experienced, and devoted officials who, except in rare moments of electoral aberration, determined themselves on the basis of equity, without any partisan considerations. There was nothing to change in this admirable mechanism; it provided freedom with a strong underpinning that protected it from sudden and violent shocks.[245]

Yet in the same volume he later complained bitterly about the authoritarian Bonapartists who had fought a rearguard battle against his reformist government from within the administration: "Since the Bonapartist party had long been at the helm, it could find men of influence who were willing to assist it in all branches of the administration."[246] That the same administration could contain professional excellence and political bias was central to the liberal view, but none of the critics of the Empire paused to ask whether these two conceptions of the bureau-

---

[244] Adolphe Thiers, *Histoire du Consulat et de l'Empire* (Paris: Paulin, 1863), 20:730.
[245] Ollivier, *L'Empire libéral*, 12:248.
[246] Ibid., 343.

cracy were intellectually compatible. Hence the unresolved tension in their minds about the necessary scope of administrative reforms.

Such a strong attachment to the unity and cohesion of the administration also had important consequences for the liberal conception of local self-government. It meant that a local government regime was worth changing only to the extent that it did not undermine the public-interest functions of the bureaucracy. Because these functions were particularly important in times of political crisis, it followed that no significant administrative change was desirable while the threat of radical revolution remained potent.

Liberals commonly claimed to prefer the despotism of central government to that of a local administrative overlord. Yet, as their ambivalence concerning the administration confirmed, they judged the local despotism of a prefect to be eminently preferable to that of a republican mayor. In other words, faced with the choice between paternalism and certain forms of democracy, the instinctive liberal preference still went to the former.

The Contradictions of Liberal Self-Government

By the time the Empire collapsed in September 1870, a number of general conclusions could be drawn about the position French liberals had reached on local liberty and self-government. First, it was worth asking what broader impact the liberal proposals had. The general consensus is that even though the liberal movement failed to win over the Bonapartist regime to its proposals on decentralization, at least it helped (together with the legitimists) place the issue of local liberty at the center of national political debate.[247]

It is also undeniable that the regime met some specific liberal demands. Thus, the Nancy manifesto's proposal that mayors be chosen from their respective councils was ratified in the liberal Empire's municipal law in 1870. In broader terms, the ideological buoyancy of liberalism was undeniable during the 1860s; indeed, it extended far beyond the question of decentralization. As we noted at the beginning of the chapter, on such essential matters as the protection of individual freedom, the advocacy of the rule of law, and the practice of constitutional government, liberal doctrines gained widespread currency during the second decade of the Empire. This influence extended not only to public opinion but also to the attitudes and norms of the Bonapartists, republicans, and even legitimists.

---

[247] Louis Greenberg, *Sisters of Liberty: Marseille, Lyon, Paris, and the Reaction to a Centralized State, 1868–1871* (Cambridge: Harvard University Press, 1971), 64–65.

It is true that this extension of liberal norms occurred to some extent at the expense of the political and intellectual core of liberalism. None-theless, liberals made a positive contribution to the emergence of post-monarchist constitutional norms in modern France, even though — as I will argue later — this contribution fell considerably short of their maxi-malist objectives.

Equally worthy of acknowledgment from an internal perspective was the evolution of the structure of liberalism during the Second Empire. Liberal political thought did not remain static during this period; the question of decentralization forced a reconsideration of its attachment to the centralized state and prompted a reevaluation of the social (as opposed to individual) dimension of political action — an aspect rather neglected by the classical liberal tradition in France. In particular, the focus on local liberty as one of the preconditions of effective citizenship was a significant departure from the somewhat complacent attitudes of the July Monarchy elites on the matter. Thanks in no small measure to the authoritarian Empire, French liberals came to realize that the proper definition of a political community required not only a conception of the state but also a theory of citizenship.

Although they did not fully succeed in articulating such a theory, as we will see later, liberal pamphleteers at least offered many interesting contributions on the issue of sociability in their discussions of local lib-erty during the 1860s. The criticisms of those who saw in the liberalism of the Second Empire a regression from the style and substance of their predecessors during the first half of the nineteenth century are thus wide of the mark.[248]

While noting these advances in liberal thought during the Second Em-pire, this chapter has also sought to highlight the internal ambivalences in its position on self-government. These elements of ambiguity stemmed from two different sources: political and ideological.

At the political level, liberals were divided in their appreciation of the evolution of the imperial regime in 1870 and the necessary response to the rise of radical republicanism. In the Legislative Corps elected in 1869, a majority of liberals welcomed the reforms announced by the regime; only a vocal minority continued to refuse to support the Empire until all "necessary" liberties had been promulgated.[249] These cleavages were manifested most graphically during the campaign for the May 1870 plebiscite, in which liberals confronted each other from opposite

[248] See, for example, Georges Burdeau, *Traité de Science Politique* (Paris: Librairie Gén-érale, 1953), 5:198.
[249] See Girard, *Les élections de 1869*, vii.

sides.[250] Liberal converts and sympathizers included Ollivier, Guizot, Barrot, Laboulaye, Albert de Broglie, Charles de Rémusat, Barante, Sacy, Prévost-Paradol, and many others.[251] Some even accepted official positions in the new administration. In many parts of France, local Orleanist notables rallied entirely to the Bonapartist camp.[252]

This evolving political situation triggered a number of interrogations among liberals about the validity of the principle of self-government. These hesitations were in a sense latent in the value system of French liberals, as we have seen earlier, but the political conjuncture of the late 1860s brought them out into the open. After the events of 1870–71, these doubts hardened into new certainties. As a result of this reconsideration of their position, many liberals eventually altered their conceptions of the social and political prerequisites of citizenship and thus abandoned their commitment to decentralization.

My contention in this chapter is that the developments of 1870–71 effectively did not cause this change; rather, these events revealed and aggravated a number of contradictions in the liberal position as it had developed by the late Second Empire. I have highlighted these doubts and uncertainties about the validity of decentralism throughout this chapter and will summarize them here.

First, liberals retained a powerful attachment to the ideal of a unitary state—an attachment that was inconsistent with their discourse about the importance of minimizing the state's role. Despite a rhetoric that sometimes suggested otherwise, liberals set very strict limits to the extent of self-government they were prepared to concede to communes and departments, even under optimal political circumstances. This circumspection was particularly reflected in their attitude to federalist doctrines. Such approaches were rejected not only as a violation of the sacred principles of legal, administrative, and political unity produced by the 1789 Revolution but also because of a continuing perception of the unsuitability of provinces for substantive self-government. Communes were often inhabited by weak, ignorant, and credulous populations; deliberative assemblies were too easily manipulated by the sophistry of the clergy or the neofeudal authority of the local aristocracy; local populations remained enmeshed in a web of language, custom, and ritual that could potentially inhibit their broader identification with the

---

[250] For an exposition of the reasons liberals should rally to the Empire, see Auguste Pougnet, *Le parti libéral en 1870* (Paris: Germer Baillière, 1870).

[251] Girard, *Les libéraux français*, 208–10.

[252] For the case of the Allier, see J. Cornillon, *Le Bourbonnais à la fin de l'Empire et sous le Gouvernement de la Défense Nationale* (Moulins: Imprimerie du Progrès de l'Allier, 1924), 9.

civilizing values of the French center. Thus, behind the rejection of federalism and affirmation of the principle of national unity, there continued to lurk a persistent liberal attachment to a paternalistic vision of society.

This paternalism was also in evidence in the defense of key aspects of the practice of administrative centralization. Throughout the debate on decentralization, liberals strongly attacked the actions of an imperial administration that was variously seen as corrupt, inequitable, arbitrary, aloof, and wasteful. Liberal pamphleteers denounced the pervasiveness of the "bureaucratic spirit," and such language suggested an uncompromisingly negative view of the bureaucracy. In his letter of support to the Nancy manifesto, Montalembert went so far as to urge his fellow countrymen to dispense with "this colony of administrators which represents a sort of dominant and conquering caste that is entrusted, as the English in the Hindustan, with speaking and acting for the incapable indigenous peoples."[253]

Yet, paradoxically, liberals also retained an almost hypnotic sense of attachment to the notion of administrative excellence. Thiers was the epitome of this sentiment, and he defended it vigorously (and successfully) during his confrontation with the decentralization commission in April 1871.[254] But he was by no means an isolated case. For example, the journalist Georges Guéroult, although an advocate of decentralization, nonetheless asserted that "the present administrative system, inspired by our military organization, is extraordinarily strong and effective."[255]

This fixation was visible in three ways: in the consistent (if rather contradictory) praise heaped on central administrative institutions, often portrayed as a paradigm of responsibility, impartiality, and sagacity; in the sturdy defense of the functions (as opposed to the practices) of the central and territorial administrations and a tendency to regard the administration's problems in terms of personnel rather than structure; and, finally, in the continuing preference for administrative supervision and regulation of local government institutions and an instinctive suspicion of deliberative assemblies, especially at the communal level. In sum, the liberal notion of self-government was constrained by a high regard for the principles of centralized administrative excellence, the application of which could only undermine the scope for effective self-government.

---

[253] *Un projet de décentralisation*, 204–5.

[254] The full text of his harangue against decentralization is in Arch. Nat. C2866 (Commission de Décentralisation).

[255] *L'Opinion Nationale*, 20 March 1870.

Also prominent was the continuing suspicion of universal suffrage. Despite suggestions that the liberalism of the 1860s successfully shed the antidemocratic legacy of the July Monarchy,[256] my evidence, on balance, points in the opposite direction. Throughout this chapter I have noted the liberal ambivalence about the mass vote, which remained entirely unresolved by the late 1860s; in fact, the events of 1870–71 served only to accentuate it.[257] At one level, there was a widespread sense among liberals (especially those of a progressive disposition) that mass involvement in politics was an irreversible feature of the political process. However serious their reservations about the phenomenon, there was therefore little sense in opposing the inevitable. And indeed, it is true that a small number of liberals such as Thiers and Waddington adapted very successfully to the exigencies of universal suffrage after 1871.[258]

Furthermore, some liberals believed that universal suffrage could in theory act as a mechanism for controlling the actions of central and local government, as well as inducting the citizenry into a responsible (as opposed to petulant) practice of politics. The manifesto of the Ligue de la Décentralisation underlined the point: "It is by giving universal suffrage the opportunity to exercise itself often and freely that it will come to regulate itself."[259] Nonetheless, a number of negative considerations remained and indeed outweighed those mentioned earlier. Some progressive liberals voiced their concerns sotto voce, or else in allusions and understatements; thus Nefftzer noted that universal suffrage was perfectible.[260]

Others, however, were much more forthright. Nowhere were these doubts better articulated than in the following passage from Charles de Rémusat's memoirs:

Universal suffrage was repeatedly used in a continual cycle of elections, especially rural elections, which were of little importance in themselves. It was abandoned to voters who understood neither its rules nor its principles, and who acted without any control, sometimes with complete irresponsibility and sometimes under the influence of strong local passions. All

[256] See, for example, Tombs, *France, 1814–1914*, 420.

[257] On this aspect of Thiers's career, see Pierre Guiral, *Adolphe Thiers* (Paris: Fayard, 1986), 533.

[258] In 1875 Dupont-White described universal suffrage as "an instrument that excels in destruction." See *Politique actuelle* (Paris: Guillaumin, 1875), 326. There is an interesting dossier on Waddington's career in the 1870s in the Archives de la Préfecture de Police, BA-1 1296, Dossier Waddington.

[259] *Statuts de la Ligue de la Décentralisation* (Paris: Dubuisson, 1870), 4.

[260] *Le Temps*, 5 February 1870. See also the article by Dupont-White in the issue of 16 February 1870.

of this has put us in the habit of regarding this manner of voting either as a ridiculous comedy or as an instrument of deception whose use has to be mastered.[261]

This disdainful assessment of the gullibility of the rural electorate was not simply a criticism of the Empire's practice of universal suffrage, as is commonly argued.[262] It was also an expression of instinctive liberal discomfort with the very notion of the mass vote. In theory, liberals believed that regular electoral participation could prove to be a useful instrument of political socialization. But this was a case where theory did not tally with intuition. As one liberal confessed, "Direct universal suffrage for political elections cannot be defended by common sense or reason or even experience."[263] In fact, the principle of universal suffrage seemed questionable at a time when the majority of the electorate was ill educated and therefore susceptible to manipulation.

As we have noted, liberals were irked by the manner in which universal suffrage was practiced under the Second Empire, in particular, by the constant intervention of the administration in electoral campaigns and the cynical exploitation of the vote for partisan purposes (as typified by the May 1870 plebiscite). Most alarming, there remained a niggling sense among liberals that they were temperamentally unsuited to the passions and turbulence of mass politics; such feelings of self-doubt were amplified by the poor showing of many leading Orleanist notables in elections to the Legislative Corps. Liberal candidates were vulnerable on a number of counts: individually, they often lacked the common touch; they were too easily portrayed as men of the past; their resentment of universal suffrage was widely known and carefully exploited by their opponents; and their resolute defense of bourgeois interests rendered them suspicious in the eyes of rural and working-class voters alike.[264]

Prévost-Paradol's unfortunate experiences in the legislative elections of 1863 and 1869 were in this sense exemplary. Running in the first constituency of the Dordogne (which included the town of Périgueux) in 1863, he managed a derisory score; the entire town of Périgueux gave him only one vote.[265] Six years later he moved to Nantes, where he trailed the republican socialist candidate Ange Guépin by more than

---

[261] Charles de Rémusat, *Mémoires de ma vie*, 48.

[262] See, for example, Georges Ferriere, "Les libéraux devant le suffrage universel sous le Second Empire," in *Réflexions idéologiques sur l'Etat: Actes du Colloque d'Aix-en-Provence, 25–27 Septembre 1986* (Aix-en-Provence: Presses Universitaires d'Aix-Marseille, 1987), 129–50.

[263] Mony, *De la décentralisation*, 143.

[264] La Gorce, *Histoire du Second Empire*, 4:195–97.

[265] Jacques Lagrange, *La vie en Périgord sous Louis-Napoléon III* (Périgueux: Pilote 24, 1992), 68.

nine thousand votes; the official candidate Gaudin eventually won the seat on the second ballot.[266] His cousin Ludovic Halévy, who had traveled from Paris to offer moral support, captured the sense of devastation in the liberal camp.

There are shouts of "Long Live Guépin!" and some republican song is bleated. The campaign is over, and how over. . . . Not even two thousand votes! I spent the evening with the principal members of the committee that had sponsored the candidacy of Paradol. I cannot describe the pain of these honest folk. Businessmen, industrialists, wealthy landowners, they all felt crushed. The legitimate and patriotic influence they had exercised until then at Nantes was annihilated, destroyed. . . . They were insignificant nothings, crushed by universal suffrage.[267]

Little wonder that universal suffrage often appeared to liberal elites as an uncertain and unreliable political instrument, whose effects needed to be corrected by the steady hand of paternalism. Here again one can find the liberal advocacy of the principle of self-government undermined by higher-order principles. For alongside the political preconditions of local liberty was also a social imperative: that the practice of self-government should be operated by a distinct social elite.[268] The liberal demand for local autonomy appeared under these conditions as little more than a call for bourgeois empowerment.

Liberalism seeks control and discussion, as well as the progressive extension of political rights and the ever greater participation of the citizenry in government, but it does not admit a priori the government of all by all. . . . It desires that citizens be masters of themselves and their affairs, but it only admits them to the management of these affairs on the basis of established or presumed titles.[269]

The liberal commitment to enlightened paternalism also undermined its claim to advance the cause of citizenship. As noted throughout this chapter, part of the rationale for local liberty was to enable members of local communities to realize their individuality. Released from the petty constraints of an omnipotent administration, individuals could thus be encouraged to develop their social and civic senses in a manner consistent with the liberal conception of citizenship. In an entry in his diary in 1860, Ollivier noted: "The only true way to decentralize is by increas-

---

[266] On the circumstances of his candidacy, see Léon Séché, "Prévost-Paradol, candidat-député," *Revue Politique et Parlementaire* (April 1901): 119–29.

[267] Ludovic Halévy, *Carnets* (Paris: Calmann Lévy, 1935), 1:195–96.

[268] On the bourgeois sense of "calling," see Adeline Daumard, *Les bourgeois et la bourgeoisie en France depuis 1815* (Paris: Flammarion, 1991), 237–38.

[269] Nefftzer, "Libéralisme," 119.

ing the autonomy of the commune, to broaden even more the sphere of individual initiative. This is genuine decentralization."[270] Saint-Marc Girardin eloquently mapped out these laudable objectives: "True decentralization consists in suppressing such and such administrative tiers, and indeed in replacing them with nothing, in allowing individuals to do alone what the administration formerly did for them, and in resigning oneself to see the child stumble by consoling ourselves that we all learned to walk by not being afraid of falling down."[271]

Yet what some liberals gave gracefully with one hand was snatched away by the other. For decentralization was also portrayed as a means of reinforcing traditional controls over local communities. These controls could be political, as noted in the example of local bourgeois notables. But at a deeper level—and especially in the eyes of conservative liberals—they also needed to be moral, in order to impose a prescribed set of social and cultural values on members of society. For this reason liberals often appealed to the Bonapartist regime to accept their proposals for decentralization, because both political groups were seen to be working toward the same objective: preventing revolutionary upheavals in France by defending the social and moral status quo. In the words of a liberal notable:

> What is today our motivation for asking the Empire to take a new step toward decentralization? Is it the desire to set up a niggardly opposition in departmental councils so as to obstruct its progress? No one can seriously believe this. It is, on the contrary, based on a sincere desire to give our country order and stability and to provide the government with new powers against any revolution that might threaten its existence.[272]

In his letter to the minister of the interior at the conclusion of his commission's work, Barrot also spelled out the social conservatism of the liberal conception of decentralization: "Religious sentiments to be revived by freedom, family ties to be strengthened, the authority of its head to be reinforced . . . here are as many ways of substituting material strength with moral force. *Indeed, decentralization is nothing else.*"[273] The promotion of religiosity, the protection of the family, and the preservation of traditional hierarchies: such objectives clearly went against the thrust of individual emancipation, at least as most progressive and rationalist liberals claimed to understand it. At best, they freed individuals from the clutches of administrative tyranny only to hand them over

---

[270] Ollivier, *Journal*, 1:448.

[271] *Journal des Débats*, 26 March 1870.

[272] Robert de Nervo, "Quelques mots sur le projet de Nancy," in *La décentralisation en 1829 et 1833*, by Prosper de Barante (Paris: Douniol, 1866), 59.

[273] Odilon Barrot, in *Le Temps*, 1 July 1870; emphasis added.

to an even more constraining set of social institutions. The "society open to all aptitudes, efforts, and ambitions"[274] promised by liberals thus turned out to be highly policed.

THE LIBERAL FAILURE AND THE LIMITS OF THE PROJECT FOR SELF-GOVERNMENT

Historians of French liberalism have attempted to portray the emergence of the new republican order after 1875 as a victory of liberal ideology.[275] In his study of Guizot, Pierre Rosanvallon goes so far as to argue that the entire political project of Third Republic opportunists was merely the logical extension of the ideological framework forged by doctrinaire liberals under the Restoration and July Monarchy.[276]

This claim that the new republican order was a liberal creation can certainly be defended with reference to some aspects of the 1875 constitution, which represented a compromise between republican and liberal principles.[277] From a broader perspective, as noted previously, there is no denying that the creation of the Republic in France was partly the result of the repeated attacks waged against the imperial order by (among others) liberal publicists, particularly over questions of civil and political liberty. Liberals and republicans also shared a number of principles, most notably a disposition toward rationalism, secularism, and even anticlericalism, and these values were strongly represented in the political order that emerged after 1877.[278] There was even a sense in which liberals and republicans could be said to have influenced each other during their long years of opposition to imperial power: the republicans moderated their Jacobinism and considerably toned down their redistributive proposals, whereas the liberals made some efforts— even if they turned out to be insufficient in the end—to come to terms with the social and political realities of mass democracy.[279]

But it is a considerable overstatement to proclaim the period after

---

[274] Charles de Rémusat, "Le parti libéral et le mouvement Européen," *Revue des Deux Mondes*, November 1866, 16.

[275] See, for example, Jardin, *Histoire du libéralisme politique*, 402–14.

[276] Pierre Rosanvallon, *Le moment Guizot* (Paris: Gallimard, 1985), 370.

[277] See Girard, *Les libéraux français*, 266. For a sense of the debate on the 1875 constitution in the early Third Republic, see Louis Blanc, *Histoire de la constitution du 25 février 1875* (Paris: Charpentier, 1882); Ferdinand-Dreyfus, "La Constitution de 1875," *Revue Politique et Parlementaire* (March 1899): 465–74; and Léon Duguit, "Le fonctionnement du régime parlementaire en France depuis 1875," *Revue Politique et Parlementaire* (August 1900): 363–74.

[278] Félix Ponteil, *Les classes bourgeoises et l'avènement de la démocratie* (Paris: Albin Michel, 1989), 380.

[279] Léon Séché, *Jules Simon, sa vie et son oeuvre* (Paris: Dupret, 1887), 81–82.

1870 as a liberal victory. It is not to be forgotten, after all, that the "liberalism of fear" prevailed in the late 1860s and early 1870s, and that in this context many conservative liberals pinned their hopes on a constitutional monarchy after the fall of the Second Empire. The new republican state clearly represented a further advance in the direction of popular sovereignty than most of them desired. Edouard Hervé described these liberals' program: "There exists in France a great party, which is neither red nor white and which aspires neither to revolution nor to counterrevolution, neither to a return to the old social order nor to the destruction of the present one."[280] This was a far cry from the vibrant and forward-looking language of the republican elites who triumphed after 1877. Furthermore, although largely sympathetic to bourgeois interests, the new republican regime was neither subservient to nor exclusively focused on them; its conception of the state could in no way be characterized as minimalist, either in the economic or in the social sphere; and, perhaps most important, its commitment to universal suffrage was much more categorical than has been seen to be the case with the liberal elites of the Second Empire. In all these respects, the republican order of the Third Republic departed significantly from the canons of French liberalism.

Therefore, from the point of view of both personnel and political values, one can argue that the collapse of the liberal Empire and the subsequent emergence of a republican order represented a defeat for the liberals with whom this chapter has been primarily concerned. Indeed, as mentioned earlier, many had viewed the liberal Empire with considerable benevolence and voted with the Bonapartists in the plebiscite of May 1870. These men also went down with the liberal Empire in August 1870 and the failed conservative reaction in the ensuing years. Although the temporary ascendancy of the "République des ducs" gave a fillip to conservative liberal hopes, it was the republicans who increasingly determined the social and political agenda and eventually took control of government after the 1877 elections.[281] Liberals were left behind, either to rally quietly to the Republic like Laboulaye, who was eventually forgiven his adhesion to the liberal Empire,[282] or, like Saint-Marc Girardin, to spend the last years of their lives waging a bitter and frantic battle against the resurgence of republicanism.[283] Perhaps nothing epitomized this liberal failure better than the fate of two men:

[280] Edouard Hervé, in *Journal de Paris*, 1 February 1872.
[281] On this period, see Daniel Halévy, *La République des ducs*.
[282] In May 1870 his lectures at the Collège de France had to be interrupted after constant heckling by republican students. See *Le Temps*, 25 May 1870.
[283] See Laurence Wylie, *Saint-Marc Girardin* (New York: Syracuse University Press, 1947), 142–51.

Lucien Prévost-Paradol, the talented publicist who committed suicide after hearing of the outbreak of the Franco-Prussian War,[284] and Emile Ollivier, the ex-republican turned liberal who spent the rest of his long life ostracized by his former colleagues, attempting to justify the fateful series of decisions that effectively ended his political career in the summer of 1870.[285]

What were the reasons for this liberal defeat? Lamenting the repeated misfortunes of the liberal idea at the end of the nineteenth century, the political economist Leroy-Beaulieu ventured that "the fault, or rather the mistake, of liberalism was that it was too speculative, too dogmatic, and too optimistic."[286] Although it is perefectly true that the gilded salons of the French Academy did not provide an ideal setting for observing the realities of social and political life, my account of the liberal movement between 1851 and 1870 suggests the need to explore other avenues. The particular events between 1870 and 1877 are no doubt significant here, notably the role of key individuals such as Thiers, who left his Orleanist friends "in the lurch" after 1871.[287] But liberalism also failed because its political project was inadequately attuned to the imperatives of its time, and to understand how and why this proved the case the period of the Second Empire is critical.

We have seen that liberals lacked secure ideological moorings in the political culture of nineteenth-century France and that their elites were vulnerable and inexperienced in their practice of universal suffrage. More broadly, one can also argue that the discourse of liberals during the 1850s and 1860s was unsuited to the social and political evolution of the times, in two important senses.

First, the liberal emphasis on accommodation and consensus failed to capture the public imagination at a time when political opinion was becoming increasingly polarized. In this respect, the secret of the republican success, as we will see in the following chapter, was that many of its elites were able to respond to this ideological polarization while producing a vision of the future that was dynamic and imaginative yet at the same time moderate and incremental.

Second, one can argue that the liberals failed in the 1870s because one of their key premises about the problems produced by centralization was flawed. The oft-repeated liberal assertion that France suffered from a crisis of sociability was in many ways contradicted by the actual

[284] Guiral, *Prévost-Paradol*, 706–26.

[285] For Ollivier's life and a defense of his political career, see Theodore Zeldin, *Emile Ollivier and the Liberal Empire of Napoleon III* (Oxford: Clarendon Press, 1963).

[286] Anatole Leroy-Beaulieu, *La révolution et le libéralisme* (Paris: Hachette, 1890), 213.

[287] J.P.T. Bury and R.P. Tombs, *Thiers, 1797–1877* (London: Allen and Unwin, 1986), 250.

awakening of civil society in France under the Second Empire — especially during the 1860s. In the place of the dormant and stagnant country they expected to find, liberal politicians and intellectuals were increasingly confronted with active and vibrant social structures (mostly in urbanized parts of France). Liberals were twice removed from these forms of social dynamism; their language was not attuned to the needs of its new strata; and their social ideology had an insufficient place for the groups clamoring for greater inclusion in the political process. It was the republicans, again, who successfully took over these constituencies as their own in the 1870s and 1880s.

All of this brings us back to my central focus: liberalism failed after 1870 because its underlying conception of citizenship — as already defined by liberal elites during the Second Empire — was riddled with contradictions. As we have seen throughout this chapter, in the 1860s liberals waved the banner of local liberty and rights-based citizenship with great fervor. But these professions of faith were constantly subverted by different and often conflicting priorities. Declarations in favor of communal liberty and autonomous citizenship were not consistent with a continuing attachment to the ideal of a unitary state, an admiration for the expertise embedded in the administration, an entrenched suspicion of universal suffrage, a sense of confidence in the natural superiority of bourgeois rule, and a defense of traditional social institutions.

These contradictions were produced by the different ideological preferences of liberals, all of which served to dilute the substance of their adhesion to decentralist objectives. In this sense, the divide between centralist liberals such as Thiers and Dupont-White and their decentralist counterparts was perhaps less significant than it seemed; liberals rejected their conclusions and rhetoric but essentially continued to agree with their premises.

At the same time, social and political conditions also played a key role in defining the priorities of liberals, and in this context their attachment to self-government was further undermined by the threat of social revolution. As noted earlier, many liberals were concerned with the rise of radical republicanism. By the late 1860s, most of them believed that serious political unrest was ineluctable.[288] We have seen how this conclusion led some liberals to abandon their belief in the prophylactic quality of self-government. Convinced in the early 1860s that decentralization constituted the most effective way to avert the threat of revolution, many liberals eventually came to hold the opposite view. This fear directly inspired many individual decisions to rally to the liberal Empire. Even before his public adhesion to the regime, Prévost-Paradol

---

[288] Charles de Rémusat, *Mémoires de ma vie*, 251.

gave a clear sense of his principal motivations in a letter: "There is indeed a great difference between not liking the Empire and preferring anything to the Empire, including civil war, anarchy, and socialism."[289]

In short, the promotion of self-government was made to depend on what might be called a fear principle: the absence of inimical political conditions at the center. When these conditions were deemed to be troubled or unfavorable, the priority given to local liberty was correspondingly reduced.

This effectively placed the question of decentralization on a slippery slope, on which it rolled down farther and farther after 1870. Whereas a few publicists and liberal reviews continued to argue for local emancipation along self-governing lines in 1871,[290] the majority of liberals became increasingly reserved. After the Paris Commune, many liberals flatly rejected the principle of decentralization altogether.[291] Even those who continued to proclaim its importance introduced significant qualifications to its application. One pamphleteer, although making the case for greater local liberty in 1871, thus suggested that municipal councils be denied the right to discuss political questions: "True municipal freedom does not lie in politics."[292]

In many individual cases, this reaction against "low" politics drove liberals to question the very necessity of local democracy. In a letter to his daughter in May 1871, Silvestre de Sacy noted soberly that "the recent municipal elections have witnessed in our big cities the triumph of men who dream only of mayhem and destruction." He then added: "Why hold municipal elections at all under such conditions?"[293]

Such positions entirely negated the substance of the earlier liberal commitment to decentralization. For many men who had done so much to bring the issue of local liberty to the forefront of political debate, this was an inherently paradoxical position to end up with. But such paradoxes followed naturally from the dualism that, as we have seen throughout this chapter, was at the heart of the liberal condition in nineteenth-century France.

The positive side of this dualism was in many senses typified by

---

[289] Letter dated 25 October 1869, in *Lettres posthumes*, by Prévost-Paradol, 12.

[290] See, for example, Lucien Arréat, *La décentralisation et la loi départementale* (Paris: Lacroix, 1871); Aimé Boutarel, *La décentralisation: Réformes administratives et financières* (Paris: Guillaumin, 1871); Léon de Saint-Pulgent, *Programme de réformes administratives par la décentralisation* (Saint-Etienne: Théolier, 1871); and *Essai sur l'organisation municipale et la liberté des communes* (Nantes: Etiembre, 1871).

[291] A. Esparbié, *Lettre à M. Thiers sur la décentralisation politique* (Lille, 1871), 21–22.

[292] Mony, *De la décentralisation*, 172.

[293] Silvestre de Sacy, "Lettres à ma fille," *Revue des Deux Mondes*, 1 November 1926, 149.

Tocqueville, a noble spirit who always doubted himself but nonetheless — and perhaps despite his better judgment — felt that "beyond the horizon where our gaze stops there is something infinitely better than what we can now see."[294] The darker side of the liberal idea was embodied by the likes of Barrot and Thiers. The latter never abandoned his pessimistic philosophy of human nature, which had long led him to the conclusion that "pain is the universal condition of mankind."[295]

That Thiers outlived Tocqueville was not just an unfortunate historical accident but a telling metaphor of the resurgence of the liberalism of fear by the end of the Second Empire. For not only did Tocqueville's El Dorado not materialize during the second half of the nineteenth century, but events took a savage turn for the worse with the collapse of the liberal Empire, the catastrophic Franco-Prussian War, and the no less calamitous Paris Commune.

These events vindicated the fears of the pessimistic liberals, and it was entirely fitting that it was Thiers who returned to the helm in 1871 to steer the French ship through the troubled transition from Empire to Republic. But the liberal principles that guided his steps were far removed from the optimistic hopes and dreams of liberal publicists in the 1860s; let us not forget that Thiers never described local freedom as a "necessary liberty." Indeed, the events of 1870–71 inoculated many in the liberal movement against the decentralist virus for many decades. Writing in 1895, at the twilight of a long career, Albert de Broglie presented a striking reevaluation of the liberal commitment to self-government under the Second Empire.

The question we never really confronted was to discover whether, when a great revolution has made a clean sweep of local, communal, and provincial institutions[,] . . . these could be replaced arbitrarily by new ones that have no roots, and whether, in a word, when a body has lost its joints and the energy of its muscles, forcible constraint is not the only way to keep it upright. Unfortunately, this is what experience has taught me to believe.[296]

[294] Letter to Rémusat, September 1857, quoted in "De l'esprit de réaction," by Charles de Rémusat, *Revue des Deux Mondes*, 15 October 1861, 805.

[295] Thiers, *De la propriété*, 426.

[296] Albert de Broglie, *Mémoires du Duc de Broglie*, 348–49.

Chapter 4

THE PATH BETWEEN JACOBINISM AND
FEDERALISM: REPUBLICAN MUNICIPALISM

REPUBLICANISM has suffered least from the benign neglect that has afflicted the history of the Second Empire in modern times. In recent years a number of stimulating contributions have helped to deepen our understanding of the political and intellectual life of the republican movement in the nineteenth century, particularly during the 1850s and 1860s.[1]

Yet, granted that we now know a lot more about the history and even the symbolism of the republican tradition,[2] the richness of its ideology during this period remains surprisingly undervalued. Historians of modern French republicanism tend to divide the analysis of their subject between a classical, or "revolutionary," phase (dealing with the development and consequences of the Revolution) and a "modern" phase (focusing on the emergence of liberal democratic notions in France). For instance, in Claude Nicolet's magnificent work *L'idée républicaine en France*, the first phase appears to last from 1789 to the mid-nineteenth century, and the second is seen to begin in 1875.[3] But there is little sense of how, why, and at what intellectual cost the transition was made from the classical phase to the modern one. The implicit assumption is that this change was the direct and necessary product of the victory of the republic over its constitutional alternatives during the 1870s.

In presenting the emergence of a new paradigm of republican citizenship during the Second Empire, this chapter offers a radically different chronology and explanation of this momentous intellectual transition. Central to this explanation is the significant reappraisal of republican notions of democracy, territoriality, and citizenship which took place

[1] Notable contributions include Raymond Huard, *Le mouvement républicain en Bas-Languedoc* (Paris: Presses de la Fondation Nationale des Sciences Politiques, 1992); François Furet and Mona Ozouf, eds., *Le siècle de l'avènement républicain* (Paris: Gallimard, 1993); Hamon, *Les républicains sous le Second Empire*; Robert Alexander, "Restoration Republicanism Reconsidered," *French History* (December 1994): 442–69; Pamela Pilbeam, *Republicanism in Nineteenth-Century France* (London: Macmillan, 1995); and Nord, *The Republican Moment*.

[2] See, in particular, Maurice Agulhon, *Marianne au combat: L'imagerie et la symbolique républicaines de 1789 à 1880* (Paris: Flammarion, 1979) and *Marianne au pouvoir: L'imagerie et la symbolique républicaines de 1880 à 1914* (Paris: Flammarion, 1989).

[3] Nicolet, *L'idée républicaine en France*.

between 1852 and 1870. Here, too, a number of conventional assumptions need to be reconsidered, more particularly those entrenched in historical accounts of the period. The question of the republican approach to local politics and government in the 1860s and 1870s has generally been represented through the prism of subsequent developments, most notably the advent of the Paris Commune in 1871. Recent scholarship has contributed enormously to our understanding of the political and intellectual origins of the commune, as well as its provincial dynamics in 1871.[4]

This predominant focus on the communalist movement and its ramifications has also somewhat distorted our understanding of Second Empire republicanism. The abiding image of the republican community is that of a divided and fractious movement, in which radical, socialist, and revolutionary elements held preponderant positions until the final defeat of the communalist movement in 1871.[5] The positions and especially the doctrinal influence of moderate and reformist republicans have been correspondingly undervalued, if not altogether ignored.[6]

On the question of decentralization, the orthodox view revolves around two broad claims. First, it is argued that the republicans remained deeply divided over the validity of decentralization, with a majority actually opposing the notion.[7] Second, it is alleged that many of those who apparently subscribed to ideas of local autonomy did so

---

[4] See, in particular, Greenberg, *Sisters of Liberty*; Jeanne Gaillard, *Communes de province, Commune de Paris, 1870–1871* (Paris: Flammarion, 1971); on the organization of radical republican groups in Paris in 1868–70, see Alain Dalotel, Alain Faure, and Jean-Claude Freiermuth, *Aux origines de la Commune: Le mouvement des réunions publiques à Paris* (Paris: Maspéro, 1980). See also Martin Phillip Johnson, *The Paradise of Association: Popular Culture and Popular Organizations in the Paris Commune of 1871* (Ann Arbor: University of Michigan Press, 1996).

[5] For an example of this view of republican weakness and division in the late 1860s, see Philippe Vigier, "Le parti républicain en 1870," in *L'esprit républicain: Colloque d'Orléans*, ed. Jacques Viard (Paris: Klincksieck, 1972).

[6] A rare exception is Pierre Barral's excellent work *Les fondateurs de la Troisième République* (Paris: Armand Colin, 1968), which by a judicious selection of speeches and writings of leading republican figures traces the emergence of an "ideologically coherent" doctrine from the 1860s to the 1880s. Considerably less appealing is Sanford Elwitt's *The Making of the Third Republic* and its sequel, *The Third Republic Defended: Bourgeois Reform in France, 1880–1914* (Baton Rouge: Louisiana State University Press, 1986), both rather crude neo-Marxist attempts to present republicanism as an ideological justification of "bourgeois class rule." By far the best work in this tradition remains Enna Jéloubovskaïa's epic narrative *La chute du Second Empire et la naissance de la Troisième République en France* (Moscow: Editions des Langues Etrangères, 1959).

[7] The republican opposition to the Empire is described as "essentially Jacobin and centralist" in *Nationalité et Nationalisme, 1860–1878*, by P. Benaerts et al. (Paris: Presses Universitaires de France, 1968), 33. See also Loppin, *Le self-government local en France*, 104.

mainly for tactical reasons.[8] This chapter will qualify the first and strongly dispute the second claim.

On the question of republican division, it would be sheer folly to ignore the breadth and variety of the republican ideological spectrum after 1851. The republican party was always a broad church, and at perhaps no other time in its history were its doors opened as wide as in the days of the Second Empire. There were a number of distinct views on communal emancipation, as indeed on many other substantive matters, but this diversity was not synonymous with fragmentation. In fact, in this chapter I will trace the emergence of a rich and inventive republican theory of municipal self-government, which was defined in opposition to both Jacobinism and federalism and was accepted by a majority of moderate and constitutionalist republicans.[9] I will argue that this doctrine was fully formed by the end of the Second Empire and that in many ways it anticipated the practice of republican elites after 1870.

More complicated is the question of whether republicans took an essentially tactical view of decentralization. Much of the evidence for this claim lies in the self-justifications of opportunist and radical statesmen during the Third Republic, when they were forced to explain why they seemed to have discarded a doctrine they had expounded so ardently in their youth. The answer, quite plausibly, was that decentralization had never been a key republican value; it was merely a political instrument with which to challenge the electoral hegemony of the Second Empire. In most later republican recollections of their opposition to the Bonapartist regime, the republicans' commitment to decentralization was completely passed over in silence. For example, in an address to a meeting of the Ligue Française de l'Enseignement in 1910, Camille Pelletan gave an eloquent and often moving account of the men who had done battle against the Empire and of the principles underlying their actions. The struggle for local democracy and municipal liberty was not even mentioned.[10]

Such retrospective justifications and omissions need to be treated with caution. This chapter will show that decentralism was defined as a core principle by a majority of constitutionalist and socialist republicans, and indeed that to ignore this fact would be to misconstrue fundamen-

---

[8] See, for example, Nicolet, *L'idée républicaine*, 148–49.

[9] For an examination of the constitutional doctrines of the republicans during this period, see Charles Grangé, *Les doctrines politiques du parti républicain à la fin du Second Empire* (Bordeaux: Cadoret, 1903).

[10] Camille Pelletan, "L'opposition républicaine sous l'Empire," conference given on 26 January 1910, *Revue Politique et Parlementaire* (May 1910): 211–35. On the two Pelletans, see Georges Touroude, *Deux républicains de progrès: Eugène et Camille Pelletan* (Paris: L'Harmattan, 1995).

tally the idealist components of republican doctrine during the Second Empire. However, we will observe that the republican party was divided over how far the decentralist principle should be advanced; in this respect, there was a fundamental opposition between federalist conceptions and the unitary approach that municipalist republicans favored.

THE ANTI-BONAPARTIST FOUNDATIONS OF REPUBLICAN UNITY

Before discussing some of these differences among republicans, it is important to start with the factors that united them. The most profound source of republican unity between 1852 and 1870 was its unrelenting hostility to the Second Empire. Whether of the generation of 1848 or of 1869, liberal or socialist, radical or revolutionary, Jacobin or federalist, metaphysical or positivist, bourgeois parliamentarian or working-class activist, each and every republican was nurtured by a culture of primary anti-Bonapartism. Leaving aside the purely political aspect of this clash — Bonapartists were in government, republicans in opposition; the latter's support was primarily urban, whereas the former relied heavily on the peasant vote — republican objections to the Second Empire were based on a fundamental rejection of the origins, principles, and values of the regime.

First, it was never forgotten that the Empire had been produced by a coup d'état against the Second Republic. At the Baudin trial in 1868, Léon Gambetta consciously equated the Bonapartist tradition with the systematic violation of republican legality: the dates of 18 Brumaire and 2 December were thus to be eternally consigned to the annals of historical infamy.[11] Bonapartists often justified the 1851 coup by invoking the subsequent plebiscites that legitimized the new political order. Throughout the 1850s and 1860s, republicans responded that not even a unanimous public endorsement could justify the state's desecration of legality. The respect of law was thus a principle that transcended even universal suffrage.[12]

In addition, the imperial regime constantly bore the stigma of its repressive actions against its republican opponents. Although severely crushed at the time, republican pamphleteers in exile commemorated popular resistance to the 1851 coup in Paris and the provinces during the 1850s and 1860s.[13] In the later years of the Empire, a number of publications in France brought home to younger generations the extent

[11] See Léon Gambetta, *Discours et plaidoyers politiques*, ed. Joseph Reinach, vol. 1 (Paris: Charpentier, 1880). See also J. J. Weiss, "Plaidoyer dans l'Affaire Baudin," in *Combat constitutionnel* (Paris: Charpentier, 1893), 1–43.

[12] Paul Lacombe, *La République et la liberté* (Paris: Le Chevalier, 1870), 66–67.

[13] Eugène Sue, *La France sous l'Empire* (London: Jeffs, 1857), 17–24.

of Bonapartist repression in the aftermath of the coup.[14] This repression continued in various forms throughout the years of the authoritarian Empire. Republican intellectuals such as Jules Michelet and Jules Simon lost their academic position for refusing to swear an oath of allegiance to the emperor, and institutions such as Freemasonry were purged of their republican elements.[15] After Orsini's failed assassination attempt against the emperor in 1858, large numbers of republican activists and sympathizers were arbitrarily arrested.[16] More generally, political movements, associations, and newspapers had to operate under a strict regime of administrative controls, which set often draconian limits to the freedom of expression of the republican movement. Even in the late 1860s, a public meeting could be dissolved at the mere mention of a proscribed republican figure.[17]

Republicans also cast an overwhelmingly negative appreciation on the founding myths of Bonapartism. Before the advent of the Second Empire, republican pamphleteers often cited the Napoleonic legend as an illustration of the vitality of the French national spirit.[18] In the early days of the 1848 revolution, cries of "Long live Napoleon" were often heard after ritual invocations to the republic.[19] After 1852, however, the mere mention of the initiator of the Napoleonic tradition could cause even the most unimpassioned republicans to splutter with indignation. Thus, Jules Favre caused a storm in the Legislative Corps in 1870 when he ridiculed those who adored the "genius" of Bonaparte, "the man who gave our country an ephemeral glory and led it to ruin and humiliation."[20] A republican historian approvingly quoted Fichte's summary

---

[14] Most notably, Eugène Ténot's two works, *La province en Décembre 1851* (Paris: Le Chevalier, 1868) and *Paris en Décembre 1851* (Paris: Le Chevalier, 1868); see also Charles Dupont, *Les républicains et les monarchistes dans le Var en Décembre 1851* (Paris: Germer Baillière, 1881). For a more recent perspective, see Luc Willette, *Le coup d'Etat du 2 Décembre 1851* (Paris: Aubier, 1982).

[15] See Iouda Tchernoff, *Le parti républicain au coup d'état et sous le Second Empire* (Paris: Pedone, 1906), 320–21. Written from a socialist republican perspective, this classic text remains the best general book on the subject.

[16] Vincent Wright, "La loi de sûreté générale de 1858," *Revue d'Histoire Moderne et Contemporaine* (July–September 1969).

[17] In 1869 an electoral meeting to support the candidacy of Bancel in Paris was dissolved by the police after one of the speakers uttered the name of Victor Hugo. See Jean-Marie Lazare Caubet, *Souvenirs, 1860–1889* (Paris: Cerf, 1893), 33. More generally, see Georges Weill, *Histoire du parti républicain en France* (Paris: Alcan, 1900), 473–77.

[18] See, for example, Edgar Quinet's epic poem *Napoléon*, in *Oeuvres complètes de Edgar Quinet* (Paris: Pagnerre, 1857), 8:135–326; and Henri Martin, *De la France, de son génie et de ses destinées* (Paris: Furne, 1847), 253–54.

[19] André-Jean Tudesq, "La légende napoléonienne en France en 1848," *Revue Historique* (September 1957): 65–66.

[20] Speech of 22 June 1870, in *Annales du Sénat et du Corps Législatif: Compte-rendu analytique des séances* (Paris: Journal Officiel, 1870), 156.

execution of Bonaparte's character: "Never did the slightest sense of the moral destiny of mankind enlighten his spirit."[21]

By the end of the Second Empire, similar pleasantries were being directed at his nephew. The Parisian journalist and deputy Henri Rochefort was prosecuted for declaring that the Bonapartes were a family "in which murders and ambushes are a hallowed tradition."[22] Republicans were particularly incensed by the Bonapartist claim to represent the true heritage of the French Revolution. Bonapartism, let us remember, celebrated 1789 as a critical moment in the formation of French national consciousness. The constitution of the Second Empire proclaimed the regime's adherence to the revolutionary principles of popular sovereignty and civil equality; the regime also restored universal suffrage in 1851.[23]

These considerations have led many commentators to remark on the formal similarities between the core values of republicanism and Bonapartism. Maurice Agulhon thus argues that during the Second Empire Bonapartism was the political family whose values were closest to those of the republicans.[24] This is a debatable view. There is no denying that republicans and Bonapartists were the only two movements that unequivocally endorsed universal suffrage; furthermore, nationalism and anticlericalism could be just as virulent in their Bonapartist expressions as in their republican forms. More fundamentally, the Empire recognized the political and juridical significance of 1789 and regarded itself as the inheritor of its values. But, as we will subsequently note, some liberals and legitimists also accepted the heritage of the Revolution. The essential question was how this heritage was defined and put into practice, and on this matter republicans and Bonapartists operated under quite different assumptions.

On the question of definition, there was a yawning gap between the republican conception of the Revolution, with its emphasis on freedom and justice, and the Bonapartist approach, which stressed the importance of civil equality, order, and charismatic leadership. Eugène Pelletan summarized the conceptual difference well: republicans placed liberty above authority, whereas in the Bonapartist scheme of things the priorities were reversed.[25]

---

[21] Hippolyte Carnot, *La révolution française* (Paris: Dubuisson, 1867), 167.

[22] *La Marseillaise*, 11 January 1870. Rochefort lampooned the regime in his journal *La Lanterne*. See also J. E. Horn, *Le bilan de l'Empire* (Paris: Dentu, 1868), and Auguste Morel, *Napoléon III* (Paris: Le Chevalier, 1870).

[23] See chap. 1.

[24] For example, Maurice Agulhon, "Les républicains sous le Second Empire," in *Dictionnaire du Second Empire*, ed. Tulard, 1114.

[25] Eugène Pelletan, *Droits de l'homme* (Paris: Pagnerre, 1867), 87.

But it was not merely a matter of ideological priorities. In the eyes of the republicans, the Second Empire paid lip service to the principles of 1789; the regime's true colors were revealed in its political and administrative practices.[26] True, these were often in glaring contradiction with the regime's ideological principles. The Second Empire claimed to venerate the patriotic spirit of the Revolution, but it proscribed one of its most famous emblems, the "Marseillaise."[27] It asserted its belief in the sovereignty of the nation but vested supreme power in the hands of a monarch whose actions were not subjected to any institutional controls. It made a great case of its restoration of universal suffrage but subjected the electoral process to overt manipulation for partisan ends. Last but not least, it affirmed its acceptance of the revolutionary legacy of civil equality but reinstituted the award of noble titles in January 1852 and showered the country with honors and titles for the duration of the Empire.[28]

After 1852, accordingly, republicans overwhelmingly rejected the claim that they shared a political heritage with the Bonapartists, or any other party for that matter. As the radical Henri Allain-Targé asserted in a letter to his father in 1867, "Bonapartism brings to Orleanism its hatred of true liberty, just as Orleanism brings to Bonapartism its hostility toward democracy."[29] For the republican socialist Arthur Arnould, "The Empire and the Republic thus truly represent two opposing principles, which cannot be reconciled, and divergent interests, which cannot be combined."[30]

This divergence in political culture between republicanism and Bonapartism was aggravated by antithetical constitutional philosophies. For the republican movement, sovereignty of the people signified the supremacy of representative institutions within their respective spheres of competence at national and local levels. The National Assembly was the supreme lawmaking body for all matters pertaining to the general interest, and the municipal and departmental councils were sovereign bodies on questions bearing on their local concerns. In the classical institutional hierarchy of the Second Empire, as we saw in chapter 1, representative bodies were subordinated to their administrative counterparts:

[26] Maurice Joly, *Les principes de 89* (Paris: Dentu, 1865).

[27] Louis Fiaux, *La Marseillaise, son histoire dans l'histoire des Français depuis 1792* (Paris: Charpentier, 1918), 241–54.

[28] For typically disapproving republican views of the imperial honors system, see Auguste Scheurer-Kestner, *Souvenirs de jeunesse* (Paris: Charpentier, 1905), 19; Eugène Pelletan, *L'ombre de 89: Lettre à Monsieur le duc de Persigny* (Paris: Pagnerre, 1863), 16.

[29] Quoted in François Henri René Allain-Targé, *La République sous l'Empire* (Paris: Grasset, 1939), 103.

[30] Arthur Arnould, *Une campagne à la Marseillaise* (Paris: Le Chevalier, 1870), 185.

the Legislative Corps to the Council of State, the municipal and departmental councils to the prefects. Under these circumstances, most republicans derided the claim that the Bonapartist regime was a genuine emanation of popular sovereignty.[31]

In this respect, even the advent of the liberal Empire in 1869 did little to change the republican view of Bonapartist institutions. Jules Ferry noted in a letter to the liberal journalist Nefftzer: "Do not call a parliamentary government a system that entrusts power to both the Crown and the Chamber. It is antagonism organized, parliamentarianism discredited, liberty compromised; it is the development, all at once, of confusion and impotence."[32] Citizenship for the Empire thus entailed celebrating the superiority of established political and administrative hierarchies; for the republicans, however, it was attained through active collective participation in shared values.

Finally, republicans never ceased to censure what they regarded as the immorality and lack of integrity of the Bonapartist regime. For the austere and somewhat puritanical elites of the republican movement, the imperial carnival was a symbol of the regime's spiritual decadence. Pelletan thus railed against the "despotism of luxury" that had emerged in France (particularly in Paris) under the Second Empire.[33] Georges Coulon added: "Corruption is the principle of the Empire."[34] Contrasting markedly with the republican attachment to reason, morality, and high culture, the Second Empire offered a polity based on cynicism, manipulation, and deceit — in short, an anti-intellectual and antirationalist conception of politics. "Intelligence frightens you all," sneered Jules Simon in a parliamentary speech directed at the government benches.[35]

The practices and values of the Second Empire were thus an important source of negative unity among republicans, and this anti-Bonapartism remained as intense in 1869–70 as in the immediate aftermath of the coup d'état. Bonapartism provided a clear benchmark against which the republicans could define and order their own ideological norms. At the same time, the practices of the imperial regime underlined the significant differences between Bonapartism and the moral and philosophical principles of the republican value system. We now turn to these values.

[31] Gustave Chaudey, *L'Empire parlementaire est-il possible?* (Paris: Le Chevalier, 1870), 23–25.

[32] Letter dated 8 August 1869, quoted in *Discours et opinions de Jules Ferry*, by Jules Ferry, ed. Paul Robiquet (Paris: Armand Colin, 1893), 1:577.

[33] Eugène Pelletan, *La nouvelle Babylone* (Paris: Pagnerre, 1863), 79–85.

[34] Georges Coulon, *Lettres républicaines* (Paris: Germer Baillière, 1873), 74.

[35] Arch. Nat. 87 AP 9, Papiers Jules Simon, notes on elections under the Second Empire (undated).

Fig. 9. Jules Simon (1814–96), lithography Perdriau et Leroy, Bibliothèque Nationale, Paris. Political philosopher, journalist, moralist, deputy, and intellectual guide of the republican movement under the Second Empire, Simon became one of the key figures in the early Third Republic.

JUSTICE AND FREEDOM: REPUBLIC AND REVOLUTION

The first and incontrovertible value of republicanism was the ideal of
the republic. To be a republican was not simply to believe in a particular form of government; it was also to assert — particularly against the
agnosticism of conservative and progressive liberals alike — that the issue of constitutional form was an essential object of political discussion:
"Questions of form, in politics, are crucial, essential."[36]

Republican institutions were distinguished in both formal and substantive terms. The republic was first a system of government that negated the monarchical principle: "The monarchy has as its principal
features selfishness, arrogance, pride, and hypocrisy; it generally takes
root among the vain, the schemers, the deceivers, and the corrupt and
venal characters."[37] The republic was different, first in terms of the political process itself: "The Republic is the state of a People that obeys
only men it has chosen."[38] But the republic also represented a number of
fundamental principles, which were typically expressed in the traditional trinity of liberty, equality, and fraternity. In particular, there was a
strong equation of republican institutions with the notion of the rule of
law. In the words of the republican socialist Pierre-Joseph Proudhon,
the republic was "a government in which Law and Freedom play
a primordial role, in contrast with all other forms of government,
founded on the preponderance of Authority and Reason of State."[39]

In a similar vein, the socialist republican Auguste Vermorel identified
three necessary conditions for designating a government as republican:
"That it is the administration of our interests by ourselves, that it
should be an inexpensive form of government, and above all that it
offers freedom."[40] To all its followers the republic was thus the embodiment of freedom, democracy, and the rule of law.

Along with their identification with a particular constitutional form,
all republicans were bound by a common attachment to the 1789 Revolution, particularly to its key principles: political liberty, civil equality,
national sovereignty, the separation of powers, the secularization of the
clergy, and the sanctity of private property.[41] In short, as a republican

---

[36] Chaudey, *L'Empire parlementaire est-il possible?*, 18.

[37] *Esquisses d'institutions républicaines, par un des comités insurrectionels de Paris*
(Brussels, 1862), 8–9.

[38] Charles Renouvier, *Manuel républicain de l'homme et du citoyen* (Paris: Pagnerre,
1848), 10.

[39] Pierre-Joseph Proudhon, *Essais d'une philosophie populaire* (Brussels, 1860), 171.

[40] Auguste Vermorel, *Qu'est-ce que la République?* (Paris: Fayard, 1871), 12.

[41] For the quirky Proudhon, the Revolution's greatest moment was the decree of 10

Freemason put it at a meeting of his lodge in 1869, "With the Revolution came justice in the spheres of religion, social relations, and politics."[42] True, in the political culture of the 1850s and 1860s, this was no longer a distinctive trait. As we saw in previous chapters, much of the social, political, and juridical heritage of the Revolution was accepted by Bonapartists and Orleanist liberals; even liberal legitimists readily embraced the Declaration of the Rights of Man, the principle of a constitutional monarchy, and the abolition of privileges.

However, there were three distinct senses in which the revolutionary tradition remained exclusive to the republicans. First, the Revolution constituted their primary (and in effect unique) founding myth. The legitimists harked back to the prerevolutionary age; liberals often offered Britain and the United States as model polities; as noted earlier, the Bonapartist lineage acknowledged the significance of the Revolution but celebrated its ultimate transcendence by the First Empire. The republicans, for their part, defined the revolutionary period as the only valid historical experience for the construction of a just polity; their key political concepts, historical allusions, and metaphors were consciously drawn from the revolutionary saga.

Second, republicans held the Revolution as the source of promises that were yet to be fulfilled. The contrast was striking in this respect with conservative liberals and especially Bonapartists, who saw it as their primary duty to end the period of political upheavals initiated by the French Revolution.

Finally, the republicans were distinct in regarding the principles and values of 1789 as universal in scope. This messianic dimension of their philosophy was based on a progressive conception of history, which was popularized in the writings of idealist historians such as Jules Michelet. Simon presented an image of humankind's confident march toward its destiny with appropriate fervor: "This date of 1789 is the great event for all peoples. . . . In the practice and speculation of all countries we find thereafter the trace of the French Revolution. The writers and publicists who fight it come under its influence despite themselves; they are as if illuminated by its genius."[43]

But the Revolution was nothing if not the product of the people who made it. Republicans shared in various degrees a particular appreciation of the essential characteristics of human nature. In the formulation of

---

November 1793, which instituted the cult of reason. See his *Essais d'une philosophie populaire*, 149.

[42] Désiré Bancel, *Les origines de la Révolution* (Paris: Degorce-Cadot, 1869), 5.

[43] Jules Simon, *La liberté* (Paris: Hachette, 1859), 1:42.

the poet Leconte de Lisle, all human activities were geared toward self-perfection: the satisfaction of affective senses and the cultivation of intellectual faculties.[44] Rationality was the essence of man; this attribute distinguished him from all other creatures.[45] Hence the particular emphasis republicans gave to artistic and cultural life and to the dissemination of popular education.[46]

Sociability was also an important feature of the human spirit. Republican ideologues saw the emergence of society as a derivation of human nature: "The social organism is formed because of the fundamental nature of man himself."[47] But what distinguished republican writings on human nature was an emphasis on its Promethean quality. Man was not simply destined to develop his rational faculties in society in a general sense; this development was itself an expression of a particular conception of the good life. "The social state has as its goal the creation of moral and intellectual man."[48] In short, to be rational and sociable was not sufficient; man also needed to be free. The mystical republican Marie d'Agoult spelled out this radical conception of the human telos in vivid terms:

> From the first day of his appearance on the earth, man has never ceased to struggle against tyrannical forces that held him captive. He has gradually succeeded in liberating himself from their clutches. Using at times cunning, and at times violence, he has untied or broken one by one the multiple links that bound his spirit and body. Then he resolutely marched toward the conquest of the universe.[49]

Freedom was defined in many dimensions: the possession of individual and collective, social and political, legal and moral rights.[50] Indeed, one of the characteristics of republicanism between 1852 and 1870 was its radical and almost unqualified embrace of the idea of liberty. Orleanist liberals also affirmed the imperative of liberty; Thiers symbolized their hopes in his formulation of the notion of "necessary liberties."[51] But republicans went one step further: "Freedom does not suffer dis-

---

[44] Charles-Marie Leconte de Lisle, *Catéchisme populaire républicain* (Paris: Lemerre, 1870).

[45] Charles Renouvier, *Essais de critique générale*, 4 vols. (Paris: Ladrange, 1854–64).

[46] This was a recurrent theme in republican conferences during the 1860s. See, for example, the public lecture given by Jules Simon, *L'instruction populaire* (Reims, 1869).

[47] Leconte de Lisle, *Catéchisme*.

[48] Maria Chenu, *Le droit des minorités* (Paris: Degorce-Cadot, 1868), 36.

[49] Daniel Stern [Comtesse Marie d'Agoult], *Esquisses morales et politiques* (Paris: Pagnerre, 1849), 6–7.

[50] Paul Lacombe, *Mes droits* (Paris: Germer Baillière, 1869).

[51] See chap. 3.

tinctions; it is or is not; one and indivisible, like the Republic."[52] The intensity of this profession of faith in freedom was a direct consequence of the political authoritarianism of the Second Empire. Shortly after the coup d'état, a group of republican exiles published a pamphlet in London which exalted the virtues of freedom.

> Freedom is the natural right to develop one's faculties and to satisfy one's needs. The free man is master of himself and of his resources and has the capacity to develop all his faculties, exercise all his rights, in a word, to accomplish his destiny; the free man depends neither on space, nor on time, nor on need, nor on error, nor on anyone or anything; this free man is sovereign and therefore equal to all other men and a brother to them all. Complete freedom necessarily brings with it equality and fraternity.[53]

Republican freedom was defined not simply in negative terms, as in the possession of certain social and political rights. Nor could freedom be confused with license: liberty was obtained only when man cultivated those values which were true to his nature. This goal-directed conception of freedom was typified in the importance of intellectual and critical thought to the republican tradition: "Freedom of thought, freedom of speech, freedom to write and publish, are among the most important liberties."[54] In this sense, no man could be entirely free if his decisions were based on underdeveloped intellectual faculties. Republican writers repeatedly stressed this link between freedom and education: "Without doubt an enlightened man is truly more free than an ignorant one: in this sense, to spread education is to develop liberty, in the same way as to obstruct the progress of science, or necessary forms of progress such as elementary education, which are at the source of everything, is to attack freedom at its core."[55]

POPULAR SOVEREIGNTY AND UNIVERSAL SUFFRAGE

Just as distinctive as its attachment to freedom and justice was the republican commitment to the principle of popular sovereignty and its institutional corollary, universal suffrage. The people played a central role in the myths of the republican tradition. Michelet's writings offered a vibrant (if sometimes controversial) celebration of the active role of the masses in the decisive moments of French history. For many republicans the people were the instruments of a particular historical purpose:

[52] Bancel, *Les origines de la Révolution*, 30.
[53] Félix Pyat, Caussidière, and Boichot, "Lettre au peuple" (August 1852), quoted in *Les révolutions du XIXeme siècle* (Paris: EDHIS, 1988), 1:6.
[54] Renouvier, *Manuel républicain*, 15.
[55] Simon, *La liberté*, 1:15–16.

"The democratic element is emerging in all parts; it will be its destiny to transform the world."[56]

During the first half of the nineteenth century, republicans of all persuasions constantly invoked the interests of the people as a justification for their actions. These references were given philosophical expression in the principle of popular sovereignty, the cornerstone of republican constitutional theory. In the words of a republican pamphleteer, "Popular sovereignty is the supreme law. All citizens, having equal rights, can lay claim to the same titles in the exercise of political power."[57] At times of political crisis, many sought refuge in the sagacity of the people, a collectivity endowed with a transcendental form of wisdom. In the hopeful words of a group of republican exiles after the 1851 coup: "The people alone are sovereign. Neither we nor others have anything to dictate to the nation, to France, to the sovereign people. The people will know better than us what will need to be done; it will wish for and seek more than we can; it will be more enlightened, more revolutionary, and stronger than any of us."[58]

This faith in the salutary capacities of collective action was also attributed to universal suffrage. Writing in 1863, at the height of the Second Empire's cynical manipulation of the electorate, Ferry nonetheless affirmed his faith in the principle of universal suffrage, "the honor of multitudes, the guarantee of the disinherited, the reconciliation of classes, and the promise of legality for all."[59] An important function of universal suffrage in the eyes of the republicans was to enable the constant confirmation of the contract between the people and the state. In this sense, no constitution could be fixed in perpetuity; every generation had the right to redefine the terms of the relationship between the collectivity and public authority.[60]

However, life was rather more untidy than republican constitutional axioms would allow, and the celebration of the ideal virtues of the people did not blind the republicans to their very real deficiencies. Indeed, there was an uncomfortable dualism in their writings, for alongside a discourse that stressed its benevolent characteristics could also be found a conception of the people as a deficient and faltering collectivity. The working classes were in need of education and moralization, and many

[56] Stern, *Esquisses morales et politiques*, 205. "Democracy" and "democratic" were often used as sociological categories to designate the working classes.

[57] Louis Joly, *La fédération, seule forme de la décentralisation dans les démocraties* (Paris: Garnier, 1866), 10.

[58] Pyat, Caussidière, and Boichot, "Lettre au peuple," 3.

[59] Ferry, *La lutte électorale*, 105.

[60] Chaudey, *L'Empire parlementaire est-il possible?*, 27.

republican writers did not hesitate to underline the depraved character of popular mores.[61]

The peasantry was a particular object of contempt among republican pamphleteers. Some remembered the heroic resistance of peasants against the 1851 coup,[62] and others celebrated the role of rural masses during the revolutionary era;[63] a small number even saw peasants as a potential source of republican regeneration.[64] But most republicans rarely bothered to hide their scorn. Ferry noted that "the logic of the countryman is as brutal as his natural surroundings";[65] then he deplored the peasants' complete subservience to established order: "So heroic in battle, these peasants tremble in their houses like leaves."[66] In Pelletan's evocation of the rural world condescension was mixed with derision.

> Up at dawn and asleep by sunset, the peasant lives alone, most of the time, in his hut or near his pastures. He makes conversation only with his dog or his herd. . . . What does he know about politics? He is vaguely aware that he has a sovereign, because he sees his profile on his coins and banknotes. He has even heard it rumored that there are high dignitaries who command the army and administer the country. But he has never been able to distinguish one from the other, and even less the living from the dead.[67]

During the Second Empire the political docility of the rural world even led some republicans to question their instinctive faith in the redemptive properties of universal suffrage. "Universal suffrage is the worst instrument of tyranny when it is not honestly organized," noted Edouard Lockroy soberly.[68] Etienne Vacherot warned that "ignorance, superstition, immorality, and misery can endanger and even pervert the exercise of popular suffrage."[69] Simon recognized that "if there is an objection against universal suffrage, it is precisely that all votes being equal, the ignorant's counts as much toward the result as the wise man's."[70]

In 1863 Proudhon, although acknowledging the philosophical validity of the principle of universal suffrage, argued that republicans

---

[61] Stern, *Esquisses morales et politiques*, 149, 166–68.

[62] See, for example, Arthur Ranc, *Souvenirs-Correspondance, 1831–1908* (Paris: Cornély, 1913), 25–26.

[63] E.-A. Erckmann-Chatrian, *Histoire d'un paysan: 1789* (Paris: Hetzel, 1868).

[64] Eugène Sue, *Le républicain des campagnes* (Paris: Librairie Internationale, 1851).

[65] Ferry, *La lutte électorale*, 84.

[66] Ibid., 15.

[67] Eugène Pelletan, *Aide-toi le ciel t'aidera* (Paris: Pagnerre, 1863), 7. See also Eugène Ténot, *Le suffrage universel et les paysans* (Paris: Librairie Centrale, 1865), 23–24.

[68] Edouard Lockroy, *A bas le progrès!* (Paris: Librairie Internationale, 1870), 117.

[69] Etienne Vacherot, *La démocratie* (Paris: Chamerot, 1860), vii.

[70] Arch. Nat. 87 AP 9, Papiers Jules Simon.

should abstain from the electoral process in protest against the inequitable conditions under which the vote was held.[71] Revolutionary republicans such as Auguste Blanqui invoked the ignorance and credulity of the masses as a justification for bypassing universal suffrage and parliamentary action: "How can we not see that the political manifestation of a people will always be the reflection of the ideas it has been showered with, and that after twenty years of despotism, of servitude, and of systematic stupefaction, the seeds sown in the public's mind can be the only harvest of an election?"[72] To this the constitutionalist republican Ernest Picard replied: "We represent law and not violence, power but especially moral power, which is based on hard work and discussion."[73] The radical Alfred Naquet went further: "Universal suffrage and the Republic are one and the same."[74]

The mainstream of the republican movement thus retained its belief in the validity of universal suffrage, but by the end of the Second Empire great emphasis was placed on the value of political education as well. Many republicans also argued that the electoral system should be reformed to provide effective representation for as broad a range of social and economic interests as possible.[75] Both propositions represented clear acknowledgments that the doctrine of the inherent goodness of the people could no longer serve as a sufficient foundation for republican political practice.[76]

FRATERNITY AND PEACE

One of the most distinctive traits of Second Empire republicanism was its commitment to the ideals of fraternity and international peace. The two objectives were closely related in the republican mind: the latter condition was one of the key expressions of the former principle.

Although a conceptual legacy of the revolutionary period,[77] the principle of fraternity was not entirely uncontroversial in republican ranks. Vacherot, for example, made it clear that he did not place this precept

---

[71] Pierre-Joseph Proudhon, *Les démocrates assermentés et les réfractaires* (Paris: Dentu, 1863), 8.

[72] Blanqui, in *La Patrie en Danger*, November 1870; quoted in *Les idées politiques et sociales d'Auguste Blanqui*, by Maurice Dommanget (Paris: Marcel Rivière, 1957), 222.

[73] Bib. Nat. NAF 24369, Papiers Ernest Picard, letter to Ferrouillat, 4 June 1863.

[74] Alfred Naquet, *La république radicale* (Paris: Germer Baillière, 1873), 16.

[75] Chenu, *Le droit des minorités*, 23–26.

[76] For an analysis of the concept of the "people" in the writings of nineteenth-century republicans (especially Hugo, Michelet, Sue, Georges Sand, and Blanqui), see Alain Pessin, *Le mythe du peuple et la société française du XIXeme siècle* (Paris: Presses Universitaires de France, 1992).

[77] See Marcel David, *Fraternité et Révolution Française, 1789–1799* (Paris: Aubier, 1987).

on an equal footing with the cardinal principles of liberty and equality: "Liberty and equality are principles, whereas fraternity is merely a sentiment. But a sentiment, however powerful, profound, and general, is not a right; and it cannot therefore serve as a basis for justice."[78]

To most republicans, however, fraternity remained an indisputable principle, even though it was grounded in different philosophical systems. Charles Renouvier's definition of fraternity was based on explicitly Christian teachings: "Never forget that the most certain means of knowing how you love God is to work with all your energies for the good of your brother for whom Jesus Christ himself gave his life."[79] At the opposite end of the republican ideological spectrum, Blanqui defined fraternity as the realization of communism: "Fraternity is the impossibility of killing one's brother."[80] Neo-Kantians such as Jules Barni derived the notion of duty to others from the precepts of natural law.[81] His teacher Simon expressed the moral law in terms that would be appealing to both Christian and secular republicans: "The strict, absolute, and universal obligation, imposed on us by morality, to serve men with our wealth, with our time, with our knowledge; to be on all occasions not an enemy or even indifferent but a brother."[82]

Seen from this angle, fraternity was also embodied in the principle of patriotism, defined by Barni as "the devotion to public life." For republican thinkers, the love of one's fellow countrymen necessarily found its continuation in a sense of identification with the public institutions that served and protected their interests.[83] Patriotism and fraternity were sharply distinguished from aggressive nationalism, which moderate and socialist republicans, especially those of the younger generation, viewed with some misgivings.[84] A minority of socialist republicans such as Proudhon rejected the nationality principle altogether, regarding it as a mere pretext used by despotic leaders to create unitary military and economic agglomerations.[85] Many federalist thinkers deplored the racist implications of the principle of nationality.[86]

International peace was therefore one of the highest expressions of

---

[78] Vacherot, *La démocratie*, 9.

[79] Renouvier, *Manuel républicain*, 7.

[80] Auguste Blanqui, *Critique sociale* (Paris: Alcan, 1885), 2:98–99.

[81] Jules Barni, *La morale dans la démocratie*, 2d ed. (Paris: Alcan, 1885), 19–20.

[82] Jules Simon, *Le devoir* (Paris: Hachette, 1854), 320.

[83] Barni, *La morale dans la démocratie*, 123.

[84] This disillusionment with conventional nationalism is strongly marked in Gustave Flourens et al.'s *Appel de la Rive Gauche à la jeunesse Européenne* (Brussels, 1866).

[85] Proudhon, *Essais d'une philosophie populaire*, 146–47.

[86] Louis Joly, *Du principe des nationalités* (Paris: Garnier, 1863), 23–24. For a curious (and profoundly unconvincing) neo-Proudhonist attempt to present federalism as part of the cultural heritage of the Latin race, see Louis-Xavier de Ricard, *Le fédéralisme* (Paris: Sandoz, 1877).

the ideal of fraternity. Peace required an active struggle on both the domestic and the international front; in the latter, the creation of an international body campaigning for the end of militarism, and in the former, the establishment of a democratic state and the reduction of military institutions' role in society. From this angle, the republicans systematically advocated the suppression of permanent armies[87] and a reduction of the French military budget.[88] But the most radical expression of republican antimilitarism during the Second Empire came from their international campaigns against war. With the exception of the Italian campaign, which they generally applauded, republicans condemned the military expeditions of Napoleon III as costly and useless exercises in personal aggrandizement.[89] They also undertook propaganda activities against war during the 1860s and participated in the International Congresses for Peace held in Geneva in 1867, Bern in 1868, and Lausanne in 1869.[90]

At the first of these meetings, the French delegation provided a complete cross section of the republican ideological spectrum; in attendance were dignified elders (Albert, Jules Favre, Victor Schoelcher, Hippolyte Carnot), artistic and literary eminences (Victor Hugo, Edgar Quinet, Auguste Barbier), romantics (Jules Vallès, Gustave Flourens), democratic socialists and libertarians (Louis Blanc, Elisée Reclus), positivists (Emile Littré, Grégoire Wyrouboff), radicals (André Lavertujon, Henri Brisson, Alfred Naquet), and moderates (Jules Simon, Jules Ferry).[91]

It was an article of faith among all shades of republican opinion that international peace depended on the domestic constitutions of states. Frédéric Morin noted:

> The international relations of peoples are fatally determined by their internal institutions. With feudal governments, local wars were inevitable, and wars between peoples are no less certain with governments dominated by the principle of authority. If European nations today yearn for some peace

---

[87] See Jules Simon, *La politique radicale* (Paris: Lacroix, 1868), esp. 179–247.

[88] Paul Lacombe, *La République et la liberté*, 107–8.

[89] See Félix Pyat, *Lettre à Juarez et à ses amis* (London, 1865); Eugène Spuller, *Petite histoire du Second Empire* (Paris: Le Chevalier, 1870), 18–19; see also André Bellesort, *La société française sous Napoléon III* (Paris: Perrin, 1932), 330.

[90] Sandi E. Cooper, *Patriotic Pacifism: Waging War on War in Europe, 1815–1914* (New York: Oxford University Press, 1991), 37–42.

[91] The full list is given by Scheurer-Kestner, *Souvenirs de Jeunesse*, 108–9. For contrasting assessments of the Geneva meeting by two participants, see the positive view of Charles Lemonnier, *La vérité sur le Congrès de Genève* (Geneva, 1868), and the criticisms of Grégoire Wyrouboff, "Le Congrès de la Paix," *Revue de Philosophie Positive* (November–December 1867). See also A. Larrieu, *Guerre à la guerre* (Paris: Guillaumin, 1868); Jules Clamageran, *Correspondance* (Paris: Alcan, 1906), 291–4.

and quiet, they should appreciate that they will get them only by rallying to democratic and liberal ideas.[92]

In their speeches at the congress, a number of French speakers, most notably Barni, suggested the existence of a close correspondence between centralized government and militarism.[93] This was a commonplace assumption in republican circles during this period. In an enthusiastic letter of support addressed to the signatories of the Nancy manifesto in 1865, Ferry had expressed categorical views on the matter: "Do you wish to be the most compact, warlike, and dangerous nation for world peace? If so, you should be the most centralized. . . . But if you wish to be a hardworking people, free and peaceful, have nothing to do with a *strong state*. Break it down, in order to weaken it."[94]

It was therefore not surprising that the Geneva Congress reserved its greatest ovation for Mikhail Bakunin's intervention, in which he posited an explicit link between peace and decentralization.

Universal peace will be impossible as long as existing centralized states remain. We must therefore hope for their dissolution, so that, on the ruins of these violent entities, organized from above by means of authority and conquest, we can build free units, organized from below by the free federation of communes into provinces, of provinces into nations, and of nations into the united states of Europe.[95]

Republicanism and Religion

The promotion of republican citizenship required a number of social and institutional transformations, as identified in previous sections. But the achievement of this goal also necessitated the removal of all obstacles that stood in the way of individual and collective emancipation. The Second Empire represented a political obstacle of mighty proportions, but the Catholic Church posed an arguably even greater challenge to the republican project. The Second Republic had seen a brief flowering of harmony between republicans and the church. Thus in 1849 the republican socialist Ange Guépin could describe the republican impera-

---

[92] "Le Congrès de Genève" (September 1867), in *Politique et philosophie*, by Frédéric Morin (Paris: Germer Baillière, 1876), 18.

[93] The full text is in the appendix of Barni, *La morale dans la démocratie*, 259–63.

[94] Quoted in *Discours et opinions*, by Ferry, 1:558.

[95] Quoted in *Annales du Congrès de Genève*, ed. Jules Barni (Geneva, 1868), 248. Charles Longuet, one of the French delegates, also focused his address on the same theme (250–57).

tive in the following terms: "I want our laws to be illuminated by the spirit of the Gospel."[96]

After 1852, however, the new regime forged a close alliance with the ecclesiastical authorities in France. As we saw in chapter 2, the church enjoyed a privileged position in the hierarchy of Bonapartist institutions, in exchange for which it readily gave the Second Empire its blessing, encouraging its clergy to enhance the regime's prestige in the eyes of the faithful. This alliance appeared most overtly during national and local elections and contributed to the overwhelming hegemony the Second Empire enjoyed in the countryside.

In response to this alliance of Bonapartists and clericalists, republicans highlighted the importance of rationalism and individual conscience. In this context the Second Empire saw the rise of freethinking movements (often operating in close association with Freemasonry) that were often at the vanguard of the battle against political and religious obscurantism.[97] Republican freethinkers bitterly acknowledged the social and moral influence of the church on the peasantry. Simon noted that "the clergy controls all women, as well as children, the handicapped, and the old. Most of the faithful are incapable of distinguishing politics from religion, and in obeying their priest, they believe they are obeying God."[98] Henri Rochefort was equally forceful: "Vicars are agitating, bishops are writing, cardinals are speaking, priests are proliferating. Today the clergy holds France in its iron grip."[99]

However, the reality on the ground was rather more complex. The peasantry often identified with Bonapartism for reasons that had little to do with religion; the Empire also appeared as the guarantor of the material interests of rural workers and the defender of their rights against the claims of the local aristocracy. In addition, Catholicism was too large and diverse an institution to act in a monolithic fashion, especially after the Second Empire alienated the church by supporting the principle of Italian reunification. Thus, during the 1860s the clergy in many parts of France supported independent Catholics, whose vigorous campaigns against official candidates were often noted approvingly by republicans.[100] In certain regions, electoral alliances were forged be-

---

[96] Ange Guépin, *Les élections* (Nantes, 1849). See also Ranc, *Souvenirs*, 22–23.

[97] On the development of freethinking associations during the Second Empire, see Jacqueline Lalouette, *La libre pensée en France, 1848–1940* (Paris: Albin Michel, 1997), 30–39.

[98] Arch. Nat. 87 AP 9, Papiers Jules Simon.

[99] *La Lanterne*, 6 June 1868.

[100] For the case of Brittany, see Ferry, *La lutte électorale*, 21.

tween royalists, republicans, and the clergy against the Bonapartists, to the great alarm of local administrative authorities.[101]

Despite these occasional alliances, at a deeper level the Catholic Church continued to pose a central problem for republican thinkers throughout the Second Empire. What was at stake was nothing less than the capture of the hearts and minds of the people, and in this contest Catholicism and republicanism were competing for the same social constituency.

To most republicans, this was a zero-sum game, for the values and principles that Catholicism espoused (especially in its ultramontane form) were seen as completely antithetical to those of republicans. There was a long history of mutual antagonism between the church and the republican movement, dating back to the Revolution. In republican writings, the church was often presented as a treacherous and counter-revolutionary institution, which had historically been the loyal ally of monarchical absolutism and feudalism.[102] The flames of these historical animosities were still burning in the middle of the nineteenth century. "Catholicism and despotism are brothers," thundered Vacherot in 1860, obviously smarting from the years of harmonious collaboration between church and state under the Second Empire.[103] Equally objectionable was the ultramontane rejection of reason, illustrated most dogmatically in the reassertion of papal infallibility in the *Syllabus*.[104] Protestant republicans such as Pelletan argued that the refusal to allow any critical discussion of Christian principles encouraged a form of religiosity that favored hypocrisy and deceit.[105]

Despotic and inflexible, the Catholic faith also perverted the human mind by encouraging feelings of fatalism and resignation among its subjects. In this respect there was a sharp contrast between republican and Catholic doctrine. Republicans were optimistic voluntarists who believed in both the possibility and the desirability of happiness. In contrast, Catholics were thought incapable of aspiring to felicity on earth. In the words of Simon, "Catholic religion considers life as a mere ordeal, and its constant goal is to teach us to repudiate it and leave it behind. It does not content itself, like stoicism, to deny pain; pain, in its eyes, is desirable, provided it is suffered in a spirit of penitence; and of all the acts that can make the heavens rejoice, the most glorious is mar-

[101] Ibid., 132–33.

[102] See, for example, Edgar Quinet, *Le christianisme et la révolution française* (Paris: Pagnerre, 1865).

[103] Vacherot, *La démocratie*, xxvii.

[104] Henri Martin, *La séparation de l'Eglise et de l'Etat* (Paris: Dentu, 1865), 1–8.

[105] Eugène Pelletan, *Droits de l'homme*, 193–94.

tyrdom."[106] As these lines suggest, many republicans were not entirely insensitive to the magnificent spiritual force embodied in the Catholic faith. But they believed that this force was rapidly nearing the end of its historical journey. According to a Proudhonist socialist, Catholicism was destined to follow the evolution of all religions: "In the beginning, all religions are eminently progressive and revolutionary; then they become simply conservative, until the moment when they become truly retrograde."[107]

But if there was an element of consensus over the analysis of Catholicism as a religion, there was much less agreement over the appropriate republican response to the church. Revolutionary republicans generally called for the wholesale destruction of Catholicism and its replacement by the teaching of science.[108] At the 1867 Geneva Congress, a delegate from the London-based Association of French Workers consciously equated the church with military institutions.

> Every religion is a form of despotism that also has its permanent armies: the priests. Have these armies not inflicted upon the people wounds that are even deeper than those that are received on the battlefield? Of course! These armies have perverted what is right and attacked reason itself. Do not clear out the barracks in order to replace them with churches. Make a clean sweep of both.[109]

The revolutionary republican Blanqui managed in one fell swoop to equate religion with sexual depravity, capitalist domination, moral indoctrination, and female exploitation.

> The brothels and the convents are brothers in opulence and in politics. Gold flows into both from the same source, capitalism. It enables the first to revel in their despicable pleasures, and the second to stupefy the masses to increase their own sense of security and power. Nun or prostitute, the woman is its instrument and victim.[110]

In contrast, most moderate, radical, and socialist freethinking republicans contented themselves with advocating the separation of church and state. Such a move was seen to be in the interests of both institutions. For the state, it represented the achievement of secularism prom-

---

[106] Simon, *Le devoir*, 405.

[107] Justin Dromel [Ecorcheville, pseud.], *La loi des révolutions* (Paris: Didier, 1862), 508.

[108] See, for example, Henri Verlet, *1793–1869: Le peuple et la Révolution, l'athéisme et l'Etre Suprême* (Paris: Librairie de la Renaissance, n.d.).

[109] Eugène Dupont, quoted in *Annales du Congrès de Genève*, ed. Barni, 171.

[110] Auguste Blanqui, "Le travail des couvents" (September 1869), in *Critique sociale*, 2:85.

ised by the French Revolution.[111] For the church, it offered the possibility of greater independence, and indeed the means of testing the intellectual strength and validity of its core principles. In the words of Vacherot, "Only when the Catholic religion will have no authority except that of its word, no prestige other than its origin and tradition, will we be able to assess its intrinsic degree of virtue."[112]

The bulk of the republican movement therefore was not intrinsically hostile to religion, only to what it saw as its most dogmatic political and intellectual manifestations. Thus the ultimate ideal was not the elimination of religion in society but the flowering of religious and spiritual diversity. Pelletan made the case for a society governed by the principle of religious pluralism: "A diverse society requires diverse religious forms, which can match the diversity of attitudes and everywhere give satisfaction to religious sentiment."[113]

This individualist approach was synthesized in the efforts of Henri Martin, Carnot, Buisson, and Pelletan himself to effect a fusion between republicanism and Protestantism.[114] Liberal Protestantism was an open, tolerant, and individualistic faith thought by many to be the perfect spiritual appendage to republicanism. In the following peroration by the republican Freemason Bancel, the radiant future was represented as a triumphant reconciliation of republican, Catholic, and Protestant doctrines:

> We will make of every people a living reformer. . . . We will all be united in equality and justice. Then will be accomplished the reconciliation of Catholicism and the Reformation. This church of labor, of honesty, of friendship and peace, will unite all men in a vast association, in which all individual efforts, guided by education and moderated by law, will constitute the harmony of the human race.[115]

Citizenship and the Commune

Membership in a political community provided the republican citizen with both rights and duties. Political freedom and civil and political equality were among the most precious rights enjoyed by all citizens; their duties included obedience to the laws of the republic and a commitment to defend it against any external threat to its integrity.[116] Re-

[111] Naquet, *La république radicale*, 153–54.
[112] Etienne Vacherot, *La religion* (Paris: Chamerot, 1869), 459.
[113] Pelletan, *Droits de l'homme*, 205.
[114] Tchernoff, *Le parti républicain*, 307–8. See also Clamagéran, *Correspondance*, 131–32, 192–200, 275.
[115] Bancel, *Les révolutions de la parole*, 301–2.
[116] Renouvier, *Manuel républicain*, 13.

Fig. 10. Pierre Clément Eugène Pelletan (1813–84), lithography Perdriau et Leroy, Bibliothèque Nationale, Paris. A liberal Protestant and Freemason, Pelletan was a deputy, as well as one of the leading theorists of republican municipalism under the Second Empire.

publicans strongly believed that a number of basic social and political values should be shared by all members of the community; hence the primordial importance of the concept of patriotism in their vocabulary. A patriot was in many senses the paradigm of republican citizenship. He was all at the same time a person who loved his country, identified with its political institutions, participated actively in their operation, and cultivated his intellectual faculties: "What is the native land elevated to its supreme power, if not a communion of all its spirits developing toward their greatest potential of intelligence and morality?"[117]

The nurture of patriotic sentiments among the political community was therefore an essential component of the republican project, along with the creation of a web of associational institutions.[118] In this context the commune assumed its central significance in republican ideology. The commune was a microcosm of the entire collectivity, and as such it enjoyed all the rights bestowed on its members. In the words of Proudhon, 'The commune is in essence like man, like the family, like all individual, free, moral, and collective intelligences, a sovereign being."[119] The commune was not simply a territorial unit among others, however; it possessed certain characteristics that gave it a special status in the hierarchy of republican political institutions. Simon explained:

A city has its history, its pride, its own patriotism; it has its particular habits, its customs; it has important interests to defend and properties to manage. Everyone knows each other and meets each other frequently, not only as fellow citizens but also as neighbors. Citizens are part of the same national guard, send their children to the same school, and take advantage in equal measure of roads, canals, libraries, and museums. The commune is a collective being recognized by law but which comes from the nature of things, their very essence. Political laws find the commune; they do not create it.[120]

In common with liberal and legitimist accounts of local community life, Simon's depiction stressed the value of sociability and common interests. But it also spelled out a number of key features of communal identity that were distinctive in the republican tradition. First, it is highly symbolic that his example of communal sociability was the urban collectivity: the town and the city were the prime bearers of the

[117] Pelletan, *La nouvelle Babylone*, 121.

[118] On the importance of associational life in republican political culture, see Nord, *The republican moment*, 217.

[119] Pierre-Joseph Proudhon, *De la capacité politique des classes ouvrières* (Paris: Dentu, 1865), 291.

[120] Simon, *La liberté*, 2:248–49.

values of republican citizenship, not the village.[121] This reinforces the point made earlier about the suspicion with which republicans regarded the rural world throughout the Second Empire. In 1871 some republicans even proposed a system of special political representation for towns and cities in order to counterbalance the preponderance of rural interests in the National Assembly.[122]

Equally significant in Simon's account is the absence of an institution that figured prominently in most legitimist and liberal depictions of the commune: the church. There was a recognition of the existence (indeed, the necessity) of a moral and spiritual dimension to the locality, but for most republicans this ethical life could not be anything but resolutely secular. Hence Simon's emphasis on the role of cultural institutions such as schools, public libraries, and museums, which were seen as missionaries of the republican moral purpose.

Finally, it is worth noting the dialectical nature of the notion of republican citizenship that Simon advanced. He posited a strong sense of complementarity between local and national civic identities. Patriotism was derived not only from an identification with general principles and institutions but also from an attachment to particular norms, values, and collectivities. Far from being incompatible with the practice of patriotism, a rich communal life was one of its foundations. Simon articulated this thought in a speech at the Legislative Corps: "It is through the love of one's poor commune that one comes to be a citizen who loves his country."[123] His colleague Pierre-Joseph Magnin echoed: "The love of one's locality marks the beginning of the love of one's country."[124]

A wide range of social and political virtues were associated with an active communal life in republican writings. In the private sphere, the commune enabled groups of citizens to nurture the development of family life, to which republicans assigned great importance: "Patriotic sentiment makes the citizen, and communal sentiment makes man, together with familial feeling."[125] The family was an essentially patriarchal unit; only a few republican writers advocated any significant equality in gender roles.[126] Most republicans remained deeply attached to the preemi-

---

[121] For another pessimistic republican view of rural life, see Ferdinand de Lasteyrie, *Le paysan, ce qu'il est, ce qu'il devrait être* (Paris: Le Chevalier, 1869), 14–16.

[122] See, for example, Edgar Quinet's proposals in May 1871, in *La République: Conditions de la régénération de la France* (Paris: Dentu, 1872), 301–10.

[123] Jules Simon, "Discours sur l'élection des maires," 5 April 1865, Arch. Nat. 87 AP 15, Papiers Jules Simon.

[124] Speech of 8 April 1867, in *Annales du Sénat et du Corps Législatif: Compte-rendu analytique des séances* (Paris: Panckoucke, 1867), 272.

[125] Vacherot, *La démocratie*, 241.

[126] See, for example, Eugène Pelletan, *La femme au XIXeme siècle* (Paris: Pagnerre,

nence of men, who were seen as beings endowed with superior moral and intellectual qualities. Thus, Marie d'Agoult equated patriotism with masculinity:

> Man most particularly represents the idea of *patrie*. The woman's sentiment rarely rises above the love of the soil. She cherishes her place of birth and the horizons under which she grew up. Man's spirit is more attuned to broader intellectual horizons where his thought can develop. He loves and can feel in himself the collectivity of invisible elements that make up the race, the nation, and the ideal fatherland.[127]

Women, by contrast, were thought to lack the capacity for abstract thought: "The spirit of woman is made for observation, in the elaborate sense of the term, rather than for analysis, which demands method and profound thought."[128] Proudhon, more brutally, affirmed the physical, intellectual, and moral inferiority of women.[129] Republican advocates of feminine rights tended to argue that greater education would help women acquire more self-confidence and thus emancipate themselves from the comfortable delusions of religion and superstition.[130] But even for such enlightened souls the social mission of women continued to be defined in essentially patriarchal terms: "To be a wife and mother."[131]

Just as important were the public virtues promoted by a communal existence. There was a strong emphasis on the civic and educative functions of the commune. To quote Simon again: "It is in the commune that the citizen learns to elevate himself above his personal interests and to know what is a community. He discovers how one ought to love freedom and be ready to sacrifice oneself for it. It is in the commune that man is truly initiated into political activity."[132] The accent was both on rights and on duties. Communal life was not about the promotion of individualism but about the emergence of a sense of solidarity and public-spiritedness. The republican citizen was thus expected not only to receive a set of goods from the collectivity but also to devote himself to the public cause — even (when necessary) at the expense of his immediate personal interests.

1869), 13; Juliette Adam, *Idées anti-proudhoniennes sur la femme, l'amour et le mariage* (Paris: Taride, 1858), 85.

[127] Stern, *Esquisses morales et politiques*, 13; emphasis is in the text.

[128] Vacherot, *La démocratie*, 132.

[129] Proudhon's views on women are gathered in *La pornocratie ou la femme dans les temps modernes* (Paris: Lacroix, 1875).

[130] Eugène Pelletan, *La charte du foyer* (Paris: Pagnerre, 1864), 18–20.

[131] Jules Simon, *La famille* (Paris: Degorce-Cadot, 1869), 34.

[132] Simon, "Discours sur l'élection des maires."

Bourgeois and Popular Republicanism

So far, I have characterized the republican community of the Second Empire in terms of its uniting features: an anti-Bonapartist culture, a sense of devotion to the Revolution, and an attachment to the values of freedom and fraternity and the principles of popular sovereignty and patriotism. Also common, as we have just noted, was entrenched hostility toward the institutions and norms of Catholicism; this rejection was often accompanied by a search for alternative forms of spirituality. But there were also important lines of division within the republican movement, which I will now examine. However, I will make little mention of some of the differences traditionally recognized in the literature. For example, the generational clash between the *quarante-huitards* who had been active during the Second Republic and the Young Turks who came of age under the shadow of Bonapartism was intense and often dramatic. But it was essentially a conflict of temperament, style, and personal ambition, not of principle or ideology.

What, then, did matter? In 1869 the Proudhonist socialist Ecorcheville brought out a book entitled *Bourgeois et socialistes*. It was not merely an account of the current state of the republican party but an examination of why the 1848 revolution had failed. He offered three main reasons: Paris had tried to assert its will against the provinces; the bourgeoisie had systematically ignored the interests of the working classes; and the republicans had exercised power by authoritarian means, instead of seeking to govern through social consensus and political accommodation.[133]

Although not identified as such by the author, these cleavages also represented the three major fault lines within French republicanism during the Second Empire: between centralist and decentralist conceptions of the state; between bourgeois and proletarian (or, broadly speaking, liberal and socialist) notions of the republic; and finally, and more generally, between authoritarian and democratic political cultures.

However, this is something of an oversimplification; the elements of each polarity contained internal subdivisions. For example, there were different manifestations of republican liberalism and republican socialism, and, as we will subsequently note, a variety of ideas both about maintaining centralism and promoting decentralized institutions. Also, these cleavages cut across each other; thus, there were centralist and decentralist liberals, as well as centralist and decentralist socialists. Finally, not all centralists recognized themselves in the authoritarian political culture of Jacobinism, and by no means all decentralists embraced the tenets of liberal republicanism.

---

[133] Justin Dromel [Ecorcheville, pseud.], *Bourgeois et socialistes* (Paris: Le Chevalier, 1869), 19.

My argument, however, is that once all these elements of diversity are meticulously dissected, there remain in essence two contrasting oppositions within the republican movement, the first vertical and the second horizontal. In the latter case, there was a clash between centralizing and decentralizing undercurrents, which I will explore in the rest of this chapter. This opposition was sometimes complicated by a second element of conflict: the vertical division between the bourgeois elites of the party and its proletarian followers.

The clash between bourgeois and popular conceptions of French republicanism was not born in 1851. During the First and Second Republics, a moderate and consensual conception of the republican idea was often challenged by more radical and egalitarian notions.[134] However, this clash was given a decisive impetus by social and ideological transformations that gained momentum during the second half of the nineteenth century. The Second Empire's rapid industrialization policies significantly altered the character of working-class life in France.[135] When concentrated in large industrial concerns in such cities as Paris and Lyon or in regions such as Saint-Etienne, this proletariat was class-conscious and often militant in the articulation of its rights.[136] At the same time, its avenues of individual and collective self-expression were severely impeded.[137] This obstruction stemmed from the Second Empire's denial (until May 1864) of workers' right to form coalitions and its more general restrictions on freedom of association (until 1868). But it also arose from a growing sense of working-class frustration with the elites, values, and institutions of mainstream republicanism.

This conflict was about both the ends and the means of political action. In conceptual terms, one of the main bones of contention was the force to be ascribed to the republican notion of social equality. For popular republicanism, the main object of politics was "the social question":[138] the defense and promotion of the interests of the working classes, hitherto condemned to eking out a miserable existence under

[134] On the formulation of these divisions in republican popular literature in the 1840s and early 1850s, see Ronald Gosselin, *Les almanachs républicains: Traditions révolutionnaires et culture politique des masses populaires de Paris, 1840–1851* (Paris: L'Harmattan, 1992).

[135] Georges Duveau, *La vie ouvrière en France sous le Second Empire* (Paris: Gallimard, 1946); Tony Judt, *Marxism and the French Left* (Oxford: Clarendon Press, 1986), 33.

[136] See Michael P. Hanagan, *Nascent Proletarians: Class Formation in Post-Revolutionary France* (Oxford: Blackwell, 1989).

[137] See Alain Cottereau, "Working-Class Cultures, 1848–1900," in *Working-Class Formation: Nineteenth-Century Patterns in Western Europe and the United States*, ed. Ira Katznelson and Aristide R. Zolberg (Princeton: Princeton University Press, 1986), 143.

[138] Pierre-Joseph Proudhon, *La révolution sociale démontrée par le coup d'état du 2 décembre* (Paris: Garnier, 1852), 11.

the dark shadows of pauperism.[139] Hence the socialist argument that republicans could not rest content with demanding greater democracy: the republic could not be achieved without greater social equality and social justice.[140]

In contrast, the traditional republican conception of society was largely impervious to class distinctions. Insofar as they were mentioned, social classes were regarded as sources of unnecessary division and conflict, which needed to be transcended in order to attain the promised land of the republic.[141] The republican socialist Guépin spelled out this unitary and consensual conception of popular class relations: "The mass of French society consists of the three classes: workers, farmers, and the petite bourgeoisie. If they were united, all social institutions would have happiness as their goal. Divided, they are easily vanquished, one by one, by the aristocracy, which sets them against each other in order to dominate them more easily."[142]

It was typically assumed that workers and middle classes had fundamentally convergent interests; under these circumstances, some republicans disputed the very rationale for the existence of classes. Vacherot concluded that in a "democratic" society (by which — *censure impériale oblige* — he meant a republic) "social classes have disappeared."[143] In the eyes of Coulon, "Social substances [classes] have been mixed to such an extent that it has become impossible to recognize them. They now form a community that is united by a common bond, and this bond is nothing other than democratic France."[144]

Bourgeois republican social policy accordingly limited the scope of the principle of equality to questions of access and opportunity: for example, the promotion of universal primary education or the guarantee that public officials would be recruited exclusively on the basis of merit.[145] Beyond this, there was simply nothing to discuss; as Gambetta would famously declare later, "There is not a social question."[146]

---

[139] For a typically Proudhonist division of the world between rich and poor, see Jules Lermina, *Histoire de la misère* (Paris: Décembre-Alonnier, 1868) and *Plus de loyers* (Paris: Alcan-Lévy, 1870).

[140] Auguste Vermorel, *Le peuple aux élections* (Paris, 1868), 19–23.

[141] Elwitt, *The Making of the Third Republic*, 41–44.

[142] Ange Guépin, *Le socialisme expliqué aux enfants du peuple* (Paris: Sandré, 1851), 36–37.

[143] Vacherot, *La démocratie*, 30.

[144] Coulon, *Lettres républicaines*, 28.

[145] Ibid., 39–45.

[146] "Il n'y a pas une question sociale" (speech at Le Havre, April 1872, quoted in *Les fondateurs de la Troisième République*, by Barral, 262). On the republican ambivalence toward the strikes of the late 1860s, see Fernand l'Huillier, *La lutte ouvrière à la fin du Second Empire* (Paris: Armand Colin, 1957), 74–75.

An equally powerful source of opposition between bourgeois and popular conceptions of republicanism was the representation of working-class interests. The traditional elites of the republican party were men of bourgeois origins and affiliations. This was not a contingent sociological occurrence. The social and moral ideals of the party elite were circumscribed within the comfortable world of the bourgeoisie, which was seen as the bearer of the core values of republicanism. The strong representation of middle-class interests was also reflected in the occupational origins of the republican party leadership, particularly in the predominance of lawyers.[147] In the early 1860s, however, this hegemony of the middle classes increasingly came to be challenged by an autonomist faction within the republican movement. Largely influenced by Proudhonist ideas, it argued that the bourgeois elites of the party were incapable of representing the interests of the proletariat: "The working classes have distinct interests from the bourgeoisie. They should therefore follow a different political strategy."[148]

In consequence, it was felt that workers should present their own candidates in national and local elections (although, as noted earlier, Proudhon recommended abstention)[149] and organize themselves on a separate corporate basis in order to protect their own interests.[150] In 1863 these ideas were articulated in the *Manifeste des Soixante*, signed by a group of *mutuelliste* workers who sought to force the republican establishment to promote labor's interests.[151] Proudhon, in one of his final works, powerfully articulated this critique of the middle classes and cruelly underlined the degeneracy of the bourgeoisie.

> In turn revolutionary and conservative, legitimist, doctrinaire, and middle-of-the-road; at one moment captivated by representative and parliamentary forms, at another losing every sense of its existence; never knowing from one hour to the next which system and form of government it prefers; valuing a government only for the profits it brings and holding on to it only by the fear of the unknown and the preservation of its privileges . . . the bourgeoisie has lost all its character: it is not a powerful, hardworking, and

---

[147] See Pierre Jacomet, *Avocats républicains du Second Empire* (Paris: Denoël, 1933) (mainly on Favre and Gambetta); Nord, *The Republican Moment*, 115–38.

[148] Proudhon, *De la capacité politique*, 440.

[149] See Proudhon, *Les démocrates assermentés*, 44.

[150] For a development of these themes, see "La Mutualité, Journal du Travail, 1865–66," in *Les révolutions du XIXeme siècle*, vol. 9.

[151] "Manifeste dit des soixante: Candidatures ouvrières" (1863), quoted in *Les révolutions du XIXeme siècle*, 4:48. See also H. Tolain, *Quelques vérités sur les élections de Paris* (Paris: Dentu, 1863), and Lefrançais, *Souvenirs d'un révolutionnaire*, 267–68.

intelligent class, which produces and reasons; it is a small minority, which speculates and flutters.[152]

This was a far cry from the bourgeois republican vision of enlightened provincial notables. These conflicts within the republican movement over social equality and representation became more deeply entrenched during the second half of the nineteenth century. Bourgeois republicans became divided between conservative opportunists and reformist radicals, and the emergence of Marxism, anarchism, and anarcho-communism further complicated the picture on the extreme Left.

In addition, for much of our century debates over the same questions underlay the ideological divide between communism and socialism in France. But we should not exaggerate the extent of these divisions during the Second Empire. In the late 1860s socialists of all descriptions (Proudhonist, Blanquist, Fourierist, Cabetist, Saint-Simonist, and followers of the International) constituted only a minority within the republican movement.[153] This was a vocal and sometimes angry minority, but one that in the main still saw itself as part of the broader republican community, even though it fiercely denounced its "bourgeois" leaders.[154]

Furthermore — or perhaps a different way of making the same point — workers remained overwhelmingly loyal to the bourgeois elites of the party in national and local elections during the 1860s. In departments that were overwhelmingly Bonapartist, such as the Charente-Inférieure, the urban working-class vote remained solidly supportive of the republican party during the Second Empire, enabling the election of a moderate republican deputy in the urban constituency of Rochefort in 1857, 1863, and 1869.[155]

Moreover, as recent studies have emphasized, rapid industrialization was by no means a sufficient condition for the development of militant republican or socialist organizations in French cities during this period.[156] The evidence also suggests that anticlericalism was a much more fundamental component of republican political culture than the class struggle

[152] Proudhon, *De la capacité politique*, 68–69.

[153] Dromel, *Bourgeois et socialistes*, 40–42.

[154] On the role of Blanquism during this period, see Maurice Dommanget, *Blanqui et l'opposition révolutionnaire à la fin du Second Empire* (Paris: Armand Colin, 1960). For an evocation of the atmosphere within the radical republican camp in the late 1860s, see Lefrançais, *Souvenirs d'un révolutionnaire*, 308–24.

[155] Dupont de Bussac in 1857; Bethmont (Paul) in 1863 and 1869. See André Baudrit, "Le mouvement républicain à Rochefort sous le Second Empire" (Ph.D. diss., University of Paris, 1957), 31–35, Bib. Nat. LK7-56144.

[156] For the case of Rouen, see Ronald Aminzade, *Ballots and Barricades: Class Formation and Republican Politics in France, 1830–1871* (Princeton: Princeton University Press, 1993), 174–208.

during the Second Empire, and, indeed, this remained so for several decades after 1870. The division between bourgeois and popular republicanism was thus significant and portentous, but in the final analysis it was contained by the imperatives of the political struggle against the Second Empire.

The Critique of Imperial Centralization

The republicans were in effect a highly decentralized movement under the Second Empire; in the absence of a firm connection with the seat of power in Paris after 1851, the movement fragmented into a "mosaic of disparate organizations."[157] Nonetheless, institutional and ideological elements of commonality remained, as we have just noted.

This was also the case over the question of centralization. Whether Jacobin, liberal, or federalist in their philosophy of the state, all republicans were united in severely condemning the theory and practice of local government under the Second Empire. At the level of principle, there were three major objections: first, the regime's limited conception of communal competence; second, its depoliticized notion of local public life and its intentional reliance on feelings of apathy and disillusionment among the local electorate; and, third, its imperfect application of the principle of universal suffrage.

The regulatory framework for local government laid down in the 1852 decree on decentralization and the 1855 municipal law was condemned as unduly restrictive for communal institutions. Communal authorities could decide very few matters without referring to their local administrative authorities. The burden of this tutelle was further aggravated by the repressive powers devolved to the administration. Municipal councillors could find their deliberations annulled by the prefect or the mayor—a situation that the republican deputy Paul Bethmont regarded as inconsistent with the principles of universal suffrage: "When municipal councils are faced with a prefect and a mayor who have the power to overrule their deliberations, no one should pretend that universal suffrage is honored by the election of municipal councils; no, it is in fact a deferral to authority to allow it to transcend the consequences of these elections."[158]

Even worse, the 1855 law allowed the prefect to suspend municipal councils if they were deemed incapable of exercising their functions adequately. Suspended municipalities were replaced by administrative coun-

[157] Huard, *Le mouvement républicain*, 86.
[158] Speech at the Legislative Corps, 8 April 1867, in *Annales du Sénat et du Corps Législatif: Compte-rendu analytique des séances* (Paris: Panckoucke, 1867), 270.

cils appointed by the prefect. This measure was generally used against republican councils that were unable to reach a modus vivendi with the appointed mayor.[159] Bethmont also roundly condemned these powers of suspension: "Municipal councils are too often fearful of being replaced by an administrative commission; this is a sword of Damocles that, held above their heads, completely takes away their freedom."[160]

The republican doctrine of the commune, let us remember, also attached great significance to the participation of the citizenry in local public life. Communal self-government was a recipe for better administration but was also intended to foster a civic sense among local populations, as well as greater social harmony among classes. In the republican scheme of things, therefore, local government was an eminently political institution, in its functions no less than in its process and outcomes.

In contrast, as we noted in chapter 1, the Second Empire's theoretical view of local public life was strictly apolitical. Elected councils were treated as administrative bodies, and as such they were denied the right to express political views. More broadly, the Empire's paternalistic philosophy repudiated any strong notion of public involvement in the management of the locality's affairs. Hence the frequent republican complaint that the regime's treatment of local institutions generated widespread feelings of apathy and disillusionment with politics. It was believed that far from being an accident, this was a deliberate strategy on the part of imperial authorities to maintain order and stability in the provinces. Instead of fostering a participant culture, republicans argued, the Bonapartist regime cynically encouraged the atrophy of local political life.[161] Simon summarized the shortcomings and potential perils of this situation as follows:

> The result is that elective functions are not sought after, because they are not seen as powerful; municipal elections are conducted in a languid atmosphere, because citizens feel that they will not really be administered by their elected representatives[.] . . . [T]herefore we find utopian and illusory views spreading about what is possible, useful, and just in matters of government.[162]

Another fundamental republican criticism of Bonapartist local government centered on its flawed conception of universal suffrage. As noted earlier, the Second Empire proclaimed its belief in the principle of

[159] See chap. 1.
[160] Speech at the Legislative Corps, 22 June 1870, in *Annales du Sénat et du Corps Législatif: Compte-rendu analytique des séances* (Paris: Journal Officiel, 1870), 187.
[161] Maurice Joly, *Réflexions utiles à propos de la session des Conseils Généraux* (Paris: Bourdier, 1864).
[162] Simon, *La liberté*, 2:258.

popular sovereignty; hence it restored universal suffrage for national and local elections in 1851. However, the regime's practice in this respect seemed contradictory in at least three senses. First, although it claimed to accept the principle of public accountability, it insisted on manipulating the voters' choices through the selection of "official" candidates and the overt intervention of administrative agents in the electoral process. As one republican mayor put it, "If the government and the nation are one and the same thing, there is no need to appoint controllers. But if they are different, as is obvious, if executive power is not the master but the servant of the nation, how can it have the temerity to choose those responsible for controlling its actions?"[163]

Second, not only did the Empire appear to distort the local (and indeed national) electoral process through intimidation and repression, it also denied communes what republicans of all ideological persuasions regarded as their most sacred right: the designation of their first magistrate. Throughout the Second Empire, mayors were appointed by political and administrative authorities. According to the 1855 municipal law, mayors could even be chosen from outside the municipal council, a provision that republican deputies condemned severely.[164]

Although by the late 1860s first magistrates were generally chosen from within the municipal council, republicans deplored the apparent contradiction in the Empire's conception of universal suffrage: citizens were allowed to elect their deputies directly, but this right was not extended to the designation of mayors.[165] The explanation was the regime's underlying view of the mayor as an administrative agent rather than a representative of the commune. Republicans subscribed to the contrary principle, which Vacherot expressed in typically unambiguous terms: "In a democratic society the mayor is the first elected representative of the city; his authority requires no nomination; it comes directly and entirely from his election."[166] The deputy Bethmont made the same point: "The mayor should do nothing other than execute the wishes of the municipal council. The council must be free, because it alone is responsible before universal suffrage."[167]

Third, the Empire was also inconsistent in the scope given to universal suffrage. The 1855 municipal law established the electoral and regu-

[163] Edouard Ordinaire, *Des candidatures officielles et de leurs conséquences* (Paris: Le Chevalier, 1869), 4.

[164] See, for example, Ernest Picard's speech of 8 March 1862, in *Discours parlementaires*, by Ernest Picard (Paris: Plon, 1882), 1:180–81.

[165] Jules Brisson, *De l'organisation communale* (Paris: Dumineray, 1861), 20–21.

[166] Vacherot, *La démocratie*, 309.

[167] Speech at the Legislative Corps, 9 April 1867, in *Annales du Sénat et du Corps Législatif: Compte-rendu analytique des séances* (Paris: Panckoucke, 1867), 290.

latory framework within which communes should operate but deprived
Paris and Lyon of the right to elect their own municipal councils. Municipal authorities were designated by the emperor, and executive power
in both cities was assumed by the prefects. Republicans viewed this situation as the source of numerous injustices. They vehemently denounced
Haussmann's rule in Paris as the reign of corruption and financial unaccountability.[168]

The absence of elected municipal councils was also a violation of the
principle that citizens should not be taxed without proper representation. On a more practical level, the situation was deemed responsible
for the neglect of the infrastructure in many poorer parts of both cities.
Simon thus noted that although Haussmann's construction sites were
transforming its central areas, the roads, pavements, and bridges in the
outer parts of Paris were in a deplorable state of disrepair.[169] Proudhon
sounded an apocalyptic warning about the consequences of denying
Parisians the right to their elected municipal council: "Give Paris back
its municipal independence; otherwise, I am telling you, Paris, the imperial city, cosmopolitan and sensuous, the city of prostitution and intrigue, Paris with all its luxury, will be nothing but a Babylon; and like
Babylon it will end."[170]

Republican publicists also objected strongly to many of the Empire's
arbitrary practices in local government. Imperial mayors were often
seen to rely on authoritarian methods to govern their communes, a situation that for republicans was largely a consequence of their lack of a
popular mandate. Commenting on the resignation of the entire municipal council of the village of Soubise (Charente-Inférieure) in the early
1860s, the republican journalist Jules Castagnary noted: "Arbitrary acts
on the part of mayors are increasing in a worrying fashion. As long as
mayors continue to be appointed by the government, they will consider
themselves not representatives of communes but agents of central government, and they will act accordingly."[171]

The Second Empire all too often forced its mayors to act as electoral
agents for official candidates. To achieve their ends, these mayors often
resorted to threats and intimidation against local populations, who
were often too frightened to stand up to the forces of officialdom. For
Edouard Ordinaire, the mayor of the commune of Maisière (Doubs),
votes obtained under these conditions were fraudulent, based as they
were on coercion and fear: "Among the voters thus won over to the

[168] See Jules Ferry, *Les comptes fantastiques d'Haussmann* (Paris: Le Chevalier, 1868).
[169] Jules Simon, *Paris aux Parisiens* (Paris: Degorce-Cadot, 1869), 10–12.
[170] Proudhon, *Les démocrates assermentés*, 47.
[171] Jules Castagnary, *Les libres propos* (Paris: Lacroix, 1864), 23–24.

official candidate, how many are in fact prompted by the secret terror that representatives of power and authority always provoke among the ignorant, who only have a vague sense of their rights and are always fearful of giving the state a reason or a pretext to torment them?"[172] He thus invited all his republican colleagues to decline to act as the Empire's electoral agents.[173] The evidence of the 1860s suggests that mayors — and not only republican ones — increasingly adopted this line of resistance to official injunctions.

But the ultimate source of imperial local power lay in the administration, and the republicans concentrated a barrage of criticism against its agents. The hated symbol of administrative despotism in the eyes of all republicans was the prefect. In the words of Renouvier, "Distant despot, obeying the orders of another despot, the prefect either ignores the particular interests of the commune or overlooks them for political or personal reasons; furthermore, he is in no way entrusted with defending the great moral, intellectual, and material interests of those he administers."[174]

For Proudhon the commune was no longer an autonomous entity but merely a "branch of the prefecture."[175] The inflation of the state bureaucracy appeared as a leitmotiv in republican writings. For the republican socialist Arnould, "There will never be a serious decentralization as long as central government has at its total control an army of bureaucrats who depend on and only know it, and represent only its wishes and its preponderance."[176] Simon offered a succinct summary of republican complaints: "Freedom has three grievances against French administration: it administers too much, with too many agents, and by too many subordinate agents."[177]

The sheer number of public servants was a cause of political inequity and administrative incompetence, both of which were injurious to the cause of liberty: "There is clearly a fundamental incompatibility between these two notions: a nation of functionaries and a free nation."[178] In an address to the mayor of a large maritime town, Proudhon colorfully represented the overwhelming preponderance of the administration in the local life of the commune.

[172] Ordinaire, Des candidatures officielles, 5.
[173] Edouard Ordinaire, Lettre électorale d'un maire de village à ses collègues (Paris: Le Chevalier, 1868), 5–6.
[174] Charles Renouvier et al., Organisation communale et centrale de la République (Paris: Librairie Républicaine, 1851), 33.
[175] Proudhon, Les démocrates assermentés, 43.
[176] Arnould, Une campagne à la Marseillaise, 174.
[177] Simon, La liberté, 2:199–200.
[178] Ibid., 223.

Let us talk about your freedom, and your municipal autonomy. You are oppressed in all your faculties (1) by the prefect; (2) by the public prosecutor; (3) by the police commissioner; (4) by the rector of the academy; (5) by the general of the local division; (6) by the archbishop; (7) by the bank; (8) by the tax collector; (9) by the railway; (10) by the dock. Your city is, for the state and all the privileged bodies that rely on it for their precarious existence, a barrack, an office, an agency, a branch, a school, a prosecutor's unit, a station, a shop; but none of this is for you, you are nothing. Show even a small measure of autonomy, and the general will besiege you, the archbishop will excommunicate you, the prefect and commissioner will denounce you, the prosecutor will adjourn your case, the bank will withdraw its credit, and the railway all its carriages. You will be nothing but a pile of old rocks, a ruin.[179]

The republican condemnation of the Second Empire's local government regime was thus universal. Furthermore, the regime's timid moves toward promoting greater local liberty in the 1860s found little favor among republicans. In the judgment of Bethmont, "The decentralisation that is being undertaken by the government is nothing but a decentralization in favor of the prefects and with a view to the forthcoming elections."[180] The Jacobin newspaper *L'Avenir National* opined: "All the actions of the imperial government are in complete contempt of the sovereignty of the commune."[181]

In 1870 the republicans thus refused to take part in the deliberations of the commission of decentralization appointed by Ollivier, believing that the liberal Empire had little to offer in terms of municipal freedom. In broader terms, most republican pamphleteers tended to focus their critical attention on communal liberty. The role of the General Councils was typically passed over in silence, except by republicans who ran for office in cantonal elections.[182] Some republicans even envisaged the abolition of the department.[183]

The reasons for this distinct focus were twofold. The commune represented the microcosm of the republican polity, and its defense against imperial manipulations was partly a matter of principle. But, as we have noted, the main political and electoral strength of the republican party during the Second Empire resided in urban centers. The protection of

---

[179] Proudhon, *Essais d'une philosophie populaire*, 82–83.

[180] Speech at the Legislative Corps, 8 April 1867, in *Annales du Sénat et du Corps Législatif: Compte-rendu analytique des séances* (Paris: Panckoucke, 1867), 270.

[181] *L'Avenir National*, 24 June 1870.

[182] For example, see Paul Bethmont, *Des préfets, des conseils généraux, et du suffrage universel* (Rochefort, 1864).

[183] Pyat, Caussidière, and Boichot, "Lettre au peuple," 10; Renouvier et al., *Organisation communale*, 49–50.

cities and towns (and, by extension, of all communes) was thus also a matter of self-interest for republicans of all ideological persuasions.

However, there ended the consensus. Indeed, the process of offering a coherent intellectual response to the encroachments of the Bonapartist regime on local life was problematic for the republican party. Although united in its rejection of the Second Empire's practices, the republican community appeared fundamentally divided over the alternative solutions to be proposed. Jacobins merely offered a restatement of their classic principles; radical decentralists made the case for a fundamental restructuring of the local government system along federal lines; and, between these two extremes, municipalist republicans argued for a moderate form of self-government, in which individual territorial units would retain substantive affiliations with the center. We will examine each of these conceptions in turn.

The Jacobin Rejection of Decentralization

Although they willingly endorsed the earlier critique of imperial institutions, a number of republican politicians and intellectuals rejected the decentralist solutions offered by their liberal and libertarian colleagues. This rejection was expressed in a critique of decentralization and a forceful restatement of traditional centralist principles.

The centralist culture of French republicanism was first defined by the Jacobins, a movement that dramatically shaped the course of the French Revolution. During the 1790s Jacobin republicanism was the standard-bearer of the unitary thrust of 1789; it was a popular, egalitarian, nationalist, collectivist, and authoritarian movement, which invoked the principle of popular sovereignty and governed by methods that were purposeful and often violent.[184] It celebrated the principle of political and administrative unity and emphasized the primordial role of the state in defining the general good. It had a definite vision of the future and saw history as a process that unfolded clearly toward the achievement of its ends.[185] Second Empire Jacobins saw themselves as the direct bearers of the heritage of the 1789 tradition, and this revolutionary fetishism was epitomized by Charles Delescluze's newspaper *Le Réveil*, which was dated according to the revolutionary calendar.[186]

By the middle of the nineteenth century, however, the concept of Jac-

---

[184] See Gaston-Martin, *Les Jacobins* (Paris: Presses Universitaires de France, 1945), 85–86.

[185] For an examination of the political philosophy of Jacobinism, see Lucien Jaume's *Le discours jacobin et la démocratie* (Paris: Fayard, 1989).

[186] René Arnaud, *La Deuxième République et le Second Empire* (Paris: Hachette, 1929), 273.

obinism had become intellectually fragmented, with diverse appreciations being expressed about the movement's political heritage both
within and outside the republican community.[187] During the Second Republic many republican movements were constituted on a basis that
was directly inspired by Jacobin centralist principles.[188]

At a broader level, the Jacobin notion of the political and cultural
unity of France was accepted and even celebrated by most mainstream
political movements — in particular, the Bonapartists, liberals, and republicans.[189] However, many other features of the heritage of the 1790s
were much more contentious. Indeed, a thorough analysis of the significance of the concept of Jacobinism during the Second Empire is complicated by the fact that the term appears in a variety of discursive contexts. For historians within the republican movement, the term tended
to be used in its literal sense to denote the institutions and characters of
the revolutionary drama during the 1790s. This historical evaluation
became the source of furious intrarepublican controversy after the publication in 1865 of a violently anti-Jacobin book about the Revolution
by Edgar Quinet.[190]

At the same time the concept of Jacobinism intruded on contemporary political debates, in at least four different settings. Throughout the
Second Empire the term was used by some to represent the intellectual
principles of republicanism. Thus, for the Bonapartist Eugène Loudun,
the works of Michelet, Renan, and Taine symbolized the revival of "materialist" Jacobin thought in France — a renewal that in his view threatened the very fabric of Christian civilization.[191]

Within the republican movement itself, liberals and libertarians reserved the label Jacobin for all those suspected of adoring power for its
own sake. Thus Proudhon denounced as Jacobins those republicans

---

[187] For an overview of the fate of Jacobinism in the nineteenth century, see François
Furet, *La Révolution, 1770–1880* (Paris: Hachette, 1988), and "Révolution française et
tradition jacobine," in *The French Revolution and the Creation of Modern Political Culture,* ed. Colin Lucas, vol. 2 (Oxford: Pergamon Press, 1988).

[188] For example, Solidarité Républicaine, an association set up by Martin-Bernard, Per-
diguier, and Delescluze in November 1848. It warned that republicans were not being
given the "protection to which they were entitled" in the departments; hence the imperative of "political unity," which was the only means to defend the republic against its
enemies. See *Solidarité Républicaine: Association pour le développement des droits et des
intérêts de la démocratie* (1849).

[189] Royalists also celebrated French unity but traced its sources back to the absolutist
monarchies of the sixteenth and seventeenth centuries.

[190] Edgar Quinet, *La Révolution,* 2 vols. (Paris: Lacroix, 1865).

[191] Eugène Loudun [Jules Amigues], *Les nouveaux jacobins* (Paris: Dillet, 1869).

(moderate and socialist alike) who ran for office in the 1863 legislative elections.[192]

Others still deployed the concept to define, and most often to criticize, a specific theory of the state. In the decentralist literature, especially in legitimist writings, there was sharp criticism of the Jacobin doctrine of the state as the exclusive guardian of the collective good and self-appointed purveyor of public happiness.[193] In this context, the Jacobin ideal of the state was represented as one of the intellectual sources of the Second Empire's failings in local liberty.

Finally, and more broadly, some liberals portrayed Jacobinism as a state of mind, or even a distinct political culture. Ferry asserted the fundamental duality of Jacobinism: "It appears sometimes as a sentiment, and sometimes as a system."[194] In Ollivier's conception, Jacobinism was not an ideology that was the exclusive preserve of a particular republican sect; it was an antiliberal manner of politics, which could be found among republicans, but also royalists, Catholics, Protestants, and atheists: "Jacobinism is a method and not an opinion; all opinions have used it for their own ends."[195]

Jacobinism was first and foremost a doctrine about power and its necessary use. For the Blanquist Gustave Tridon, centralization was the medicine that could heal the French nation of its secular disorders:

> Centralization is here with its flowing arteries, its vigorous muscles, and its admirable circulation; yesterday perhaps an instrument of death, but tomorrow an instrument of life. Thanks to it, the burden of secular errors and superstitions will fade away, freedom will flow from the heart to all parts of the body, and progress will multiply its strength and purpose. Only centralization will tear society away from the Middle Ages, support the weak against the powerful, flood Europe with light, and save the world. It is the Archimedean lever.[196]

This exaltation of the state's liberating role was common to all Jacobins, from the revolutionist Tridon to the eminently moderate and pragmatic Favre. But the self-styled Jacobin republicans of the Second Empire were not systematically committed to violence. Revolutionist republicans such as the Blanquists were the exception, and their invocation of the revolutionary violence of the 1790s was intended to inspire

[192] Proudhon, *Les démocrates assermentés*, 72.
[193] Muller, *La légitimité*, 174, 179.
[194] Ferry, "Polémique avec Peyrat," in *Discours et opinions*, 1:101.
[195] Ollivier, "Lettres sur 'La Révolution Française' par E. Quinet," 345–46.
[196] Gustave Tridon, "Gironde et Girondins," in *Oeuvres diverses de Gustave Tridon* (Paris: Allemane, 1891), 130–31.

contemporary political action.[197] In the immediate aftermath of the 1851 coup, a number of Jacobin groups thus plotted the assassination of the emperor and the establishment of a dictatorial republic; these attempts were easily foiled by the police.[198] But most of the Jacobins who defended the methods used by the Revolution in the 1790s were constitutionalist republicans, who sought to achieve their ends through legal and peaceful means. Their Jacobinism was in part a means of establishing a distinct historical lineage and defining their specific identity in relation to other political undercurrents within the republican party.

Second Empire Jacobins identified with the revolutionary governments' successes in creating a sense of unity and national identity after 1789 and in defending the country against both domestic and external forces of counterrevolution. In the opinion of the journalist Alphonse Peyrat, all the measures taken by the Revolution to defend itself against its enemies were justified, including the Terror. Political and administrative centralization was thus seen as essential to protecting the Revolution's achievements.[199]

Steeped in a particular reading of history, Jacobin republicans were ardent practitioners of analogical reasoning: their interpretation of the past was often a direct inspiration for their contemporary political views. The question of local liberty was a case in point. Making an argument against an autonomous regime for local government institutions in 1851, the socialist republican Louis Blanc rhetorically inquired whether any of the major gains of the Revolution could have been made under a decentralized regime.

> Would any of these things have been possible with 37,000 microscopic assemblies, each claiming to speak in the name of the sovereign, embarrassing each other with their internal divisions, dissipating their enthusiasm in petty quarrels, replacing the striking effect of a common unitary will with the uncertainty of probable dissension, open to intrigue, and tormented by village influences?[200]

The answer was of course negative. A system of strong municipal and departmental autonomy could therefore lead only to "the fragmentation

---

[197] See, for example, Gustave Tridon, *Les Hébertistes*, in *Oeuvres diverses de Gustave Tridon*, 3–93.

[198] For a detailed example of the activities of one such group, see Arch. Préfecture de Police (Paris), Série A-A/434 (Attentats et Complots Second Empire), Dossier 4029: "Comité Révolutionnaire organisé par Raynaud et Biotère."

[199] Alphonse Peyrat, *La Révolution et le livre de M. Quinet* (Paris: Michel Lévy, 1866), 192. On Peyrat's political philosophy, see Joseph Reinach, "Un journaliste républicain: Alphonse Peyrat," *Revue Politique et Parlementaire*, 10 February 1910, 293–327.

[200] Louis Blanc, *La République une et indivisible* (Paris: Naud, 1851), 81.

of popular sovereignty, the destruction of national unity, and the unco-ordinated clash of local pretenses and jealousies."[201] This was, in short, the slippery slope to federalism, and federalism was in the Jacobin mind a certain recipe for social and political chaos: "Federalism has always been for all peoples the source of bloody quarrels and the principle of inevitable ruin."[202]

Analogical reasoning sometimes also involved a transposition of the political situation in France under the Second Empire back to the tor-mented decade of the 1790s. From this perspective, France was not the strong and healthy nation celebrated by Bonapartist propagandists, but a weak and frail community threatened by external and internal turbu-lence. In the face of this potential threat of social disintegration, only a strong centralized state could advance the cause of republicanism. In a work published shortly after the 1851 coup d'état, a Jacobin theorist defined the proper domain of state action in these extensive terms:

> The state is called upon by its very essence to intervene in all spheres of human activity. Nothing that impinges on the material and moral destiny of individuals and peoples could be totally indifferent to it. Whether in reli-gion, education, science, art, industry, credit[,] . . . the state should be pre-sent, not to direct these great and powerful manifestations of human en-deavor, but to remove any obstacles that might obstruct their providential accomplishments.[203]

The Jacobin state was neither absolutist nor (to use modern political terminology) totalitarian; it did not purport to direct and control the thoughts and actions of all citizens. But its conception of the good life was clear and unambiguous, and it saw it as its unquestionable duty to lead the citizenry toward its telos. Indeed, the core functions of the state were not a matter for political debate.

One of the distinctive features of Jacobin theory was its emphasis on the transcendental nature of state institutions. Like absolutist royalists (Joseph de Maistre's admiration of Jacobinism was no accident), Jac-obin constitutionalists argued that the fundamental nature and purpose of the state did not vary according to time, place, or circumstance. Dur-ing the Second Empire, Jacobins viewed the wide-ranging discussion about reformulating the relationship between state and society with considerable distaste. In the reproving words of Vacherot, "The domain of the state cannot be at the mercy of fashionable opinions that some-

---

[201] Ibid., 16–17.

[202] Louis Blanc, *L'Etat et la commune* (Paris: Librairie Internationale, 1866), 33.

[203] Pascal Duprat, *De l'Etat, sa place et son rôle dans la vie des sociétés* (Brussels, 1852), 32–33.

times seek to restrain it, and at others to expand its limits."[204] The Jacobin state was the only effective instrument for promoting the general interest, and it was the guarantor of principles that were eternally and universally valid: national independence, order, justice, freedom, and equality. To quote Vacherot again: "Military unity is the condition of national independence. Political unity is the prerequisite for internal order. Unity of legislation and taxation are the conditions of civil equality. Indeed, what would remain of a nation if it had no independence, no order, and no equal justice for all?"[205]

Jacobins also dismissed the notion that France could learn anything from other countries; their conception of internationalism was merely the dissemination of French patriotic values throughout the world. In the words of a very hopeful socialist Jacobin in 1869:

> The perfect happiness that the founders of religions promised to their faithful, this freedom, this equality, this fraternity that the Conventionalists of 1792 wished to impose by violence, it is we, the men of 1869, who are destined to make it reign on earth. It is in France, in Paris, that this social renovation will begin, and from here it will spread to neighboring countries, eventually pervading the entire universe.[206]

Jacobin republicans feigned not to understand why their conception of a strong state inspired such trepidation and fear.

> In what way is centralization so threatening to the freedoms of individuals, cities, and districts? The state does not take away any of these liberties, but merely watches over their development, in order to guarantee that they remain consistent with the general interest. Popular sovereignty suffers neither despots in the great centers nor petty tyrants in the small ones. With the complete freedom of universal suffrage, the spread of enlightenment, the strengthening of laws, what a powerful force for the good can centralization become![207]

Particular weight was given to the state's duty to promote and protect individual freedom. Gambetta made it clear that opposition to the authoritarianism of the Second Empire was no excuse to cripple the essential functions of the state.

> Once it is democratically organized, the state has the strict duty to enable the citizen to enjoy his rights and cultivate his faculties. It is one of its three

[204] Vacherot, *La démocratie*, xxii.
[205] Ibid., 260.
[206] Tony Moilin, *La liquidation sociale* (Paris: 1869), 25–26.
[207] Henri Marchegay, *La liberté des proudhoniens, des libéraux, c'est l'esclavage* (Paris, n.d.), 10.

or four great social obligations. By an excessive reaction against the administrative despotism of the defeated monarchies and the two Bonapartist regimes, we must under no circumstances go along with the idea of suppressing the idea of the state, of a social government, Initiator and Protector.[208]

In opposition to liberals who defined freedom in terms of the absence of state interference in the citizenry's affairs, Vacherot underlined that centralization was an indispensable precondition for the universal enjoyment of liberty: "We are in favor of centralization, of course, not only as a principle of order but especially as a principle of justice. Individual freedom is a sacred and priceless value, but only when it is founded on justice. Otherwise the freedom of some will be the servitude of others."[209] This was echoed by Louis Blanc: "What will happen if we allow the most intelligent or the strongest to prevent the development of the faculties of those who are less intelligent or strong? It will happen that freedom will be destroyed. How should this crime be prevented? By making all the power of the people intervene between the oppressor and the oppressed."[210]

To express the point in different terms, Jacobin republicans subscribed to the values of both liberty and equality but accorded greater weight to the latter: "We want freedom, all freedoms, but we want the same freedom for all. And for this we want everyone to have the power to use freedom."[211] This formula expressed one of the core values of Jacobinism but at the same time deeply ambiguous. In its weak form, it signified that liberty was valuable, but only if every citizen could enjoy some measure of it. More strongly (and therefore controversially), it could be taken to mean that liberty existed only when it was enjoyed by every citizen in equal amounts. Liberal, radical, and socialist Jacobins generally subscribed to the weak view, whereas revolutionist Jacobins adhered to the strong.

Brazen about the validity of its principles, and sometimes messianic in its quest to convert the rest of humankind to its vision of the good life, Jacobinism was at one level a confident and even complacent doctrine. For one of its republican critics, its maxims consisted of simple certainties: "Popular sovereignty as a principle, the happiness of the people as a goal, and absolute equality as an end."[212]

[208] Letter to André Lavertujon, 30 August 1869, in *Lettres de Gambetta, 1868–1882*, by Léon Gambetta, ed. Daniel Halévy and Emile Pillias (Paris: Grasset, 1938).

[209] Vacherot, *La démocratie*, xxiv.

[210] Louis Blanc, "De l'Etat," in *Histoire de la Révolution de 1848* (Paris: Lacroix, 1870), 2:236. Blanc makes the same point in *L'Etat et la commune*, 27.

[211] Jules Labbé, *Le manifeste de Nancy et la démocratie* (Paris: Dentu, 1865), 30.

[212] Simon, *La liberté*, 1:216.

Yet this sanguine posture was merely a facade, behind which the demons of suspicion and self-doubt roamed freely. Jacobin republicans were constantly haunted by the fear of conspiracy. In their Manichaean view of history, a sinister coalition of interests was always preparing to destroy the Revolution's achievements. During the 1790s, this implacable logic gave birth to the doctrine of public safety. By the time of the Second Empire, the inherent suspiciousness of jacobinism was still strongly in evidence, albeit articulated in somewhat different forms.

First, it was trapped in a profoundly pessimistic conception of human nature. This was commonly expressed in the belief that little good could come from the spontaneous will of the people. The Jacobin Adolphe Guéroult expressed this bleak vision powerfully: "If power has assumed such exaggerated proportions in our country, the fault lies for the most part in the ignorance, levity, and lack of application that afflict ninety-nine hundredths of the French population. It is in ourselves that the evil resides."[213]

Without the intervention of public authority, therefore, people would remain rooted in a state of nature — a condition in which the weak were mercilessly crushed by the strong. Hence the Jacobin reluctance to abandon localities to their own interests and proclivities.[214] In Vacherot's formula, "There is no worse tyranny than that of the commune."[215]

From this followed the second key feature of the defensive armory of Jacobinism: authoritarian paternalism. Because the people were incapable of identifying those goals and values which were true to their nature, these aims had to be defined for them by the state. And, some revolutionist Jacobins added, if the people were unwilling to follow the road to liberty, then they had to be forced to be free. In the words of the Blanquist Tridon, "Without force, nothing can be founded."[216] This sort of reasoning gave Jacobinism its sinister reputation in liberal circles. Here is Ollivier's scathing portrait:

> The Jacobins do not discuss, they condemn, and if one persists, they excommunicate. Whoever does not think like them is at the very least a traitor. . . . They have one law for themselves and another for their opponents, one doctrine for defeat and another for victory. When it is for them, there is never enough freedom; but there is always too much of it for others; when

[213] Adolphe Guéroult, in *L'Opinion Nationale*, 30 June 1870.
[214] See Emile Littré, "La Centralisation," in *Fragments de philosophie positive et de sociologie contemporaine* (Paris: Philosophie Positive, 1876), 229.
[215] Vacherot, *La démocratie*, 224.
[216] Gustave Tridon, "La Force," in *Oeuvres diverses*, 97.

they are weaker, they cry persecution; but they oppress when they are the stronger.[217]

Intellectually dogmatic and often strident, Second Empire Jacobins were dismissive of proposals for greater decentralization. Some writers saw the demands for greater local liberty as a red herring, in the same way as French Marxists would later dismiss republican anticlericalism as an unnecessary diversion from the real interests of the people. In the scathing words of Blanqui:

> The individual is the key element of humanity, like the stitch in knitted fabric. In consequence, beyond individual education, there is nothing. Administration, centralization, decentralization, and combinations and accommodations of power are all silliness and corruption. With individual education, we can have everything. Without it, nothing. Light or darkness, life or death.[218]

Other critics were more ferocious, thereby displaying one of the essential features of the Jacobin mind: the tendency to impute the worst possible motives to their political opponents. In this context, the doctrine of decentralization was sometimes rejected not so much for its content but because of the political identity and values of those who proclaimed it. One Jacobin pamphleteer thus warned that the liberal opposition's pleas for decentralization were dangerous to the cause of liberty, because they left the republican party open to infiltration by "the supporters of bourgeois monopoly, the Orleanists, transformed into liberals, who fraudulently introduce themselves in the ranks of democracy to take advantage of its loyalty or its weaknesses."[219] For another republican writer: "In 1847 we would have said decentralization is a legitimist conception; in 1865 we say it is a Catholic notion."[220] Above all, decentralization appeared to many Jacobins as a conspiracy to turn the clock back to the prerevolutionary era. For the Blanquist Tridon, "Federalism, under its modern label of decentralization, represents dispersal and disarmament; in the face of an organized and rallied reaction, this is defeat and ruin. To decentralize is to kill the provincial worker, to hand him over, gagged and bound, to the Jesuits and the clan chiefs, and to return to the darkness of the Middle Ages."[221] The 1865 Nancy manifesto was similarly presented by a Jacobin pamphleteer as

---

[217] Ollivier, "Lettres sur 'La Révolution Française' par E. Quinet," 346–47.
[218] Blanqui, Critique sociale, 2:116.
[219] Marchegay, La liberté des proudhoniens, 6.
[220] Labbé, Le manifeste de Nancy, 18. Needless to say, this was not a compliment.
[221] Gustave Tridon, "Gironde et Girondins," 130.

"the reorganization of feudalism across the entire surface of the country";[222] another denounced its disfranchisement of "the popular communities of small farmers, daily workers, and artisans."[223] Its authors and supporters (including the republican signatories of the document) were vigorously harangued.

> Today, under the pretext of provincial liberty, you wish to surrender France to the triple oppression of the church, the castle, and the factory, and thus make impossible any economic or moral emancipation. You want the inhabitants of town and country, governed by your oligarchic councils, to be incapable of liberating their spirits from the yoke of ultramontanism, and their labor from the yoke of financial feudalism. You want to dismantle the heritage of 1789, 1792, 1830, and 1848. We refuse this; we will have none of it.[224]

The apocalypse was thus never far removed from the Jacobin mind, and it was both poetic and tragic that its instincts were played out in the drama of the Paris Commune in 1871. Jacobinism did not offer a philosophical solution to the problems posed by imperial centralization. From the perspective of its own logic, however, this was entirely consistent. Because Jacobins believed that their theory of the state was eternally and universally valid, a reaffirmation of the orthodoxy was their only conceivable response to the decentralization debate during the 1860s.

As a political culture, Jacobinism represented the darker side of the French republican tradition. In lieu of the latter's benevolent spirit, it was sectarian, ungenerous, and sometimes harsh with its political and intellectual adversaries. In contrast with the republican faith in human nature, it was pessimistic and suspicious about the aptitudes and inclinations of people. Its conception of the state was messianic and its ends authoritarian, because in the final analysis it could not bring itself to trust the temperament and instincts of the people in whose name it aspired to exercise power.

This suspiciousness is well conveyed by the moderate republican journalist Hector Pessard, here describing a disconcerting encounter with the Jacobin Charles Delescluze in the mid-1860s:

> The Jacobin Delescluze one night ceased to return my greeting, and I learned from [Arthur] Ranc that he was in this way expressing his horror at one of my articles in the *Courrier du Dimanche*. Had I insulted the gods,

[222] Labbé, *Le manifeste de Nancy*, 26.
[223] Paul Joly, *Opinion du citoyen Paul Joly sur la décentralisation* (Tours: Ladevèze, 1866), 7.
[224] Ibid., 30–31.

vilified Robespierre, or praised a tyrant? I had done worse. A firm advocate of administrative decentralization, along with Jules Simon, Jules Ferry, Carnot, and hundreds of other liberal and independent republicans, I had applauded a manifesto published in Nancy recommending liberal reforms. Such an infamy constituted an inexpiable crime in the eyes of a Jacobin such as Delescluze. For my punishment, I was no longer greeted, and six years later Delescluze, delegate of war, was killed on a communalist barricade, the final expression of an exaggerated form of decentralization.[225]

THE FEDERALIST SOLUTION AND ITS LIMITS

Against this Jacobin perspective stood a democratic and self-governing culture, which tended toward liberty rather than paternalistic or dictatorial authority. In opposition to the Jacobin focus on the state, it addressed the questions of power and authority from a social perspective and sought to identify the appropriate sociological conditions for democratic governance. It was patriotic as opposed to nationalist, and it adopted a consensual approach in politics, in contrast to the conflictual postures of Jacobinism. It was tolerant and open to experimentation and innovation, in sharp distinction with the Jacobin confidence in the certainty of its goals and values. Suspicious of parochial forms of nationalism, it readily borrowed from the political and constitutional experiences of other developed societies and subscribed to a genuine form of internationalism.[226]

This democratic and self-governing culture idealized the role of local institutions and associational life and stressed the vital importance of the individual in the attainment of the republican ideal. Above all, it was deeply attached to the principles of federalism, which it regarded as offering the only viable solution to the problems posed by centralization.

Like Jacobinism, republican federalism was not a unitary doctrine. In the diverse and pluralistic intellectual atmosphere prevailing in the republican community during the 1860s, it could manifest itself in a variety of ideological forms; there were thus democratic, socialist, libertarian, and even Communist forms of federalism.[227] However, all its adepts were united in their adherence to a number of core attitudes and principles. One of their defining characteristics was the very acceptance of the label federalist. As we have noted throughout this book, political

[225] Pessard, *Mes petits papiers*, 109–10. On Delescluze, see Iouda Tchernoff, *L'extrême-gauche socialiste révolutionnaire en 1870–1* (Paris: Action Nationale, 1918), 7–10.

[226] Desmarest, *Les états provinciaux*, 164.

[227] For an example of the latter, see Edouard de Pompéry, *La question sociale dans les réunions publiques* (Paris: Degorce, 1869).

concepts in nineteenth-century France were often laden with historical significance, and none more so than the notion of federalism. Although it still enjoyed some positive connotations in republican circles, by the mid-nineteenth century federalism was principally associated with the legend of the Girondin movement, which during the 1790s sought to assert the power of provincial towns against the Parisian center.[228]

Many republican federalists of the Second Empire warmly endorsed the Girondin project, and rightly rejected claims that it had threatened the unity and integrity of the Revolution.[229] In addition to this common historical ancestry, all republican federalists were defined by the significance they assigned to local liberty in their scheme of values. If all Jacobins were committed to the principles of unity and equality, federalists believed that decentralization was the most important organizing principle of social order, and that all political values ultimately stemmed from it.

Proudhon, who was the recognized standard-bearer of the federalist cause within the republican community, expressed this point simply: "All my political views can be expressed in this single formula: political federation or decentralization."[230]

Furthermore, whatever the political content they chose to give to their federal republic, all were agreed in defining its form. In Proudhon's words:

> In the federation the attributions of central government become specialized and more restricted . . . as the confederation develops by the accession of new states. In centralized governments, by contrast, the attributions of supreme power are multiplied. From this there results a compression under which all liberty disappears, not only at the communal or local level but even in the individual and national spheres.[231]

The federation was a freely contracted alliance of communes, all of which enjoyed the full trappings of sovereignty within their jurisdictions. The extensive competence attributed to each component within the federation was again highlighted by Proudhon:

---

[228] See Mona Ozouf, "Fédérations, fédéralisme et stéréotypes régionaux," in *Federalism: History and Significance of a Form of Government*, ed. J. C. Boogman (The Hague: Martinus Nijhoff, 1980), 217–41; Alan Forrest, "Regionalism and Counter-Revolution," in *Rewriting the French Revolution*, ed. Lucas, 152–53; François Furet and Mona Ozouf, eds., *La Gironde et les Girondins* (Paris: Payot, 1991).

[229] Paul David, *La confédération française* (Périgueux: Dupont, 1870), 4.

[230] Pierre-Joseph Proudhon, *Du principe fédératif et de la nécéssité de reconstituer le parti de la révolution* (Paris: Dentu, 1863), 116.

[231] Ibid., 70–71.

The commune is in essence, like man, like the family, like any intelligent individual or collectivity, an ethical, free, and sovereign being. In this quality the commune has the right to govern itself, to levy its taxes, to dispose of its properties and revenues, to build schools for its youth, to appoint its teachers, to create its own police force, to nominate its magistrates, to have its own newspapers, meetings, particular societies, warehouses, and banks. The commune, in short, issues directives and promulgates decrees: who would prevent it from going so far as to give itself laws?[232]

The question was rhetorical: most political groups rejected federalism as an impractical and even dangerous utopia. In response, republican federalists offered a critique of the key institutional values and assumptions of their adversaries. The Bonapartist subjugation of communal life by an omnipotent and oppressive bureaucratic hierarchy was severely condemned for its underlying operating principle: the tutelle of communes by a higher body. In the federalist scheme of things, communes had to be treated as adults and could therefore not be subjected to any hierarchical supervision. The only limits to their autonomy were set by the natural interests of their neighbors. Potential conflicts of interest between communes were to be settled through a framework of legal regulations; there was no need for the Second Empire's arsenal of "tutelage, hierarchy, and destitution."[233]

Federalist republicans were also strongly critical of legitimist schemes for local autonomy. At first glance, legitimists and federalists appeared to share an attachment to a substantive measure of decentralization. However, this similarity was misleading. Republican federalists regarded democracy as a necessary corollary of decentralization, whereas legitimists (as we noted in the preceding chapter) were in fact attached to an aristocratic conception of local autonomy.

This contrast appeared most clearly in the federalist critique of the 1865 Nancy manifesto, which was heavily influenced by legitimist priorities. In the eyes of republican federalists, a genuine form of decentralization should not enable the systematic transfer of power to local notables; even less should it encourage multiple office-holding. Far from threatening these two features, however, the Nancy project seemed positively to encourage them, to the great indignation of many federalists: "Who would indeed prevent the same person from becoming mayor of an important commune, president of the cantonal council, and member of the general council? Is this accumulation of influences, of honors, of powers, really compatible with the principle of democratic decentralization?"[234]

---

[232] Proudhon, *De la capacité politique*, 291.
[233] Louis Joly, *La fédération*, 20.
[234] Ibid., 28.

Federalism was thus a rejection of both the authoritarian hierarchy of the Bonapartists and the inegalitarian and paternalistic community envisaged by the legitimists. But its sharpest rebuke was directed at the Jacobin project of defining and enforcing the values of the republic from above. For the socialist republican Vermorel, such an approach represented an inversion of the proper relationship between the state and the localities:

> In a republic unity must not come from the center and be imposed by an arbitrary order; it should result from the free will of groups and their harmonious adhesion to common principles, which are the guarantee of the greatness, independence, and prosperity of the nation. It is the communes and the departments that, instead of receiving their instructions from central government, should direct it. Central government, indeed, has no separate existence, independent of local groups, and it is in no way superior to these groups; it is only their delegate and representative, and in consequence, it is essentially their subordinate.[235]

This was a complete rejection of the intellectual foundations of Jacobinism. The interests of the whole were not greater than those of individual communities; membership in a wider national entity had to be based on choice, not coercion; and power flowed from the communes and departments up to the central state, not the reverse. Most fundamentally, the state had no justifiable moral or political purpose of its own; all its legitimate functions were merely expressions of the particular wills of the localities. One could not assert a more contrary doctrine to the Jacobin faith in the transcendental authority of the state.

Finally, and contrary to the beliefs of many of its critics, unity was also recognized as a necessary feature of a federalist polity. In the words of Proudhon, "Unity, in any political organism, is, at the risk of destruction, inviolable."[236] But the unity that federalists celebrated was not the same as that proposed by the advocates of the "one and indivisible republic." Federalist unity was based on liberty, political equality, and patriotic sentiment; its members were free agents, who treated each other as equals and were united in a common sense of identification with the values of the republic. Most important, this unity was founded on the voluntary nature of the federalist contract, which was in itself a guarantee of its survival in the long term: "The aggregation of parts, based on adhesion, voluntary alliance, and contractual commitment, is much more solid and generates a much more energetic form of patrio-

---

[235] Vermorel, *Qu'est-ce que la République?*, 25.
[236] Pierre-Joseph Proudhon, *Théorie du mouvement constitutionnel* (Paris: Lacroix, 1870), 109.

tism than an annexation or absorption that is simply the product of coercion."[237]

Federalism thus represented a powerful and coherent ideological alternative to Jacobinism. It was strongly idealistic in some respects, notably in its emphasis on the possibility of cooperation within society and its faith in the redemptive attributes of communal freedom. But not all federalists were naive utopians. Communal autonomy was not always viewed as sufficient in itself; communes had to possess the instruments and aptitudes necessary to enjoy their freedom. It was recognized, for instance, that in their current state many rural communes lacked the material and intellectual means to exercise full self-government. For this reason, arguments for extensive decentralization were often accompanied by proposals for a systematic reorganization of communes. These suggestions were aimed at eliminating the significant disparities between large and small communes, thus enabling all members of the national community to enjoy similar rights. More cynically, perhaps, such proposals were also intended to compensate for the political weakness of the republican movement in rural communes. In this light, the democratic socialist Félix Pyat argued for a radical reduction in the number of communes and their regroupment into larger entities.

> Most of the communes vegetate and languish, far from the center, slaves of the prefect, of the large landowner and the priest, in ignorance, poverty, and isolation, under the triple oppression of authority, usury, and superstition. There is therefore atrophy, paralysis, and servitude on one side; obstruction, excess, and tyranny on the other. It is thus necessary to reconstitute all the communes, so that they may each — as is their right — have a share in our collective life; so that they may all have an independent will, a proper measure of autonomy, and a genuine existence.[238]

Thus, during the 1860s, a federalist culture flourished within the republican movement. Throughout the decade, democratic, socialist, and libertarian republican organizations advanced a plethora of federalist and quasi-federalist schemes in books, journals, and pamphlets.[239] This self-governing and democratic tendency represented an intellectual challenge to two phenomena that were often conflated in federalist writings: the ideological prominence of Jacobinism within the republican party and the despotic centralism of the Second Empire. The intellectual potency of this culture came into full view after the collapse of the Second

---

[237] Chaudey, *L'Empire parlementaire est-il possible?*, 48.
[238] Pyat, "Lettre au peuple," 11.
[239] See, for example, *Esquisses d'institutions républicaines*, 73.

Empire, with the emergence of the Paris Commune and federalist republican movements in the provinces.[240]

But, as would be tragically confirmed by the ultimate fate of these movements in 1871, the federalist cause was also inhibited by a number of weaknesses. As a movement, federalism was fragmented into diverse ideological undercurrents, each possessing different and sometimes conflicting aspirations, for example, on the questions of property ownership and redistribution. The death of Proudhon in 1865 deprived the federalist cause of its most articulate (if not necessarily coherent) advocate and created a growing fracture within the socialist movement between different conceptions of revolutionary change. Within the broader republican community, federalism (in its dominant Proudhonist form) was further undermined by two serious — and related — weaknesses.

First, it still suffered from the pejorative connotations associated with the Girondin legacy, most notably, the fear of the disintegration of French national unity. That this apprehension remained so potent more than seventy years after the Revolution was a measure of the affective strength of the Jacobin myth in the historical memory of Second Empire republicans.

Second, these fears of separatism were also fueled by the social exclusivism of the Proudhonists, typified in their conscious efforts to separate the working class from the bourgeois leadership of the republican party. In a large part due to the influence of Proudhon, the federalist message thus came to be conflated with the doctrine that workers should seek political dissociation from the elites of the nation — a doctrine that was in complete contradiction with the unitary sociological assumptions of federalism. But neither Proudhon nor his followers were particularly noted for their consistency.

From an ideological point of view, the principles of federalism coincided with the generous aspiration that was embodied in the republican spirit. In particular, they carried the republican demands for political liberty and self-government during the Second Empire to their logical conclusion. If freedom was to be the defining characteristic of the republic, then it surely followed that each and every commune should be entitled to enjoy it in the most extensive possible terms. But there were important respects in which the federalist approach was problematic. Most critically, federalist writers tended to idealize the commune and overestimate the extent to which republican values were already embraced by French society. A federation of communes, let us remember,

---

[240] On the communes in Paris and the provinces, see *Les révolutions du XIXeme siècle*, vols. 7 and 8.

was to be generated on the basis of the voluntary adhesion of its individual members. This acceptance, in turn, was meant to rest on a common identification with the principles and values of republicanism.

However, the latter postulate represented a confusion of means with ends. It was one thing to hope that adhesion to the federation would facilitate the promotion of republican values in society. But it was quite another to expect a predominantly rural, largely illiterate, and deeply conservative society to embrace the principles of republican federalism even prior to the institutional emancipation of communes. In short, republican federalism was faced with a dilemma. Either society was not yet ready to accept the principles and values of republican self-government — in which case the federalist solution would simply have to wait — or these norms had to be formulated and codified in the absence of a broad consensus — in which hypothesis there would be a violation of the federalist principle of voluntary adhesion.

In addition to idealizing the commune, federalist discourse manifested a profound ambiguity over the question of freedom. In their critique of Jacobin, legitimist, and Bonapartist authoritarianism, federalist writers tended to project a liberal and pluralist conception of freedom. The state's imposition of its moral and political values on localities was thus presented as a violation of the rights of communes to exercise their free will as sovereign agents.

The implications of this proposition were that the aspirations of communes were not one but multiple, and that this diversity was both a legitimate and a valuable feature of the republican project. Yet at the same time, some federalist writers presented liberty as a goal to be realized. In this eminently republican conception freedom was defined not in terms of acting according to one's will but rather as a progression toward achieving a predetermined set of moral and political ends. From such a perspective, ethical and ideological diversity was not a manifestation of freedom but unnecessary and potentially dangerous impediments to its realization. There was only a short step from this inference to the conclusion that these obstacles should be removed in the very name of freedom.

REPUBLICAN MUNICIPALISM, OR THE DEMOCRATIC SELF-GOVERNMENT OF THE COMMUNE

Pitched between the two extremes of Jacobinism and federalism stood the republican doctrine of municipalism.[241] Municipalism argued for the democratic self-government of the commune within the framework of a

[241] Municipalism was a concept Ferry used in his letter to the signatories of the Nancy manifesto. See Ferry, *Discours et opinions*, 1:558.

politically centralized state. Its doctrine consciously borrowed elements
from the two other traditions. In common with Jacobin culture, it affirmed the necessity of the principle of centralization, defined in terms
of a unitary political, military, juridical, and financial framework for the
nation. But it also recognized with the federalists that the overextension
of state functions was damaging to the civic health of the polity. Just as
important, it accepted the federalist intuition that democracy was not
simply an institutional process but a political culture. Fostering democratic institutions in France was therefore not just a matter of formally
practicing universal suffrage; it required establishing the conditions for
the emergence of an open, tolerant, enlightened, and participant community. The democratic self-government of the commune was seen as
an essential instrument for achieving this goal.

Republican municipalism defined itself as a product of the French
revolutionary tradition but located itself firmly within its liberal and
antidespotic inspirations. In the passionate debate over the role and utility of the Terror during the 1790s, municipalist republicans sided firmly
with Quinet against the Jacobins. In a heated polemic with Peyrat, Ferry
affirmed that "the doctrine of public safety is the last bastion of despotism," before concluding: "Jacobins are the casuists of freedom."[242] The
Revolution was worthy of celebration because it had brought to France
the idea of justice; people who had violated its principles could not
therefore be accepted as rightful members of the republican community.
In the words of Pelletan, "The men of the Jeu de Paume had taken upon
themselves the initiative of the revolution because they saw in it the
reign of justice, and by carrying it out they hoped to found it. However,
to violate justice on the pretext of saving the Revolution, what is it,
except to turn the effect against the cause and keep the word while
destroying the idea?"[243]

This attachment to political liberalism was also in evidence in the
municipalist conception of the state, which rested on a key distinction
between its essential and superfluous functions. To begin with, the validity of the principle of centralization was recognized, even if it was
sharply distinguished from the Second Empire's conception and practice: "Centralization is needed to found the unity of the government, of
its territory, legislation, justice, and system of taxation. Anything that
goes beyond is harmful, and it is because centralization goes beyond the
limits of the acceptable that we are forced to demand more freedom."[244]

[242] Jules Ferry, *Le Temps*, 6 January 1866.
[243] Pelletan, *Droits de l'homme*, 46–47.
[244] Simon, "Discours sur l'élection des maires."

A republican government would therefore demarcate itself from the authoritarianism of the Bonapartist tradition:

> Instead of suffocating municipal freedoms under a system of administrative centralization, the republican state will favor their development. But at the same time it cannot suffer, under the pretext of communal independence, that the rights of citizens and the public interest should be endangered. At this double condition, the commune will be what it should be, and only what it should be: a free collectivity in a free society.[245]

In short, the sovereignty of the commune was defined and circumscribed by the principle of general interest: "Theoretically, the commune is as sovereign in the sphere of communal interests as the state is in the domain of the general interest."[246] In the early 1870s the radical Naquet also defined the strict limits of communal and departmental liberty by invoking the distinction between general and local interests:

> We cannot accept that a department should be able to modify at its will the organization of the army, the financial system of the country, the laws that govern property and the family . . . nor should it be able to obstruct the construction of a railway or a public utility located on its territory; it is also unacceptable that a department or commune should have the right to adopt a regime of free trade while its neighbor takes the protectionist approach to its limits by imposing internal tariffs. . . . These are all questions that interest the inhabitants of the Republic in equal measure, and over which no fraction of these inhabitants should have the right to enact laws. In a word, the broadest form of decentralization consistent with the most complete form of unity, this is the system that is suitable for our country.[247]

The municipalist notion of democratic self-government accordingly presupposed a distinct type of republican state: neither the passive and subordinate aggregation of local interests that federalists advocated nor the imperious and transcendental agent of popular sovereignty Jacobins promoted. In opposition to the latter, Simon rejected the notion that the state should concern itself with industrial policy:

> We can accept a state that governs and decides; but when it takes, among private citizens, the demeanor of a private citizen, having its own businesses, its own properties that it buys and sells, its own houses and roads that it builds, its own manufactures where it competes against other indus-

---

[245] Jules Barni, *Manuel Républicain* (Paris: Germer Baillière, 1872), 23–25.
[246] Ferry, letter to the signatories of the Nancy manifesto, in *Discours et opinions*, by Ferry, 1:560.
[247] Naquet, *La république radicale*, 138–39.

trialists, the state obviously departs from its appointed and dignified role; it becomes oppressive.[248]

There were therefore important areas of public and private life which municipalist republicans believed should remain impervious to state penetration.

At the same time — and this was its critical distinction from both Jacobinism and federalism — the democratic self-governing state was not weak. Somewhat carried away by his youthful enthusiasm for the decentralist cause, Ferry had once gone so far as to subscribe to the view that "France needs a weak state."[249] This was a crude and somewhat misleading formulation of the municipalist position. It was superficially true in the sense that, in the 1860s at least, the doctrine of democratic self-government rejected the Jacobin emphasis on the physical attributes of state power. This was particularly manifest in the republican denunciation of imperial administrative coercion and political repression, but also in its general hostility to the army, as well as its opposition to the bellicist foreign policy of Napoleon III.[250]

However, rejecting the notion of a strong government was not the same as subscribing to the idea of a weak state. For, in the eyes of the advocates of democratic self-government, there was an essential distinction between power and authority. A republican state could under no circumstances assert its legitimacy on the basis of brute force, as the Second Empire had done. But it was just as inconceivable that the republicans should abdicate their moral and spiritual authority over the nation. Municipalist republicans thus rejected the idea of a strong government but at the same time subscribed to the view that the state should exercise a robust measure of authority over the citizenry. Simon underlined the point firmly: "The more a state is free, the more its authority is limited; the more this authority is limited, the more indispensable it is that it should be strong."[251] As we will subsequently note, this conception of authority played a central role in the municipalist approach to local order.

Municipalist doctrine also highlighted the beneficial consequences of communal self-government for the development of a republican sense of citizenship. First, collective participation in local public life was seen as

[248] Simon, *La liberté*, 2:220.
[249] See his letter to the signatories of the Nancy manifesto, in *Discours et opinions*, by Ferry, 1:558.
[250] On public attitudes to foreign policy, see Lynn M. Case, *French Opinion on War and Diplomacy during the Second Empire* (Philadelphia: University of Pennsylvania Press, 1954).
[251] Simon, *La liberté*, 1:263.

a crucial means of giving sense to the republican principle of political equality. In the words of the radical Allain-Targé, "By the frequent exercise of political rights alone, by the discussion of collective interests in all places where three men are gathered, in towns and villages, all men will rise to the conception of solidarity, justice, and law! All will be united in human dignity and will be equal."[252]

In addition, citizenship would be strengthened through the substantive interactions produced during the political process. Addressing the imperial government during the discussion of the 1867 municipal law, the republican deputy Magnin underscored the broader range of values that could be promoted through a strong regime of municipal liberty.

> The commune should be the training school of public administration. When municipal councils will have the influence they should really possess, citizens will learn, by looking after their communal business, how important it is to participate in public life. They will shake off the spineless egoism that is one of the plagues of our time; a sense of public-spiritedness will emerge in the commune, from where it will spread throughout the territory and will find itself, if necessary, ready to the task in the hour of need. One will attach oneself to the commune, to the native soil, when it will be realized that one can exercise a positive influence to do good and prevent harm.[253]

An active municipal life would bring the citizenry into the public arena and thus generate a healthy public spirit. In addition, it would make individual citizens reason not only in terms of their own selfish interests but also with regard to the needs of others; hence, in conclusion, the promotion of the spirit of fraternity and the logical progression from an attachment to the commune to the love of the *patrie*.

Participation in the life of the city performed another essential ideological objective in the municipalist republican project: fostering a sense of common identity that transcended class boundaries. The following lyrical passage by Ferry represented this notion of communal class solidarity in its most idealistic form:

> Nothing is more conducive than an active and strong communal life to engendering this fusion of classes which is the goal of democracy, to shorten and attenuate the distances and inequalities between social groups by the indefinite availability of local functions and the exercise of offices that are not complicated but honored and important; to make the rich

---

[252] Letter to his father, 6 February 1867, in *La République sous l'Empire*, by Allain-Targé, 104.

[253] Speech of 8 April 1867, in *Annales du Sénat et du Corps Législatif: Compte-rendu analytique des séances* (Paris: Panckoucke, 1867), 272.

more generous and the poor less bitter; and finally to awaken among the wider sections of society a feeling of political reality and respect for the law.[254]

A broad regime of municipal liberty was also seen as offering a more efficient system of local government than the Bonapartist structure of administrative paternalism. To quote Magnin again: "Local populations want to be something; they do not want the bureaucrats to continue to be what they are at present, which is everything."[255] But, although obviously important, administrative competence was not a paramount concern of republican municipalism. More significant was an active local political culture, in which citizens could learn to develop a sense of civic responsibility, to tolerate opinions contrary to their own, and to settle their differences through discussion and compromise. The end was nothing, the movement everything: obtaining the "correct" administrative outcome was of much slighter consequence than promoting public participation in local life. Many municipalists even insisted on the value of making mistakes, because administrative science could be learned only through trial and error. In the estimation of the republican journalist Pierre Lanfrey, "Decentralization consists in developing everywhere a sense of life, activity, and initiative among all citizens; to allow them even to make mistakes, because mistakes are necessary for truth to emerge, and we all make them; because indeed it is not a question of never being wrong but of being active and alive."[256]

However, this recognition of the heuristic value of experimentation in local politics was hardly an invitation to joyful anarchy. Indeed, municipalist republicans were passionately devoted to political and administrative stability, and precisely in order to prevent local government institutions from collapsing into confusion and chaos did they advocate retaining many existing elements of the political and administrative framework of central controls.

Thus, again with the exception of the overzealous Ferry,[257] municipalist republicans tended to oppose the dismantling of the prefectoral institution. The prefect was the legitimate representative of the state in each department, and it was his duty to see to it that communes did nothing

[254] Jules Ferry, letter to the authors of the Nancy manifesto (1865), in *Discours et opinions*, 1:559.

[255] Ibid.; it is interesting to hear, in the speech of a republican, the exact echo of the Nancy manifesto's formula about the domination of the citizenry by the bureaucracy.

[256] Pierre Lanfrey, *Chroniques Politiques, 1860–1865* (Paris: Charpentier, 1883), 1:151–52. For a study of Lanfrey's political and historical writings, see Othenin d'Haussonville, "P. Lanfrey: Sa carrière de polémiste et d'historien," *Revue des Deux Mondes*, October 1880.

[257] See his letter to the signatories of the Nancy manifesto, in *Discours et opinions*, 562–63.

to impugn the general interest.[258] At the same time, it was an essential feature of the municipalist approach that local political stability could not be maintained by regulatory action alone, as had been attempted by the Second Empire. Furthermore, stability could come neither through the Jacobin deployment of the resources of centralist power nor through the federalists' irresponsible and turbulent invocation of the absolute liberty of communes. Municipalism, in short, was an attempt to reconcile order and liberty. Simon provided the formula that would later become one of the guiding themes of the opportunist republic: "The true party of order is the party of freedom."[259]

A key figure in maintaining republican order in the commune was the mayor, and here the municipalist school offered a notable contrast with both Jacobinism and federalism. The former circumscribed the mayor's attributions in the name of the general interest, and the latter extended them almost without limits by appealing to a radical notion of political liberty. The municipalist mayor preserved communal order by appealing to the notion of authority—a key attribute in the municipalist scheme of values. The mayor's personal authority was derived not merely from his election by the commune but from his social reputation and occupational respectability.

The essential place of these values in the definition of municipalist authority is well represented in Pelletan's portrait of the ideal republican mayor, which again in many ways anticipated the emergence of the Third Republic's *notable*.

> This man, whoever he is, and who is generally a doctor, a notary, a businessman, veterinary, cultivator, farmer, a man of independent means, liberal by character, having no ambition other than to cultivate his assets and bring up his family; he has no need to seek influence, influence comes to him naturally; he attracts it and holds on to it; whenever advice is needed, everyone turns to him; and when there is a quarrel to be settled, he is the one chosen to adjudicate it.[260]

This passage represents the distinctive character of municipal republicanism in all its ambiguity. The attempt to reconcile the principles of order and liberty created two significant tensions within its core value system, the first social and the second political. In the invocation of Ferry, as previously noted, class differences were to be eroded and even eliminated through an active municipalist culture. This was a classic formulation of the republican dream of a society in which class differ-

[258] Renouvier et al., *Organisation communale*, 61.
[259] Simon, *La liberté*, 2:270.
[260] Pelletan, *Droits de l'homme*, 282.

ences had no significant political consequences. Yet, paradoxically, municipalist republicanism also sought to recognize and even confirm existing class differences by appealing to the social authority of established elites.

A political contradiction followed directly from this tension. On one hand, municipalist republicanism aspired to create an active and participant local political culture, in which citizens would treat each other as equals and settle their differences by the compromises of universal suffrage. On the other hand, and alongside this democratic framework, municipalists expected to promote a distinct bourgeois elite, which would owe its political fortunes mainly (if not exclusively) to the social esteem it enjoyed among the local population. The latter point was clearly spelled out by Pelletan, who prefaced the remarks quoted earlier by acknowledging — *contra mores republicani* — the preeminence of social distinction over democratic choice: "One thing is often forgotten, which is that one does not create a mayor; a mayor *already exists*."[261] In other words, the commune's designation of the mayor merely involved giving legal expression to a form of "natural" social leadership. But if this was true, universal suffrage was not so much a means of leveling the social field, as proclaimed in traditional republican doctrine, as simply an instrument for granting political legitimacy to an emerging social elite. Here again, this was a portentous development: the opportunist republic's celebration of the "couches nouvelles" (new social strata) was fully anticipated in the social theory of municipalist republicanism.

Municipalism was an original and highly successful attempt to define a position between the extremes of Jacobinism and federalism. Although it borrowed broad principles from each approach, it departed significantly from the values and assumptions of both. Federalists saw communal emancipation as an end in itself; municipalists regarded it primarily as a means of promoting key republican goals and institutions such as liberty, civic responsibility, and democracy. Federalists completely rejected the principles of political and administrative centralization, as well as their institutional corollary for communes, the tutelle; municipalists distinguished between administrative centralization, which needed to be weakened (but not abolished entirely), and political centralization, which was a valuable and irreversible achievement of the Revolution.

In the federalist scheme of things, the impulsion for political action came from below, through the particular wills of self-governing communes; for the municipalists, the central state remained the only legitimate guardian of the general interest, as well as the necessary bearer of

---

[261] Ibid., 281; my emphasis.

a civilizing moral and cultural purpose. Indeed, there was a fundamental opposition over the notion of the state: federalists asserted that the state possessed only such authority as was vested in it by local institutions. In this sense, the federalist republican state was entirely subordinate to its local authorities. By contrast, the municipalist state was more than the mere sum of its parts. It enjoyed substantive regulatory and coercive powers but, even more important, was expected to exercise an independent moral authority over its citizens.

There was, furthermore, a striking contrast between federalism and municipalism over the character of social life in the commune. Federalists often (but admittedly not always) depicted social relations in the commune in entirely nonconflictual terms. Indeed, in the more utopian federalist writings, the federation of self-governing communes appeared to generate social harmony by the mere fact of its existence. Conflicts of interest between social classes and occupational groups seemed to vanish; even the dreaded figures of the nobleman and the priest ceased to loom large over the local political horizon. Municipalist republicans, however, recognized the existence of class conflict but believed (somewhat inconsistently, as we have seen) that it could be contained and even arrested through their system of municipal enfranchisement. Federalists were also suspicious of local notabilities and sought to create a political system in which decentralized power was exercised by the people themselves, through their elected representatives. In the more radical federalist schemes, public office was subjected to the imperative mandate; local officials could thus be constantly controlled and even revoked if necessary.

Nothing could be further removed from the staid assumptions of the municipalist scheme. Local power was exercised in the name of the people but by bourgeois notables, who were furthermore entitled (and indeed expected) to hold office at higher levels. Their legitimacy was derived not only from their election but also from their social standing among the local population. Federalism, in short, was a popular (and at times populist) variant of republicanism, which sometimes openly embraced the rural way of life, whereas municipalism represented its elitist and urban expression, which was somewhat wary of the deep provinces.

We can therefore conclude that in many ways municipalist republicanism contained the radical thrust of federalism by appealing to quasi-Jacobin arguments. At the same time, however, municipalists carefully demarcated themselves from both the style and the substance of Jacobin politics. This was particularly manifest in relation to radical expressions of Jacobinism such as Blanquism. None of the Jacobins' crude admiration and celebration of centralized power appears in the writings of the municipalists. For the latter, political power was to be wielded cautiously, and it was mainly used to create opportunities that could then be exploited by the talents and energies of men. It was not the business of the state to go beyond this enabling function. For jacobin republicans, however, the municipalist state was insufficiently armed (literally as well as metaphorically) to face up to its social and political challenges. For socialist and Communist jacobins, it was the duty of the state to create social equality through radical redistributive measures.

From this angle, there emerged a wide rift between municipalism and radical forms of jacobinism, based on different conceptions of equality. Municipalists were political liberals, who worked for the establishment of a gradualist and socially conservative republic, which would constitute civil and political equality, respect property rights, and encourage a modest element of social mobility through equality of opportunity — a "tempered republic."[262] On the other side stood the radicalism of socialist and Communist Jacobins, who advocated a democratic and social republic that would eliminate class and status differences through extensive (and if necessary coercive) redistribution. This ideological difference also conditioned the respective attitudes toward space and time. Radical Jacobins looked to the cities for liberation: "If the big cities so wish, we can all be delivered without any difficulty";[263] they were contemptuous of the provinces and especially of rural France, where, in Louis Blanc's expression, "idiocy is complete";[264] they also always acted and sounded as though they were in a hurry.

This sense of haste was in part generated by their estimation of the distance needed to be traveled to fulfill the egalitarian promises of the Revolution. But it was also based on an expectation of strong public opposition to its objectives, coupled with an intuition (generally justified) that its grasp of the reins of power would be tenuous and ephemeral. Political change, when it came, therefore had to be swift and comprehensive. Municipalists, however, operated on the basis that time was on their side. The republic would eventually emerge across all of France (and not just in its cities), through a slow and consensual process, during which social and political antagonisms would gradually abate and the rights and interests of all citizens would be fully safeguarded.[265] Be-

---

[262] Gustave de Molinari, *La république tempérée* (Paris: Garnier, 1875).

[263] A. Rogeard, *La crise électorale de 1869* (Brussels: Briard, 1869), 51.

[264] Blanc, *L'Etat et la commune*, 32.

[265] This gradualist notion is fully developed in Emile Littré, "De la durée de la République," *Revue de Philosophie Positive* (November–December 1879).

tween these two cultures, the opposition was complete and irreconcilable, as would be demonstrated after the fall of the Second Empire.

Municipalists also contrasted themselves with moderate Jacobins. The latter operated on the assumption that their conception of the state was valid a priori; from this perspective, discussions about altering the distribution of power within state institutions were simply a waste of time. For municipalists, however, the state was an evolving institution, which needed to be constantly adapted to its changing social environment. This attentiveness to changing circumstances was enhanced by the influence of positivism on the social and political thought of many municipalist republicans.[266]

From this followed another key difference concerning political knowledge. In the Jacobin mind-set, all important political truths were articulated by state elites in the name of popular sovereignty and the general interest; local elites were there merely to reinforce the centralist message. For municipalist republicans, however, local elites enjoyed full sovereignty within their legitimate sphere of power; furthermore, with the encouragement given to multiple office-holding, these local elites could even exercise a significant measure of influence at the state level.

There was, finally, an important contrast between Jacobin and municipalist assumptions about human nature. Jacobins, as we have noted, were suspicious and generally pessimistic about the attributes of their fellow human beings. Municipalist republicans, although rejecting the utopian conceptions of the federalists, were much more positive and even optimistic about the possibilities of human development through education and political participation.

THE EMERGENCE OF A PRACTICAL DOCTRINE

By the end of the Second Empire, municipalism had become the mainstream republican doctrine of local government. Even before the tragic events of 1871 had ended the utopian dreams of both radical Jacobinism and federalism, a majority of republicans had come to accept the notion of the democratic self-government of the commune within the framework of a unitary state.[267] With nuances of style and presentation, municipalism was espoused by most of the republican party's parliamentary and intellectual elites, as well as the majority of its elected local

---

[266] On Ferry, see Louis Legrand, *L'influence du positivisme dans l'oeuvre scolaire de Jules Ferry* (Paris: Marcel Rivière, 1961). See also John Eros, "The Positivist Generation of French Republicanism," *The Sociological Review* (December 1955): 255–77.

[267] Jean-Michel Gaillard, *Jules Ferry* (Paris: Fayard, 1989), 210–11.

councillors. Thus, for example, the 1869 Belleville manifesto was profoundly municipalist in spirit.[268] The vast majority of the twenty-five-odd republican deputies elected to the Legislative Corps in 1869 subscribed to municipalist views,[269] repeatedly making the case for local government reform along municipalist lines during parliamentary debates on decentralization;[270] only a very small minority of republican parliamentarians advocated radical and quasi-federal schemes.[271]

However, the ideological tide had not turned only among the national elites of the republican party. In the late 1860s and particularly in 1870, a large number of republican municipalities sent petitions to the Legislative Corps demanding greater communal liberty. The proposals were characteristic expressions of the municipalist spirit: sober and measured, they advocated a moderate form of decentralization and generally included the specific demand that communes be allowed to choose their mayors.[272] In the concluding part of this book, I will explain how and on what basis this intellectual hegemony was achieved. There were four main reasons for this preponderance: the inherent weaknesses of Jacobinism and federalism; the ideological unity of municipalism; its successful attempt to offer a coherent and appealing intellectual alternative to both extremes; and the municipalist synthesis of theoretical and practical concerns.

As noted earlier, the intellectual atmosphere of the late Second Empire was inimical to both Jacobinism and federalism, for rather different reasons. Federalism still suffered from the pejorative connotations associated with the term in the political mythology of republicanism. Jacobinism, for its part, was constrained by the unfortunate fact that it shared almost all its key intellectual assumptions with Bonapartism (and indeed, more often than not, with authoritarian Bonapartism). Jacobin and Bonapartist conceptions of centralization were not identical; in particular, all Jacobins fully accepted the notion that mayors should be appointed by the commune, in contrast with most Bonapartists. But there were nonetheless many intellectual convergences between the two

---

[268] The full text of the manifesto is quoted in *Democracy in France*, by Thomson, 250–52.

[269] Because of the fluidity of party and ideological labels, it is difficult to be extremely precise. In Louis Girard's estimate, the figure of twenty-five represents an absolute maximum. See his *Elections de 1869*, vii.

[270] For an example, see the heated discussions on the designation of mayors in May–June 1870 in *Annales du Sénat et du Corps Législatif: Compte-rendu analytique des séances* (Paris: Journal Officiel, 1870).

[271] Raspail and Rochefort advocated a scheme for the complete emancipation of the commune. See Georges Weill, *Histoire du parti républicain*, 507.

[272] For an example of such demands, see *Petition au Corps Législatif pour l'élection des maires* (Lyon, 1870).

cultures. However, in a political climate in which there emerged a broad agreement about the need to trim the sails of the state, and where liberty and liberal values were overwhelmingly supported, the Jacobin emphasis on centralization could appeal only to the most obdurate and unreconstructed republican minds.

It is in this respect interesting to note that some erstwhile Jacobins underwent a dramatic conversion to decentralism during the 1860s. The most spectacular case was Vacherot, the inflexible censor of communal self-government, who added his name to the list of republican endorsements of the Nancy manifesto in 1865. He stated that he fully maintained his beliefs in political radicalism but added somewhat sheepishly: "I have become very liberal."[273]

Second, municipalism was more cohesive than its intellectual alternatives. This did not mean that it was entirely consistent; as we have noted, there were serious internal tensions and even contradictions in the municipalist project, notably in its conception of the relationship between social and political democracy. But it was ideologically homogeneous, in the sense that all its adepts (whether moderate, radical, or even socialist) subscribed to the core values of moderate republicanism: individual freedom, constitutional government, civil and political equality, a law-governed state, and the defense of private property.

Jacobinism and federalism, as the fate of the Paris Commune would show, were both undercut by serious clashes between moderate and extreme elements over the political content to be given to their respective constitutional structures.[274] Municipalism was also able to transcend many of the basic cleavages of the republican movement under the Second Empire: it found support on the moderate Left as much as on the moderate Right of the party, among the aging *quarante-huitards* and the Young Turks of the 1860s, in Paris as well as in the provinces, and among bourgeois notables as well as working-class activists.

In part, this underlying ideological unity enabled municipalist republicans to define a doctrine that stood in clear contrast to Jacobinism and federalism. The appeal of the municipalist approach in the republican

---

[273] *Un projet de décentralisation*, 222. This intellectual evolution continued under the Third Republic. In his political testament *La démocratie libérale* (Paris: Calmann Lévy, 1892), Vacherot offered a strong defense of conservative principles and even called for the restoration of the monarchy.

[274] Jacques Rougerie, *La Commune* (Paris: Presses Universitaires de France, 1988), 86. On the struggle between the authoritarian radical majority and the socialist minority, see Georges Weill, *Histoire du mouvement social en France* (Paris: Alcan, 1924), 147. For a more general analysis of the philosophical differences within the communalist movement, see Charles Rihs, *La Commune de Paris, sa structure et ses doctrines* (Geneva: Droz, 1955), pt. 2.

community (and even beyond) was partly based on its "reasonable" nature and its rejection of the impractical aspects of the alternative schemes. But the fact that it occupied a middle position between two intellectual extremes should not lead to the conclusion that municipalism was devoid of idealistic and even utopian elements. On the contrary, its success also rested on its ability to combine elements of moderation with an ideological self-representation as the legitimate heir of the revolutionary tradition. Municipalism not only embraced the core ideals of the republican movement but presented itself as an important instrument in achieving its broad objectives: civil and political equality, individual freedom and education, secularism, democracy and universal suffrage.

These goals were often given a strongly utopian coloring: municipalist republicans also embraced peace and antimilitarism, accepting the radical claim of a correspondence between centralization and militarism. Furthermore, they recognized the centrality of class conflict and sought to provide an institutional mechanism for its containment at a local level. Finally, and perhaps most significant, municipalism fully assumed the Promethean vision of man that was at the heart of the republican project. As a police report noted of a leading municipalist intellectual, "He is a moderate and sensible republican, but by no means a bashful one."[275] In short, municipalist doctrine was also appealing because it continued to offer a utopia, albeit a reasonable and practical one. "In order to govern France, we need violent words and moderate actions"; this eclectic but effective mixture of idealism and realism was celebrated by Gambetta in his writings on local government and administration after 1871.[276]

If municipalism represented an inventive alternative to Jacobinism and federalism, its emergence as the mainstream republican doctrine of local government went considerably further than its successful theoretical articulation. The fourth and final reason for its triumph was that it was grafted onto an ongoing set of political practices in republican communes. Federalists were too utopian and Jacobins too aggressive to make much of an impact in local elections during the Second Empire. Municipalist republicans, by contrast, slowly but surely began a process of capturing local government office which would reach its climax under the Third Republic during the 1870s and 1880s. This process was facilitated by their political style and values. Municipalists were open

---

[275] Report on Jules Barni, 3 January 1872, in Arch. Préfecture de Police, BA1 946, Dossier Jules Barni.

[276] See especially his two "Lettres à un Conseiller Général" (September–October 1871), in *Discours politiques de Gambetta, 1871–1873* (Paris: Leroux, 1875), 11–39.

and tolerant of the opinions of other parties, and indeed they often collaborated with them. This cooperation assumed a variety of forms: political and intellectual exchanges (particularly favored at international conferences, where moderate republicans could meet members of the liberal opposition without incurring the wrath of "irreconcilable" elements of the party); tactical alliances against the Empire during national elections, such as the Union Libérale formula in 1863; ideological convergences on specific issues such as decentralization, as expressed in the long list of municipalist republicans who publicly endorsed the Nancy manifesto;[277] and, most concretely, political collaboration with anti-imperial opposition groups in hundreds of French municipalities during the 1850s and particularly the 1860s. Finally, the cross-class nature of these alliances should be noted: municipalists made it a point to extend their appeal to working-class voters and win them over to their synthetic notion of republicanism.

All the evidence suggests that these ideological and sociological alliances were already bearing fruit by the late 1860s. This was demonstrated by the special cases of Paris and Lyon, where the republican writ ran large, but also in legislative and municipal elections in Marseille, Bordeaux, Lille, Nantes, Toulouse, Reims, Saint-Etienne, and a host of middle-size French towns.[278]

The legislative elections of 1869 saw the victory of municipalists such as Favre (in Paris), Picard (in the Hérault), Simon (in the Gironde), and Gambetta (in Marseille) in constituencies where the republicans formed broad cross-class and ideological alliances.[279] This urban hegemony often assumed awesome proportions. For instance, in the municipal elections held in Toulouse in October 1869, republican candidates won no

[277] The endorsements appear in the appendix of the second edition of the Nancy manifesto (75–237); they include letters of support from Bethmont, Carnot, Clamagéran, Desmarest, Ferry, Garnier-Pagès, Lanfrey, Lasteyrie, Magnin, Pelletan, and Simon. See also Clamagéran, *Correspondance*, 287–88.

[278] See F. Hérold, "Le vote des villes," *Le Siècle*, 7 December 1863; C. Terme, *Les élections municipales à Saint-Etienne en 1865* (Paris, 1865); on the republican advance in Marseille, see Norbert Rouland, *Le conseil municipal Marseillais et sa politique de la IIeme à la IIIeme République (1848–1875)* (Aix-en-Provence: Edisud, 1974), 249–50; for the case of Lille, see Pierre Pierrard, *La vie ouvrière à Lille sous le Second Empire* (Brionne: Montfort, 1965), 475–76; on Reims and Saint-Etienne, see Gordon, "Industrialization and Republican Politics: The Bourgeois of Reims and Saint-Etienne under the Second Empire," in *French Cities in the Nineteenth Century*, ed. John Merriman (London: Hutchinson, 1982), 132–38; for the case of Limoges, see Corbin, *Archaïsme et modernité*, 899–900. Even in the 1870 plebiscite, which was comprehensively won by the Empire, the "no" vote (which was predominantly republican) triumphed in many urban centers such as Toulon, Béziers, Creuzot, Mâcon, Avignon, Vienne, Châlon, Brives, Beaune, Arles, Alençon, and Lunéville. See *Le Temps*, 12 May 1870.

[279] Girard, *Les élections de 1869*, xi.

CORPS LÉGISLATIF 1869
SALLE DES CONFÉRENCES

DÉPUTÉS DE LA SEINE
2ME ÉLECTION

Fig. 11. Corps Législatif, 1869, Députés de la Seine. Photograph by Appert, Bibliothèque Nationale, Paris. The republican and liberal opposition deputies elected in Paris in 1869. *From left to right*: Emmanuel Arago, Adolphe Crémieux, Alexandre Olivier Glais-Bizoin, Henri Rochefort, Antoine Garnier-Pagès, Adolphe Thiers, Jules Favre, Jules Ferry, and Eugène Pelletan.

less than eight thousand of the ten thousand votes.[280] After the municipal elections of August 1870 at Le Havre, the entire council was made up of republicans; the same was true in Carcassonne, Nîmes, and numerous other towns.[281] This trend was accentuated in the municipal

[280] See Ronald Aminzade, *Class, Politics, and Early Industrial Capitalism: A Study of Mid-Nineteenth-Century Toulouse* (Albany: State University of New York Press, 1981), 218–19.

[281] For further analysis of the municipal elections of 1870, see Jéloubovskaïa, *La chute du Second Empire*, 342–45.

elections of May 1871, which saw further republican advances in cities and towns across France.[282]

Theoretical and practical considerations were thus mutually reinforcing. Municipalism sought to capture the hearts and minds of French localities through an inclusive and pragmatic approach, and the practical imperatives of governing republican communes gave municipalist theory a tolerant and consensual edge. Municipalist politics were in this sense a perfect microcosm of the republic — not so much in substantive terms (the communes of the Second Empire had relatively little margin of maneuver) but in its process: the creation of a civic culture through the patient practice of local democracy. In a letter to a local newspaper in June 1870, Gambetta clearly underlined this incrementalist territorial strategy: the republic, in his words, had to be "practically demonstrated in the very details of the everyday life of the people, in the individual, the commune, the department, and the state."[283]

Despite its imperfections, therefore, the local democracy of the Second Empire acted as an effective conduit for republican ideals. This surprising conclusion — which stood in sharp contrast with the official rhetoric of the republican party[284] — ultimately represented the most radical difference between municipalism and its two conceptual alternatives. Like all republicans, Jacobins and federalists shared the premise that republican institutions would have to be created by a clean break with the imperial order. Municipalists agreed with this end but saw the distinct possibility of working toward (and even accelerating) its achievement through the existing institutions of local government. A faith in the civic and educational properties of communal politics shines through the following account of the 1865 municipal elections by the provincial republican journalist Léonide Babaud-Laribière:

> The recent municipal elections deserve to be cited for the alacrity with which citizens voted and for the order that presided over electoral operations. . . . If I were to follow the operation of popular sovereignty from commune to commune, I would no doubt be pained by the abuses and unfortunate pressures, as well as by the sight of many a disturbing and grotesque scene. But I would also have the gentle satisfaction of noticing a genuine development of our public spirit, a softening of attitudes as well as a more elevated appreciation of human dignity, and a better and more gen-

[282] Edmond Chevrier, *Histoire des partis politiques en France et du parti républicain en particulier* (Macon: Protat, 1873), 299–300.

[283] Letter to *Le Réveil du Dauphiné*, 24 June 1870, in Arch. de la Préfecture de Police, Série BA-1 917, Léon Gambetta, 1869–71.

[284] For a traditional republican account of the abuse of universal suffrage under the Second Empire, see Jules Clère, *Histoire du suffrage universel* (Paris: Sagnier, 1873), 113–207.

eral sense of the civic rights that the 1848 revolution has given to all Frenchmen. Our political education is long in coming, but it is nonetheless advancing. As primary education is becoming common and private interests are spreading, the excellence of the great principles of 1789 are better appreciated, and everyone understands that these principles are the safeguard of the wealth and happiness we have conquered at the cost of so many efforts.[285]

"Ah! How beautiful was the Republic under the Empire."[286] Edouard Durranc's sense of beauty was later overshadowed by darker considerations. Indeed, it is now a commonplace assumption among historians of the Third Republic that the republican generation of the Second Empire was surprised by the sudden collapse of the Bonapartist regime in 1870 and was therefore unprepared for the exercise of power. It is true that many contemporaries were pessimistic about the future of the party in the later days of the Empire. In a letter written after the 1869 elections, Jules Clamagéran affirmed: "The Empire is falling apart. After it there is a general sense that only the Republic is possible. But the Republic with whom? We lack leaders."[287] According to the republican socialist Emile Acollas, the intellectual condition of the party was no better: "Up to this day, why not start by confessing to it? The republican idea has not reached its full development; it has not managed to present a body of doctrine; it is lost in many a cloud and suffers from many shortcomings."[288]

In broad terms, neither estimate was entirely inaccurate. There were still some battles to fight (both within the republican party and without) before the republicans would overcome what Littré called their "sociological infirmity"[289] — the intellectual transition from the status of a sectoral opposition movement to a party representing the interests of all sections of society; in this process, the ideological morphology of republicanism would also need further refinement.

But this chapter has shown that the political tide had already turned by the late Second Empire; in this respect, my argument departs somewhat from those accounts which highlight the fragmented and disunited

[285] Report dated 28 November 1865, in *Lettres Charentaises*, by Léonide Babaud-Laribière (1866; reprint, Marseille: Laffitte, 1979), 2:132–33. An active member of the Grand-Orient de France during the Second Empire, Babaud-Laribière was elected as its grand master in 1870; see Pierre Chevallier, *Histoire de la Franc-Maçonnerie Française* (Paris: Fayard, 1974), 2:483–84.
[286] Quoted by Camille Pelletan, "L'opposition républicaine sous l'Empire," 234.
[287] Letter to Herold, 1 August 1869, in *Correspondance*, by Clamagéran, 318.
[288] Emile Acollas, *Guerre aux monarchies* (Geneva, 1869), 9.
[289] Emile Littré, "D'une infirmité sociologique du parti républicain en France," *Revue de Philosophie Positive* (March–April 1880).

character of republicanism in the late 1860s.[290] By this time the elites of
the republican party were already in possession of a well-defined notion
of the state, a clearly formulated doctrine concerning its relations with
the communes, and an ideological justification of the social authority of
its elites. The basic principles of republican citizenship — political participation, education, rationalism, public-spiritedness, tolerance, and patriotism — were also precisely delineated in the writings of municipalists. It
was on these fundamental pillars that the edifice of the Republic would
be successfully constructed in subsequent decades.

[290] For this view of the (Parisian) republican elite, see, for example, Philip Nord, "The
Party of Conciliation and the Paris Commune," *French Historical Studies* 15, no. 1
(spring 1987): 1–35.

Conclusion

THE SECOND EMPIRE AND THE EMERGENCE
OF REPUBLICAN CITIZENSHIP

THREE MAJOR problems dominated the politics of the late Second Empire: the question of regime transition and change, the place of religion in society, and the issues of territoriality and citizenship. Whereas the importance of the first two questions has been generally recognized, the third has been ignored or undervalued. This book has attempted to redress the balance in this respect and to point to the emergence of a vibrant democratic political culture in France before 1870. As Philip Nord has rightly noted, "The idea and even the practice of democratic citizenship were in place before a republican Third Republic existed to give them sanction."[1] Nord's explorations have highlighted the important role that republican groups and organizations played in this flowering of modern French civic culture. The argument of this book is that many other actors contributed to this process, and indeed that the Second Empire represented an important stage in the emergence of modern democratic norms and values in France.

Before its untimely interruption by the Franco-Prussian War and the collapse of the Second Empire, the debate on the question of local liberty occupied a central position in French public life, especially between 1865 and 1871. Even in the summer of 1871, as France nursed its wounds after the traumatic events of the first half of the year, Léon Gambetta could still describe decentralization as a "burning issue."[2] This question could be described in such terms — even by a republican who was by no means sympathetic to any substantive notion of departmental autonomy[3] — because the debate was not merely about local government and territorial administration. As we have seen throughout this book, the issue of decentralization went to the heart of a number of

[1] Nord, *The Republican Moment*, 216.

[2] Léon Gambetta, *Discours de Bordeaux* (Paris: E. Lachaud, 1871).

[3] Gambetta was never forgiven by liberals and conservatives for his brutal dissolution of all general councils in September 1870; they were all replaced by administrative committees appointed by the government. See Maurice Deslandres, *Histoire constitutionnelle de la France* (Paris: Armand Colin, 1937), 17. On the state of mind of the new government of 4 September concerning local democracy, see Jules Simon, *Souvenirs du 4 Septembre: Le Gouvernement de la Défense Nationale* (Paris: Michel Lévy, 1875), 43–50.

critical problems about the nature of public life in France: the role and functions of the state; the place of democracy and universal suffrage in the political system; the social dynamics and underpinnings of political power; and, above all, the definition of the principles of good citizenship.

To engage in a thorough comparative evaluation of the different positions participants took on these various matters would not be productive at this stage. I would simply reiterate the point made in the introduction: these contrasting perspectives and arguments conclusively point to the richness and dynamism of the Second Empire's political culture. For example, one theme that emerges at various points of my analysis, which has not been systematically explored, is the phenomenon of urbanization. In a broad sense, much of the material in this book may be read as theoretical and philosophical responses to the growth of urban and semiurban population centers in France during the second half of the nineteenth century. This growth produced, and was partly an expression of, a number of socioeconomic developments such as large-scale industrialization, the slow but inexorable depopulation of the rural world, the increasing confidence of the bourgeoisie, the appearance of working-class communities, and the emergence of new forms of sociability and political organization.[4]

As this book has shown, these developments also produced a wide-ranging and contradictory debate about the social and political underpinnings of urban existence. Some celebrated the city as the necessary and even exclusive site of civilization and progress, whereas others reviled it as the source of all the evils of the modern world. In a short but blistering pamphlet written in 1869, a provincial cleric blamed the urban way of life for introducing all forms of moral and material corruption into the quiet pastures of rural France: politics, newspapers, fashion, novels, intellectual activity, capitalism, and its dialectical opposite, "the revolutionary spirit."[5]

One overall conclusion emerges. The demands for greater municipal franchises were expressions of political cultures that recognized and sometimes even celebrated the urban condition, as was the case with the republicans and (somewhat more grudgingly) the liberals. Conversely, the rejection of substantive urban political autonomy was often predicated on provincialist and rural views of the world, as we saw with the legitimists and many elements of the Bonapartist movement.

I do not wish to overplay this contrast, but it is difficult to ignore its

---

[4] See Charle, *Histoire sociale*.

[5] Abbé Rigaud, *La dépravation du village, cause principale de la dépopulation des campagnes et de l'encombrement des villes* (Aix, 1869).

portentous character. On one hand, the political forces that accepted urbanization, and indeed sought to build their social and political futures around it, proved to be precisely those which would lead France into the modern age. On the other hand, groups that were suspicious and fearful of the political voice (or rather voices) of the towns and cities eventually came to be marginalized from the political system. The Second Empire's debate on decentralization was in this sense, as in many others, a harbinger of the political future of modern France.

THE SECOND EMPIRE AND THE QUESTION OF CITIZENSHIP

Some of the broader themes and findings of the debates of the 1860s are also worth drawing out briefly. The question of decentralization was, above all, a debate about the nature of citizenship in France. It can be analytically separated into two distinct sets of arguments, the first concerned with problems and the second with solutions.

There was a large measure of agreement on the first. It was generally suggested that France lacked a stable civic culture, and that this absence posed many problems: political order was constantly threatened by revolution; state institutions were perceived as arrogant, unaccountable, and overbearing; enthusiasm for public life seemed to be declining; associational activity remained weak; and political elites often appeared lacking in dignity, honesty, and integrity. Whether all these representations were entirely accurate is a somewhat different matter, which again cannot be explored in depth. It is obvious, for example, that the relationship between the state and the citizenry was deeply problematic. This was an old story in France, but there were particularly aggravating circumstances after the middle of the nineteenth century: the increase in the political salience of the state, as well as the growth of the size and functions of its central and territorial bureaucracies.[6]

Other elements of the decentralist diagnosis, however, were more contestable. In overall terms, the argument of this book is that a sense of citizenship was already quite strongly developed in France by the end of the Second Empire; indeed, this is (perhaps somewhat paradoxically) borne out by the broad elements of convergence among political elites over the very issue of decentralization. Other elements also point to the limits of the decentralist diagnosis. For example, the claim that associational activity was weak in France is not entirely supported by the evidence, especially during the 1860s. As we noted in the introduction, this was, after all, the period of the expansion of France's inter-

[6] See Guy Thuillier and Jean Tulard, *Histoire de l'administration française* (Paris: Presses Universitaires de France, 1994), 46–49.

nal market and the development of its road and rail networks.[7] This era was also marked by the multiplication of nonpolitical associations and societies, among provincial and rural communities no less than in urban centers.

So why the recurrent complaints from political elites? Part of the answer was that the diagnosis of associational weakness was often filtered through ideological lenses. For instance, republicans did not generally approve of manifestations of religious sociability (which were extremely plentiful during this period,[8]) any more than Catholics and legitimists welcomed the growth of clubs, salons, and freethinking discussion groups,[9] or secular associations such as Freemasonry.[10] Sociability was thus a valuable commodity, but its appreciation was almost invariably colored by deeper ideological principles and beliefs.

As far as the solutions were concerned, there were obviously significant differences among the various political traditions (and also, as we noted in the Bonapartist and republican cases, within them). Yet it is possible to identify something of a formal convergence over three broad areas. First, there was a widespread notion that a strong and healthy sense of citizenship could not be defined in opposition to the center. Bonapartists, liberals, most legitimists, and the majority of republicans were in agreement on the irreversibility of French political unity; federalist and quasi-federalist schemes were overwhelmingly rejected. This meant that however differently they might be defined in substantive terms, the key values that gave sense and meaning to the notion of citizenship had to be national in origin and character.

It is particularly interesting to note the legitimist position on this question. Whatever private misgivings they may have harbored against the revolutionary legacy of unity and indivisibility, their public discourse on citizenship remained substantively centralist. Another way of making the same point is to note the weakness of explicit theorizing about provincial or regional identities during the Second Empire.[11] Evidence suggests that several decades before the Third Republic's allegedly forcible conversion of peasants into Frenchmen, a strong (if not explic-

[7] See Price, *The Modernization of Rural France.*

[8] See Pierre Pierrard, *Histoire des curés de campagne* (Paris: Plon, 1986), 168–235.

[9] On the development of republican salons during the later Second Empire, see Sylvie Aprile, "La République au salon: Vie et mort d'une forme de sociabilité politique, 1865–1885," *Revue d'Histoire Moderne et Contemporaine* (July–September 1991): 473–87.

[10] On the growth of the Grand Orient de France during the 1860s, see André Combes, *Les trois siècles de la Franc-Maçonnerie française* (Paris: Edimaf, 1987), 112–13.

[11] The term *regionalism* entered French political discourse only in the mid-1870s, and the regionalist movement developed fully only two decades later. See Philippe Vigier's chapter in *Régions et régionalisme en France*, by Gras and Livet, 162–63.

itly articulated) sense of national community and togetherness was already present in French society during the 1850s and 1860s.[12]

Second, there was a consensus on the importance of the public realm in contrast to the private one. Citizenship was not only about the satisfaction of individual or self-interested needs but also a matter of recognizing the significance of normative and collective concerns in the life of the community. How this public sphere was intellectually articulated was again a source of ideological controversy: Bonapartists emphasized technical and administrative norms in opposition to political ones; republicans highlighted self-governing and participatory values; liberals stressed the importance of reasonable and enlightened political intercourse; and legitimists invoked the social and moral allegiances created by tradition.

However, despite these divergent views, there was a common appreciation of the need to strengthen the link between the individual and the public sphere and to prevent members of society from retreating into the gentle comfort (or anomic despair) of private life. Again, it is worth stressing that this was not merely a republican or liberal view; as we saw in chapter 2, many legitimists had become convinced by the 1860s that their treasured principles and values could be saved only by greater political and civic activity. Centralization and decentralization were in this sense powerful metaphors, the first a symbol of death and "decadence"—a term already beginning to make its appearance in French political discourse[13]—and the second a portent of the nation's civic revival and regeneration.

Third, and last, the commune was universally identified as the privileged site at which the institution of citizenship could be constructed. If the citizen acquired many of his—for it was an all-male affair—important values from the nation and the state, it was in his locality that he could learn to cherish and nurture them. In this respect the role of the education system was pivotal, as the elites of the opportunist and radical Republics would recognize.[14] Their conception of republican patriotism attempted to reconcile particularistic and universal forms of sociability, and thus to strike a balance between the citizen's loyalty to the state, the protection of his individual rights, and the development of his

[12] On the weakness of federalist ideas in nineteenth-century France, see Maurice Agulhon, "Conscience nationale et conscience régionale en France de 1815 à nos jours," in *Federalism*, ed. Boogman, 254–55.

[13] For a comprehensive analysis of the concept from antiquity to modern times, see Julien Freund, *La décadence* (Paris: Sirey, 1984).

[14] On this theme, see Albert Thibaudet, *La République des Professeurs* (1927; reprint, Geneva: Slatkine, 1979), and Jacques Ozouf and Mona Ozouf, *La Republique des Professeurs* (Paris: Gallimard, 1992).

capabilities and talents in civil society. Local in form, national in substance: such were the two principal formal attributes of the notion of citizenship as they were generally agreed on by mainstream political elites by 1870 — a formal convergence that would later underpin the emergence of the new republican order after the Second Empire. Many lucid contemporary observers noted this point; Maurice Joly, writing in 1872, declared that "deep down, parties are divided only on the form of government, not on its substance."[15]

DEMOCRATIC CONCERNS AND ADJUSTMENTS

Another theme that featured prominently throughout the debate on decentralization was the role of democracy and universal suffrage in French public life. A number of general concerns were expressed here.

In terms of the process of local politics, important questions were raised about the agency of power. The entire issue of local liberty was couched in terms of the dichotomy between elected and nonelected forms of local power. Authoritarian Bonapartists were alone in defending the view that local democracy could operate effectively without a significant redistribution of authority from the administration to elected officials in the communes and departments. All the other parties and movements demanded an extension of the powers of municipal and cantonal representatives. As we noted in the introduction, there was a substantive measure of agreement on extending the attributions of the mayor. However, the functional powers of local institutions continued to be the object of much disagreement — and this a long time after the participants in our debate had left the stage. Indeed, despite the significant changes to the system of territorial government introduced by the Socialists in the 1980s, the debate about devolution and regional government still resurfaces periodically in France.[16]

Also entirely unresolved was the question of the social and occupational prerequisites of local power. There was an interesting convergence among federalist republicans, liberals, and legitimists, who opposed the "notabilization" of local politics. All three traditions emphasized not only the importance of local roots in selecting municipal and cantonal elites but also the necessity of a rigid separation between local and national political representation.

For Bonapartists and municipalist republicans, by contrast, multiple office-holding was accepted, and even welcomed, as a means of strengthening the social and political links between the center and the periphery,

---

[15] Maurice Joly, *Le tiers-parti républicain* (Paris: Dentu, 1872), 62.
[16] See, for example, Jacques Amalric, "Exception Française," *Libération*, 5 May 1996.

providing a territorial power base for national elites and at the same time affirming the political values of the center. The model of the provincial elected notable, defender of the interests of the "small" peasants and landowners against the "powerful," was also in this sense a strong element of continuity between the Second Empire and the Third Republic.[17]

Other concerns were also expressed about the role of the main instrument of democratic politics: universal suffrage. As I argued in the introduction, the Second Empire represented an important founding moment in the institutionalization of universal suffrage in France. This development required all political movements to adjust their perspectives to the requirements of mass democracy. The debates over local democracy demonstrated that these adjustments were made in different ways and at somewhat varying rates. Legitimists and conservative liberals remained suspicious of the mass vote, even though they came to recognize the ineluctability of democratic politics by the late 1860s. For their part, Bonapartists, progressive liberals, and municipalist republicans endorsed universal suffrage in principle and were united in regarding it as a potential instrument of order and social conservation. This represented a significant change from the attitudes of the late 1840s and early 1850s, when many liberal and conservative politicians railed against the unpredictable nature of the mass vote. The Second Empire thus constituted a discernible phase in France's democratic learning curve.

Indeed, one can argue that one of the most interesting features of the debates of the 1860s was the emerging sense that universal suffrage could be controlled by political elites and made to serve their institutional and ideological purposes. This comes across very clearly in the Bonapartist theory of local democracy, as we saw in chapter 1. But this instrumental conception of democracy also transpired in the persistent efforts of liberals, legitimists, and municipalist republicans to conceive of local democracy as a vehicle for furthering a distinct range of social and economic interests. In other words, democracy was not just a process to be suffered fatalistically; it was a malleable institution that could be made to serve specific, and if necessary partisan, needs.

Here, too, the republicans were not slow to appreciate the adroit mixture of cajolery, dexterity, and brutality with which the Bonapartists successfully held their vote across provincial and rural France between 1852 and 1870. This lesson would prove useful in the 1870s and 1880s,

---

[17] See Philippe Vigier, "Quelques aspects de l'évolution politique régionale au XIXeme siècle," in *Révolution et Traditions en Vicomté de Turenne: Haut-Quercy et Bas-Limousin de 1738 à 1889* (Saint-Céré: Association des Amis du Passé de Saint-Céré, 1989), 315.

when it would be the Republic's turn to placate the conservative instincts of rural France.[18] This further underscores my claim about the pivotal role of the Second Empire in the transition from elite to mass politics in France.

THE SECOND EMPIRE AND REPUBLICAN CITIZENSHIP

The final issue to be settled is the intellectual impact of the debates of the 1860s on subsequent developments in France, particularly the emergence of the new republican order after 1875. Three reasons have conspired to bury—or at least to neglect—this essential legacy. First, modern French historians, especially those of a republican disposition, have generally overlooked the broader significance of the Second Empire. As we noted in the introduction, only over the last two decades does this unarticulated but powerful taboo in French historical culture appear to be lifting.[19]

Second, the 1860s have been ignored because of the distinct way in which the political and ideological origins of the Third Republic have been narrated. In modern republican historiography, there is a measure of elasticity concerning the birth of the new republic; temporal estimates thus vary from 1870 (the year the Second Empire collapsed) to 1884 (when Ferry promulgated the liberal legislation on individual and collective rights).[20] Nonetheless, the common view is that the new order was essentially a product of postimperial (and postCommunal) circumstances. Its ideological debts to earlier republican generations are acknowledged, but in a somewhat ritualistic fashion, rather in the way in which dignified ancestors are honored. Until recently, however, the notion of an explicit element of continuity between the political culture of the 1860s and the birth of the Third Republic has rarely been pursued systematically.

A third, and no less important, reason for the neglect of the Second Empire era is the subsequent fate of the idea of decentralization. After the French defeat by Prussia and the Paris Commune, the atmosphere of nationalistic and patriotic fervor rendered the adoption of substantive

[18] On the later republican view of the peasantry, see, for example, Emile Littré, "La composition de la société française et la République," *La Nouvelle Revue*, 1 February 1880.

[19] The most recent evidence of this transformation is the June 1997 issue of the popular French review *L'Histoire* (no. 221), which tantalizingly asks: "Faut-il réhabiliter Napoléon III?" (Should Napoleon III be rehabilitated?).

[20] For a review of the historiographical debates during the first half of the twentieth century, see Auguste Soulier, "La Troisième République entre dans l'Histoire," *Revue Internationale d'Histoire Politique et Constitutionnelle* (1955): 151–72.

legislation on decentralization all but impossible. It was true that the anti-Parisian mood that followed the Commune was partly conducive to the idea of devolving greater power away from France's large cities. Also, the monarchist wave that engulfed the National Assembly in the elections of February 1871 contained a built-in majority in favor of some form of decentralism. But the fear of social revolution, which would continually haunt the corridors of power in France for at least the next seventy years, was not particularly compatible with the idea of fragmenting power at the center. In addition, the humiliating experiences of occupation and military defeat heightened elite awareness of the benefits of centralization.

Ferry, the erstwhile advocate of a weak state, later acknowledged that the events of 1870–71 had completely transformed his Weltanschauung: "One had to be blind to the events of 1870 and 1871 not to see that during those terrible and painful ordeals, neither the honor nor the integrity of France could have been saved but for two things: the persistent sentiment of national unity and the little that remained of a unitary and centralized state."[21]

Thus, from the point of view of the debates of the 1860s on local liberty, the period after 1870 appears to belong to a completely different epoch. During the discussions leading up to the law of August 1871 on the General Councils, for example, it was the republicans who provided the staunchest defense of the role and functions of the prefects.[22] Equally paradoxically, a predominantly monarchist majority voted the April 1871 law retaining the government's prerogative to appoint mayors in communes of more than twenty thousand inhabitants.[23] Furthermore, some of the core values of republicans underwent significant changes after the Franco-Prussian War and the Paris Commune. After 1870, the mainstream republican movement completely abandoned the instinctive antimilitarism that had been central to its political identity during the Second Empire.[24] Even more dramatically, the republican laws of March 1882 and April 1884 on communal administration seemed to show little evidence of the generous decentralist spirit of the 1860s. The attributions of the municipal authorities were not substantively widened; the prefectoral tutelle was maintained over the communes' administration of their finances; and the denial of an elected mayor to the city of Paris was

[21] Jules Ferry, "Discours de Bordeaux" (30 August 1885), in *Les fondateurs de la Troisième République*, ed. Barral, 319–20.

[22] See, for example, Ernest Picard's robust defense of the prefectorate, in *Discours parlementaires*, 3:138–39.

[23] See Hanotaux, *Histoire de la fondation de la Troisième République*, 1:216.

[24] See Georges Goyau, *L'idée de patrie et l'humanitarisme: Essai d'histoire française, 1866–1901* (Paris: Perrin, 1902), x.

confirmed.[25] Compared with the expansive ideas about local autonomy that municipalist republicans floated in the 1860s, the legislation of the early Third Republic seemed disappointingly tame.

THE ORIGINS OF THE THIRD REPUBLIC RECONSIDERED

However, this is one way of looking at this story, and by no means the most helpful. The central argument of this book is that there were profound elements of continuity between the 1860s and the 1880s, and that the modern republican order that emerged in France was deeply indebted to the political culture of the Second Empire. This legacy is apparent in several dimensions. First, the local government legislation of the early Third Republic was in many respects faithful to the aspirations of municipalist republicans. The latter, let us remember, attached a considerable importance to the promotion of wide and cross-class participation in local affairs. In the words of a municipalist pamphleteer, "In a municipal council we must have honest and intelligent workers, small businessmen and farmers, as well as industrialists . . . it is necessary that the spirit of caste be swept away by the egalitarian result of a sincere election."[26]

Central to the municipalist design was this conception of political equality based on civic participation and identification with the public sphere, independently of considerations of class and religion. The local government reforms of 1882 (on the election of mayors) and 1884 (on the attributions of municipal councils) remained faithful to this project of drawing the public into the political process.[27] It is true that these local authorities were "independent without being sovereign";[28] their political liberty remained conditioned by the higher imperatives of order and the general interest. This formula was criticized by some radical republican advocates of communal emancipation as insufficient;[29] some contemporaries even denounced a return to Jacobinism.[30]

But the importance of communal institutions was unmistakable. It was recognized in the creation of a unified legislative framework for their operation, the stipulation of the principle of the sovereignty of the

---

[25] Jean Leduc, *L'enracinement de la République, 1879–1918* (Paris: Hachette, 1991), 28.

[26] Jules Hue, *Les élections municipales* (Péronne, 1873), 11, 13.

[27] See Ferdinand-Dreyfus, *Manuel populaire du conseiller municipal, texte et commentaire pratique de la loi du 5 avril 1884* (Paris: Quantin, 1884).

[28] Jules Clamageran, *La France républicaine* (Paris: Germer Baillière, 1873), 110.

[29] Edouard Portalis, *Les deux républiques* (Paris: Charpentier, 1880), 323–41.

[30] For example, Edouard de Marcère, "La République et les Républicains," *La Nouvelle Revue* (October 1884): 688–94.

municipal council on all matters that were purely of communal interest, and the adoption of the principle of publicity for all communal deliberations.[31] Above all, the mayor emerged as the central embodiment of the new civic order; his election by the municipal council—the culmination of the long battles fought by the liberal and republican opposition during the Second Empire—was a further symbol both of the greater political responsibility accorded to the communes[32] and of the essential function of the municipality as the link between the locality and the political center.[33] At the same time republican writings emphasized that of the mayor's executive, judicial, and representative functions, the first and second took precedence over the third—again, a fulfillment of the municipalist goal of reconciling local liberty with local order.[34]

The patient practice of municipal democracy was also central to the republican strategy for capturing power after 1871.[35] Loyal participation in communal politics would, in Gambetta's formula, enable urban and rural populations to recognize the republican party's "zeal, devotion, spirit of sacrifice, and commitment to the interests of the greatest number."[36] Indeed, Gambetta was so obsessed with the growth of the republican party at the local level that he compiled a complete list of republicans in each and every municipal council of France.[37]

This conception of local politics also went to the heart of the modern republican conception of politics as a public, collective, and essentially

[31] Louis Rouchon, "La décentralisation municipale et la loi du 5 avril 1884" (Ph.D. diss., University of Lyon, Le Puy, 1900), 35–39. On the development of this legislation before 1914, see Edmond Soulage, "La décentralisation au profit des communes depuis la loi du 5 avril 1884" (Ph.D. diss., University of Montpellier, 1910).

[32] On the festive and commemorative dimensions of the communal order in the early Third Republic, see Olivier Ihl, La fête républicaine (Paris: Gallimard, 1996), esp. 181–222.

[33] Maurice Agulhon, "La Mairie," in Les lieux de mémoire, ed. Nora, 1:167–93. For an illustration of the key role municipalities played in the new republican order, see Bruno Dumons and Gilles Pollet, "Fonctionnaires municipaux et employés de la ville de Lyon (1870–1914): Légitimité d'un modèle administratif décentralisé," Revue Historique (1992): 105–25.

[34] See Georges Lamy, Eléments d'éducation civique et sociale (Paris: Picard, 1902), 136–37.

[35] On the importance of municipal and cantonal elections during the early 1870s, see Daniel Daëron, L'idée républicaine en Seine-et-Marne de 1870 à 1878 (Le Mée-sur-Seine: Amatteis, 1989), esp. 52–60.

[36] Speech at Abbeville, 25 September 1872, in Discours et plaidoyers politiques de Gambetta, ed. J. Reinach (Paris: Charpentier, 1881), 3:70–71.

[37] Gambetta mentioned this list in a letter dated 24 October 1874 to Juliette Adam. See Juliette Adam, Nos amitiés politiques avant l'abandon de la revanche (Paris: Lemerre, 1908), 185.

rational activity.[38] Its purpose was to involve the citizens in public life and help them settle their differences through political competition, reasoned and public discussion, and the display of tolerance, which, as Edgar Quinet reminded his colleagues in 1870, was "the virtue that we most lack in France."[39] Eugène Spuller spelled out this republican notion of political activity succinctly:

> True political action is not conducted in isolation; on the contrary, it is action based on common deliberation, over which one has agreed with one's friends, one's neighbors, and about which one has exchanged opinions with others, outlined one's ideas, faced a number of criticisms: if we wish to be a truly free people, we must not hesitate to take the habits of freedom.[40]

The continuity between the 1860s and the republicanism of the early Third Republic went much deeper. It has been my argument that the liberal political culture of the later Second Empire played a decisive role in the emergence of republican municipalist notions of the good life. To repeat, between 1852 and 1870 the mainstream republican movement made the momentous transition from the classical problematic of Revolution to the concerns of democratic modernity. It was in these years, in other words, that priority was given within the overall republican ideological paradigm to the defense of civil and political liberties, the protection of property, and the creation of a polity that was both orderly and progressive.

This intellectual modernization of republican norms was not merely the accomplishment of the municipalists, who triumphed over their Jacobin and federalist rivals within the republican party; it was in a very fundamental sense the product of the political culture of the Second Empire. In this respect, there is an unmistakable line of continuity between municipalist norms and the liberal republican legislation of the early 1880s, which introduced key reforms in education, press freedom, associative rights, and communal administration. It was no accident that one of the leading young municipalists of the 1860s, Ferry, made the most telling contribution to the promulgation of these reforms.[41]

---

[38] Marquis A. Montaigu, *Manuel politique du citoyen français* (Paris, 1881), 323–24.

[39] Edgar Quinet, "Réviser la Tradition Française," letter from Geneva, May 1870, in *Le livre de l'exilé* (Paris: Germer Baillière, 1880), 357.

[40] Eugène Spuller, *La tradition républicaine* (speech to the Association Nationale Républicaine, 29 June 1893) (Paris: Association Nationale Républicaine, 1893), 12.

[41] Serge Berstein, "Jules Ferry," in *Les opportunistes: Les débuts de la République aux républicains*, ed. Léo Hamon (Paris: Editions de la Maison des Sciences de l'Homme, 1991), 263–67. See also the classic articles by Jean Dietz: "Jules Ferry: Sa première Présidence du Conseil," *Revue Politique et Parlementaire* (10 October 1935): 98–109, and

Even more significant was the continuity between the 1860s and the early Third Republic over the definition of the principles of good citizenship. The municipalist paradigm, to summarize, contended that republican citizenship could not be founded on sectional identities (class, religion, or an exclusive loyalty to a region); it aspired to create a society governed by an enlightened and secular elite, which was politically liberal but socially conservative; furthermore, this elite was to preside over a cohesive collectivity that was public-spirited, respected the laws of the land, and rejected violence as a solution to conflicts of interest.

Republican municipalists also highlighted the centrality of territorial institutions in the formation of citizenship — hence the importance assigned to the commune, the fulcrum of sociability for all members of the political community. These notions were all defined by the late 1860s, and many of them were borrowed from the broader political culture of the Second Empire.

All these features of the debates of the 1860s were directly incorporated into the Third Republic. Indeed, its thinkers and political elites came to define membership in the political community in terms that bore a striking resemblance to the municipalist paradigm: the same emphasis was placed on the development of democratic and representative government, the defense of property, the creation of a civic sense of patriotism, the promotion of rational individualism, and the practical virtues of hard work and social compromise.[42] Above all, this modern republican notion of citizenship highlighted the unity of France, both in its historical and in its contemporary sense. Historically, any artificial separation between positive and negative phases in French history was rejected: "In our collective past, there is not a period in which we do not have something to treasure. All these memories, close or remote, are part of our common patrimony."[43] Also disavowed were all notions that sought to distinguish one group of French citizens from another. Rejecting the age-old division between an urban and a rural France, Gambetta thus declared: "There are not two Frances, a rural France and an urban France; there is only one France, the France of those who work and toil to make their native land free and prosperous internally and strong and powerful externally."[44]

"Jules Ferry: Sa seconde Présidence du Conseil," *Revue Politique et Parlementaire* (10 November and 10 December 1935): 288–311 and 500–501.

[42] On the latter notions, see Bruno Dumons and Gilles Pollet, "Une distinction républicaine: Les médailles du travail au tournant des XIXeme et XXeme siècles. Eclairages sur le modèle républicain de citoyenneté," in *Cultures et folklores républicains*, ed. Maurice Agulhon (Paris: CTHS, 1995), 69–81.

[43] Louis Havet, *Le devoir du citoyen français* (Paris: Stock, 1899), 6.

[44] Speech at Chambéry, 24 September 1872, in *Discours et plaidoyers*, ed. Reinach, 3:14–15.

Indeed, one can affirm that this eclectic and "agnostic"[45] ideological heritage of Second Empire republicanism was much more important than the influence of positivist doctrines in the elaboration of mainstream republican values after 1870.[46] The republicanism whose emergence I am tracing here was not a particular legal or constitutional philosophy, a general theory of culture, the ideology of specific groups such as the opportunists or the radicals, or even the specific articulations of republican intellectuals. It was something less than all of these, in terms of the range of issues it covered; but, at the same time, it was something much broader. What this "republican synthesis"[47] represented most of all was a way of defining the essential contours of what held the French political community together while allowing for the inevitable differences and conflicts of "normal" political intercourse in a democracy. This republicanism attempted to stipulate the precise bounds of what was acceptable and unacceptable in public life and articulated the range of issues over which reasonable individuals could come to different conclusions and hence settle their differences by compromise.[48]

This sense of compromise was bounded by the imperative of preserving the Republic and its core values. To put it more strongly, the new elites made little attempt to placate congregationists, anarchists, integral nationalists, striking workers, and other "overt enemies" of the republic.[49] Nor were the liberal juridical credentials of this political system entirely impeccable; in this respect too there were unfortunate elements of continuity with the Second Empire.[50]

Despite the strictures against the institutional absolutism of this new

[45] For a depiction of opportunist republican philosophy in these terms, see Pierre Deluns-Montaud, "La philosophie de Gambetta," *Revue Politique et Parlementaire* (February 1897): 241.

[46] Nicolet emphasizes the centrality of positivism in the ideological modernization of republicanism after 1870. See *L'idée républicaine en France*, esp. 191–248.

[47] This term was used by Stanley Hoffmann in 1963; I am defining it very differently here, but I completely share his sense of the political and intellectual *mélange* that went into making the Third Republic. See Stanley Hoffmann, ed., *In search of France* (Cambridge: Harvard University Press, 1963), esp. 3–21.

[48] It is important to distinguish this minimalist and essentially procedural republicanism from its broader ideological formulations by opportunists, radicals, and socialists; for further discussion, see my "Republican Tradition," in *Political Traditions in Modern France*, 65–97.

[49] On this theme, see Jean Rivero, "Le libéralisme à l'épreuve," in *Centenaire de la Troisième République: Actes du Colloque de Rennes, 15–17 Mai 1975* (Paris: Editions Universitaires Jean-Pierre Delarge, 1975), 43–45.

[50] The full list is drawn up in Jean-Pierre Machelon's *La République contre les Libertés? Les restrictions aux libertés publiques de 1879 à 1914* (Paris: Presses de la Fondation Nationale des Sciences Politiques, 1976).

republican order,[51] the Republic founded after 1875 did succeed in uniting a broad cross section of French society under a minimalist consensus. It was a conception of citizenship "open to all men of goodwill
... without any party preconditions,"[52] an ecumenical construct that centered around the idea of a law-based state, constitutional government, basic civil and political freedoms, and a certain patriotic notion of "being French," which celebrated both the local and national character of national unity.[53] The municipalist emphasis on separating religion from civic life was given its ultimate accolade in Renan's celebrated definition of the nation as a "daily plebiscite," and more particularly in his claim that "religion can no longer constitute a sufficient basis for the establishment of a modern form of nationality."[54] Renan's political and civic conception of the nation was repeatedly emphasized by republican orators in the early decades of the Third Republic.[55]

Conversely, this open form of republican citizenship eschewed class conflict, rejected political violence, condemned authoritarianism and strong individual leadership, and opposed any substantive alienation of individual and national sovereignty. Most of all, it offered a system of government that was open to modification and change; in the words of one of its young positivist advocates, "The republic is the form of government that, by its sheer elasticity, is best adapted to the incessant modifications of modern times."[56]

This flexibility was inherent in the internal structure of republican ideology itself; after all, the very same principles of liberty, equality, and fraternity could be invoked to legitimize a particular form of power and subvert it at the same time. Hence the almost cyclical feature of intra-

[51] See Odile Rudelle, *La République absolue, 1870–1889* (Paris: Publications de la Sorbonne, 1986).

[52] Emile Littré, "Passage de la République Provisoire à la République Définitive," *Revue de Philosophie Positive* (May–June 1875).

[53] On this "open" notion of republicanism, see Edgar Quinet, "L'esprit de coterie" (1871), in *La République*, 286–88.

[54] Ernest Renan, "Qu'est-ce qu'une nation?" (1882), in *Discours et conférences* (Paris: Calmann Lévy, 1887), 301. For a different view of Renan and the broad republican conception of the nation, see Zeev Sternhell, "The Political Culture of Nationalism," in *Nationhood and Nationalism in France*, ed. Robert Tombs (London: HarperCollins, 1991), esp. 30–37.

[55] See, for example, Eugène Spuller's speech to the departmental and regional congress of the Ligue Française de l'Enseignement, Nancy, 18 November 1883, in *Ligue de l'Enseignement: Conférence de M. Spuller* (Paris: Chaix, 1884), 47.

[56] L. Gensoul, *La République au-dessus du suffrage universel* (Paris: Lacroix, 1871), 46. See also P. J. Stahl [Pierre-Jules Hetzel], *Entre bourgeois actionnaires de la même société et citoyens du même pays* (Paris: Hetzel, 1872), 25.

republican debate after 1870, with new elites and thinkers constantly
questioning and challenging the certainties of the older generation.[57]

None of this may sound terribly dramatic. Indeed, it was positively
and purposefully unheroic, giving further credence to the liberal (and
later populist) view that the republic was merely a "regime of democratic mediocrity."[58] And it is no doubt paradoxical to offer this open
and synthetic representation of republican citizenship at a time when
furious political battles were beginning to unfold—notably over the
questions of regime and religion, without forgetting the reemerging issues of class and social justice. But the ultimate argument of this book is
that the intellectual articulation of what held the French political community together was mostly completed by the time many of these battles had even begun. In other words, it was very probably because this
broad sense of citizenship was not only accepted but also practiced by a
very wide section of society by the late 1860s that the republic was able
to establish itself, in the measured words of Littré, as "the regime that
best allows time to keep its just preponderance."[59]

[57] For an example of a late-nineteenth-century republican critique of republicanism, see
Jean-Louis de Lanessan, *La République démocratique* (Paris: Armand Colin, 1897).

[58] Edmond Scherer, *La démocratie et la France* (Paris: Librairie Nouvelle, 1883), 48–49.

[59] Emile Littré, *De l'établissement de la Troisième République* (Paris: Philosophie Positive, 1880), x.

BIBLIOGRAPHY

PRIMARY SOURCES

Archives Nationales, Paris

BB30-368, reports of procureurs-généraux, 1849–63
BB30-389–90, reports of procureurs-généraux, 1868–70
BB30-426, reports of procureurs-généraux on the elections of 1857, 1859, 1861, 1862, and 1863
C 2866, Commission of Decentralization, 1871
F1a 49, Ministry of Interior circulars, 1861–69
F1c IV 8, Ministry of Interior reports on elections to General Councils, 1852
F7 12243, prefectoral reports: summaries, 1861–62

Archives de la Préfecture de Police, Paris

Série A-A/434, Attentats et Complots du Second Empire
Série BA-1 86 and 621, reports to the minister of the interior on local elections and the general political situation (1871)
Série BA-1 1621, dossier on the French press, 1871–75
BA-1, individual dossiers (from the late Second Empire to the early Third Republic)
866, Louis Blanc
871, Comte de Chambord
917, Léon Gambetta
946, Jules Barni
1158, Emile Littré
1232, Edgar Quinet
1237, Claude-Marie Raudot
1267, Auguste Scheurer-Kestner
1270, Jules Simon
1280, Adolphe Thiers
1296, William Waddington

Private papers

Archives Nationales
Papiers Odilon Barrot
271 AP 1 and 29, letters and notes on the Second Republic and the Second Empire
Papiers Auguste Nefftzer
113 AP3, correspondence, 1860–70
Papiers Eugène Rouher
45 AP 5 and 11, press reports, ministerial notes, and correspondence, 1852–70

45 AP 19, municipal administration of Paris, 1864
Papiers Jules Simon
87 AP 9, elections and political activities, 1848–70
87 AP 15, Second Empire speeches
Archives Départementales Loire-Atlantique
  Papiers Billault 20 J 18, 20, 26, and 59: notes and correspondence, 1851–63
Bibliothèque Nationale
  Papiers Persigny NAF 23066: letters to Napoleon III, 1858–65
  Papiers Ernest Picard NAF 24369: letters, 1858–77
  Papiers Adolphe Thiers NAF 20658: reports of the prefect of police, 1871–72
Fondation Thiers
  Papiers Baroche 1119–1132: ministerial circulars and reports on elections, 1852–69
Newspapers and Periodicals Consulted (Second Republic, Second Empire, and early Third Republic)
  Annales des Chemins Vicinaux; L'Ariégois; L'Avenir National; La Bourgeoisie, Journal des Amis de l'Ordre; Le Correspondant; Courrier de Saint-Etienne; Courrier du Dimanche; La Décentralisation (Lyon); La Décentralisation Littéraire et Scientifique; L'Electeur Libre; Le Français; Gazette de France; Journal de Paris; Journal de la Ville et des Campagnes; Journal des Débats; Journal des Economistes; La Lanterne; Le Libéral; La Liberté Electorale; Le Lien; Le Lorgnon; La Marseillaise; Le Napoléon; L'Opinion Nationale; Le Pays; La Presse; Le Réveil; Revue Contemporaine; Revue de Philosophie Positive; Revue des Deux Mondes; Revue Européenne; Revue Libérale; Revue Nationale; Revue Politique et Parlementaire; Revue Provinciale; Le Temps; L'Union; L'Univers
Official Publications
  Annales du Sénat et du Corps Législatif, 1861–70
  Annales de l'Assemblée Nationale, 1871–75
  Annuaire du Ministère de l'Intérieur, 1852–55
  Bulletin Officiel du Ministère de l'Intérieur, 1861–70
  Enquête Parlementaire sur l'Insurrection du 18 Mars 1871
  Journal Officiel, 1865–70
  Rapport sur la situation financière des communes de l'Empire, 1862

SECONDARY SOURCES

Acollas, Emile. *Guerre aux monarchies.* Geneva, 1869.
Adam, Juliette. *Idées anti-proudhoniennes sur la femme, l'amour et le mariage.* Paris: Taride, 1858.
———. *Mes sentiments et nos idées avant 1870.* Paris: Lemerre, 1905.
———. *Nos amitiés politiques avant l'abandon de la revanche.* Paris: Lemerre, 1908.
Adhémar, Comte Alexandre d'. *Du parti légitimiste en France.* Paris: Dentu, 1843.
———. *La raison monarchique devant la France.* Paris: Lacroix, 1871.

Agulhon, Maurice. *La république au village: Les populations du Var de la Révolution à la Seconde République*. Paris: Plon, 1970.

———. *Marianne au combat: L'imagerie et la symbolique républicaines de 1789 à 1880*. Paris: Flammarion, 1979.

———. *Marianne au pouvoir: L'imagerie et la symbolique républicaines de 1880 à 1914*. Paris: Flammarion, 1989.

———, ed. *Histoire de la France urbaine*. 4 vols. Paris: Editions du Seuil, 1983.

———, et al. *Les maires en France du Consulat à nos jours*. Paris: Publications de la Sorbonne, 1986.

Alexander, Robert. "Restoration Republicanism Reconsidered." *French History* (December 1994).

Allain-Targé, François Henri René. *La République sous l'Empire*. Paris: Grasset, 1939.

Allier, Raoul. *La formation du futur citoyen à l'école primaire publique*. Paris: Fernand Nathan, 1924.

Amigues, Jules [Eugène Loudun]. *Les nouveaux jacobins*. Paris: Dillet, 1869.

———. *La politique d'un honnête homme*. Paris: Lachaud, 1869.

———. *Lettres au peuple*. Paris: Amyot, 1872.

———. *Les aveux d'un conspirateur bonapartiste*. Paris: Lachaud, 1874.

Aminzade, Ronald. *Class, Politics, and Early Industrial Capitalism: A Study of Mid-Nineteenth-Century Toulouse*. Albany: State University of New York Press, 1981.

———. *Ballots and Barricades: Class Formation and Republican Politics in France, 1830–1871*. Princeton: Princeton University Press, 1993.

Angle-Beaumanoir, Marquis Tristan de l'. *Etude administrative*. Paris: Dupont, 1865.

Appel à la France contre les divisions des opinions. Paris: Gazette de France, 1831.

Aprile, Sylvie. "La République au salon: Vie et mort d'une forme de sociabilité politique, 1865–1885." *Revue d'Histoire Moderne et Contemporaine* (July–September 1991).

Arbaud, Léon. "Tocqueville." *Le Correspondant* 31 (January 1866).

Ariès, Philippe. *Histoire des populations françaises*. Paris: Editions du Seuil, 1971.

Armailhac, Louis d'. *La légitimité et le progrès*. Poitiers: Oudin, 1871.

Arnaud, René. *La Deuxième République et le Second Empire*. Paris: Hachette, 1929.

Arnould, Arthur. *Une campagne à la Marseillaise*. Paris: Le Chevalier, 1870.

Arréat, Lucien. *La décentralisation et la loi départementale*. Paris: Lacroix, 1871.

Asselain, Jean-Charles. *Histoire économique de la révolution industrielle à la première guerre mondiale*. Paris: Presses de la Fondation Nationale des Sciences Politiques, 1985.

Association Normande. Comité de décentralisation: Organisation cantonale. Caen: Le Blanc, 1871.

Association pour l'émancipation politique et la réforme parlementaire contre le serment, le monopole et la centralisation administrative. Paris: Gazette de France, 1833.

Aubert, Jean-René. *Enquête sur la décentralisation artistique et littéraire.* Paris: Bibliothèque de l'Association, 1902.

Aubiers, V. des. *De l'administration et de ses réformes.* Paris: Dupont, 1852.

Aubry, Dominique. *Quatre-vingt-treize et les Jacobins: Regards du dix-neuvième siècle.* Lyon: Presses Universitaires de Lyon, 1988.

Aubry, Octave. *Le Second Empire.* Paris: Club du Livre, 1956.

Aucoc, Léon. "Les controverses sur la décentralisation administrative." *Revue Politique et Parlementaire* (April and May 1895).

Aulard, Alphonse. "Origines du mot *centralisation.*" *La Révolution Française* (July–December 1902).

———. "La centralisation napoléonienne." In *Etudes et leçons.* Vol. 7. Paris: Alcan, 1913.

Aumale, Duc d'. *Ecrits politiques, 1861–1868.* Brussels: Briard, 1869.

Auspitz, Katherine. *The Radical Bourgeoisie: The Ligue de l'Enseignement and the Origins of the Third Republic, 1866–1885.* Cambridge: Cambridge University Press, 1982.

Babaud-Laribière, Léonide. *Lettres Charentaises.* 2 vols. 1866. Reprint, Marseilles: Laffitte, 1979.

Bacot de Romand, Claude Réné. *Observations administratives.* Paris, 1822.

Bailleux de Marisy, Alexis. *Transformation des grandes villes de France.* Paris: Hachette, 1867.

Bancel, Désiré. *Les origines de la Révolution.* Paris: Degorce-Cadot, 1869.

———. *Les révolutions de la parole.* Paris: Degorce-Cadot, 1869.

Barail, Général François du. *Mes souvenirs.* 3 vols. Paris: Plon, 1913.

Barante, Prosper de. *La décentralisation en 1829 et 1833.* Preface by Robert de Nervo. Paris: Douniol, 1866.

———. *Souvenirs du Baron de Barante, 1782–1866.* 7 vols. Paris: Calmann Lévy, 1890–1901.

Barbalet, J. M. *Citizenship: Rights, Struggle, and Class Inequality.* Stratford, England: Open University Press, 1988.

Barbès, André. *Les traditions nationales autrefois et aujourd'hui dans la nation française.* Paris: Douniol, 1873.

Barbey d'Aurevilly, Jules. *Les quarante médaillons de l'Académie.* 1863. Reprint, Paris: Armand Colin, 1993.

Bardoux, Agénor. *La bourgeoisie française, 1789–1848.* Paris: Calmann Lévy, 1886.

Barginet, Alexandre-Pierre. *De la centralisation.* Paris: Delaunay, 1828.

Barni, Jules. *Manuel Républicain.* Paris: Germer Baillière, 1872.

———. *La morale dans la démocratie.* 2d ed. Paris: Alcan, 1885.

———, ed. *Annales du Congrès de Genève.* Geneva, 1868.

Baroche, Madame Jules. *Second Empire: Notes et souvenirs.* Paris: Crès, 1921.

Barral, Pierre. *Les agrariens français de Méline à Pisani.* Paris: Armand Colin, 1968.

———, ed. *Les fondateurs de la Troisième République.* Paris: Armand Colin, 1968.

Barrot, Odilon. *De la centralisation et de ses effets.* Paris: Dumineray, 1861.

Barthélémy, Charles. *Histoire du Deuxième Empire.* Paris: Blériot, 1874.

Bartillat, Christian de. *Histoire de la noblesse française*. 2 vols. Paris: Albin Michel, 1988.

Basdevant-Gaudemet, Brigitte. *La commission de décentralisation de 1870*. Paris: Presses Universitaires de France, 1973.

Baudrit, André. *Le mouvement républicain à Rochefort sous le Second Empire*. Ph.D. diss., 1957, Bibliothèque Nationale (henceforth abbreviated as Bib. Nat.) LK7-56144.

Beau de Loménie, Emmanuel. *Les responsabilités des dynasties bourgeoises*. 5 vols. Paris: Denoël, 1943–73.

Beaumont-Vassy, Vicomte Edouard-Ferdinand de. *Histoire intime du Second Empire*. Paris: Sartorius, 1874.

Béchard, Ferdinand. *Essai sur la centralisation administrative*. Paris: Hivert, 1836.

———. *De l'administration de la France: Essai sur les abus de la centralisation*. 2 vols. Paris: Perrodil, 1845.

———. *De la réforme administrative et électorale: Réponse à M. Duvergier de Hauranne*. Paris: René, 1848.

———. *La commune, l'Eglise et l'Etat dans leurs rapports avec les classes laborieuses*. 2 vols. Paris: Giraud, 1849–50.

———. *Du projet de décentralisation administrative annoncé par l'Empereur*. Paris: Gazette de France, 1864.

———. *Les élections en 1869: Lettre aux Nîmois*. Nîmes, 1869.

Belcastel, Gabriel de. *La citadelle de la liberté*. Toulouse, 1867.

Bellamy, Richard. *Liberalism and Modern Society*. Oxford: Polity Press, 1992.

Bellesort, André. *La société française sous Napoléon III*. Paris: Perrin, 1932.

Belleval, Marquis René de. *De Venise à Frohsdorf: Souvenirs et récits*. Paris: Dentu, 1880.

———. *Souvenirs de ma jeunesse*. Paris: Lechevalier, 1895.

Beltran, Alain, and Pascal Griset. *La croissance économique de la France, 1815–1914*. Paris: Armand Colin, 1994.

Benaerts, P., et al. *Nationalité et Nationalisme, 1860–1878*. Paris: Presses Universitaires de France, 1968.

Benedetti, Ange. *La décentralisation et la commission départementale*. Aix: Barthélémy, 1897.

Benoid, Jules. *Des avantages de l'hérédité: Etude politique*. Paris, 1870.

Bernard, Henri. *La décentralisation ou la province: Comédie en cinq actes*. Montpellier: Boehm, 1862.

Bernardi, Gustave de. *La vérité divine et l'idée humaine*. Paris: Sarlit, 1870.

———. *La Révolution*. Paris: Albanel, 1875.

Berryer, Antoine. *Oeuvres de Berryer*. 8 vols. Paris: Didier, 1872–76.

Bersot, Ernest. "La Décentralisation." In *Questions actuelles*. Paris: Didier, 1862.

Berstein, Serge, and Odile Rudelle, eds. *Le modèle républicain*. Paris: Presses Universitaires de France, 1992.

Bert, Paul. *L'instruction civique à l'école*. Paris: Picard-Bernheim, 1883.

Berton, Henry. *L'évolution constitutionnelle du Second Empire*. Paris: Alcan, 1900.

Bethmont, Paul. *Des préfets, des conseils généraux, et du suffrage universel.* Rochefort, 1864.

Billet, Henri-Auguste. *De la décentralisation administrative.* Arras: Courtin, 1866.

Birnbaum, Pierre, and Jean Leca, eds. *Sur l'individualisme: Théories et méthodes.* Paris: Presses de la Fondation Nationale des Sciences Politiques, 1986.

Blanc de Saint-Bonnet, Antoine. *Notion de l'Homme tirée de la notion de Dieu.* Paris: Pitois-Levrault, 1839.

———. *De la restauration française.* Paris: Hervé, 1851.

———. *Politique réelle.* Paris: Bailly, 1858.

———. *La loi électorale.* Paris: Casterman, 1875.

Blanc, Louis. *La République une et indivisible.* Paris: Naud, 1851.

———. *L'Etat et la commune.* Paris: Librairie Internationale, 1866.

———. *Histoire de la Révolution de 1848.* 2 vols. Paris: Lacroix, 1870.

———. *Histoire de la constitution du 25 février 1875.* Paris: Charpentier, 1882.

Blanchard, Marcel. *Le Second Empire.* Paris: Armand Colin, 1956.

Blanchet, Didier, and Denis Kessler. "La mobilité géographique de la naissance au mariage." In *La société française au XIXeme siècle*, edited by J. Dupaquier and D. Kessler. Paris: Fayard, 1992.

Blanqui, Auguste. *Critique sociale.* 2 vols. Paris: Alcan, 1885.

Blayau, Noël. *Billault Ministre de Napoléon III.* Paris: Klincksieck, 1969.

Bled, Jean-Paul. *Les lys en exil.* Paris: Fayard, 1992.

Bluche, Frédéric. *Le bonapartisme: Aux origines de la droite autoritaire.* Paris: Editions Latines, 1980.

———. *Le bonapartisme.* Paris: Presses Universitaires de France, 1981.

Bodineau, Pierre, and Michel Verpeaux. *Histoire de la décentralisation.* Paris: Presses Universitaires de France, 1993.

Boinvilliers, Edouard. *Le programme de l'école libérale de 1830.* Paris: Dubuisson, 1864.

———. *Paris souverain de la France.* Paris: Dubuisson, 1868.

———. *La chute de l'Empire.* Paris: Dubuisson, 1887.

Boisson, Abbé. *Essai sur le libéralisme en réponse aux libéraux catholiques.* Besançon: Tubergue, 1869.

Boissy, Marquis Hilaire Etienne Octave de. *Mémoires du Marquis de Boissy, 1798–1866.* 2 vols. Paris: Dentu, 1870.

Boom, Cornelius de. *Une solution politique et sociale: Confédération, décentralisation, émigration.* Paris: Michel Lévy, 1864.

———. *Unité Européenne.* Paris: Toinon, 1867.

Borderie, A. de la. *Les élections départementales de 1867: Lettres à un électeur.* Rennes: Catel, 1867.

Bornecque-Winandy, Edouard. *Achille Fould, Ministre de Napoléon III.* Neuilly, 1989.

Bosq, Paul. *Les royautés du jour.* Paris, 1867.

Bosselet, H. *Lettres de Monsieur Journal.* Paris: Dentu, 1860.

Bouchage, Auguste. *Sauvons la France.* Toulouse: Delboy, 1871.

Boulay, Gustave. *Réorganisation administrative.* Paris: Michel Lévy, 1840.

Bourgeois, J. *Le catholicisme et les questions sociales.* Paris: Poussielgue, 1867.

Bourgnon de Layre, Baron Antonin. *Les minorités et le suffrage universel.* Paris: Dentu, 1868.

Bourillon, Françoise. *Les villes en France au XIXeme siècle.* Paris: Ophrys, 1992.

Bourjol, Maurice. *Les institutions régionales de 1789 à nos jours.* Paris: Berger-Levrault, 1969.

Boutarel, Aimé. *La décentralisation: Réformes administratives et financières.* Paris: Guillaumin, 1871.

Boutry, Philippe. *Prêtres et paroisses au pays du curé d'Ars.* Paris: Cerf, 1986.

Bouvet, Francisque. *Du principe de l'autorité en France et de la limite des pouvoirs.* Paris: Pagnerre, 1839.

Boyer de Sainte Suzanne, Baron Emile Victor Charles de. *La vérité sur la décentralisation.* Amiens: Jeunet, 1861.

Brisson, Jules. *De l'organisation communale.* Paris: Dumineray, 1861.

Broder, Albert. *L'économie française au XIXeme siècle.* Paris: Ophrys, 1993.

Broglie, Albert de. "Un réveil libéral en province." *Revue des Deux Mondes* 33 (October 1863).

————. "Les candidatures officielles." *Le Correspondant* (1868).

————. *Mémoires du Duc de Broglie.* Paris: Calmann Lévy, 1938.

Broglie, Victor de. *Vues sur le gouvernement de la France.* 2d ed. Paris: Michel Lévy, 1872.

————. *Souvenirs, 1785–1870.* 4 vols. Paris: Calmann Lévy, 1886.

Broise, Henri de la. *Le vrai et le faux libéralisme.* Paris: Lethielleux, 1866.

Brotonne, Léonce de. "Les partis monarchistes sous le Second Empire." *La Nouvelle Revue* (November–December 1885).

Brubaker, Rogers. *Citizenship and Nationhood in France and Germany.* Cambridge: Harvard University Press, 1992.

Buisson, Ferdinand. *Le christianisme libéral.* Paris: Cherbuliez, 1865.

Burdeau, François. *Libertés, libertés locales chéries!* Paris: Cujas, 1983.

————. *Histoire de l'administration française du XVIIIeme au XXeme siècle.* Paris: Editions Montchrestien, 1989.

Burdeau, Georges. *Traité de Science Politique.* 7 vols. Paris: Librairie Générale, 1949–1957.

————. *Le libéralisme.* Paris: Editions du Seuil, 1979.

Bury, J.P.T., and R. P. Tombs. *Thiers, 1797–1877.* London: Allen and Unwin, 1986.

Cadoudal, Georges de. *Esquisses morales, historiques et littéraires.* Paris: Sarlit, 1861.

Calonne, Alphonse de. "Le projet de loi sur les chemins vicinaux." *Revue Contemporaine* 62 (March–April 1868).

————. "Les partis dans la nouvelle Chambre." *Revue Contemporaine* 72 (November–December 1869).

————. "De la décentralisation." *Revue Contemporaine* 74 (March–April 1870).

Carné, Louis de. "Le problème de 89." *Revue des Deux Mondes,* October 1852.

Carnot, Hippolyte. *La révolution française.* Paris: Dubuisson, 1867.

Caron, François. *De l'Empire à la République.* Paris: Fayard, 1985.

Case, Lynn M. *French Opinion on War and Diplomacy during the Second Empire*. Philadelphia: University of Pennsylvania Press, 1954.

Casimir Perier, Auguste Victor Laurent. *Les finances et la politique*. Paris: Michel Lévy, 1863.

———. *L'article 75 de la Constitution de l'an VIII sous le régime de la Constitution de 1852*. Paris: Le Chevalier, 1867.

Castagnary, Jules. *Les libres propos*. Paris: Lacroix, 1864.

Castries, Duc René de. *La monarchie interrompue*. 3 vols. Paris: Taillandier, 1983.

Caubet, Jean-Marie Lazare. *Souvenirs, 1860–1889*. Paris: Cerf, 1893.

Cavenne, Ferdinand. *Un mot sur la décentralisation*. Paris: Dentu, 1863.

Cere, Paul. *La décentralisation administrative*. Paris: Dentu, 1865.

Challamel, Augustin. *Histoire de la liberté en France*. 2 vols. Paris: Jouvet, 1886.

Chambord, Comte Henri de. *Correspondance de 1841 à 1871*. Geneva: Grosset et Trembley, 1871.

———. *Manifestes et programmes politiques de M. le Comte de Chambord*. Paris: Sauton, 1873.

Chambrun, Joseph Dominique Pineton, Comte de. *Fragments politiques*. Paris: Garnier, 1871.

Chandernagor, André. *Les maires en France*. Paris: Fayard, 1993.

Changy, Hugues de. *Le soulèvement de la Duchesse de Berry, 1830–1832*. Paris: Albatross, 1986.

Charency, Comte de, H. Gaidoz, and Charles de Gaulle. *Pétition pour les langues provinciales au Corps Législatif de 1870*. Paris: Picard, 1903.

Charle, Christophe. *Naissance des "intellectuels," 1880–1900*. Paris: Editions de Minuit, 1990.

———. *Histoire sociale de la France au XIXeme siècle*. Paris: Editions du Seuil, 1991.

———. *Les intellectuels en Europe au XIXeme siècle*. Paris: Fayard, 1996.

Charléty, Sébastien. *Histoire du Saint-Simonisme*. Paris: Hachette, 1896.

Charriaut, Henri. *Enquête sur la décentralisation*. Paris: Nouvelle Revue Internationale, 1895.

Chastenet, Jacques. *L'enfance de la Troisième République, 1870–1879*. Paris: Hachette, 1952.

———. *La République des républicains*. Paris: Hachette, 1954.

Chateaubriand, Alphonse de. *Mémoires d'outre-tombe*. 3 vols. Paris: Librairie Générale, 1973.

Chaudey, Gustave. *L'Empire parlementaire est-il possible?* Paris: Le Chevalier, 1870.

Chavane, Alfred. *Les assemblées de province et les conseils généraux*. Paris: Wittersheim, 1870.

Chenu, Maria. *Le droit des minorités*. Paris: Degorce-Cadot, 1868.

Chérot, Ernest. *La bourgeoisie et l'Empire*. Paris: Dentu, 1860.

Chevalier, Michel. *Lettres sur l'organisation du travail*. Paris: Capelle, 1848.

———. *Les questions politiques et sociales*. Paris: Revue des Deux Mondes, 1850.

———. *Examen du système commercial connu sous le nom de système protecteur.* Paris: Guillaumin, 1852.

———. *Le progrès dans la société et dans l'état par les libertés économiques.* Paris: Guillaumin, 1867.

Chevallier, Pierre. *Histoire de la Franc-Maçonnerie Française.* 3 vols. Paris: Fayard, 1974.

Chévillard, Jules. *Etudes d'administration: De la division administrative de la France et de la centralisation.* 2 vols. Paris: Durand, 1862.

Chevrier, Edmond. *Histoire des partis politiques en France et du parti républicain en particulier.* Macon: Protat, 1873.

Citron, Suzanne. *Le mythe national: L'histoire de France en question.* Paris: Editions Ouvrières, 1989.

Civrac, Albert. *Réponse à M. Mie.* Périgueux, 1868.

———. *Le masque arraché.* Périgueux, 1869.

Clamagéran, Jules. *La France républicaine.* Paris: Germer Baillière, 1873.

———. *Correspondance.* Paris: Alcan, 1906.

Claremont-Weybridge. *Notes et souvenirs, 1848–1866.* Dinan: Peigné, 1871.

Claudin, Gustave. *Mes souvenirs, 1840–1870.* Paris: Calmann Lévy, 1884.

Claveau, Anatole. *Souvenirs politiques et parlementaires d'un témoin, 1865–1870.* Paris: Plon, 1913.

Clère, Jules. *Histoire du suffrage universel.* Paris: Sagnier, 1873.

Clozel de Boyer, A. *Monarchie ou anarchie.* Paris: Garnier, 1851.

Cochin, Augustin. *La ville de Paris et le corps Législatif.* Paris: Douniol, 1869.

———. *Paris et la France.* Nantes: Forest et Grimaud, 1870.

Coëtlognon, Comte Emmanuel de. *Appel aux Bretons pour la revendication des principes monarchiques et des libertés nationales.* Paris: Sapia, 1844.

Colet, Louise. *Ces petits messieurs.* Paris: Dentu, 1869.

Combes, André. *Les trois siècles de la Franc-Maçonnerie française.* Paris: Edimaf, 1987.

Comment d'après la religion et la morale doit-on comprendre la légitimité? Paris: Montdidier, 1858.

Compayré, Gabriel. *Eléments d'éducation civique et morale.* Paris: Garcet, 1880.

Constant, Vincent. *De la décentralisation dans la commune.* Aix: Niel, 1905.

Cooper, Sandi E. *Patriotic Pacifism: Waging War on War in Europe, 1815–1914.* New York: Oxford University Press, 1991.

Coquille, Jean-Baptiste-Victor. *Politique chrétienne.* Paris: Palmé, 1868.

———. *La royauté française.* Paris: Lecoffre, 1874.

Corbin, Alain. *Archaïsme et modernité en Limousin au XIXeme siècle.* 2 vols. Paris: Marcel Rivière, 1975.

Cormenin, Louis de. *Recueil sur l'administration municipale.* Paris: Dupont, 1838.

———. *Le maire de village.* Paris: Pagnerre, 1848.

Cornillon, Jean. *Le Bourbonnais à la fin de l'Empire et sous le Gouvernement de la Défense Nationale.* Moulins: Imprimerie du Progrès de l'Allier, 1924.

Cosnac, Comte Gabriel-Jules de. *De la décentralisation administrative.* Paris: Dentu, 1844.

———. *Discours à la Commission de décentralisation.* Paris: Dentu, 1870.

Cottereau, Alain, "Working-Class Cultures, 1848–1900." In *Working-Class Formation: Nineteenth-Century Patterns in Western Europe and the United States,* edited by Ira Katznelson and Aristide R. Zolberg. Princeton: Princeton University Press, 1986.

Coulon, Georges. *Lettres républicaines.* Paris: Germer Baillière, 1873.

Couret, Emile. *Le pavillon des princes: Histoire complète de la prison politique de Sainte-Pelagie.* Paris: Flammarion, 1891.

Curzon, Emmanuel de. *Documents contemporains pour servir à la restauration des principes sociaux.* Poitiers, 1851.

Daëron, Daniel. *L'idée républicaine en Seine-et-Marne de 1870 à 1878.* Le Mée-sur-Seine: Amatteis, 1989.

Dagail, Louis. *De la décentralisation administrative.* Paris: Dentu, 1871.

Dalotel, Alain, Alain Faure, and Jean-Claude Freiermuth. *Aux origines de la Commune: Le mouvement des réunions publiques à Paris.* Paris: Maspéro, 1980.

Dansette, Adrien. *Du 2 Décembre au 4 Septembre.* Paris: Hachette, 1972.

Darimon, Alfred. *L'opposition libérale sous l'Empire, 1861–1863.* Paris: Dentu, 1886.

Daumard, Adeline. *Les bourgeois et la bourgeoisie en France depuis 1815.* Paris: Flammarion, 1991.

David, Marcel. *Fraternité et Révolution Française, 1789–1799.* Paris: Aubier, 1987.

David, Paul. *La commune rurale au point de vue administratif et social.* Toulouse: Paul Savy, 1858.

———. *La commune rurale.* Toulouse: Savy, 1863.

———. *La confédération française.* Périgueux: Dupont, 1870.

De la nomination des maires, par un ancien député. Nîmes: Clavel-Ballivet, 1870.

Debbasch, Charles, and Jean-Marie Pontier, eds. *Les Constitutions de la France.* Paris: Dalloz, 1989.

Decazes, Duc Louis-Charles-Elie-Amanieu. *La liberté et les conservateurs.* Paris: Schiller, 1868.

Décentralisation, par un bourguignon. Dijon: Lamarche, 1863.

Defrance, Jean-Pierre. "Janvier de la Motte." *Administration,* no. 160 (1993).

Dejob, Charles. *Le réveil de l'opinion dans l'Université sous le Second Empire.* Saint-Cloud, 1914.

De la décentralisation et des partis. Paris: Dentu, 1865.

De la décentralisation: Objections au projet du Comité de Nancy par un ancien préfet. Paris: Librairie Centrale, 1866.

De Lanzac de Laborie. "L'amitié de Tocqueville et de Royer-Collard." *Revue des Deux Mondes,* July 1930.

Delaroa, Joseph, ed. *Le Duc de Persigny et les doctrines de l'Empire.* Paris: Plon, 1865.

Delord, Taxile. *Histoire illustrée du Second Empire.* 6 vols. Paris, 1880–83.

Déloye, Yves. *Ecole et citoyenneté: L'individualisme républicain de Jules Ferry à Vichy.* Paris: Presses de la Fondation Nationale des Sciences Politiques, 1994.

Deluns-Montaud, Pierre. "La philosophie de Gambetta." *Revue Politique et Parlementaire* (February 1897).

Denis, Michel. *Les royalistes de la Mayenne*. Paris: Klincksieck, 1977.

Deschanel, Paul. *La décentralisation*. Paris: Berger-Levrault, 1895.

Descola, Edouard. *L'émancipation départementale*. Paris: Maillet, 1869.

Des Garets, Comte. *Mémoires sur l'administration*. Paris: Le Normant, 1821.

Desjardins, Albert. *La nomination des maires dans l'ancienne France*. Paris: Douniol, 1870.

Desjoyeaux, Claude-Noël. *La fusion monarchique, 1848–1873*. Paris: Plon, 1913.

Deslandres, Maurice. *Histoire constitutionelle de la France*. Paris: Armand Colin, 1937.

Desmarest, Ernest. *Les Etats provinciaux: Essai sur la décentralisation*. Paris: Librairie Internationale, 1868.

Devillers, Christian, and Bernard Huet. *Le Creusot: Naissance et développement d'une ville industrielle*. Seyssel: Champ Vallon, 1881.

Deyon, Pierre. *Paris et ses provinces: Le défi de la décentralisation*. Paris: Armand Colin, 1992.

Dietz, Jean. "Jules Ferry: Sa première Présidence du Conseil." *Revue Politique et Parlementaire* (10 October 1935): 98–109.

———. "Jules Ferry: Sa seconde Présidence du Conseil," *Revue Politique et Parlementaire* (10 November and 10 December 1935): 288–311 and 500–518.

Dino, Dorothée de Courlande, Duchesse de. *Chronique de 1830 à 1862*. 3 vols. Paris: Plon, 1910.

Domazon. "La Décentralisation." *Annales des Chemins Vicinaux* (March 1859).

Dommanget, Maurice. *Les idées politiques et sociales d'Auguste Blanqui*. Paris: Marcel Rivière, 1957.

———. *Blanqui et l'opposition révolutionnaire à la fin du Second Empire*. Paris: Armand Colin, 1960.

Dosne, Madame Elise. *Mémoires de Madame Dosne, l'égerie de M. Thiers*. 2 vols. Paris: Plon, 1928.

Douniol, Charles. *La politique d'un provincial: Lettres d'un oncle à son neveu*. Paris, 1869.

Dreux-Brézé, Marquis Henri-Scipion-Charles de. *Quelques mots sur les tendances du temps présent*. Paris: Vaton, 1860.

———. *La Révolution, l'unité de son but, sa logique et ses contradictions*. Paris: Vaton, 1863.

Dromel, Justin [Ecorcheville, pseud.]. *La loi des révolutions*. Paris: Didier, 1862.

———. *Bourgeois et socialistes*. Paris: Le Chevalier, 1869.

Dubois, Jean. *Le vocabulaire politique et social en France de 1869 à 1872*. Paris: Larousse, 1962.

Du Boys, Albert. *Des principes de la révolution française considérés comme principes générateurs du socialisme et du communisme*. Lyon, 1851.

Duby, Georges, and Armand Wallon, eds. *Histoire de la France rurale*. 4 vols. Paris: Editions du Seuil, 1976.

Du Camp, Maxime. *Souvenirs littéraires*. 2 vols. Paris: Hachette, 1883.

―――. *Souvenirs d'un demi-siècle, 1830–1870*. Paris: Hachette, 1949.

Duchêne, Albert. *Un ministre trop oublié: Chasseloup-Laubat*. Paris: Société d'Editions Géographiques, Maritimes, et Coloniales, 1932.

Dufeuille, Eugène. *Réfléxions d'un monarchiste, 1789–1900*. Paris: Calmann Lévy, 1901.

Duguit, Léon. "Le fonctionnement du régime parlementaire en France depuis 1875." *Revue Politique et Parlementaire* (August 1900).

Dumons, Bruno, and Gilles Pollet. "Fonctionnaires municipaux et employés de la ville de Lyon (1870–1914): Légitimité d'un modèle administratif décentralisé." *Revue Historique* (1992).

―――. "Une distinction républicaine: Les médailles du travail au tournant des XIXeme et XXeme siècles. Eclairages sur le modèle républicain de citoyenneté." In *Cultures et folklores républicains*, edited by Maurice Agulhon. Paris: CTHS, 1995.

Dunoyer, Charles. *Le Second Empire et une nouvelle restauration*. 2 vols. London: Tafery, 1864.

Dupeux, Georges. *Aspects de l'histoire sociale et politique du Loir-et-Cher, 1848–1914*. Paris: Mouton, 1962.

Dupont, Charles. *Les républicains et les monarchistes dans le Var en Décembre 1851*. Paris: Germer Baillière, 1881.

Dupont-White, Charles. *L'individu et l'état*. Paris, 1856.

―――. *La centralisation, suite à l'individu et l'Etat*. Paris: Guillaumin, 1860.

―――. "L'administration locale en France et en Angleterre." *Revue des Deux Mondes*, February 1863.

―――. *La liberté politique considérée dans ses rapports avec l'administration locale*. Paris: Guillaumin, 1864.

―――. *Des candidatures officielles*. Paris: Guillaumin, 1868.

―――. *Le progrès politique en France*. Paris: Guillaumin, 1868.

―――. *La République conservatrice*. Paris: Guillaumin, 1872.

―――. *Politique actuelle*. Paris: Guillaumin, 1875.

Duprat, Pascal. *De l'Etat, sa place et son rôle dans la vie des sociétés*. Brussels, 1852.

Dupray de la Mahérie. "Notre profession de foi en matière de décentralisation littéraire et scientifique." *La décentralisation littéraire et scientifique* 1 (October 1863).

Durand. *Projet de réorganisation des mairies des grandes villes*. Bordeaux, n.d.

Durieux, Joseph. *Le Ministre Pierre Magne, 1806–1879*. 2 vols. Paris: Champion, 1929.

Duruy, Victor. *Notes et souvenirs*. 2 vols. Paris: Hachette, 1901.

Duval, Jules. "Les fonctions économiques de l'Etat." *Journal des Economistes* (January–March 1870).

Duveau, Georges. *La vie ouvrière en France sous le Second Empire*. Paris: Gallimard, 1946.

Duvergier de Hauranne, Ernest. *La coalition libérale*. Paris: Le Chevalier, 1869.

Duvergier de Hauranne, Jean-Marie. *Réflexions sur l'organisation municipale et sur les conseils généraux de département*. Paris: Delaunay, 1818.

Duvivier, J. H. *L'Empire en province*. Paris: Dentu, 1861.

Echard, William. *Historical Dictionary of the French Second Empire*. London: Aldwych, 1985.

Les élections dans le département de la Moselle. 2 vols. Metz: Faculté des Lettres et Sciences Humaines de Strasbourg, 1971.

Elleinstein, Jean, ed. *Histoire de la France contemporaine*. 6 vols. Paris: Editions Sociales, 1979.

Elwitt, Sanford. *The Making of the Third Republic*. Baton Rouge: Louisiana State University Press, 1975.

———. *The Third Republic Defended: Bourgeois Reform in France, 1880–1914*. Baton Rouge: Louisiana State University Press, 1986.

Englund, Steven. "Le Théatre de la Démocratie Française." In *Une histoire de la démocratie en Europe*, by Antoine de Baecque. Paris: Editions Le Monde, 1991.

Erckmann-Chatrian, Emile and Alexandre. *Histoire d'un paysan: 1789*. Paris: Hetzel, 1868.

Eros, John. "The Positivist Generation of French Republicanism." *The Sociological Review* (December 1955).

E.S. *Causeries avec mes concitoyens des villes et des campagnes*. Compiègne, 1869.

Escamps, Henry d'. *Du rétablissement de l'Empire*. Paris: Plon, 1852.

Esparbié, Alfred. *Lettre à M. Thiers sur la décentralisation politique*. Lille, 1871.

Esquisses d'institutions républicaines, par un des comités insurrectionels de Paris. Brussels, 1862.

Essai de décentralisation administrative pratique. Paris: Lainé, 1861.

Essai sur l'organisation municipale et la liberté des communes. Nantes: Etiembre, 1871.

Eugène Rouher: Journées d'étude, 16–17 Mars 1984. Clermond-Ferrand: Institut d'Etudes du Massif Central, 1985.

Faguet, Emile. "Tocqueville." *Revue des Deux Mondes*, February 1894.

———. *Le libéralisme*. Poitiers: Société Française, 1902.

Falloux, Alfred de. *Le parti catholique: Ce qu'il a été, ce qu'il est devenu*. Paris: Ambroise Bray, 1856.

———. *Mémoires d'un royaliste*. 2 vols. Paris: Perrin, 1888.

Farat, Honoré. *Persigny, un ministre de Napoléon III*. Paris: Hachette, 1957.

Fauchois, Yann. "Centralisation." In *Dictionnaire critique de la Révolution Francaise: Idées*, edited by François Furet and Mona Ozouf. Paris: Flammarion, 1992.

Favé, General Ildefonse. *La décentralisation*. Paris: Dentu, 1870.

Feher, Ferenc, ed. *The French Revolution and the Birth of Modernity*. Berkeley: University of California Press, 1990.

Féral, Pierre. *La Société d'Agriculture du Gers sous le Second Empire*. Auch, 1973.

Ferdinand-Dreyfus. *Manuel populaire du conseiller municipal, texte et commentaire pratique de la loi du 5 avril 1884*. Paris: Quantin, 1884.

———. "La Constitution de 1875." *Revue Politique et Parlementaire* (March 1899).

Ferrand, Joseph. *Un avant-projet de décentralisation administrative.* Amiens: Jeunet, 1895.

Ferraz, Martin. *Histoire de la philosophie en France au XIXeme siècle: Spiritualisme et Libéralisme.* Paris: Perrin, 1887.

Ferriere, Georges. "Les libéraux devant le suffrage universel sous le Second Empire." In *Réflexions idéologiques sur l'Etat: Actes du Colloque d'Aix-en-Provence, 25–27 Septembre 1986.* Aix-en-Provence: Presses Universitaires d'Aix-Marseille, 1987.

Ferry, Jules. *La lutte électorale en 1863.* Paris: Dentu, 1863.

———. *Les comptes fantastiques d'Haussmann.* Paris: Le Chevalier, 1868.

———. *Discours et opinions de Jules Ferry.* Edited by Robiquet. 7 vols. Paris: Armand Colin, 1893.

Fèvre, Justin. *Mission de la bourgeoisie.* Paris: Douniol, 1864.

Fiaux, Louis. *La Marseillaise, son histoire dans l'histoire des Français depuis 1792.* Paris: Charpentier, 1918.

Fitzpatrick, Brian. *Catholic Royalism in the Department of the Gard, 1814–1852.* Cambridge: Cambridge University Press, 1982.

Fleury, Comte Maurice, and Louis Sonolet. *La société du Second Empire.* Paris: Albin Michel, 1914.

Florent-Lefebvre, Louis. *De la décentralisation.* Paris: Marescq, 1849.

Flourens, Gustave, et al. *Appel de la Rive Gauche à la jeunesse Européenne.* Brussels, 1866.

Foblant, Maurice de. "L'Union Libérale." *Le Correspondant* 77 (1869).

Fontana, Biancamaria. *The Invention of the Modern Republic.* Cambridge: Cambridge University Press, 1994.

Fontarèches, Baron de. *Monarchie et liberté.* 2d ed. Paris: Dentu, 1861.

———. *Révolution et despotisme.* Paris: Dentu, 1861.

———. *Libéralisme et révolution.* Paris: Dentu, 1862.

———. *La souveraineté du peuple.* Paris: Dentu, 1865.

Ford, Caroline. *Creating the Nation in Provincial France: Religion and Political Identity in Brittany.* Princeton: Princeton University Press, 1993.

Foucher de Careil, Armand. *De la centralisation politique.* Paris: Lainé et Havard, 1865.

———. *La dépopulation des campagnes.* Paris: Lainé, 1867.

Fournier, Ernest. *Les réformes nécéssaires.* Paris: Guillaumin, 1869.

Un Français d'Alsace. *Le libéralisme catholique.* Paris: Douniol, 1874.

Freeden, Michael. *Ideologies and Political Theory: A Conceptual Approach.* Oxford: Oxford University Press, 1996.

Freund, Julien. *La décadence.* Paris: Editions Sirey, 1984.

Freycinet, Charles de. *Souvenirs, 1848–1878.* Paris: Delagrave, 1914.

Fumeron d'Ardeuil, M. *La décentralisation.* Paris: Plon, 1866.

Furet, François. *La gauche et la révolution au milieu du XIXeme siècle.* Paris: Fayard, 1986.

———. *La Révolution, 1770–1880.* Paris: Hachette, 1988.

Furet, François, and Pierre Rosanvallon. *La république du centre.* Paris: Calmann Lévy, 1988.

———. Furet, François, and Mona Ozouf, eds. *La Gironde et les Girondins.* Paris: Payot, 1991.

———. *Le siècle de l'avènement républicain.* Paris: Gallimard, 1993.

Gaillard, Jean-Michel. *Jules Ferry.* Paris: Fayard, 1989.

Gaillard, Jeanne. *Communes de province, Commune de Paris, 1870–1871.* Paris: Flammarion, 1971.

Galembert, Louis-Charles-Marie de Bodin, Comte de. *De la décentralisation et du transfert en province de la capitale politique de la France.* Tours: Mame, 1871.

Gambetta, Léon. *Discours politiques de Gambetta, 1871–1873.* Paris: Leroux, 1875.

———. *Lettres de Gambetta, 1868–1882.* Edited by Daniel Halévy and Emile Pillias. Paris: Grasset, 1938.

Gardane, Comte Alfred de. *De la souveraineté nationale.* Paris: Le Chevalier, 1868.

Garnier, Joseph. *Tableau des causes de la misère et des remèdes qu'on peut y apporter.* Paris: Garnier, 1858.

Garrigou, Alain. *Le vote et la vertu: Comment les Français sont devenus électeurs.* Paris: Presses de la Fondation Nationale des Sciences Politiques, 1992.

Gaston-Martin. *Les Jacobins.* Paris: Presses Universitaires de France, 1945.

Gavardie, Edmond de. *Etudes sur les vraies doctrines sociales et politiques.* Pau: Veronese, 1862.

Gaxie, Daniel, ed. *Explication du vote: Un bilan des études électorales en France.* Paris: Presses de la Fondation Nationale des Sciences Politiques, 1985.

Gazeau, Luc. *L'évolution des libertés locales en France et en Belgique au cours du XIXeme siècle.* Paris: Pedone, 1905.

Genoude, Eugène de, and Henri de Lourdoueix. *La raison monarchique.* Paris: Sapia, 1838.

Gensoul, L. *La République au-dessus du suffrage universel.* Paris: Lacroix, 1871.

Gibson, Ralph. "The French Nobility in the Nineteenth Century." In *Elites in France,* edited by Jolyon Howorth and Philip Cerny. London: Pinter, 1981.

Gildea, Robert. *Barricades and Borders: Europe, 1800–1914.* Oxford: Oxford University Press, 1987.

———. *The Past in French History.* New Haven and London: Yale University Press, 1994.

———. *France, 1870–1914.* 2d ed. Harlow: Longman, 1996.

Girard, Louis. *La politique des travaux publics du Second Empire.* Paris: Armand Colin, 1952.

———. *Les élections de 1869.* Paris: Rivière, 1960.

———. *Les conseillers généraux en 1870.* Paris: Presses Universitaires de France, 1967.

———. "La Cour de Napoléon III." In *Hof, Kultur, und Politik im 19. Jahrhundert,* edited by Karl Ferdinand Werner. Bonn: L. Rohrscheid, 1985.

———. *Les libéraux français.* Paris: Aubier, 1985.

———. *Napoléon III.* Paris: Fayard, 1986.

Girardin, Mme. Emile de. *Lettres Parisiennes*. Paris: Charpentier, 1843.

Giraudeau, Fernand. *Nos moeurs politiques*. Paris: Dentu, 1868.

———. *Vingt ans de despotisme et quatre ans de liberté*. Paris: Lachaud, 1874.

Gobineau, Arthur de. "La centralisation devant l'Assemblée Nationale." *Revue Provinciale* 1 (1848).

———. *Ce qui est arrivé à la France en 1870*. Paris: Klincksieck, 1970.

Godard, Abbé Léon. *Les principes de 89 et la doctrine catholique*. Paris: Lecoffre, 1863.

Goguel, Francois. *La politique des partis sous la Troisième République*. Paris: Editions du Seuil, 1956.

Goncourt, Edmond, and Jules de Goncourt. *Journal*. 9 vols. Paris: Flammarion, 1935.

Gosselin, Ronald. *Les almanachs républicains: Traditions révolutionnaires et culture politique des masses populaires de Paris, 1840–1851*. Paris: L'Harmattan, 1992.

Goueffon, Jean. "La candidature officielle sous le Second Empire: Le rôle des considérations locales." In *Les facteurs locaux de la vie politique nationale: Colloque*, edited by Albert Mabileau. Paris: Pedone, 1972.

Goyau, Georges. *L'idée de patrie et l'humanitarisme: Essai d'histoire française, 1866–1901*. Paris: Perrin, 1902.

Grammont, Marquis Ferdinand de. *Discours sur les candidatures officielles*. Paris: Dupont, 1868.

Grange, Annie. *L'apprentissage de l'association, 1850–1914*. Paris: Mutualité Française, 1993.

Grangé, Charles. *Les doctrines politiques du parti républicain à la fin du Second Empire*. Bordeaux: Cadoret, 1903.

Granier de Cassagnac, Adolphe. *Souvenirs du Second Empire*. 3 vols. Paris: Dentu, 1883.

Gras, Christian, and Georges Livet, *Régions et régionalisme en France*. Paris: Presses Universitaires de France, 1977.

Greenberg, Louis. *Sisters of Liberty: Marseille, Lyon, Paris, and the Reaction to a Centralized State, 1868–1871*. Cambridge: Harvard University Press, 1971.

Grothe, Gerda. *Le Duc de Morny*. Paris: Fayard, 1966.

Guépin, Ange. *Les élections*. Nantes, 1849.

———. *Le socialisme expliqué aux enfants du peuple*. Paris: Sandré, 1851.

Guignard, Alfred. *Le self-government ou la décentralisation*. Paris: Ligue Nationale de Décentralisation, 1897.

Guillaume, Pierre. "L'accession à la nationalité: Le grand débat, 1882–1932." In *Citoyenneté et nationalité*, by Dominique Colas, Claude Emeri, and Jacques Zylberberg. Paris: Presses Universitaires de France, 1991.

Guiomar, Jean-Yves. *Le Bretonisme: Les historiens bretons au XIXeme siècle*. Rennes: Société d'Histoire et d'Archéologie de Bretagne, 1987.

Guiral, Pierre. *Prévost-Paradol, 1829–1870: Pensée et action d'un libéral sous le Second Empire*. Paris: Presses Universitaires de France, 1955.

———. "Réfléxions sur la justice du Second Empire." In *La France au XIXeme siècle*. Paris: Sorbonne, 1973.

———. *Adolphe Thiers*. Paris: Fayard, 1986.

Guizot, François. "La génération de 1789." *Revue des Deux Mondes*, February 1863.

Guyard, Auguste. *Lettres aux gens de Frotey sur une commune modèle.* Paris: Dentu, 1863.

Halévy, Daniel. *La fin des notables.* Paris: Grasset, 1930.

———. *La République des ducs.* Paris: Grasset, 1937.

Halévy, Ludovic. *Carnets.* 2 vols. Paris: Calmann Lévy, 1935.

Hamon, Léo, ed. *Les opportunistes: Les débuts de la République aux républicains.* Paris: Editions de la Maison des Sciences de l'Homme, 1991.

———. *Les républicains sous le Second Empire.* Paris: Editions de la Maison des Sciences de l'Homme, 1993.

Hanagan, Michael P. *Nascent Proletarians: Class Formation in Post-Revolutionary France.* Oxford: Blackwell, 1989.

Hanotaux, Gabriel. *Histoire de la fondation de la Troisième République, 1870–1873.* 2 vols. Paris: Plon, 1925.

Hauser, Pierre. *De la décentralisation.* Paris: Paulin, 1832.

Haussmann, Baron Georges. *Mémoires.* Paris, 1890.

Haussonville, Comte Othenin d'. *Lettre au Sénat.* Paris: Dumineray, 1860.

———. *Souvenirs et mélanges.* Paris: Calmann Lévy, 1878.

———. "P. Lanfrey: Sa carrière de polémiste et d'historien," *Revue des Deux Mondes*, October 1880.

Havet, Louis. *Le devoir du citoyen français.* Paris: Stock, 1899.

Hazareesingh, Sudhir. *Political Traditions in Modern France.* Oxford: Clarendon Press, 1994.

———. "A Jacobin, Liberal, Socialist, and Republican Synthesis: The Original Political Thought of Charles Dupont-White (1807–1878)." *History of European Ideas* (1998).

Henrion de Pansey, Baron Pierre-Paul-Nicolas. *Du pouvoir municipal.* Paris: Barrois, 1820.

Hervé-Bazin, Ferdinand-Jacques. *La décentralisation provinciale.* Grenoble, 1889.

Hesse, Alexandre. *L'administration provinciale et communale en France et en Europe, 1785–1870.* Amiens: Caron, 1870.

Higgs, David. *Nobles in Nineteenth-Century France.* Baltimore: Johns Hopkins University Press, 1987.

Hobsbawm, Eric. *Echoes of the Marseillaise.* London: Verso, 1990.

Hobsbawm, Eric, and Terence Ranger, eds. *The Invention of Tradition.* Cambridge: Cambridge University Press, 1983.

Hoffmann, Stanley, ed. *In Search of France.* Cambridge: Harvard University Press, 1963.

Holmes, Stephen. *Benjamin Constant and the Making of Modern Liberalism.* New Haven: Yale University Press, 1984.

Horn, J. Edouard. *Le bilan de l'Empire.* Paris: Dentu, 1868.

Huard, Raymond. *Le suffrage universel en France, 1848–1946.* Paris: Aubier, 1991.

———. *Le mouvement républicain en Bas-Languedoc.* Paris: Presses de la Fondation Nationale des Sciences Politiques, 1992.

————. *La naissance du parti politique en France*. Paris: Presses de la Fondation Nationale des Sciences Politiques, 1996.

Hue, Jules. *Les élections municipales*. Péronne, 1873.

Hugo, Victor. *Napoléon-le-Petit: Histoire d'un crime*. Paris: Ollendorf, 1907.

Huillier, Fernand l'. *La lutte ouvrière à la fin du Second Empire*. Paris: Armand Colin, 1957.

Hutchinson, John, and Anthony D. Smith. *Nationalism*. Oxford: Oxford University Press, 1994.

Igersheim, François. *Politique et administration dans le Bas-Rhin, 1848–1870*. Strasbourg: Presses Universitaires, 1993.

Ihl, Olivier. *La fête républicaine*. Paris: Gallimard, 1996.

Imbart de La Tour, Jean. "Décentralisation et liberté dans la commune." *Revue Politique et Parlementaire* (October 1899).

Jacomet, Pierre. *Avocats républicains du Second Empire*. Paris: Denoël, 1933.

Jacquier, Bernard. *Le légitimisme dauphinois, 1830–1870*. Paris: CRHESI, 1976.

Jardin, André. *Histoire du libéralisme politique*. Paris: Hachette, 1985.

Jaume, Lucien. "Citoyenneté et souveraineté: Le poids de l'absolutisme." In *The French Revolution and the Creation of Modern Political Culture*, edited by Keith Michael Baker. Vol. 1. Oxford: Pergamon Press, 1987.

————. *Le discours jacobin et la démocratie*. Paris: Fayard, 1989.

Jéloubovskaïa, Enna. *La chute du Second Empire et la naissance de la Troisième République en France*. Moscow: Editions des Langues Etrangères, 1959.

Johnson, Martin Phillip. *The Paradise of Association: Popular Culture and Popular Organizations in the Paris Commune of 1871*. Ann Arbor: University of Michigan Press, 1996.

Joire, Abel. *Questions industrielles et questions sociales*. Paris: Masson, 1870.

Joly, Louis. *Du principe des nationalités*. Paris: Garnier, 1863.

————. *La fédération, seule forme de la décentralisation dans les démocraties*. Paris: Garnier, 1866.

Joly, Maurice. *Réflexions utiles à propos de la session des Conseils Généraux*. Paris: Bourdier, 1864.

————. *Les principes de 89*. Paris: Dentu, 1865.

————. *Maurice Joly par lui-même*. Paris: Lacroix, 1870.

————. *Le tiers-parti républicain*. Paris: Dentu, 1872.

Joly, Paul. *Opinion du citoyen Paul Joly sur la décentralisation*. Tours: Ladevèze, 1866.

Jonglez de Ligne, Alexandre. *Une province sans départements*. Paris: Dentu, 1868.

Judt, Tony. *Socialism in Provence, 1871–1914: A Study in the Origins of the Modern French Left*. Cambridge: Cambridge University Press, 1979.

————. *Marxism and the French Left*. Oxford: Clarendon Press, 1986.

Kale, Steven. "The Monarchy According to the King: The Ideological Context of the *drapeau blanc*, 1871–1873." *French History* 2, no. 4 (December 1988).

————. *Legitimism and the Reconstruction of French Society, 1852–1883*. Baton Rouge: Louisiana State University Press, 1992.

Keller, Emile. *Aux électeurs de Vendée*. 1869.

Kelly, George Armstrong. *The Humane Comedy: Constant, Tocqueville, and French Liberalism*. Cambridge: Cambridge University Press, 1992.

Kergorlay, Louis de. *Etude littéraire sur Alexis de Tocqueville*. Paris: Douniol, 1861.

Kuntz de Rouvaire. *La décentralisation*. Paris, 1859.

Kymlicka, Will, and Wayne Norman. "Return of the Citizen: A Survey of Recent Work on Citizenship Theory." In *Theorizing Citizenship*, edited by Ronald Beiner. Albany: State University of New York Press, 1995.

Labbé, Jules. *Le manifeste de Nancy et la démocratie*. Paris: Dentu, 1865.

Laboulaye, Edouard. *Histoire politique des Etats-Unis*. 3 vols. Paris: Durand, 1855–66.

———. *Etudes morales et politiques*. Paris: Charpentier, 1862.

———. *L'Etat et ses limites*. Paris: Charpentier, 1863.

———. *Le parti libéral, son programme et son avenir*. Paris: Charpentier, 1864.

———. "Les Deux Politiques." *Revue Nationale* (1867).

Lachaud, Georges. *Bonapartistes blancs et bonapartistes rouges*. Paris: Dentu, 1885.

Lacombe, Charles de. *De l'arbitraire dans le gouvernement et dans les partis*. Paris: Douniol, 1864.

———. *Les préfets en tournée de révision*. Paris: Sauton, 1869.

Lacombe, Paul. *Mes droits*. Paris: Germer Baillière, 1869.

———. *La République et la liberté*. Paris: Le Chevalier, 1870.

La Gorce, Pierre de. *Histoire du Second Empire*. 7 vols. Paris: Plon, 1903.

Lagrange, Jacques. *La vie en Périgord sous Louis-Napoléon III*. Périgueux: Pilote 24, 1992.

Lajoga, P. E. *Economie et décentralisation: Comment pourrait-on les réaliser en France?* Paris: Lachaud, 1870.

Lallier, François. *L'élection municipale et le suffrage universel*. Paris: Le Clère, 1873.

Lalouette, Jacqueline. *La libre pensée en France, 1848–1940*. Paris: Albin Michel, 1997.

Lambert, Gustave. *Rénovation administrative*. Bayonne: André, 1863.

Lamy, Etienne. *Le tiers parti*. Paris: Librairie Internationale, 1868.

———. *Etudes sur le Second Empire*. Paris: Calmann Lévy, 1895.

Lamy, Georges. *Eléments d'éducation civique et sociale*. Paris: Picard, 1902.

Lançon, Romain. *Le régime parlementaire et la centralisation*. Paris: Garnier, 1870.

Lanessan, Jean-Louis de. *La République démocratique*. Paris: Armand Colin, 1897.

Lanfrey, Pierre. *Chroniques Politiques, 1860–1865*. 2 vols. Paris: Charpentier, 1883.

Langeron, Edouard. *La question communale*. Dijon, 1865.

Larcy, Roger de. *Des vicissitudes politiques de la France: Etudes politiques*. Paris: Amyot, 1860.

———. "La décentralisation de 1789 à 1870." *Le Correspondant* 46 (1870).

La Rochefoucauld Doudeauville, Duc Louis-François-Sosthène de. *La vérité au peuple*. Paris: Poussielgue, 1851.

———. *Cri d'alarme*. Paris, 1861.

———. *La fontaine miraculeuse de Lourdes.* Paris: Racon, 1964.

La Rochejaquelin, Marquis Henry-Auguste-Georges Du Vergier de. *La France en 1853.* Paris: Simon, 1853.

Larrieu, A. *Guerre à la guerre.* Paris: Guillaumin, 1868.

Lassez, Georges. *La vérité sur le deux décembre.* Paris: Le Chevalier, 1874.

Lasteyrie, Ferdinand de. *Le paysan, ce qu'il est, ce qu'il devrait être.* Paris: Le Chevalier, 1869.

Latour du Moulin, Pierre-Célestin. *Autorité et liberté.* 2 vols. Paris: Hachette, 1874.

Laurentie, Sébastien. *Mélanges: Religion, philosophie, morale.* Paris: Vivès, 1865.

———. *L'athéisme social et l'Eglise.* Paris: Plon, 1869.

———. *Souvenirs inédits.* Paris: Ploud, 1892.

Laveleye, Emile de. *Un précurseur: Charles Dupont-White.* Paris: Imprimerie Nationale, 1888.

Lavergne, Léonce de. *La constitution de 1852 et le décret du 24 novembre 1860.* Paris: Dumineray, 1860.

Lavoie, Elzéar. "La décentralisation discutée dans la presse politique Parisienne de 1860 à 1866." Ph.D. diss., Paris, 1963.

———. "La révocation des maires, 1830–1875." In *Europe et Etat: Actes du Colloque de Toulouse, 11–13 Avril 1991.* Aix-en-Provence: Presses Universitaires d'Aix-Marseille, 1992.

Lazare, Louis. *La France et Paris.* Paris: Bibliothèque Municipale, 1872.

Lebon, Félix. *La décentralisation.* Cannes, 1870.

Le Bras, Hervé, and Emmanuel Todd. *L'invention de la France.* Paris: Librairie Générale, 1981.

Le Brun, Henri. *Essai de politique administrative.* Paris: Didier, 1902.

Leca, Jean. "La citoyenneté en question." In *Face au racisme*, edited by Pierre-André Taguieff. Vol. 2. Paris: Editions La Découverte, 1991.

Leclercq, Emile. *La guerre de 1870: L'esprit Parisien, produit du régime impérial.* Brussels: Claasen, 1871.

Leçon de décentralisation, de garde nationale, d'horlogerie et d'archéologie comparées en Deux Actes et Sept Tableaux, par le rural Petitjean-Bonaventure-Grospierre. Nantes: Libraros, 1871.

Le Clère, Bernard, and Vincent Wright. *Les Préfets du Second Empire.* Paris: Armand Colin/Presses de la Fondation Nationale des Sciences Politiques, 1973.

Leconte de Lisle, Charles-Marie. *Catéchisme populaire républicain.* Paris: Lemerre, 1870.

Le Cour Grandmaison, Olivier. *Les citoyennetés en révolution, 1789–1794.* Paris: Presses Universitaires de France, 1992.

Leduc, Jean. *L'enracinement de la République, 1879–1918.* Paris: Hachette, 1991.

Lefevre, Georges. *Napoléon.* Paris: Presses Universitaires de France, 1969.

Lefrançais, Gustave. *Souvenirs d'un révolutionnaire.* Brussels: Hautstont, 1902.

Legoyt, Alfred. *De la centralisation administrative.* Paris: Revue Administrative, 1849.

———. "Du mouvement de la population en 1854." *Journal des Economistes* (April–June 1858).

———. *Du progrès des agglomérations urbaines et de l'émigration rurale en Europe et particulièrement en France.* Marseille, 1867.

Legrand, Louis. *L'influence du positivisme dans l'oeuvre scolaire de Jules Ferry.* Paris: Marcel Rivière, 1961.

Lehning, James. *Peasant and French: Cultural Contact in Rural France during the Nineteenth Century.* Cambridge: Cambridge University Press, 1995.

Lemonnier, Charles. *La vérité sur le Congrès de Genève.* Geneva, 1868.

Lequien, Félix. *Recherches sur la situation financière des départements et des communes.* Paris: Assemblée Nationale, 1850.

———. *Du fonds commun des départements.* Paris: Imprimerie Administrative, 1854.

Lermina, Jules. *Histoire de la misère.* Paris: Décembre-Alonnier, 1868.

———. *Plus de loyers.* Paris: Alcan-Lévy, 1870.

Leroy-Beaulieu, Anatole. *La révolution et le libéralisme.* Paris: Hachette, 1890.

Leroy-Beaulieu, Paul. *De l'état moral et intellectuel des populations ouvrières.* Paris: Guillaumin, 1868.

———. *L'administration locale en France et en Angleterre.* Paris: Guillemin, 1872.

Liberté municipale: Nomination des maires par les électeurs. Saint-Germain, 1866.

Littré, Emile. "Passage de la République Provisoire à la République Définitive." *Revue de Philosophie Positive* (May–June 1875).

———. "La Centralisation." In *Fragments de philosophie positive et de sociologie contemporaine.* Paris: Philosophie Positive, 1876.

———. "De la durée de la République." *Revue de Philosophie Positive* (November–December 1879).

———. *De l'établissement de la Troisième République.* Paris: Philosophie Positive, 1880.

———. "La composition de la société française et la République." *La Nouvelle Revue* (1 February 1880).

———. "D'une infirmité sociologique du parti républicain en France." *Revue de Philosophie Positive* (March–April 1880).

Locke, Robert R. *French Legitimists and the Politics of Moral Order in the Early Third Republic.* Princeton: Princeton University Press, 1974.

Lockroy, Edouard. *A bas le progrès!* Paris: Librairie Internationale, 1870.

Logue, William. *From Philosophy to Sociology: The Evolution of French Liberalism, 1870–1914.* Dekalb: Northern Illinois University Press, 1983.

Loppin, Paul. *Le self-government local en France.* Paris: Pedone, 1908.

Loris, Jean de. *L'idée de la décentralisation.* Besançon: Imprimerie du Progrès, 1900.

Lourdoueix, Henri de. *La révolution c'est l'orléanisme.* Paris: Dentu, 1852.

———. *Conseils de la sagesse d'un père à un fils.* Paris, 1869.

Loyseau, Jean. *Pouvoir et liberté.* Paris: Dillet, 1872.

Lucas, Colin, ed. *Rewriting the French Revolution.* Oxford: Clarendon Press, 1991.

Lucay, Comte Hélion de. *La Décentralisation*. Paris: Guillaumin, 1895.

M. *Qu'est-ce que l'orléanisme?* Paris: Dentu, 1870.

Machelon, Jean-Pierre. *La République contre les libertés? Les restrictions aux libertés publiques de 1879 à 1914*. Paris: Presses de la Fondation Nationale des Sciences Politiques, 1976.

Mailly-Nesle, Marquis Adrien-Augustin-Amalric de. *La révolution est-elle finie?* Paris: Dentu, 1853.

Un maire à M. Prévost-Paradol: Réponse à sa lettre circulaire. Paris: Dentu, 1869.

Malo, Henri. *Thiers, 1797–1877*. Paris: Payot, 1932.

Marcère, Edouard de. "La République et les Républicains." *La Nouvelle Revue* (October 1884).

Marchegay, Henri. *La liberté des proudhoniens, des libéraux, c'est l'esclavage*. Paris, n.d.

Margadent, Ted. *French Peasants in Revolt: The Insurrection of 1851*. Princeton: Princeton University Press, 1979.

———. "Tradition and Modernity in Rural France during the Nineteenth Century." *Journal of Modern History* (December 1984).

Margerie, Amédée de. *La morale et la politique*. Nancy, 1862.

Marion, Edouard. *Les maires de village aux prochaines élections*. Paris: Le Chevalier, 1869.

Marmier, Xavier. *Journal, 1848–1890*. 2 vols. Geneva: Droz, 1968.

Martin, Henri. *De la France, de son génie et de ses destinées*. Paris: Furne, 1847.

———. *La séparation de l'Eglise et de l'Etat*. Paris: Dentu, 1865.

Marx, Karl. *Le dix-huit brumaire de Louis Bonaparte*. Paris: Editions Sociales, 1979.

Maugny, Comte Albert de. *Souvenirs du Second Empire*. Paris: Kolb, 1889.

Maupas, Charlemagne Emile de. *Mémoires sur le Second Empire*. 2 vols. Paris: Dentu, 1885.

Maurain, Jean. *Baroche, ministre de Napoléon III*. Paris: Félix Alcan, 1936.

Maurice, Etienne. *Décentralisation et décentralisateurs*. Paris: Librairie Nouvelle, 1859.

Maurras, Charles. *L'idée de décentralisation*. Paris: Revue Encyclopédique, 1898.

Mazade, Charles de. "Chronique de la Quinzaine." *Revue des Deux Mondes*, 1 April 1870.

———. *L'opposition royaliste: Berryer, de Villèle, de Falloux*. Paris: Plon, 1874.

McMillan, James. *Napoleon III*. London: Longman, 1991.

Ménager, Bernard. *Les Napoléon du peuple*. Paris: Aubier, 1988.

———. "1848–1871: Autorité ou Liberté." In *Histoire des droites en France*, edited by Jean-François Sirinelli. Vol. 1. Paris: Gallimard, 1992.

Mendras, Henri. *La seconde révolution française, 1965–1984*. Paris: Gallimard, 1988.

Mérimée, Prosper. *Lettres à M. Panizzi, 1850–1870*. 2 vols. Paris: Calmann Lévy, 1881.

Merriman, John, ed. *French Cities in the Nineteenth Century*. London: Hutchinson, 1982.

Merruau, Charles. *Souvenirs de l'Hôtel de Ville de Paris, 1848–1852.* Paris: Plon, 1875.

Merson, Ernest. *Confessions d'un journaliste.* Paris: Savine, 1890.

Michel, Henry. *L'idée de l'Etat en France.* Paris: Hachette, 1898.

Michelet, Jules. *Histoire de la Révolution Française.* 2 vols. Paris: Robert Laffont, 1979.

Mille-Noé, H. "La Paix Perpétuelle." *Revue Libérale,* 10–25 August 1867.

Miquel, Pierre. *La Troisième République.* Paris: Fayard, 1989.

Moilin, Tony. *La liquidation sociale.* Paris, 1869.

Molinari, Gustave de. *La république tempérée.* Paris: Garnier, 1875.

La monarchie démocratique. Paris: Lachaud, 1871.

Monnet, Emile. *Histoire de l'administration provinciale, départementale et communale en France.* Paris: Rousseau, 1885.

Montaigu, Marquis A. de. *Le maire de village, conseils aux habitants de sa commune.* Lille, 1863.

———. *Manuel politique du citoyen français.* Paris, 1881.

Montalembert, Charles de. "La Décentralisation." *Le Correspondant* 24 (1865).

Montégut, Emile. "Du génie de la race anglo-saxonne." *Revue des Deux Mondes,* September 1859.

Monti de Rézé, René. *Souvenirs sur le comte de Chambord.* Paris: Emile-Paul, 1931.

Mony, Stéphane. *De la décentralisation.* Paris: Dupont, 1871.

Moreau, Henry. *Les élections des conseils généraux.* Paris, 1861.

Morel, Auguste. *Napoléon III.* Paris: Le Chevalier, 1870.

Morienval, Jean. *Les créateurs de la grande presse en France.* Paris: Spes, 1934.

Morin, Frédéric. *Politique et philosophie.* Paris: Germer Baillière, 1876.

Moulin, Annie. *Les paysans dans la société française.* Paris: Editions du Seuil, 1992.

Mouline, Virgile. *Etude sur la centralisation, son origine et ses résultats.* Dijon: Lamarche, 1863.

Moulins, Charles des. *Du provincialisme et de ses inconséquents.* Bordeaux: Gounouilhou, 1864.

Muller, Charles. *La légitimité.* Paris: Dentu, 1857.

———. *L'Empire et les légitimistes.* Paris: Dentu, 1864.

Muret, Charlotte. *French Royalist Doctrines since the Revolution.* New York: Columbia University Press, 1933.

Muret, Théodore. *A travers les champs.* 2 vols. Paris: Garnier, 1858.

Nadaud, Martin. *Mémoires de Léonard ancien garçon maçon,* edited by Maurice Agulhon. Paris: Hachette, 1976.

Napoléon, Louis [Napoléon III]. *Oeuvres de Napoléon III.* 5 vols. Paris: Plon, 1856–69.

———. *Discours, messages, et proclamations de l'Empereur.* Paris: Plon, 1860.

Napoléon, Prince Jérôme. *Choix de discours et de publications du Prince Napoléon.* Paris, 1874.

———. *Economie politique: Discours et rapports du Prince Napoléon.* Paris, n.d.

Naquet, Alfred. *La république radicale.* Paris: Germer Baillière, 1873.

Nefftzer, Auguste. "Libéralisme." In *Oeuvres de A. Nefftzer*. Paris: Librairie du Temps, 1886.

Nicolet, Claude. *Le métier de citoyen dans la Rome républicaine*. Paris: Gallimard, 1976.

———. *L'idée républicaine en France*. Paris: Gallimard, 1982.

Noailles, Jules de. "De la décentralisation en Angleterre." In *Essais de politique contemporaine*. Paris: Amyot, 1869.

Nora, Pierre, ed. *Les lieux de mémoire*. 3 vols. Paris: Gallimard, 1982–1992.

Nord, Philip. "The Party of Conciliation and the Paris Commune." *French Historical Studies* 15, no. 1 (spring 1987).

———. *The Republican Moment: Struggles for Democracy in Nineteenth-Century France*. Cambridge: Harvard University Press, 1995.

Notaras, J. *De la centralisation*. Paris: Mocquet, 1861.

Oechslin, Jean-Jacques. *Le mouvement ultra-royaliste sous la Restauration, son idéologie et son action politique*. Paris, 1960.

Ohnet, Jean-Marc. *Histoire de la décentralisation française*. Paris: Librairie Générale, 1996.

Ollivier, Emile. *Démocratie et liberté*. Paris: Librairie Internationale, 1867.

———. *L'Empire libéral*. 18 vols. Paris: Garnier, 1895–1916.

———. *Journal, 1846–1869*. Paris: Julliard, 1961.

Oppenheimer, H. *Le libéralisme français au début du XIXeme siècle*. Paris: Sirey, 1930.

Ordinaire, Edouard. *Lettre électorale d'un maire de village à ses collègues*. Paris: Le Chevalier, 1868.

———. *Des candidatures officielles et de leurs conséquences*. Paris: Le Chevalier, 1869.

———. *Du perfectionnement de la race préfectorale*. Paris: Voitelain, 1870.

Ornano, Comte Rodolphe d'. *De l'administration de l'Empire*. Paris: Dentu, 1860.

Ory, Pascal, and Jean-François Sirinelli. *Les intellectuels en France, de l'Affaire Dreyfus à nos jours*. Paris: Armand Colin, 1986.

Osmond, Comte Th. d'. *L'Etat par la province*. Nevers: Michot, 1871.

Ozouf, Jacques, and Mona Ozouf. *La République des professeurs*. Paris: Gallimard, 1992.

Ozouf, Mona. "Fédérations, fédéralisme et stéréotypes régionaux." In *Federalism: History and Significance of a Form of Government*, edited by J. C. Boogman. The Hague: Martinus Nijhoff, 1980.

Pain, Maurice. "Le Second Empire et ses procédés de gouvernement." *Revue Politique et Parlementaire* (June 1905).

Payne, Howard C. *The Police State of Louis Napoleon Bonaparte, 1851–1860*. Seattle: University of Washington Press, 1966.

Pelletan, Camille. "L'opposition républicaine sous l'Empire." *Revue Politique et Parlementaire* (May 1910).

Pelletan, Eugène. *Aide-toi le ciel t'aidera*. Paris: Pagnerre, 1863.

———. *La nouvelle Babylone*. Paris: Pagnerre, 1863.

———. *L'ombre de 89: Lettre à Monsieur le duc de Persigny*. Paris: Pagnerre, 1863.

————. *La charte du foyer.* Paris: Pagnerre, 1864.

————. *Droits de l'homme.* Paris: Pagnerre, 1867.

————. *La femme au XIXeme siècle.* Paris: Pagnerre, 1869.

Penanrun, David de. *Décentralisation: Le passé, le présent, l'avenir.* Caen: Le Blanc, 1870.

Perceau, Henri. *Le Sénat sous le Second Empire.* Paris: Jouve, 1909.

Perint, Charles. *De la nomination des maires.* Paris: Dentu, 1870.

Persigny, Fialin de. *Mémoires du duc de Persigny.* Paris: Plon, 1896.

Pessard, Hector. *Mes petits papiers, 1860–1870.* Paris: Calmann Lévy, 1887.

Pessin, Alain. *Le mythe du peuple et la société française du XIXeme siècle.* Paris: Presses Universitaires de France, 1992.

Petitfils, Jean-Christian. *La Droite en France de 1789 à nos jours.* Paris: Presses Universitaires de France, 1989.

Peyrat, Alphonse. *La Révolution et le livre de M. Quinet.* Paris: Michel Lévy, 1866.

Picard, Ernest. *Discours parlementaires.* 4 vols. Paris: Plon, 1882–90.

Picherit, Abbé Louis. *Moralisation des classes ouvrières.* Angers, 1856.

Pierrard, Pierre. *La vie ouvrière à Lille sous le Second Empire.* Brionne: Montfort, 1965.

————. *Histoire des curés de campagne.* Paris: Plon, 1986.

Pilbeam, Pamela. *Republicanism in Nineteenth-Century France.* London: Macmillan, 1995.

Pinard, Ernest. *Mon Journal.* 2 vols. Paris, 1892.

Pinaud, Pierre-Francois. "La vie quotidienne de l'Inspection des Finances sous le Second Empire." *Revue Historique* (January–March 1987).

Plessis, Alain. *The Rise and Fall of the Second Empire, 1852–1870.* Cambridge: Cambridge University Press, 1987.

Poitou, Eugène. *La liberté civile et le pouvoir administratif en France.* Paris: Charpentier, 1869.

Polignac, Jules de. *Considérations politiques sur l'époque actuelle.* Paris: Pinard, 1832.

————. *Etudes historiques, politiques et morales.* Paris: Dentu, 1844.

————. *Réponse à mes adversaires.* Paris: Dentu, 1845.

Pompéry, Edouard de. *La question sociale dans les réunions publiques.* Paris: Degorce, 1869.

Ponteil, Félix. *Napoléon 1er et l'organisation autoritaire de la France.* Paris: Armand Colin, 1956.

————. *Les institutions de la France de 1814 à 1870.* Paris: Presses Universitaires de France, 1966.

————. *Les classes bourgeoises et l'avènement de la démocratie.* Paris: Albin Michel, 1989.

Pontmartin, Armand de. *Lettres d'un intercepté.* Paris: Hachette, 1871.

Portalis, Edouard. *Les Etats Unis, le self-government et le césarisme.* Paris: Le Chevalier, 1869.

————. *Les deux républiques.* Paris: Charpentier, 1880.

Pougnet, Auguste. *Hiérarchie et décentralisation.* Paris: Germer Baillière, 1866.

————. *Le parti libéral en 1870.* Paris: Germer Baillière, 1870.

Poujoulat, Jean-Joseph-François. *Etudes et portraits*. Paris: Lefort, 1868.

Pouthas, Charles. *Histoire politique du Second Empire*. Paris: Sorbonne, 1956.

Pouthas, Charles, et al. *Démocratie, réaction, capitalisme, 1848–1860*. Paris: Presses Universitaires de France, 1983.

Pradalié, Georges. *Le Second Empire*. Paris: Presses Universitaires de France, 1969.

Prévost-Paradol, Lucien-Anatole. *Les anciens partis*. Paris: Dumineray, 1860.

———. *Quelques pages d'histoire contemporaine*. 4 vols. Paris: Michel Lévy, 1862–66.

———. *Quelques réflexions sur notre situation intérieure*. Paris: Michel Lévy, 1864.

———. *La France nouvelle*. Paris: Calmann Lévy, 1868.

———. *Aux maires des 38000 communes de France: Lettre circulaire*. Paris: Le Chevalier, 1869.

———. *Lettres posthumes de Prévost-Paradol*. Brussels, 1871.

Price, Roger. *The Modernization of Rural France: Communications Networks and Agricultural Market Structures in Nineteenth-Century France*. London: Hutchinson, 1983.

———. *A Social History of Nineteenth-Century France*. New York: Holmes and Meyer, 1987.

Prignet, Jules. *Souvenirs: Le Comte de Fourmestraulx-Saint-Denis*. Valenciennes, 1867.

Programme démocratique libéral. Paris: Racon, 1868.

Un projet de décentralisation. 2d ed. Nancy: Vagner, 1865.

Proudhon, Pierre-Joseph. *La révolution sociale démontrée par le coup d'état du 2 décembre*. Paris: Garnier, 1852.

———. *Essais d'une philosophie populaire*. Brussels, 1860.

———. *Les démocrates assermentés et les réfractaires*. Paris: Dentu, 1863.

———. *Du principe fédératif et de la nécéssité de reconstituer le parti de la révolution*. Paris: Dentu, 1863.

———. *De la capacité politique des classes ouvrières*. Paris: Dentu, 1865.

———. *Théorie du mouvement constitutionnel*. Paris: Lacroix, 1870.

———. *La pornocratie ou la femme dans les temps modernes*. Paris: Lacroix, 1875.

Pyat, Félix. *Lettre à Juarez et à ses amis*. London, 1865.

Quentin-Bauchard, E. *Etudes et Souvenirs*. 2 vols. Paris: Plon, 1902.

Quesnet, Edouard. *Les élections municipales depuis 1763 jusqu'à nos jours*. Rennes, 1870.

Quinet, Edgar. *Oeuvres complètes*. 11 vols. Paris: Pagnerre, 1857–74.

———. *Le christianisme et la révolution française*. Paris: Pagnerre, 1865.

———. *La Révolution*. 2 vols. Paris: Lacroix, 1865.

———. *La République: Conditions de la régénération de la France*. Paris: Dentu, 1872.

———. *Le livre de l'exilé*. Paris: Germer Baillière, 1880.

Rainneville, Joseph de. *Catholiques tolérants et légitimistes libéraux*. Paris: Michel Lévy, 1862.

Ranc, Arthur. *Souvenirs-Correspondance, 1831–1908*. Paris: Cornély, 1913.

Rattier, Paul-Ernest de. *Paris n'existe pas*. Bordeaux: Balarac, 1857.

Raudot, Claude-Marie. *De la décadence de la France*. Paris: Amyot, 1850.

———. *La décentralisation*. Paris: Douniol, 1858.

———. "La Décentralisation." *Le Correspondant* (1861).

———. *Mes oisivetés*. Avallon, 1862.

———. *L'administration locale en France et en Angleterre*. Paris: Douniol, 1863.

———. "La décentralisation en 1870." *Le Correspondant* (1870).

Reclus, Maurice. *Ernest Picard, 1821–1877*. Paris: Hachette, 1912.

Réflexions sur l'organisation municipale par un membre de la Chambre des Députés. Paris: Delaunay, 1818.

Regnault, Augustin. *La France sous le Second Empire, 1852–1870*. Paris: Vanier, 1907.

Reinach, Joseph, ed. *Discours et plaidoyers politiques de Gambetta*. 11 vols. Paris: Charpentier, 1880–85.

———. "Un journaliste républicain: Alphonse Peyrat." *Revue Politique et Parlementaire* (February 1910).

Rémond, René. *Les droites en France*. Paris: Aubier, 1982.

———. *L'anticléricalisme en France de 1815 à nos jours*. Brussels: Complexe, 1985.

Rémusat, Charles de. *Politique libérale, ou fragments pour servir à la défense de la Révolution française*. Paris: Michel Lévy, 1860.

———. "De l'esprit de réaction." *Revue des Deux Mondes*, October 1861.

———. "Situation politique de la France." *Revue des Deux Mondes*, October 1864.

———. "Le parti libéral et le mouvement Européen." *Revue des Deux Mondes*, November 1866.

———. *Mémoires de ma vie*. Edited by C.-H. Pouthas. Paris: Plon, 1958.

Rémusat, Paul de. *De la dissolution du Conseil Municipal de la ville de Toulouse*. Paris, 1867.

Rémy, Alexandre. *La faction orléaniste*. Paris: Desloges, 1852.

Renan, Ernest. "L'école libérale et ses principes." *Revue des Deux Mondes*, August 1858.

———. "La monarchie constitutionnelle en France." *Revue des Deux Mondes*, November 1869.

———. "Qu'est-ce qu'une nation?" In *Discours et conférences*. Paris: Calmann Lévy, 1887.

———. *Oeuvres complètes*. 10 vols. Paris: Calmann Lévy, 1947–61.

Renouvier, Charles. *Manuel républicain de l'homme et du citoyen*. Paris: Pagnerre, 1848.

———. *Essais de critique générale*. 4 vols. Paris: Ladrange, 1854–64.

Renouvier, Charles, et al. *Organisation communale et centrale de la République*. Paris: Librairie Républicaine, 1851.

Revelière, Louis. *De la vanité des institutions*. Paris: Lecoffre, 1880.

Les révolutions du XIXeme siècle. 4th ser., 10 vols. Paris: EDHIS, 1988.

Rials, Stéphane. *Le légitimisme*. Paris: Presses Universitaires de France, 1983.

———. *Révolution et contre-révolution au XIXeme siècle*. Paris: Albatros, 1987.

Ribbes, Charles de. *La nouvelle école libérale et la décentralisation*. Marseille: Olive, 1859.

Ricard, Louis-Xavier de. *Le fédéralisme*. Paris: Sandoz, 1877.

Rigaud, Abbé Pierre. *La dépravation du village, cause principale de la dépopulation des campagnes et de l'encombrement des villes*. Aix, 1869.

Rihs, Charles. *La Commune de Paris, sa structure et ses doctrines*. Geneva: Droz, 1955.

Rioux, Jean-Pierre. *La révolution industrielle, 1780–1880*. Paris: Editions du Seuil, 1971.

Rivero, Jean. "Le libéralisme à l'épreuve." In *Centenaire de la Troisième République: Actes du Colloque de Rennes, 15–17 Mai 1975*. Paris: Editions Universitaires Jean-Pierre Delarge, 1975.

Roche, Hippolyte. *Napoléon et les communes*. Paris: Lainé, 1869.

Rogeard, Auguste. *La crise électorale de 1869*. Brussels: Briard, 1869.

Rondelet, Antonin. *Les mémoires d'Antoine*. Paris: Didier, 1860.

Rosanvallon, Pierre. *Le moment Guizot*. Paris: Gallimard, 1985.

———. *L'Etat en France de 1789 à nos jours*. Paris: Editions du Seuil, 1990.

———. *Le sacre du citoyen: Histoire du suffrage universel en France*. Paris: Gallimard, 1992.

Rothney, John. *Bonapartism After Sedan*. New York: Cornell University Press, 1969.

Rouchon, Louis. *La décentralisation municipale et la loi du 5 avril 1884*. Ph.D. diss., Le Puy, 1900.

Rougerie, Jacques. *La Commune*. Paris: Presses Universitaires de France, 1988.

Rouland, Norbert. *Le conseil municipal Marseillais et sa politique de la IIeme à la IIIeme République (1848–1875)*. Aix-en-Provence: Edisud, 1974.

Rousseau, A. *L'idée décentralisatrice et les partis politiques sous la restauration*. Vannes: Lafolye, 1904.

Royer, Clémence. "Moyens d'améliorer le sort des classes ouvrières." *Journal des Economistes* (January–March 1869).

Rudelle, Odile. *La République absolue, 1870–1889*. Paris: Publications de la Sorbonne, 1986.

———. "La tradition républicaine." *Pouvoirs*, no. 42 (1987).

Ruggiero, Guido de. *The History of European Liberalism*. London: Oxford University Press, 1927.

Rulof, Bernard. "Popular Culture, Politics, and the State in Florensac (Hérault) during the Second Empire." *French History 5*, no. 3 (September 1991).

Sabran-Pontèves, Duc de. *A travers les champs de la pensée*. Paris: Librairie Catholique, 1869.

Sacy, Silvestre de. "Lettres à ma fille." *Revue des Deux Mondes*, November 1926.

Saint-Clou, Comte de. *Des maux produits par la centralisation*. Paris: Dentu, 1831.

Saint-Marc Girardin. *Souvenirs et réflexions politiques d'un journaliste*. Paris: Michel Lévy, 1859.

Saint-Pulgent, Léon de. *Programme de réformes administratives par la décentralisation*. Saint-Etienne: Théolier, 1871.

Saint-Victor, Paul de. *Barbares et Bandits*. Paris: Michel Lévy, 1871.

Sarcus, Vicomte Félix-Hyacinthe de. *Lettre d'un provincial à propos du vote du Conseil Général de l'Oise sur la décentralisation*. Dijon, 1864.

Savary, Charles. *Alexis de Tocqueville*. Paris: Retaux, 1870.

Scherer, Edmond. *La démocratie et la France*. Paris: Librairie Nouvelle, 1883.

Scheurer-Kestner, Auguste. *Souvenirs de jeunesse*. Paris: Charpentier, 1905.

Schnapper, Dominique. *La communauté des citoyens*. Paris: Gallimard, 1994.

Schnerb, Robert. *Rouher et le Second Empire*. Paris: Armand Colin, 1949.

Séché, Léon. *Jules Simon, sa vie et son oeuvre*. Paris: Dupret, 1887.

———. "Prévost-Paradol, candidat-député." *Revue Politique et Parlementaire* (April 1901).

Sède, Baron Gustave de. *Le choix des maires*. Arras: De Sède, 1870.

Séguin, Philippe. *Louis Napoléon le Grand*. Paris: Grasset, 1990.

Ségur, Mgr. Louis-Gaston-Adrien de. *La Révolution*. Paris: Tolra et Haton, 1861.

Seignobos, Charles. *Histoire de la France contemporaine*. Vol. 7. Paris: Hachette, 1921.

Senior, Nassau William. *Conversations with Distinguished Persons during the Second Empire, 1860–1863*. 2 vols. London: Hurst, 1880.

Serman, William. "La Noblesse dans l'Armée Française au XIXeme siècle." In *Les noblesses européennes au XIXeme siècle*. Rome: Ecole Française, 1988.

Serment, Jacques Henri. *Le libéralisme*. Paris: Cherbuliez, 1860.

Sewell Jr., William. "Activity, Passivity, and the Revolutionary Concept of Citizenship." In *The French Revolution and the Creation of Modern Political Culture*, edited by Colin Lucas. Vol. 2. Oxford: Pergamon Press, 1988.

Siedentop, Larry. *Tocqueville*. Oxford: Oxford University Press, 1994.

Siguier, Auguste. *Les légitimistes et les orléanistes*. Paris: Philippe, 1837.

Silverman, Max. "The Revenge of Civil Society." In *Citizenship, Nationality, and Migration in Europe*, edited by David Cesarani and Mary Fulbrook. London: Routledge, 1996.

Simiot, Alexandre. *Centralisation et démocratie*. Paris: Dentu, 1861.

Simon, Jules. *Le devoir*. Paris: Hachette, 1854.

———. *La liberté*. 2 vols. Paris: Hachette, 1859.

———. *La politique radicale*. Paris: Lacroix, 1868.

———. *La famille*. Paris: Degorce-Cadot, 1869.

———. *L'instruction populaire*. Reims, 1869.

———. *Paris aux Parisiens*. Paris: Degorce-Cadot, 1869.

———. *Souvenirs du 4 Septembre: Le Gouvernement de la Défense Nationale*. Paris: Michel Lévy, 1875.

———. *Le livre du petit citoyen*. Paris: Hachette, 1880.

Simonot, Edme. *Le suffrage universel et l'existence communale sous le régime de la loi de 1855*. Paris: Firmin Didot, 1861.

Smith, William H. C. *Napoléon III*. Paris: Hachette, 1982.

Solidarité Républicaine: Association pour le développement des droits et des intérêts de la démocratie. 1849.

Soltau, Roger. *French Political Thought in the Nineteenth Century*. London: Ernest Benn, 1931.

Sonnier, Edouard de. *Un Conseil Général sous l'Empire*. Blois: Marchand, 1871.

Soto, Jean de. "Edouard de Laboulaye." *Revue Internationale d'Histoire Politique et Constitutionnelle* (1955).

Souchet, Guillaume. *Napoléon III Empereur des Français: L'administration municipale, la ré-édification des peuples, le progrès et la science*. Nîmes, 1864.

Soulage, Edmond. "Le décentralisation au profit des communes depuis la loi du 5 avril 1884." Ph.D. diss., Montpellier, 1910.

Soulier, Auguste. "La Troisième République entre dans l'Histoire." *Revue Internationale d'Histoire Politique et Constitutionnelle* (1955).

Souvenirs et impressions de 1851 à 1870. Paris, 1879.

Sparwasser, Reinhard. *Zentralismus, Dezentralisation, Regionalismus und Föderalismus in Frankreich*. Berlin: Duncker und Humblot, 1986.

Spuller, Eugène. *Petite histoire du Second Empire*. Paris: Le Chevalier, 1870.

———. Speech to the departmental and regional congress of the Ligue Française de l'Enseignement, Nancy, 18 November 1883. In *Ligue Française de l'Enseignement: Conférence de M. Spuller*. Paris: Chaix, 1884.

———. *La tradition républicaine*. Paris: Association Nationale Républicaine, 1893.

Stahl, Pierre-Jules [Pierre-Jules Hetzel]. *Entre bourgeois actionnaires de la même société et citoyens du même pays*. Paris: Hetzel, 1872.

Statuts de la Ligue de la Décentralisation. Paris: Dubuisson, 1870.

Steeg, Jules. *Instruction morale et civique*. Paris: Fauvé et Nathan, 1883.

Stern, Daniel [Comtesse Marie d'Agoult]. *Esquisses morales et politiques*. Paris: Pagnerre, 1849.

Strieter, Terry W. "The Faceless Police of the Second Empire: A Social Profile of the *Gendarmes* of Mid-Nineteenth Century France." *French History* 8, no. 2 (June 1994).

Sue, Eugène. *Le républicain des campagnes*. Paris: Librairie Internationale, 1851.

———. *La France sous l'Empire*. London: Jeffs, 1857.

Taine, Hippolyte. *Carnets de voyage: Notes sur la province, 1863–1865*. Paris: Hachette, 1897.

———. *Les origines de la France contemporaine*. 2 vols. Paris: Robert Laffont, 1986.

Tallès, Maximilien. *L'Empire c'est la souveraineté du peuple*. Paris: Garnier, 1852.

Tassin, Charles. *Un mot à l'enquête ouverte sur la question de décentralisation*. Troyes: Dufey-Robert, 1866.

Tchernoff, Iouda. *Le parti républicain au coup d'état et sous le Second Empire*. Paris: Pedone, 1906.

———. *L'extrême-gauche socialiste révolutionnaire en 1870–1*. Paris: Action Nationale, 1918.

Ténot, Eugène. *Le suffrage universel et les paysans*. Paris: Librairie Centrale, 1865.

———. *Paris en Décembre 1851*. Paris: Le Chevalier, 1868.

———. *La province en Décembre 1851*. Paris: Le Chevalier, 1868.

Terme, C. *Les élections municipales à Saint-Etienne en 1865*. Paris, 1865.

Thévenot, Arsène. *De la décentralisation intellectuelle et des progrès des arts, des sciences, et des lettres en province*. Paris: Dentu, 1864.

Thibaudet, Albert. *Les idées politiques de la France*. Paris: Stock, 1932.

————. *La République des professeurs*. 1927. Reprint, Geneva: Slatkine, 1979.

Thiers, Adolphe. *Histoire du Consulat et de l'Empire*. 21 vols. Paris: Paulin, 1845–69.

————. *De la propriété*. Paris: Paulin, 1848.

————. *Discours sur les libertés politiques*. Paris: L'Heureux, 1865.

————. *Discours parlementaires de M. Thiers*. 16 vols. Paris: Calmann Lévy, 1879–89.

Thomson, David. *Democracy in France*. London: Oxford University Press, 1946.

Thuillier, Guy, and Jean Tulard. *Histoire de l'administration française*. Paris: Presses Universitaires de France, 1994.

Thureau-Dangin, Paul. *Le parti libéral sous la Restauration*. Paris: Plon, 1876.

Le tiers parti et les libertés intérieures. Paris: Dentu, 1866.

Tilly, Charles. "The Emergence of Citizenship in France and Elsewhere." *International Review of Social History* 40, no. 3 (1995).

Tocqueville, Alexis de. *De la démocratie en Amérique*. Paris: Gallimard, 1961.

————. *l'Ancien régime et la révolution*. Edited by J.-P. Mayer. Paris: Gallimard, 1967.

Tolain, Henri. *Quelques vérités sur les élections de Paris*. Paris: Dentu, 1863.

Tombs, Robert. *France, 1814–1914*. London: Longman, 1996.

————, ed. *Nationhood and Nationalism in France*. London: HarperCollins, 1991.

Touroude, Georges. *Deux républicains de progrès: Eugène et Camille Pelletan*. Paris: L'Harmattan, 1995.

Trannoy, André. "Notes et lettres de Montalembert, 1848–1852." *Revue Historique* (October–December 1946).

Tridon, Gustave. *Oeuvres diverses de Gustave Tridon*. Paris: Allemane, 1891.

Troisier de Diaz, Anne, ed. *Regards sur Emile Ollivier*. Paris: Sorbonne, 1985.

Tudesq, André-Jean. "La légende napoléonienne en France en 1848." *Revue Historique* (September 1957).

————. "La Décentralisation et la droite en France au XIXeme siècle." In *La Décentralisation, Colloque d'Histoire*, Faculté des Lettres et Sciences Humaines d'Aix-en-Provence, 1–2 December 1961. Aix-en-Provence: Editions Ophrys, 1964.

————. "L'influence du romantisme sur le légitimisme sous la Monarchie de Juillet." In *Romantisme et Politique, 1815–1851*. Paris: Armand Colin, 1969.

Tulard, Jean, ed. *Dictionnaire du Second Empire*. Paris: Fayard, 1995.

Turckheim, Baron Alfred de. *Lettre à sa majesté l'Empereur Napoléon III sur une application du principe des spécialités à l'organisation municipale*. Colmar: Hoffmann, 1856.

Turner, Brian, and Peter Hamilton, eds. *Citizenship*. 2 vols. London: Routledge, 1994.

Vacherot, Etienne. *La démocratie*. Paris: Chamerot, 1860.

———. *La religion.* Paris: Chamerot, 1869.

———. *La démocratie libérale.* Paris: Calmann Lévy, 1892.

Vaillant, Nicolas Gabriel Victor. *La décentralisation à l'oeuvre.* Metz, 1863.

———. *Décentralisation et régime représentatif.* Metz, 1863.

———. *Congrès décentralisateur de Lyon: Nos réserves.* Metz, 1870.

Valori, Vcte. Henry de. *Essai sur la noblesse.* Paris: Didiot, 1855.

———. *L'unité politique et la décentralisation en Europe.* Paris: Dentu, 1865.

Vanel, Gabriel. *Le Second Empire.* Paris: Marigny, 1936.

Varia: Les départements et les provinces. Nancy: Vagner, 1860.

Varia: Morale, Politique, Littérature. Paris, 1860.

Varia: Aristocratie et democratie. Nancy: Vagner, 1861.

Varia: De l'éducation politique de la France. Nancy: Vagner, 1863.

Ventavon, Edouard de. *Essai sur la décentralisation.* Paris: Dentu, 1870.

Véran, Guillaume. *La question du dix-neuvième siècle.* Paris: Dentu, 1866.

Verlet, Henri. *1793–1869: Le peuple et la Révolution, l'athéisme et l'Etre Suprême.* Paris: Librairie de la Renaissance, n.d.

Vermorel, Auguste. *Le peuple aux élections.* Paris, 1868.

———. *Qu'est-ce que la République?* Paris: Fayard, 1871.

Vernon, Richard. *Citizenship and Order: Studies in French Political Thought.* Toronto: University of Toronto Press, 1986.

Véron, Eugène. *Lettres Parisiennes.* Grenoble, 1866.

Véron, Louis. *Mémoires d'un bourgeois de Paris.* 5 vols. Paris: Librairie Nouvelle, 1856.

———. *Nouveaux Mémoires d'un Bourgeois de Paris.* Paris: Librairie Internationale, 1866.

Veuillot, Louis. *Le parti catholique: Réponse à M. le Comte de Falloux.* Paris: Vivès, 1856.

———. *L'illusion libérale.* Paris: Palmé, 1866.

———. *Les odeurs de Paris.* Paris: Palmé, 1867.

———. *Mélanges religieux, historiques, politiques et littéraires.* 3d ser., 6 vols. Paris: Vivès, 1876.

———. *Correspondance de Louis Veuillot.* 7 vols. Paris: Palmé, 1884–87.

Veyland, M. *Moralisation des classes indigentes.* Metz, 1854.

Viard, Jacques, ed. *L'esprit républicain: Colloque d'Orléans.* Paris: Klincksieck, 1972.

Viel-Castel, Comte Horace de. *Mémoires sur le règne de Napoléon III.* 6 vols. 1883–84. Reprint, Paris: Le Prat, 1979.

Vigier, Philippe. *La Seconde République dans la région alpine.* 2 vols. Paris: Presses Universitaires de France, 1963.

———. "Le bonapartisme et le monde rural." In *Le bonapartisme, phénomène historique et mythe politique,* edited by Karl Hammer and Peter Claus Hartmann. Munich, 1977.

———. "Quelques aspects de l'évolution politique régionale au XIXeme siècle." In *Révolution et Traditions en Vicomté de Turenne: Haut-Quercy et Bas-Limousin de 1738 à 1889.* Saint-Céré: Association des Amis du Passé de Saint-Céré, 1989.

Vignes, R. "A propos de la décentralisation." *Journal des Economistes* (October–December 1865).

Vigreux, Marcel. "Les élections de 1869 dans le Morvan nivernais." *Revue d'Histoire Moderne et Contemporaine* 25 (July–September 1978).

Villèle, Jean-Baptiste. *Projet d'organisation municipale, départementale, et régionale.* Paris: Plon, 1874.

Waldinger, Renée, Philip Dawson, and Isser Woloch, eds. *The French Revolution and the Meaning of Citizenship.* Westport, Conn.: Greenwood Press, 1993.

Warshaw, Dan. *Paul Leroy-Beaulieu and Established Liberalism in France.* Dekalb: Northern Illinois University Press, 1991.

Weber, Eugène. *La fin des terroirs.* Paris: Fayard, 1983.

Weill, Alexandre. *Questions brûlantes: République et monarchie.* Paris: Dentu, 1848.

———. *De l'hérédité du pouvoir.* Paris: Dentu, 1849.

———. *Génie de la monarchie.* Paris: Dentu, 1850.

Weill, Georges. *L'école Saint-Simonienne.* Paris: Alcan, 1896.

———. *Histoire du parti républicain en France.* Paris: Alcan, 1900.

———. "Les Saint-Simoniens sous Napoléon III." *Revue des Etudes Napoléoniennes* 3 (1913).

———. *Histoire du mouvement social en France.* Paris: Alcan, 1924.

———. *Le journal.* Paris: La Renaissance du Livre, 1934.

Weiss, Jean-Jacques. "Plaidoyer dans l'Affaire Baudin." In *Combat constitutionnel.* Paris: Charpentier, 1893.

Welch, Cheryl B. *Liberty and Utility: The French Idéologues and the Transformation of Liberalism.* New York: Columbia University Press, 1984.

Willette, Luc. *Le coup d'Etat du 2 Décembre 1851.* Paris: Aubier, 1982.

Wright, J. *Un intermédiaire entre l'esprit Germanique et l'esprit français sous le Second Empire: Camille Selden.* Paris: Champion, 1931.

Wright, Vincent. "La loi de sûreté générale de 1858." *Revue d'Histoire Moderne et Contemporaine* (July–September 1969).

———. *Le Conseil d'Etat sous le Second Empire.* Paris: Armand Colin, 1972.

Wylie, Laurence. *Saint-Marc Girardin.* New York: Syracuse University Press, 1947.

Wyrouboff, Grégoire. "Le Congrès de la Paix." *Revue de Philosophie Positive* (November–December 1867).

Zeldin, Theodore. *The Political System of Napoleon III.* London: Macmillan, 1958.

———. *Emile Ollivier and the Liberal Empire of Napoleon III.* Oxford: Clarendon Press, 1963.

———. *France, 1848–1945.* 4 vols. Oxford: Oxford University Press, 1979.

Zévaès, Alexandre. *L'Histoire de la Troisième République.* Paris: Georges-Anquetil, 1926.

INDEX

Note: Page numbers in bold type denote figures.

absolutism 100, 143, 216, 253; institutional 319–20; monarchical 120, 121, 253; political 120, 162; religious 111
abstention(ists) 135, 136, 263
Académie Francaise 169, **170**, 204, 229
accountability 61, 71, 107, 162, 216; apparent absence of any mechanism of 196; local 56, 67; ministerial 63; political 11, 13; proper 174; public 267
Acollas, Emile 304
Adam, Edmond 206n
Adam, Juliette 316n
Additional Act (1815) 10
Adhémar, Comte Alexandre d' 109, 120
administration 32, 33, 52, 138, 142, 212; accountability of 107, 162; admirable 179; affront to legitimacy 71; agents 45, 56, 70, 71, 122; benevolent functions 76; better, self-government recipe for 266; Bonapartist system 88; committees appointed by government 306n; communal 138, 317; complaints about intervention in local elections 58–9; conservatism of 64; contradictions of the system 33; "correct" outcome 292; councils appointed by prefect 265–6; crisis 61; delays suffered by rural communes 55; departmental 33; dependency 212; dominant mores should be changed 66–7; dysfunctions 122; efficiency of 77; free and independent 140; greater involvement of citizenry in 139; growing public opposition to 58; hierarchy 34; inefficiency 53, 60, 67; inherent superiority 75; institutions 4, 41; interference 92; internal political fragmentation of 92; municipal councils fearful of 266; omnipotent 225; patronage 47; political reliability 59; powers taken away from 141–2; powers transferred from 83; problems

53, 62; provincial 72, 141–2, 208; radical objection to activities 99; reduced ability to interact fruitfully with citizen 77; reorganization of 99; reports on election (1863) 54; resistance of centralists 70–3; role of 59, 73, 123–4, 131, 214–19; rules 17; structure created by the Revolution 112; territorial 94, 139, 222; threats to 70; training school of 291; tyranny 162; ultimate source of imperial local power 269; vertical chain of command in 51; withdrawal from local politics 71; writings on 300. *See also* administrative power; centralization; decentralization; local administration
administrative powers 102; of appointment 41, 44; arbitrary exercise of 195; desirability of enhancing 53; excessive concentration of 205; handed over to elected councils 18; increased 45; municipal and departmental 206; prefects 134; real devotees of 43; seeping away to elective bodies 91; tyranny of 131–4
agglomerations 50, 54, 64, 249
agitators 41, 47, 54n
agnostics 187
Agoult, Comtesse Marie d' 244, 259
agriculture 64, 129; centralized system disastrous for 130; departmental interests 128; development of 98; local, improved conditions 50; ministers for 56; plight of workers 102; revenues 21
Agulhon, Maurice 238, 310n
Alexander, Robert 233n
Algiers 114n
Allain-Targé, Henri 239, 291
allegiance 173; academic positions lost for refusing to swear an oath of 237; emphasis on 161; political 186; social and moral 310

alliances 158, 284; antirevolutionary 80; Bonapartists and clericalists 252; communes 282–3; cross-class nature of 301; electoral 252–3; ideological 301; royalists, republicans, and clergy against Bonapartists 253; sociological 301; tactical 301

Alsace 68, 86, 138

Amigues, Jules 62–3, 100

Aumale, Duc d' 169

anarchy 25, 72, 106, 149, 153, 231, 264, 319; joyful 292; liberty without 175; social 188, 205

Ancenis 52

ancien régime 10, 13, 121, 156

Andelarre, Jules François Jacquot-Rouhier, Marquis d' 45, 52n

Angers 111, 124

Anglophilia 183

Anjou 124

anthropology 117, 121, 172

anticlericalism 31, 65, 171, 227, 264, 279; almost Jacobin form of 187; virulent 238

antimilitarism 250, 300, 314

apathy 54, 56; Empire's reliance on feelings of 265; social 199–202; widespread sense of 266

Arago, Emmanuel 302

arbitrariness 168, 185, 195, 216, 222

"Arcadians" 36

Ariège 39

Ariès, Philippe 21

aristocracy 37, 44, 116, 157, 179, 262; advocacy of rule 158–9; celebration of virtues of 99; common aversion to 169; complaints against the appropriation of public offices by 132; conception of local autonomy 283; demise of 146; grim picture of society deprived of 115; ideally suited to local office 145; leadership promoted 137; legitimist 98; local 221, 252; moral 123; morally corrupt and politically incompetent 147; most important duty 117; origins of elites 100; practice of empowering 145; provincial 14; social mores 159; sociological reality 147

armies 39, 44, 98, 250, 254

Arnould, Arthur 239, 269

Arras 207

artisans 168, 280

arts 5, 60, 204, 205, 250

assemblies 64, 197, 215; attributions of 82; deliberative 77, 222; departmental/cantonal 51, 59, 82–3, 91, 141, 142, 215; elected 139; local 137–8, 141, 157, 158; manipulated by the sophistry of the clergy 221; microscopic 274; municipal/communal 51, 97; provincial 62. See also National Assembly

Association of French Workers 254

associational activity 67, 70, 115, 151, 187, 281

atheism 105, 119, 125, 273

Aucoc, Léon 81

Aulard, Alphonse 13–14

Austria 106

authoritarian Bonapartism/Bonapartists 36, 76n, 289; endorsement of decentralization 62, 63; local democracy and 311; mayors and 52–3, 58; Ollivier's complaint about 218; opposition to administrative despotism 64; press 86; sense of territorial hierarchy 284. See also Persigny

authoritarianism 11, 29, 31, 36, 57, 176, 195, 220, 237, 276, 271, 280; administrative 60, 189; Bonapartist 287; centralist 54, 71; condemned 89, 320; Jacobin 287; legitimist 107, 287; liberalism and 37; as method of governing communes 268; paternalist 278; political 189, 245; prefectoral 77; republican 260. See also authoritarian Bonapartism

authority 32, 36, 42, 47, 52, 161, 194, 250; abdication of doctrines of 59; central(ized) 154, 195; challenged 60; communal order preserved by appealing to 293; convenient means of challenging 167; deferral to 265; entrenched 90; essential distinction between power and 290; legal 88; mayoral 71; measures compatible with principle of 63; monarchic 135; moral 295; municipalist 293; neofeudal 221; political 67, 71; prefects' 205; preponderance of 242; public 83, 177, 246, 278; questions addressed from a social perspective 281; reciprocal independence of liberty and 43; redistribution of 311; regime committed to 94; representatives of 269; republicans placed liberty above 238; royal 105; social 18, 22, 98, 294, 305; sovereign 56; state 284, 290, 295; transcendental 284; tyranny of 208; weakened 64, 79

autonomy 68, 70, 131, 156; claims from the periphery 209; communal 54, 71, 72, 76, 156, 193, 226, 285; denial of 195; departmental 54, 71, 156, 274, 306; dissolution of all forms of social activity 123; endorsed for mainly tactical reasons 234–5; individual 133; moral 160; municipal 270, 274; political 69, 71, 76, 191, 307; provincial 131, 193. *See also* local autonomy

Auxerre 41n

Azy, Baron Benoist d' 81

Babaud-Laribière, Léonide 303–4

Bakunin, Mikhail 251

Bancel, Desiré 237n, 255

Barante, Prosper, Baron de 14, 212, 221

barbarians 123–7

Barbier, Auguste 250

Barni, Jules 249, 251

Baroche, Jules 91, 186n

Baroche, Mme Jules 51

Barral, Pierre 234n

Barrot, Odilon 80, 188, 198, 203, 205–6, 221, 232; condemns omnipresence and omnipotence of state 199; definition of decentralization 193; writings: *De la centralisation* 199, 202; letters to *Le Temps* 88n, 226

Barthélémy, Charles 29

Baudin, Jean Baptiste Alphonse Victor 236

Beau de Loménie, Emmanuel 163

Béchard, Ferdinand 107, 132–3, 148, 155

Béhic, Louis Henri Armand 56

Belcastel, Gabriel de 133, 150

Belleval, René, Marquis de 145

Belleville manifesto (1869) 298

Bern International Congress for Peace (1868) 250

Bernard, Henri 16

Bernaret, Abbé 130

Berryer, Antoine 107, 117, 136, 150

Berton (mayor of Saint-Vaize) 48n

Besançon 149

Bethmont, Paul 265–6, 267, 270, 301n

Billault, Adolphe 39, 41, 51, 53, 54n, 91, 93

birth rate 130

Blanc, Edmond 81

Blanc, Louis 250, 274, 277

Blanc de Saint-Bonnet, Antoine 159; *Notion de l'Homme tirée de la notion de Dieu* 119; *Politique réelle* 111, 117, 118, 123, 125, 147, 149; *De la restauration française* 103, 115, 118, 124, 146

Blanchard, Marcel 27

Blanqui, Auguste 248, 249, 254, 279

Blanquism/Blanquists 264n, 273, 278, 279, 295

Bluche, Frédéric 30–1

Boilay, F. 36

Bonald, Louis G. A., Vicomte de 98, 120

Bonaparte, Napoleon Joseph Charles Paul, Prince Napoleon 29, 67–8, 70

Bonaparte family 238. *See also* Napoleon

Bonapartism/Bonapartists 16, 20, 24, 97, 100, 178, 260, 272, 307, 309, 310; acknowledge the significance of the Revolution 238, 243; administrative despotism of 277; alienated Catholics from regime 110; alliance between royalists, republicans, and clergy against 253; appealed to by liberals 226; attitudes and norms of 219; centralism 14, 32, 37–44, 81; conception of the mayor as an agent of central government 211; conservative 158, 186n; constitutionalist minority 216; coup (December 1851) 135, 185, 236, 237; decentralization 18, 32, 33, 35, 37, 61–3, 69, 156, 207; departments' overwhelming support for 264; elites 203; encouraged atrophy of local political life 266; encroachments on local life 271; equated with systematic violation of republican legality 236; founding myths of 237; "hermaphrodite" notion 105; immorality and lack of integrity 240; importance of the legacy 179; important legitimist objection to practice 159–60; Jacobinism shared almost all its

Bonapartism/Bonapartists (*cont.*)
key intellectual assumptions with
298; left-wing 25; legitimists' relationship with 101; liberal 25, 62, 66,
70, 73, 87, 151, 165, 168n, 210; liberal critique of 207; local democracy
theory 312; minority of legitimists
rallied to the regime 106; moderate
181; Orleanist notables rallied to
221; over-centralization denounced
124; peasantry often identified with
252; political ends 136; propagandists
275; rapprochement between legitimists and 65, 66; reform attempts
(1850s and 1860s) 207; repression
237; republican opposition to 235;
stereotypical view of Orleanism 168;
subcultures within 19, 25; subjugation of communal life 283; sudden
collapse (1870) 304; *tiers parti* 166;
tyranny 185; unity and diversity of
35–7; views of local life 194, 195;
views of public authority 159; votes
in plebiscite (May 1870) 228. *See
also* authoritarian Bonapartism
Bonjean, Louis-Bernard 62, 67, 70, 81
Bordeaux 41n, 57, 66n, 86, 191, 199;
ideological and sociological alliances
in 301; public prosecutor of 98
Borderie, Arthur de la 128
Boulatigner, Joseph 81
Bourbons 10n, 96, 99, **113**, 152; deposed
106; restoration of 107
bourgeoisie, bourgeois 5, 19, 146, 179,
279; articulating the interests of 167;
attack on privileged position 132;
"class rule" 234n; defense of interests
165; degeneracy of 263; dominant 7,
55; elites 22, 294; emancipation of
190; empowerment of 225; increasing
confidence of 307; interests 224, 228;
leadership 286; natural superiority of
230; notables 226, 295; provincial
193; and republicanism 260–5; universality of 167–71; urban 152
Bouteiller, Ernest de 36
Boyer de Sainte Suzanne, Emile Victor
Charles de, Baron 75
Brie 90
Brisson, Henri 250
Britain 44, 46n, 182

Brittany/Bretons 7n, 128, 190
Broglie, Albert, Duc de 169, **170**, 174,
176, 221, 232
Broglie dynasty 169, 185–6
Broglie, Victor, Duc de 169, **170**, 181,
192, 204, 208, 212–13, 217
brothels 254
Brumaire (18) 236
Buisson, Ferdinand 255
bureaucracy 12, 64, 73, 209; accountability of 216; Bonapartist 91; campaign to enhance responsiveness to
public concerns 56; central and territorial, functions of 308; conservatism
of 67; criticism of 57, 69; division
into separate administrative corps
133; domination of citizenry 292n;
enhancing the effectiveness of 66; expansionary, irksome, and all-powerful
78; growth of 214; hallmarks of 55;
inflation of 269; local agencies 18;
lower levels 122; national 159; op-
pressiveness deplored 13; Parisian 53;
perceived as an instrument of administrative excellence 218; pretensions
of 132; provincial 159; public-interest
functions of 219; several features a
source of concern to liberals 214–15;
transferring powers to local administration 77; two conceptions of 218–
19; uncompromisingly negative view
of 222; unnecessary expansion of
132; war against red tape 67; waste
and financial profligacy 203
Burgundians 128
burial rights 151

Cahors 168
Cajarc 168
Calonne, Alphonse de 142, 143, 148
cantons, cantonal 27, 37, 47, 48, 51, 92,
97, 191; attributions 82; councils
283; extension of powers of representatives 311; prefectural functions in
141; residence requirements 155.
See also departmental/cantonal elections
capitalism 254, 307
Carcassonne 86, 302
Carné, Louis de 181
Carnot, Hippolyte 250, 255, 281, 301n

Casimir Perier, Auguste Victor Laurent 198, 216
Cassagnac, Adolphe Granier de 36, 38
Cassagnac, Paul Adolphe Marie de 36
Castagnary, Jules 268
castes 222, 315
Castelbajac, Vicomte de 120
Catholicism/Catholics 9, 11, 66, 100, 128, 138, 157, 193, 309; abhor working on Sunday 126; antiliberal manner of politics found among 273; call for the wholesale destruction of 254; challenge to republican project 251; competing with republicanism for the same social constituency 253; conception of territoriality 109; consensus over the analysis of 254; decentralization seen as ideology of 158, 279; devout 109; divided into two cross-cutting cleavages 110; entrenched hostility toward the institutions and norms of 260; excluded from Third Republic 26; Gallican 110; independent 252; intransigent 108, 111, 149; journalists 95; liberal 110, 166, 187, 192; modern defenders of 171n; notion of freedom 150; pamphleteers 105; party 166; provincial 65; reliance on the spirit of France 114; secular liberal opinion often suspicious of 187; spiritual force embodied in 254; territories of the West 107; too large and diverse an institution to act in a monolithic fashion 252; triumphantly reconciled with republicanism and Protestantism 255; ultramontane 110, 253; unity with legitimism 109–15
census (1866) 44
centralism 7, 73, 83, 186; authoritarian 71; Bonapartist 37–44, 81; conception of state 260; continuing strength of feeling 88; crushing oppression of 210; culture of republicanism 271; defense of 162n; despotic 285; dysfunctions of 51–60; ideas about maintaining 260; ills of 199; institutional purposes of state 214; liberal critique of 195; need to emancipate localities from 138; power 293; principles 272; resistance of supporters of

70–3; Saint-Simonian economic justification of 77; utility of 44–51
centralization 37, 38, 68, 70, 78, 199; Bonapartist 14, 32, 37–44; correspondence between militarism and 300; corruptive social consequences of 124; critiques of 99, 119–23, 131, 195–7, 265–71; debates (1860s) on 94; defended by Thiers 218; dilemmas of 206–7; electoral dimension of 198; elite awareness of the benefits 314; emphasis on 299; excessive 64, 68, 69, 125, 163, 195; fervent advocate of 74; held responsible for a wide range of social ills 200; imperial 265–71, 280; indispensable precondition for universal enjoyment of liberty 277; intellectual opposition to 96; intimately linked to incidence of revolution 200; Jacobin and Bonapartist conceptions 298; legitimist definition of 15; liberal fixation with 222; medicine that could heal the nation of its secular disorders 273; as metaphor of death and decadence 310; monarchical 120, 121; most effective auxiliary to 154; most extreme manifestation of 196; necessity of the principle of 288; pernicious effects on the rural world 127; plurality of factors attributable to the pressures of 202; political 14, 37, 38, 75, 162, 274, 294; power 94, 141; powerful force for good 276; principle of 209; problems with 88, 208, 229, 281; progress resides in 204; shortcomings of 13; some inefficient aspects of 77; threat of 130, 276; unrelenting hostility toward 96
Challamel, Augustin 29
Chambéry 47
Chambord, Henri Charles Dieudonné, Comte de 54, 106–9, 110, 135–6, 143, 161; Correspondance 147; "Manifeste de 1852" 114n; Manifestes et programmes politiques 144, 148
change 166, 204; concrete suggestions for 214; constitutional 166; economic 21, 23n, 167; incremental 188; obsession with 202; political 81, 166, 167,

change (*cont.*)
183–4, 207, 296; revolutionary 123, 286; social 21, 23n, 112–13; system of government open to 320
Charencey, Comte de 128
Charente-Inférieure 48n, 264, 268
charity 102, 116, 150, 176; misappropriated by the state 15; souls who aspire to 127
Charles X, king of France 101, 114n
Charter (1830) 10
Chateaubriand, Alphonse de 145
Chevalier, Michel 186
Chevandier de Valdrôme, Eugène 61, 80
Chévillard, Jules 75, 139
children 106, 252
Chinese expeditions 177
Christianity 102, 119, 127, 139
church 100, 130, 149; detestation of 187; enjoyed a privileged position in hierarchy of Bonapartist institutions 252; expropriation of 124; oppression by 280; possibility of greater independence 255; role of 5; Second Empire and 110; state and 35, 101, 111, 177, 253, 254
cities 94, 131, 214, 264; devolving power away from 314; groups suspicious and fearful of political voice of 308; handed over to forces of subversion 86; impossible to administer 78; large(r) 40n, 91, 92, 213, 231, 296, 314; mass migration into 21, 22, 129; mayors of 40n; participation in the life of 291; population estranged from each other 50; population growth 21; protection of 270–1; republican advances across France 303; small 78; special political representation for 258; ungrateful 95; united with royalty 140; values of republican citizenship embodied in 257–8
citizenship 3–28, 115; autonomous 230; commune and 139, 255–9; cultivation of genuine feeling of 68; debates over 188–9; decentralization and 17–20; defining attribute of 171; depoliticized conception of 90; divisions over the nature of 37; effective 208, 220; fostering a distinct type of 42; in historical perspective 8–13; individual, administrative, and economic aspects of 69; liberal conceptions of 167, 196, 230, 225; liberal recognition of need for theory of 220; modern 3, 4, 12n, 89, 161; normative theory of 4; political 135, 221; prerequisite for 190, 221; promoting a more positive and open conception 89; redefining 13–17, 99, 103, 147, 156, 158; republican 3, 4, 99, 233, 257–8, 290, 305, 306–21; rights-based 230; strengthened 190, 291. *See also* "good" citizenship
civic life 11, 14, 266; Bonapartist projects for restoring 88, 90; consensus about status and functions of mayor 94; French political culture and 199–202, 306, 308; mass participation in 13, 36, 89; prompted by 1848 revolution 304; revived and regenerated 310; separating religion from 320; social responsibility 123, 191, 292, 294; under Third Republic 9; virtues of 25, 42, 163
Civil Code 144, 151–2
civil equality 25, 107, 112, 239, 242, 255, 276, 296, 299, 300; adherence to 238; aspect of Bonapartist tradition attached to 36; introduction of 35; involvement of citizenry on the basis of 18; preservation of 89; respect for 209; upholding the principles of 43
civil service 132
Clamagéran, Jules 304, 301n
class. *See* social class
clergy 194, 253; agitation during elections (1863) 54n; controls all women 252; deliberative assemblies too easily manipulated by the sophistry of 221; hostile activities of 46n; leadership of legitimist party recruited from 114; party of 45; political attitudes of 45–6; rejection of influences 209; secularization of 242; support of 98; ultramontane, antagonism between regime and 65
clericalism/clericalists 31, 35, 36, 54, 66, 100, 204; alliance of Bonapartists and 252; Dupont-White's scathing views on 171n; intransigent 112
Clovis 3

Clozel de Boyer, A. 103, 155
clubs 309
Cochin, Augustin 192, 203
coercion 48, 51, 268, 290; as basis for political unity 285; as a means of redistribution 296; mayors' use of 122
cohesion 44, 70, 100; administrative 219; collective 178; political and ideological 114; social 43, 207
Colet, Louise 29
collective life 12, 115; accomplishments 30; action, salutary capacities of 246; attempts to form associations 199; basic principles, reconsideration of 13; first laws of 137; interests 62, 291; mentalities 21, 22. *See also* identity
collectivities 258, 259; cohesive 318; commune as microcosm 257; decadence of 119; deficient and faltering, people as 246; entitlements and guarantees of 4; free 289; local 109; political 13; urban 257
Collège de France 228n
colonialism 114, 163n
comedians 154
commercial exchanges 22
Commission of Inquiry (1870) 33, 35, 61n, 62, 66, 67, 143, 193, 212, 222, 270; frustrations of 79–88; part of a strategic calculation 64
commissions mixtes 60
common good 176
common interest(s) 42, 172, 184, 193, 257; appeal to 188; search for 190
common sense 100, 154, 176, 224
communes 37, 47, 48n, 64, 109, 140, 191, 197, 282, 314; administration of 33, 76, 138, 155; adversarial politics in 90; alliance of 282–3; assistance to 49; attributions of 82; authoritarian methods to govern 268; autonomy of 54, 71, 72, 76, 85, 156, 193, 226; citizenship and 255–9; civic and egalitarian character 194; competence of 265; deferential and loyal 213; democratic self-government of 287–97; denied their most sacred right 267; deprived of management of own affairs 210; division into sections 41; elected institutions of 213, 311; elec-

toral and regulatory framework 267–8; emancipation of 63, 76 120, 143, 211, 235, 287, 315; empowerment of 143; enabled to establish autonomous religious associations 150; executive powers of 40; family likened to 139; federation of 286–7; financial profligacy of 77; franchises of 84; free federation into provinces 251; freedom and rights of 148; government 151; greater political responsibility accorded to 316; idealization of 286; identified as the privileged site at which citizenship could be constructed 310; identity of 139; immaturity of many 76, 154; importance assigned to 318; important 283; independence 207; instruments and aptitudes necessary to enjoy freedom 285; interests 217; intrinsically unfit for self-government 195; key agents in 60; large and small, disparities between 285; led by aristocracy 158; liberation of 158; liberty of 142; limited range of rights to 14; local solidarized 143; many incapable of self-administration 76; mayors 198, 210, 211, 298; moralizing 136; new decentralized order in 158; no longer an autonomous entity 269; no worse tyranny than 278; number of inhabitants (1866) 44n; overwhelming preponderance of the administration in local life of 269–70; political and intellectual origins 234; political conflict in 42; potential conflicts of interest between 283; power flowed from 284; power to the populations of 155; prefects 45, 83, 141; principal symbol of local political life 190; problems faced by 137; protection of 270–1; province primary location of 129; republican 266, 303; rival factions in 51–2; rural 39, 44, 55, 70, 86, 210, 285; schoolteachers 143; selecting the executive agent of 212; smaller 141; sole representatives of political authority in 71; sphere of citizenship 139; state's relations with 305; well administered 145; zeal of the citizen for the interests of 192

communism 62, 264; as form of federalism 281; Jacobin 296; realization of 249

communitarianism 9, 11

compromise 111, 112, 135, 137, 319; differences settled through 292; ideological 158; republican and liberal principles 227; social 318; through universal suffrage 294

Concordat 111

congregationists 319

conservatism/conservatives 31, 37, 68, 84, 166; administrative 64; Bonapartist 86, 158; bureaucratic 67; canons of 100; distinction between liberalism and 188n; elites 65; excellent instrument for protecting interests 152; failed reaction (1870s) 228; functional virtues of hierarchy 116–17; Gambetta never forgiven by 306n; imperial 73; instincts 102, 313; institutional 88; leading figure 170; legitimists 101; liberals 80, 81; major forces 66; majorities 154; notion of order 175; opportunists 264; politicians 312; rejected 188; religions 254; rural 313; social 36, 63, 145, 153, 226, 318; strong defense of principles 299n; true 183

Constant, Benjamin 10n, 163–4

constitution 10, 101–2nn, 173, 216, 227, 238; allegiance to 173; substance much more important than form of 174; monarchical, republican, and imperial 173

Conventionalists 276

convents 254

Coquille, Jean-Baptiste 116, 117, 128, 144, 150, 154

Cormenin, Louis de 71n

corruption 203, 216, 222, 268; heritage of 168; intellectual 125; magistrate guilty of 216; material 307; moral 126, 146, 205, 307; political 132; practice leading to 141; "principle of the Empire" 240; social 125; social and political purposes of bureaucratic expansion 133; of state's functions 198

Cosnac, Comte Jules de 125, 143

"couches nouvelles" 294

Coulon, Georges 240, 262

Council of State 43, 61, 76, 91, 140; councillors 34; generously salaried piece of inconsequence 133; inherent bias against provinces 217; members 81; political role of 215; prelegislative role sharply criticized 216; representative body subordinated to 239–40; review of decentralization 53; some liberals opposed to political and legislative functions of 217

councillors 154; departmental/cantonal 98, 142, 226, 283; elected 52, 93, 266, 297–8; freely chosen 210; general 42, 91, 155; hostile 197; local 141, 192, 297–8; local communities deprived of the right to elect their own 196; municipal 90, 142, 265; oligarchic 280; prefectoral 140; sanction against 196. See also Council of State; departments (administrative councils); General Councils; municipal councils

counterrevolution 101, 107, 183, 202, 209, 228; Bonaldian doctrines 98; domestic and external forces of 274; political instrument 153; as tradition 131

coup d'état (1851) 41, 44, 46–8 passim, 60, 64, 185, 274, 275; justification of 236; Persigny's pun on emperor's warning after 71; repression in the aftermath of 237; republican exiles after 246

Crémieux, Adolphe 302

criminal proceedings 216

culture(s) 297; as basis for national unity 209; civic 199–202, 303, 306, 308; democratic and self-governing 281; of dependency 199; differences between English and French 182–3; excellence 204, 205; federalist 285; high 240; historical, unarticulated but powerful taboo in 313; Jacobin 288; modern notion of Frenchness 7; municipal 28, 293. See also political culture(s)

cynicism 187, 240, 246

David, Jérôme 36, 43

decadence 146, 189, 203; centralization as symbol of 310; class 131; collectivities 119; directly associated with development of industry 130–1; of modern society 102; spiritual 240

Decazes, Duc Louis-Charles-Elie-Amanieu 183

decentralism 19, 32, 67; Bonapartist 88–95; conception of state 260; dramatic conversion to 299; one of the dominant campaigning themes of 83; radical 15, 271

decentralization 3, 60, 64, 66, 269, 301; antirevolutionary aspect 68; attempt to cement an alliance of conservative forces resisting political change 81; Bonapartist 18, 32, 33, 35, 37, 61–3, 69, 83; citizenship and 17–20; classic 19th-century juridical account of 17n; commitment to 33, 80, 235; convergence among political elites over 308; Council of State's review 53; dangerous myth 78; debates on 298, 308, 311; democracy a necessary corollary of 283; described as a "burning issue" 306; economic 90; either undesirable or impossible 76; Empire's record on 90; explicit link between peace and 251; extensive arguments for 285; favored 71; genuine form of 105; hindered 70; history of 13–17; imperial, proper limits of 67; in favor of prefects 270; Jacobin rejection of 271–81; "judicious" 182; legitimist conceptions 96–161; liberal conceptions 162–232; measured degree of 100; moderate form of 298; most important organizing principle of social order 282; political 63–6, 72, 78, 79, 87–8, 134–8; powerful metaphor 310; prefects and 73–9; question of 308; range of opinions on 82; republicans and 234, 235; rural society 63, 64, 68; substantive legislation on 313–14; symptomatic of a number of critical problems 306–7; tactical view of 235; true form of 73; unwieldy instrument for discussing 87; validity of 234. See also Commission of Inquiry (1870)

Declaration of the Rights of Man (1789) 118, 243

degeneration 119, 145–6, 183; racial 130, 131

Delescluze, Charles 271, 280–1

delocalization 78

demagoguery 50, 72

democracy 216, 279, 300; American 189; Bonapartist conception of 42–43; choice between paternalism and certain forms of 219; citizenship and 3–28; communal 206; concerns and adjustments 311–13; emergence of 26–8, 246; goal of 291; hostility toward 239; imperial, political, and social reaction to 167; mass 161, 227, 312; means of promoting 294; municipal 316; necessary corollary of decentralization 283; place in the political system 307; political 5, 288, 299; republic the embodiment of 242; republican notions of 233–4; social 299; socialist argument for greater 262; sociological category to designate the working class 246n; tide sweeping all modern societies toward 186. See also local government

department stores 22

departmental/cantonal elections 66, 92, 154, 156, 270; frequent 27; ideological conflict in 51; official candidates 47, 48; proposals to depoliticize 158

departments 33, 37, 39, 46, 64, 91, 140, 191, 197, 221, 284; arbitrary divisions of 121; assemblies of 42, 51, 59, 82–3, 141, 142, 213, 215, 226, 239, 240; attributions of 82; autonomy 54, 71; coordinating common projects among 141; decentralization 73; demands for reestablishment of territorial division above 206; deprived of management of own affairs 210; distribution of power within 83; elected officials 311; emancipation of 141n; envisaged abolition of 270; executive powers of 40; franchises 79, 84; freedom and rights 148; funds available to 142; independence of 207; interests 78, 128, 217; key agents 60; led by the aristocracy 158; legitimist political representation in 157; new decentralized order in 158; overwhelmingly Bonapartist 264; political conflict in 42; power flowed from 284; prefects and 51, 77, 141,

departments (*cont.*)
292; reforms 138; residence require-
ment 155; Seine 80n; well administered 145
depoliticization 18, 39, 58, 69, 89, 90, 94,
194, 265; local government institutions 137; logic of 158
depopulation 130, 131
deportation 60n
deputies **34**, 39, 91, 210–11, **241**, **256**;
Bonapartist 72; citizens allowed directly to elect 267; liberal **302**; nomination of 154; "persecuted" by
prefects 51; republican 54, 264, 265,
267, 291, 298, **302**
Desmarest, Ernest 301n
despotism 62, 105, 149, 248, 253; administrative 64, 269, 277; Catholicism
and 253; centralism 285; every religion is a form of 254; exposure to
123; government 219; last bastion of
288; leaders of 249; "of luxury" 240;
of mayors 143; opposition to 185;
order without 175; prefectoral 219;
provincial 197; republican 120,
219
Desquennoy (mayor of Lawarde-Mauger)
48n
determinism 121
dialectic 102
dialects 128
Dijon 70, 183, 200
Dino, Dorothée de Courlande, Duchesse
de 126, 129
disfranchisement 280
distribution: goods 178, 184; power 80,
297; resources 198, 203; social benefits 178
diversity 69, 184–9, 128, 235, 261; associations 22–3; Bonapartist 32, 35–7;
cultural 121, 151; ethical 287; ideological 11n, 106, 176, 287; intellectual 31; legitimist manifestations 100;
political 106; religious and spiritual
255; social 31, 151; temperamental
151; territorial 121
divine right 107
divorce 103
dogmatism 279
Dordogne 224
Doubs 268

Dreux-Brézé, Henri-Scipion-Charles, Mar-
quis de 130
Dromel. *See* Ecorcheville
Dubois, Jean 10
Dubois de Jancigny, Alfred Louis Marie
59
Du Boys, Albert 156
Du Camp, Maxime 80n, 81, 87
Dufaure, Jules 169, 188, 198
Dupont-White, Charles 81, 122; defender
of centralization 162, 230; scathing
views on clericalism 171n; sociological determinism of 121; writings: *La
centralisation* 171, 172, 177, 204;
L'individu et l'état 178; *La liberté
politique* 209; *Le progrès politique en
France* 183
Durkheim, Emile 25n
Durranc, Edouard 304
duty 12, 56, 71, 93, 99, 101, 109, 117,
159, 178, 249, 255; accent on 259;
civic 200; freedom as 148, 151; individual and collective 4; middle class
193; moral 161; "patriotic" 192; reciprocal 10; religious 102, 112n, 136;
state 296; unquestionable 275
Duval (mayor of Soncourt) 48n
Duvergier de Hauranne, Jean-Marie 14
Duvernois, Clément 62

Ecorcheville, (Justin Dromel) 260
education 42, 148, 192, 208, 246, 255,
259, 300, 305; belief in the necessity
of 168; elementary 245; freedom of
175; higher 80n; individual 279; key
reforms in 317; link between freedom
and 245; moral 150; political 190,
191, 194, 248, 304; positive bias toward 169; possibilities of human development through 297; primary 262,
304; promotion of 25; religious 150,
158–9; republican system 7; role of
the system 310; secular 103; spread
of 36; universal 262; working classes
in need of 246
egalitarianism 261; promises of Revolution 296; result of sincere election
315; rhetoric of 194; social 145
election, elections 155, 228, 263, 270; city
213; corrupt practices in 28; cynical
manipulation of electorate 246; de-

feats suffered by mayors 71; evidence that officials campaigned for opposition 59–60; frequent 90, 191; General Council 58, 59; growing proportion of mayors who ran for 92; importance of municipal and cantonal 316n; indirect method of 211; legislative 93–4; legitimists' political success in 98; movement of opinion 52; presidential (1848) 65; recriminations against role of administration particularly vehement during 122; regime's tendency to rely on mayors during campaigns 83; rural 51, 223; sincerity in 174, 199, 315; workers tossed in storm of 192. See also legislative elections; local elections; national elections

elites 30, 100, 186, 310; administrative 49, 132; aristocratic 100, 146; arrogant 187; artistic 203; awareness of the benefits of centralization 314; Bonapartist 32, 37, 64, 89, 203; bourgeois 22, 261, 263, 264, 294; cantonal 311; centralist 73; conservative 65; cultural 203; enlightened and secular 318; established 294; government in the hands of 117; imperial 67; intellectual 10, 14, 80, 297; journalistic 23; July Monarchy 220; legitimist 98, 110, 112; local 12–13, 46, 52, 64, 147, 209, 297; municipal 311; national 12–13, 298, 312; natural, government of 144–7; new 319, 321; opportunist 11; Orleanist 49, 186; Parisian 16, 23; parliamentary 297; provincial 71; radical 11; recruitment 190; republican 194, 228, 229, 235, 263, 305; social 36, 43, 225, 294; state 297; workers should seek political dissociation from 286; working-class frustration with mainstream republican 261. See also political elites

emancipation 142, 287; bourgeois 190; collective 251; communal 120, 143, 211, 235, 294, 315; departmental 141n; from delusions of religion and superstition 259; individual 160, 226, 251; local 231; municipal 142, 212; of provinces 160; of slaves 150

empiricism 32, 173
England 181, 182–3
Enlightenment 187
equality 50, 65, 282, 320; absolute 277; access of all groups of citizens to positions of honor 159; complete freedom necessarily brings 245; different conceptions of 296; fraternity not on an equal footing with 248–9; of gender roles 258; Jacobin republicans subscribed to 277; of opportunity 25, 159, 262, 296; treatment of all religious faiths 177; true 118. See also civil equality; political equality; social equality

executive branch 40, 67, 83; power of 217, 267, 268; nomination of mayors 85

Faguet, Emile 163
Falloux, Comte Alfred de 107, 108, 113, 137; writings 159, 161; Le parti catholique 112; Mémoires d'un royaliste 124, 129, 135–6, 146, 153–4
family 101, 111, 116, 194; children call themselves heads of 106; defense of 112n, 136; destructive consequences of social changes on 112–14; development of 258; dissolution of 106; linked to commune 139; protection of 226; ruin and dispersal 193; threatened 114; ties strengthened 226; unbroken chain linking the individual to 139
farmers 262, 315; small 280
fatalism 112, 253
Favé, Gen. Ildefonse 67, 81
Favre, Jules 84, 237, 250, 273, 301, 302
fear 230, 231, 268, 276, 278; "liberalism of" 188, 189, 228, 232; of social revolution 314
federalism/federalists 265, 317; argument against 178; liberal attitude to 179, 221; path between Jacobinism and 233–305; Proudhonist 286; rejection of 207–10, 222, 309; solution and limits 281–7
female exploitation 254
Ferry, Jules 165, 250, 281, 290, 293, 302, 313; writings: 240, 251, 273, 287n, 291–2, 301n, 314, 317; La lutte électorale 246, 247

feudalism 15, 250, 253, 280; abolition of 35; financial 280; Nancy manifesto presented as reorganization of 279–80

Fichte, J. G. 237–8

finance 37, 208, 268

Finance Inspectorate 30

First Empire (1804–15) 14n, 218

First International (1864–76) 143, 264

First Republic (1792–1804) 261

Flourens, Gustave 250

Folies-Belleville 206

Fontarèches, Baron de 140, 154

Forcade, Jean Louis Victor Adolphe 94n

foreign affairs 201

Foucher de Careil, Armand 130, 131

Fould, Achille 91

Fourmestraulx-Saint Denis, count of 90

Fournier, Ernest 200

Franco-Prussian War (1870–1) 6, 33, 82, 86, 94, 131, 232, 306, 313, 314; talented publicist who committed suicide after hearing of the outbreak 180, 229

fraternity 242, 260, 276, 320; complete freedom necessarily brings 245; definition based on explicitly Christian teachings 249; peace and 248–51; promotion of the spirit of 291

free love 103

free trade 46n, 177, 186

free will 284

freedom 116, 161, 164, 183, 190, 191, 260, 317; ambiguities inherent in conceptions of 151; of association 16, 18, 148, 261; casuists of 288; civil 105, 151, 165, 175; clear notion of the concept 17–18; communal 64, 105, 285; of conscience 151; constitutional 158; contingent view of 149; conviction that it is valuable and beneficial 187–8; defenders of 213; definition of 101; departmental 64, 105; education 175; electoral 63; emphasis on 238; of expression 18, 110, 148, 237; "external" 118; general exercise of 194; granted by French Revolution 179; how one ought to love 259; incompatible conceptions of 99; individual 13, 63, 99, 175, 276, 277, 299, 300; justice and 242–5; legiti-

mists' strong attachment to 148; liberal notion of 175, 176, 287; local 62, 232; municipal 270, 289; national 105; order before 210; party of 293; pluralist conception of 287; political 11, 63, 118, 139, 149, 150, 155–6, 151, 160, 165, 175, 255, 320; power to use 277; press 61, 63, 149, 317; profession of faith in 245; profound ambiguity over the question of 287; religious 112, 150, 151, 175, 226; republican 242, 245; social 118, 175; souls who aspire to 127; of speech 245; of thought 245; three grievances against administration 269; ultimate 152; virtues of 245; of writing and publishing 245

Freemasonry 242–3, 252, 256, 309; purged of republican elements 237

freethinking movements 252, 254, 309

Fréminville, chevalier de 101

French Academy. See Académie Francaise

French Revolution (1789) 3, 8, 96, 101n, 304; administrative power created by 200–2; administrative reorganization promulgated by 121; attempt to locate centralization in theory and practices of 120; Bonapartist acknowledgement of significance of 243; centralization as product of 13; creation of liberal tradition 26; critique of type of society created by 112–13; cultural, political, and social legacy 161; damaging legacy 123; destruction of aristocratic privileges 146; development and consequences of 233; dismantling of social, political and administrative legacy 209; dramatically shaped by Jacobins 271; heritage of 5, 13, 24–5, 238, 243, 271–2, 280; ideological legacy of 178; inalienable rights sanctified by 151; Jacobins who defended the methods used by 274; key values and principles of 25, 35; legitimists' interpretation of 101; modern national citizenship an invention of 12n; patriotic spirit of 239; people always opposed to 153; project that threatened unity and integrity of 282; republicans bound by common attachment

to 242; royalists' support of local liberties under 19; secularism promised by 254–5; sense of devotion to 260; social, political, and juridical heritage 243; through liberal eyes 178–84; Tocqueville's study of 200–2; unity produced by 221; valuable and irreversible achievement of 294; viewed as a key stage in the development of liberal principles 178
Freycinet, Charles de 81
Frohsdorf 106, 109, 156
frugality 184
"functionocracy" 133
Furet, François 233n

Gaidoz, H. 128
Galembert, Louis-Charles-Marie de Bodin, Comte de 157n
Gallican Church 111, 171n
Gallicanism 110, 171, 187
Gambetta, Léon 165, 236, 262, 276–7, 300, 301, 303, 306, 316, 318
Gard 59
Garnier, Charles 66, 81
Garnier-Pagès, Antoine 301n, 302
Gaudin, E. F. 225
Gaulle, Charles de 128
General Councils 40, 41–2, 54, 140, 197, 215, 283; authoritative analysis of 97; budgetary attributions of 89–90; dangerous to admit legitimists to 57; departmental liberty 42–3; elections to 58, 59; establishment of permanent executive commission 79, 82; external pressures 137; Gambetta's brutal dissolution of 306n; greater local liberty to 64; law on 82; leading members of 91; legislative role 43n; legitimists elected (1852) 135; Loire-Inférieure 97–8; modest increases in competences of 61; prefects appointed by 215; prerogatives relinquished to 141; principal instrument of provincial emancipation in the eyes of the legitimists 142; role of 270; should be given greater latitude to make policy 134; suggestion that they be allowed to express political views 83; tasks devolved to 77
Geneva International Congress for Peace 250, 251, 254

Girard, Louis 167, 298n
Gironde 48, 301
Girondin movement 282, 286
Glais-Bizoin, Alexandre Olivier 302
Gobineau, Arthur de 96, 120, 131, 132
God 18, 109, 114, 118, 150; denial of 119; obeying 252; outrage against 126; revolt of man against 105; wonder at the complex ways of 111
Godard, Abbé Léon 119
Goncourt brothers 203
"good" citizenship 10, 12, 13, 112n; definition of the principles of 307, 318; favorable conditions for the development of 206; pedagogy of principles 9n; reconciling subjectivity with 186; values of 162
Gorce, Pierre de la 165
government 13, 38, 48, 91, 96; administrative committees appointed by 306n; agents of 142; aristocratic 157; attributions become specialized and more restricted 282; best and most durable 174; centralization needed to found the unity of 288; centralized 282; communal 151; conception of municipal reform 84–5; conditions deemed politically inimical to 213; constitutional 107, 179–81, 219, 299, 320; contempt of sovereignty of commune 270; delegating certain attributions of 71; democratic 318; departmental 40, 151; despotic 219; devotion to 42; dictatorial 185; electoral triumph for 54; elites and 117, 144–7; failings of local administration blamed on 60; feudal 250; general theory of the nature of 103; good, conditions for 189; ideal of local life put forward by 41; initiative contained within reasonable limits 175; interference in local matters 67; lampooned 17; lightening the burden of 62; mayors and 16, 45, 268, 211, 314; mechanism for controlling the actions of 223; most abominable and most absurd 185; natural, of provinces 159; obstructionism 89; official candidacies of 51, 57, 58, 59, 60; parliamentary 91, 240; parties divided only on the form of 311; pa-

government (*cont.*)
  tronage 49; power 104–5; prefects
    should no longer be appointed by
    141; quality of 177; reformist 218;
    regional 141, 157, 311; rejection of
    decentralization 19; representative
    112, 318; royalist 14; social 277;
    strong 290; system open to modifica-
    tion and change 320; territorial 3, 16,
    25, 138, 206, 311; transfer of powers
    to prefects 56, 70; tyranny of 208;
    undue importance given to the form
    of 174n. *See also* local government;
    self-government; state
Grammont, F., Marquis de 59
grand corps 78
"Great Debate" (1820s) 14
Guépin, Ange 224–5, 251, 262
Guéroult, Adolphe 168n, 278
Guéroult, Georges 222
Guizot, François Pierre Guillaume 13,
    80n, 172, 179, 221, 228
Gussignies 90

Halévy, Daniel 6
Halévy, Ludovic 225
Hamon, Léo 233n
happiness 119, 120, 262, 277; can depend
    on the choice of a mayor or the com-
    position of a municipal council 135;
    guarantees of 147; perfect 276; possi-
    bility and desirability of 253; safe-
    guard of 304; state as self-appointed
    purveyor of 273; universal 134
Harris, Ruth 26n
Haussmann, Georges Eugène, Baron 21,
    48, 58, 72, 125–6; liberals (and re-
    publicans) infuriated by the reign of
    196; rule in Paris denounced 268; ur-
    ban renovation project for Paris 127
Haussonville, Comte Othenin d' 29, 169,
    174
health 124, 199, 208
hedonism 129
hegemony 252, 301; achieved by munici-
    palist republicans 298; of middle
    classes 263
Hérault 301
heredity 66, 96, 103–6, 139, 153
heritage 3, 168; cultural 249n; eclectic and
    "agnostic" 319; political 112, 272; Rev-

olutionary 5, 13, 24–5, 89, 172, 238,
    271–2, 280; Roman conquest 122
Hervé, Edouard 228
hierarchy 39, 43, 53, 111, 252; adminis-
    trative 34, 44, 91, 194, 240; authori-
    tarian 284; based on power and
    authority of traditional social forces
    194; of Bonapartist institutions 239;
    bureaucratic 132, 283; conservative
    emphasis on the functional virtues of
    116–17; emphasis on 161; natural
    129, 144; omnipotent 283; omnis-
    cient 194; oppressive 283; overthrow
    of 153; Parisian Bonapartist 91; polit-
    ical 240; republican political institu-
    tions 257; social 26, 117, 194;
    traditional, preservation of 226
history 18, 24, 166, 209, 271; administra-
    tive 17; artificial separation between
    positive and negative phases rejected
    318; as cyclical process 112; destruc-
    tion of the achievements of 153;
    Manichaean view of 278; people be-
    came the subjects of 179; political
    163; progressive conception of 243
Hoffmann, Stanley 319n
honesty 112n, 115, 129
honor 115, 116, 147, 156, 200, 314;
    equal access of all groups of citizens
    to positions of 159; sold cheaply 205
Huard, Raymond 233n
Hugo, Victor 20, 237n, 248n, 250
human nature 18; contrasting assumptions
    about 186; essence of 118–19; evil in
    117; inherent unreasonableness of 188;
    Jacobin and municipalist assumptions
    297; liberalism deeply suspicious of
    188; negation of the true principles of
    117; pessimism about 99, 102, 232,
    278; rejection of positive anthropologi-
    cal assumptions concerning 172; re-
    publican writings on 244

ideas 154, 248; articulation and presenta-
    tion of 23; cultural 24; democratic
    251; of elites 263; federalist 209,
    310n; liberal 163, 165, 189, 251;
    maintaining centralism 260; political
    23, 24, 40; preconceived 182–3; Ro-
    man 171n; Saint-Simonian 38; uncer-
    tain 111

identity: civic 9, 258; collective 7, 12, 78; common 291; communal 139, 257; cultural 128; historical 190; ideological 135; local 258; national 4, 7n, 13, 258; negative 169; political 3, 12, 19, 25, 129, 274, 279, 314; provincial and regional 128, 309; religious 129; republican 13; sectional 318; social 128, 129, 165, 167; territorial 12

ideologies, ideological thinking 3–4, 7, 8, 11, 24, 26, 42, 147, 229; administrative 45; Bonapartist 30, 31, 32, 36, 39, 45, 50; coherent 137, 234n; compromises 158; conflicting 51; convergent 13, 25, 301; core 31, 187; countervailing influences 102; critical modernization 9; decentralization and citizenship 17–20; different 64, 65, 185, 230, 296; diversity of 6, 87, 176, 281; divide between communism and socialism 264; imperatives 33; influence on sociability 309; justification of centralization 38; lack of clarity 161; legacy of French Revolution (1789) 178; legitimist 99, 111, 116, 137, 138, 159; liberal 166, 172, 219, 227, 228, 230; opposition to administrative machinery of the state 131; political 168; powerful and coherent alternative to Jacobinism 285; principles 31, 167, 239, 309; profound contradictions 167; republican 234n, 235, 249, 250, 313, 317, 320; royalist 119–20; self-representation 300; shift in 189; social 230; source of controversy 310; superiority of imperialism 63; transformations of 261; unity 298, 299

illiteracy 169

immorality 131, 200, 240, 247

immortels 169n

imperial court 50

imprisonment 46, 60

independence 192; municipal/communal 268, 289; national 276

Index 171n

individualism 7, 9, 11, 101, 187, 225, 259; liberal 115; political 124; Protestant 106; rational 318; strong emphasis on 179

industry, industrialists 129–31, 168, 193, 225, 289–90, 315

industrialization 22, 16, 289–90; large-scale 307; rapid 264, 261

information 46, 137n

injustices 183, 268

instability 104, 205

Institut de France 204

insurrection 149

integrity 205, 314; external threat to 255; mayors 212; political 196, 308; public standards 177, 214; territorial 75

intellectual, intellectuals 10, 13, 14, 22, 31, 125, 186, 257, 285; articulation of what held the French political community together 321; coalition of 25; distinct type in provinces 128; diverse and pluralistic atmosphere 281; dogmatic 173, 255; elite 80; exchange 174; flexibility 172; foundations of Jacobinism 284; leading figures 204; legitimist 98, 147; liberal 162, 164, 202, 203, 230; men endowed with superior qualities 259; moral and material corruption of 307; municipalist 300; notables 186; notion of 24; opposition to centralization 96; paradigm for relationship between individual and state 208; progenitor of 7; provincial, second-rate 203; republican 237, 271–2; success 156; supremacy 204; transition from sectoral opposition to party representing the interests of all 304; uncertainty about application of universal suffrage to local politics 152

intelligence 153, 186, 240, 257

internal market 21, 308–9

International Congresses for Peace: Bern (1868) 250; Geneva (1867) 250, 251, 254; Lausanne (1869) 250

internationalism 276, 281

interpellation, ministerial 61, 63

Italian reunification campaign (1859) 54, 110, 177, 250, 252

Jacobinism/Jacobins 7, 14, 106, 178, 227, 317; administration 151; "all are brothers" 181; centralism 119; commitment to unitary conception of state 43; constitutionalist 275; doctrine 120; intrarepublican debate on 24n; legitimist critique of 131, 134;

Jacobinism/Jacobins (*cont.*)
  moderate 297; newspaper, *L'Avenir National* 270; not so much a doctrine as a method of politics 181–2; path between federalism and 233–305; principle of popular sovereignty 105; publicly declared conversion to liberal values 166; radical 277, 296; republican approach to politics 173; return to 315; revolutionist 277; scathing denunciation of 181; taken for granted 32; thinkers inspired by tradition 162
Jéloubovskaïa, Enna 234n
Jesuits 279
Jeu de Paume 288
Joan of Arc 3
Joly, Maurice 311
Jonglez de Ligne, Alexandre 78n
journalism/journalists 23, 99, 222, **241**, 274; Catholic 95; legitimist 103, 107n, 114, 120–1, 126, 143, 150–1, 154; liberal 240; republican 268, 280, 292, 303–4; royalist 103; talented 108
journals 88n, 151, 166, 204, 166, 285
Jouvelle 45
judiciary 45, 140, 216. *See also* justice
Judt, Tony 23n
July Monarchy (1830) 14, 40, 101, 107n, 120, 152; antidemocratic legacy of 223; complacent attitudes of elites 220; ideological framework forged by doctrinaire liberals under 227; legitimist advocacy of local liberty throughout 156; Orleanist elites socialized into politics 186; political heritage of 168; mayors dismissed by 41
justice 18, 46n, 198, 208, 255, 277, 291; administrative 140, 215, 216, 217; emphasis on 238; equal 276; freedom and 242–5; in place of violence 184; individual 25; parallel and arbitrary system 216; republican attachment to 245; Revolution had brought the idea of 288; sentiment of fraternity not a basis for 249; social 262, 321; souls who aspire to 127
justices of the peace 59

Kale, Steven 99n
Keller, Emile 138

labor 116, 129, 280
Laboulaye, Edouard 164, 187, 188, 198, 221, 228; indictment of ultramontanism 171n; writings: *Histoire politique des Etats-Unis* 176, 182; *L'Etat et ses limites* 208; *Paris en Amérique* 189; *Le parti libéral* 168, 175, 189, 196, 216
landowners 75, 155, 193; big 76; concerns over depopulation 130n; legitimist 98; rich/wealthy 64, 127, 225; "small" 312
Lanfrey, Pierre 292, 301n
Larcy, Roger de 131
La Rochefoucauld Doudeauville, Louis-François-Sosthène, Duc de 106
La Rochejaquelin, Henri-Auguste-Georges Du Vergier, Marquis de 106
La Rochette (radical republican) 81
Lasteyrie, Ferdinand de 301n
Latin races 122, 249n
Laurentie, Sébastien 109, 111, 116, 126–7, 155
Lausanne International Congress for Peace (1869) 250
Laval (municipality) 56
La Valette, Charles 58
Lavergne, Léonce de 213
Lavertujon, André 250
law(s) 50, 53, 85, 87, 89–90, 142, 248, 255, 291; administrative 216; common 175; communal administration 314; divine 103, 150; equal application of 65, 75, 179; family 116; General Councils 82, 314; governing relations between church and state 111; ill suited to the needs and aspirations of the public 216; illuminated by the spirit of the Gospel 252; impartiality in administering 177; moral 150, 151, 249; natural 145, 184, 249; political 257; positive 17; on press freedom 61; public 102n; publicizing 44; religious 150; respect for 236, 292, 318; strengthening of 276; supreme 246; universal application of all 76; what should remain protected

by 118. *See also* municipal laws; rule of law

Lawarde-Mauger 48n

lawyers 263

leadership/leaders; "bourgeois" 264, 286; charismatic 238; despotic 249; effective 192; "natural" social 294; political 156; republican party, occupational origins of 263; strong individual 320; successful, qualities required for 147

Le Clère, Bernard 17, 40n

Leconte de Lisle, Charles-Marie 244

Le Creusot 22n

Lefèvre-Pontalis, Antonin 210–11

Lefrançais, Gustave 90

Left, Left-wing 7; Bonapartist 25, 31; Center 211; extreme 264; moderate 299; radical and revolutionist 25; voting regions 6

legality 215, 216, 246

Legion of Honor 48

legislation 42, 90, 288, 316n; civil, revision of 148; decentralist 33, 313–14; liberal 313; liberal republican 317; local government 82, 315; social 20; Third Republic 315; unity of 276

Legislative Corps 16, 22n, 38, 39, 59, 62, 83, 84, 85, 94n, 197, 212, 220, 258; elected representatives 91; election of president 82; formation of ministry truly responsible to 215–16; institutional conservatism abetted by 88; legislation prior to discussion and adoption 215; ministerial interpellation 61; official candidacies 51, 57; petition sent to (1870) 128; poor showing of many leading Orleanist notables in elections 224; powerful members of 91; ranked in Bonapartist hierarchy 43; representative bodies subordinated to 239–40; republican support for municipalist views in (1869) 298; Seine deputies (1869) 302; speech criticizing Empire 63; storm (1870) 237

legislative elections 51, 54, 198, 273; official candidates 47, 57, 92; Prévost-Paradol's unfortunate experiences in 224–5; voter choices 154

legitimation/legitimacy 25, 33, 52, 58, 69, 71, 106, 236, 294–295

legitimism/legitimists 10n, 11, 15, 16, 96–161, 113, 114–15, 166, 173, 307, 309–12 *passim*; accounts of local community life 257; attitudes and norms 219; dangerous to bestow influence on 57; depictions of commune 258; historically divided against Orleanists 65; ideologies of 31; inegalitarian and paternalistic community envisaged by 284; liberal 25, 66, 107, 113, 136, 151, 152, 156, 165, 194; no substantive quarrel with Empire 65–6; political and organizational strength undermined 44; public discourse on citizenship 30; rapprochement between Bonapartists and 65, 66; rejecting notion of local depoliticization 194; revival of participation in electoral process 54; schemes for local autonomy 283; subcultures within 19, 25; views of local life 194; worthy object of Empire's attentions 65

legitimist writings/writers 123, 144, 148, 152, 157, 158, 273; grim picture of society without aristocracy 115; played down significance of monarchical absolutism 120; rejection of rationalism 117; and Tocqueville's *l'Ancien Régime* 121

Le Havre 86, 302

Le Play, Frédéric 61, 81

Leroy-Beaulieu, Anatole 184, 229

Leroy-Beaulieu, Paul 164, 182

Le Temps 41n, 59n, 86n, 88n, 93n

liberal pamphlets/pamphleteers 182, 214, 217, 231; Catholic 193; denounced pervasiveness of "bureaucratic spirit" 222; importance of the commune in 191; interesting contributions on sociability 220; leading 166; provincial 172–3; significance of the commune 190. *See also* Broglie (Victor); Prévost-Paradol

liberalism/liberals 11, 16, 18, 36, 43, 97, 100, 138, 153, 244, 265, 272, 296, 301, 307, 309, 311, 318; accounts of local community life 257; authoritarianism and 37; "bastardized" 59;

liberalism/liberals (*cont.*)
  Bonapartist 25, 62, 66, 70, 84, 87,
    151; centralist 204, 230, 260; concep-
    tion/depictions of the commune 194,
    258; conservative 80, 81, 181, 183,
    188, 226, 228, 312; and decentraliza-
    tion 134, 260, 156, 162–232, 279;
    definition of 165; demands 64; di-
    lemmas of 25–6, 206–7; elective
    principle favored by 104; evolution of
    Empire 62–3; feeling that local gov-
    ernment reexamination necessary 61;
    few justifiable grounds for extensive
    state intrusion 134; "flatteries of"
    107; freedom defined in terms of the
    absence of state interference 277;
    Gambetta never forgiven by 306n;
    ideologies 31; Jacobin 277, 278; legit-
    imist 99, **113**; Orleanist 25, 151, 244;
    political, attachment to 288; political
    opposition to Second Empire 24; por-
    trayal of Jacobinism 273; progressive
    188, 189, **201**, 205, 211, 223, 226,
    312; republican 112, 260; subcultures
    within 19, 25; traits denounced by
    124; view that the republic was
    merely a "regime of democratic
    mediocrity" 321
liberalization 24, 61, 71, 85
libertarians 250, 272, 281; republican or-
    ganizations 285
liberty 10, 63, 94, 161, 179, 238, 242,
    281, 320; attempt to reconcile order
    and 293; centralization indispensable
    precondition for universal enjoyment
    of 277; civic 150, 151; civil 63, 160,
    174, 227, 317; collective 148; com-
    munal 42, 62, 142, 213, 230, 270,
    289, 298; departmental 42, 89, 289;
    factors injurious to the cause of 269;
    federalist unity based on 284; frater-
    nity not on an equal footing with
    248–9; goal to be realized 287; indi-
    vidual 18, 25, 99, 148; Jacobin re-
    publican conception of 277; legitimist
    conception of 118; malevolent 149;
    means of promoting 294; most im-
    portant 245; municipal 89, 211, 230,
    291, 292; Napoleonic theory and the
    problem of 43; national 43; necessary
    220, 232, 244; not to be confused

  with liberal notions 118; over-
    whelmingly supported 299; private
    175; property the fruit of 175; pro-
    vincial 280; public 133; radical and
    almost unqualified embrace of 244;
    rule of law and 174–6; seen as a
    good in itself 176; social, precondi-
    tions of 147–52; unconditional val-
    idity of 166; without anarchy 175.
    See also local liberty; political liberty
licentious art/literature 204
Ligue de la Décentralisation 184, 223
Ligue Française de l'Enseignement 235
Lille 41n, 57, 301
Limoges 67
Limousin 92
literacy 22, 23
litigation 216
Littré, Emile 250, 304, 313n, 321
local administration 33, 144; apolitical
    nature of 51; attempt to wrest power
    away from 79; discouraged 55; exec-
    utive tasks fulfilled by 77; failings
    blamed on government 60; heavy-
    handed intervention of 92; imple-
    menting Nancy manifesto would
    serve only to disorganize 78–9; ma-
    chinations of 91; overloaded 53; par-
    liamentary commission (1851) 80;
    prefects and 46; transferring powers
    to 77, 78
local autonomy 33, 79, 143, 167, 225;
    aristocratic conception 283; expansive
    ideas about 315; legitimist schemes
    for 283
local elections 57, 107, 252, 264, 267,
    300; administrative interference in
    58–9, 71–2; adversarial 54; apolitical
    44; candidate selection for 40, 45,
    46–7, 48, 52; efforts to depoliticize
    58; manipulated 16; mass vote unsui-
    table for 155; "official" candidates at
    national and 197–8; theme that dom-
    inated campaigns 49; workers should
    present own candidates in 263. *See
    also* departmental/cantonal elections;
    municipal/communal elections
local government/democracy 11, 19, 26,
    306n, 311; American system 182;
    apolitical 138, 159; arbitrary prac-
    tices in 268; argument against auton-

omous regime for 274; aristocracy and 144, 145; assemblies 51; attempt to preserve apolitical nature of 69; attempt to use the system to promote a distinct type of citizenship 90; authoritarian conception of 57; Bonapartist 266, 312; British 182; case for fundamental restructuring of 271; centralist 43, 44, 49, 56; competence in 77; condemnation of 265, 270; consensual 159; contending conceptions of 17; contradictions in 52, 60; councils 155; debates over 312; deficiencies 195; denounced 200; depoliticized 18, 137; drastic reorganization of 82; effective and impartial 78; English system of 61, 182; extraparliamentary commission of inquiry into 212; inconsistent with commitment to universal suffrage 210; institutions of 89, 232; internal failings 60; legislation 82, 315; legitimist 144, 157, 158; liberalization in regime's dealings with 71; liberals and 194, 196, 231; mainstream republican doctrine of 297; management of 71; mechanism for controlling the actions of 223; more efficient system 292; paternalistic regime 28; patient practice of 303; peasants turning institutions into instruments of mutual antagonism 76; politicization of 78–9, 197–9; publication of a program on 137; reform 15, 61, 69, 139, 298, 315; regime inaugurated by Napoleon III 39–40; relationship between central and 13; reorganization of 99; requirements 70; structures of 148; struggle for 235; unity and stability 73; winning the confidence of local population 48; writings on 300. See also departmental/cantonal elections; local administration; municipal/communal elections; municipal councils

local liberty 150, 151, 159–60, 220, 230, 210, 274, 311; according greater priority to 214; advocacy of 32, 195; Bonapartists' commitment to 37; debate on 162, 219, 306, 314; demands for return to prerevolutionary forms of 120; discussions of 220; ethically

regenerative potential of 194; failings in 273; genuine 140; golden age of 120; greater 81, 193, 213, 231, 270; legitimists and 96, 99, 103; liberals and 167, 176, 178, 195; municipalities and General Councils 64; part of the rationale for 225; part of wider scheme of values 18; political preconditions of 225; practice of 207; priority reduced 231; promise of 61; promoting 33, 207, 209, 270; reconciled with local order 316; republican federalists defined by significance assigned to 282; rhetorical commitment to 214; royalists' support under Revolution 19; skepticism about sincerity of Empire's commitment to 80; why one scheme was preferable to any other 17–18

local notables 48, 49, 64, 73, 90, 283, 295; bourgeois 226; political ambitions 191; social and political entrenchment 92

local politics 33, 44, 90, 316; leading role for privileged social constituency 192; nonantagonistic conception of 138; "notabilization" of 311; republican approach to 234; seen as a partisan instrument 137; universal suffrage application to 154

Lockroy, Edouard 247

Loire 43n

Loire-Inférieure 52n, 97–8

Loir-et-Cher 66

London 254

L'Opinion Nationale 168n, 213–14

Lot 168

Loudun, Eugène 272

Louis-Philippe, king of France 106, 170

Louis Napoleon. See Napoleon III

Lourdes 111

lower classes 172

loyalty 39, 56, 93, 94, 147, 279; exclusively pledged to a region 318; to state 310

Lyon 16, 40, 55, 86, 109, 138; deprived of the right to elect own municipal council 268; elected municipalities in 206; election of mayors 84; Empire's political position in 57; ideological and sociological alliances in 301;

Lyon (*cont.*)
placed under special administrative regime 196; proletariat of 261

magistrates 51, 212, 216
Magnin, Pierre-Joseph 258, 291, 292, 301n
Mailly-Nesle, Adrien-Augustin-Amalric, Marquis de 146
Maisière 268
Maistre, Joseph de 275
Mariology 111
Marmier, Xavier 29
marriage 114
Marseillaise 239
Marseille 41n, 57, 86, 301
Martin, Henri 255
martyrdom 253–4
Marx, Karl 20
Marxism/Marxists 264, 279
masses 169, 213; ignorance and credulity of 248; opinions of 207; rioting 124; rural 247; stupefied 254; votes of 223, 224, 312
materialism 200
Maupas, Charlemagne Emile de 85
Mayenne, Jean de 138
mayoral appointments 16, 44, 82, 88n, 94, 268, 314; designation 192, 294; entitlement 211; freedom to elect 86, 210; increasingly difficult to establish authority on the basis of 52; municipal councils' right 134, 143, 213; nominations 40–1; opposition figures 57; outside municipal council 87; by political and administrative authorities 267; reform of 212; state prerogative 40, 85, 195, 196–7; through universal suffrage 69, 71, 155, 211, 213
mayors 39, 42, 72–3, 91, 85, 92, 95, 134, 135, 143, 158, 265, 266, 283; agreement on extending attributions 311; arbitrary acts 268; authority compromised 60, 71; communes should be allowed to choose 298; debate on the question of 88; deliberations annulled by 265; denounced 45; deputy 40, 48, 90, 122, 197; despotism 143; dismissed 41, 93; functions of 44, 206, 212, 316; happiness can depend on

choice of 135; imperial 268; integral members of municipal councils 53; integrity of 212; key figure in maintaining republican order in the commune 293; lowly place assigned to 34; material and moral responsibilities of 198; politicization 58; problems faced by 57; repression carried out by 51; republican 219, 267; role of 83, 122, 198, 212; rural 48, 70, 86; suppression of 213. *See also* mayoral appointments
Mérimée, Prosper 37
merit 144, 147, 262
Metz de Noblat (decentralist) 81
Metz (town) 36
Michelet, Jules 179, 237, 243, 245, 248n, 272
Middle Ages 145, 273, 279; monastical orders of 111
middle classes 117; convergent interests with workers 262; countering the enforced idleness of 193; duties of 193; growth of 22; hegemony 263; historical vocation of 193; lower 169; political centrality of 184; Proudhon's critique of 263–4; representation of interests 263; right to be granted equal access to privileges enjoyed by the aristocracy 179; strength of any community resides in 168; as subversive social category 153
Midi 107
migration 21, 22, 68, 126, 129
militarism 36, 222, 250; correspondence between centralized government and 251, 300
Ministry of Justice 27, 46, 59
Ministry of Public Instruction 55
Ministry of the Interior 27, 46, 48, 55, 70, 95; head of division 162n. *See also* Billault; Chevandier de Valdrôme; La Valette; Pinard
mob rule 124
modernity: democratic 8, 317; dichotomy between tradition and 161; political 152
modernization: ideological 9; policies 94; political culture/life 6, 89; production methods 22; revolutionary heritage 24–5; rural 8n

monarchists 45, 65, 166; conservative 98; liberal 194; *ralliement* of 49; wave that engulfed National Assembly 314. *See also* royalists

monarchy, royalty 109, 135, 239; abolition of 181; absolute 120, 121, 253, 272n; Bourbon 96; call for restoration of 299n; Capetian 3; case for affirming centrality of 140; constitutional 107, 181, 228; defeated 277; guaranteed constitutional freedoms 157–8; hereditary 103–6, 139, 153; indifference to 174; legitimist attachment to 99, 100; Orleanist 14n; political attributions of 101; strong equation of the religious cause with 114; unacceptable dilution of principle 152. *See also* July Monarchy

Montalembert, Charles de 169, 176, 185, 205, 222

Montégut, Emile 183

Montpellier 16

Montricoux 45

moral, morality 18, 20, 36, 86, 115, 137, 226, 257; aristocracy 146; of Catholic liberals 187; certainties 111; constraints 99; corruption 124; freedom without 150; indoctrination 254; interests 178; men endowed with superior qualities 259; personality of the commune 139; principles 134, 159; rectitude 205; republican attachment to 240; republican purpose 258; social 150; universal obligation imposed by 249; working classes in need of 246

Morin, Frédéric 250–1

Morny, Charles Auguste Louis Joseph, Duc de 51, 64, 66–7, 91

Moselle 36

"movement" 48, 87, 117, 205

Muller, Charles 65, 112; *L'Empire et les légitimistes* 66; *La légitimité* 103, 114, 116, 124, 132, 147, 152

multiple office-holding 141, 158, 198, 283; accepted and even welcomed 311; encouragement given to 297

municipal/communal elections 66, 72, 86, 87, 92, 154–6 *passim*, 197, 231, 265, 303; campaign (1865) 192; frequent 27; ideological conflicts in 51; official candidates in 47; prefect's division of Marseille 41n; proposals to depoliticize 158; quiescent 33; regime opposed all demands for 40; Toulouse republican majority 301–2

municipal councils 16, 18, 40, 41, 70, 79, 83, 134, 155, 195, 196, 197, 239, 315–16; "banned from municipality" 45; call for prerogatives to be restored to 84; dissolved 42, 61n; elected, absence of 268; enhanced powers 53; fearful of being replaced by administrative commission 266; hard to find local figures willing to serve in 52; influence of 291; mayors chosen from within 211, 267; nominated by emperor 55; power to suspend and dissolve 196; right to elect own 268; sovereignty of 315–16; subordinated to prefects 240; suffer bureaucratic delays in rural areas 55. *See also* mayors. *Also under the following headings prefixed* "municipal"

municipal laws: (1855) 195, 265, 267; (1867) 62, 72, 76, 83n, 291; (1870) 210–11, 212, 219

municipalities 16, 40, 43, 54–6 *passim*, 124, 140, 301; council banned from 45; emancipation of 142; essential function of 316; greater local liberty to 64; incompetent 72; key role in the new republican order 316n; medieval system 145; modest increases in competences 61; Orleanist legislation on 14n; republican 298; suspended 265–6; wider franchises for 167

Muret, Théodore 107n

Nancy program/manifesto (1865) 70, 75, 76, 79, 84, 85, 134, 195, 203, 210, 281; advocated retention of executive's nominating prerogative for mayors 83; campaign for abolition of prefectoral councils 216; demanded that universal suffrage be applied to the selection of mayors 211, 219; federalist critique of 283; Ferry's letter to the signatories of 251, 287n, 290n, 292n; Montalembert's letter of support to 222; objectives of 65; permanent executive commission of

Nancy program/manifesto (*cont.*)
departmental assembly mooted by
215; prefect depicted as the supreme
instrument of imperial malevolence in
197; presented as reorganization of
feudalism 279–80; republican endorsements of 299
Nantes 17, 224–5, 301
Napoleon I Bonaparte, emperor of France
10, 14, 35, 48, 122; second abdication (1815) 173
Napoleon III, Charles Louis (Napoleon)
Bonaparte, emperor of France 20, 29,
30, 33, 41, 46n, 72n, 174, 215n; assassination attempt against 237, 274;
centralism 47; coup (1851) 36, 185;
decentralization 61, 65; foreign policy
290; "Idées Napoléoniennes" 63; influence of Saint-Simonian ideas on
38; letters to Rouher 53–4, 56; local
government regime inaugurated by
39–40; military expeditions condemned by republicans 250; Persigny
and 59, 71n, 73, 74, 87n, 89, 110;
rehabilitation of 313n; reluctance to
form a distinct Bonapartist party 31,
48
Napoleonic dynasty 153
Naquet, Alfred 248, 250, 289
National Assembly (1871–1876) 239; decentralization commission of 15;
monarchist wave that engulfed 314;
preponderance of rural interests in
258
national elections 65, 252, 301; bourgeois
elites 264; frequent 27; legitimists
voting for Bonapartists 107; manipulated 16; rallying political support 57;
theme that dominated 49; universal
suffrage restored for 267; workers
should present own candidates in
263
national guard 168, 257
national interests 177, 208
national unity 210, 314; affirmation of the
principle 222; attachment to 178,
207; destruction of 275; fear of disintegration 286; highlighted 318; local
and national character 320; preservation of 218; principal architects of 6;
sustaining a sense of 167

nationalism 24, 31, 313; aggressive 249;
conventional, disillusionment with
249n; integral 319; parochial forms
of 281; virulent 238
nationality: conception codified 9; racist
implications of the principle of 249;
rejected 249; religion no longer a sufficient basis for modern form of 320
Nefftzer, Auguste 59n, 197, 223, 240
Negroes 154
Neo-Kantians 249
neolegitimism 31
Nervo, Robert de 14n
newspapers 39, 59, 192, 197, 206, 271,
283; banned 46; cheap 23; corruptive
151; Jacobin 270; legitimist 66, 107,
137, 138; liberal 204; local 23, 303;
moral and material corruption introduced by 307; official legal announcements in 82–3; operating under strict
regime of administrative controls 237;
provincial 137. *See also Le Temps*
Nicolet, Claude 233, 319n
Nièvre 23–4nn
Nîmes 86, 87, 302
Noailles, Jules, Duc de 182
nobility 5, 36, 45, 115, 168, 194; British
44; declining social homogeneity of
146; dominant role reserved for 145;
equation of legitimism with 98; interests of 144; leading role in local institutions 147; legitimist 97, 107n, 117;
persecution of 124; perversion and
depravity of 159; profound social and
moral crisis 145; rejection of influences 209; titles 239
Nord, Philip 233n, 306
Nord (department) 78n, 90
Normans 128, 190–1
norms 91, 134, 136, 219, 258; Catholic
260; coercive 151; constitutional 174,
220; core 100; cultural 12; family
116; legitimist 157; liberal 220; modern democratic 306; moral 157, 160;
municipalist 317; oppressive 151; political, technical, and administrative
310; republican, intellectual modernization of 317; social 157, 160
notabilism/notables 31, 37, 39, 221, 295;
Bonapartist 70, 86; bourgeois 226,
295, 299; conservative 86; decentral-

ist 73; departmental 82; elected 51, 91, 312; enlightened 264; greater powers given to 69; intellectual 186; liberal 226; provincial 264, 312. *See also* local notables
nuns 254

official candidates 46–7, 48, 211, 225, 267, 268–9; in national and local elections 197–8; unpopularity of 92; vigorous campaigns against 252. *See also* mayoral appointments; prefectorate
Ollivier, Emile 185, 188, 212, 221, 229, 273, 278–9; appointment during liberal Empire 61, 66; speeches 173, 175; decentralization commission (1870) 66, 80, 88, 270; proposed reforms 62, 131–2; writings: *Démocratie et liberté* 178–9, 181–2; *L'Empire libéral* 80, 85, 91–2, 218; *Journal* 213, 225–6
opportunism 11, 32, 264
opposition parties/groups 16, 24–5, 32, 46, 55, 122, 196, 215–16; activism of 54; antirevolutionary dimension of 69; anti-imperial coalition of 166, 301; building bridges with 65; candidates severely defeated 198; clamors for greater civil and political liberties 63; compromise with 51; constant theme in writings 200; constitutional 138; evidence that Bonapartist officials campaigned for 59–60; powers used to undermine and frustrate 41; steady progression of support for 63–4, 85–6; sympathy for 59; visceral hostility to prefects 134
oppression 277, 290; bureaucratic 13; centralist 210; church 280; triple 285
order 18, 36, 47, 75, 90, 184, 206, 226, 238; arbitrary 284; attempt to reconcile liberty with 293; civic 316; comes before freedom 210; communal 293, 316n; conservative notion of 175; deliberate strategy to maintain 266; desire to preserve 33; established, subservience to 247; financial 218; immutability of 103–4; imperial 227, 303; inescapable means of maintaining 183; instinctive attachment to 63;

instrument for the promotion of 194; internal, prerequisite for 276; local 290, 316; new 60n, 311, 313, 316; oppressive 205; other forces of 80; party of 58; people's primary instincts highly favorable to 153; potential instrument of 312; public 46, 84, 106, 208, 218; regime committed to 94; republican 7, 20, 25, 227, 228, 311, 313; restoring 65; social 89, 101, 103, 104, 105; souls who aspire to 127; state mission to preserve 134; symbolic 39; true party of 293; without despotism 175. *See also* political order
Ordinaire, Edouard 268
Orleanism/Orleanists 14n, 25, 29, 31, 80, 183, 239, 279; constitutional opinions of 172; description of 1848 events 181; dismissed as the attitude of monopoly and exploitation 168; elites socialized into politics under July Monarchy 186; former 49, 211; growth of forces 54; leading 170, 198; left "in the lurch" 229; legitimists historically divided against 65; liberal 151, 168, 244; notables rallied to Bonapartist camp 221; older generation of figures 188; political and organizational strength undermined 44; "providential" defeat of 106
Orléans 86
Orsini, Felice 237
overregulation 177
Ozouf, Mona 233n

paganism 120, 133
Pamard, Paul 72–3
pamphlets/pamphleteers 16, 24, 106, 145, 199; Bonapartist 35, 36n, 63, 67; Catholic 105; federalist schemes outlined in 285; imperial 88; Jacobin 279–80; legitimist 215; short but blistering 307. *See also* Clozel de Boyer; Favé; liberal pamphlets/pamphleteers; Muller; republican/pamphleteers
Paris 21, 40, 55, 73, 91, 202–6, 213, 225, 240, 299; absence of firm republican connection with the seat of power in 265; bureaucracy 53, 78; condemna-

Paris (*cont.*)

tion of the noxious role of 99; "decapitalization" 63, 157; denial of elected mayor to 84, 314–15; denied elected municipal authority 16, 28, 206, 268; distribution of power between provinces and 80; elites of 16, 23; Empire's political position in 57; Haussmann's grandiose plans for renovation of 126; Hôtel de Ville 124; ideological and sociological alliances in 301; information flow from provinces to 46; infrastructural development 126; legitimists' condemnation of 124; liberals in 186; movement which sought to assert the power of provincial towns against 282; placed under a special administrative regime 196; popular resistance to the coup (1851) 236; press 16; proletariat 261; reconstruction of 126; relationship with provinces 47; religious ignorance in 125; republican and liberal opposition deputies 302; revolutionary impetus coming from 81; right to elect its municipal council 192; rural and provincial demonology of 22; severe condemnation of 157; suppression of the central municipality 124; tried to assert its will against provinces 260; vacuousness and frivolity of lifestyle 187; working population seen as the embodiment of barbarity 127. *See also* Ligue de la Décentralisation

Paris Commune (1871) 157, 202, 231, 232, 297, 313, 314; advent of 234, 286; fate of 28, 299; Jacobin instincts played out in 280

parliament: constitutional government responsible to 179–81; debates on decentralization 298; justification for bypassing action 248; preserving a majority in 198; right to elect members of 210. *See also* Legislative Corps; Senate

Parliamentary Commission of Inquiry on the causes of the Commune (1871) 202

participation 36, 61, 160, 161, 225, 292; civic 89; collective 240, 290–1; deliberate but restrained 136; electoral 192, 224; legitimists' revival in electoral process 54; loyal 316; mass 11, 13; political 135–6, 297, 305; voluntary abstention from 44

Pastoret, Amedée David, Marquis de 106

paternalism 28, 38, 188, 195, 278, 284; administrative 292; authoritarian 278; Bonapartist 160; enlightened 212, 225; following instincts 207; impulsions of liberal elites 167; persistent liberal attachment to 222; philosophy 266

patriarchy 116, 129, 161, 258, 259

patrimonies 144, 318

patriotism 68, 191, 276, 281, 305; cultivated through local politics 190; derivation of 258; equated with masculinity 259; fervor for 313; fraternity embodied in the principle of 249; more energetic form of 284–5; primordial importance of 257; republican conception of 310, 320; sentiments of 257, 258, 284

patronage 47, 49, 73; state 91, 198

PCF (Parti Communiste Français) 5

peace 250, 300; fraternity and 248–51; guarantees of 147; state mission to preserve 134; world 251

peasantry/peasants 22, 50, 76, 128, 309; Church influence on 252; histories of 6–7; later republican view of 313n; often identified with Bonapartism 252; particular object of contempt among republican pamphleteers 247; pauperization of 130; physical degeneration of 131; "small" 312; true 154; vulnerable and dependent 122

Pelletan, Camille 235

Pelletan, Pierre Clément Eugène 256, 301n, 302; writings: *Aide-toi le ciel tíaidera* 247; *Droits de l'homme* 238, 255, 288, 293, 294; *La nouvelle Babylone* 240

penitence 114, 253

Périgord 98

Périgueux 224

Persigny, Jean Gilbert Victor Fialin, Duc de 54, 65, 72, 76, 87, 91–2; advocacy of authoritarian centralism 70–1; circular to prefects (1860) 48–9; denounces powers of bureaucracy 78;

introductory report on decentralization decree (1861) 55; Napoleon III and 59, 71n, 73, **74**, 87n, 89, 110; political instincts of 36; sketches comparison with British nobility 43–4; speech drawing contrast between urban and rural public opinion 50
Pessard, Hector 88n, 280–1
Peyrat, Alphonse 274
philosophical anthropology 117
philosophy 5, 17, 38, 173, 203; nihilism in modern society 119
Picard, Ernest 80, 248, 301, 314n
piety 115, 125
Pilbeam, Pamela 233n
Pinard, Ernest 62, 68
pleasures 126, 146, 187, 196; common 190; despicable 254; innocent 157; material 199; pastoral 129; unseemly 131
plebiscite, plebiscites 27, 37, 60, 66, 92, 95, 220–1, 228, 236; "daily," nation as 320
police 14, 30; assassination attempts foiled by 274; commissioners of 59, 168, 197; electoral meeting dissolved by 237n; repression carried out by 51; rural 59
Polignac, Jules de 105
political culture(s) 202, 229, 288, 313, 315; attachment to and entrenchment within 165; authoritarian and democratic 260; celebrating the urban condition 307; of democracy and citizenship 3–28; distinct 273; divergence in 239; guaranteeing sacred principles of Catholic faith 158; intellectual convergences between 298–9; Jacobin 280; liberal 317; local 292, 294; notions borrowed from Second Empire 318; republican, fundamental component of 264; richness and dynamism of 307; vibrantly democratic 306
political elites 10–11, 13, 14, 26, 147, 154, 318; aspiring 191; Bonapartist attempts to recruit from 64; lacking in dignity, honesty, and integrity 308; overrepresentation of liberal professions among 169–71; powers of patronage 49; recruitment of 192;

recurrent complaints from 309; universal suffrage could be controlled by 312
political equality 255, 291, 296, 299, 300; based on civic participation 315; federalist unity based on 284; involvement of citizenry on the basis of 18; upholding the principles of 43
political liberty 160, 175, 227, 242, 286; defense of 317; demands for extension of 148; essential component of liberal society 149; genuine 105; greater 63, 70, 163, 174; philosophical ambiguity about 152; social privilege and 155; training school for 211
political order 158, 189, 205; alternative conceptions denied 105; constantly threatened by revolution 308; counterrevolutionaries and 101; intelligibility of 4; liberal values strongly represented in 227; liberty as one of the foundations of 149; new 179, 236; respect for 168; superior principle of 103
political rights 25, 171, 245; defense of 175; of expression and association 18; frequent exercise of 291; local communities' deprivation of 160; positive 151; progressive extension of 225
political values 287, 300, 312; constitutionalist 23; legitimist 109, 130, 161; liberal 25, 167, 195, 206, 228
politics, political: accountability 11, 13; adversarial 54, 90, 93; agents 45; anti-intellectual and antirationalist conception 240; antiliberal manner found among atheists 273; based on general principles 116; of Bonapartist centralism 37–44; certainties 111; cleavage between urban and rural 55; cohesion 114; communal 303, 316; conservative forces resisting change 81; contradictions 18, 33, 39; core characteristics of French 13; crisis 61; democratic 33, 312; disillusionment with 266; diversity 106; docility of rural society 247; dogmatic 255; electoral, history of 27; Empire's relationship with provinces 48; expression of preferences 27; General Councils for-

politics, political (*cont.*)
bidden from expressing views 42; growing importance of the nation-state in 12; heritage 168, 243; "high" 116, 158, 184; imperatives of decentralization 63–6, 134–8; imperial system 14; intellectualization of 24; intervention 172; Jacobin 173, 295; legitimist 110; local factors 92; "low" 231; management of provinces 46; mass 186, 188, 223, 224, 313; moral and material corruption into 307; most of the faithful incapable of distinguishing religion from 252; movements 46; municipalist 303; municipal, modern 93; nationalist 24; necessity and legitimacy of 58; obscurantism 252; preferences 175; problems 62; proper relationship between religion and 110; protest 214; provincial loyalty 94; reality 293; "reasonable" 188; reform of 18; relationship between Paris and provinces 90–1; reorganization of 99; republican 24; revolution, containing and preventing spread of 213; road to social and moral salvation 147; technical conception of 37; territorial 17, 19; turmoil 124, 126. *See also under various headings,* e.g., Bonapartism; centralization; decentralization; government; Jacobinism; legitimism; liberalism; parliament; political culture(s); political elites; republicanism; universal suffrage. *Also under headings above prefixed* "political"
popes 110, 114; infallibility of 253
popular sovereignty 106, 120, 121, 139–40, 260, 271, 276, 277; adherence to revolutionary principles of 238; all important political truths articulated in the name of 297; belief in 266–7; claim that the Bonapartist regime was a genuine emanation of 240; fragmentation of 274–5; further advance in the direction of 228; imperious and transcendental agent of 289; Jacobin principle of 105; republican notion of 179, 245–8
popular suffrage 115–16. *See also* universal suffrage

population growth 21
populism/populists 9, 31
positivism 173, 297, 250, 320; centrality of 319n
power(s) 32, 46, 47, 77, 153, 174, 194, 254, 280; adored for its own sake 272; centralized 54, 120, 141, 293, 295–6; coercive 295; collective 68; consolidated 48; convenient means of challenging 167; decentralized 295; decision-making 18, 67; deductive 203; devolution of 67, 69; distribution of 80, 297; doctrine about 273; elected assemblies 139; excessive concentration of 202; executive 40, 142, 217, 267; fragmenting 314; given to populations of communes 155; government 104–5, 207; handed over to the "beardless tramps" of society 155; hope of recapturing 168; imperial 227, 269; important questions about the agency of 311; legal 216, 217; legitimists alienated from centers of 97; legitimized and subverted 320; local 49, 51, 69, 193, 269, 295, 311; love of 80; material 120; monarchical 239; moral 248; of municipal delegates 143; patronage 73; of the people 277; peripheral forms of 92; Persigny's denunciation of 78; petty 122; political 102, 246, 296, 307; preservation of 209; principal feature of Bonapartist society 38; questions addressed from a social perspective 281; representatives 269; repressive 265; republican generation unprepared for the exercise of 304; revolutionary 202; royal 105; scope of 132; state 81, 120, 131, 132, 196, 290; superstition of 202; supreme 257, 282; taken away from central and provincial administrations 141–2; tenuous and ephemeral 296; territorial base 312; too much given to the people 148–9; transfer of 18, 56, 70, 73, 78, 83, 207, 283; ultimate 104; uncertain 111; unnecessary 143; wide-ranging 82; wielded arbitrarily 197. *See also* administrative power; prefectoral powers
pragmatism 47, 135, 147, 273, 303; Gallican 187; monarchist 106

prefectoral councils 217, 292; Nancy program campaign for abolition 216

prefectoral powers 134, 197; abuse of 216; concentrating further 73; considerable 40n; decreasing 206; devolution to 69; executive 142, 268; extension of 61; liberal solution to the problem 215; nomination of mayors made through 40–1; progressively challenged 91; transferred 56, 70, 207; weakened 71. *See also tutelle*

prefectorate/prefects 30, 40, 42n, 43, 47, 53n, 64n, 65, 67n, 93, 168, 268; administrative commissions appointed by 196, 265–6; ambiguous relationship between councillors of state and 34; appointed by General Council 215; authority 205; Bonapartist 79; centralized control over local, political, and administrative life 91; challenge to 60; concerns of 73–9; decentralization in favor of 270; deliberations annulled by 265; denunciation of role 57; departmental councils subordinated to 240; deputies "persecuted" by 51; despotism 219; fate of the corps 140–1; former 139; hated symbol of centralization 269; institutional value system 75; legitimate representative of state in each department 292; lightening administrative burdens of 78; likened to old and outdated material 133; limitation of the role of 82; major criticisms levelled at competence of 77; mayor denounced to 45; municipal councils subordinated to 240; pernicious role of 122; Picard's robust defense of 314n; portrayed in 1865 Nancy program as the supreme instrument of imperial malevolence 197; presence a guarantee of fairness 76; public-interest functions of 141; public salaries of 132; reduced role of 90; reports to regime 46; repression carried out by 51; republicans' defense of the role and functions of 314; resentment directed at 45; selection of official candidates by 48; strong opposition to measures that might weaken their hold on local administrative system 88; structural conflict between General Council and 79; symbol of institutional perversion 215; tactical withdrawal from electoral arena 59. *See also* prefectoral councils; prefectoral power; subprefects

prejudices 8, 153, 209, 214

press 137n; authoritarian Bonapartist 86; freedom of 149, 317; Gallican legitimist 110–11nn; liberal 166; liberalization of strict controls on 24; Parisian 16; political 125; provincial 16; right of discussion in 174; ultra-Catholic 111

Prévost-Paradol, Lucien-Anatole 81, 84, 164, 169, 171, 179, 180, 188, 212, 215n, 216, 221, 230–1; writings: *La France nouvelle* 191, 199, 206, 210; *Quelques pages d'histoire contemporaire* 185, 186, 189, 192, 198, 200

privilege(s) 145–6, 179, 252; aristocratic 146; attack on 132; of communes 158; preservation of 263; social 155

procureurs-généraux 46, 93; Agen 62, 64, 84n; Aix 50; Angers 66n, 84n; Besançon 66n, 82, 84n; Bordeaux 66n, 86n; Bourges 84n; Caen 52, 66n; Colmar 47; Lyons 55; Nîmes 59n; Rennes 60; Riom 57; Rouen 55; Seine-et-Marne 45; Toulouse 58, 66n

professions/professionals 169–71, 177

progress 36; agricultural 128; belief in 187; necessary forms of 245

proletariat. *See* working class

property, properties 155; alienation of 15; communal 12, 86; defense of 299, 318; freedom to own 148; ownership 171, 175, 179, 286; private 101, 114, 242, 299; protection of 317; rights 296; small- and large-scale owners 167–8; territorial 117

prosecution 238; immunity from 140, 216

prosperity 22, 62, 65; agricultural 21; economic 106

prostitution 254, 268

protectionism (economic) 186

Protestantism/Protestants; antiliberal manner of politics found among 273; blamed for the origins of French ab-

Protestantism/Protestants (*cont.*)
solutism 120; corruptive influence of 101; fusion between republicanism and 255; liberal 25, 187, 255, **256**; "political" 106; republicans 253; seditious spirit engendered by 121

Proudhon, Pierre-Joseph 286; writings: *De la capacité politique des classes ouvrières* 257, 282–3; *Les démocrates assermentés et les réfractaires* 247–8, 268, 269–70, 272–3; *Essais d'une philosophie populaire* 242, 249; *La pornocratie ou la femme dans les temps modernes* 259; *Théorie de mouvement constitutionnel* 284

providence, providentialism 111, 118, 133

provinces 50, 62, 140, 160, 206, 295, 299; administration of 72; aristocracy in 14; autonomy of 131, 193; Bonapartists and 36, 312; bourgeoisie in 193; Catholics in 65; claim to represent natural government of 159; Council of State's inherent bias against 217; deliberate strategy to maintain order and stability in 266; despotism of 197; distinct type of intellectual in 128; distribution of power between Paris and 80; electoral influence of Empire in 85; elites 71; emancipation of 142, 160; Empire's political relationship with 48, 92; federalist republican movements in 286; foot soldier of the regime in 45; free federation into nations 251; governors 141; identification with 128; ignorance and superstition of 203; institutions 232; key role assigned in the social and political value system of legitimism to 127; liberals 186–7, 189; linked to monarch 139; management of 46, 51, 53, 60; means of fortifying 205; natural entities formed by historical affinities 121; nonpolitical associations in 309; Paris and 22, 46, 47, 78, 80, 90–1, 203, 260; political loyalty of 94; prefects' stewardship of 77; press 16; primary location of commune 129; promotion of greater artistic and cultural excellence in 204; public life in 41; radical Jacobins contemptuous of 296; republican support

in 23; restoration of 64, 120, 141, 157; royalists 65; servility of 205; social and moral atrophy of 157; towns 282; transfer of artistic and cultural resources to 204; unsuitability for substantive self-government 221; writers 16. See also rural society

prudence 42, 143, 171–4, 183, 184, 206; worship of 168

Prussia. See Franco-Prussian War

public expenditure 177

public interest 32, 71, 83, 142, 289; bureaucratic functions 219; institutions devoted to 217; mayoral functions 212; regard for 197

public offices 35. See also deputies; mayors; prefectorate; *procureurs-généraux*; senators

public opinion 32, 50–1, 60, 63, 149, 207, 219; ill-educated and volatile 188; impatient 82; inflamed by radical republican groups 214; more knowledgeable than Council of State 216

public prosecutors 98, 111

public safety 44, 278, 288

public-spiritedness 259, 305

public works 55, 150

Puy-de-Dôme 42

Pyat, Félix 285

quarante-huitards 260, 299

Quentin-Bauchard, Ernest 72

Quinet, Edgar 250, 272, 288, 317

race 121; degeneration of 130, 131; implications of the principle of nationality 249; superior 122

radical republicanism 81, 181, 211, 214, 234, 264n; condemnation of 143; fear of 188; liberals apprehensive about rise of 167; menace of 75, 136; reemergence of 66; rise of 212–13, 220, 230; threat of 205

radicalism 296; federalist schemes 295; Jacobin 277; political 143, 299; popular 152; reformist 264; urban 143

rail networks 21, 22, 49, 309

Rainneville, Joseph de 153

Rambouillet 79

Ranc, Arthur 280–1

Raspail, François-Vincent 298n

rationalism, rationalist 117–18, 187, 227, 305, 317; approach to moral and political issues 171; thought 100, 119

Raudot, Claude-Marie 66 107, 128; writings: *L'administration locale en France et en Angleterre* 121, 122, 123, 142; "L'avenir des nations" 114n; "La décentralisation" (*Correspondant* articles) 124, 130, 133, 140, 141, 142

reason, reasoning 102, 187, 224, 278; analogical 274, 275; deductive 166; limit between faith and 171n; public 188; republican attachment to 240; superiority of 203; ultramontane rejection of 253

Reclus, Elisée 250

redistribution 178, 286, 296; of authority 311; forcible 144, 296; republican proposals for 227

Reformation 255

reforms 87, 189, 190; administrative 140, 214, 219; of communal institutions 210; decentralist 131–2, 167; economic 61, 62; education, key 317; intended 207; judicial 217; legislative 158; liberal 32, 46, 73, 281; liberals' cautious optimism at the prospect of 131–2; local government 15, 61, 69, 139, 298, 315; mayoral appointments 84, 212; moderate 84; municipal 84–5, 206; opposition to 73; political 18, 61, 63, 156, 157; rejected 83; social 156, 157; structural 215; substantive 88; territorial 156; universal suffrage 63

regicide 103, 124

regionalism 46, 309n

regulation(s): excessive 124; legal 283; of local government institutions 222; reduced and streamlined 140

Reims 301

relativism 176

religion, religious 36, 42, 86, 112, 134, 139, 152, 176, 318, 321; belief in redemptive potential of 187; central position in social and political value system of legitimists 109; conception of social life 159; defense of 137; duty 102; emancipation from delu-

sions of 259; equal treatment of all faiths 177; freedom and 150; freedom of 112, 151; institutions 37, 99, 136; "mediating" influence in making of national identity 7n; moral certainty 114; no longer a sufficient basis for modern form of nationality 320; obligation 161; obscurantism 252; place in society 306; promotion of 226; republicanism and 26, 251–5; separation of politics from 110; threat 114; tolerance and pluralism 26; true 109–10; ungodly and ridiculous 125; values 99. *See also* Catholicism; Protestantism

Rémond, René 30, 32n

Rémusat, Paul de 196, 198

Rémusat, Charles de 162, 174, 178, 198, 200, **201**, 221; memoirs 215n, 223–4

Rémusat dynasty 186

Renan, Ernest 164, 205, 272, 320

Renouvier, Charles 249, 269

representation 258, 264; effective 248; perversion of the principle of 197–8; no taxation without 268

repression 41, 46, 48, 51, 237, 267; *commissions mixtes* 60; political 290

republican pamphleteers 215, 246; in exile 236, 245; focus on communal liberty 270; often cited the Napoleonic legend 237; peasantry particular object of contempt among 247

republican socialists 25, 234, 237n; decentralism endorsed by 235; democratic organizations 285; freethinking 254; not content with demanding greater democracy 262. *See also* Acollas; Blanc (Louis); Ecorcheville; Guépin; Proudhon

republicanism/republicans 16, 80, 97, 166, 173, 196, 230; ambition to involve the citizenry in local public life 192; attitudes and norms of 219; autonomist faction within 263; bitter and frantic battle against resurgence of 228; bourgeois and popular 260–5; Catholic Church challenge to 251; celebration of Vendée atrocities by 103; Christian and secular 249; citizenship 4, 99; conception of popular sovereignty 179; conception of state

republicanism/republicans (*cont.*)
228; condemned military expeditions of Napoleon III 250; consistently argued for abolition of state's practice of appointing mayors 83–4; consistent progress in urban areas 85–6; constitutionalist 235, 248; criticism of views of public authority 159; decentralists 134; defense of role and functions of prefects 314; demanded return of elected municipalities 206; demonology of imperial authoritarianism 89; despotism 120, 219; dominant political group in France 167; elective principle favored by 104; federalist 311; good relations between legitimists and 102n; growth of forces 54; ideologies 31; indifference to 174; internal history of 25; Jacobin 273; legacy of centralization denounced by 124; liberal 25, 112, 165, 194; liberals less suspicious of 186; mayoral candidates 93; men of honor 102; militant 264; moderate 25, 151, 181, 188, 249, 301, 234, 264, 280, 299; moderated Jacobinism 227; modern 4, 7, 9n, 116; municipalism 11, 18, 26, 233–305, 312; new order 228; opposition to law (1867) 61n; opposition to Second Empire 24; placed liberty above authority 238; political and organizational strength undermined 44; political subversion 137; "providential" defeat of 106; *ralliement* of 49; reactionary majority 27; reformist 234; religion and 251–5; revolutionary 248, 254, 273; secret of success 229; stress on civic and participationist advantages of universal suffrage 36; subcultures within 19, 25; support for 64; values 5, 7; writings on human nature 244; zealous 48. *See also* radical republicanism; republican pamphleteers; republican socialists; Second Republic; Third Republic
"République des ducs" 228
resources 204, 245, 293
respect 39, 50, 111, 184; for law 236, 292, 318
Restoration 14, 119–20, 227

Revue de la Decentralisation 194
Revue des Deux Mondes 162, 166, 214
Rhône 41
Rials, Stéphane 110
Right, Right-wing; Bonapartist 31, 32; Center 211; moderate 299; religious and counterrevolutionary 25; voting regions 6
rights 12, 14, 29, 50, 63, 99, 101, 105, 136, 255, 276; accent on 259; associative 151, 160, 317; burial 151; citizens' 289; civil 25, 175; collective 4, 144, 313; communal 257; denied 266; electoral 61, 152; equal 179, 194, 246; of expression 160; feminine 259; freedom as a set of 148; fully safeguarded 296; inalienable 149, 151, 161, 179; individual 4, 144, 310; legal 144; militantly articulated 261; natural 132, 245; property 296; public 10; social 144, 245; uncertain 111; vague sense of 269; violation of 287; voting 152. *See also* Declaration of the Rights of Man; political rights
riots 124, 202, 213
roads 21, 22, 50, 55, 86, 257, 268; construction of 90; development of 309; local 142; maintenance of 90, 196
Robespierre, Maximilien de 281
Rochefort, Henri 238, 252, 298n, **302**
Rochefort (urban constituency) 264
Roman question 46n, 177
Rosanvallon, Pierre 27n, 228
Rothney, John 31
Rothschild, James D., Baron 90
Rouher, Eugène 37, 42, 43, 53, 54n, 56, 58, 91, 186n
Rousseau, Jean-Jacques 116, 118
Royal charter (1814) 112
royalism/royalists 9, 14, 99, **113**, 114, 253; absolutist 275; antiliberal manner of politics found among 273; Bourbon 113; celebration of French unity 272n; flag 101; ideology 119–20; journalist 103; mainly articulated by legitimists 96; optimistic 124; party driven by the force of inertia 112; political activism urged by Falloux 136; provincial 65; "reflective" 107; support of local liberties 19
royalty. *See* monarchy

Royer-Collard, Pierre 14
rule of law 184; advocacy of 219; defense of 174; liberty and 174–6; liberty could be enjoyed only under 175; quality of government 177; republic the embodiment of 242; tendency to subvert for partisan purposes 207; unconditional validity of 166; upholding 175
rural society/communities 31, 36, 51, 95, 98, 316; age-old division between urban and 318; Bonapartists successfully held vote across 312; bourgeois habits and attitudes seeping into 169; collective virtues of 50; complaint against effects of centralization 99; conservative instincts of 313; decentralization 63, 64, 68; decline of 102; depopulation 21, 130, 307; devastating effects of urbanization on 157; feelings of resentment 22; gullibility of the electorate 224; interests 258; largely illiterate and deeply conservative 287; masses 247; material interests of workers 252; mayors 48, 86; menace to 127–31; migration 21, 68; modernization of 8n; moral and material corruption 307; nonpolitical associations in 309; police 59, 197; politics 55; radical Jacobins contemptuous of 296; republican support 23; strategic importance of cultivating 35; strong links with imperial state 49; suspicion with which republicans regarded 258; traditionalism and backwardness 199; understanding of traditionalist concerns and practices of 171; voters 152, 199, 224; way of life openly embraced by republican federalists 295. See also agriculture; communes
Russia 200

Sacy, Silvestre de 169, 221, 231
Sagan 129
Saint Vincent of Paul Society 111
Saint-Aulaire, Louis de 185
Saint-Étienne 71, 86; ideological and sociological alliances in 301; proletariat of 261
Saint-Marc Girardin, Louis Claude de 189, 226, 228

Saint-Simonian, Saint-Simonist 31, 37, 38, 77
Sainte-Beuve, Charles 187
Sainte-Pelagie (prison) 102
salons 309
Sand, Georges 248n
Savoie 47
Saxon peoples 122
Say, Jean Baptiste 163n
Schneider, Eugène 22
Schoelcher, Victor 250
schoolteachers 40n, 45, 59, 122, 143, 197
science 245; experimental 173; teaching of 254
Second Republic (1848–52) 9, 15, 101, 260; Barrot's career under 80; brief flowering of harmony between republicans and the church 251; legitimists support for local liberty throughout 156; Jacobin influence during 272; moderate and consensual conception of the republican idea 261. See also coup d'état (1851)
secularism 5, 7, 9, 11, 227, 258, 300, 309; often suspicious of Catholicism 187; promised by French Revolution 254–5
Sedan 29, 89
Segris, Alexis Emile 57n
Ségur, Louis de 105, 112n, 114, 136, 148
Seine 72, 80n; communes of 40
self-government 122, 190, 208, 210, 220; all forms founded on the Catholic principle 150; claim that the French were culturally unfit for 121; commitment to the principle of 214; communes intrinsically unfit for 72, 195; demands for 286; democratic 287–97; greater, promoting the cause of 84; liberals and 210, 219–32; material and intellectual means to exercise 285; moderate form of 271; municipal, republican theory of 235; promoting 184, 209; recipe for better administration 266; requires fortunes 145; requires men of leisure 144; Vacherot as inflexible censor of 299
Senate 16, 43, 62, 83, 133; commission of decentralization (1858) 53; institutional conservatism abetted by 88; role of 43n

senators **34**, 85
sensuality 173
sentiments 102, 257; communal 258; patriotic 257, 258, 284; religious 255
separation of powers 242
separatism 286
servility 200, 205
servitude 176, 248, 277, 285
sexual issues 130, 254
shopkeepers 168
Simon, Jules 57n, 165, 240, 247, 249,
252, 253, 281, 301; academic position lost for refusing to swear an oath
of allegiance 237; key figure of the
Third Republic **241**; letter of support
for Nancy manifesto 301n; writings:
"Discours sur l'élection des maires"
258; *La famille* 259; *La liberté* 243,
257, 266, 269, 289–90, 293; *Paris
aux Parisiens* 268; *La politique radicale* 250
slavery 143, 150
small business owners 168, 315
smallholders 193
sociability 12, 38, 220; communal 257;
crisis of 229; cultural 139; emergence
of new forms of 307; expression of
190; farewell to a form on the verge
of extinction 157; fulcrum of 190,
318; important feature of the human
spirit 244; institution for promoting
191; liberal pamphleteers' contributions 220; local and national, meeting
point between 190; natural source of
190; particularistic and universal
forms of 310; religious 309; value of
257
social class(es) 42, 132, 157, 291, 318,
321; agricultural 50; conflict among
50, 75, 167, 295, 300, 320; differences eroded and eliminated 293,
296; divisions 5; equality among 179;
exclusive 100; harmony of 184, 266;
inspiration to other 144; lower 154;
most numerous and least fortunate
178; propertied 63, 144, 155; reconciliation of 246; regarded as sources
of unnecessary diversion and conflict
262; republican conception of 293–4;
structure of 22; struggle 264–5. *See
also* bourgeoisie; middle classes; peas-

antry; proletariat; upper classes;
working class(es)
social equality 5, 194, 261, 262; conflicts
over 264; duty of state to create 296;
radical, condemned 160; restricted
definition of 179
social mobility 296
social order 100, 282; best guarantees of
137, 145; decentralization the most
important organizing principle of
282; destructive passions within 167;
distinct conception of 116; legitimist
115; maintenance of 175–6, 218; old
228; preservation of 144, 193, 207;
regenerating 193; threat to 127, 214;
victory of nihilism over 125; violation
of the fundamental laws of 126
social revolution 25, 50, 66; fear of 314;
menace of 214; Paris the abode of
203; threat of 126, 190, 230
socialism/socialists 31, 79, 126, 157, 231,
281, 311; Blanquist, Fourierist,
Cabetist, Saint-Simonist 264; centralist and decentralist 260; democratic
25, 250, 285; growing fracture within
the movement 286; ideological divide
between communism and 264; Jacobin 276, 296; militant 264; moderate 25; municipal 212–13;
Proudhonist 254, 260, 264; revolutionary 43, 80, 209. *See also* republican socialists
socialization 192; individual and group
191; political 64, 224
society 38, 63, 110, 130; bourgeois spirit
gradually pervading 169; civil 68,
189, 230; complete disintegration of
202; cooperation within 285; created
by French Revolution 112–13; defense of interests of certain sections of
155; degeneracy of 124; democratic
262, 267; described as facing a "state
of siege" 214; diversity within 255;
example of social and moral excellence to 145; exercise of power and
influence in the best interests of 193;
free 175, 176, 289; governed in the
best interests of all 194; liberal 149;
modern 102, 119, 161; moral and
material conditions of 176; nobility
presented as a valuable model for

147; organic 62, 99, 115–17; place of religion in 306; political 116; privileged sections of 192; ranks ordered in accordance with ability and merit 144; relationship between state and 190, 275; revolves around heredity 103; Taine's horticultural metaphor for 171; traditional republican conception of 262. *See also* rural society

Solidarité Républicaine 272n

solidarity 39, 100, 104, 184; class 291; emergence of a sense of 259; social 67, 68, 190

Somme 48

Soncourt 48n

Soubise 268

sovereignty 105, 177, 270, 282–3; belief in 239; of commune 289; full, local elites enjoyed 297; individual and national 320; of municipal council 315–16; national 242; temporal 110. *See also* popular sovereignty

spirituality 260

Spuller, Eugène 317

stability 33, 56, 226; administrative 292; deliberate strategy to maintain 266; economic 168; local government 73; political 43, 137, 173, 292, 293; social and political institutions that promoted 101

state 67–8, 148, 150, 190, 107, 211, 260, 292; active intercession of 177; administrative appointments 40; agents of 71, 175; authority 295; broad agreement about need to trim sails of 299; building 5; burdensome presence of 69; centralized 79, 209–10, 214, 275, 288, 294–5, 314; church and 35, 101, 111, 177, 253, 254; citizen and 16; commune comes before 14; conceptions of 32, 43, 87, 88, 159, 166, 220, 228, 288, 297; confirmation of contract between people and 246; conflicts of interest between different branches 33; democratic 250; desecration of legality by 236; dissolution of 106; duty of 178, 296; employees of companies 59; entirely subordinate to local authorities 295; everything depends on 56; excessive

enthusiasm for intervention of 96; excuse to cripple the essential functions 276; extension of the family principle to 116; frugal 176–8, 184; functions of 307; fundamental nature and purpose of 275; growing importance in local society and politics 12; ideal 177; imperial 16, 33, 49; increase in political salience of 308; intellectual paradigm for relationship between individual and 208; intervention of 275; intrusion into public and private domain 176; Jacobins' theory of 280; law-governed 299, 320; legitimists' concern with the consequences of actions 132; liberal 177; liberating role of 273; local populations' collaboration with 49; localities and 284; loyalty to 310; mayoral appointments by 44, 84, 85, 87, 195, 196–7; minimalist 208; mission to preserve order/peace 134; monarchy as restraining influence on 105; obsession with controlling all aspects of social life 60; omnipotence of 133, 199, 207; overbearing presence of 131; paternalistic view of role 38; patronage 73, 91, 198; philosophy of 265; power 120, 131, 132, 196; providential 159; reason of 242; represents a divine power 103; republican 228; resource distribution 203; revenues arbitrarily taken by 15; role of 167, 221, 271, 290, 307; security 54, 62; sharp criticism of Jacobin doctrine of 273; social purposes 134, 244; society and 190, 275; strong 13, 251, 275, 276; subjects pretend to govern 106; suppressing the idea of 277; surveillance 207; tutelage of 211; unitary 230, 297, 314; upper classes' function in 66; weakening of 167, 290; well-defined notion of 305

strikes 214, 319; republican ambivalence toward 262n

subprefects 45, 52, 59, 91, 92; diligence of 77; mayors described as worse than 83; proposals to abolish the function 140; proposals to elect by universal suffrage 215; public salaries 132 subversion 43, 63, 101, 153, 230; cities handed over to forces of 86; freedom as form of 149; political 50, 137; republican 137; social 106; threat of 47, 75

Sue, Eugène 248n

suffrage. *See* popular suffrage; universal suffrage

superiority: of aristocracy 145–6; of bourgeois rule 230; of French administration 75; of imperialist ideology 63; of reason 203

superstition 247, 259

surveillance 41, 84, 207

syndicalists 46

Syrian expeditions 177

Taine, Hippolyte 5, 162, 171, 182–3, 272

Tarn-et-Garonne 45

taxation 35, 75, 196, 288; local 141, 208; revenues from 141; unity of 276

technocracy 31

tenors 60

territoriality 109, 306; Catholic conception 109; republican notions 233–4

Terror (1790s) 274, 288

Thibaudet, Albert 163

Thiers, Adolphe 83 162, 169, 185, 188, 222, 223, 229, 230, 232, 244, **302**; writings: *Discours sur les libertés politiques* 63, 179; *Histoire du Consulat et de li'Empire* 218

thinkers. *See* thought

Third Republic (1870–1940) 6, 7, 174, **201**, 315–21; abrasive and reactionary character of Bonapartism under 89; allegedly forcible conversion of peasants into Frenchmen 309; anticipated by doctrinaire liberals 227; commonplace assumption among historians of 304; elites of 11; emergence of its *notables* anticipated by Second Empire 293; excludes women, workers, and Catholics 26; height of the liberal regime 163; intellectual evolution under 299n; liberal juridical credentials of 319; municipalist republicans capturing local government office 300; nationality conception codified 9; one of the key figures **241**;

part played in emergence of modern polity 8; political and ideological origins of 313; political dreams of legitimism ended in 161; powers of prefects 40n; republican notion of citizenship 20; republican order departed significantly from the canons of French liberalism 228; self-justifications of opportunist and radical statesmen 235; strong element of continuity between the Second Empire and 312; troubled transition from Empire to 232

Thomson, David 8

thought/thinking/thinkers 318; bourgeoisie identified by a particular way of 168; federalist 249; freedom of 245; inspired by Jacobin tradition 162; intellectual and critical 245; legitimist 99, 114, 117, 119; liberal 14n, 162, 164, 178, 189, 193, 206, 220; "materialist" Jacobin 272; new 321; political 14n, 24, 117, 220, 297; rationalist 100, 119; republican 253; social 117, 178, 297; survival of modes of 128; "systematic" 100; women believed to lack the capacity for 259

Thuillier, Guy 32

Tocqueville, Alexis Charles de 13, 96, 163–4, 182, 188, 232; writings: *L'ancien régime et la revolution* 121, 200; *De la démocratie en Amérique* 186

tolerance 26, 305, 317

Toulouse 57, 58, 66n, 86; ideological and sociological alliances in 301; municipal council dissolved (1867) 196

Tournon 91

towns 291; estranged from each other 50; groups suspicious and fearful of political voice of 308; large(r) 50, 55, 91, 92, 94, 130, 213, 214; mass movement into/migration to 21, 22, 129; population growth of 21; prime bearers of values of republican citizenship 257–8; protection of 270–1; provincial 282; republican advances across France 303; small(er) 40n, 55; special political representation for 258. *See also* municipalities

tradition 35; change and 96–161; of Catholic religion 255; classical liberal

189; constraint of 25–6; liberal 26, 209; revolutionary 288
tribunals 10n, 216
Tridon, Gustave 273, 278, 279
tuning forks 60
turbulence 137, 172, 205, 218, 224, 275
tutelle 76–7, 83, 143, 265, 283; maintained over communes' administration of their finances 314; rejected by federalists 294
tyranny 278, 285; administrative 162, 226; Bonapartist 185; centralizing 168; communal 278; opposition to 184–5; petty 122; political 106; submissive 205; threat of 123; worst instrument of 247

ultramontanism 105, 110, 280; instinctive dislike of 171; intransigent 111n; rejection of reason 253
uniformity 133, 176, 178
Union Libérale 136–7, 166, 301
United States 182
unity 75, 184–9, 282, 298; administrative 178, 271, 219, 221; Bonapartist 35–7; cultural 272; functional 43; ideological 298; legal 221; of legitimism with Catholicism 109–15; local government 73; moral 178; must not come from the center 284; political 121, 178, 208, 215, 221, 271, 272, 276, 309; recognized as a necessary feature of federalist polity 284; republican, anti-Bonapartist foundations of 236–41; revolutionary government's successes in creating a sense of 274; social 121, 178; territorial 43. *See also* national unity
universal suffrage 23, 27, 42–3, 47, 49, 51, 68, 101, 181, 191, 236, 288, 300; affront to the principle inherent in hereditary monarchy 153; Bonapartists' view of 36, 37, 73; commitment to 228; complete freedom of 276; compromised 160, 294; continuing of 223; credulous theoreticians of divine right combined with 100; deep-seated suspicion of 212; election of subprefects by 215; Empire's attachment to 90; endorsed in principle 312; faith in salutary capacities of

collective action attributed to 246; flawed conception of 266; foundations shaken 72; important founding moment in the institutionalization of 312; justification for bypassing 248; legitimation by 52, 69; liberals and 224, 225, 229, 230; limits of 93, 152–6; local authorities freely chosen by 67; local government regime inconsistent with commitment to 210; mayors and 69, 71, 158, 211, 213; only two movements that unequivocally endorsed 238; "personalization" of 154n; philosophical validity of the principle 247; place in the political system 307; political competition through 18; popular sovereignty and 245–8; practice of 89; preference for 211; principle seemed questionable 224; qualified by introducing restrictions based on property and residence 160; redemptive properties of 247; reform of 63; republicans' stress on civic and participationist advantages 36; restoration of 23, 27, 238, 239, 267; role in public life 311; subjecting "lieutenants of the army of order" to the vagaries of 87; unease about 86; validity of 248; violation of the spirit of 197; widespread political competition at local level through 94
upheavals/unrest: political 75, 105, 174, 205, 230; revolutionary 202, 226
upper classes 66, 172
urban areas 54, 63, 171, 316; age-old division between rural and 318; Bonapartist support in 60; bourgeoisie 152; constituency of Rochefort 264; development of 21; electoral strength of the republican party 270; as focus of republicanism 257; municipal councils granted freedom to elect mayors 86; municipalism 295; politics 55, 214; proletariat 22; republicans' consistent progress in 85–6; republican hegemony in 301; way of life 125, 127; working-class vote 264
urbanization 230, 307; critique of 125; devastating effects on rural communities 157; legitimist approach to 126;

urbanization (*cont.*)
policies 94, 130; political forces that accepted 308
utopias/utopians 16, 295; conceptions rejected 297; demented 155; elements 300; imperial 175; impractical and dangerous 283; naive 285; social 5

Vacherot, Etienne 165, 248–9, 253, 255, 262, 267, 275–6, 277, 278, 292, 299
Vaillant, Victor 145, 149
Vallès, Jules 250
values 117, 135, 146, 148, 189–94, 236, 253, 258, 278, 279, 281; aristocratic code of 159; authoritarian 73; Bonapartist 90; broader range that could be promoted 291; capitalist 186; civilizing 222; collective 190; constitutionalist 23; cultural 190, 226; defined and enforced from above 284; disseminated by the modern state 134; of Enlightenment 187; essential to a civilized society 129; family 116; formalistic 101; of good citizenship 162; ideological 8; individual 106; institutional 283; key 7, 25, 166, 283, 293; legitimist 99; liberal 25, 165, 166, 207, 299; local liberty as part of wider scheme of 18; metaphysical 101; modern democratic 306; moral 190, 200, 287; municipalist scheme of 293; patriotic 276; religious 99; republican 261, 284, 286, 287, 319; sacred and priceless 277; shared 240; social 17, 109, 130, 226; traditional 100; treasured 310; true to nature 245. See also political values. Also under various headings, e.g., authority; democracy; equality; fraternity; freedom; hierarchy; order; political liberty; secularism; social equality
vanities 145–6, 173, 199
Varia 193–4, 199, 210
Vatican 110, 177
Venice 106
Vermorel, Auguste 242, 284
Veuillot, Louis 108, 111n, 117, 137; writings: *L'illusion libérale* 119, 136; *Les odeurs de Paris* 152–3; *Mélanges religieux . . .* 95, 109, 122, 128, 129–30, 150, 153, 154

Villèle, Jean-Baptiste 120
Vincent, Charles Louis Marie, Baron de 41n
violence 153; expressions of political protest 214; justice in place of 184; political 320; rejected 318; revolutionary 273–4
virtues 120, 147, 171–4, 187, 245; administrative 145; aristocratic 99; cardinal 168; Christian 129; civic 25, 42, 163, 199; collective 50; false 73; "honest" 154; ideal 169, 246; liberal 183; moral 117, 131; political 65, 258; practical 318; public 218, 259; social 115, 117, 131, 145, 159, 258
Vosges 48n
voting/votes/voters 267; manipulation and intimidation of 160; mass 223, 224, 312; in regions 6; rural 224; working-class 224, 301
Vuitry, Adolphe 83

Waddington, William-Henry 223
Waldeck-Rousseau, Pierre 165
war 250, 281
wealth 123, 147, 192; accumulation of 203; distribution 75; inherited 145; safeguard of 304
Weber, Eugène 6
women 26; clergy controls all 252; excluded from Third Republic 26; physical, intellectual and moral inferiority of 259
workers 20, 40; agricultural 130; conditions of 64; daily 280; denied right to form coalitions 261; excluded from Third Republic 26; honest and intelligent 315; indisputable 154; intelligent 192; landowner support of 193; middle classes' convergent interests with 262; migrant 126, 129; *mutuelliste* 263; overwhelmingly loyal to bourgeois elites 264; provincial 279; should present own candidates in national and local elections 263; should seek political dissociation from elites 286; striking 214, 319; victims of social justice 127
working class(es) 22, 117, 125, 168, 192, 264, 286, 299; appearance of communities 307; bourgeoisie system-

atically ignored the interests of 260; corrupt 203; defense and promotion of the interests of 261, 263; democracy as sociological category to designate 246n; habitats 22; industrial 102; in need of education 246; life significantly altered 261; militancy of 143; threat from 169; voters 301

Wright, Vincent 17, 40n

writings/writers 24, 244, 279, 300; federalist 285, 286, 287, 295; liberal 166, 189, 200; municipalist 296, 305; provincial 16; republican 247, 253, 258, 279, 316. *See also* legitimist writers

Wyrouboff, Grégoire 250

Young Turks 260, 299

Zeldin, Theodore 6, 27

Zorn de Bulach, Baron 68–9, 86

About the author

SUDHIR HAZAREESINGH is an Official Fellow and Tutor in Politics at Balliol College, Oxford. He is the author of *Political Traditions in Modern France*.

DATE DUE
